The Heart of Art Education:
Holistic Approaches to Creativity, Integration, and Transformation

ABOUT NAEA

The National Art Education Association is the world's largest professional visual arts education association and a leader in educational research, policy, and practice for art education. NAEA's mission is to advance visual arts education to fulfill human potential and promote global understanding.

Membership includes elementary and secondary art teachers, middle school and high school students in the National Art Honor Society programs, artists, administrators, museum educators, arts council staff, university professors, and students from the United States and several foreign countries. It also includes publishers, manufacturers, and suppliers of art materials; parents; students; retired art educators; and others concerned about quality art education in our schools.

NAEA publishes *Art Education, Studies in Art Education,* and other professional papers on art education; holds an annual convention; conducts research; sponsors a teacher awards program; develops standards for student learning, school programs, and teacher preparation; and co-sponsors workshops, seminars, and institutes on art education. For further information, visit our website at www.arteducators.org.

© 2012 by National Art Education Association
1806 Robert Fulton Drive, Suite 300, Reston, VA 20191

To order a copy of this book or obtain additional information, contact National Art Education Association: www.arteducators.org or 800-299-8321.

Order No. 315
ISBN 978-1-890160-54-8

Cover: Kate Elkins' Color Wheel Identity Map, page 177.
From "Artist/Researcher/Teacher: A Holistic Approach to Art Teacher Preparation."

The Heart of Art Education: Holistic Approaches to Creativity, Integration, and Transformation

Laurel H. Campbell and Seymour Simmons III

NATIONAL ART EDUCATION ASSOCIATION

CONTENTS

Karen Lee Carroll

For me, the heart is a metaphor for the core beliefs and values that inspire and guide one's actions. "The heart" might also be said to reflect a spiritual dimension, as in the breath that animates our actions. What's in the heart should represent an alignment of ideas, values, and actions.

In the more than 40 years that I have been involved with art education, the field has grown in depth, breadth, and complexity. The notion of making a positive difference in the lives of others through art, which was once inspirational, has developed over the years into a complex network of ideas. These ideas are at times closely knit together, and then again expanding in an elastic manner. Many of these ideas have been validated by research. To give a better sense of what I believe constitutes the heart of art education, I'd like to mention some of the thinkers and experiences that have contributed to enlarging and strengthening the values I hold for the profession.

My best experiences making art have been akin to a journey that took off into unknown territory, surprised me, engaged me, pulled me along, and led to insights and ideas that in some way personally transformed me. The study of art and culture likewise provided a pathway into the world, and I note how new critical perspectives have allowed my perceptions, questions, and understandings to evolve over the years. My goal as an art teacher was to create the conditions that would allow others to find art an avenue for adventure, discovery, reflection, inquiry, and empowerment. Although I may not have used words such as "empowerment" when I first started to teach, it seems a very appropriate name today for the manner in which working with materials, learning how to represent ideas, thinking through a medium, and engaging with works of art can produce a personal sense of power and capacity.

The scholarship of Ellen Dissanayake (1995) gave validation to the notion of art as a human behavior selected for survival. She identified various human propensities that artists can draw upon. Among them, three are especially relevant here: (1) The need to make special, especially when a person or event matters a great deal; (2) the attraction human beings have for the novel, the mastery of tools, and communication with others; and (3) the act of building a sense of "group one-heartedness" (p. 222). Based on this vision, I began to think of teaching art as developing human capacities that have their roots both in infancy and the nature of the human species. I still feel it is the responsibility of art educators to foster the development of visual language (although I would say that visual-spatial-temporal language continues to expand as artists continue to invent new forms of representation); to frame investigations of materials that reveal the ways in which materials can communicate meanings; and to encourage creative, visual, spatial, and temporal modes of thinking and knowing.

While Dissanayake's biobehavioral theory rendered art as species-centric, the research of Rudolph Arnheim, Claire Golomb, Howard Gardner, David Baker, and Judith Burton provided another way of thinking about art as a language that could be developed. From this perspective, art is a language pulled forward at times by the possibilities of representation, and at other times by the narrative impulse and the possibilities of visual storytelling. The research of Brent and Marjorie Wilson, Al Hurwitz, and Janet Olson validated the notion of the narrative construction of meaning through art, providing a more significant way of speaking about

ABOUT THE AUTHOR

Karen Carroll serves as the Dean for Center for Art Education at the Maryland Institute College of Art, and holds the Florence Gaskins Harper Chair in Art Education. She has written on gifted education in the arts, cultivating artistic behaviors, holistic theory and practice, and teacher preparation. She is one of seven co-authors for *Creating Meaning through Art: Teacher as Choice-Maker*; co-author (with Al Hurwitz) of *Memory and Experience: Thematic Drawings from Qatari, Taiwanese, Malaysian and American Children*; and author of *Better Practice in Visual Arts Education*. Her accomplishments have been recognized with several national awards from NAEA, including the 2004 Lowenfeld Award and 2009 National Art Educator of the Year award. Her doctorate was earned at Teachers College, Columbia University.

self-expression. The construction of self-identity through the development of coherent personal narratives is an integrative process that helps make sense out of the world of experience.

Holistic theory has been helpful to me in several ways. It offers a way of thinking about development as moving in the direction of greater mastery of a medium, greater complexity of ideas, and greater ownership of the creative process (Carroll, 2006, p. 24). It also helps define learning as "transformational" in the sense that previous notions have been deconstructed, reconstructed, and reintegrated with more depth, complexity, and understanding. Peter London's (2003, 2004) contribution to both theory and practice has been of particular value to me, and certain of his ideas continue to hold my attention. For example, he asserts the importance of a caring environment (what some would call a safe community for learning), positive mutual regard (between teacher and student and among members of a learning community), and existential or self-reflective questions (what some might call questions of inquiry). In addition, I am interested in ways in which deeper engagement can be fostered. London's work with a study group at the Maryland Institute in 2001 inspired pedagogical innovations, as K-12 art teachers tested ways to more deeply engage learners. Several members of that original study group have continued to perform research and write from their investigations into holistic teaching pedagogy. Two are included in this anthology (see Chapter 10, by J. Castro; and Chapter 35, by S. McKenna).

Does my own practice of teaching qualify as holistic? In some ways, I would say yes. More accurately, I aspire to a comprehensive approach drawing on three sources: (1) the learners—their needs and the windows of opportunity presented in their development; (2) the discipline of art, with its rich repertoire of possibilities for engagement, exploration, and challenge; and (3) large ideas and significant questions that appear to be relevant, meaningful, timely, and worth pursuing. What happens in the classroom? Hopefully, a dynamic relationship is created wherein the intersection of learner, art, and ideas provide a seductive and challenging journey that leads to multiple dimensions of development, if not transformational learning.

The authors appearing in this anthology present a comprehensive vision of art education, incorporating both theoretical perspectives and practical applications for a variety of settings: preK-12, community art programs, and art teacher education. Together, they help create a contemporary vision of art education with the whole child in mind, while also accommodating the connections that link the child to the school, community, and environment. In the time since I was first inspired by the writings of Viktor Lowenfeld (1957), the field has grown significantly in research, theory, and practice. Developments along the way in learning theory and new research in neuro-education validate a learner-centered approach as well as the importance of the arts. A learner-centered approach appears to be developmentally essential for building the capacity for empathy and the will to entertain different points of view, challenge assumptions, and think critically. In short, these developments and possibilities, and the attention this anthology brings to the question, give me great heart.

REFERENCES

Carroll, K. L. (2006). Development and learning in art: Moving in the direction of a holistic paradigm for art education. *Visual Arts Research, 32*(1), 16-28.

Dissanayake, E. (1995). *Homoaestheticus: Where art comes from and why.* Seattle: University of Washington Press.

London, P. (2003). *Drawing closer to nature: Making art in dialogue with the natural world.* Boston, MA: Shambhala.

London, P. (2004). Toward a holistic paradigm in art education. In P. London & The Study Group for Holistic Art Education (Eds.), *Toward a Holistic Paradigm in Art Education*, pp. 1-5. [Center for Art Education Monograph No. 1]. Baltimore: Maryland Institute College of Art.

Lowenfeld, V. (1957). *Creative and mental growth*, 3rd. ed. New York, NY: Macmillian.

Laurel H. Campbell and Seymour Simmons III

Over the past quarter-century, art education has expanded in many directions to encompass an ever-widening array of content, concerns, disciplines, and standards. In the process, the arts have established themselves nationally as core subjects equivalent to the academic domains, and thus as necessary components in every student's education. While celebrating this important accomplishment, however, many art educators may have sensed that something essential was lost along the way—namely, the emphasis on meeting the holistic needs of children and young adults.

This anthology seeks to redirect the attention of the field to that important goal by viewing holistic art education through a variety of lenses, including studying, critiquing, and reflecting upon the art of many cultures. It provides a particular focus on meaning-making involving creativity as well as transformative and integrated learning.

Such active and experiential learning made education through art, craft, or design unique and uniquely valuable, largely because it engages and integrates multiple dimensions of the individual. Depending on the goal of the lesson and the way it is taught, these may include physical/sensory, emotional, and cognitive functions, as well as social, moral, and even spiritual attributes. We call this focus on comprehensive, or holistic, development through meaning-making "the heart of art education." We believe it always has been, and still remains, a primary concern for a majority of art educators, despite competing trends within the field and conflicting demands upon the time allotted for art in schools.

While we recognize these and other challenges facing art educators today, we nonetheless argue that holistic considerations should become increasingly emphasized in art classes as well as in art teacher preparation in response to the personal, societal, and environmental problems young people must be prepared to solve, today and in the future. A growing body of literature has been promulgated in general education on holistic teaching and learning, but relatively little specifically for art educators. This volume seeks to redress this situation and bridge the gap between holistic educators at all levels, from P-12 teachers, to university faculty, researchers, and those involved in community art centers and museums. By presenting diverse views on the subject, we hope to provide a broader and more inclusive definition of contemporary holistic art education. We also hope to lay a theoretical foundation for the holistic approach in the context of postmodernism, while offering guidelines and examples for teaching holistically in the visual arts.

The response to our call for submissions demonstrated promise in meeting our goals. Chapters came from researchers and practitioners alike, and included extensive theoretical discussions as well as briefer vignettes that demonstrate how such theories relate to visual art curriculum development, pedagogy, and assessment. Others addressed teacher preparation and the ongoing advancement of art teachers as educators, artists, and researchers. Together, these chapters offer varying ways to more fully meet the needs of young people today, while contributing to ongoing conversations about new directions for art education in years to come.

LOOKING BACK AND MOVING FORWARD

As several of these essays explain, holistic education in theory and in practice is hardly a new trend—rather, it is one that has been around for centuries in general education and in art. Holistic considerations in general education can be traced back to the ancient Greek system of *Paideia*, while more-recent formulations are found in the theories of Rousseau, Montessori, and Dewey, among others. In the visual arts, holistic education begins with the recognition, now widely accepted, that each dimension of the individual can be educationally involved in making and/or studying art.

For example, on the physical plane, art education is known for its role in developing perception, skill, and craftsmanship, thereby building confidence and competence in the particular art form. At the emotional level, art education has been recognized for its ability to cultivate empathy, facilitate expression, and encourage reflection that can, in turn, foster understanding and communication among people despite apparent divisions of gender, age, race, religion, ethnicity, and culture. Cognitive considerations include ways art education fosters creative problem-solving, conceptual understanding, and critical thinking, including capacities to describe, analyze, interpret, and evaluate.

Literature addressing moral, social, and spiritual aspects emphasizes how making and studying art that is concerned with universal themes and issues of enduring importance can help build character and prepare students for a life of thoughtful engagement grounded in their deepest values. This anthology promotes each of these aspects of art education and hopes to demonstrate ways they can be mutually developed and integrated to promote outer connectedness and inner wholeness. Thus described, contemporary holistic art education can contribute both to comprehensive personal growth and the social good.

Admittedly, our position refers back to earlier, "child-centered" progressive philosophies. Nevertheless, we do not intend to retrace the significant steps art education has taken in the immediate past, nor do we wish to revive an approach that was best suited to another time. Rather, our concern is to draw upon the best aspects of previous models along with contemporary approaches in order to construct a *new* vision that is appropriate to current conditions and grounded in postmodern understandings of art, education, and human development. To differentiate this transformative model of learning from earlier methods, we call it "student-connected" (Miller, 1993), not only because it brings together the different facets of the individual and helps unite students with the wider world, but also because it connects educational experiences more directly with the needs of children and young adults. This new vision is presented here. We have tried to construct it in a way that will resonate with our readers, personally as well as professionally.

Our goal as editors is to document the history and philosophical underpinnings of holistic education and consider its potential implications for art education today while taking into account the vast array of content, skills, and experiences encompassed by the domain. The chapters and vignettes included here will address a variety of issues and approaches such as visual culture, art as research, transformative learning in the arts, new media and technology, globalization, ecology, social justice, service learning, and multicultural studies. Based on these examples, we hope that the reader will find ways to holistically connect the visual arts with other art forms and with fields of knowledge across disciplines.

CONTRIBUTIONS TO THE FIELD

As mentioned, this book comes at a time when art education has been established as a core subject area. Art is also touted by representatives of business, industry, and government as an essential means to address problems in our society. Means to these ends include holistic attributes addressed in the book—cultivating creative problem-solving skills that engage both sides of the brain, fostering collaborative learning, working for the common good, and establishing common ground among peoples of diverse backgrounds. Equally important, holistic approaches apply here to address the needs of children and young people, who must find their own way in a world of international terrorism, environmental degradation, economic crises, violence in schools, and drug abuse.

Still, this book is not intended to provide a definitive formulation of "contemporary holistic art education," nor does it pretend to provide reliable recipes for teaching visual art in a holistic manner. Instead, its larger purposes are to raise interest in the subject, provide multiple perspectives from art educators on the topic, address some of the controversies attached to it, and encourage further research about established and emerging approaches. Toward these ends, we invite comments from our readers so that the conversation and debate can widen, with greater depth and variety. With continued experimentation and erudition, we hope that a holistic perspective will provide a viable way of looking at ourselves (as educators), our students, our research, and our practice as we engage with the visual arts in the 21st century.

REFERENCE

Miller, J. P. (1993). *The holistic teacher*. Toronto, ON: The Ontario Institute for Studies in Education.

ABOUT THE EDITORS

Seymour Simmons III is an associate professor of Fine Arts at Winthrop University, where he coordinates the undergraduate art education program and teaches drawing. Prior to coming to Winthrop, he taught at the Massachusetts College of Art, and did research at Harvard Project Zero (in particular, on the Arts PROPEL project).

Laurel H. Campbell is an assistant professor of Art Education and Director of Art Education at Indiana University-Purdue University Fort Wayne. She has been an art educator since 1996 and a metalsmith since 1974. Her research interests include reflective practice, preservice teacher education, and holistic art education.

Foundational Approaches to Holistic Art Education

As art educators, we must understand fundamentally—not just academically—the profound significance of interdependence, for example, between self-other, and thought-feeling. We must revamp old thinking and seize upon the interconnectedness of biology, culture, art, and empathy, working to explore the interactions through classroom activities intended to build peak performance learning communities and promote collective flow. The practice of taking the perspective or role of others would be valued by teachers and students alike as imaginative, empathic, and creative acts.

—Carol S. Jeffers, p. 35

CHAPTER 1

The Configuration of Meaning: Learner-Centered Art Education Revisited

Judith M. Burton[1]

The arts, it has been said, cannot change the world, but they may change human beings, who might change the world.

—Maxine Greene

Most of us tend to take for granted that children are at the heart of our teaching and have a natural proclivity to learn. But the very notion of child-centered education is now long outmoded, a casualty of the challenges presented by new knowledge and the demand for complex social and technological skills. Even as neuroscience is opening insights into the human mind and the processes whereby learning takes place, we are more perplexed than ever about the nature of knowledge and what learning is likely to be most worthwhile. What assumptions do we now make about childhood and adolescence? How do we position young people as learners in our classrooms? How do we conceive of the visual arts as a critical domain of generativity and new knowledge?

It is perhaps timely to revisit one of the most enduring "chestnuts" to have given life and controversy to the field of art education. In this chapter, I want to bring together some threads of new—and not so new—thinking in order to place the child or adolescent learner more securely at the heart of our discipline. In short, I want to move art education from a child-centered to a learner-centered position. I suggest that the traditional theory of mind that has long informed the notion of child-centeredness is both too simplistic and too exclusionary to be a useful guide to teaching and instruction in art education. The concept of learner-centeredness, albeit it in updated garb, will challenge the demands of a scripted curriculum tied to a narrowly conceived assessment that drives contemporary education in the visual arts, as in all other subject domains. Education, as it is practiced in so many schools today, excludes recognition of the richness and generativity of children's minds.

This argument raises questions about the theories we hold in art education and how they are rooted in the actuality of classroom experiences for many young people. As my colleague at Teachers College, Maxine Greene (2001), pointed out, young people are often bored in schools because we do not offer them meaningful challenges; we do not invite them to bring their own experiences into the arena of learning; we do not offer them competencies that serve the kind of reflection on and exploration of possibilities that engage their thinking; and we do not offer them insights and skills in those non-verbal languages of the arts where imagination can open up new corners of reality.[2] In the end, of course, we do not help them construct continuity between their own creative efforts and the culture in which they live in a way that accords distinction and respect to each.

Perhaps we do not offer them these things because, somewhere along the way in education, we have actually lost sight of child and adolescent learners; we have disengaged them from the heart of the educational enterprise. We have made young people the objects of education, rather than inviting them as participants into a shared enterprise that involves exchanges between young and old, experienced and inexperienced. Put differently, we have not always grounded learning in contexts that are meaningful to contemporary youth. In losing sight of the needs of the learner, we also may have lost sight of the significance of learning in and through the arts. The kinds of visual narratives youngsters construct not only make meaningful their own sense of self, but also establish continuity between their personal lives and the experiences of the world they share with others. Therefore, in losing sight of the learner, we may have also abandoned the belief that the construction of meaning in visual form is a fundamental feature of being human, and that art itself is a normative function of the human mind.

CHILD-CENTEREDNESS

Theories about how children think and learn have been proffered and debated by philosophers, psychologists, and educators for centuries. Indeed, historical influences that have shaped contemporary views of children and their artistic learning can be traced back to ancient Greece. We still debate, for example, whether the artistic content in children's works derives from historical precedent or individual experience, the degree to which socio-cultural or psycho-dynamic forces determine artistic style, and the relative status of sensory against conceptual knowledge in the fashioning of visual images.

We also have been endlessly perplexed about outcome, or telos, and whether it assumes singular or multiple forms. Is there a normative strand to artistic development which stretches into adolescence and, perhaps, beyond? If so, how are the upper reaches of development constituted—by styles such as realism or abstractionism, or by less-obvious underlying structures of thought conceived in terms of complexity or simplicity, or repertoires of possibility? Such perceptions, ideas, and theories about children, art, and learning have dictated the ways in which we have thought about teaching and education.

Threading through such debates has been the perennial issue of "child centeredness" in art education, along with various conjectures about what schools should do to promote (or, sometimes, combat) this notion. Harking back 200 years to Rousseau and Locke, protagonists have inherited the dichotomous views that children are naturally creative if left alone and untrammeled by social and educational influences or, alternatively, are creative only if predispositions are nurtured by the direct intervention of teaching. Variants of these two positions have emerged over time as the naturalist view and found support from the emerging field of psychoanalysis and, later, psychology. In education, these views have become centered in studio practice and work with materials. The interventionist view tended to draw heavily on learning from art history and the past, and more recently from information theory. The interventionist view of learning also centered largely on the acquisition of proven techniques for appreciation and the acquisition of conventions for graphic rendering.

For the most part, the more "naturalist" view has framed what came to be called child-centered art education. Holders of this view tended to believe, perhaps naively, that children's art, left "unsullied" by external forces, either offered a road map of children's inner mental life or directly mirrored their emotional concerns. Neither of these orientations was informed by clear understanding of art as a distinctive symbolic domain, and only relatively recent research has offered insights into artistic development as a quasi-coherent process governed by rules, phases, and influences. Similarly, child-centered art education has always played an important role within Progressive Education—where, unfortunately, it often became linked to laissez-faire methods and the exhortation that teachers downplay their influence in the classroom. Notwithstanding these caveats, holders of the child-centered view of art education nonetheless claimed studio practice to be the perfect arena in which the mental, emotional, and social life of the child could be best expressed.[3]

Criticism of the Child-Centered Approach

Criticism of the child-centered approach to art education swung back and forth throughout the 20th century, and has been multi-pronged. While the approach has been taken to task for offering a "psychological" rather than "artistic" view of learning, proponents have been seen either to romanticize the child as "natural artist" or adopt a deficit model as "immature adult artist." Similarly, as this view has been linked to studio practice and free expression with materials, its appropriateness has been seen as dubious in the years beyond childhood, where expressive capacities were assumed to decline. As products of child-centered art education, adolescents were often seen to become bored, lacking the expertise to create the kinds of images they desired, and having little or no insight into the larger world of art that was lost to them. Furthermore, even in the earlier years of childhood, free expression was often viewed as subject to the intervention of simplistic media-dominated images. This occurrence was not only seen to curtail youngsters' own imaginative efforts, but also (in the absence of any pedagogical intervention to the contrary) had the effect of cutting them adrift from the larger world of aesthetic insight and understanding.

There is no doubt that child-centeredness, as an approach clearly linked to the romantic notion of the young person as an autonomous artist who can develop naturally with simple encouragement and lots of materials, has too frequently given rise to poor practice. Nevertheless, we now have other ways of understanding children's artistry; its psychological, artistic, and cultural origins; and its outcomes as measured by the ways in which young people in schools construct ideas and "re-present" their worlds. We are grasping not only important insights about artistic development, but also a deeper understanding of development in light of the symbolic processes involved in the construction of meaning in and through visual materials. In addition, we are learning more about the diverse shaping mechanisms of the cultures in which children grow up and learn. We know more about what is distinctive to learning in and through the arts than we perhaps realize, or take into account in our teaching.

NEW PERSPECTIVES

Let me bring into view some of the salient ideas that have emerged in our discipline in recent years, and argue for their contemporary relevance in re-centering the child at the heart of learning.[4] In what follows, I show how ideas about experience, body, and mind interweave as they find voice in and through action on visual materials. Basically, I will argue that artistic development is normative, occurs in all human beings, and progresses with some regularity across the life span.

This argument is based on three important assumptions. The first is that works of art (whether created by children, adolescents, or adults,) are multi-layered; that is, they consist of interweavings of many, often divergent and inconsistent, dimensions of thought and feeling. The second is that responses come into being over time and are not of necessity subsumed by later responses, but rather coalesce with them into flexible repertoires of thought and action. In the normal course of events, responses are both recursive and regressive, and they are energized by the ever-shifting sands of experience and the challenges of the culture. The third is that the outcome of artistic development is not subsumed by any single end point or style; rather, development proceeds in complexity in the sense that young people construct evolving "repertoires of possibility," which they place in the service of an increasing variety of artistic/aesthetic needs. This view of development can be linked to a way of teaching that is centered in dialogue that both supports the journey of learning and unblocks artistic stagnation. Dialogue provides the holding environment and creates the space in which focused and open-ended interchange, reflection, and learning can occur between two learners—teacher and pupil—to the benefit of each.

What follows reflects my own stance on child- and adolescent-centered art education. It is, inevitably, an eclectic approach. This is not meant to be a comprehensive survey; rather, it is an effort to understand how children interpret their worlds in and through visual materials, as well as how we (as artists, educators and scholars) enter into this world of learning in a way that allows us to understand youngsters' interpretations. This discussion also explores the implications these measures have for our own pedagogical practices.

THE ROLE OF EXPERIENCE IN ART

Artists throughout time have created works from the "stuff" of their experience. Art history is less a record of dates and periods than a continuity of how human beings across the centuries have encountered and experienced their worlds. It also captures the interplay of personal and/ consensual values and beliefs they have found therein. A recent exhibition at the British Museum in London showed works created by British and American artists made in response to sculptures on display in the Egyptian Gallery. Many concepts were extraordinary about this intermingling of the contemporary and ancient; not only could one experience artists in dialogue with each across almost five millenia, but also identify their shared human concerns. In this sense, art history is linear only in a temporal sense; the experiences it embodies are recursive. But as Dewey (1934) tells us, experience is not just a spectacle observed from the outside; it is something that immerses us, within which we are situated, and its features engender thoughts, feelings, and sensory resonances. As Victor Lowenfeld was to write in his seminal text *Creative and Mental Growth* (1947), we do not paint and draw objects in our world; instead, we paint and draw our "relationships" with them. Thus, when we talk of art as experience, we comment on the experience of relationships borne out of constellations of feelings, thoughts, and sensory responses. Interestingly, later feminist writings also argued for the central power of this kind of relational thinking in forming higher-order judgments about morality, caring, and justice.[5] Similarly, from the myriad writings of artists themselves, we learn that the experience of all manner of relationships—with objects, people, events, and surroundings—provide the deeper narratives of their art.

This view of experience embedded in relationship includes two additional dimensions not always factored into the equation: the artist's relationship to his or her material, and the artist's relationship to his or her work as a "reflected upon" experience is transformed into a "re-presented" experience (Burton & Hafeli, 2010). In the process of re-presentation, and through the agency of a particular material, experience is reflected upon, possibilities are entertained, selections and combinations are constructed, and transformative experiences occur, often, as the work itself comes into being—the world and self are known differently. In short, through the process of re-presentation, the artist constructs meaning and, in so doing, becomes the generator and narrative author of his or her own knowledge.

Multi-layered exploration of relationship also occurs for children, who bring their experiences of daily life into the classrooms with them—experiences often colored with strong feelings and fantasy. As they engage in painting or drawing, they learn that their materials have particular properties and qualities that resonate more fully with some aspects of their experiences than others. As children explore and discover ever-new possibilities in materials, this new learning resonates, calling forth particular aspects of their actual lived experience (thoughts, perceptions, feelings, sensory responses), and making these available as possibilities for new exploration and elaboration. A great deal of learning takes place through this dialectic involving active, hands-on, bodily manipulations of material. As materials bring responses into focus for the mind, they simultaneously act as vehicles of reflection, provoking new shades of meaning and enriching the immediate significance of the originating thought, memory, or event.

This ongoing dialectic (between interaction with a material and reflection on the outcome) engages thinking, feeling, and sensing that, over time, are brought into new integrative constellations through the exercise of the imagination. In turn these evolutions, in Maxine Greene's (1995) terms, allow children to ask questions of, and to construct narrative about, their lives as ordinarily lived. It is the material that transforms an inner event (an experience apprehended by the mind) by taking it on a journey outward into a new kind of re-presented reality; it is the role of the imagination along this journey to interplay the different and divergent threads of this experience and intensify the outcome.

INVITED ACTS AND VOICES OF MATERIALS

The dialectic between reflection on experience and action with materials is undergirded by yet another set of considerations. Much has been written about the presence of the body in art and its pervasiveness in working with visual materials. Meaning and aesthetic presence, one might argue, are the eloquent records of the artist's body; for through the body come powerful ideas, feelings, and moods seeking wordless forms of expression. One thinks of the strong presence of the maker's body-in-action in many artworks, such as a Michelangelo dying slave, a Noguchi standing rock, a Voulkos ceramic, and, especially in the wonderful, witty-yet-serious installations in the recent Abracadabra exhibition in London's Tate Gallery. Addressing the world of everyday life and using an eclectic-hybrid attitude toward materials, the exhibition was set in an open and continuous space that, involved strong participation of the viewer's body in sharing and connecting the real and the imagined experiences of the artists. As audience to such works, permitted to wander in and out of fantastical constructions, one felt the palpable pull of body, the stirrings of the senses, the mind's ability to play in the body, to meet the maker at the place where he or she began—in action.

The role of body action and the sensory system in art and in experience also has been a topic of interest to other scholars with a more psycho-scientific purpose. Thinkers such as Piaget (1971), Bruner (1966), and Vygotsky (1978) share with Dewey the view that the foundations of mental processes lie in action on and in the world, and that embodied learning continues throughout development to be a fundamental feature of human intelligence. Moreover, Bruner (1966) and Vygotsky (1978) argue that the ability to symbolize experiences, as in language and the arts, emerges from physical-sensory action, and that representational capacities facilitate the emergence over time of complex thought.

Traditionally, development has been set forth in terms of an increasingly unified system of logical operations of the mind; nevertheless, this has largely been derived from analysis of the context and content of mathematical, philosophical, and scientific reasoning. In the context of other domains of thinking, such as the arts, we are required to think differently about the content, experiences, and operations of mind that give distinction to the complexity of human thought.

A re-casting of stage theory likewise suggests that development occurs in smaller, overlapping phases wherein new behaviors emerge over time but are not necessarily structured in equal graphic complexity. The products of these phases include specific skills, practices, and accomplishments that can be called upon flexibly in the process of creative practice. New skills enter into adolescents' artistic repertoires as they emerge, widening and deepening their constructive and expressive potential. Thus, challenges prompted by youngsters' expanding world views inspire subject-matter ideas that call into being a range of graphic possibilities; these in turn provide a reflective lens on the subject matter, provoking new thoughts and feelings for expression. This kind of flip-flop interplay between experience and repertoire is made possible by the imagination, which invites experimentation, testing, and play as possibilities are explored (Arnheim, 1974; Franklin, 1973; Greene, 1995; Smith, 1983; Wener & Kaplan, 1963). Here, imagination comes into play to inform creative intelligence and generate new meanings.

THE ROLE OF EXPERIENCES IN CHILDREN'S CREATIVE DEVELOPMENT

As we now envision it, development might be understood at one level in terms of phases, or even as gradual transitions in creative behaviors, as these are layered in complexity over time. At another level, development might also be seen in terms of what David Feldman (1994) has called "crystallizations," or the integration of phases for increasingly complex constructive and expressive purposes. Here, a range of earlier and later graphic skills may be called forth in response to a youngster's experience or idea, and may crystallize as a constructive-expressive vehicle. While such crystallizations may often be temporary, they nonetheless introduce new skills and possibilities into the young person's existing repertoire.

This conception of development would more adequately explain how children and adolescents, quite naturally and happily, appear to draw upon differently organized groups of creative behavior in single works, and how actions vary from material to material. For example, a 10-year-old may combine a complex feel for pattern and design in depicting a human figure, yet place the figure on a simple baseline more typical of a younger child. The same child working with clay may ignore pattern and design completely in favor of a concentration on the spatial volume and action of the figure. It also explains how, from time to time, creative practice appears recursive, as if youngsters need to revisit past possibilities in order to explore their potential for further growth.

DIMENSIONS OF MIND

What we now know and understand about the characteristics of artistic thinking helps to envision development in terms of an array of different capacities within a different conception of logical thought, perhaps something more akin to "sensory logic."[6] Conceived of in terms of dimensions of the mind, these capacities include motor, sensory, affective, and cognitive modes of responding; most constructive acts in the arts call forth an interplay of body sensations, feelings, and thought. More important, however, is that these dimensions of mind do not emerge only to disappear or reappear with age; rather, they emerge and continue to play increasingly complex and interdependent roles in the structuring of visual symbolic outcomes. Moreover, and again drawing upon the way artists work, we might perhaps envision these dimensions of mind emerging in terms of layers, one interpenetrating the other, framing larger and more complex constellations of thought and action over time, giving rise to evolving repertoires of possibility. The idea of sensory logic as a mechanism of the mind, is useful in providing a concept for understanding how complex constellations of mind might be held together meaningfully, while retaining their rootedness in the life and energies of the body. In simpler terms, a serviceable metaphor might be that the phases of development in the arts look rather like the layers of a painting!

TOWARD A NARRATIVE CONSTRUCTION OF THE WORLD: EARLY CHILDHOOD

Critical to our understanding of development is that it does not proceed independently of experiences in the larger world, active and purposeful engagements with materials, and teaching that is respectful of the learner yet challenging and nurturing. Given this, I draw upon what Bruner (1996) calls a "narrative construction of reality" to capture the presence of the child and adolescent at the heart of their own artistic and aesthetic experiences. I would like to think that what I present here has some universal validity—if not in these precise forms and stories that follow, then in terms of what they tell us about the underpinnings of young people's artistic interests and developmental capacities.

The ability to make visual forms and symbols emerges in children all over the world. From Africa to Alaska, children between the ages of 2 and 6 entwine scraps of wood, swoosh paint, or pummel clay and announce that the outcomes are *something*. This occurrence is a momentous and mysterious step in children's development, for in taking one thing and using it to embody or refer to some other, experiential, content, a child opens myriad possibilities for knowing the world beyond the self—and thus the self—in entirely new and exciting ways. Such a step is not a casual one, and the symbols do not emerge overnight. On the contrary, visual images are born out of a lengthy period of preparation and learning.

From the moment when infants achieve hand-eye coordination and realize that they are responsible for the markings on paper or the pileup of "stuff" that mysteriously appear before their eyes, they also learn that they have created *"something* where nothing was before." From this point onward, the excitement of discovery, linked to body action, urges an ordered journey of exploration characterized by a growing ability to perform acts of transformation on whatever materials are at hand. As children change blobs of paint into lines, and from lines into masses of "stuff;" as they change balls of clay into pancakes or combine one strip of paper with many; they become aware that all materials have distinct and distinguishing physical properties and sensory qualities. They learn, for example, that the plasticity of clay is different from that of paint; the texture of cloth different from paper; the density of line made by pencil, crayon, or chalk varies according to the pressure and speed of the hand and arm. Thus materials show their hand at the dawn of development. Materials invite motor actions, linking discovery to imagination in what will become an inexhaustible interplay guiding artistic growth and development.

Acting on and changing materials from one state of being into another leads to other kinds of learning. For instance, children learn that scattered markings or balls of clay may be grouped within "target areas" and that target areas may become surfaces that can be thought of as continuous or divisible in myriad and marvelous ways. Within or on these surfaces, young children learn they can create marks, lines, and dabs, and compile masses of "'stuff" which over time become elements to be grouped and fashioned into shapes, patterns, and relationships of infinite variety and complexity. Moreover, as children begin to order and organize their body actions purposefully, they learn that they can transform their materials in many different ways. Over time, they become attentive to dynamic and tactile properties: Lines on paper can go fast and swoosh, or slowly and drag; clay can be silky, soft, poked, and stretched; paper itself can be crumpled, piled, slotted, and woven. At the same time, young children discover that change in the physical properties of materials leads to infinite kinds of changes in their visual appearance as well. For example, every time children exert pressure in making a line, explore mixing a new color, squeeze out a clay configuration, or pile up paper and straws, they learn about such things as thickness, vibrancy, surface rhythms, and balance.[7]

Early learning is carried out with much intensity, vigor, body involvement, and evident excitement. That this excitement may well be contingent upon young children beginning to recognize a direct connection between their actions, the outcomes of their actions in the materials they use, and the inner sensations and experiences this evokes within them. Children will often accompany their activities with delightful running commentaries that describe their lines as fast, slow, wiggly, or pointy; their clay as fat and bendy; as coils dancing with each other. Over time, this act of expressive naming is soon joined by a new type of commentary, which attributes a diverse range of feelings and moods to actions and their outcomes. Children will frequently state, for example, that their lines, marks, clay, or paper shapes, are tired, happy, sad, excited, scared, or even in love. Although this kind of naming may reveal no more than a direct and instantaneous connecting of children's own immediate feelings with the products of their actions, it is nonetheless a prelude to something more momentous. Over time, children will set out with the goal of selecting certain kinds of body actions to produce lines and shapes and organize them in the creation of configurations, or whole works, which express happenings in the world colored by excitement, tiredness, happiness, and love.

STORIES OUT OF ACTION ON MATERIALS

At this early time of symbolic or representational development, children learn to create representations by naming configurations in clay, paint, paper, or crayon after they are made. The subject matter of these early proto-symbolic works is usually very fluid; quite often, names or stories are announced only to change 5 minutes later, and then to change again 5 minutes after that. The next step in this sequence of development involves naming in the process of making; a familiar configuration or design will suddenly become a "doggie with fierce teeth" or "a boat with wind and clouds." Frequently, this idea too will be amended as the work progresses, and what was a doggie could well become the story of a fight between an ant and a spider, or even end up as a clay piece called "my mom with an alligator in her pocket." Over time, children set out with a stated goal or idea in mind, which directs the course of their actions on whatever materials they use and results in an outcome reflective of an intended purpose or idea.

It is important to remember that this new occurrence in development, as young children begin to create their first re-presentations, does not override the dynamic-affective-body responsivity that had served them until this moment. Creating re-presentations is not something young children do instead of exploring and expressing their immediate feelings directly through lines, colors, and forms; rather, they begin to discover new and more complex means to articulate the imaginative and objective interplays of affective experiences in their social worlds. In short, re-presentation heralds a new layer of possibility in which meaning originating in embodied experiences becomes imaginatively structured and extended in symbolic forms. Perhaps even more critically, this new possibility allows for the mentally constructed meanings that images express to become available to reflection and further imaginative interpretation. In the process of transforming materials, new journeys are taken from an inner world of private meaning to an outer socio-cultural world within which the private expressive voice is elaborated. In short, young children become the authors of their own knowledge.

KEEPING THE DIALOGUE ALIVE: MIDDLE CHILDHOOD

It has almost become a leitmotif of artistic development, and indeed of pedagogical theory, that the years of middle childhood herald a slow decline in the dynamic responses to materials that are characteristic of earlier childhood. With attention increasingly focused on acquiring the representational conventions of the culture in drawing, painting, clay, and collage, the natural artistry and craft of the young child is subsumed by interest in technique and skill acquisition as determined by teachers and even parents. As children acquire the skills of their culture by early adolescence, this is thought to override their personal and idiosyncratic artistic expressivity, except that which is in the wayward imaginations of the specially gifted and talented.

It may sound perverse, but art education in schools too often actually closes down options and choices for children, rather than opening them up. One might argue that this is the direct result of the way we think about the role of the body and senses in art and in thought, and about materials in the shaping of ideas and responses. For centuries, the western mind has dichotomized mind and body and found little use for imagination in the construction of human meaning, even in art. Yet, and intriguingly, artistic learning can be kept alive in situations where teachers do recognize the importance of embodied responses to materials and where the environment intercedes to support the kind of thoughtful play and inquiry out of which visual ideas are born and meaning is constructed.

Where pedagogy intercedes to support development, one glimpses new and more-complex kinds of interplay between body orientation, sensory responses, and thinking. What we see by mid- to late childhood in children's engagements with different materials is the interweaving of several new levels of competence. At one level, a culture-specific set of skills comes into being in structuring or composing visual ideas; at another level comes the inclusion of increasingly complex visual details in capturing the particular character or nuance of an idea or subject; yet another level involves personal responses to the sensory-feeling qualities of materials, which carry the expressive import of the final piece. Taken together, these layers of responses offer new repertoires of possibility for the construction and expression of new kinds of meaning. Children in these middle years are curious about a world in which they are becoming active and participating members. They explore what it means to be expert at things such as sports, and how it feels to be involved in social groupings and outings. They are also increasingly skilled observers of their social world, noting in their artworks new details of the structured and human environment in which they live. They also explore more complex relationships among phenomena, testing new positional stances and vantage points.

Children's sensibilities and understandings of their world, however, are always and inevitably mediated by patterns of embodied experiences that emerge from invitations to act on materials. Aesthetic presence is endowed in the imaginative transformation of ideas from inner to outer realities, made possible by the engagements of materials and the mind, and makes so compelling the final outcome.

ADOLESCENCE: BODY, CULTURE, AND SELF

Contemporary theorists and educators demonstrate an ongoing concern about the developmental continuity of artistry into the adolescent years and beyond. One of the most difficult problems, however, is to characterize the upper reaches of artistic development and determine the nature of the journey to get there. At present, no agreement has been reached about the psychological, aesthetic, or artistic underpinnings of mature artistry. Moreover, while not all children will become artists, all are capable of constructing and expressing ideas, thoughts, and feelings through visual images.

We may have been looking for light in all the wrong places; we may have been blinded to continuing issues in artistic development by searching for symptoms of good and bad art, of talent, or of the demise of creativity. A case may be made for re-examining the issue of developmental continuity as it moves forward by looking closely at what young people *actually* accomplish in the passage from childhood to adolescent artistry, and what makes these accomplishments special.

Looked at developmentally—and in light of questions about rightness, realism, and the representation of the third dimension that youngsters themselves pose—we encounter another set of considerations. What we encounter is a rather lengthy, often idiosyncratic, and unpredictable, transitional period in artistic development when new ideas, questions, skills, and interests emerge but find no resonance within the young person's symbolic repertoire, which often remains glued to the certainties of childhood practices.

Adolescence is a time when confused thoughts and feelings emerge about place-in-the-world and about self as simultaneous subject and object of contemplation. A new intensity emerges, involving identity-related questions as disruptions to the safe continuities of childhood occur. In the arts, we are beginning to realize that two things come adrift and are polarized: the technical skills of structuring or composing visual ideas, as these are determined by the culture; and personal-idiosyncratic responses deriving from new body-sensory orientations to materials. Central to this is a resurgence of embodied responses of a kind and power last encountered in early childhood. These responses, as they re-emerge in development, implicate body perceptions intimately and directly, and often provoke wild and messy explorations in materials. The search for expressive means through which to contextualize this newly fragmented sense often results in imagery that is difficult, frightening, and sometimes deeply offensive.

In addition to their more personal forays into new ways of using visual materials, the powerful affective and dynamic roots of these new experiences also compel young people to search for more-conventional means of visual organization. It is not surprising, therefore, that their attention turns to what the culture might offer as means for organizing new and more-complex ideas about themselves and their worlds. One of the most compelling graphic conventions to grip adolescents' interests is, of course, perspective, that makes possible the representation of three-dimensional space on a flat surface. Yet we make an error of developmental judgment if we see in youngsters' struggles with perspective the desire to conquer an artistic convention or, as is often the case, a reflection of their inability to do so. Developmentally, the desire for competence in perspective is neither to create static views and vistas in the mathematical-optical-renaissance sense nor to hijack the visual clichés of the culture. Rather, the intention is to use lines and forms to transform flat surfaces into spaces that enclose living, dynamic forms.

To do this, youngsters need to be able to explore concepts of representation such as occlusion, depth, distance, movement, and directionality; further, they must understand how multiple concepts come into ever-changing relationships depending upon position and vantage point. In addition, they also need to understand that, in the arts, they can transcend the conventions of the culture; through the use of the imagination, they can bend them to their own expressive purposes. The connection of these representational struggles to youngsters' own dilemmas of locating a new physical self-in-space is not arbitrary. In the search for new means of representation during the adolescent years, perspective becomes part of the story, not an incidental cultural attachment.

SOME PERVASIVE HABITS OF MIND

Evidence suggests that the provision of arts experiences over time and in depth impacts young people's artistic learning. For example, we know that a number of specific cognitive abilities come in to being in early artistic development, and play increasingly complex roles in fashioning the kinds of experiences set forth above.

According to the Champions of Change Report (Burton, Horowitz & Abeles, 1999), four abilities, in particular, appear to play pervasive roles in artistic development: elaboration, originality, fluency, and resistance to closure. The capacity for elaboration enables youngsters to be attentive to parts and details of their perceptions and ideas, explore and bring into play further information, and in general to entertain different possibilities on an idea, problem, or experience. Originality involves seizing some of these different possibilities and reconceiving them in fresh and new ways; originality undergirds independent thinking about things, about making the familiar strange, and vice versa. Fluency engages the ability to make ideas flow, to move them forward, and to sift out and interweave ideas and responses into new unities. Resistance to closure, of course, implies the ability to keep an open and independent mind, consider possibilities, and move thinking forward into new domains of insight and understanding. Young people who have been exposed to arts education for considerable periods exhibit these abilities.

Filtering through these creative-thinking abilities are more-general competencies of thought, such as imagination, risk taking, and expressivity. If the mind is at work considering and filtering possibilities, and making leaps and jumps as part of the forward/backward movement of thought, then this dynamic is fueled by the imagination, which allows the mind to entertain the not-yet-known and open up the possibility of taking some risks and entertaining ambiguity. Despite this, it seems that, as young people reflect upon the content of their experiences, these capacities—imagination, risk taking, and expressivity—do not act as single cognitive units. Rather, they interweave, to form more broadly based habits of mind. For example, they inform youngsters' abilities to conceive of or imagine different and divergent vantage points on an idea, event, or problem. They interweave as these vantage points offer possibilities to be considered in the fashioning of an idea or question. They interweave as possibilities are layered in thought, creating new unities of meaning. They interweave to help sustain focused perception over time, and they offer a base in thought from which children can feel competent in expressing their ideas and feelings openly and thoughtfully. These habits of mind, activated through the agency of particular materials, allow experience to be reflected upon, possibilities entertained, selections and combinations constructed. As a work itself comes into being, transformative experiences often occur, whereby the world and the self are known differently.

The question of developmental continuity, and what it involves, will no doubt perplex us for some time to come. We have much to learn from thoughtful analysis of the principles and practices that guide mature artists; at the same time, we must recognize that their efforts emanate from talents, learning, and choices not accessible to young people. Anecdotal evidence shows that, if supported in education, clear-cut artistic development appears to accompany all children into adolescence, as ideas about self and world and ideas about materials and their organization come into new relationships. The forward movement of development is at times both recessive and regressive—moving backward, forward, and across in sometimes idiosyncratic and spiral motions. Over time, young people form repertoires of increasing possibility which allow them to encompass and integrate concepts and meanings that reflect responses to their changing experiences. The representational images of adolescents, and their stated reasons for making them, quite clearly distance them from childhood. It now remains for future research to offer a more fully articulated vision of the continuities and upper reaches of normative artistic development.

CONDUITS TO THE CULTURE

Perhaps because we have for so long confused aesthetic and artistic issues with developmental issues, many well-meaning observers propose that, during the adolescent years, young people should not be engaged in studio practice, but instead should develop the critical and aesthetic insights they will need as audience members within the culture. Looked at from a different (and developmental) perspective, as I argued here, a more refined approach includes acknowledging the need to shape profound and conflicting ideas about self and world through the agency of materials and visual images, coupled with the need to construct narratives of meaning and purpose that is so urgent among young people and yet so unattended to in most art education programs. From this perspective, I argue that the omission of studio practice from curricula at this stage of development is nothing short of reprehensible.

The "studio experience," a critical aspect of the environment that facilitates artistic development, is itself part of a larger constellation of influences. Equally important is that the culture, in all its forms, plays a central role in shaping human minds and action. The culture offers the tools and establishes the larger climate within which young people construct ideas about themselves and their worlds in visual materials. An examination of developmental issues not only reveals much of critical importance about the artistic and aesthetic needs of the individual during the child and adolescent years, also tells us that, from the beginning, youngsters' image-making capacities integrate ideas, techniques, systems of organization, and values drawn from the socio-political and cultural world in which they live. Their image-making capacities and the meanings they enshrine are, like experience itself, essentially culturally situated in the particular forms of private meaning that provide the basis for cultural exchange.

As young people grow and develop, however, they appear not to borrow already-formed cultural conventions instead, they distill elements, features, and details useful to their own representational concerns. Interestingly enough, contemporary research on the development of youngsters' understandings of adult artworks is beginning to reveal that their own developing artistic concerns play an important role in shaping the way they perceive and respond to works of mature artistry.[8] Youngsters' own artistic preoccupations, drawn from the world of their experience, become conduits to new aesthetic considerations. These preoccupations radiate outwards to the study of mature works, and return in the form of new insights and understandings that influence personal efforts. We are beginning to identify a number of issues that derive from young people's own image-making concerns offer bridges to the way they make overtures to mature works of art, whether from their own or other cultures.

For example, in responding to portraits in painting, a sequence of content-defined responses emerges and appears to be layered over time. These responses begin in early childhood with issues surrounding questions of identity, proceeding later to questions about character, relationship, affectivity, social position, self, and worldview. As each dimension emerges in development—in creating art as well as making or appraising the work of others—it appears to offer expanding networks of possible responses for youngsters to draw upon. Other kinds of responses, such as responses to the role and effects of color, texture, expressivity, and aesthetic value, also emerge in layered sequence and combine with content responses to guide youngsters' relationships with mature works. Such responses are also found in youngsters' work with new media, where deeply personal image-making not only draws upon contemporary cultural resources, but also becomes the conduit to critical appreciation. The kinds of confused identity-based images adolescents have traditionally created in painting, drawing, and sculpture now find a home in digital technology. Nevertheless, the kinds of cultural distillations and critical appraisals associated with both new and traditional art forms remain linked directly to youngsters' own experiential worlds. It seems that young people construct important relationships between their own personal knowledge and interests, and what the larger culture presents to them, by way of images and artifacts made by others. In this way, personal aesthetic judgments are framed by what is known and valued from the past or practiced in the present, and form a continuum of understanding. In a very direct manner, young people lend their lives to the interpretation and appraisal of the work of others.

We know that even very young children can unravel the symbolic meaning of adult works as this relates to themselves and their own interests. We know, too, that this kind of evolving rich and layered repertoire of responses (to their own work and to that of others) lead young people to fashion complex relationships with their cultural environment. We also know that the construction of this subtle and important network of relationships can easily be demolished by teaching that does not honor what children and adolescents themselves bring to the pursuit of their own learning,

THE FACILITATING ENVIRONMENT

It is necessary to reiterate that this developmental picture will not occur to any degree of fullness if the facilitating environment does not intercede in its support. Artistic development will not occur in any richness and depth in situations where it is assumed that simple "exposure to materials" is all that is needed to direct children's efforts. However much children and adolescents may seem to learn on their own in creating images and in their quests for meaning, they cannot accomplish this by themselves unaided. For development to occur, experiences in the arts must be provided in schools, and teachers must be encouraged to learn from young people that which in their experience most compels them, and what drives their aesthetic interests.

Here, the role of the teacher becomes crucial. For it is the task of the teacher to read development, promote learning, and create a classroom atmosphere of trust and caring in which exploration and learning can take place. It is critical that teachers are knowledgeable enough about development and contemporary culture to help each child in their classes contextualize and situate learning in the context of their own experience. Also crucial to success is the notion that teachers provoke imagination and critical reflection and are able to evoke situations and experiences of profound import to the youngsters they teach. If learning is situated in compelling personal contexts, then it will take hold and be grounded enough to inform the emergence of new ways of knowing, thinking, and re-presenting. Only when learning is grounded in a personal context will it demonstrate a shared salience.

One way in which teachers can both challenge and nurture development is through classroom dialogue. It was, of course, Plato in the guise of Socrates who argued that dialogue is the rational path to knowledge of Truth, Goodness, and Beauty as well as the highest form of teaching. Reframed around a broader conception of knowledge, dialogue has come to mean an open-ended communication, investigation, or inquiry between teachers and learners and/or among learners, instead of conveying knowledge as static, the sole possession of the teacher, and something to be passed on to and acquired by the learner. Teaching through dialogue presupposes a free and continuous interchange of ideas that is actively directed toward reflection, discovery, and new understanding. Teaching through dialogue also embodies a recognition that children and adolescents are thinkers who are fully able to marshal their ideas and imaginations in the service of developing their own visual symbolic capacities. In short, teaching through dialogue not only opens children to new ways of thinking, but it also empowers their understanding and sense of agency, and gives them insights into the ways in which knowledge emerges and is constructed and expressed in and through visual images.

Teaching through dialogue is not a laissez-faire pedagogical practice, nor is it a simple free-for-all conversation. For dialogue to be successful in promoting learning, it needs to be thoughtfully structured around a sequence of questions that advances the learning of the lesson. Sometimes a dialogue may be more narrowly structured with specific learning in mind, and at other times more open-ended, to lead toward exploration and discovery.

Regardless of whether the dialogue is narrowly focused or broadly phrased, it requires that the teacher knows enough about children's perceptions to pace the interchange to their needs, capacities, interests, and levels of understanding. Equally important is that the teachers themselves need to have a rich inventory of insights and experiences in the arts, a nuanced repertoire they can call upon in the service of responding to young people's reflections and questions as the dialogue moves forward. Teachers need to be able to engage children's reflective capacities in a way that allows new learning to first be grounded within existing schemas of understanding and action, then challenged to move toward new insights, responses, and imaginative applications.

Many virtues and values attach to the practice of teaching through dialogue in the arts. In the first place, it inhibits the kind of dreary uniformity of outcome in making and appraising that is the consequence of "telling and demonstration." It also does not presume that children's minds are blank slates or empty buckets waiting to be filled. An effective dialogue will allow an interweaving of personal sensory, affective, and cognitive responses as youngsters reflect on their experiences and, through imaginative reconstruction, give them voice in and though visual materials. A provocative dialogue will also promote self-reflection, recognition, and tolerance for diversity, as well as an ability to listen to and learn from the ideas and thoughts of others. In addition, a thoughtful dialogue will offer youngsters insights into how ideas are made, how they relate to each other in sequence, and how they build in complexity to larger ideas or concepts. A challenging dialogue is just that—it gives meaning in terms of an individual's personal development by opening the person to the powers of scrutiny, investigation, inquiry, and questioning. By the same token, the teacher must be able to offer through dialogue insights and understandings about materials, techniques, and visual ideas that meet the learner where he or she is in the process of personal meaning making.

A FINAL WORD

Many threads form the tapestry of artistic development as it flows from infancy to adolescence and perhaps, beyond—some of which I have attempted to sketch this chapter. I have presented a picture of youngsters' minds as they engage in the arts, through both making and critical appraisal, become centered within their experiences of self/world and relationships. Youngsters' minds consist of inextricable mixtures of personal and cultural dimensions; and engagement in the arts offers them the means to construct the kinds of narratives they need in order to make a complex world meaningful to them. In their aesthetic presence and the demands they make upon the imagination visual images become compelling and open the mind to new corners of reality. This vision of mind and of art places children at the heart of their own lived experiences, but these experiences are themselves culturally formed and involve the actions and perceptions of others. For this reason, the child-centered notion of mind that has informed art education for so long is inadequate. Also inadequate is the belief in laissez-faire teaching, which does not honor youngsters' needs to be taken seriously as thinkers and to be challenged as artists. If learning is to occur, and visual symbolizing capacities are to do their work, then focused experiences with materials must be paced to interests and capacities. Similarly, personal studio experiences must offer bridges toward understanding the narratives of others, just as they in turn are enriched by new insights provided by those others.

We sometimes forget that we are not born knowing how to get ideas into materials, or how materials can be manipulated to shape ideas and meaning. These are constructs of the human senses and mind, and thus need to be nurtured in a thoughtful and disciplined way. In our anxiety to initiate children and adolescents into the norms and conventions of the culture, we sometimes overlook the fact that culture exists only through the personal expressive endeavors of individuals working with materials, going beyond cultural norms. By acting on materials to transform them, ideas become form, imagination is engaged to this end, and the form assumes particular aesthetic presence. Through using materials, children carve a niche for themselves in time, space, and human culture, becoming participants in an ancient ritual.

We forget much too much. Perhaps this is why young people are so bored?

ENDNOTES

1   Parts of this chapter first appeared in "The Configuration of Meaning: Learner-centered Art Education Revisited," *Studies in Art Education, 41*(4), Summer 2000.

2   Maxine Greene begins her preface to the new edition of John Dewey's *How We Think* (1999) by pointing out how far we are from the kind of educational vision offered by Dewey in 1933.

3   This section on development draws on the work and writings of Margery Franklin, Nancy R. Smith, Heinz Werner, and Bernard Kaplan, along with many studies on artistic development I have carried out with my students over the past 20 years or so at Boston University and Columbia University Teachers College.

4   This was a theme Viktor Lowenfeld introduced in the first edition of *Creative and Mental Growth* (1947) and which re-occurred in the next three editions, but became somewhat lost in subsequent re-writings.

5   This focus is found particularly well developed in the writings of Carol Gilligan and Nel Noddings.

6   I first used the term "*sensory logic*" in the Developing Mind Series I authored for *School Arts* in 1980-81. In the second article, "The First Visual Images," I used the term to show how these early images obeyed a certain kind of aesthetic-sensory organization while confounding traditional rules of visual appearance. The term seems particularly apt in this context. The idea of sensory logic was further developed in "The Integrity of Personal Experience, or the Presence of Life in Art" as it appeared in the *International Journal of Arts Education (3*(2), 2005).

7   This behavior has typically been called "scribbling"—a term that does disservice to the serious and organized learning that is taking place.

8   This section draws on the findings of several small interview studies carried out over a 10-year period at Columbia University Teachers College. The studies involved groups of adolescents who were invited to share, with an interviewer, responses to their own paintings and to those made by mature artists. To date, more than 100 adolescents have been interviewed. These studies are being prepared for publication.

REFERENCES

Arnheim, R. (1974). *Art and visual perception*. Berkeley, CA: University of California Press.

Bruner, J. (1996). *The culture of education*. Cambridge, MA: Harvard University Press.

Bruner, J. (1966). The growth of representational processes in children. *Proceedings of the 18th. International Congress of Psychology,* Moscow, 1966.

Burton, J. M., & Hafeli, M. (2012). *Conversations in art: The dialectics of teaching and learning*. Reston, VA: NAEA.

Burton, J., Horowitz, R., & Abeles, H. (1999). Learning in and through the arts: Curriculum implications. In Edward B. Fiske (Ed.), *Champions of change: The impact of the arts on learning*. Washington, DC: Art Education Partnership.

Burton, J. M. (2002). Regarding Madame Matisse: Conversations across worlds. Unpublished paper, Teachers College Columbia University.

Dewey, J. (1934). *Art as experience*. New York, NY: Capricorn Books.

Feldman, D. (1994). *Beyond universals in cognitive development*. Norwood, NJ: Ablex.

Franklin, M., & Kaplan, B. (1994). *Development and the arts: Critical perspectives*. Hillsdale, NJ: Erlbaum.

Franklin, M. (1973). Non-verbal representation in young children. *Young Children, 33-52.*

Gilligan, C. (1993). *In a different voice: Psychological theory and women's development*. Cambridge, MA: Harvard University Press.

Greene, M. (2001). *Variations on a blue guitar*. New York, NY: Teachers College Press.

Greene, M. (1995). *Releasing the imagination*. San Francisco, CA: Jossey-Bass.

Lowenfeld, V. (1947). *Creative and mental growth*. New York, NY: Macmillan.

Noddings, N. (2003). *Caring: A feminist approach to ethics and moral education*. Berkeley, CA: University of California Press.

Piaget, J. (1971). *The language and thought of the child*. New York, NY: Meridian Books.

Smith, N. (1983). *Experience and art: Teaching children to paint*. New York, NY: Teachers College Press.

Werner, H., & Kaplan, B. (1963). *Symbol formation*. Hillsdale, NY: Erlbaum.

Vygotsky, L. S. (1978). *Mind in society*. Cambridge, MA: Harvard University Press.

ABOUT THE AUTHOR

Judith M. Burton is Professor and Director of Art & Art Education at Columbia University Teachers College. Before that she was Chair of Art Education at Boston University and taught at the Massachusetts College of Art. Burton received her EdD from Harvard University. Her research focuses on the artistic/aesthetic development of children, adolescents, and young adults. She co-founded the Center for Research in Arts Education at Teachers College, and founded the Heritage School in Harlem, NY— a comprehensive high school featuring the arts. She has received the Edwin Ziegfeld Award; the Manuel Barkan Award; and the Lowenfeld Award, all from National Art Education Association (NAEA). Burton is a Fellow of the Royal Society for the Arts in Great Britain, a Distinguished Fellow of NAEA, and Distinguished Visiting Professor at the Central Academy of Fine Arts in Beijing, China. She was recently nominated as a Trustee of the Maryland Institute College of Art.

CHAPTER 2

Art Practice as Relational and Transformative Research

Graeme Sullivan

In her acclaimed performance as Blanche DuBois in the 2009 Brooklyn Academy of Music production of Tennessee Williams' play, *A Streetcar Named Desire*, Cate Blanchett suggests that Blanche reminds us of what we've lost. Written in the late 1940s, when America was flexing its military muscle, the macho optimism that swept the country could be seen and felt everywhere, even in the provincial world of Stanley Kowalski, where every man was king of his castle. But it is Blanche who helps us see beyond the limits of what can be controlled, consumed, or conquered. When interviewed on National Public Radio, Cate Blanchett explained that, as seen through Blanche's "prism," part of the past that's been lost is the "death of poetry, the death of idealism, the death of that sort of reality–the validity that someone can actually create something ephemeral and beautiful, that one can't touch and hold and has no monetary value" (Lunden, 2009, para. 15). She added, "they're very different states that both exist within America, but maybe it's a time where we can re-evaluate those fragile things we've lost."

Though social and political conditions have obviously changed since the play's release more than 60 years ago, its themes resonate today. It is often what is lost that has particular import to the field of education in general, and art education in particular. When reflecting the concerns of the larger society, for instance, the prism currently used to cast light on education reflects a vision that tries to control the consumption of knowledge in order to conquer the onslaught of the information economy—often at the expense of other, non-material, needs of young people, such as the concerns for holistic development addressed in this anthology. Under these circumstances, it may be opportune to look at what we've lost in the past as a way to anticipate what we may need in the future. If it is acknowledged that present-day reality is shaped not only by information that is fleeting (and understanding that is fluid), but also by experience that is fundamental, then it can be argued that the arts play a most vital role in helping us respond to the uncertainties of the age.

In reflecting on the challenges facing art education, it is necessary to heed Cate Blanchett's advice and look backward and forward at the same time. The caution sometimes etched on the side mirror of a car reads: "Objects in the mirror are closer than they appear." This saying can also be used as a guide to see if things from the past loom larger than they really are, and to consider whether they have the capacity to overtake us and lead to new ways to think about what lies ahead. The desire to chart different directions in response to new challenges is at the heart of art education; nevertheless, enduring artistic concepts and practices continue to sustain art learning as a critical and creative agency of human understanding. Sensing the possible is what art educators do best, but achieving goals that are both unanticipated and expected means that what might be seen to be an illusion from the past may need to be brought into full view if enduring values and beliefs are to shape the creative and critical practices necessary to build a new vision of art education for this young century.

One enduring truth that is sometimes lost amid the rhetoric of justifying art education is the very reason why most of us found our way into the field in the first place: We were entranced by the experience of making art from a very early age, and, somewhere along the way, someone else valued what we did. Since then, most of us have felt the need to share our passion, and so we became enamored by the opportunity to excite others about art. Yet this generous impulse can overwhelm us, absorbing our time and diverting our creative energies entirely toward teaching and away from making. I argue that something of the original impulse must be held in reserve, cherished, nurtured, and developed; the life of an art educator ceases to exist if the person stops making art. This is certainly true, for those who choose to make art for a living; they have an unmitigated need to create things that they believe sustains their very being. A recent study on aging artists in New York showed that artists never "retire" in the conventional sense; they continue to make art as long as they are "above ground" (Jeffri, 2007). Jeffri's study shows that aging artists, unlike the stereotype of people becoming more isolated as they age, tend to remain passionate and display high self-esteem and life satisfaction because of their active art practice. Artists stay engaged and productive well past retirement age, and if given the chance to select their profession over again, they would not choose differently. Much can be learned from this belief and commitment because it reflects the capacity of art to satisfy deeply felt human needs. Similarly, those who teach art take as their mantra the goal of immersing others in the experience of art. Through personal passion and a profound appreciation of the importance of the creative and critical imagination in human development, art teachers take on a purposeful educational role so that young people continue to develop to their full potential as they grow. The challenge, then, is to keep growing as artists ourselves. Those involved in art in teacher-education institutions and university settings are similarly challenged to sustain the life-long artistic development of future teachers. Despite these responsibilities, university-based art educators need to maintain their creative selves through the acts of making that keep them grounded in their original motivations and purposes, ideally integrating their various roles as teachers, researchers, and makers to the benefit of all.

Responding to the challenge of keeping an eye on past visions while addressing new realities, this chapter focuses on issues surrounding theories and practices of research that are relational and transformative, and thereby central to teaching and learning practices in art education. The purpose of the chapter is to review some research strategies used by artists and art educators to inquire into issues, ideas, and problems, as well as how these creative and critical practices can influence what is done in classrooms, institutions, and communities. At the center of inquiries undertaken in artistic contexts is the desire to create new knowledge and understanding. Whether encountered as the imaginative explorations of the very young, the reflective incursions of adolescents, or the conceptual excursions of mature artists, the artistic impulse is motivated by a need to relate and transform things.

Artistic insights inform us about what we don't know, and therefore change what we *do* know. This process is both reflective and reflexive in that we not only think differently by experiencing art, but we are impelled as well to act on these impulses by making art or talking about it with others. Similarly, artistic insights derive from artistic inquiry and encourage further investigations into unfamiliar terrain. Artistic inquiry, thus defined, has important individual, communal, and cultural outcomes; in looking backward and forward, past strengths and future prospects alike are considered. In this way, new understandings emerge by building on what is "known" to add new insights and perspectives; here, the creative pursuit involves moving from the "known to the unknown." On the other hand, arts practitioners are also intensely interested in the possibility of the unknown because fresh ideas are often found from a position unburdened by tradition or convention; here, the creative pursuit involves moving from the "unknown to the unknown."

Linking all art practitioners—whether they are artists, teachers, researchers, theorists, students, or participants (or all of the above)—is an awareness that art can connect us, and it can change us. In other words, art is a creative and critical practice that has the capacity to transform individual and collective understanding. Art practice in its various forms therefore makes use of approaches that are imaginative in their reach and eclectic in their scope, yet are no less rigorous in their procedural demands and applications than other forms of disciplined inquiry. Drawing on such principles, recent arguments have positioned artmaking at the center of the research and teaching process (Biggs & Karlssohn, 2011), Macleod & Holdridge, 2006; Smith & Dean, 2009; Sullivan, 2010). This chapter draws on this research to present art practice as a relational and transformative mode of inquiry that is similar to, but different from, more-mainstream methods of research. To support this argument, a parallel narrative illustrates how art practice can be seen as relational and transformative research that has individual significance and community impact. Together, these narratives suggest certain implications for teacher training and P-12 art education. At particular points throughout the chapter, artist Frank Shifreen joins me in this discussion to exemplify the role of art as an agency of communication and change. Extended quotes by Frank accompany the captions for the images used throughout the chapter.

Frank Shifreen has lived in New York for a long time, working along the fringes of the art world in those "in-between" community spaces where artists' collectives thrive and where the art is passionate, prolific, and public. Frank is a certified art teacher who has extensive experience teaching in community centers, hospitals, and jails, and particularly with homebound students, yet he manages to create a seamless connection among the many educational and artistic roles he takes on. He is also a doctoral candidate whose research interests involve theorizing notions of non-institutional art through his practice. Frank continually looks to involve artists in projects that have community interest and invest in social transformation. Often personal and always political, the art he creates and curates is of the moment. Many projects are site-based community actions; Frank has been initiating these events since the 1970s. Some are referenced throughout this chapter, and open up ideas about art practice as relational and transformative inquiry.

ARTISTIC INQUIRY THAT CONNECTS AND CHANGES

The discussion introducing this chapter brings to mind an old question often asked about art education theory: Is art valued for its intrinsic or its instrumental impact? Past arguments variously assert that one is educated "through" art (Read, 1949) or educated "in" art (Eisner, 1972). In that perspective, art learning is believed to be a means to help achieve broad goals aimed at a range of developmental, discipline, and social interests; or it is acknowledged that there is merit in experiencing art because of its unique individual and cultural significance.

In retrospect, this distinction offers a false choice. The educational outcomes that are generated from the making and understanding of art emerge from a range of changing relational and transformative practices that take place "between," "around," "within," and "across" theories and practices of art; that is, between and around issues and ideas that encompass what art is about, and within and across the forms of artistic inquiry that artists use. To appreciate the breadth and depth of these spaces where art practice flourishes, it is necessary to ditch past dichotomies that separate art from life. Similarly, to continue to isolate what art teachers do from what artists do, or what art theorists do from what art practitioners do, has little rhetorical appeal and certainly no practical merit.

About the only place where we are still constricted by past descriptions of the differences among "art teachers," "art students," "artists," or "artist-teachers" is in schools and universities, where the safety of discipline boundaries and social mythologies about reclusive artists keeps these populations comfortably apart. Yet in a wider sociocultural reality, when the challenge of new times requires different ways of thinking and acting, the art practitioner blends the best from the past as it is reinvented in the present. Even a quick review of radical changes within contemporary art, cultural production across new global geographies, research collaborations between the arts and sciences, and innovative changes around digital technologies reveals rich environments where artists are taking on new research and pedagogical roles.

Given this current reality, for the purpose of this chapter I use the term "artist-researcher" to describe a practitioner who is driven by a profound belief in the importance of art as a means of inquiring into the world around us, with an understanding that making and encountering art is an intensely educational act. This term encompasses the seemingly disparate occupations listed here, potentially linking artists, teachers, and art students together in a similar pursuit. For example, when we make art and place it in a public space (be it a gallery, community, classroom, or a virtual setting), the artwork opens up an opportunity for others to respond. This is an enduring human form of engagement, and the places (actual or virtual) in which this engagement occurs can be considered "learning spaces," regardless of whether they involve formal instruction. In the remainder of this chapter, I explore these potential creative and critical learning spaces and the theoretical and methodological constructs that surround them, once again, in conversation with the artist Frank Shifreen.

ART PRACTICE AND RELATIONAL CONTENT

Several important relational features are formed "between" and "around" visual arts practices, as artist-researchers respond to concerns addressing what art is about and how this content can be explored. These relational features reflect the evolving nature of art and its place in contemporary society. As such, they influence what we do in the diverse artistic and pedagogical roles we take on. For instance, when investigating the relational aspects "between" theories, artist-researchers look at connecting ideas and issues through practices of problem-finding, meaning-making, and creative and critical questioning, while those involved in teaching use these practices themselves as well as guide others to apply them in widely differing situations. On the other hand, when exploring relational issues and ideas "around" theories, artist-researchers look outward at the surrounding contexts that bring order to the complex realities faced. Similarly, art educators prepare future art teachers to take such contexts and realities into account as they enter the classroom. These two relational areas of art practice are explored below.

Relating Issues and Ideas "Between" Theories

A function of theory is to explain things. Theories are summaries of the way we understand how the world works. Nevertheless, theories come in many forms that are themselves the outcomes of different research approaches. Irrespective of the theoretical questions that are addressed, there will be a range of content and methods within which any idea or inquiry can be positioned. Often it is imagined that the realm of theory and the realm of practice are worlds apart, especially in the arts. Likewise, art teachers may take little interest in educational theories. Yet, in pursuing a relational research practice, artist-researchers engage directly with theoretical concerns that can be investigated in studio and classroom contexts. Problem-finding, for instance, tends to draw together ideas and issues that emerge from situational factors, while the meaning-making that occurs when creative links are made between informing theories tends to rely on broader interpretive and hermeneutical processes. Similarly, oppositions are often drawn between creativity and critical thinking. Despite this, a generic approach in responding to topical issues that has a long tradition within visual arts is evident in the work of artists who use their creative insight to pursue a critical stance. Invoking a critical perspective often is directed by personal passions, yet tempered by the creative tension seen between issues and ideas that bring theoretical views into sharp relief. In this way, content that is grounded in particular theoretical frameworks is opened up to critical gaze and creative interpretation by artists as well as art teachers.

An instance where an artist-researcher critiques particular theoretical perspectives that were prominent in the field of art and art education at the time is seen in a project led by Frank Shifreen in the early 1980s called *The Monument Defined*. From his early days as an artist and teacher in New York City, Frank pursued a transgressive art practice that unfolded on the fringes of the art world and outside formal educational settings. Eschewing the burgeoning commercial Soho art market of the time, Frank and a community-minded colleague, Scott Silken, sought to claim a sense of artistic autonomy and purpose for art that had collective agency. They put together a loose coalition of publicly spirited artists, and reclaimed large tracts of disused local space, murky, stagnant Gowanus Canal in south Brooklyn, New York, as a huge exhibition site for public art. Their contention was that "public art today has lost its content, its social responsibility to communicate" (cited in Glueck, 1982, p. 27).

The site of this public art project was a five-acre abandoned lot adjacent to the canal, which was once the location of an active barge waterway community. Far from being dispirited by the toxic area, Frank, who lived locally among a small but active artist community, was enthralled by the potential of art to inhabit these disused spaces. The result was provocative. *New York Times* art critic Grace Glueck described it this way:

> The left bank of the Gowanus Canal, an unlovely piece of real estate in South Brooklyn, seems hardly the most propitious site for an outdoor art show. Yet there, at Smith and Fifth Streets, on a five-acre former dump rife with weeds, trash middens and expired auto bodies, blooms the Gowanus Memorial Art Yard. A city-owned facility preempted for the moment by sculptors, it—along with two other indoor locations—serves as a setting for "The Monument Redefined," a vastly ambitious show with more than 150 participants, whose stated aim is to encourage new interpretations of the public monument. (1982, p. 27)

FIGURE 1. *The Monument Redefined Poster.* 1982. Design by Frank Shifreen, Scott Siken, Scott Lloyd. An artist-organized project situated along the Gowanus Canal, Brooklyn, New York. In reflecting on his long-term interest in community-based art, Frank Shifreen described his practice in terms of cultural inquiry:

> *My interest is investigating the actions, groupings and patterns of artists outside the gallery, museum and the academic system. There are no impermeable barriers to those systems, and artists cross the borders at various times. The anthropologist Victor Turner (1969) studied the counterculture, and coined the term* liminoid, *and noted many characteristics that seemed to accurately portray the society of artists in this demi-monde. Unlike the* liminal, *which refers to being part of society, the liminoid is a break, a rupture. Turner believed the liminoid to be essential to highly charged, creative societies, which are constantly changing and evolve in a state of flux between structure and anti-structure. (2007, p. 2)*

A sense of local community spirit of the kind that Frank Shifreen encouraged is captured in a blog excerpt by a community-minded resident, Katia Kelly, who posted an exchange with Frank in the wake of debates about the Gowanus Canal being declared a superfund polluted site and plans for redevelopment.

> There has been so much talk of late about the future of the Gowanus Canal. The area is ready to become just another high rise, high prized condo neighborhood if our politicians and developers have their way. And with that, we are loosing [sic] one more New York City enclave where artists thrived and created. How rich and fertile artistically the shores of the Gowanus were as far back as the early 1980s became clear to me when I received an email from artist Frank Shifreen. Frank used to live near the Gowanus Canal at 3rd and 3rd, in his words "in the greatest (I thought) loft in the city." Using this great space, Shifreen started opening his doors and exhibited his works as well as those of fellow artists. By around 1979, these art happenings allowed the creative community to come together and to thrive in the unlikely area around the Gowanus. The shows were such a success that he decided to set his sights on an even bigger space. The heavily polluted "Public Space" site on Smith and Fifth Street was just big enough for what he had in mind. Securing grants from the Brooklyn Council On the Arts, with help from Gowanus Canal Community Development Corporation and the Carroll Gardens Association, Shifreen curated the "Monumental [sic] Redefined Show." He asked 150 artists to contribute works, gave each a lot of 20 by 20 foot and turned the 5 acre abandoned lot into the coolest art space. His purpose was to encourage artists to push the limits of public art, to communicate socially and to engage the public. "The ideas I was trying to discuss, art in the community, political art: 'messages', not didactic," Shifreen wrote to me in an email. It must have been quite an event. Hundreds of people came to this remote area of the Gowanus Canal to see the "Monument Redefined Show." It was hailed as the event of the season. For many months, the works of art could be seen from the F train as it came out of the ground at the Carroll Street Station en route to Park Slope. Shifreen wrote that some of the art work was still there until the 1990's. (Kelly, 2007, para. 2-4)[1]

Not only did the Gowanus project give Frank Shifreen and his cadre of artists an opportunity to invigorate local consciousness, but it also served as an example of art practice undertaken outside the bounds of formal discourse. The New York art world in the early 1980s was a curious place where artists, galleries, and critical discourse were all seemingly becoming part of the Manhattan real estate boom and best seen for their commercial value. Critics were replaced by gossip columnists, and collectors by investors, while hype and self-promotion became the distinctive means used by the new art stars on the block. It was as if the art world re-created itself as a sealed, self-congratulatory space, while any serious theorizing became sequestered within the walls of the academy.

The field of art education at the time also was undergoing a fundamental transformation—in this case as a result of the powerful critique of American education captured in *A Nation at Risk* (National Commission of Excellence in Education, 1983), which called for a drastic return to the basic elements of *reading, 'riting,* and *'rithmetic.* The response was to shift the emphasis in school-based art curricula to a subject-centered focus where learning "about" art became the primary goal, and this meant drawing content from the disciplines that informed the teaching of art (Greer, 1984). For some art educators, past expressive traditions grounded in studio experience were an anathema to what art education should be about. Ralph Smith suggested the "single purpose" (1986, p. 18) of art education was aesthetic knowing, while for Vincent Lanier (1982) it was important to respond to the new technologies of visual culture, but this could be done without the help of any studio practice. Considering theoretical perspectives about art and art education at the time, the community-based art practice of artist-researchers such as Frank Shifreen may appear to have been part of a romantic counter-culture from the past. Instead, his work "in-between" theories reflected the very heart of art and art education as an original and purposeful response to perceived needs. The importance of the creative impulse as a challenge to assumed attitudes, values, and beliefs, as well as a hinge to link valid cultural theories and significant practices, is even more relevant today when local necessity is being swamped by global overreach.

Relating Issues and Ideas "Around" Theories

If relating issues and ideas "between" theories brings aspects of content into critical focus, then drawing attention to the broader conceptual landscape "around" theories increases the scope and responsibility of art practice to contribute to how we understand things. By its very nature, creating and exhibiting art is a personal and public act, and therefore takes on a communicative and educational role, irrespective of whether an artist intends to do so. An important outcome of working "with" art and experiencing it is to realize the range of opportunities that arise for others as a consequence of artmaking. For those teaching art in schools or those training art teachers, this means taking a closer look at the nature and purpose(s) of displaying student art and visiting galleries or museums. By doing so, they may recognize that the theories and practices that emerge from encounters and discussions about art open up new meanings, offer alternative interpretations, and precipitate responses and actions. In the past, this role has been energetically taken up by cultural theorists, art historians, critics, and the like.

These days, it is artists themselves who often take up the task of "theorizing" their practice by placing their work in broader socio-cultural and political contexts. This can be seen, for example, in the number of contemporary artists who adopt the role of artist-curators as part of their art practice, whereby they readily position contemporary art within broader realms of discourse and theory. The tradition of artists taking elements like theory into their own hands is, of course, not new; it was taken up by many avant-garde modernists when they were unable to gain entry into established salons and chose to make their own statements. Translating this tradition into the contemporary classroom, teachers may increasingly expect their students to be able to frame their work within broad sociocultural contexts. Similarly, art education students are now expected to be able to discuss their work from a variety of perspectives as part of their Praxis II certification requirement.

Another feature of the broadening of the theoretical areas opened up by artists is evident in the way the "studio" has been reinvented to embrace a much more expansive notion of where art is made and viewed. Part of the conceptual challenge to modernist views of the mythology of the artist as a studio-bound individual was the move to a post-object position, where the creative process could be enacted in just about any available space, no matter how impermanent. By the same token, the definition of art has expanded to include non-permanent, or ephemeral, objects, as well as non-objects such as conceptual and performance art. Given such circumstances, it becomes difficult to categorize artist-researchers such as Gabriel Orozco by national identity, artist-type, or distinctive stylistic practice because the places and circumstances that inform his practices, the settings and audiences for his work, and the forms he creates and annotates resist classification (Temkin, 2009). The points of reference upon which his art touches continually change through different histories, politics, art theories, and cultural geographies. Teaching about art nowadays requires more flexible thinking along with an expansive knowledge base in order to consider artists and their work in relation to the larger contexts in which they live. Similarly, students must also be able to look reflectively at their own art in the context of increasingly complex relationships including family, community, environment, and the multiplicity of cultures.

FIGURE 2. Frank Shifreen. *Art Against War Poster.* 2003. Digital image. The poster was used in the first of the series of Art Against War exhibitions in the Macy Gallery at Teachers College, Columbia University; and the New York Arts Space Gallery in Soho. The poster was updated in August 2003 with additional exhibition sites. Shifreen states:

> This is about information and sharing it. The idea of the Art Against War show was posters. I believe in clarity. That is the beauty of a poster. It was interesting to read the history of posters and they started as indulgences for the church, to fund the war against the Sultan. The idea of having artists make posters that were clear and to the point was telling. What was nice was that the show was open to anyone: students, professional artists and non-artists. The poster got a lot more play in some of the other venues around the world than it did in the galleries in New York. I think the viral nature of it was interesting as a research project and as an art exhibition in eight galleries around the world and back and forth into the web. Shows were staged from June, 2003, to 2005, culminating in Mumbai Social Forum IV. (Personal communication, March 10, 2009)

Artist-run collectives in recent decades also present examples of art practice being used for its relational capacity to embrace broad content and to excite theoretical discourse that is mostly outside mainstream debate. These are often anti-establishment responses that not only critique the art world and institutional systems, but also often bring broader sociopolitical issues into debates about art, culture, and education. An example is the "Art Against War"[2] project initiated by Frank Shifreen and a growing collection of artists that began in 2003 as a critique of the United States' invasion of Iraq. Bringing his well-known sociocultural consciousness and belief in the political responsibility of artists, Frank curated an exhibition of anti-war posters that overflowed in two galleries in New York City in 2003. The response continued with more artists from around the US and overseas sending in work, so the exhibition grew and travelled and also took on a presence online as a parallel Internet exhibition. Frank described the idea behind the project this way:

> The exhibition consists of printed and handmade posters, video and sound works. It is being shown concurrently in two New York galleries and on three independent and connected website exhibitions. The show is an example of a new kind of community collective combining digitally assembled and traditionally curated art. Over 40 artists contributed work. In addition to pieces developed by local artists, there are works submitted by artists from across the country and from thirteen other countries from around the world... The dynamic between these two forms [verbal text and visual image] conveys impressions on an emotional as well as an intellectual level even though some of the pieces in the show do not have words. Certain messages, impulses, perceptions, or narratives can be conveyed and appreciated without the use of language. I hope that the ambiguity of the works will be evocative as well as mysterious. This dichotomy reflects our contemporary life in that a narrative can be understood without any language whatsoever. (2003, n.p.)

ART PRACTICE AND TRANSFORMATIVE INQUIRY

An important feature of art practice is that it is not only viewed as a set of relational approaches to issues and ideas, but also serves as a form of transformative inquiry; as artist-researchers immerse themselves in their creative and critical practice, they are also changed by this process. This means that the creative and critical process of making art and encountering art follows a recursive pattern, and constantly undergoes change as new experiences "talk back" to the artist and the viewer. Similar patterns of transformation emerge from the interchanges between the art teacher and the art student. This transformative nature of art practice is best seen in its reflexivity and post-discipline structure. I describe these as "braided" and "self-similar" systems (Sullivan, 2010), and they are explored more fully in this section.

Transformative Inquiry "Within" Braided Practices

It may be argued that art practice as a form of inquiry not only has the potential to yield important human insights, but also has the power to change the way we come to understand our lifeworlds. It is based on several claims that can be defended. First, as post-modernism affirms, there is a need to reject the tendencies of the past that squeeze art through filters looking for its "essence"—be it educational outcomes, social agency, communicative power, or cultural language. When an experience "with" art is profound, the capacity to learn can reach in many directions in response to individual passions, proclivities, or prompts. Second, artistic inquiry embodies a reflective and reflexive quality that "works against" existing theories and practices, and offers the possibility of seeing phenomena in new ways. This is an "infolding" inquiry process that is directed by creative insight and knowledge and requires an artist-researcher to "see through" existing information and contexts so as to be open to alternative conceptions and imaginative options. Therefore the artist-researcher has the capacity to see things in a critical and transparent manner and responds in a creative way.

Issues-based inquiry of this kind not only identifies problems, but also opens up areas whereby participants become responsive to potential change. For example, artist-researchers working within formal educational settings are challenged to help younger students recognize and eventually participate in this messy, experimental, non-linear form of working through visual ideas, especially as they seek their own artistic identities. This is evident, for example, in the personal projects required for high school Advanced Placement courses and students studying in International Baccalaureate programs, as well as in the portfolios of those aspiring to higher education in visual art. But even those who are less advanced or less committed as art learners could be presented with this more complex vision of the creative process by looking at the many patterns of change that occur when making artworks, and the different pathways followed in the life of an artist. As artist-researchers ourselves, we can draw upon personal examples by tracing the history of our own work, acknowledging the problems that hampered our progress, and the unexpected influences or discoveries that set us off on different paths, contributing to our own transformations as artists. The structural metaphor that most adequately captures this dynamic process of artistic inquiry is "braiding." I have described the use of the braid this way:

> The metaphor that best represents the idea presented here–that visual arts research is a simple and complex liquid structure with powerful generative potential for change– is the image of the braid. Metaphors help us to see things differently as we further our understanding of relationships and networks, influences and connections, and this can intrigue visual arts researchers. What is proposed is that the braid, with its infolding and unfurling form that disengages and reconnects with core themes while continually moving into new spaces, serves as a useful metaphor that captures the dynamic complexity and simplicity of art practice as research. (Sullivan, 2010, p. 112)

Frank Shifreen represented an "infolding" inquiry into some of the private worlds that shape his art practice in two examples from exhibitions that were particularly personal. The first exhibition, True Stories of Dreams and the Paranormal (2005), explored many of the private narratives that have been a central part of his work. A second exhibition, Speech-Acts: Art Responding to Language, Rhetoric and Politics (2008), took a more-public theme that had its own histories and theories within the language arts and the humanities. Frank's work

FIGURE 3. Frank Shifreen. *Elevated.* 2005. Acrylic on wood. From the exhibition True Stories of Dreams and the Paranormal, Macy Gallery, Teachers College, Columbia University. Shifreen states:

The show came up quickly after agreeing to do it in May. My father died on July 25th and I had no new work. I always wanted to do art with stories. My dreams have always felt important and have marked my emotional life. This painting is not about one dream but a long series of dreams that lasted for over 7 years. I kept dreaming about riding the elevated subway line almost every night. Sometimes I would get off the train at Coney Island and go to the sea. A wave 100 feet high—a wall of water—would be standing there still, not moving. It was scary about what would happen if that water should crash. I would get back on the train.

For the show I wanted to share the stories that had lived under the surface. That is the motor, the machine that keeps things going. These were experiences that I lived with, and except for a few friends or therapists—and often not even then—I did not share these experiences.... I stayed at my mom's house in Hartford. The family secrets that I had to live with almost destroyed me and I felt that what was bubbling up from dreams, shamanic journeys, or other mental events must have a kind of truth. It was a risky maneuver, a big risk. I am not sure if the show was successful in any terms, but I am proud of taking the risk to reveal these hidden stories and my inner life. (Personal communication, March 10, 2009).

portrayed artistic investigations that opened up lines of inquiry within the fringes of existing discourse. The artworks created in these contexts emphasized personal accounts and nudged open other ways of seeing and thinking about personal issues by sharing them in public.

Transformative Inquiry "Across" Self-Similar Structures

Art practice can be a transforming process of inquiry that is informed by particular structural and methodological influences, but it retains a fluid and flexible state. This perspective further exemplifies how a creative and critical process can be simple and complex at the same time. This is not a contradiction; rather, it is an acknowledgement that the realities faced in everyday life and the ordered means used to organize our social worlds do not conform to some stable, foundational structure upon which our informational and operational systems are built. Reductionism and Euclidean notions of space are powerful systems that have a strong historical legacy in guiding inquiry in the arts and sciences alike. The assumption is that a change in scale reveals new information so that the more things can be reduced to their basic essence, the better the chance of figuring out how they work.

Nature and human design, however, resist such simplistic solutions. It is not so much an investigation of underlying structures that holds promise, but rather it is the capacity to

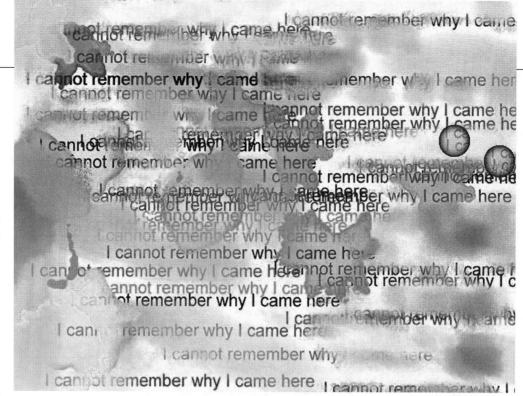

FIGURE 4. Frank Shifreen. *Cannot remember why I came here.* (2008). Arches paper, printed digitally, watercolor added. From the exhibition Speech-Acts: Art Responding to Language, Rhetoric and Politics, Dudley House, Lehman Hall, Harvard University, Boston, April 3-25, 2008. Shifreen states:

Each piece from the show reflected a different aspect of my understanding of the show's themes about language, rhetoric and politics. This piece reflects on longing for certainty. Memory is how we hope to carry knowledge to the future, yet part of the equation is missing — the self who remembers but who is lost in the facts of the world. Why did I come here? How can we identify our purpose and meaning as an educator, teacher as well as a student? It is not about facts, but about being. (Personal communication, March 10, 2009)

embrace realities that are both the simple and the complex at the same time. "Self-similarity" is a construct that exhibits these properties. Self-similarity is a concept that has its origin in the mathematics of fractal geometry developed by Benoit Mandelbrot (1983). Fractal structures have become very influential in theory across many fields to describe iterative patterns found in natural forms and human designs that appear both simple and complex, yet generally look regular, and possess the capacity for radical change over time. James Gleick (1988) explains:

> Self-similarity is symmetry across scale. It implies recursion, pattern inside of pattern... self similarity is an easily recognizable quality. Its images are everywhere in the culture: in the infinitely deep reflection of a person standing between two mirrors, or in the cartoon notion of a fish eating a smaller fish eating a smaller fish eating a smaller fish. (p. 103)

The concept of self-similarity nicely captures the way that transformative artistic inquiry takes place "across" practices, as the inquiry process endlessly divides and builds upon itself. This reflects how artist-researchers respond creatively and critically to issues, actions, and change at all levels of theory and practice. This characteristic means that visual arts inquiry is independent of scale, which suggests it has a similar structure if undertaken in studios, in classrooms, in communities, or within cultures. With self-similarity, there is no underlying structure upon which more-detailed systems are built. Instead, no matter whether viewed at the micro- or macro-level, the structure has similar properties and characteristics—it is simple, complex, and dynamic all at the same time.

The claim made here is that knowledge, beliefs, and values are aspects of human knowing that are independent of scale. What we know and believe doesn't change all that much; it is irrespective of the personal or public places in which it is expressed. Therefore, being able to move "across" academic areas allows artist-researchers interested in seeing things anew to reveal the transformative potential of exploring what might be possible. Maxine Greene suggests that the social imagination is an agency for new possibility that emerges in tenacious response to constraints and controls. Maxine reminds us that "to resist such tendencies is to become aware of the ways in which certain dominant social practices enclose us in molds or frames, define us in accord with extrinsic demands, discourage us from going beyond ourselves, from acting on possibility." (1995, p. 112).

Public education is among the institutions that can be considered in this light, particularly at a time when political forces like the "No Child Left Behind" legislation seem to dictate almost every aspect of what is taught. Yet creative people (including, in this case, artist-researchers) are notorious for finding ways around such constraints, particularly in response to the genuine, holistic needs of students. In doing so, we can set an example not simply of evading constraints, but also in working creatively within or beyond them. Similarly, we need no longer think of the domain of art as being cast within firm disciplinary or institutional boundaries, but instead as a more fluid and flexible system evolving as part of a changing world.

Consequently, there is merit in thinking about institutional conditions as non-linear and non-foundational, and as being capable of new, emergent possibilities. Opportunities for inquiry can be seen to be informed by existing knowledge structures, but not to be a slave to them. For professionals, art teachers, and art students alike, artistic inquiry helps to open up new ways of responding to pressing issues, and to see the impact of challenging existing information structures such as those imposed by the limits of discipline tradition. "Post-discipline" practice describes the way art practice can take place within and beyond existing discipline boundaries as theories are explored and imaginative forms of inquiry developed. For instance, in completing projects within an academic setting, the methods used by an artist-researcher will center on artmaking and be surrounded by different discipline perspectives and practices. When planning and undertaking inquiry, artists make informed choices about imaginative and intellectual approaches, just as they do when they create and respond to art. Various theories of human processes, communal practices, and cultural agencies abound, and these serve as both a grounded set of conditions and an interpretive framework for approaching inquiry. These domains of known content, however, can limit the capacity to see beyond them. Notwithstanding the necessity of making use of diverse forms of knowing, working creatively and critically in a way that is unencumbered by the constraints of knowledge boundaries can open up new possibilities.

Searching out knowledge and understanding across the gaps of the unknown and the known involves selecting, adapting, and constructing ways of working and ways of seeing. To do this, one has to construct the tools of inquiry from an array of practices on hand. Just as these processes are exemplified by contemporary artists (as well as artists from the past), art teachers have the equally creative challenge to help translate such ways of working so that they apply to the level of the students in their classrooms, providing authentic experiences based on what happens in the field. This makes it all the more important that art teachers retain their own practice as artist-researchers, sustaining and evolving their particular lines of inquiry and supporting their own continuing transformations. In this regard, their work can be continually informed by close examination of contemporary artists like Frank Shifreen, who are constantly reshaping the boundaries of what we think we know as art.

When working from a base in contemporary art, discipline parameters are seen to be open-ended, yet the opportunity for imaginative re-interpretation is at hand. In these circumstances, the artist-researcher is seen to be participating in a post-discipline practice whereby the infolding and unfurling braided process of inquiry might follow a self-similar pattern as simplicities and complexities are explored. Here there is little reliance on a prescribed content base; rather, it is the use of a suitable approach to inquiry that supports the questions being asked, which may take the artist-researcher beyond existing content boundaries. When viewed as an educational rationale, this line of open-ended inquiry captures the best of what meaningful learning hopes to achieve. The exhibition—Speech-Acts: Art Responding to Language, Rhetoric and Politics—described earlier gave Frank Shifreen an opportunity to respond in a creative and critical way to systems of language and forms of engagement that opened up possibilities that Maxine Greene would enjoy.

FIGURE 5. Frank Shifreen. Doorway to "Yes" and "No." 2008. Timber door-frame, hinged door. From the exhibition Speech-Acts: Art Responding to Language, Rhetoric and Politics, Dudley House, Lehman Hall, Harvard University, Boston, April 3-25, 2008. Shifreen states:

I used to design sets for the theater and liked how a theater set can be a playground, a symbolic space, a machine for drama or action for further action. A door to 'yes' and 'no' can be called a logic gate. The doorway can be a prop to rehearse, propagate, and investigate decisions and decisive action. By going thru the 'no' door the actor embraces negation. He or she decides. The 'no' door leads to the 'yes' space and vice versa. Doors with signs identify and exclude the other class: The men's room; Employees only; Exit, Entrance. It is empowering to make a decision. In Ulysses, by James Joyce, the last chapter is Molly Bloom's soliloquy where she reflects on her life and world in contrast to the mental and intellectual world of the male characters in the book. Her monologue is bracketed by 'yesses,' which Joyce called the female word, not in the negative, but the end of all resistance, or acceptance. (Personal communication, March 11, 2009)

CONCLUSION

Ephemeral or illusionary images from the past may be assumed to have little value in a cultural economy that fixes borders around objects of desire. Nevertheless, there is merit in looking backward and forward at the same time; even though the past cannot be changed, the way we interpret history can. A basis for better understanding of what art means, and how it is implicated in the very core of human knowing, is the acceptance that art practice is a relational and transformative process of continual renewal. Through creative and critical inquiry that cuts "between," "around," "within," and "across" theories and practices, the artist-researcher takes on responsibilities that are personal and public, artistic and educational, and local and global. In this essay, Frank Shifreen participated in the manner of an artist-in-residence, as his art practice exemplified many of the issues and ideas discussed, and displayed many of the attributes of a contemporary artist-researcher whose imaginative energy cannot be constrained for long by existing intellectual, social, or cultural limits. In the same way, Frank's work was offered as an example of ongoing artistic development that drew upon the range of attributes sometimes addressed under the heading "holistic." Most these attributes, most evident were the continuities among the intellect and the emotions, between the community and the individual. As such, he exemplifies qualities that can be carried into the classroom at every level in the appreciation and the practice of art, while encouraging art teachers in their own explorations as artist-researchers. And his relentless re-searching continues; Frank's most recent public art projects continue to expand the notion of community and take place in online environments, a creative space that has a new capacity to draw together individuals who share a common purpose. Frank explains these emerging art communities this way:

> Local self-contained artist communities that drew artists into cities and artist colonies have given way to disparate individual artists connecting in cyberspace. Technical

problems have largely been solved with the result being that large amounts of image and text can be readily stored online. I am part of a nonprofit group that has developed an artists' network website. The entire site, www.cultureinside.com, has a parallel structure in three languages, French, German and English, with Spanish soon to be added... Differences in languages have long been a barrier to effective communication and access to open knowledge. Language translation programs now have the capability to allow for substantial communication exchange and are getting better all the time. (Personal communication, March 6, 2009)

The prospect of widespread access and communication across community spaces is an image that holds the best from the past in view alongside the most intriguing that looms ahead. This is a fitting description on which to conclude and to begin.

REFERENCES

Biggs, M., & Karlssohn, H. (Eds.) (2011). *The Routledge companion to research in the arts*, pp. 99-119. New York, NY: Routledge.

Eisner, E. W. (1972). *Educating artistic vision*. New York, NY: Macmillan.

Gleick, J. (1988). *Chaos: Making a new science*. London, England: Sphere Books.

Glueck, G. (1982, October 3). Gallery Viewing: Drawing a bead on public monuments. *New York Times*, Section 2, p. 27.

Greene, M. (1995). Texts and Margins. In R. W. Neperud (Ed.), *Context, content, and community in art education: Beyond postmodernism* (pp. 111-127). New York, NY: Teachers College Press.

Greer, D. W. (1984). Discipline-Based Art Education: Approaching art as a subject of study. *Studies in Art Education, 25*(4), 212-218.

Jeffri, J. (2007). *Above ground: Information about artist III: Special focus New York City aging artists*. New York, NY: Trustees of Teachers College Columbia University/Research Center for Arts and Culture.

Kelly, K. (2007, October 16, para. 2-4). Once upon a time on the shores of the Gowanus: Frank Shifreen and "The Monument Defined" Show. Retrieved from http://pardonmeforasking.blogspot.com/2007/10/once-upon-time-on-shores-of-gowan-us.html

Lanier, V. (1982). *The arts we see: A simplified introduction to the visual arts*. New York, NY: Teachers College Press.

Lunden, J. (2009, December 5). Blanchett's Blanche, at the heart of a new 'Streetcar.' Retrieved from www.npr.mobi/templates/story/story.php?storyId=121090904

Macleod, K. & Holdridge, L. (Eds.) (2006). *Thinking through art: Reflections on art as research*. New York, NY: Routledge.

Mandelbrot, B. B. (1983). *The fractal geometry of nature*. San Francisco, CA: W. H. Freeman.

National Commission on Excellence in Education. (1983). *A nation at risk: The imperative for educational reform*. D. Pierpont Gardner (Chairman), Washington, DC: National Commission on Excellence in Education.

Read, H. (1949). *Education through art*. New York, NY: Pantheon Books.

Shifreen, F. (2003). *Art against war: Exhibition statement,* June 9-27, 2003, Macy Gallery, Teachers College Columbia University.

Shifreen, F. (2007). Purposive, expansive and inclusive art learning in a community: A case study of a political art exhibition. Unpublished paper, Art and Art Education Program, Teachers College, Columbia University, New York, NY.

Smith, H., & Dean, R. T. (Eds.) (2009). *Practice-led research, research-led practice in the creative arts*. Edinburgh, UK: Edinburgh University Press.

Smith, R. A. (1986). *Excellence in art education: Ideas and initiatives*. Reston, VA: National Art Education Association.

Sullivan, G. (2010). *Art practice as research: Inquiry in visual arts* (2nd ed.). Thousand Oaks, CA: Sage.

Temkin, A. (2009). Open studio. In Ann Temkin (Ed.), *Gabriel Orozco* (pp. 11-21). New York, NY: Museum of Modern Art.

ENDNOTES

1   From Katia Kelly, (2007, October 16, para. 2-4). Once upon a time on the shores of the Gowanus: Frank Shifreen and "The Monument Defined" Show. Retrieved from http://pardonmeforasking.blogspot.com/2007/10/once-upon-time-on-shores-of-gowan-us.html

2   The Art Against War exhibition was held concurrently at the Macy Gallery, Teachers College, Columbia University and NY Arts Space, New York, from June 9-27, 2003; and over the following year, it was exhibited in various forms at the Detroit Museum of New Art; the Presbyterian College, South Carolina; Comma Gallery, Orlando, Florida; the Roubaix Musee de L'art et Industrie, France; Magelis/Takoma, France, and the World Social Forum IV, Mumbai, India. Internet exhibition sites included: Digitalmuseum.org, Detroit (www.digitalmuseum.org), and Retiform.net (http://retiform.net).

ABOUT THE AUTHOR

Graeme Sullivan is the Director of the School of Visual Arts and Professor of Art Education at Penn State University. His scholarly interests center on the creative and critical thinking processes and methods of inquiry used in visual arts; these ideas are described in *Art Practice as Research: Inquiry in Visual Arts*. Graeme maintains an active art practice, and his Streetworks have been installed in several international cities and sites over the past 15 years.

CHAPTER 3

Engaging Mind, Body, and Soul: Essential Connections for Art Education

Carol S. Jeffers

Artists of all ages often are caught up in the bonds forged between themselves and their work. Rooted in the body, these bonds are deeply resonant, soulful, even existential or transcendental in nature. Similar connections also can develop between a viewer and an especially meaningful piece, or among viewers sharing experiences of profound encounters with works of art. A testament to the union of mind, body, and soul, these connections spring from the human capacity for empathy and lie at the heart of art education.

This chapter explores these empathic connections—a resonant connectedness—and some implications for holistic learning by integrating personal accounts of such connectedness with the findings of recent research on the nature of human consciousness, inter/intrapersonal relations, and empathy. One author's spiritual journey into a Rembrandt painting is considered, along with Rembrandt's own journey, and the resonance I felt for the author, artist, and painting upon reading this moving account. In addition, I use the connections that my students and I shared in an embodied, yet collective response to a classroom presentation of a metaphorical work to illustrate holistic learning in light of neuroscientific research on the mirror neuron system; I also examine other studies of emotional intelligence, flow, and the interdependent self-other. Lastly, the chapter argues for curriculum reform in art education that would open the way to educating whole and resonant beings.

THE CLASSROOM

The 2nd-grade classroom seems to vibrate as children dance around their tables, chattering all the while about their plans and ideas for paintings soon to emerge. I am there as a university supervisor ostensibly to observe a student teacher, but my attention is drawn to one child in particular and I cannot take my eyes off of her. She seems unaware of me or of the others, even of herself, for that matter, so utterly absorbed is she by her work. Her eyes are wide and sparkling, yet focused intently, almost trance-like, on what is for her the glorious fluidity of the paint, its lusciousness flowing from her brush. The 7-year-old is sublime, her face relaxed, lips parted in a wisp of a smile; it is clear to me that she is deeply immersed in the process, enraptured by it, and resonating with it. It is as if her creative achievement, her very being, depends on this single-minded immersion. Process and being seem to fuse; they are neither cognitive nor affective, but a union of mind and body that outstrips any Cartesian categories. Indeed, the child is one with the brush, the colors, their magical flow; I am certain now that through her intense, intimate connections, she has entered into a state of grace and self-forgetting, a state of "flow" itself, as Mihaly Csikszentmihalyi (1994), describes it. She is alive in the moment—mind, body, and soul—and, feeling her resonance, I, too, am vitalized. Her sense of joy has become my own, and in that moment, there is no sense of self, no other; there is only this resonant, electrifying connectedness.

Whether working in a loft studio, a computer lab, or the 2nd-grade classroom, artists of all ages can experience flow, a state that puts them in "the zone" and finds them, like the 7-year-old painter, so captivated by what they are doing that they lose track of time, space, self, and other. Like the world-class athletes, chess masters, and rock-climbers that Csikszentmihalyi also studied, artists in flow are highly motivated and work harder than usual, staying in the "peak moment" that allows them to achieve their peak performance. Intense concentration also allows them to be more fully conscious without becoming *self*-conscious. Moreover, they seem able to balance the powers of mind and body, to integrate thought and feeling, as if they understand implicitly that thought *requires* feeling and feeling requires the *body*—just as the eminent cognitive neuroscientist, Antonio Damasio, describes in his now classic work, *Descartes' Error* (1994). From this mind/body balance, artists (and others) can remain open, without need of ego defenses.

This is not to imply that creativity does not equally involve hard work and struggle. Even for young artists like our 7-year-old, there can be long moments of frustration when things do not seem to go as planned, where messes are made, and failure is felt. Nevertheless, the extra effort it takes to get beyond such temporary setbacks often is the very thing that gets us into that state of flow in which discouragement gives way to a state of exhilaration, and frustration dissolves into feelings of ecstasy, spontaneous joy, and transcendence. At this point, too, creativity seems no longer merely an individual event. Instead, it is sometimes experienced as going beyond the self to become part of what Csikszentmihalyi (1994) characterizes as a larger energy, a team, a harmony. In a very real sense, the concept of this energy-harmony seems remarkably similar to that which the 2nd-grade painter and I shared in her lively classroom—what I describe as a resonant connectedness.

Similarly, intimate, resonant connections can develop between viewers and works of art—for example, in museum or classroom settings. Viewers who are enthralled by a particular work, who may identify with its narrative or are profoundly moved by the meaning it holds, can lose touch with the reality of these settings. Henry Nouwen (1992), for instance, wrote about his encounter with Rembrandt's *The Return of the Prodigal Son* (1669) in St. Petersburg's Hermitage Museum, an experience so utterly absorbing that he was unaware 3 hours had passed and the museum was closing. Regardless of whether Nouwen's experience constitutes a state of flow, such connectedness does involve a laser-like focus, deep immersion, and self-transcendence. It requires a fusion of mind and body that is sometimes manifested in what Hubard (2007) describes as an intense physical response, an "embodied" response. To an outsider—perhaps a museum educator or gallery attendant—such responses may appear to be involuntary. Take, for example, the 5-year-old child who is so riveted by the sight and gestures of a woman's bloody hands featured in an Ana Mendieta video that she must emulate the movements with her own hands, or the young adult who, standing before a crucifixion, flinches and exclaims, "ouch," as if she, too, feels the pain, experiences the suffering of the wounded Christ figure (Hubard, 2007).

In an only slightly different way, a student in one of my elementary art-methods courses also experienced a particular work physically, as well as conceptually. This became clear as she explained to the class why she had chosen the Baroque figure painting *Saint Cecilia* (1606), by Guido Reni, to serve as her personal metaphor. The classroom fell silent as the 20-something preservice teacher stood before us, erect, her eyes intense, giving a determined look. In effect, Cecilia had chosen the preservice teacher, we learned, calling out from her place on the museum wall—not as the patron saint of music she was—but with her eyes, uplifted, yet intense, transfixed. In that moment, the student herself seemed transfixed, as if becoming Cecilia, her own eyes turned upward. Then we understood that the student was, at the same time, modeling for us the very pose her dying father had taken, his eyes lifted heavenward, as he begged for a miracle from God.[1] Ever since that particularly resonant presentation more than 6 years ago now, when I find myself in front of Saint Cecilia at the Norton Simon Museum of Art, I still feel my student's sorrow, the angry sobs she choked back. My eyes well up, remembering how her classmates and I cried together for the young woman who lost both her father and her faith. Student-to-painting, daughter-to-father, audience-to-student, classmates-to-instructor, instructor-to-painting; this embodied connectedness resonates to this day.

EMPATHY AND EMBODIED SIMULATION

Such soulful connectedness evidently involves something familiar to every human being: empathy, that biological capacity within us that enables us to step outside of ourselves and to identify with others, including those depicted in works of art. Integral to self-awareness and emotional intelligence (Goleman, 1995, 2005), empathy also allows us to understand the meanings of actions, language, and metaphor. It also allows us to experience Csikszentmihalyi's larger energy, the harmony, that holds the potential for developing new and better relationships with others through a "collective flow" that, ultimately, must hold the human community together.

To understand the nature of this energy-harmony, we need only to examine our capacity for empathy, and to locate it not in the stardust of the cosmos or in a Jungian concept of the collective unconscious, but in the cells of the human body and the synapses of its brain.

Indeed, recent research has yielded compelling explanations of the neural mechanisms for empathic understanding and connection—which, incidentally, serve to reinforce Damasio's earlier findings that the body is required for feelings and feelings are required for thoughts. With the mid-90s discovery of the mirror neuron system in the human brain, the neurological basis for empathy—its mechanism—was revealed at last (Carr, Iacoboni, Dubeau, Mazziotta, & Lenzi, 2003; Rizzolatti & Craighero, 2004). It is this "strange" class of neurons (Gallese, 2006) that "create[s] some kind of magical connection between people" (Iacoboni, 2007) that, ultimately, allows us to step outside ourselves, and to imagine walking in the shoes of others; that is, to identify with the other as a second self, and thus understand another's situation.

Originally discovered in the motor region of the brain (area f5 of the ventral premotor cortex), mirror neurons have since been found to be involved not only in the body state associated with action, but also in those related to emotion and sensation. In each body state, these cells allow us to mirror other people, and thus to understand implicitly their gestures, graphic signs, and facial expressions. This occurs because mirror neurons in the premotor and somatosensory cortices are activated both when an action or expression is performed by one human being *and* when observed by another. Noted neuroscientist Marco Iacoboni succinctly explained the mirroring mechanism this way: "When I see you grasping something, the same [motor] cells in my brain are activated, so it's almost like I'm in your mind" (2007). Through such activation, the mirroring mechanism allows human beings to experience their own actions, sensations, and emotions, as well as those of others in what another neuroscientist, Vittorio Gallese (2006), termed an "embodied simulation." Representing the body states at an abstract level, embodied simulation is the mechanism that, according to Gallese (2006), "allows our body to resonate along with the bodies of others." And as Damasio makes clear:

> When you have the possibility of generating your own simulated body state because you can represent the body on line all the time in the brain, then you have the possibility of

generating the body states of others, all the way from the emotional to the muscular-skeletal. You can go from the body of the self to the body of another and through the body, into the mind of another. (Damasio, 2006)

With clarity, even eloquence, Damasio addresses philosophical issues involving inter-subjective relations between self and other, human consciousness, the nature of empathy, and the age-old question of how it is possible for human beings (who physically have access only to their own thoughts and feelings) can mentally/emotionally access the minds of others. Likewise, Iacoboni and Gallese were quick to grasp the existential implications, understanding that empirical evidence of the mirroring mechanism must supplant at last the Cartesian duality of mind and body, and related dualities like "self" versus "other" so pervasive in Western thought since the 17th century. Establishing a kind of "existential neuroscience," they advocate a more interdependent approach that understands self and other as "two sides of the same coin" (Iacoboni, 2008). As Iacoboni sees it, "mirror neurons put the self and other back together," creating a "sense of us" (p. 155). For Gallese (2003), the interconnected self and other define each other in terms of their physical encounters—their embodied experiences—that both shape and situate them in a "we-centric shared space." In his view, mirror neurons "instantiate a supramodal intentional shared space" allowing human beings "to appreciate, experience, and implicitly and prereflexively understand the emotions and sensations we take others to experience" (p. 177). He also notes that French philosopher Marcel Merleau-Ponty (1964) accurately, if succinctly, captured this view of an embodied, interdependent self-other: "I live in the facial expression of the other, as I feel him living in mine" (p. 146).

These embodied interactions of self-other, whether described from a neuroscientific or philosophic standpoint, explain the resonant connectedness experienced, for example, in the art-methods classroom, with our empathic bodies resonating along with those of Saint Cecilia, the preservice teacher, and her supplicant father. Classroom experiences like this appear to support Iacoboni's (2008) claim that "the interdependence between self and other that mirror neurons allow shapes the social interactions between people, where the concrete encounter between self and other becomes the shared existential meaning that connects them deeply" (p. 265).

The elegant circuitry of the mirror neuron system that allows us to develop a "sense of us" and to empathize with others has also made it possible to develop social systems and moral codes, as well as to share cultural beliefs and practices. Empathy arises in the inter-face of nature and culture. At a species level, it both explains and facilitates the human need for storytelling (manifested originally in oral forms), from which culture emerged. We are story-sharing creatures who use myth, art, dance, music, and ritual as metaphors to share our various emotional states in social and physical ways. These art forms are physical entities in their own right, presenting themselves in the same physical space that becomes a "we-centric shared space."

Lying at the heart of culture, the arts develop our capacity for empathy, even as they amplify experience and invite us to make meaning. Empathy, like the arts, prompts us to imagine, to project, and thus to feel with others. It is empathy, particularly *narrative* empathy (Keen, 2007), that allows us to interact—even with portrayals of others—through the imaginative acts of perspective-taking, role-taking, metaphor, and character identification. Within story-telling societies, narrative empathy has broad impact that can apply not only to the reader's experiences with the literary arts, but also to the viewer's with the visual arts. Henry Nouwen's (1992) life-changing encounter with Rembrandt's *The Return of the Prodigal Son* involved a kind of narrative empathy that is especially resonant and created a "shared existential meaning" that connected him to the painting's biblical characters, to Rembrandt, and to the residents of the L'Arche community where Nouwen lives and works.

Nouwen's memoir recounts a spiritual journey that began more than 20 years ago and took the former Harvard professor into the lives and roles of each of the characters (figures) depicted in Rembrandt's magnificent interpretation of the parable—from the younger son who returns ragged and ashamed to a glorious homecoming, to the dutiful older son, clearly resentful, who remains stiff and aloof, to the elderly father, who, bathed in a divine light, is all-forgiving and welcomes the prodigal, clasping his shoulders with joy and compassion. From the moment he first caught sight of the painting reproduced in a poster pinned to an office door, Nouwen found himself spellbound, touched so deeply that he wanted to laugh and cry at the same time. Rembrandt had brought to consciousness his yearning for a new home, a lasting one, and Nouwen knew he would be drawn into the quest to find the place that called him home. His was a journey of becoming a self interconnected with others. This interdependent self showed him the way to move beyond the two sons, to become the father at last; the one who welcomes, forgives, and offers compassion. Nouwen's is a story about learning to give of the self, giving freely and generously to others—who, as second selves, are embodied within and define the first self. At journey's end, Nouwen embraced a kind of empathic kinship with others and found himself at home among a community of adults with developmental disabilities (L'Arche), where he now serves as pastor and where Rembrandt's *The Return of the Prodigal Son* graces his wall.

Along the way, Nouwen developed empathy for Rembrandt and the artist's own spiritual struggle. Spending time with the painting, and through study of the master's life and body of work, Nouwen came to believe that Rembrandt presented the inner drama of his soul, and his own move from maintaining a hedonistic focus on an exterior world to developing an inner-directed orientation filled with an interior light. In Nouwen's eyes, such a transformation was prompted by a tragic series of personal and financial losses that turned the once calculating, vengeful artist known for his obnoxious personality into someone wiser and more chastened. Painted near the end of his life, *The Return of the Prodigal Son* revealed to Nouwen how Rembrandt had been both the younger and the older son, embodying their traits at different points along the way. Later, he would take comfort in his own spiritual homecoming. Nouwen resonates along with Rembrandt, recognizing unmistakable bonds that, according to his interpretation, connect his own life story to the artist's. Such resonance also comes from the pastor's deep appreciation for and empathic insight into Rembrandt's remarkable skill in creating and developing the father and sons, and in enveloping them in light, as if endowing them with life.

The details, the simple cues that drew Nouwen into their story, and thus into his own—the prodigal's shaven head and broken sandal; the father's rich, red cloak; and above all else, his arthritic hands, one strong, masculine, the other more feminine, loving, and compassionate—are what drew me to the pastor and the artist alike. Through Nouwen, the painting has been embodied within me, and as he once did, I feel a strong urge to travel to the Hermitage to spend some time with the original work. Until then, I feel privileged to have visited Rembrandt's house in Amsterdam and to have shared the existential meaning that connects Nouwen, Rembrandt, and me deeply.

EDUCATING WHOLE BEINGS AND THE NEED FOR CURRICULUM REFORM

Offered as examples of meaningful engagement, resonant connectedness, and holistic-embodied learning, the stories presented in this chapter—the 2nd-grade painter, the 5-year-old museum visitor, the preservice teacher, and the L'Arche pastor—could indeed become the narrative for the field of art education. These kinds of intense existential experiences could occur more regularly and frequently in art classrooms if the field were to dedicate itself to educating whole beings (which is to say, empathic and engaged beings) who seek to understand themselves and others and make sense of the world through the bodily sensations and feelings that inform their cognitive processes. Such a commitment would require the field to apply, at long last, the clear, compelling results of the mounting body of neuroscientific research—and to grasp the pedagogical-curricular implications. As art educators, we must understand fundamentally—not just academically—the profound significance of interdependence, for example, between self-other, mind-body, and thought-feeling. We must revamp old thinking and seize upon the interconnectedness of biology, culture, art, and empathy, working to explore their interactions through classroom activities intended to build peak-performance learning communities and promote collective flow. The practice of taking the perspective or role of others would be valued by teachers and students alike as imaginative, empathic, and *creative* acts.

This effort would not replace art teaching as it is commonly practiced; instead, it would build upon it. As noted earlier, flow requires the skills and understandings necessary to meet challenges and to overcome difficulties in concept development, visual communication, self-expression, design, and craftsmanship. Equally, students do not automatically understand how to respond to works of art, whether of the past or present. Empathetic appreciation often requires rigorous study, encompassing traditional training in description, analysis, interpretation, and evaluation. Yet skills like these become merely "academic" without the ultimate concern of encouraging resonant connectedness between the artist and the subject, the viewer and the work.

Should this project of curriculum reform be undertaken, we would need to begin at the beginning: We must engage in what Noddings (2003) refers to as "aims talk," taking on the question of what are we educating for, and reflecting upon what we believe to be the meaning and purpose of (art) education. In so doing, we must have the courage to cast aside the narrow and reductive aim predominant in a No Child Left Behind environment, which, as Noddings (2003) points out, is to educate for a global (market) economy. What if art educators were to step up to challenge this aim and its ideological economic self-interest? What if we assumed an activist role, determined and driven by shared social and humanistic concerns? Indeed, we are the ones who must take responsibility for educating whole beings and preparing the way for a just and empathic society. Ours is the commitment to make, the project that would move us closer to the heart beating within our own field.

REFERENCES

Carr, L., Iacoboni, M., Dubeau, M., Mazziotta, J., & Lenzi, G. (2003). Neural mechanisms of empathy in humans: A relay from neural systems for imitation to limbic areas. *Proceedings of the National Academy of Sciences U.S.A. 100*, 5497-5502.

Csikszentmihalyi, M. (1994). *Flow*. New York, NY: Nightingale–Conant Corp, Simon and Schuster.

Damasio, A. (1994). *Descartes' error*. New York, NY: Putnam (Grosset Books).

Damasio, A. (2006, March 24). Lecture at the Forum on Art and the New Biology of Mind, sponsored by the Italian Academy for Advanced Studies in America at Columbia University, New York. Retrieved from www.columbia.edu/cu/news/media/06/421_neuroBioArts/

Gallese, V. (2006, March 24). Lecture at the Forum on Art and the New Biology of Mind, sponsored by the Italian Academy for Advanced Studies in America at Columbia University, New York. Retrieved from www.columbia.edu/cu/news/media/06/421_neuroBioArts/

Goleman, D. (1995/2005). *Emotional intelligence*. San Francisco, CA: Jossey-Bass.

Hubard, O. (2007). Complete engagement: Embodied response in art museum education. *Art Education, 60*(6), 46-52.

Iacoboni, M. (Interview). (2007, July 25). Interview with Larry Mantle, KPCC's *Air Talk*. [Audio podcast]. Retrieved from www.publicradio.org/tools/media/player/kpcc/shows/airtalk/2007/07/20070725_airtalk2?start=00:28:28&end=00:52:31

Iacoboni, M. (2008) *Mirroring people: The new science of how we connect with others*. New York, NY: Farrar, Strauss and Giroux.

Keen, S. (2007). *Empathy and the novel*. New York, NY: Oxford University Press.

Merleau-Ponty, M. (1964). *The primacy of perception* (J. M. Edie, Trans). Evanston, IL: Northwestern University Press.

Noddings, N. (2003). *Happiness and education*. Cambridge, England: Cambridge University Press.

Nouwen, H. (1992). *The return of the prodigal son: A story of homecoming*. New York, NY: St. Anthony Messenger Press.

Rizzolatti, G., & Criaghero, L. (2004). The mirror neuron system. *Annual Review of Neuroscience, 27*, 169-192.

ENDNOTE

1   For a more detailed description of the preservice teacher's experience and her classmates' responses, please see "Within Connections: Empathy, Mirror Neurons, and Art Education," by Carol S. Jeffers, published in *Art Education, 62*(2), March 2009, pp. 18-23.

ABOUT THE AUTHOR

Carol S. Jeffers is currently professor of art education at California State University, Los Angeles. Her research focuses on empathy, resulting in the publication of a series of articles in *Art Education, International Journal of Education and the Arts, Journal of Cultural Research in Art Education*, and *Journal of Aesthetic Education*. She currently is working on a book exploring significant connections between empathy and the image.

CHAPTER 4

Holistic Education and the Role of Transferred Values: John Dewey's Socially Instrumental Practice at the Barnes Foundation as Precedent for 21st-Century Skills

Margaret Johnson

[T]here is a difference between the art product (statue, painting or whatever), and the work of art. The first is physical and potential; the latter is active and experienced.

John Dewey (1980/1934, p. 162)

Among the roots of holistic education is Progressive Education, as demonstrated by John Dewey. Adherents believed that education should provide for more than passive transfer of knowledge to develop future factory workers; it should actively cultivate the moral, physical, psychological, emotional, and spiritual dimensions of students. Dewey valued the interconnection of home, school, and community, as well as the child's first-hand experience in learning. Dewey also championed the arts in general education for their ability to infuse spiritual meaning into activities and processes of daily living by providing artistic (making) and aesthetic (viewing) experiences. Progressive Education did emphasize learning by doing, but, unfortunately, fell short of Dewey's focuses on cooperative learning as social activity as well as on the thorough integration of art into the overall curriculum (Althouse, Johnson, & Mitchell, 2003).

One context in which Dewey was able to develop his ideas about the social dimension of learning and the interrelationship between aesthetic education and life was through his work at the Barnes Foundation. This chapter will give an overview of Dewey's and the Barnes Foundation's involvement and ideas, then focus on *transferred values,* a little-known concept employed at the Barnes Foundation, which was a key to the holistic perspective in art education as practiced there. An understanding of the development and application of this concept will indicate ways that looking at and talking or writing about works of art can contribute to holistic art education. Such a practice can help students of all ages to develop 21st-century skills, such as creative and critical thinking, and essential human qualities, such as sensory awareness, emotional receptivity, and empathy. These qualities can be developed not only in studying the so-called "fine arts," but also from works of craft, design, and artifacts, as well as from nature. In this broadening of appreciation and awareness, art education that addresses transferred values also contributes to the democratic spirit so important to both Dewey and the Barnes Foundation.

AESTHETIC EXPERIENCE AND SCIENTIFIC METHOD AT THE BARNES FOUNDATION

Albert Barnes established an art education program at The Barnes Foundation in 1924, and he asked John Dewey to become the first President and Director of Education. Barnes's and Dewey's original mission in their educational program at the Foundation was a socially instrumental pedagogy that should provide all people with the means to intelligently reflect upon and evaluate their decisions, actions, and resultant work and lives in a participatory democracy through critical and creative thinking. They developed a concept of "transferred values" and applied it to Barnes' collection of (then) modern art.

Barnes and Dewey enjoyed a sustained and fruitful partnership with regard to aesthetic experience and scientific theory as applied to education in the presence of Barnes's great collection at his foundation and abroad. The relationship between Albert Barnes and John Dewey lasted for more than a quarter of a century. Barnes's appreciation of Dewey is stated explicitly in the dedication to his book *The Art of Painting*. In turn, in the preface to *Art as Experience,* Dewey wrote:

> My greatest indebtedness is to Dr. A. C. Barnes... Whatever is sound in this volume is due more than I can say to the great educational work carried on in the Barnes Foundation. That work is of a pioneer quality comparable to the best that has been done in any field during the present generation, that of science not excepted. I should be glad to think of this volume as one phase of the widespread influence the Foundation is exercising. (Dewey, 1980/1934, p. viii)

FIGURE 1. John Dewey, Albert C. Barnes, and Fidèle seated in the Gallery beside "After the Concert" (BF862), 1941. Photograph collection, The Barnes Archives. Reprinted with permission.

SOCIALLY INSTRUMENTAL SCIENTIFIC METHOD IN EDUCATION AT THE BARNES FOUNDATION

Among the common social and educational values that Barnes and Dewey shared, as I argued in "Democracy and Education at the Barnes Foundation" (Johnson, 1987), was a serious and abiding interest in educating "the masses." They shared a deep involvement in bringing art to many people in a way that affects their lives by integrating the aesthetic with ongoing experience. Moreover, Dewey's socially instrumental scientific approach to learning was the

SECTION 1 | **FOUNDATIONAL APPROACHES TO HOLISTIC ART EDUCATION** | THE HEART OF ART EDUCATION educational method implemented at the Barnes Foundation (Johnson, 1987). Barnes had determined in an earlier experiment in education at his Argyrol Factory that Dewey's *How We Think* (1910), with its five-step analysis of reflective thinking, enabled his adult learners (in this case, factory workers) to adapt their reading (works by William James, John Dewey, George Santayana, and Bertrand Russell) to their own experiences. Similarly, Barnes intended that his 1925 book *The Art in Painting* would be used as a text to correspond with the use of the principles of scientific method in education. Dr. Barnes made this point very clear in the preface to the first edition of the book, stating "...this book is an experiment in the adaptation to plastic art of the principles of scientific method" (Barnes, 1925, p. 11). Barnes wrote about this method:

> The method comprises the observation of facts, reflection upon them, and the testing of the conclusions by their success in application. It stipulates that an understanding and appreciation of paintings is an experience that can come only from contact with the paintings themselves. It emphasizes the fact that the terms *understanding, appreciation, art, interest,* and *experience,* have precise meanings that are inseparable parts of the method (p. 9).

Art educators familiar with John Dewey's ideas and meanings through their reading of *Art as Experience* realize that, to Dewey, the words *appreciation* and *experience* were best understood more as verbs than as nouns. Yet another term that Dewey mentions in *Art as Experience* is not commonly used in the field: *transferred values.* This concept is the focus of this chapter as it relates to holistic education and curriculum integration.

Transferred values are understood as aesthetic attributes or affective qualities of objects that pass from one thing to another, among objects, artifacts, works of art, the environment, and our experiences. Transferred values enable us to see and experience visual metaphors in art and life. On one hand, for example, I might describe Renoir's 1879 painting *Mussel Fishers at Berneval* (until recently located in Gallery 14 at the Barnes Foundation in its original, Merion, Pennsylvania site) as a sentimental genre scene; but on the other hand, my immediate aesthetic experience of the work is enhanced by transferred values as I recall the scents and sounds of low tide, coupled with an eldest daughter's impatience with her younger siblings. Transferred qualities are carriers of the familiar from life to art and art to life, and they enhance our experience of both.[1]

The concept of transferred values was developed after the first edition of *The Art in Painting* (Barnes, 1925), and built upon the author's art theory regarding plastic and human values in relation to decoration and expression in painting. According to Barnes, plastic values are qualities common to all perceived things (colors, lights and shadows, contours, spatial intervals); they are formed in works of visual art (plastic) and are not literary or moral values. Human values, as part of human nature, are qualities that evoke the feelings of the same general kind as the emotions of everyday life, such as tenderness, pride, dignity; transferred values, on another hand, are qualities sensed or perceived in reciprocal manner among works of art and human experience.

According to Barnes, transferred values add expression/decoration to objects or situations to provide aesthetic unity. Barnes elaborated on the concept in the third edition of *The Art in Painting*: "Esthetic unity requires the presence of both decoration and expression... Intermediate between expression and decoration stand what may be called transferred values. These are values which do not belong to an object in its intrinsic nature, but serve to enrich and diversify the perception of it" (1976/1937, p. 18). Between 1925 and 1937, this topic had been addressed in detail in a book co-authored by Barnes and his associate, Violette de Mazia, titled *The Art of Henri Matisse* (1933):

> If an object has been part of an experience having emotional value, another object resembling the first may subsequently attract to itself at least a part of the original emotion. Such values we have termed "transferred values": they often exist even when there is no conscious recall of the original experience. (p. 31)

The conversation between Barnes and Dewey about transferred values may have begun early in 1934, when Dewey sent Barnes a copy of *Art as Experience*. In a letter to Dewey about the book, Barnes critiqued several passages. He questioned whether "seeing" a Picasso in the snow was an example of aesthetic expressiveness. Dr. Barnes wrote, "It is not a misunderstanding of the nature of an aesthetic experience, nor is it entirely a matter of transferred values. The man who finds out what it is has a better head than mine. The clue might lie in letting incubate your 'isolation of the act of expression from the expressiveness of the object' etc. on page 82" (Letter, Albert C. Barnes to John Dewey, 29 March 1934). Dewey's return letter continues a discussion of the topic:

> There is one point I didn't touch on which may have made the difference between us seem bigger than it is—in fact it may not exist at all. You have been a painter and anyway have a much greater experience with pictures than I have. Consequently your reconstructive processes in perception of either a natural object or a picture are much more pronounced than mine. You would make an art product out of a natural object much more completely than I would, tho [*sic*] of course as far as I have an esthetic experience at all I make an art object of it to some extent. I wasn't denying this, but was concentrating on the peculiar change of attitude that comes when we find when we have been, as you say, "cheated"—so I guess we agree about that too. But the whole problem involved is a very interesting one and I think new.

In a postscript, Dewey adds the following:

> I doubt for instance whether I would have seen the Picasso in the snow picture tho [*sic*] I might have seen a picture. (Letter, John Dewey to Albert C. Barnes, 30 March 1934).

Barnes responds in return that "[i]t is possible that the root of the matter lies in fitting in the concept of transferred values to the aesthetic response to natural objects" (Letter, Albert C. Barnes to John Dewey, 30 March 1934). Barnes continues to write at length about the matter related to his perception of the "Picasso in the snow," but adds, "About your feeling of a waterfall, I can show it to you in many Renoirs and Cézannes that have all the vital aesthetic power of a real waterfall increased a thousand fold; does this latter idea link the problem up with transferred values?" (Letter, Albert C. Barnes to John Dewey, 30 March 1934).

This exchange of letters between Barnes and Dewey likely influenced Dewey to add the following to the published version of *Art as Experience*: "Dr. Barnes has pointed out that not only are intellectual meanings carried over from past experiences to add expressiveness, but so are qualities that add emotional excitation, whether the excitation be of serenity or poignancy" (1980/1934, p. 118). Dewey goes on to quote Barnes:

> "There are," as he says, "in our minds in solution a vast number of emotional attitudes, feelings ready to be reexcited when the proper stimulus arrives, and more than anything else it is in these forms, this residue of experience, which, fuller and richer than in the mind of ordinary man, constitute the artist's capital. What is called the magic of the artist resides in his ability to transfer these values from one field of experience to another, to attach them to the objects of our common life, and by his imaginative insight make these objects poignant and momentous." (p. 118)

Furthermore, in a footnote, Dewey points the reader to the chapter on transferred values in *The Art of Henri Matisse* in which Dr. Barnes demonstrates the unconscious transference of emotional values connecting tapestry, tiles, stripes, and so on in Matisse's paintings.

Dr. Barnes referred again to transferred values in this third edition of *The Art in Painting* (1976/1937) when he wrote about the work of Henri Matisse, noting that the "general decorative quality of Matisse's design is greatly enhanced by the fact that it effects the transfer of values from one realm of experience to another" (p. 366). Barnes gave an account of his concept of transferred values especially apparent in Matisse's work. He listed tapestries, posters, rosettes, and fireworks as having decorative qualities also found in Matisse's art, no matter the subject matter, figure, or landscape. "To this essential realism," Barnes wrote, "[Matisse's] transferred values add a further expressive effect: they invest the most prosaic objects with the attributes of tapestries or banner, flowers or jewels" (pp. 366-367). Conversation with Dewey led Barnes to recognize that transferred values were a phenomenon associated not only with the "fine arts," but also with decorative arts and crafts. This recognition in turn resulted in the expansion of Barnes' collection, as well as his educational approach.

REARRANGING THE COLLECTION TO CORRESPOND WITH A THEORY OF TRANSFERRED VALUES

Dewey's observation in the letter to Barnes dated 30 March 1934 that "the whole problem involved is a very interesting one and I think new" may not have simply been a way to avoid an argument with Barnes, but perhaps was an extension of an intriguing philosophical question between the two men. In the 1930s, while Dr. Barnes was continuing to collaborate closely with John Dewey as the "philosopher applied his instrumentalism to the realm of aesthetics in *Art as Experience,* Barnes was inspired to expand his collection again, to include decorative arts, rearranging the rooms in his gallery to illustrate his new theory of Transferred Values (Bahr, 1999, p. xxvii). It would seem that this "new" problem opened new fields for Barnes to plow in his gallery and in his educational practice. Thus, while Barnes had collected paintings and sculptures in the 1920s, by 1935 he was adding such items as wrought iron, furniture, and pottery (Bahr, 1999, p. xxvii). With these additions to his collection, we begin to see Dewey's broadly social instrumentalism exemplified in the practice of an institution concerned with education in art. This is especially apparent in a poster that hangs in the coatroom of the Barnes Foundation, on a wall opposite the lockers where for a quarter, visitors store their bags, books, and purses. The poster reads:

> ...Art is not a phase of life apart from the work-a-day world, to which one may turn in moments of leisure or perhaps in the name of so-called 'culture,' or in a spirit of worship. In the Foundation's courses, art is taken out of its usually detached, esoteric world and is linked up with life itself because all the qualities which give painting its value are those which are found in various phases of everyday life; and art has value only because it expresses those qualities. In other words, 'art is a fragment of life presented to us enriched in feeling by means of the creative spirit of the artist.'... We do not teach students how to paint, for that would be like teaching an injured person how to scream. We teach them how to learn to see; that is, to perceive the meanings in the events of everyday life, as well as in paintings, sculpture, music, furniture, objects in wrought iron, trees and flowers. (Poster, coatroom, Barnes Foundation)

Being able to "perceive the meanings in the events of everyday life, as well as in the paintings" is a faculty developed, according to Barnes, through awareness of the existence of transferred values in the act of appreciating works of art, artifacts, and nature.

In her unpublished 1999 dissertation, *Transferring Values: Albert C. Barnes, Work and the Work of Art,* Megan Bahr wrote that Barnes began to expand his theory of transferred values to a method in art education in 1935, and continued to do so for the rest of his life.

> For the last 16 years of his life, he was preoccupied with developing a method to teach his students how to transfer the value of their aesthetic experiences of perceiving ideal

forms in the Foundation galleries, to enhance their pleasure of their observations of objects and situations in the mundane world. (Bahr, 1999, p. 280-281)

By 1950, Barnes "had systematically rearranged all of the displays in the galleries 'in accordance with a new and more proper sense of 'Transferred Values'" (Bahr, 1999, p. 282). The implication is that a student's appreciation of aesthetic qualities in works of art would be more apparent to him or her when seen in relation to well-designed, decorative, and utilitarian objects from ordinary life; and in turn, the viewer's perception of objects and situations in the "mundane" world would be enhanced and developed by becoming aware of any expressive qualities in works of art.

TRANSFERRED VALUES AND DEMOCRACY

In a participatory democracy, all individuals, no matter their status or education, should be given opportunities to think (and act) intelligently, and this is what Barnes and Dewey envisioned for the Barnes Foundation and its educational program. Dr. Barnes did this with his factory workers and his paintings long before he took a class with Professor Dewey, before he read Dewey's 1916 book *Democracy and Education*, and before John Dewey became the first Director of Education at the Barnes Foundation. And so, when Dewey and Barnes met, their ideas about democracy, education, and art resonated with each other, just as they resonate today, nearly a century later, as we hear calls for education reform and a need for 21st-century skills to focus on creativity and critical thinking in education (see, for example, the Partnership for 21st Century Skills and the Whole Child organization; in addition, National Center on Education and the Economy, 2007; Pink, 2006; Friedman, 2006).

Perhaps the best way to understand transferred values is not simply to read about them, but instead to experience them directly. Such experiences were had when visiting the Barnes Foundation in Merion, where transferred values are apparent in the wall ensembles, the architecture, and the surrounding grounds, including the horticulture. However, the collection is moving to Philadelphia's Center City and is scheduled to reopen in May 2012, so it is quite possible that the current Barnes Foundation, with Dr. Barnes's mission of integration of art, architecture, and context (environment: the arboretum and grounds), will trade holistic educational value for common tourist value. According to Nicolai Ouroussoff (2009),

> The new Barnes will include many of the features that have virtually mandated in the museum world today—conservation and education departments, temporary exhibition space, auditorium, bookstore, cafe—making it four times the size of the old Barnes.

Yet even as the actual collection is moved and transformed, much can be gained from reflection on the value to education today of Barnes's and Dewey's original mission in their educational program at the Barnes Foundation: a socially instrumental pedagogy that should provide all people with the means to intelligently reflect upon and evaluate their decisions, actions, and resultant work and participation in a participatory democracy through critical and creative thinking. Albert Barnes died in 1951, John Dewey in 1952. We are left to wonder if transferred values could have value today to holistic and interdisciplinary education. If so, what works of art and artifact would we place in our galleries and their environments? What lessons would we and our students draw about art and about life? With their emphasis on the interaction of language, culture, society, and politics, I suggest that postmodern art and contemporary art theory provide us with venues to do so. And, as we consider our arts programs in light of postmodern concerns as well as earlier "progressive" ones, we can recognize opportunities to deliver an integrated, holistic curriculum that celebrates interrelationships of art and of life through transferred values.

Docents leading classroom tours of the Barnes Foundation galleries help students recognize and relate to human values in individual portrait and family paintings, expressions of tenderness, aloofness, and so on. The docents point to the way repeated shapes underscore these expressed feelings as they draw students' attention to the way curvilinear or angular aspects of metalwork (latches) on the walls, or imagery on painted chests, are repeated in adjacent paintings. Observing a tour for a group of third-grade students in November 2007, I heard the docent state, "Dr. Barnes wanted to show the work of workers. He considered these pieces artwork too." In this way, docents convey an understanding of transferred values while they emphasize Barnes's democratic and egalitarian philosophy regarding the art he collected and promoted in the Foundation's art education program.

In like manner, teachers of young children point out the parallels between stripes in a painting with stripes on a shirt; colors seem warm or cool; patterns are recognized around a classroom as they are studied in works of art; baskets of fruit are set out on a table by a still life of the same, while slices of fruit are served for snack. Even our youngest students can connect what they see and feel in works of art to human values, such as one kindergartener did when he pointed out that the images in Hicks's *Peaceable Kingdom* made him think that the artist wanted us to "not fight and all be friends on the playground." Teachers and students evoke memories of experiences and rekindle emotions to help describe and interpret works of art.

Other examples demonstrate this. Following an appreciative examination of Burchfield's *Gateway to September* in art class, a 7th-grade student's reflective art criticism (Johnson, 1988, 1992) demonstrates the kind of critical thinking and an integration of life with art that Barnes and Dewey would applaud:

> *Gateway to September* is a watercolor painting. It is a Asymmetrical [*sic.*] painting, The yellow and green give the painting unity. There are a lot of straight, curved, and squiggled lines. The rythem [*sic.*] is the lines making sounds.
>
> I see clouds in the Background. I see the tree frowning, and a praying mantis on the tree. I see a mountain, and in the middle of it I see negative space that looks like a person. They are yellow with another world in them. There are faces in the leaves and masks on the trees.
>
> I like the painting. When I look at it, it makes me feel peaceful. I [*sic.*] reminds me of the movies when people enter a portal to another world. It blends with the peace and stress of life. It could be a land with mirrors of what you [*sic.*] past and what the future is.
>
> When I look at this painting I hear nature all around me, and see the dangers and positives of life. But there are some things I dislike about the painting. When I see the power lines in the middle of the page it seems like now—when we use up the sun's energy and release bad carbons. It's a creepy painting because of the way we can translate to what we go through every day. When I see the trees all mean I translate it to stress. When I see the new wold [*sic.*] I translate it to peace.
>
> I see a lot more stuff each time I look at it—like the criket [*sic.*] and the trees in the far-grounds [*sic.*]—Like the dragon fly or maybe the owl. Or the flowers 20, 30, 62. I can't count how many I find. This is the neverending painting.
>
> *Gateway to September* is the most touching painting I've seen in the 7th grade. It is the neverending painting. It relates to the peace and stress of everyday lives and is a very succesful [*sic.*] painting.
>
> —K.S., Rawlinson Road Middle School, Rock Hill, SC (Susan Cooper, art teacher)

Spelling errors aside, this example of written art criticism reflects the higher-order critical and creative thinking that middle-school teachers in any subject area would want their students to achieve. More than mere intellectual effort is evident in this paper; it also reflects the student's holistic engagement, demonstrating the integration of perception, feeling, thought, and spirit. Such comprehensive learning is perhaps uniquely provided by the experience of transferred values, even as it demonstrates the interrelationship of art with experience.

Transferred values are apparent throughout the Barnes Foundation as of this writing—in the wall ensembles, the architecture, and the surrounding grounds, including the horticulture. As discussed previously, transferred values are apparent throughout the Barnes Foundation in its original site. It is possible that the previous Barnes Foundation collection, with Dr. Barnes's and Dr. Dewey's mission of integration of art, architecture, and context (environment), may trade the collection's holistic educational value in Merion, Pennsylvania for tourist value 5 miles away in Philadelphia. It is vitally important that art educators understand the role that transferred values may play not only in holistic education but also in a participatory democracy.

ABOUT THE AUTHOR

Margaret Johnson retired in 2011 as director of the art education program at the State University of New York in New Paltz. Johnson spent a recent sabbatical year (2007-2008) studying at the Barnes Foundation in Merion, Pennsylvania.

REFERENCES

Althouse, R., Johnson, M. H., & Mitchell, S. T. (2003). *The colors of learning: Integrating the visual arts into the early childhood curriculum*. New York, NY: Teachers College Press.

Bahr, M. (1999). *Transferring values: Albert C. Barnes, work and the work of art*. (Doctoral dissertation, The University of Texas at Austin, 1999). Dissertation Abstracts International, (UMI No. 9936964).

Barnes, A. C. (1925). *The art in painting*. New York, NY: Harcourt Brace & Company.

Barnes, A. C. (1976/1937). *The art in painting* (3rd ed., fourth printing). Merion Station, PA: The Barnes Foundation Press.

Barnes, A. C., & de Mazia, V. (1933). *The art of Henri Matisse*. Merion, PA: The Barnes Foundation.

De Mazia, V. (Autumn 1978). Transferred values: Part I—introduction. *Journal of the Art Department of The Barnes Foundation, IX*, no. 2.

De Mazia, V. (Spring-Summer, 1979). Transferred values: Part II. *Vistas. Journal of The Art Department of The Barnes Foundation, I*, no. 1.

De Mazia, V. (1983). *The Barnes Collection: The display of its art collection*. Merion Station, PA: The Barnes Foundation.

Dewey, J. (1980/1934). *Art as experience*. New York, NY: G. F. Putnam.

Dewey, J. (1966/1916). *Democracy and education*. New York, NY: Macmillan.

Dewey, J. (1910). *How we think*. Boston, MA: D.C. Heath.

Friedman, T. L. (2006). *The world is flat: A brief history of the twenty-first century* (updated and expanded). New York, NY: Farrar, Straus and Giroux.

Johnson, M. H. (1987). Democracy and education at the Barnes Foundation. *The Bulletin of the Caucus on Social Theory and Art Education, 8*, 62-69.

Letter, Albert C. Barnes to John Dewey, 29 March 1934. Administration, Presidents' Files, Albert C. Barnes Correspondence. The Barnes Foundation Archives, Merion, PA. Reprinted with permission.

Letter, Albert C. Barnes to John Dewey, 30 March 1934. Administration, Presidents' Files, Albert C. Barnes Correspondence. The Barnes Foundation Archives, Merion, PA. Reprinted with permission.

Letter, John Dewey to Albert C. Barnes, 30 March 1934. Administration, Presidents' Files, Albert C. Barnes Correspondence. The Barnes Foundation Archives, Merion, PA. Reprinted with permission.

National Center on Education and the Economy. (2007). *Tough times or tough choices: The report of the new commission on the skills of the American workforce*. Washington, DC: Author.

Ouroussoff, N. (2009). Architects reimagine the Barnes collection. *The New York Times, Architectural Review*, October 7, 2009.

Partnership for 21st Century Skills. (2004). *Framework for 21st century learning: Skills framework*. www.21stcenturyskills.org.

Pink, D. H. (2006). *A whole new mind: Moving from the information age to the conceptual age*. New York, NY: Riverhead Press.

The Barnes Foundation.(2009), *About the Barnes*. www.barnesfoundation.org/h_main.html.

The Barnes Foundation. (2003). *A passion for art: Renoir, Cezanne, Matisse, and Dr. Barnes* [DVD]. The Barnes Foundation and Corbis Publishing. www.barnesfoundation.org.

ENDNOTE

1   Violette de Mazia wrote extensively about transferred values in the Barnes collection in several articles. There are two articles in *Vistas*, a publication of the Journal of the Art Department of The Barnes Foundation,: Autumn 1978 (pp. 3-33) and Spring-Summer 1979 (pp. 3-39). She also wrote about transferred values in a 1983 pamphlet, *The Barnes Foundation: The display of its art collection*.

CHAPTER 5

Aesthetic Behaviors and Cultural Transaction

Eleanor Weisman and Jay Hanes

I know the feeling
I know it from before
Descartes through Hegel,
Belief is never sure.
　　　　　—Lou Reed (1990),
　　　　　　Dime Store Mystery

BIOLOGY AND CULTURAL CONSTRUCTS OF A WHOLE HUMAN BEING

The purpose of this chapter is not to build a case for why the arts are important in holistic education, but rather to advocate that educators recognize themselves as cultural workers.[1] We urge all educators to consider *how* the arts are used or excluded as both process and subject matter within the learning institution. In our advocacy, we include all categories of the arts, visual and material culture as well as performing arts. We define *aesthetic behaviors* as deeply felt and sensed processes that engage the full person. The whole human is assumed to include the physical, emotional, and intuitive or spiritual as well as the intellectual or rational aspects of being. The aesthetic experience itself can occur when doing—making or performing—as well as when observing or witnessing. We then draw on neuroscience to explore the biological foundation for aesthetic behaviors, and we call on cultural studies for demonstrating the range of values and beliefs that can be taught or transmitted through aesthetic experience. Finally, the chapter concludes with a plea for educators to question themselves, their cultural assumptions, and the effect their pedagogy has on students in the 21st century, the environment that is now. Because educational systems either promote a status quo or guide students toward social reconstruction, teaching and learning can be seen as an important cultural transaction that reflects and conveys society's values. Holistic education serves the needs of an evolving society, providing opportunities for aesthetic transactions to develop human potential.

Our inquiry commences by asking what differentiates people from other beings. What does it mean to be human? Scholars from neuroscience (Damasio, 1999; Lewis, Amini, & Lannon, 2000) and cultural studies (Dissanayake, 2000; Small, 1998) have addressed this question, giving new meaning and direction for education in the 21st century. We interpret these studies as helping to reinforce the importance of the aesthetic experience in the quest for the identity of the individual, for building relationships with others in community, and for coping with the natural environment. In effect, when creating or receiving art, aesthetic behaviors are not only essential aspects of holistic human experience, but may even be seen as our birthright.

Elders have taught that the questions one asks determine the answers one receives. This chapter questions how culturally determined attitudes toward aesthetic experience and arts-based learning influence human values, beliefs, and behaviors. While one might assume that human biology is universally the same, one also accepts that cultures around the globe exhibit vastly differing values and beliefs. Simply because human cultures evolve at the confluence of biology and environment, groups of people will develop various adaptations to the extremes of the natural world. Yet, if cultural behaviors, including artistic or aesthetic experiences, vary so greatly, how does the common biology influence the construction of human culture?

INTEGRATED BRAIN FUNCTIONS

Developmentally, one common influence is the fact that, in every culture, human infants are dependent on adults to support, guide and maintain their existence. Meredith Small (1998), in her cross-cultural study of parenting, referred to research that demonstrates the depth of that infant dependency. Young babies even learn how to stabilize their very breath through contact with a mature human body. Perhaps most relevant to the discussion in this chapter is the work of Ellen Dissanayake. In her book *Art and Intimacy* (2000), Dissanayake built the case that it is through the "rhythm and modes" of mutuality in the human infant to adult relationship that the arts appear as crucial to the development of humanness. The bodily movement and vocalizations that occur in basic human interaction lay the groundwork for behaviors referred to as dance and music. The playful use of materials and the joy of creative making-of-things lead directly to aesthetic material culture that reveals the values and mores of a human social group. If one defines the aesthetic experience as a state of deep feeling and sensing in the moment, as well as thinking about and intuiting the meaning of the act, then perhaps it is the aesthetic experience that uniquely inhabits and animates the whole human being. We will continue the examination of aesthetic behaviors as integrated brain functions through the findings of neuroscientists.

Research on the human brain reveals new understandings of its complexity. Knowledge of human neural networks establishes that thinking and feeling are activities that involve the body, emotions are physically determined, and the human brain is patterned through both nature and nurture. People rely on movement, whether through the action potential of the neuron, or through full-bodied travel through space, to experience themselves and others as fully human. These ideas once again link the deeply felt and sensed aesthetic experience to the consciousness of being human.

Neuroscientist Antonio Damasio titled his book, *The Feeling of What Happens* (1999), with the subtitle *Body and Emotion in the Making of Consciousness*. He demonstrated that human consciousness is a result of neural connections of the physical, emotional, and intellectual aspects of the human self. Human consciousness is richly complex simply because it is an embodied experience. Perhaps the arts in their engagement of these three aspects of being, are what make us human. In addition, the mystery of the intuitive, commonly known as the fourth attribute of Jungian psychology, is enhanced through aesthetic experience. At the least, aesthetic knowledge may be closely related to the unexplainable. Neuroscience provides more details that support this theory in identifying what has been called the "triune" or "three-part brain."

Triune Brain

As early as the 1980s, neuroscientists were using the model of a three-part brain, based on the work of Paul MacLean (1973). This model (see Figure 1) described the spinal cord and cerebellum or brain stem as the reptilian brain, necessary for maintaining vital functions of organs and transmitting information to the skeletal-muscular system. Damasio (1999) elaborated on

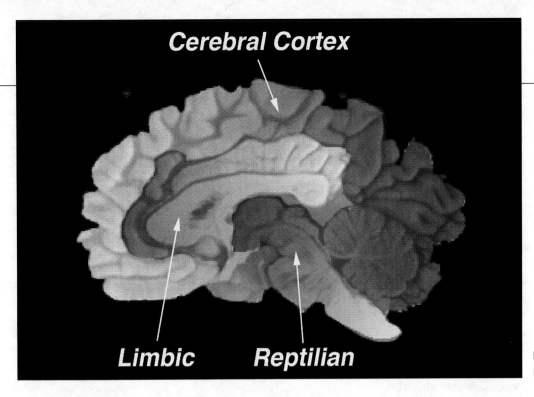

FIGURE 1. The triune brain. Illustration by Jay Hanes.

the role of the reptilian brain in the "core consciousness" (p. 82) of the human being. Mammals are distinguished from other species by a well-developed limbic brain, housed deep in the skull and nestled on top of the cerebellum. The limbic brain is the seat of the emotions, connected to memory and responses to stimuli that are evolutionarily necessary for survival, such as fear. Structures in the limbic brain receive crucial patterning lessons during infancy, that period when Dissanayake's rhythms and modes of interaction with adults are so important. The third portion of the brain is the cerebral cortex, surrounding the limbic brain as a mantle.

The cerebral cortex is generally considered to be the rational, problem solving brain that analyzes, manipulates language, and supports distinctly human activities, such as mathematical calculations. Although the cerebral cortex is undoubtedly essential to the activities of being human, it is only in concert with neural connections to the sensing and feeling human self that this higher brain contributes to "humanness." Thomas Lewis, Fari Amini, and Richard Lannon (2000) suggested that a "temperocentrist" approach assumes that the latest stage of evolution is the most highly advanced. They stated, "Expunge this temperocentrist bias, and the neocortical brain [cerebral cortex] is not the most advanced of the three [parts of the triune brain], but simply the most recent [development in the human brain]" (p. 31). Even within the cerebral cortex, information flows or moves throughout, passing through the core consciousness of memory and emotion and connecting into the physical experience of being.

This perspective makes all three parts of the triune brain essential for a truly whole human experience. The neural patterning that begins in infancy structures relationships that course throughout the entire human nervous system and body. In essence, the heart is connected to the head, which is connected to the hands, the navel, and the toes. When dancing, singing, decorating, and reflecting on the most appropriate choice, the whole person is engaged in aesthetic action. Digging deeper into neuroscience on the cellular level provides more information on human behavior and biology.

MONKEY SEE, MONKEY DO: MIRROR NEURONS AND LEARNING

A neuron is a specialized cell found in the brain and the nervous system. Neurons are designed to both send and receive information. The relays of information are connections among the neurons that help us to perceive, act, and know. As we learn, we make new neural patterns and connections. There are many ways that humans learn, sometimes by exploring or experimenting, through imitation, and occasionally through flashes of insight or intuition. The latter style of learning might be related to aesthetic process and is intimately connected to cultural ritual. For now, it is useful to examine the neural underpinnings of imitation.

Rizzolatti and Craighero (2004) have identified that certain neurons function when humans and primates are learning through watching and then imitating what they have seen. From copying how to draw an image or cut a carrot, many young children observe and then do in like fashion what they observed. Dance sequences and drying dishes can be learned in a similar manner. However, more importantly, social relationships depend on mirror neurons for understanding what another person is feeling. It has been suggested that empathy depends on mirror neurons and that effective therapy is a result of a therapist's well-developed ability to empathize (Pallaro, 2007). Acknowledgment of the human capacity for imitation and empathy directly relates to the use of the arts for expression, communication, and for the unique aesthetic experience. The innate mirror neuron system may account for the pleasure humans find in watching others perform as well as explain the learning style used when observing elders and peers. Human see, human do.

Massaging the Whole Brain

So, when and how is the maximum percentage of the human brain used simultaneously? Although that answer may not be known precisely, it has been suggested that when people are performing dance improvisation in community, the triune brain is called upon to work in harmony (Dale, Hyatt, & Hollerman, 2007). Mirror neurons must be used to witness and respond to what others are doing. Certainly the cerebellum and the motor cortex of the cerebral cortex are quite active, as the body is in motion. In addition, the limbic brain responds to the mood or emotional quality of the other movers and the music (if there is any) as well as to the individual's own internal feelings and sensations during movement. Other areas of the cerebral cortex are constantly judging spatial relationships, perhaps counting rhythms or moments of pause, and making choices.

Similarly, the participant in a group mural-making process may be employing all aspects of the brain. Many artistic ventures involve thinking on the spot with spontaneous decision-making that depends on previous knowledge, immediate analysis, and the ability to foresee consequences. A moment of aesthetic improvisation requires rational thought, supported by emotional memory, and the behavior itself depends on physical movement.[2] Thus, knowledge from neuroscience supports the understanding that artmaking processes are significant holistic endeavors. Groups of people all around the globe have used such rich aesthetic behaviors, usually through ritual, to transmit cultural values and beliefs, or worldviews.

ART, BODY, BRAIN, AND CULTURE

Anthropologist Victor Turner connected the role of the ritual-creative-aesthetic act and the human brain. In a discussion on the anthropological basis of ritual, Turner (1987) asked,

> If ritualization, as discussed by Huxley, Lorenz, and other ethologists, has a biogenetic foundation, while meaning has a neocortical learned base, does this mean that creative processes, those which generate new cultural knowledge, might result from a coadaptation, perhaps in the ritual process itself, of genetic and cultural information? (p. 162)

Turner's question suggests that both the biological, genetic nature of the human and the constructed knowledge of a society are evoked during ritualized creative acts. The individual is motivated to participate in community through aesthetic and artistic practices. Many groups of people have benefited from ritualized, often spiritual, community or individualized events that include dance, music, and visual expression. The range of functions that these aesthetic behaviors serve is complex, and the values they transmit are supported by the beliefs held by the people.

The Multiple Functions of Art in Culture

Zoe Strother (1995), an art historian, described one such ritual of the Central Pende of Zaire as an integration of the sister muses. The dance ritual cannot occur without the mask or the music. It is collaboration, with no one artist more important than another to the total act. The community ritual originated in the mid-1970s, and Strother further pointed out how the performance changed over time due to the influence of the audience. Strother drew on popular culture theory to build the case that rituals can change, "generating new cultural knowledge" due at least in part to the preferences and reactions of the audience (Turner, 1987, p. 162). The community impacts the enactment or "life" of the ritual. The Central Pende people value the influence of the community. This example is significant as a distinctly holistic human activity for the manner in which the sister arts are integrated and for the recognition of the interaction between artist and community. There is a social transaction demonstrated in this aesthetic ritual as the individual influences the group simultaneously with being influenced by the group.

In the book *Calliope's Sisters*, Richard Anderson (1990/2004) gave many examples of other cultural aesthetic traditions that reveal attitudes about what it means to be human. He analyzed the world-view paradigms of groups of people as suggested by their aesthetic practices. The Kung San people are exemplary in their use of art as an enhancement of life. With modernization of the sub-Saharan African continent, the San are referred to as an example of a disappearing culture. Historically, they were a nomadic people with more leisure time than most Westerners in the 21st century (Small, 1998). An infant was raised by being carried on the mother's body, was fed whenever desired throughout the day, and had very little need to cry. According to Anderson (2004), the San people danced, made music and decorated the body. The body was the main object of adornment, as material possessions were few, and those they did have needed to be portable. Human activities that now are described as "art" were part of daily life for the San.

In contrast to the San, the aesthetic behaviors of the Inuit people of North America are influenced by a colder climate. Inuit practices that could be labeled as art have what Anderson (1990/2004) discussed as a transcendent dimension. The transformation of nature[3] from the ordinary to the sacred ensures the future wellbeing of the people in a harsh environment. Inuit people instilled a supernatural, transformative quality to their artmaking. The aesthetic experience for the Inuit integrates the human with both the natural and the supernatural, or mythic and spiritual, worlds. Anderson (1990/2004) described how Inuit myths reveal the power of art processes in supernatural transformation by highlighting the aesthetic practices of song and dance, as well as crafts such as woodcarving and sewing. Anderson stated, "...art mediates the boundaries between the material, the human, and the superhuman realm" (1990/2004, p. 52). The aesthetic behaviors of the Inuit are interwoven with their beliefs surrounding the relationship and dependency of people to their environment, quite different from paradigms that view the natural world as a commodity to be consumed or controlled.

The role of the arts in a culture also reveals economic as well as political structures and attitudes. One poignant example is the Ghost Dance of the Plains Indians of North America. The atrocities committed against the native people of North America are well known, but perhaps less recognized is that the culture of the people remains vibrant, especially as resistance to a dominator culture. The Northern Plains Indians traditionally used dance for both sacred and social reasons. The complex political context of the late 19th century with non-Indian expansion into the western plains, the growth of the railroads, and the slaughter of the buffalo gave rise to this spiritual ritual. Alice Beck Kehoe (1989) described both the situational context and the reasons behind the spread of the Ghost Dance, a spiritual dance conceived of in a vision by a Paiute man, Jack Wilson, or Wovoka. The Ghost Dance, similar to the Central

Pende ritual discussed earlier, also relied on visual or material culture to complete the ritual. A specially designed Ghost Dance shirt was worn for the dance and was said to protect the wearer from harm. Performance of the Ghost Dance was a spiritual act of political resistance. Many American Indians in the 21st century have continued dancing in protest. Contemporary Native American choreographers draw on their historical heritage (Murphy, 2009) and continue to use the Ghost Dance as a resource for artistic statements in performance.

Other examples of aesthetic behaviors as expression of cultural beliefs and values abound. Anderson (1990/2004) discussed the social functions of art in the lives of the Sepik; ceremonial uses of art by the Dine or Navaho; issues of beauty and goodness in the aesthetic preferences of people such as the Yoruba; and, the value placed on the impermanent forms of music, dance, and floor drawings by the Asian Indian people. The arts have helped to make sense of an uncertain world, to make leisure more pleasurable, to instill values of human relationship, to harmonize with the natural world, and generally, to actualize what it means to be human. Studying the range of worldviews tied to aesthetic experiences and art practices can provide more options for the role of art in one's own life.

Cogito, Ergo Sum

Similarly the western world has had a variety of uses for the arts, and they too can be examined from the perspective of ethnic practices. If western culture is one's "home culture," it is a useful experience to question the assumptions about "art" as taught in educational experiences, both in school and out. When seen as such, aspects of elitism, political power, and domination will be observed to have entered in to the aesthetic practice of the western art world. Western culture has a long history, from Plato and Cartesian dualism, of placing a higher value on knowledge gleaned from the intellectual mind than from the body and emotions. This underlies western systems of belief and influences aesthetic behaviors.

The French academy established ballet as the highest form of dance in order to reinforce the reign of Louis XIV (Lee, 1999). Similarly, the positioning of painting as the highest form of visual art harkens back to Leonardo DaVinci (Capra, 2007). Symphony and opera became the epitome of music. While placing the artist on an elite pedestal does teach the audience to respect skill and discipline, perhaps it also separates the audience from the personal practice of the art. As John Berger (1972) pointed out over 35 years ago, why should anyone want to go to a museum filled with images that do not directly relate to the lives of the viewers? Perhaps a more integrated view of the arts in concert with each other mirrors the view of neuroscience that the idealization of the rational is meaningless without the support of other aspects of mind/body.

Transmission of Cultural Values Through the Arts

The examples discussed above demonstrate how the arts carry meaning and value beyond the surface. The use of art in any culture is obviously a significant form of cultural transmission and can be an effective method of education. John Chernoff (1979) in his now almost classic discussion of drumming in Ghana clearly described the transmission of social values through the dialogue between drummers and dancers. Chernoff stated,

> The development of musical awareness in Africa constitutes a process of education: music's explicit purpose, in the various ways it might be defined by Africans, is, essentially, socialization. An individual learns the potentials and limitations of participation in a communal context dramatically arranged for the engagement, display and critical examination of fundamental cultural values. (p. 154)

One can acknowledge that education takes place in all facets of life. We are constantly learning from what we see (visual culture), what we hear (media), and the social institutions that call on our participation (government, economics, politics, religion, etc.). Academic settings implicitly inhibit or promote social behaviors, often reinforcing inappropriate cultural assumptions concerning human interactions. Educators have the dual opportunity to model personal lifestyle choices and to guide social growth of students. How subject matter is taught, including classroom competition or collaboration, is as powerful as what is taught. We urge educators in the 21st century to think critically concerning their home culture values and the biases they implicitly support. The critical examination of a variety of cultural art forms, including one's own, brings up many essential issues of values concerning life in community and in the world.

HOLISTIC EDUCATION AND RECONSTRUCTING CURRICULUM: EMBODIMENT OF VALUES AND BELIEFS THROUGH AESTHETIC BEHAVIORS

Through the arts, education can address questions of self, community, and environment (Anderson & Milbrandt, 2005; Weisman & Hanes, 2002). The investigation of self is the search for a meaningful identity. The self continually changes and evolves as one matures and learns. This dynamic aspect of self, therefore, is constantly in need of self-reflection and introspection. Ritualized aesthetic practices have been used to meet this goal throughout the history of human culture. Community, which traditionally has been built upon such practices, is thus deeply interwoven with the search for self-knowledge. Contributing to one's community in beneficial ways adds to and draws upon self-knowledge. As such, it builds satisfaction and creates a meaningful life. Educational curriculum that includes community-building activities can be supported by aesthetic process. These themes of self, others, and the natural environment provide opportunities for the arts to be most relevant in developing holistic experiences for students to live full, rich lives through aesthetic behaviors.

Aesthetic education experiences that help create a sense of identity while promoting community become increasingly important in a consumerist and often-violent dominant culture. The 21st century opened with military conflict, environmental degradation, and spiritual poverty, events that confuse and cause apathy. Globalization, technology, and economic exchange bring cultures and nations closer together, yet alienate individuals. From a political and economic as well as a personal perspective, one must question the reliance of much of the population on pharmaceutical solutions to the depression and anxiety arising from stresses of the modern world. We suggest that aesthetic holistic education can provide other strategies for meeting basic human needs and environmental wellness. Educators as well as students of today must recognize that their choices and actions today affect not only themselves but also the future generations. Holistic education has the power to develop meaningful curriculum to include transformative aesthetic rituals that address self, community, and the global environment.

We challenge holistically minded educators to employ aesthetic behaviors as means to address themes of diversity and social justice, personal and environmental responsibility, local community action/service, and global/international perspectives, as well as interconnected and holistic thinking. These and other interdisciplinary themes can be explored through bringing academic or historical research into contemporary application through the aesthetic process. Art is a process of being/learning and can result in culminating products that communicate what has been learned, even if the product is non-tangible or impermanent. Aesthetic practices can bring into focus the possibility of social reconstruction through art education (Dewey, 1916, 1934; Greene, 1995, 2005). The arts in holistic education at this pivotal point in history have the potential to guide students of all ages through meaningful critical thinking, feeling, and decision-making.

One local example from our neighborhood involved a first grade classroom, a service-learning project, and college/schools collaboration. Guided by their classroom teacher, a college student, and a dance studies professor "emeritus," the children wrote haiku poetry, illustrated their writing, and choreographed accompanying dance movement. They were invited to perform their work as part of a college dance concert. Through the generosity of the first grade teacher, the children's families were brought to campus as audience members; for many of them, this was a first experience at a dance concert and as guests on a college campus. The drawings the first grade students made in response to their concert experience reflected the thrill the children felt performing on a professional stage and having their families witness the event. The presence and grace of the young performers and the sophistication of their visual, oral, and movement expression touched the college students who also were in the audience. The ritual of the performance gave voice to each individual child while strengthening bonds between the local low-income community and the more privileged student population. Perhaps the aesthetic behaviors of performers and audience created a new mode of cultural transaction that suggests possibilities of social reconstruction.

Here, the interaction among the children, families, and college community demonstrated that the human organism is hardwired to transform, through aesthetic experiences, activities that engage and integrate sensing, feeling, thinking, and doing. The human brain holistically functions to its capacity when connecting the emotional to the rational through the physical and intuitive. Equally important, through the arts, students of all ages learn values, beliefs, and behaviors of their home cultures becoming socialized as well as inspired. Educators, however, must ask what values and beliefs they want to instill because the arts have the potential to reinforce structures of power, dominance, and elitism or they can be used for empowerment of the oppressed self to build healthy communities. The latter purposes as evidenced in the example just given serve social reconstruction goals of holistic education.

It could be said that we are at a crisis point as we shift from body-centered humans (hunter gatherers, agrarian societies, into the Industrial Revolution) to brain-centered (the "Information Age"). Future challenges for educators as they develop holistic learning experiences in the years to come will include adjusting their teaching to accommodate popular culture and digital technology that exponentially change daily. Students must be prepared to deal with the world that confronts them, including the challenges of environmental change, terrorism, economic disasters, and dysfunctional cultures. Facing such challenges, holistic aesthetic practices in educational institutions can be a significant way to prepare individuals of all ages to value community and dialogue as paths to creative global problem solving. The arts have a long history in integrating the mysteries of life with daily reality; thus, the investigation of the intuitive, spiritual aspects of self, community, and the natural world are crucial to successful educational experience (Cajete, 1994). We urge educators to follow their own search for identity and to share that authenticity with students. Deeply reflective self-initiated study can provide an educator with content to teach while role modeling for students engaged in finding their own way. As both teachers and students, we must each ask ourselves what it is that we truly value and believe, trusting that our aesthetic behaviors will be fruitful, yet knowing that the inquiry may never be complete, much as an aesthetic ritual needs to be repeated and is new each time it is experienced. Throughout history, the arts have embodied the ongoing search for meaning through holistic, community-based engagement. Considering the challenges facing human beings in the years to come, such efforts cannot be left to one domain. Instead, educators across the curriculum need to engage aesthetic behaviors that guide self-actualization, community, and cultural transaction.

REFERENCES

Anderson, R. L. (2004). *Calliope's sisters: A Comparative study of philosophies of art* (2nd ed.). Upper Saddle River, NJ: Pearson Prentice Hall. (Original work published 1990.)

Anderson, T., & Milbrandt, M. K. (2005). *Art for life: Authentic instruction in art.* New York, NY: McGraw Hill Companies, Inc.

Berger, J. (1972). *Ways of seeing.* London, England: Penguin Books Ltd.

Cajete, G. (1994). *Look to the mountain: An ecology of indigenous education.* Durango, CO: Kivaki Press.

Capra, F. (2007). *The science of Leonardo.* New York, NY: Doubleday.

Chernoff, J. (1979). *African rhythm and African sensibility: Aesthetics and social action in African musical idioms.* Chicago, IL: The University of Chicago Press.

Dale, J. A., Hyatt, J., & Hollerman, J. (2007). The neuroscience of dance and the dance of neuroscience: Defining a path of inquiry. *Journal of Aesthetic Education, 41*(3), 81-110.

Damasio, A. (1999). *The feeling of what happens: Body and emotion in the making of consciousness.* Orlando, FL: Harcourt.

Danto, A. (1981). *The transfiguration of the commonplace.* Cambridge, MA: Harvard University Press.

Dewey, J. (1916). *Democracy and education.* New York, NY: Free Press.

Dewey, J. (1934). *Art as experience.* New York, NY: Penguin Group

Dissanayake, E. (2000). *Art and intimacy: How the arts began.* Seattle, WA: University of Washington Press.

Eliade, M. (1987). *The sacred and the profane: The nature of religion.* Orlando: Harcourt Brace Jovanovich. (Original work published 1959)

Greene, M. (1995). *Releasing the imagination.* San Francisco, CA: Jossey-Bass.

Greene, M. (2005). *The arts in difficult times* [Monograph]. Pittsburgh, PA: Arts Education Collaborative.

Kehoe, A. B. (1989). *The Ghost Dance: Ethnohistory and revitalization.* New York, NY: Holt, Rinehart and Winston.

Lee, C. (1999). *Ballet in western culture.* Boston, MA: Allyn & Bacon.

Lewis, T., Amini, F., & Lannon, R. (2000). *A general theory of love.* New York, NY: Vintage Books.

MacLean, P. D. (1973). *A triune concept of the brain and behavior.* Toronto, ON: Toronto University Press.

Murphy, J. S. (2009). *The people have never stopped dancing.* Minneapolis, MN: University of Minnesota Press.

Nachmanovitch, S. (1990). *Free play: Improvisation in life and art.* New York, NY: Penguin.

Pallaro, P. (2007). Somatic countertransference: The therapist in relationship. In P. Pallaro (Ed.), *Authentic movement: Moving the body, moving the self, being moved, a collection of essays volume two* (pp. 176-189). London, England: Jessica Kingsley Books.

Reed, L. (1990). *Dime store mystery* [Music Recording]. New York, NY: Sire Records Company.

Rizzolatti, G., & Craighero. L. (2004). The mirror neuron system. *Annual Review of Neuroscience, 27,* 169-192.

Small, M. (1998). *Our babies, ourselves.* New York, NY: Anchor Books.

Strother, Z. S. (1995, Spring). Invention and re-invention in the traditional arts. *African Arts, 28,* 24-33.

Trend, D. (1992). *Cultural pedagogy: Art/education/politics.* New York, NY: Bergin & Garvey.

Turner, V. (1987). *The anthropology of performance.* New York, NY: PAJ Publications.

Weisman, E., & Hanes, J. (2002). Thematic curriculum and social reconstruction. In Y. Gaudelius & P. Speirs (Eds.), *Contemporary issues in art education.* Upper Saddle River, NJ: Prentice Hall.

ENDNOTES

1   David Trend (1992) coined the term *cultural worker* to refer to teachers and artists, people whose work involves the transmission of culture. Cultural workers, especially teachers, have the opportunity to maintain the status quo of the culture or to work to change it. In this manner, they influence the values and beliefs of the people.

2   Musician and writer Stephen Nachmanovitch (1990) drew the connection between improvisational aesthetic processes and daily life. Perhaps the practice of aesthetic activities helps prepare one for the spontaneous decisions that occur moment by moment in life.

3   Mircea Eliade (1959/1987) explored this concept from the perspective of a scholar of comparative religion whereas Arthur Danto (1981) pursued a similar thread of thought while discussing the philosophy of art. Both scholars recognized the intimacy of the sacred in the arts and human aesthetic behaviors.

ABOUT THE AUTHORS

Eleanor Weisman directs the Dance and Movement Studies Program at Allegheny College where she examines cultural implications of aesthetic movement behaviors. Her work promotes collaboration and community building.

Jay Hanes is head of Art Education at Edinboro University of Pennsylvania. He is an organic gardener, raku potter, and tea practitioner. He continues to explore cultural values, issues of identity, and political implications of art and education.

CHAPTER 6

Holistic Teaching of Art with Technology: Practical Models and Enlarged Theory

Ching-Chiu Lin and Bertram C. Bruce

This chapter aims to investigate the potential of holistic teaching of art with technology, exploring how art teachers can integrate art with an array of digital media in the larger context of holistic pedagogy. Holistic education proposes nurturing the wholeness of individuals, helping learners to make sense of their lived experience and to act responsibly both to themselves and to the community. Many art educators embrace this value in their art teaching practice, believing that the unity of individuals can be cultivated through "a transformative engagement in visual arts" (Campbell, 2006, p. 29). This belief implies a model for teaching and learning which fosters inquiry into life, seeking the alignment of body, mind, and spirit through learners' visual expression and communication (Campbell, 2005; Carroll, 2006; Gradle, 2009; Kind, Irwin, Grauer, & de Cosson, 2005; London, 2006).

In response to the impact of changing information and communication technologies (ICTs), art educators and teachers are asking questions about how learners make sense of their learning experiences through an array of digital resources and media (Flood & Bamford, 2007; Freedman & Stuhr, 2004; Gregory, 2009). Approaching such questions from the perspective of the relationship between technology and literacy, some scholars have articulated an enlarged set of literacy skills and practices as a proficiency that meets societal needs (Hobbs & Jensen, 2009; Stankiewicz, 2004; Stokrocki, 2007). While research on definitions of literacy has expanded beyond a single-minded focus on linguistic proficiency to highlight multiple forms and purposes of communication in the information age, some scholars of literacy instruction are nevertheless drawn to develop sets of generic and prescriptive principles of specific competencies with an imperative that new ICTs require new literacy skills to exploit learners' potential. Although this understanding of learning and technology does offer a guideline or checklist for the integration of technology into art and other subject areas, identifying competencies or techniques in isolation does not take account of the larger context of practice and may cause educators to ignore the learning activities and environments drawn from learners' social and cultural experiences.

An alternative is to embrace a holistic understanding of technology in which the uses of ICTs are situated both in learners' personal knowledge structures and in a network of learning relationships. For example, one approach is to have classrooms in which teachers engage students in projects that integrate their work across art forms—both digital and material forms—and do not focus on skills per se. A major study of primary schools in Ireland (Casey et al., 2009) examined "a situated approach to literacy" (p. 6) and focused on the social contexts of classroom activities in which digital media were used. The study was pursued through a year-long investigation of classroom practices, interviews, and student-produced artifacts. It not only found that students' learning of technological skills was enhanced along with their participation in digital media and learning, but also reported increased, productive collaboration among teachers and community members. In fact, this study provides an illustration showing the understanding of technology in education is not merely about the individuals' competencies; more importantly, this understanding is contextual and interrelated as an inquiry into the wholeness of the learning experience in the age of digital culture.

Other recent research resonates with Casey and his colleagues' findings that a holistic approach to classroom practices involving digital media and the arts can make learners more complete, and it is relevant to all types of learning (Bruce & Reynolds, 2009; Eshet-Alkalai & Chajut, 2009; Ohler, 2008; Stasko, 2009). However, while the transformational power of art in holistic learning is recognized across disciplines (Carroll, 2006; Miller, 2006), little attention has been paid to the development of theoretical and practical understanding of technology as part of a holistic pedagogy (Bruce & Bishop, 2008; Gagel, 2006; Lankshear, Snyder, & Green, 2000; Seemann, 2003), as well as to the roles of art in relation to technology within this pedagogical framework. As a result, we have observed two major barriers to using art and technology integration in a more holistic way. One is that we lack empirical evidence to show educators and teachers what is possible and how to link everyday details to pedagogical ideals. The second major barrier is that we lack adequate conceptualizations of how technology, art, and holistic learning intersect. To address these two barriers, we present a study of three secondary art teachers' holistic engagements with digital media in their classroom practices (Lin, 2008) and a discussion of how holistic art education can be realized with new ICTs. Specifically, we identify the key characteristics derived from the three teachers' holistic engagements in teaching art and then use these concrete experiences to examine learning as lived experience, technology as means for inquiry, and learning relationships as groundwork for cultivating a unified whole.

HOLISTIC ENGAGEMENT IN ACTION
Methodology and Demographics

This study examined three secondary art teachers' pedagogical beliefs as manifested through their teaching practices with digital media. Viewing the art teachers as three unique instances of educational experience, case studies were conducted to explore the conditions of specific locations, learners, and factors that shape practices. Two major research questions were: "How do these teachers conceptualize, implement, and interpret their uses of digital media in teaching art?" and, "How do the social contexts of teaching and learning influence these teachers' teaching practices with art and technology?" From three different Midwestern secondary schools, all three participants—Liz, Chris, and Sara (pseudonyms)—shared several attributes: at least 5 years of teaching experience in art, confidence and competency in incorporating technology into their art teaching, and high regard from their communities.

Liz had taught for over 13 years in the larger of two public high schools in a university town. Chris was employed in a rural town at a high school that has a reputation for integrating technology across subject areas, whereas Sara taught in a junior high school located on the urban fringe of a mid-sized city. The study observation took place in Liz's class of Advanced Photography, Chris's Computer Graphics and Multimedia classes, and Sara's Video Documentary class. The research data consisted of field notes and records of classroom observations and a series of semi-structured interviews, as well as photographs of classroom activities and copies of teachers' teaching materials and student productions. Data analysis involved a three-stage process of coding, case report creation, and cross-case analysis that facilitated the study goal of depicting the uniqueness of the three case studies. Due to the scope of this article, only selective description about how these teachers approached their art teaching with technology in a holistic manner is presented.

Creative and Critical Inquiries

The facilitation of artistic production and critical reflection through digital media are two major components in these teachers' classroom practices. They consider the experience of making art an avenue through which learners can understand how technology serves the intents of artistic expression and communication. Sara asserted that "to be able to understand what you see, you have to understand how digital images are made" (Sara, personal communication, March 17, 2007), while Liz explained her belief "that having students exposed to the process of making digital images helps them to question the authenticity of things, like information or images" (Liz, personal communication, May 10, 2007). Liz viewed the computer and its wealth of programs as an artmaking medium just as the camera is the tool for photography. For Liz, artistic inquiry is the process of solving visual problems. She encouraged students to consider how the Photoshop effects represent their intentions by saying, "Think about the message that students can convey with the use of imagery; think about what certain things you can do to have an impact on your audience in terms of symbols, colors, or messages" (Liz, personal communication, May 4, 2007).

As digital media provide instant visual effects for students to experience the immediate trial and error of technological outcomes, the teachers are able to focus on the students' ability to inquire into their own learning processes. For Chris, such a reflective inquiry into lived experience helps to spark students' interest in art and cultivate students' artistic sensibility through their interests in digital media:

> I know that very few students will go into game design or animation, but this learning experience of 3D modeling may help them to develop an appreciation of those things that they run into, especially when they made those creatures and got to do just a few seconds with the movement. They maybe appreciate that more when later they watch movies. (Chris, personal communication, March 23, 2007)

These teachers are also interested in asking their students questions that lead students into a critical analysis of and reflection about the images they are consuming and producing. For example, Liz provided exposure to both digital and conventional photography and then encouraged students to rationalize their decisions about whether they preferred making art at the computer or in the darkroom. Using prior photographic knowledge to teach Photoshop, Liz would say, "Well, here's how your sepia tone looks in Photoshop" or "We've worked with solarization in a darkroom with the chemicals and the lights, and here's how you do it in Photoshop" (Liz, personal communication, May 4, 2007). The classroom dialogue played a large role in Liz's instruction as she constantly facilitated student discussion on the pros and cons of hands-on and digital photograph manipulation and representation, along with the constraints and potentiality of technology.

Just as Dewey (1938b) observed that knowledge is derived from the processes of continuous inquiry into experience, these teachers' practices linked knowledge transformation and construction to their students' background, potential, and experience through an interaction between creative production and critical reflection. Beyond the scope of classroom activities and art knowledge, these teachers' beliefs in and practices of art and technology integration take into account the larger contexts of teaching and learning in response to the changing development of ICTs. Their teaching knowledge is tied to situated learning contexts (Bernstein, 1996), and their act of teaching is based on their repertoires of practical understanding of what works best for their students (Clandinin & Connelly, 1995; Zhao, 2003).

Inquiry into Life

With regard to the totality of learning experience, these teachers' understanding of what students should learn does not focus merely on the imagery itself but also on how students' encounters with images as a unified learning experience can spark connections with their lives. Many of their teaching incidents engage a thematic approach to sociocultural issues and embrace learning resources "from a variety of disciplines from both within and beyond the visual arts" (Delacruz & Dunn, 1996, p. 77). By incorporating sociocultural issues into their teaching, these teachers encouraged their students to:

- explore their own strengths and identity;
- acknowledge the social and cultural connotations embedded in images
- examine the sociocultural issues in their daily existence;
- use digital media as an artistic tool for making social statements; and
- take action to voice their opinions on issues with which they are concerned.

For example, Liz wanted her students to go into their local communities and use digital cameras to portray stories about their community members, whereas Chris incorporated service learning into his computer graphics class, asking students to pitch their ideas to simulated clients, the local fire and police departments to publicize public safety. Likewise, Liz and Chris conducted a digital photography and a video project, respectively, to explore identity through the making of self-portraits:

> I'm always really interested in high school self-portraits. I think it's a great way to see what's going on in [high school students'] brains, like what's their concepts of themselves… So, [the project of digital self-portrait] forces them to think about their values, cultures, and things they care about. It's not only about self-expression; they learn to be aware of the connotations of images. It is an exercise in getting them to think about the codes and symbols that go into their visual experiences. (Liz, personal communication, May 4, 2007)

> We do a lot of projects where [students] are exploring themselves about where they are right now and their identities. We have done a music video self-portrait project [in which] they've learned to express themselves visually [and] make conscious decisions on their choices of music, images, and particular aspects of themselves. (Chris, personal communication, March 23, 2007)

Such an approach embraces a belief that "art education can make a difference in student understanding of and action in the world and that difference can enrich and improve social life" (Freedman, 2000, p. 314). Considering digital media as a powerful educational means, all three teachers take an active stance that provokes students' awareness of sociocultural issues, together with the cultivation of their ability to express themselves artistically. Derived from a "practicality ethic" (Delacruz, 2004, p. 8), these teachers strive to develop students' personal and social responsibility through their visual learning experience and believe art helps students foster the skills needed to face and manage contemporary life problems. As Liz explained, "Hopefully when [my students] get out of my classroom, when they do something in their lives, they are able to connect with their art experience or to the attitude or process they learned from art" (Liz, personal communication, May 12, 2007), a sentiment with which Chris and Sara agreed:

> I don't want to just teach the tools and programs; it's very dry. I want [my students] to be able to make connections with their lives through learning technology from art; to develop a sense of appreciation of art and their lives. (Chris, personal communication, April 17, 2007)

I'm hoping that my class raises questions that make my students start to think differently, not only in my classroom but everywhere. If they can start thinking differently everywhere, then they are going to able to ask questions about their lives. (Sara, personal communication, March 20, 2007)

REALMS OF LEARNING FOR HOLISTIC ENGAGEMENT IN ART AND TECHNOLOGY

The three teachers' practical endeavors resonate with Dewey's (1948/1981) observation that artistic activities are "manifested not just in what are regarded as the fine arts, but in all forms of life" (p. 315). Beyond developing students' visual competencies, they embrace a wholeness of experience that intersects with themes such as teacher expertise, student background, environment, teacher-student relationship, connections with lives, and social contexts of learning. Accordingly, we articulate how such themes are interrelated in an attempt to understand how holistic art education can be realized with implementations of new ICTs. We found that these three teachers' practices responded to the nature of holistic education by bringing three intersected realms of learning to the foreground, thus promoting the wholeness of individuals. These realms are learning as lived experience, technology as means for inquiry, and learning relationships as groundwork for cultivating a unified whole.

Learning as Lived Experience

Artistic practice is a form of life practice; in this sense learning through art helps us to make sense of life as artistic activities are understood within the context of lived experience. As fostering students' meaning-making capacity through artistic and aesthetic experience is central to quality art education (Darts, 2006; Gude, 2008), we view the process and creation of artistic experiences as "carriers of meaning" (Jackson, 1998, p. 111) that connect wholeness of life and artfulness. Recently, with the changing development of ICTs, this value of art has received a growing attention across disciplines in an attempt to implement technology in a more holistic way. Research shows there are increasing numbers of classroom activities and community youth projects approaching digital media as an artistic medium through which learners can express feeling, communicate ideas, and develop literacy skills (Bruce & Lin, 2009; Burn, 2009; Goldfarb, 2002; Goodman, 2005; Levy, 2008). New ICTs can then be seen as media for realizing Dewey's four instincts of the learner (Bruce & Levin, 1997, 2003; Levin & Bruce, 2003). Dewey (1916/2001) described the impulses (or instincts) of the learner as the social instinct, the instinct of making, the instinct of investigation, and the expressive impulse that sparks active learning to thrive. To participate in the digitally mediated world in which they live, individuals need to have the experience of using digital media to describe their understanding of and relationship with the world, to engage and communicate with others, and to learn to act responsibly to the self and the world.

This educational approach may seem common in general education but has become more significant in today's digital learning environments. That is, rather than following particular sets of skills or concepts in framing learning outcomes, a holistic engagement with technology indicates that learning is embedded within and around the impulses or instincts of the learner and connects to multiple aspects of lives, including social, cultural, and moral. It then results in the experience that Dewey (1934/2005) described as the "interaction of organism and environment which, when it is carried to the full, is a transformation of interaction into participation and communication" (p. 22). This transformation highlights the presence of learning, "extracting at each present time the full meaning of each present experience" (Dewey, 1938a, p. 51). As Dewey (1916/2007) explained, "the value of that experience"

(p. 61)—the full engagement in the moment when learning takes place—is more urgent than the idea of learning to prepare for the future. While the ever-evolving development of ICTs may signify a need to catch up with new skills and practices, nevertheless the significance of learning itself in the age of digital culture responds to the wholeness of life. The connections between the presence of learning and ordinary life experience help to enrich the learner's capacity of meaning-making. This enrichment is integrated, bringing along general literacy skills and participation in learning.

Technology as Means for Inquiry

Holistic teaching and learning respond to an inquiry-driven curriculum, and an artistic approach to the use of technology can facilitate this experience. Dewey's (1933, 1938b) notion of inquiry suggested that learners search for resolution of a problem-driven situation through their actions. For Dewey, inquiry into authentic questions evoked from the learners' experiences situates that learner at the center, with both the initiative and the responsibility for learning. Today's multimodal digital environment signifies a form of communication that is configured and conveyed through visual imagery, sound, gesture, animation, and the written word. The lines between learning *about* technology and learning *through* technology are starting to merge, and learners can choose from a variety of digital media to expand a wide range of learning experiences. Learning is thus driven by the individual needs and interests of learners, and technology becomes not only a medium of representation, but also a vehicle that facilitates learners' exploration and reconstruction of their cultural and social experiences. In the context of holistic pedagogy, technology tends to become invisible as it is embedded in social practices. Therefore, we shift from a notion of employing technology as a tool to accomplish a task to view the task itself as the central focus, with the technology as substrate. We also highlight the mediative function of technology, considering technology as a means for inquiry into the relations among ideas, and thus we experience a more connected way of learning.

Furthermore, like technology, art is embedded in the holistic practice of teaching and learning. While integrating art and technology, classroom activities all occur in some material or digital forms of media, which echoes Bolter and Grusin's (2000) argument that "new visual media achieve their cultural significance precisely by paying homage to, rivaling, and refashioning such earlier media as perspective painting, photography, film, and television" (back cover). Ultimately, we are not to differentiate between technology and art in relation to holistic teaching and learning, because the significant interrelation between the two can be realized in expanded ways with new meanings. For example, the study we presented shows that the three art teachers' allegiance to a studio-based art background and experience sustains their practices with digital media. Liz expressed a belief that students' decisions about their media choices develop from working with both conventional and digital media; Chris posited that learning foundational art knowledge is imperative to students' development of both aesthetic quality and craftsmanship in digital productions; Sara put forward the view that hands-on art experience contributes to student understanding of digitally visual representation. Importantly, holistic art education in the age of digital culture represents an interdependent partnership in which old media contribute to the enhancement of new media and new media reshape the meaning of old ones.

The Learning Relationship as Groundwork for Cultivating a Unified Whole

Recognized by Dewey and other holistic education advocates, the learning environment and teacher-student relationship play crucial roles in the course of holistic experience (Black, 2009; Campbell, 2006; Delacruz, 2004; Nardi & O'Day, 1999). Dewey's (1938a) idea of *continuity* explains that the character of each new experience is shaped by those that come before, suggesting the teacher's task of maintaining education continuity is to help learners reconstruct prior knowledge and present experience. In the age of digital culture, the role of the teacher has become more significant as teachers can offer strategies and practices to sustain this education continuity. In other words, to facilitate the totality of learning experience, teachers move beyond merely delivering subject content to helping students make connections with their lived experience. As a result, the role of teacher is beyond simply delivering technological knowledge, but, as in Miller's (2006) profile of a holistic educator, is someone who possesses, "a receptive, compassionate awareness, an attitude of wonder, awe and reverence for life" (p. 8).

In the cases of three selected art teachers, we found the role of teacher has changed from that of instructor to that of facilitator in their holistic practices of linking art with technology, and importantly, a continually evolving teacher-student trust and mutual respect has emerged in each learning setting. Other studies that approached art and technology in a more holistic way also indicate the need of a supportive environment and a trusting relationship (Bruce & Reynolds, 2009; Casey et al., 2009; Lin & Polaniecki, 2009, Winkler, Ide-Schoening, & Herczeg, 2007). For example, Bruce and Lin's (2009) study of making podcasts with Latino youth suggested the role of teacher has shifted from being the sole source of knowledge about content and media to sharing authority while integrating technology and art; Levy's (2007, 2008) studies of arts-based digital media education in a community setting suggested a pedagogical style move from knowledge transmission to two-way collaborative knowledge construction between the teacher and the students. In short, the teachers' teaching strategies and characteristic styles in these studies manifested a shared learning environment where interaction was based on mutual rapport built over time, where individual differences were respected, and where collaboration, rather than competition, was highlighted.

Furthermore, a trusting teacher-student relationship can not only facilitate the quality of learning, but also provide an educational source for young people that mirrors how human relationships interact and develop. We observed that the students who took classes from the three teachers appeared to be more fulfilled through a sense of participation in a nurturing learning community in which content and context both contributed to learning as a whole. Again taking into account Dewey's notion of inquiry, a learning community in school is seen by extension as part of the situation we transform into a larger community of humanity. In line with this enlarged notion of community, a highly developed level of teacher-student trust and mutual respect is vital, as this experience of human interaction nurtures all participants of that community to become a unified whole.

CONCLUSION

In sum, we present practical cases and research examples of implementing art with technology in a more holistic way, as well as discuss the strengths of engaging a holistic and contextualized learning model in education. Experiences that make sense are those that individuals construct in relation to the world in which they live. Technology then can be seen as a medium that assists individuals to construct meaning for their lives through the process of learning. Although ever-evolving ICTs continually impact our lives, our pedagogical attention is not on how much we know about the technology itself, but, more importantly, on how we can use technology to better understand the world around us, relationships between self and others, and the continuity of lifelong inquiries. Thus, embracing holistic art education in contemporary society suggests an artistic engagement with and through an array of digital media as part of contemporary lived experience in an attempt to highlight learners' contextualized involvement with community and environment.

This study of the three art teachers' holistic engagements with art and technology indicates a holistic practice which moves away from the boundaries of subject areas, a collection of competencies, or a set of situations that can be prescribed for another teacher or class; rather, it represents "a coevolution of individual, society, literacy, and technology, given coherence by the processes of construction" (Bruce, 2003, p. 337). Moreover, the three realms of learning—lived experience, inquiry, and learning relationships—are inextricably linked. Together, the three realms represent a possibility of how technology can be realized in a holistic way through individuals' endeavors for personal growth and community action. Art and technology in tandem are not simply a means to cultivate personal growth, but offer forms of reconstruction of the human experience, representing the connectedness between individuals and environments.

REFERENCES

Bernstein, B. (1996). *Pedagogy, symbolic control, and identity: Theory, research, critique.* London, England: Taylor & Francis.

Black, J. (2009). Necessity is the mother of invention: Changing power dynamics between teachers and students in wired art classrooms. *Canadian Review of Art Education, 36,* 75-118.

Bolter, J., & Grusin, R. (2000). *Remediation: Understanding new media.* Cambridge, MA: The MIT Press.

Bruce, B. (2003). In closing: What is literacy in the information age? In B. Bruce (Ed.), *Literacy in the information age: Inquiries into meaning making with new technologies* (pp. 327-338). Newark, DE: International Reading Association.

Bruce, B., & Bishop, A. (2008). New literacies and community inquiry. In J. Coiro, M. Knobel, C. Lankshear, & D. Leu (Eds.), *Handbook of research on new literacies* (pp. 703-746). New York, NY: Lawrence Erlbaum Associates.

Bruce, B., & Levin, J. (1997). Educational technology: Media for inquiry, communication, construction, and expression. *Journal of Educational Computing Research, 17*(1), 79-102.

Bruce, B., & Levin, J. (2003). Roles for new technologies in language arts: Inquiry, communication, construction, and expression. In J. Flood, D. Lapp, J. Squire, & J. Jensen (Eds.), *Handbook of research on teaching the English language arts* (2nd ed.) (pp. 649-657). Mahwah, NJ: Lawrence Erlbaum Associates.

Bruce, B. & Lin, C. (2009). Voices of youth: Podcasting as a means for inquiry-based community engagement. *E-learning and Digital Media, 6*(2), 230-241.

Bruce, B., & Reynolds, A. (2009). Technology in Docklands education: Using scenarios as guides for teaching and research. *Educational Studies, 35*(5), 561-574.

Burn, A. (2009). *Making new media: Creative production and digital literacies.* New York, NY: Peter Lang Publishing.

Campbell, L. (2005). Spiritual reflective practice in preservice art education. *Studies in Art Education, 47*(1), 51-69.

Campbell, L. (2006). Spirituality and holistic art education. *Visual Arts Research, 32*(1), 29-34.

Carroll, K. (2006). Development and learning in art: Moving in the direction of a holistic paradigm for art education. *Visual Arts Research, 32*(1), 16-28.

Casey, L., Bruce, B., Martin A., Hallissy, M., Sheil, G., Reynolds, A., Brown, C., & Coffey, L. (2009). *Digital literacy: New approaches to participation and inquiry learning to foster literacy skills among primary school children.* Dublin, Ireland: Centre for Research and Innovation in Learning and Teaching, National College of Ireland.

Clandinin, D., & Connelly, F. (1995). *Teachers' professional knowledge landscapes.* New York, NY: Teachers College Press.

Darts, D. (2006). Art education for a change: Contemporary issues and the visual arts. *Art Education, 59*(5), 6-12.

Delacruz, E. (2004). Teachers' working conditions and the unmet promise of technology. *Studies in Art Education, 46*(1), 6-19.

Delacruz, E., & Dunn, P. (1996). The evolution of Discipline-Based Art Education. *Journal of Aesthetic Education, 30*(3), 67-82.

Dewey, J. (1933). *How we think. A restatement of the relation of reflective thinking to the educative process (revised ed.).* Boston, MA: Heath. (Original work published 1910)

Dewey, J. (1938a). *Experience and education.* New York, NY: Macmillan.

Dewey, J. (1938b). *Logic: The theory of inquiry.* New York, NY: Henry Holt and Company.

Dewey, J. (1981). Foreword to the unfolding of artistic activity (Original work published 1948). In J. Boydston (Ed.), *The later works, 1925-1953: John Dewey* (pp. 315-317). Carbondale, IL: Southern Illinois University Press.

Dewey, J. (2001). *The school and society & the child and the curriculum.* Mineola, NY: Dover. (Original work published 1916)

Dewey, J. (2005). *Art as experience.* New York, NY: Perigee Books. (Original work published 1934)

Dewey, J. (2007). *Democracy and education.* Middlesex, England: Echo Library. (Original work published 1916)

Eshet-Alkalai, Y., & Chajut, E. (2009). Changes over time in digital literacy. *CyberPsychology & Behavior, 12*(6),713-715.

Flood, A., & Bamford, A. (2007). Manipulation, simulation, stimulation: The role of art education in the digital age. *International Journal of Education Through Art, 3*(2), 91-102.

Freedman, K. (2000). Social perspectives on art education in the US: Teaching visual culture in a democracy. *Studies in Art Education, 41*(4), 314-329.

Freedman, K., & Stuhr, P. (2004). Curriculum change for the 21st century: Visual culture in art education. In E. Eisner & M. Day (Eds.), *Handbook of research and policy in art education* (pp. 815-828). Mahwah, NJ: Lawrence Erlbaum Associates.

Gagel, C. (2006). Towards an authentic technological literacy. *Journal of Industrial Teacher Education, 43*(4), 69-75.

Gradle, S. (2009). Another look at holistic art education: Exploring the legacy of Henry Schaefer-Simmern. *International Journal of Education & the Arts, 10*(1). Retrieved from www.ijea.org/v10n1/

Gregory, D. (2009). Boxes with fires: Wisely integrating learning technologies into the art classroom. *Art Education, 62*(3), 47-54.

Goldfarb, B. (2002). *Visual pedagogy: Media cultures in and beyond the classroom.* Durham, NC: Duke University Press.

Goodman, S. (2005). The practice and principles of teaching critical literacy at the educational video center. In G. Schwarz & P. Brown (Eds.), *Media literacy: Transforming curriculum and teaching* (pp. 206-228). Malden, MA: National Society for the Study of Education.

Gude, O. (2008). Commentary: Aesthetics making meaning. *Studies in Art Education, 50*(1), 98-103.

Hobbs, R., & Jensen, A. (2009). The past, present, and future of media literacy Education. *Journal of Media Literacy Education, 1*(1), 1-11.

Jackson, P. (1998). *John Dewey and the lessons of art.* New Haven, CT: Yale University.

Kind, S., Irwin, R., Grauer, K., & de Cosson, A. (2005). Medicine wheel imag(in)ings: Exploring holistic curriculum perspectives. *Art Education, 58*(5), 33-38.

Lankshear, C., Snyder, I., & Green, B. (2000). *Teachers and technoliteracy: Managing literacy, technology and learning in schools.* St. Leonards, NSW, Australia: Allen & Unwin.

Levin, J., & Bruce, B. (2003). Technology as media: A learner centered perspective. In Y. Zhao (Ed.), *What should teachers know about technology? Perspectives and practices* (pp. 45-51). Charlotte, NC: Information Age Press.

Levy, L. (2007). Girls' meaning making practices and critical art education. *Journal of Cultural Research in Art Education, 25*, 129-141.

Levy, L. (2008). The skinny on This is My Body: Filmmaking as empowerment intervention and activism. *Visual Culture & Gender, 3*, 7-29.

Lin, C. (2008). *A qualitative study of three secondary art teachers' conceptualizations of visual literacy as manifested through their teaching with electronic technologies.* (Unpublished doctoral dissertation). University of Illinois, Urbana-Champaign.

Lin, C., & Polaniecki, S. (2009). From media consumption to media production: Applications of YouTube™ in an eighth-grade video documentary project. *Journal of Visual Literacy, 28*(1), 92-107.

London, P. (2006). Towards a holistic paradigm of art education. Art Education: Mind, body, spirit. *Visual Arts Research, 32*(1), 8-15.

Miller, R. (2006). Reflecting on spirituality in education. *Encounter, 19*(2), 6-9.

Nardi, B., & O'Day, V. (1999). *Information ecologies: Using technology with heart.* Cambridge, MA: The MIT Press.

Ohler, J. (2008). *Digital storytelling in the classroom: New media pathways to literacy, learning, and creativity.* Thousand Oaks, CA: Corwin Press.

Seemann, K. (2003). Basic principles in holistic technology education. *Journal of Technology Education, 14*(2), 28-39.

Stankiewicz, M. (2004). Commentary: Notions of technology and visual literacy. *Studies in Art Education, 46*(1), 88-91.

Stasko, C. (2009). *A pedagogy of holistic media literacy: Reflections on culture: Jamming as transformative learning and healing.* (Unpublished Master's thesis). University of Toronto.

Stokrocki, M. (2007). Art education avatars in cyberspace: Research in computer-based technology and visual arts education. In L. Bresler (Ed.), *International handbook of research in arts education* (pp. 1361-1380). Dordrecht, The Netherlands: Springer.

Winkler, T., Ide-Schoening, M., & Herczeg, M. (2007). Sustainable Teaching through the use of Media Art Technology. In R. Carlsen et al. (Eds.), *Proceedings of Society for Information Technology & Teacher Education International Conference* (pp. 2155-2162). Chesapeake, VA: Association for the Advancement of Computing in Education.

Zhao, Y. (2003). What teachers need to know about technology? Framing the question. In Y. Zhao (Ed.), *What should teachers know about technology? Perspectives and practices* (pp. 1-14). Greenwich, CT: Information Age Publishing.

ABOUT THE AUTHORS

Ching-Chiu Lin is a postdoctoral research fellow in the Department of Curriculum and Pedagogy at the University of British Columbia. Her research interests include issues of technology and community in art education.

Bertram C. Bruce is a Professor Emeritus in Library and Information Science at the University of Illinois at Urbana-Champaign. His research emphasizes explorations of a variety of questions regarding the nature of knowledge, democratic participation, community, technology, and literacy.

CHAPTER 7

Assessing and Teaching for Creativity

Lars Lindström

This chapter takes the visual arts as the point of departure in a discussion of how, with the help of portfolios, assessments may extend to include both the unpredictable and the ambiguous. Doing so, I challenge the notion that assessment of learning outcomes must be either limited to superficial knowledge or completely arbitrary. This claim is confirmed by a study I did of the progression of young people's creativity in the visual arts from preschool to upper secondary school. The assessment was based on both product criteria and process criteria (investigative work, inventiveness, ability to use models, capacity for self-assessment). The materials assessed were portfolios of work containing sketches, drafts and finished works, log books, sources of inspiration and videotaped interviews with the students. (The term "student" refers here to young people in general, from 5-year-olds to 19-year-olds.)

Hypotheses derived from the research findings yield concrete and practical guidelines for teaching and assessing for creativity. Moreover, the multidimensional approach, with a focus on physical, emotional and cognitive aspects, defines essential elements of a holistic approach to art education. To begin, I will review an earlier research project that influenced my ideas about assessment in the arts. In the process, I will provide an example of creative development from a holistic perspective.

ARTS PROPEL: REFLECTION FOR CREATIVE DEVELOPMENT

Being a visiting scholar at Harvard Project Zero in 1991, I had the opportunity to study Arts PROPEL, a program of curriculum development in the areas of the visual arts, music and imaginative writing (Gardner, 1989; Winner, 1991). This program encouraged students to reflect and to make their own observations about their work. Students reflected on the purpose of their work, on decisions they had made, and on their strengths, weaknesses and positive achievements.

Norman Brown, a visual arts teacher in Pittsburgh, took part in the project; Ella Macklin was one of his students. At the end of Ella's second year in high school, Norman and Ella went through her voluminous portfolio (Wolf & Pistone, 1991, pp. 42-51). It contained a book of sketches and notes and close to 20 works, accompanied by accounts of the way they had progressed. They discussed what Ella had learned while working on her "family series." She leafed through her file and pulled out an early drawing of her father, who is holding her (Figure 1). In working on this picture she had to decide which was most important: expression or a naturalistic depiction of reality. Ella remembered:

> I felt that I didn't draw the arm right. But I changed my opinion of it when we talked about Matisse in class, and I saw pictures in art magazines where the arms are somewhat distorted. My dad is just like that arm. I mean, he is really protective. (pp. 42-43)

Ella now began to recognize that she had the right to develop and alter the actual content of her family photographs. The portfolio contained a portrait of Ella and her grandmother (Figure 2).

FIGURE 1. (left) Ella's Father.

FIGURE 2. (right) Ella's Grandmother.

In my family photo album at home she's sitting on the couch in the living room, and the photo shows the whole living room. But I just wanted my grandmother and myself, so I decided to put the picture in an outdoor setting. (pp. 43-44)

Norman commented on how the open, airy landscape brought Ella and her grandmother into focus. He turned the attention towards the visual design of her drawing, and Ella remarked on the way the soft, rounded shapes conveyed a sense of shared intimacy.

> I think there is more to this picture. You see the way my grandmother's body hugs me. It is strength; it's warmth; it's caring. I think pastels help achieve that—they can be blended and they can be smoothed even. Or they can be left rough in certain areas, where you want it to be highlighted. (pp. 45)

Ella pursued what she called "this family quality," that is, the intimacy she had captured with the help of soft shades in pastel oils—a surrounding, embracing intimacy. A catalogue from a Harlem Renaissance exhibition and a visit to the Carnegie Museum sparked her imagination. Ella found other artists there, among them Giacometti, who had confronted similar problems of visual design. The visit to the museum made her question the individualization that had hitherto been a characteristic of her family portraits;

> One of the things that I noticed," she said, "was that the paintings, and even some of the sculptures, didn't have a face.... So I could interpret it; I could put myself into the picture; I could put in my own feelings.... This began the universal series that I later developed in which you have an adult holding a child, a mother holding a daughter, whoever. (p. 46)

Ella began to draw more of her figures with less detail. One was a mother holding her child on a swing, a theme that culminated in Ella's plaster sculpture of a parent lifting a child (Figure 3):

> *I liked the way the quality of Giacometti's Walking* Man was rough; it was a very rough bronze statue. I attempted to create that same roughness. Even though you have good relationships with your parents, you still have arguments. You have rough edges in a relationship. So I left that rough quality. Because to smooth everything would be very unrealistic. (p. 48)

Later, she returned to the theme of parents with children, and produced a simple line drawing and a series of prints in different colors (Figure 4).

FIGURE 3. (left) Parent with Child, 1.

FIGURE 4. (right) Parent with Child, 2.

This is an illustration of the kind of learning that occurs in creative activity, provided the students are given the opportunity to constantly make new observations and reflect on what they have done. Ella's description of her work process confirms the findings of other case studies, not only of artists (e.g., Arnheim, 1962) but also of children and young people (Wolf, 1988; Lindström, 2010). These studies show that creative work has a number of dimensions, among them the ability to adopt a variety of different stances or perspectives, to harness both cultural and social resources, and to pursue ideas for a period of time long enough to allow the sources of problems to be identified, and ways of solving them to be found.

As suggested by art educator Seymour Simmons, the creative dimensions of Ella Macklin's work could also be understood in holistic terms: *physically*, she worked inventively with materials and was responsive to tactile as well as visual experience; *emotionally*, her focus was on interpersonal family relationships, caring, and love as exemplified by her father's embracing arm; *cognitively*, she was reflective and engaged in research and problem solving, for example, dealing with the power of abstract images to reach out universally. Incidentally, it may be worth noting that Ella had relatively little art experience before taking classes with Norman Brown, which demonstrates that creativity doesn't always require a long technical apprenticeship.

WHAT CRITERIA ARE VALID?

Performance or process qualities like these can scarcely be measured objectively. Neither can we measure the "beauty" or similar qualities of the finished product. Nevertheless, as John Dewey points out in *Art as Experience* (1934), this does not prevent us from employing various *criteria* to judge the qualities we appreciate in a painting or, for that matter, in an essay, a scientific experiment or a historical study. In any of these examples, creativity is, of course, a pertinent quality, but one that is often considered difficult if not impossible to assess. Below, I describe an evaluation project intended to take on the challenge of assessing creativity on a large scale. Assessments of student portfolios were done by art teachers and art education students. The criteria and procedures used were not to be so complicated that they could not be modified to fit into almost any art classroom and applied with students at various levels. Equally important, teachers would find that, just as knowledge acquisition sometimes requires "teaching for the test," developing students' creativity in the visual arts also depends on what is being assessed and evaluated.

In 1998, I was in charge of an evaluation of Swedish students' creative performance in the visual arts, reported in Lindström, Ulriksson and Elsner (1999). The study was commissioned by The National Agency for Education. A revised edition of the final report has been translated into English and will be published by Stockholm University Press. We tested seven criteria. Three of these criteria concern finished products, while four concern the work process. The selection of criteria is based on objectives formulated in the national curricula, on qualities that are appreciated in the art world, and on research into the creative process (for a different, inductive method for defining criteria, see Lindström, 2008).

The *product criteria* comprise (1) the visibility of the intention behind the picture or pictures (the student's visual work communicates what he or she intended), (2) color, form, and composition (the student achieves desired effects with the aid of visual elements and principles), (3) craftsmanship (the student masters materials and techniques).

Process criteria describe (4) investigative work (the student pursues a problem across several works or experiments, feels challenged rather than discouraged by difficulties); (5) inventiveness (the student sets up problems, tries new solutions, is willing to take risks); (6) the ability to use models (the student actively searches out models to emulate); (7) capacity for self-assessment (the student describes and reflects on different qualities in his or her work). In addition, we included (8) an overall judgment in which the teacher takes into account what degree of difficulty the student masters, his or her capacity to work independently and other significant circumstances.

Again, the multi-dimensional approach to creativity assessment and instruction that we developed in Sweden fits seamlessly into a holistic framework (Campbell, 2011) by similarly identifying physical aspects (skill development and media experimentation, sensory input and sensitivity), emotional aspects (courage and risk taking, as well as self-expression), and cognitive aspects (self-knowledge through reflection and self-assessment, as well as problem solving, concept development, research, etc).

Approximately 500 children took part in the Swedish study of creativity in the visual arts, from preschool (5-year-olds), through the 2nd, 5th, and 9th grades (8-, 11-, and 15-year-olds) of the compulsory comprehensive 9-year school, to the final year (19-year-olds) or concluding courses in the arts program of the upper secondary school. The study was carried out in Jönköping[1] and Stockholm from 1997 to 1999. The materials studied consisted of portfolios that included, in addition to a final product, sketches and drafts, reflections in logbooks, models used as sources of inspiration, and a 10- to 15-minute videotaped interview with each student. The portfolios documented the students' work over a period of 10 hours (in the 9-year comprehensive school) or 30 hours (in the upper secondary school). The theme, which was selected by the teacher, should be of a divergent nature. That is, the students were encouraged to approach the theme in a variety of ways.

All of the students' portfolios were independently assessed by each student's own teacher and a teacher at the same grade level from another school. A general definition of what was to be assessed was formulated for each of the seven criteria. The following quotation is an extract from our description of "capacity for self-assessment":

> Creative people often possess an ability to adopt a number of different stances or perspectives. When they look at their own work, they focus alternately on the technical aspects,

the visual design, the ideas, and so on. They develop a set of standards or a checklist that directs their attention and helps them to monitor the creative process. In addition, they master a vocabulary that enables them to assess their work in multiple dimensions, so that they can pass more qualified judgements than just 'good' or 'bad.'

A capacity for self-assessment is not innate, it is something that students can develop and refine. A student with a high ability to evaluate his own work can leaf through his portfolio and reflect upon the content, on both the themes addressed and the materials and techniques, and also upon colour, form, and composition. He can point out works or parts of works that are successful or that require continued work, and he can give reasons why. He can point to decisions taken in the course of the work and explain why he chose to do something in a particular way (for example, why he chose a particular colour or arrangement). He may also be able to say how the choices he made affected his pictures and reflect upon how his future work may benefit from the experience he has gained. (Lindstrom, Ulriksson, & Elaner, 1999)

For each criterion the assessors had to choose between four rubrics, each with "plus," "medium" and "minus" (that is, a 12-point scale), presented in a teacher's manual. These rubrics describe levels of performance on an ascending scale. They correspond to the development from *novice* to *expert* outlined by the Dreyfus brothers in *Mind over Machine* (1986) and thoughts about rubric design put forward by Goodrich (1996), Wiggins (1998), and others. The development proceeds from solving simple tasks with assistance to tackling complicated problems in an independent and confident way. The progression on our process criteria corresponds particularly well to this description (Table 1). The lowest level (*novice*) is characterized by expressions such as, "[the student] does only what the teacher requires." Descriptors at the next level include the student being able to assess his or her work "with some help" and "take a problem the teacher has set and change it slightly." At the highest level, students develop the work on their own, set themselves problems to solve, actively search out models, can justify their preferences, and so on.

TABLE 1. PROCESS CRITERIA WITH RUBRICS

Process criteria	Expert	<	<	< Novice
Investigative Work	Takes considerable pains, approaches themes and problems in several different ways and uses drafts, sketches or test work to develop the work.	Does not give up in the face of difficulties, preferring to concentrate on a particular approach that he or she begins to develop and refine.	Demonstrates a degree of patience, tries out his or her own solutions and approaches, but does not develop them.	Gives up easily, does not follow his or her own ideas to completion, and only does what the teacher requires of her.
Inventiveness	Often sets up problems or reformulates the problems set by the teacher. Makes consistent progress and experiments regularly, is willing to take risks and often finds unexpected solutions to problems.	The student sometimes sets him- or herself problems. He or she develops her knowledge, experiments fairly often and sometimes finds unexpected solutions to problems.	Can take a problem the teacher has set and change it slightly. Shows tendencies to experiment and play with color, form and composition, or materials and techniques.	Does not set him- or herself any problems, shows no sign of experimenting with color, form and composition or materials and techniques.
Ability to Use Models	Actively searches out models to emulate and can use them in his or her work in a multifaceted, independent and well-integrated way.	Makes active efforts to find pictures for his or her own work. Demonstrates an ability to select images that suit his or her intentions.	The student shows an interest in other people's pictures that he or she or the teacher has found, but confines him- or herself to copying them.	Shows no interest in other people's pictures and cannot benefit from them even when the teacher has helped find them.
Capacity for Self-Assessment	Clearly identifies merits and shortcomings in his or her own work and can select sketches, drafts and works that illustrate his or her progress. Can justify opinions and explain why a particular result was obtained. Can produce qualified judgments of peers' work and contribute constructive criticism.	As a rule, manages to see for him- or herself the merits and short-comings in her work, and can select sketches, drafts and works that illustrate progress. Is beginning to produce qualified judgements of peers' work.	With some assistance, can identify his or her strengths and weaknesses and differentiate between good and less successful work. His or her views about peers' work are limited to subjective preferences (good/bad, like/dislike).	Cannot identify strengths and weaknesses in his or her own work or differentiate between good and less successful work. Has no views about the work of peers.

Good descriptive rubrics, supported by examples of both high quality and less satisfactory work, help students to assess their own work and understand the qualities of performance that the teaching aims to achieve. The rubrics should satisfy the following requirements:

- **They should be sufficiently general so that their connection with the overall goal is evident.** Rubrics that apply only to a particular assignment are, no doubt, more concrete and easier to apply. However, such rubrics may obscure the broader educational objective for which the assignment was designed, and may unnecessarily limit the freedom of students and teachers to demonstrate knowledge and skills by various means.
- **They should be descriptive.** That is, they should describe unique and typical characteristics of performance at different levels. To be informative, they should refrain from using a purely comparative and evaluative language, such as "better composition" or "poor composition."
- **Levels of performance should be described in equivalent terms.** Descriptors should make it clear that the assessment at different levels is based on the same criterion; new dimensions, explicit or implicit, should not be introduced in the transition from one level to another.
- **Rubrics should be neither too many nor too few.** There should be enough levels to separate and identify important qualities, but there should not be so many levels that they become impossible to distinguish one from another. From the educative viewpoint, three levels are perfectly adequate, says Peter Elbow (1997), who considers the important factor to be that the assessment is multidimensional, not that it differentiates many levels.

CAN CREATIVITY BE RELIABLY ASSESSED?

As noted, all student portfolios in our study were assessed independently by each student's own teacher (the class teacher) and by a teacher who taught students of the same age at a different school (the co-assessor). The assessors used a teacher's manual containing our descriptions of the seven criteria of creative ability and the four levels of performance for each of these criteria. They also judged, at each level on a criterion, whether the portfolio demonstrated performance that was slightly below, on a par with, or slightly above the average described in the manual. As a result, the level on each criterion was assessed on a 12-point scale. Such a finely-graded scale was essential for research purposes, because we wanted to make statistical comparisons of students between the ages of 5 and 19.

We compared the assessments of the class teachers and the co-assessors, applying all criteria on 458 portfolios gathered from 22 classes in 17 schools (later on, another set of 32 portfolios from 6 preschools was similarly collected and assessed). If there had been major discrepancies in the judgments, with considerable differences between assessors, the criteria and levels described above would not have been accepted as a reliable instrument to assess and judge students' creativity. Possible causes would be imprecise definitions of the criteria, inconsistencies in the criteria, inadequate quality of the material materials gathered (the portfolios), highly idiosyncratic preferences among assessors, or irrelevant circumstances affecting the assessment.

One of the methods we used to study the reliability of assessments was to calculate the frequency with which the judgements of the class teacher and the co-assessor differed by 2 steps or less. We considered a difference of 2 steps on a 12-point scale to be acceptable, particularly as the teacher's manual contained verbal descriptions of only 4 levels of performance. Assume that Leif's portfolio was assessed by applying the "Inventiveness" criterion. The class teacher gave him a score of 6 while the co-assessor scored his performance as being no better than 4.

Both judgments are compatible with the following rubric: *"The student can take a problem that the teacher has set and change it slightly. He shows tendencies to experiment and play with color, form, and composition, or with materials and techniques."* Even in cases where a difference of 2 ends up on different levels, we regard this difference as fully acceptable. After all, judgments contain a subjective element that defies precise verbal description; they presuppose that the teacher uses her or his professional judgment in interpreting criteria, levels, and the content of portfolios.

We found high agreement between class teachers and co-assessors in ratings of both the students' visual results (product criteria) and their approach to work (process criteria). In almost 3,100 comparisons between class teachers and the co-assessors from another school, there was 78 % agreement (≤ 2 steps on a 12-point scale). Given that other discrepancies between the two assessors were small and indicate an approximately normal distribution, this may be regarded as a satisfactory result. Were we to consider the differences of 3 steps or fewer as negligible, which would not seem unreasonable, then the level of inter-rater agreement would be as high as 90%. Thus, the study effectively refutes the idea that only superficial knowledge and skills can be assessed and evaluated. By using criteria related to visual design and students' work habits, we managed to evade the assessor's Scylla and Charybdis, that is, a tendency to place undue emphasis on students' skills in the use of materials and techniques on the one hand, and a judgement based solely on arbitrary preferences on the other.

The results of our study are in conflict with the view that process criteria are intrinsically difficult or impossible to assess. They suggest, however, that assessment of processes of learning requires the students' thoughts to be made accessible in a more explicit way than normally happens. It was not until we supplemented the students' logbooks with the video-taped interviews that different assessors arrived at similar results. The interviews addressed the students' capacity for self-assessment and their work processes step-by-step. The appropriate criterion, that is, the dimension of performance that a question is primarily intended to highlight, is given in parens below.

What task have you worked on? (Criterion 1: Visibility of the intention)

Choose a picture that you like. Explain why. (7: Capacity for self-assessment–quality)

Choose a picture you are less satisfied with. Why don't you like it so much? (7: Capacity for self-assessment–quality)

Choose a picture that says something about your way of expressing yourself. How can one see that it is your work? (7: Capacity for self-assessment–personal style)

What did you want your pictures to state or express? (1: Visibility of the intention–can the picture stand by itself or does it require an explanation?)

What inspired or suggested your pictures? (6: Ability to use models–how actively and independently did the student use models and cultural resources?)

What problems and difficulties did you encounter during the work? How did you go about resolving them? (4, 5, and 6: Information about the work process)

Have you attempted something you have never done before? How did you get on? (5: Inventiveness–the courage to try something new and the ability to learn from experience)

Choose a picture from which you learned something new about making pictures. What did you learn? (5: Inventiveness)

Choose a picture that you would like to change or redo. What would you do with it?
(7: Capacity for self-assessment; 4: Investigative work–the ability to develop an idea)

How much help did you get? Who helped you and how? (This question is relevant for assessment with reference to all the criteria.)

Extracts lasting about 5 minutes each, from 46 videotaped interviews, were converted to digital format and put on a CD-ROM that we produced as an appendix to the final report. Here students commented on their work, on the background of sketches, drafts and other "footprints." The CD made it possible for anyone to search for portfolios representing a specific score on a certain criterion and to compare these with portfolios from his or her own classroom. For each portfolio, there was a description of the recruitment area, the school and the class, the project and the aims of the teacher, as well as the student and the habitus of his or her family. Thus teachers would be able to use the CD, with its digitalized portfolios, not as the right answers but as a resource containing *exemplars,* i.e., samples of work illustrating qualities of processes and products in visual arts education and how they would be evaluated in a multidimensional perspective.

HOW DO ASPECTS OF CREATIVITY DEVELOP?

A high correlation between independent judges is a necessary but insufficient condition for assessment outcomes to be accepted as valid. Another condition is that the ratings on different criteria are independent. Everyday experience, as well as empirical evidence from a few similar studies (Hargreaves, Galton & Robinson, 1996; Kárpáti, Zempléni, Verhelst, Velduijzen, & Schönau, 1997), directed our attention to the risk that both the class teacher and the co-assessor form a general impression of a student's work, which then influences their assessments on each individual criterion. It would still be interesting to know whether the class teacher and the co-assessor had a similar general impression of portfolios. However, a tendency to over-generalize would make ratings on individual criteria less valid.

To examine this source of error, we recruited 30 students who were close to completing their training as art teachers. Each of them was asked to assess a large number of portfolios, including videotapes, using a single criterion. They were to ignore other aspects of the portfolios than those defined by that criterion. Thus a student art teacher judging pupils' "inventiveness" had to examine all portfolios from that viewpoint alone, and ignore, for example, how successful the final product was. The portfolios were anonymous, and were sorted in random order to make it more difficult to estimate the sex and age of the pupils.

Although this procedure took several days, it proved to be a good investment. A factor analysis (i.e., a statistical technique that allows the researcher to reduce the number of variables that represent a particular construct) supported the assumption that teachers' judgments on separate criteria were influenced by their overall impression of a portfolio. However, with the more independent judgment procedure that the student art teachers followed, we obtained two main factors: "product criteria" and "process criteria." All of the process criteria were loaded on a common factor, as were the product criteria. None of the seven process or product criteria appeared to be multidimensional, that is, to be a manifestation of qualities in both process and product. This outcome supports one of the hypotheses on which the present study is based: Creativity in the visual arts contains two main dimensions that must be considered separately when assessing students' work. The results also suggest that teachers need training in applying one criterion at a time, if they are to evaluate various qualities in their own teaching and give useful feedback to their students.

The outcome of the student art teachers' assessments indicates that pupils in the comprehensive school improve their visual design and artistic skills. That is, they make progress on two of the product criteria, one of which describes elements and principles of design, such as color, form and composition, and the other, the use of materials and techniques (craftsmanship). However, with regard to process criteria, referring to their capacity to work independently, evaluate their work, and so on, pupils in ordinary comprehensive school classes appeared to stagnate or show only insignificant improvement (Tables 2 and 3).

Since it is ultimately the products of the creative process that count in society, there may be reason to question the relevance of the process criteria. If the art works steadily improve, does it matter, then, how the improvement comes about? To answer that question, we must examine the content of the process criteria. The result for *investigative work* shows that the average student at the junior and intermediate grades "tries out [his or] her own solutions and approaches, but does not develop them" (Level 2 in the transition from "novice" to "expert," see Table 1). The same applies to boys in the final grades of comprehensive school, whereas girls at that age begin to develop the approaches they have chosen (Level 3). With regard to *inventiveness*, most students, irrespective of grade and sex, can "take a problem that the teacher has set and change it slightly;" they also show "tendencies to experiment" (Level 2). On the other hand, they do not set up problems of their own, and they have not begun to experiment regularly (Level 3).

Most students in the comprehensive school lack an advanced *ability to use models*. They show an interest in other people's pictures that they or their teacher have found, but they confine themselves to copying them (Level 2); they do not actively look for pictures or genres to find ideas, and they are unable to select what can be of particular use to them (Level 3).

TABLE 2. PRODUCT CRITERIA WITH RUBRICS

Process criteria	Expert	<	<	<	Novice
Visibility of the Intention	The student's intention is obvious from the picture(s) in a convincing way.	The student has a clear intention, but it is not obvious from the picture(s) until it is explained to the observer.	The student knows what he or she wants to achieve, but his or her intention is not visible in the picture(s).		The student has no conscious intention for what he or she is doing.
Color, Form and Composition	The picture(s) suggests that the student has acquired an understanding of fundamental principles of visual design, such as focus, variation, balance, rhythm, and so on, and can use them to achieve visual effects and a sense of unity.	The picture(s) suggests an understanding of how different visual elements may be used and combined to make a whole, but this is applied in a rather stereotyped way.	The picture(s) suggests a certain insight into how different visual elements may be used and combined to make a whole, but there are serious deficiencies in the execution.		The picture(s) suggests little or no understanding of how different elements such as lines, shapes, light and dark, color, and texture can be used to achieve visual effects. The picture(s) lacks any attempt to create a composition in which the parts contribute to the whole.
Craftsmanship	The picture(s) shows a good and flexible mastery of materials and techniques and are consistently of high technical quality.	The picture(s) shows an ability to use materials and techniques to achieve the desired visual effects, but this is applied in a rather stereotyped way.	The picture(s) suggests a certain ability to use materials and techniques, but there are serious deficiencies in the execution.		The picture(s) shows little or no ability to use materials and techniques.

TABLE 3. MEDIAN VALUES ON CRITERIA FOR CREATIVE SKILLS

	Visibility of the Intention	Color, Form, and Composition	Craftmanship	Investigative Work	Inventiveness	Ability to Use Models	Capacity for Self Assessment	Overall Judgment
Grade 9	7	7	8	7	6	6	5	8
Grade 5	7	5	5	5	5	5	5	6
Grade 2	7	3	5	6	6	5	4.5	6

The ratings on *capacity for self-assessment* show that most students in the comprehensive school can, "with some assistance," point out strengths, weaknesses and other characteristics of their work (Level 2); on the other hand, they do not achieve this on their own, nor can they select sketches, drafts, and works that demonstrate their own progress over time.

This examination of the meaning of the process criteria testifies that these criteria are significant in their own right. They show how well the school has achieved one of its overall goals: the development of students' creative skills from solving simple tasks with support to tackling complicated problems in an independent and confident way. This is the very core of the development from apprentice to master, from novice to expert in a domain. Using a terminology that underpinned one of the latest Swedish curricula, we can say that the students in our study acquired *knowledge* and *skills* regarding how to draw and paint. However, they did not develop the *understanding* and *familiarity* that is required to apply what they have learned to new situations or to rely on their own judgement.

Criterion-referenced assessment, applied by teachers and students, can draw attention to the procedural dimensions of creative work and articulate the "tacit" knowledge (Polanyi, 1962) or "dispositional" characteristics (Winner & Hetland, 2001) to which these criteria refer. To that end, guidelines for what should go into the portfolio must take into account not only the quality of the product or performance, but also the student's ability to reflect upon his or her work and choose appropriate materials, techniques, and content. A student with sophisticated reasoning and an appropriate approach may still hand in flawed or careless work, while a less sophisticated student can produce painstaking and well executed, albeit simple, work. With a multidimensional assessment, both of these students will be acknowledged for their achievements and encouraged to progress.

CAN CREATIVITY BE TAUGHT?

A multidimensional assessment gives students *feedback*, which helps them discover their strengths and identify areas in which they need to improve. The scores on such assessments can also help administrators of an educational program to review its results, consider its position and modify the course if necessary. The 1998 evaluation of the Swedish curricula indicated that both students and teachers needed to be more aware of the procedural dimensions of creative work and to reflect upon the "dispositional" qualities that are involved. The students made progress in terms of visual design, it is true; but they did not improve on those dimensions of creativity that we have summarized under the rubrics of investigative work, inventiveness, ability to use models and capacity for self-assessment.

However, there was one exception. In the very area of the process criteria, students in the final year of the comprehensive school who attended Stockholm's Bild och Formklasser (*The Stockholm Visual Arts and Craft Classes*) completely outdistanced students of the same age in ordinary classes. Some of this difference is probably attributable to the culture of learning that Stockholm's Bild och Formklasser offer. "Children are given the opportunity to get deeply involved in and complete their various projects," and the art and craft teachers, whose classes are half the size of regular classes, "are in constant dialogue with the students about their work as it evolves" (from teacher interviews). These and other observations have been documented on a video film produced as part of the 1998 evaluation. They substantiate what has been found in research on contexts and dispositions that foster creativity (e.g., Jay & Perkins, 1997; Nickerson, 1999; Cropley, 2001; Weisberg, 2006) as well as experience from Arts PROPEL (Gardner, 1989; Winner, 1991; Winner & Simmons, 1992) and other attempts to enhance creativity.

ON THE BASIS OF THESE OBSERVATIONS, I PROPOSE THE FOLLOWING HYPOTHESES ABOUT HOW SCHOOLS CAN ATTAIN THE PRESCRIBED TARGET OF HELPING STUDENTS TO DEVELOP THEIR CREATIVE ABILITY IN A HOLISTIC MANNER.

Investigative work **is fostered if students are given assignments that extend over a significant period of time and address central themes in the domain.**

The proliferation of subject matter and materials that schools are supposed to deal with and offer causes major problems. In general, it is easier to add new subject matter and extra materials, techniques, and teaching materials than to remove something. The underlying assumption appears to be that the more information the school provides and the more activities the students carry out, the better. It is easy to forget that if too much is crowded into the syllabus, teaching breaks down into small segments and knowledge becomes fragmented. Research on the psychology of learning lends support to a motto that the school reformer Theodore Sizer (1992) took from the Bauhaus School: "Less is more" (see also Dempster, 1993). The concepts, principles and perspectives addressed in schools should be central to a domain of knowledge and skills. They should be exercised in different contexts over an extended period of time to allow the students to understand their interrelationships and implications (Wiske, 1998). In order to further creativity, students should be given enough time to investigate, test and revise, to reflect and speak to peers, and to make critical assessments of their own work.

Inventivenes **is fostered if the teacher emphasizes the process as well as the product and provides ample opportunity for research, experimentation, and revision.**

Creative people have been characterized as problem-finders, since they often discover new challenges when working on a project (Csíkszentmihályi & Getzels, 1989; Jay & Perkins, 1997). They try out new solutions, often by combining ideas and suggested solutions in unanticipated ways. There is a close association between these distinctive features and what has been mentioned above, since one must get deeply involved with a work over time to discover where the interesting challenges reside, and to find ways of pursuing them. Discovery through mistakes or serendipity requires a "prepared mind" (Merton, 1957, p. 12). Yet mental readiness is not sufficient for a creative leap to take place. To reformulate problems and try new solutions, one also needs a certain degree of courage and a willingness to take risks. Experiments and risk-taking do not always bring successful results. This is inherently true. Experiments that always succeed involve no risk; they teach us nothing that we did not know already. If a student is to be adventurous and willing to take certain risks, the teacher must show appreciation and approval of the student's courage to take further something he or she did not already know or master, even if the outcome is not always the intended one.

The ability to use models **is fostered if students are encouraged to integrate production with perception and reflection.**

Without exception, studies of creativity show the importance of other people's works and ways of thinking (Weisberg, 2006). Creativity is not as private and individual a process as we often imagine. It is always part of a social and cultural context. Looking for models to emulate, and finding links between them and one's own work, is an active and complex process. This type of cultural influence should not be counteracted in school, as often used to be the case. On the contrary, it should be encouraged and appreciated, since the conditions for creative work are considerably improved if the student constantly intersperses his or her own work with observations of other people's works, and reflection upon what can be learned from them. Making active use of models means choosing what corresponds to one's own intentions and making something of one's own from it. One borrows what is useful from one or more works that have captured one's interest. This interaction between the student's pictures and those of other people is facilitated if pictures are discussed in class, if the students have ample access to pictures of various kinds, and if they get help in finding the cultural resources they need.

Capacity for self-assessment **is fostered if the students are given many opportunities to assess their own performance and to get feedback from peers and teachers; the most informative feedback originates from explicit criteria that tap the important keys to good performance.**

The creative work of students, if taken seriously, can and must be assessed and evaluated. Refusal to assess student work is a concession to those who maintain that no learning is taking place. If we accept the assumption that visual design is related to thinking and learning, and that students can develop their ability to appreciate aesthetic qualities, then it is also important to establish what they have learned. A teacher who fails to assess what the students do cannot decide whether she is contributing to or impeding their progress. If everything, however trivial it may be, receives the response, "That's good. Would you like to tell me something about it?" then the student probably will conclude that what he is doing is not particularly important. In his classic paper on "myths" in art education, Elliot Eisner (1974/2009) maintained that children respect considered evaluation and criticism, because they indicate that the teacher cares for them and is paying attention to their work.

As demonstrated in the example from Arts PROPEL as well as in the research reported above, it is not simply the finished product that should be assessed. Consideration should also be given to the work process and the students' ability to make more subtle observations and reflect on what they have done in a wider context. Assessment thus described has an important part to play in the learning process. It should not simply be a matter between teacher and student; it is at least as important that students are given the opportunity to assess what they themselves and their peers achieve. Rubrics framed in evaluative rather than descriptive terms and assessment procedures based on arbitrary criteria can, of course, divert learning and stifle creativity. However, criteria and scoring rubrics can also serve to focus students' attention on qualities of performance that are easily neglected; they give them instruments with which to reflect on and communicate about their own learning processes.

Evidently, the view presented in this chapter stands in stark contrast to the popular belief that assessment necessarily stifles the creative impulse. Instead, as I have suggested, if applied holistically, assessment can actually foster students' creative development, preparing them to apply their creativity to a wide range of problems, within and beyond the classroom.

REFERENCES

Arnheim, R. (1962). *The genesis of a painting: Picasso's Guernica.* Berkeley, CA: University of California Press.

Campbell, L. H. (2011). Holistic art education: A transformative approach to teaching art. *Art Education, 64*(2), 18-24.

Cropley, A. J. (2001). *Creativity in education and learning.* London, England: Kogan Page.

Csíkszentmihályi, M., & Getzels, J. B. (1989). Creativity and problem finding in art. In F. H. Farley & R. W. Neperud (Ed.), *The foundations of aesthetics* (p. 91-116). New York, NY: Praeger.

Dempster, F. N. (1993). Exposing our students to less should help them learn more. *Phi Delta Kappan, 74*(6), 433-437.

Dewey, J. (1934). *Art as experience.* New York, NY: Putnam.

Dreyfus, H. L. & Dreyfus, S. E. (1986). *Mind over machine.* New York, NY: Free Press.

Eisner, E. W. (1974). The mythology of art education. *Curriculum Theory Network, 4*(2/3), 89-100. Reprinted in K. Freedman (2009), *Looking back: editors' selections from 50 years of studies in art education* (pp. 5-15). Reston, VA: The National Art Education Association.

Elbow, P. (1997). Grading student writing: making it simpler, fairer, clearer. In: M. D. Sorcinelli & P. Elbow (Eds.), *Writing to learn* (p. 127-140). San Francisco, CA: Jossey-Bass.

Gardner, H. (1989). Zero-based arts education: an introduction to Arts PROPEL. *Studies in Art Education, 30*(2), 71-83.

Goodrich, H. (1996). Understanding rubrics. *Educational Leadership, 54*(4), 14-17.

Hargreaves, D. J., Galton, M. J., & Robinson, S. (1996). Teachers' assessments of primary children's classroom work in the creative arts. *Educational Research, 38*(2), 199-211.

Jay, E. S., & Perkins, D. N. (1997). Problem finding: the search for mechanism. In M. A. Runco (Ed.), *The Creativity Research Handbook*, Vol. 1 (pp. 257-293). Cresskill, NJ: Hampton Press.

Kárpáti, A., Zempléni, A., Verhelst, N. D., Velduijzen, D. W., & Schönau, D. W. (1997). Expert agreement in judging art projects—a myth or reality? Unpublished paper.

Lindström, L. (2008). Assessing craft and design: conceptions of expertise in education and work. In A. Havnes & L. McDowell (Eds.). *Balancing dilemmas in assessment and learning in contemporary education* (pp. 61-72). London, England: Routledge.

Lindström, L. (2010). Free spirit or copycat? Artistic development and comic imagery. In T. Costantino and B. White (Eds.), *Essays on aesthetical education for the 21st century.* Rotterdam, Netherlands: Sense Publishers.

Lindström, L., Ulriksson, L., & Elsner, C. (1999). *Portföljvärdering av elevers skapande i bild.* [Portfolio assessment of students' creativity in the visual arts]. Stockholm, Sweden: The National Agency for Education / Liber Distribution. (Skolverket US 98). A revised English edition, under the preliminary title *Assessing Creativity*, is forthcoming.

Merton, R. (1957). *Social theory and social structure.* New York, NY: Free Press.

Nickerson, R. S. (1999). Enhancing creativity. In: R. J. Sternberg (Ed.), *Handbook of creativity* (pp. 392-430). Cambridge, England: Cambridge University Press.

Polanyi, M. (1962). *Personal knowledge* (2nd ed.). Chicago, IL: University of Chicago Press.

Sizer, T. R. (1992). *Horace's school: Redesigning the American high school.* Boston, MA: Houghton Mifflin.

Weisberg, R. W. (2006). *Creativity: Understanding innovation in problem solving, science, invention, and the arts.* Hoboken, NJ: John Wiley.

Wiggins, G. (1998). *Educative assessment: designing assessments to inform and improve student performance.* San Francisco, CA: Jossey-Bass.

Winner, E. (1991). *Arts PROPEL: An introductory handbook.* Cambridge, MA: Educational Testing Service/Project Zero, Harvard Graduate School of Education.

Winner, E., & Hetland, L. (2001). Research in arts education: directions for the future. In E. Winner & L. Hetland (red.), *Beyond the soundbite: arts education and academic outcomes* (pp. 143-148). Los Angeles, CA: The J. Paul Getty Trust.

Winner, E., & Simmons, S. (Eds.). (1992). *Arts PROPEL: A handbook for the visual arts.* Cambridge, MA: Harvard Project Zero/Educational Testing Service.

Wiske, M. S. (1998). *Teaching for understanding: linking research with practice.* San Francisco, CA: Jossey-Bass.

Wolf, D. (1988). Artistic learning: What and where is it? *Journal of Aesthetic Education, 22*(1), 143-155.

Wolf, D. P., & Pistone, N. (1991). *Taking full measure: rethinking assessment through the arts.* New York, NY: College Examination Board.

ENDNOTE

1   Jönköping is one of Sweden's 10 largest cities. It is located in a southern region of the country known for its many successful small- and medium-sized enterprises.

ABOUT THE AUTHOR

Lars Lindström is a Professor Emeritus of Education at Stockholm University, Sweden. His research focuses on philosophy of education, creativity, assessment and education in the arts, craft and technology. He edited "Nordic Visual Arts Education in Transition: a Research Review," 2008, published by the Swedish Research Council. He received the Brian Allison Research Award, 2006, by the National Society for Education in Art & Design, UK, and the Ziegfeld Award for Outstanding Service in International Art Education, 2010, by the United States Society for Education through Art.

CHAPTER 8

Five Emerging Themes of Holistic Art Education

Laurel H. Campbell

Holistic education stems from the philosophy that everything in the universe is interconnected to everything else (J. P. Miller, 1993). Teaching with this understanding in view, therefore, aims to connect learning and daily life while engaging all dimensions of human awareness and action. These include, but are not limited to, emotional, physical, ecological, cognitive, aesthetic, social, cultural, and spiritual aspects of the person. Although often thought of as a "New Age" phenomenon, contemporary holistic education as described below is actually the continuation of a centuries-old tradition. Nonetheless, support for this approach has grown significantly in recent years as a means to address a widespread sense of personal alienation and fragmentation, along with larger societal issues like the current global economic, ecological, and spiritual crises. The evident interdependence between these internal and external conditions, as some have argued, makes a holistic approach to education all the more urgently needed today (Seymour, 2004).

Responding to the situation outlined here, educators who adopt a holistic approach promote a sense of concern and caring for teachers' and students' relationships with each other, with their community, and with the natural environment. Furthermore, holistic educators see the purpose of education as encouraging students to become intelligent, active, and engaged citizens of the classroom and the greater society, thereby preparing them to strive throughout their lives for social justice and ethical living. Holistic education, so conceived, is itself part of a larger movement in which holistic approaches have recently emerged in such diverse fields as science, medicine, psychology, and social theory. Research findings from these and other domains have, in turn, provided new insights as well as confirmation for holistic educators (R. Miller, 2000). Yet, despite the growing support for holistic values in general education, the field of art education has been relatively slow to accept holistic approaches.

The purpose of this chapter is, therefore, to expand the discussion of holistic education as applied to teaching P-12 art, as well as in the preparation of art teachers. In doing so, I will trace the history of holistic education, comparing earlier and more recent approaches. I will also address five themes that emerge when considering art education from a holistic perspective. In the process, I will draw upon literature from our field as well as from several other disciplines in order to formulate a working definition of contemporary holistic art education.

To begin, I will review some key terms to consider in formulating a holistic art curricula: *balance, inclusion* and *connection*. According to J. P. Miller (1993, 2007), *balance* refers to the correct relationship between each aspect of the person, while *inclusion* means linking together various educational orientations for authentic learning. *Connection* includes focusing on the relationships between various aspects of the person, as well as those between the person and all other living things (J. P. Miller, 2007). Balance is crucial to a successful holistic approach so that one dimension of human experience is not valued more than others. For example, analytical and mechanistic modes are respected more than other modes in many traditional educational approaches (R. Miller, 2000). Similarly, a holistic approach nurtures *synthetical moments* in the curriculum (Pinar & Grumet, 1976, as cited in Slattery, 2006), in which there is a "reconstruction of the self and an experience of solidarity of the intellect, the body, the spirit, and the cosmos, as well as an intrinsic coherence of time, place, and meaning" (Slattery, 2006, p. 242).

As mentioned, contemporary holistic theory in education, generally conceptualized for all disciplines, has important antecedents and combines several historical threads. Romantics such as Rousseau, Pestalozzi, Froebel, and Alcott, along with subsequent generations of "whole-child" theorists (e.g., Steiner, Montessori, Tolstoy, Dewey, and Ferrer), advocated for a progressive, humanistic approach to education (R. Miller, 2000). During the 1960s and 1970s, a *new paradigm holism* was influenced by the human potential movement, which represented a convergence of humanistic educators, who emphasized psychological growth, with transpersonal educators who promoted spiritual growth, all of whom operated without clear distinctions (J. P. Miller, 1996; R. Miller, 2000). This configuration has been problematic for some holistic educators (Forbes, 2003), primarily due to the fact that, as an emerging paradigm, holism frequently held onto "New Age" mysticism as a central tenet. In addition, this version lacked serious attention to cultural and political realities and failed to promote change in the lives of people who were marginalized, oppressed, abused, or exploited (R. Miller, 2000). Moreover, as R. Miller (2000) explained, the mystical, anti-intellectual orientation proposed by holistic thinkers in the 1960s and 1970s as an attempt to correct for the excessive rationality of education at the time soon took on a "messianic quality," a characteristic from which contemporary holistic educators continue to distance themselves even today (p. 44).

So described, late 20th-century *holism-as-New-Age-paradigm* may simply have represented past theories in postmodern guise. By contrast, 21st-century *holism-as-critical-theory* more fully reflects the principles of postmodern education, in which multiple perspectives are valued (R. Miller, 2000). As Reeder (2005) explained, postmodern theory has reconfigured holistic education, so that it is now

> imbued with concepts of relationship, self-organization, recursion, order emerging from chaos, and meaning making. This way of thinking values systemic relations and runs in contrast to the control and reductionistic underpinnings of the modern paradigm from which our current education system and our ideas about education have grown and developed. (p. 249)

More concretely, many current holistic educators (e.g., R. Miller, 2000; Purpel, 1998; Shapiro, 2006) promote a paradigm shift from modernist forms of schooling designed to create workers for industry to an approach that ties together the individual and society. Clearly related to this change in purpose, critical holism is characterized by a view of the person as a socially and culturally constructed being who can benefit from personal, spiritual transformation through cultural and political critique. Far from the standardized system of schooling that is now commonly imposed in classrooms across the country, context *necessarily* shapes how holistic art education is practiced. As R. Miller (2000) put it, "meaning emerges in context, in experience; holistic education is therefore essentially a responsiveness to the wholeness of experience as we live it in particular times and places" (p. 4).

In order to better define how holistic theories can be useful in the field of art education, I have identified five major themes that are emerging in holistic art education: The holistic art educator *(1) creates student-connecting experiences that place the student and art at the center of education; (2) expands one's worldview to include the human spirit as an aspect of the learning experience; (3) implements transformative models for teaching and learning through ecological education; (4) fosters a democratic, cooperative, and safe classroom environment; and, (5) creates curricula that help students learn compassion and empathy for others, thus encouraging students to work for social justice.* Each theme will be explained below in greater detail with appropriate support from holistic theorists, while also being framed by recent discussions within visual arts research and teaching.

STUDENT-CONNECTING ART EXPERIENCES

In the first theme, the educator creates student-connecting experiences that place the student and art at the center of education. This perspective replaces earlier child-centered models, which as Burton (2000) explained, tended to romanticize the notion of the child, leading to a simplistic view of artmaking as free self-expression, unfettered by social or cultural influences. By contrast, contemporary holistic educators such as J. P. Miller (1993) promote curricula that encourage "child-connecting" experiences. Moreover, within this more recent system, experiential knowledge is based on self-knowledge, where the self is understood as being complex and constantly changing while also remaining open to a myriad of possibilities as one experiences the world in connection with others (Forbes, 2003).

Like previous approaches, the student-connected model assumes that knowledge is constructed by the student through the process of making connections. Here, however, connection-making includes integration, both within the person and between disciplines. The arts are instrumental in such integrated learning, in large part, because artists have historically expressed the relationship between the *self* or *identity* and one's understanding of the world (Parsons, 2004). A holistic approach to art curricula therefore would encourage teachers and students to construct curricula based on their experiences. This has been discussed in the literature on issues-based art education (Gaudelius & Speirs, 2002), integrated curriculum (Marshall, 2005; Parsons, 2004), and utilizing themes or "big ideas" (Walker, 2003). In these instances, however, integration often means only that issues most relevant to students are used as starting points, in which dialogue and inquiry lead to new insights. Holistic art educators would go a step further in order to consider all dimensions of the person when deciding which issues/themes are deemed worthy of study. One reason for this more challenging orientation is that a goal in holistic art education is for students to become open to the complexity of their own experiences, while connecting these to the most relevant and important phenomena they wish to explore through art media, both traditional and new.

THE HUMAN SPIRIT

One of the most distinctive and highly contested aspects of holistic education is spirituality, in large part because of a widespread confusion between spirituality and religion. However, religion is not at all implied in the definition used here and elsewhere in holistic art education literature. As the topic is addressed in this chapter, an educator who expands one's worldview to include the human spirit as an aspect of the learning experience encourages mindfulness and reflective practice, both of which are necessary components of personal and social development among teachers no less than students (Campbell, 2005). Spirituality is therefore defined here in terms related to the basic tenet of holistic education stated in the first paragraph: as the awareness of the interconnectedness of all life forms. It is thus quite possible to express spirituality without the practice of religion, although there are aspects of religious practice that are decidedly spiritual. There is no attempt by holistic educators to deny the fact reported by Emmons

(2006), that historically, spirituality has not been distinguished from religion. However, the two concepts may now be addressed as separate discourses, especially in public school contexts, due to the increasing support from educators who have moved away from a dualistic, Cartesian worldview toward a contemporary version of spirituality (Griffin, 1997). Moreover, according to Griffin, most holistic educators perceive spirituality as a journey toward developing in students' lives such widely accepted values as "wisdom, compassion, loving kindness, joy, beauty, [and] peacefulness" (p. 271). Psychologists Lakoff and Johnson (1999) focus on spirituality in education using different, but equally secular terms, saying that it provides "deep insight into who we are, how we experience the world, and how we ought to live" (p. 551). Holistic art educators may incorporate this spiritual journey in their classrooms through activities such as artistic, narrative journal writing or exercises in artmaking as spiritual practice (Azara, 2002; Sanders-Bustle, 2008).

Besides these theoretical discussions and practical applications, there is a growing body of research from different disciplines to suggest that contemporary understandings of spirituality can provide scholarly grounding for a holistic worldview. These arguments can be found in positive psychology (Emmons, 2006), naturalized spirituality (Solomon, 2002), and spiritual intelligence (Zohar & Marshall, 2000). Becoming aware of one's spirituality means asking questions such as, What is my purpose in life? or How will I create meaning in my life? Conversations based on questions like these allow students to voice conflicting, paradoxical, and ambiguous ideas while they search for meaning in their complex and often difficult lives, a process Wright (1996) termed *communal spirituality*. According to bell hooks (1999), there is a place for such spirituality in education:

> To be guided by love is to live in community with all life. However, a culture of domination, like ours, does not strive to teach us how to live in community. As a consequence, learning to live in community must be a core practice for all of us who desire spirituality in education. (p. 119)

Living in community also requires that spirituality be balanced with other dimensions of experience, such as learning skills in an atmosphere of collaboration, cooperation, and tolerance. Spirituality in this context means considering the deeper meaning of the *relational self* (Taggart, 2001), and how one learns to live peacefully with others. According to Peter Abbs (2003), art education can similarly provide a venue for understanding spirituality in terms of wholeness and the connectedness of our experiences:

> In a quite fundamental way, spirituality can be conceived as part of, as an unplanned outcome of, the natural world, yet opening up within nature new dimensions of reflection, prophecy, and possibility. It is this distinctive power of consciousness attending to consciousness through sustained acts of recognition and affirmation which illuminates the true nature of spirituality. It is the spiritual in us which aspires toward wholeness, seeks connection, pattern, circumference. (p. 35)

One route to this wholeness is to give more depth and meaning to the expression of one's purpose in life, through visualizing artistically and creatively a more just and loving community. Service learning in visual arts education is one example of connecting social responsibility to action, with reflective practice as an important component of the process (Buffington, 2007; Jeffers, 2006; Taylor, 2002). Besides attending to their own, internal development, accessing their spiritual dimension as it has been defined here can help students expand rather than limit their efforts to enact meaningful change in the world and raise their level of commitment to others (Kessler, 2000).

TRANSFORMATIVE MODELS FOR TEACHING AND LEARNING

As suggested in the previous section, holistic education can serve as an impetus for social renewal, which occurs in relationship *with* the world rather than isolation *from* the world (Forbes, 2003). This, in turn, evokes a vision of education as transformative, in which students become responsible global citizens, who can then help change the world. Education for transformation begins with the assumption that both students and teachers have agency in the learning process. Yet it also acknowledges that teachers must have a holistic understanding of individual students' needs and the correct pedagogic approach for "protecting the process" of interactive education (Forbes, 2003). According to J. P. Miller (2007), this means abandoning outdated models of learning, such as the *transmission* model, where there is a one-way flow of knowledge and skills from the teacher to the student. It also opposes the *transaction* model, where there is more cognitive dialogic interaction between student and teacher, but which stresses "analysis... more than synthesis and thinking more than feeling" (p. 11). By contrast, the *transformative* model recognizes the wholeness of the child, where the student and the curriculum are connected during learning experiences. As Miller (2007) has stated,

> The teacher working from this position will use strategies such as creative problem solving, cooperative learning, and the arts, which encourage students to make various types of connections. These connections make learning personally and socially meaningful to the student. (p. 12)

Some holistic educators claim that transformation involves "waking up" to, or becoming conscious of, the interconnectedness between one's personal, cultural, and environmental identities (Hart, 2000, p. 13). Transformative educator Edmund O'Sullivan (1999) termed his particular version of this approach as *transformative ecozoic education*, because it connects "holistic education to a planetary consciousness while maintaining a critical perspective" (p. 64). In this model, spiritual and ecological awareness are simultaneously manifested through holistic teaching and learning.

If, as Shapiro (2006) believes, education is a process that shapes our humanity, transformative holistic approaches such as those described above may be crucial to the sustainability of life on earth (Gallegos-Nava, 2001; O'Sullivan & Taylor, 2004). Support for this view also comes from scientists who are involved in the "deep ecology movement." Deep ecology is an attempt to connect science and ethics with regard to the natural world and the relationship humans maintain with it (Bowers, 2005; Capra & Apffel-Marglin, 2002; Laszlo & Seidel, 2006). According to Capra (1995), deep ecologists posit that humans are a part of a network of natural phenomena, interdependent with nature rather than dominating it. Educators who share this view must first challenge their students' (and often their own) fundamental assumptions about human relationships with the environment (O'Sullivan & Taylor, 2004), then go on to pursue an "active engagement in practices that embody ecological values—connection, openness, generosity, appreciation, partnership, inquiry, dialogue, and celebration" (p. 3). These values are evidently compatible with the goals of holistic education in which all individuals are involved in an ongoing, mutually dependent process of co-creation and co-evolution (J. P. Miller, 1993).

Research in art education has also focused on environmental challenges (see Blandy & Cowan, 1997; Neperud, 1997; Stankiewicz, 1997). In particular, Candace Stout (2007), as editor of *Studies in Art Education,* published a special issue on the role art educators can assume in educating for ecological awareness. In this issue, Hicks and King (2007) wrote, "A critical, holistic response to the environmental crisis will advance an environmentally responsible culture if it links understanding of ecological harms to the natural world with awareness of the social and political impacts of those harms" (p. 335).

Practical support for art teachers with these concerns include recent examples of ecological art curricula (e.g., Gradle, 2007, 2008; Reisberg, 2008), as well as information about contemporary artists (e.g., Mel Chin, Lynn Hull, and Agnes Denes) whose work brings attention to the relationship between humans and their environment. To sum up, a holistic approach to fostering cultural and social transformation for ecological awareness should include interdisciplinary art lessons linking science and art, extensive dialogue on the ethical aspects of this debate, and hands-on instruction on how to make one's views visible to the world through imagery.

A DEMOCRATIC, COOPERATIVE AND SAFE CLASSROOM

In the fourth theme, a holistic approach to teaching art fosters a democratic, cooperative, and safe classroom environment. The discussion of this topic echoes the principles of democratic education described by curriculum theorist, James Beane (2002), who claimed that, "A vibrant, just, and ethical democracy involves the interests of individuals and those of the common good—and the possibility that the two can be integrated or at least kept in reasonable balance" (p. 26). Beane explains how student-generated questions about one's personal sense of the world can lead to connecting self-interest to the common good. Beane's approach is based on his democratic core curriculum, which, in turn, is created through collaboration and cooperation, as multiple sources of knowledge are considered (2002).

The concept of democratic art education has been well documented over the past several decades (Blandy & Congdon, 1987; Garber & Costantino, 2007). Similar to the transformative model noted above, students can initially experience democratic education with an art teacher who facilitates learning in a participatory manner. Beyond that, a democratic model of art education will also involve some degree of collaborative planning for artmaking projects, in which teachers and students, as well as experts from the greater community, determine the goals for learning. Holistic art educators who wish to encourage these practices must also establish a safe, cooperative learning environment. One aspect of feeling safe is learning about and embracing diversity (Orr, 2005). This is also important for holistic education because it encourages students to make connections with others while valuing their differences (J. P. Miller, 2007).

Linked to such specific concerns, there are two general factors involved in feeling safe in the art classroom: emotional safety and physical safety. Emotional safety relates to students feeling respected by their teachers and peers, as well as teachers receiving respect from students, parents, and administrators. Speaking in similar terms, Forbes (2003) wrote that love is "the foundation for the pedagogic relationship of holistic education; rather than the... fear many teachers have tried to engender" (p. 34). Fear is often associated with a traditional authoritative model, which contemporary educators who support a participatory model for teaching now view not only as harmful, but also as ineffectual.

The harm derived from traditional forms of discipline is one form of emotional abuse that some students report to have experienced at the hands of their teachers. McEachern, Aluede, and Kenny (2008), in their research on the topic, define emotional abuse as unsatisfactory "verbal and nonverbal interactions, discriminating behaviors, grading practices and treatment of exceptional children" (p. 3). Such practices, as the research revealed, are actually fairly common. In fact, approximately 50-60% of adults in the US reported being emotionally abused by a teacher during their schooling years. Other forms of abuse by teachers include withholding warmth or affection as well as ignoring bullying, especially if it is aimed at their least favorite students (Suckling & Temple, 2001). Even in the absence of such overt and/or intentional abuses, other less obvious forms are fairly common. Two ways teachers can avoid these common forms of emotional abuse is to learn how to fairly assess their students, as well as to critically reflect on their own teaching behaviors, identifying their inherent biases in order to eliminate them.

A second important issue is physical safety; holistic philosophy is compatible with new research on violence prevention programs that are now being used in many P-12 schools (Campbell, 2009). One-third of secondary students were involved in some type of physical violence in 2006 (www.safeyouth.org). Even though the number of homicides among students has dropped in the past 10 years, assaults still continue, and have increased among young women (Larson, 2008). Examples of bullying, or relational aggression, abound on social networking sites and in national news. According to Skiba, Boone, Fontanini, Wu, Strussell, and Peterson (n.d.), there is a relationship between students displaying incivility or having minor discipline problems and their future use of serious violence. They also reported that some students who were bullied, teased, or socially rejected are becoming violent adults, capable of killing the peers who subjected them to humiliation. Teachers and parents must stop the cycle of violence, as well as bullying, through early intervention, beginning with insisting on peaceful classrooms that promote connectedness between students. Teachers can advocate for change in the school culture by creating a sense of community in their classrooms, where transformation occurs through relationship building. Art educators can design art curricula in which students "create, critically discuss, and exhibit images of both anti- and pro-social behavior" (Bickley-Green, 2007, p. 7). Exhibiting images that evoke discussion in the school and greater community can help advance the individual teacher's goals, thereby involving parents, students, and administrators.

LEARNING COMPASSION AND EMPATHY, WORKING FOR SOCIAL JUSTICE

In the final theme, an educator utilizing a holistic approach to art education creates curricula that help students learn compassion and empathy for others and moves students to work for social justice. In this theme, educators can provide a place where students are opened to "possibilities for change through self- and societal introspection and reflection," while gaining wisdom for "making choices that can contribute to social, hence global welfare" (Yokley, 1999). First, students must learn how compassion and empathy can help them negotiate meaning with others (Mezirow, 2000). Apart from its more familiar association with calculated arrangements in business and politics, negotiation understood in the context of holistic education involves empathy, which, according to Hart (2000), is the trait that "makes us most human ... and serves as an active center for character and compassion" (p. 10). Through processes like negotiation and nurturance of others, aware and caring teachers can encourage empathic understanding in their students, which at times is spiritual in nature. As Lakoff and Johnson (1999) explained,

> It is this empathic dimension of spiritual experience that links the spiritual to the moral via nurturance—to the responsibility to care for that with which we empathize. It is thus an activist moral attitude not just toward individuals, but toward society and the world. (p. 567)

Although empathy is, at some level, an innate human capacity, there is much in society that impedes our abilities to empathize with others, especially those whom we see as somehow different from us. Given such circumstances, teachers often need to use specific activities to promote empathetic awareness and help students to become more consciously empathic.

This process includes modeling effective and appropriate responses to someone else's situation as well as helping students to identify with other people's thoughts and feelings (Hoffman, 2000). These lessons are sometimes taught through role-playing or conflict resolution exercises. However they are learned, these lessons begun in childhood and adolescence have important implications for life at school and beyond, into adult relationships. In fact, the growth of empathy need never end. DeRobertis (2008) stated that, "Growing, developing, maturing, and becoming a healthy self-with-others-alongside-things is a personal accomplishment that is carried out in and through meaningful worldly relations throughout the lifespan" (p. 11). Nor is the development of empathy and other forms of sensitivity to others merely a part of emotional life. Instead, it is an integral part of holistic development connecting with the full range of human functioning. For example, according to Lerner (2005), students and teachers should bring a spirit of compassion to critical thinking as well as to their practice of social justice.

Art education can be an excellent venue for teaching students to care through a specially designed curriculum aimed at developing empathic awareness (Stout, 1999). For example, Russell and Hutzel (2007) described instruction in art for the purpose of teaching social and emotional skills while students are engaged in service learning. Using student behavior as a topic, the authors describe how they reinforced discussion about "identifying and understanding the feelings of others, appreciating diverse perspectives, treating others with kindness and compassion, and fostering healthy, rewarding connections to individuals and groups" (p. 11). Similarly, Darts (2006) posited that the arts "can facilitate the development of an ethic of care" where students experience positive transformation (p. 7). Furthermore, Hare (2006) wrote that holistic educators should prepare each student to become an "active, participatory and critical learner who perceives and understands him/herself in a changing world and in a variety of local and global scenarios" (p. 302). Hare also found a holistic approach to self-knowledge to be especially helpful for adolescents in middle school, when questioning personal values and identity is prevalent. Practical applications for holistic art education are currently being researched and are included in this volume.

CONCLUSION

Why should art educators consider a holistic approach to teaching visual arts? The reasons outlined in this chapter and throughout the anthology are many and compelling, especially in light of the challenges that young people face today and in the future. Moreover, the integrative quality of artistic creation, involving, as Ruskin (1893) put it, head, heart and hand, makes art a natural venue for holistic teaching and learning. Based on these several factors, I believe that contemporary versions of holistic art education could not only make art a more meaningful experience for students, but could also bring the arts to the forefront as a viable model for educational reform across the curriculum. This view is confirmed by Slattery (2006), among others, who suggested that, "The arts are no longer understood to be at the periphery of the curriculum; rather the arts are the heart and soul of teaching, pedagogy, and human growth" (p. 243). Teaching young children and young adults to understand and appreciate the world of art is an important part of their general education. While teaching them to make art using concepts and techniques encourages creativity, both activities are important aspects of art education and are, of course, included in a holistic model. Yet, as suggested above, there is more to holism than this. Teachers who view art in terms of holistic development, according to Lin (2006), are equally concerned to help students create harmonious and peaceful relationships with nature and each other, a capacity that is urgently needed today.

As R. Miller (1999) has explained, holistic education "is not just a fantasy, not just a passing fad, but is something that is truly emerging" (p. 192). To keep pace with new research as well as to meet the needs of children, society, and the environment, holistic education should be addressed, and taught, in teacher education programs at the university level. As with holistic teaching in the classroom, holistic teacher education includes traditional knowledge and skill development but goes beyond these to address other aspects of the individual. Addressing other dimensions, Kessler (2000) explains how holistic teachers-in-training must begin by acquiring a *teacher presence*. This, in turn, happens through careful, continual, reflexive inquiry about their role in creating learning opportunities focused on connectedness in the curriculum (Kessler, 2000). Moreover, because most philosophies of teaching are formed during early practicum experiences, it is crucial to discuss holistic education in art teacher education programs.

The five themes described in this chapter provide a framework for both art teachers and university art educators to help envision a different kind of practice. This practice begins by creating "student-connecting" experiences, with art at the center of these learning opportunities. Through such activities, students can experience transformation that will help them connect self to the world, all with a sense of purpose at the core of their actions. Among the outcomes of this approach, as I have suggested, is that students develop empathy and compassion at deeper, spiritual levels of understanding. These understandings, in turn, potentially lead students to a greater adherence to democratic principles, to concern for the natural world, to peaceful cohabitation in schools and society as a whole, as well as to actively work for social justice. All this, however, begins with an art educator whose goals for teaching and learning represent the five themes in this chapter. Such teachers also share the belief that our future survival depends on a radical departure from our current educational goals. Finally, these teachers have the hope that future generations can create a better life for all citizens, both locally and globally.

REFERENCES

Abbs, P. (2003). *Against the flow: Education, the arts and postmodern culture.* New York, NY: RoutledgeFalmer.

Azara, N. (2002). *Spirit taking form: Making spiritual practice of making art.* Boston, MA: Red Wheel.

Beane, J. (2002). Beyond self-interest: A democratic core curriculum. *Educational Leadership, 59*(7), 25-28.

Bickley-Green, C. (2007). Visual arts education: Teaching a peaceful response to bullying. *Art Education, 60*(2), 6-12.

Blandy, D., & Cowan, D. (1997). iMagine! Yellowstone: Art education and the reinhabitation of place. *Art Education, 50*(6), 40-46.

Blandy, D., & Congdon, K. (Eds.). (1987). *Art in a democracy.* New York, NY: Teachers College Press.

Bowers, C. A. (2005). *Rethinking Freire: Globalization and the environmental crisis.* Mahwah, NJ: Lawrence Erlbaum.

Buffington, M. (2007). The big idea: Service-learning and art education. *Art Education, 60*(6), 40-45.

Burton, J. (2000). The configuration of meaning: Learner-centered art education revisited. *Studies in Art Education, 41*(4), 330-345.

Campbell, L. H. (2005). Spiritual reflective practice in preservice art education. *Studies in Art Education, 47*(1), 51-69.

Campbell, L. H. (2009). Spirituality in holistic art education: Preventing violence among youth in the United States. *Journal of Cultural Research in Art Education, 27,* 122-131.

Capra, F. (1995). Deep ecology: A new paradigm. In G. Sessions (Ed.), *Deep ecology for the 21st century: Readings on the philosophy and practice of the new environmentalism* (pp. 19-24). Boston, MA: Shamble.

Capra, F., & Apffel-Marglin, F. (2002). *The hidden connections: Integrating the biological, cognitive, and social dimensions of life into a science of sustainability.* New York, NY: Doubleday.

Darts, D. (2006). Art education for a change: Contemporary issues and the visual arts. *Art Education, 59*(5), 6-12.

DeRobertis, E. (2008). *Humanizing child development theory: A holistic approach.* Lincoln, NE: iUniverse.

Emmons, R. (2006). Spirituality: Recent progress. In M. Cskiszentmihalyi, & I. Cskiszentmihalyi (Eds.), *A life worth living: Contributions to positive psychology* (pp. 62-81). New York, NY: Oxford University Press.

Forbes, S. (2003). *Holistic education: An analysis of its ideas and nature.* Brandon, VT: Foundation for Educational Renewal.

Gallegos-Nava, R. (2001). *Holistic education: Pedagogy of universal love.* (M. N. Ríos & G. S. Miller, Trans.). Brandon, VT: Foundation for Educational Renewal.

Garber, E., & Costantino, T. (2007). Social issues in art and visual/material culture education. In L. Bresler (Ed.), *International Handbook of Research in Arts Education* (pp. 1055-1070). Dordrecht, The Netherlands: Springer.

Gaudelius, Y., & Speirs, P. (2002). *Contemporary issues in art education.* Upper Saddle River, NJ: Prentice Hall.

Gradle, S. (2007). Ecology of place: Art education in a relational world. *Studies in Art Education, 48*(4), 392-411.

Gradle, S. (2008). When vines talk: Community, art, and ecology. *Art Education, 61*(6), 6-12.

Griffin, D. R. (1997). *Parapsychology, philosophy, and spirituality: A postmodern exploration.* Albany, NY: SUNY Press.

Hare, J. (2006). Towards an understanding of holistic education in the middle years of education. *Journal of Research in International Education, 5*(3), 301-322.

Hart, T. (2000). *From information to transformation: Education for the evolution of consciousness.* New York, NY: Peter Lang.

Hicks, L., & King, R. J. H. (2007). Confronting environmental collapse: Visual culture, art education, and environmental responsibility. *Studies in Art Education, 48*(4), 332-335.

Hoffman, M. L. (2000). *Empathy and moral development: Implications for caring and justice.* New York, NY: Cambridge University Press.

hooks, b. (1999). Embracing freedom: Spirituality and liberation. In S. Glazer (Ed.), *The heart of learning: Spirituality in education* (pp. 113-129). New York, NY: Tarcher/Putnam.

Jeffers, C. (2006). *Spheres of possibility: Linking service-learning and the visual arts.* Reston, VA: The National Art Education Association.

Kessler, R. (2000). *The soul of education: Helping students find connection, compassion, and character at school.* Alexandria, VA: Association for Supervision and Curriculum Development.

Lakoff, G., & Johnson, M. (1999). *Philosophy in the flesh: The embodied mind and its challenge to western thought.* New York, NY: Basic Books.

Larson, J. (2008). Angry and aggressive students. *Education Digest, 73*(7), 48-52.

Laszlo, E., & Seidel, P. (Eds.) (2006). *Global survival: The challenge and its implications for thinking and acting.* New York, NY: Select.

Lerner, M. (2005). The spiritual transformation of education. In H. S. Shapiro & D. Purpel (Eds.), *Critical social issues in American education: Democracy and meaning in a globalizing world* (3rd ed., pp 325-348). Mahwah, NJ: Lawrence Erlbaum.

Lin, J. (2006). *Love, peace, and wisdom in education: A vision for education in the 21st century.* Lanham, MD: Rowman & Littlefield.

McEachern, A., Aluede, O., & Kenny, M. (2008). Emotional abuse in the classroom: Implications and interventions for counselors. *Journal of Counseling and Development, 86*(1), 3-10.

Marshall, J. (2005). Connecting art, learning, and creativity: A case for curriculum integration. *Studies in Art Education, 46*(3), 227-241.

Mezirow, J. (Ed.). (2000). *Learning as transformation: Critical perspectives on a theory in progress* (pp. 3-33). San Francisco, CA: Jossey-Bass.

Miller, J. P. (1993). *The holistic teacher*. Toronto, ON: The Ontario Institute for Studies in Education.

Miller, J. P. (1996). *The holistic curriculum*. Toronto, ON: The Ontario Institute for Studies in Education.

Miller, J. P. (2007). *The holistic curriculum* (2nd ed.). Toronto, ON: University of Toronto Press.

Miller, R. (1999). Holistic education for an emerging culture. In S. Glazer (Ed.), *The heart of learning: Spirituality in education* (pp. 189-201). New York, NY: Tarcher/Putnam.

Miller, R. (2000). *Caring for new life: Essays on holistic education*. Brandon, VT: Foundation for Educational Renewal.

Neperud, R. (1997). Art, ecology, and art education: Practices and linkages. *Art Education, 50*(6), 14-20.

O'Sullivan, E. (1999). *Transformative learning: Educational vision for the 21st century. New York,* NY: Zed Books.

O'Sullivan, E., & Taylor, M. (2004). Conundrum, challenge, and choice. In E. O'Sullivan & M. Taylor (Eds.), *Learning toward an ecological consciousness: Selected transformative practices* (pp. 1-4). New York, NY: Palgrave Macmillan.

Orr, D. (2005). Minding the soul in education: Conceptualizing and teaching the whole person. In J. P. Miller, S. Karsten, D. Denton, D. Orr, & I. Kates (Eds.), *Holistic learning and spirituality in education* (pp. 87-100). Albany, NY: State University of New York Press.

Parsons, M. (2004). Art and integrated curriculum. In E. Eisner & M. Day (Eds.), *Handbook of research and policy in art education* (pp. 775-794). Reston, VA: National Art Education Association.

Purpel, D. (1998). Social transformation and holistic education: Limitations and possibilities. In H. S. Shapiro, & D. Purpel (Eds.), *Critical social issues in American education: Transformation in a postmodern world* (2nd ed., pp. 355-369). Mahwah, NJ: Lawrence Erlbaum.

Reeder, S. (2005). Classroom dynamics and emergent curriculum. In W. Doll, M. J. Fleener, Truitt, D., & St. Julien, J. (Eds.), *Chaos, complexity, curriculum, and culture: A conversation* (pp. 247-260). New York, NY: Peter Lang.

Reisberg, M. (2008). Social/ecological caring with multicultural picture books: Placing pleasure in art education. *Studies in Art Education, 49*(3), 251-267.

Ruskin, J. (1893). *The two paths: Being lectures on art*. New York, NY: Maynard, Merrill & Co.

Russell, R., & Hutzel, K. (2007). Promoting social and emotional learning through service-learning art projects. *Art Education, 60*(3), 6-11.

Sanders-Bustle, L. (2008). Visual artifact journals as creative and critical springboards for meaning making. *Art Education, 61*(3), 8-14.

Seymour, M. (2004). Introduction. In M. Seymour (Ed.), *Educating for humanity: Rethinking the purposes of education* (pp. 1-10). Boulder, CO: Paradigm Publishers.

Shapiro, H. S. (2006). *Losing heart: The moral and spiritual miseducation of America's children*. Mahwah, NJ: Lawrence Erlbaum.

Skiba, R., Boone, K., Fontanini, A., Wu, T., Strussell, A., & Peterson, R. (n.d.). *Preventing school violence: A practical guide to comprehensive planning*. Bloomington, IN: The Safe and Responsive Schools Project at the Indiana Education Policy Center, Indiana University.

Slattery, P. (2006). *Curriculum development in the postmodern era* (2nd ed.). New York, NY: Routledge.

Solomon, R. (2002). *Spirituality for the skeptic: The thoughtful love of life*. New York, NY: Oxford University Press.

Stankiewicz, M. (Ed.). (1997). Art & ecology [Special issue]. *Art Education, 50*(6).

Stout, C. J. (1999). The art of empathy: Teaching students to care. *Art Education, 52*(2), 21-24, 33-34.

Stout, C. J. (Ed.). (2007). Eco-responsibility in art education [Special Issue]. *Studies in Art Education, 48*(4).

Suckling, A., & Temple, C. (2001). *Bullying: A whole-school approach*. Philadelphia, PA: Jessica Kingsley Publishers.

Taggart, G. (2001). Nurturing spirituality: A rationale for holistic education. *International Journal of Children's Spirituality, 6*(3), 325-339.

Taylor, P. (2002). Service-learning as postmodern art and pedagogy. *Studies in Art Education, 43*(2), 124-140.

Walker, S. (2003). What more can you ask? Artmaking and inquiry. *Art Education, 56*(5), 6-12. Reston, VA: National Art Education Association.

Wright, A. (1996). The child in relationship: Towards a communal model of spirituality. In R. Best (Ed.), *Education, spirituality and the whole child* (pp. 139-149). London, England: Cassell.

Yokley, S. (1999). Embracing a critical pedagogy in art education. *Art Education, 52*(5), 18-24.

Zohar, D., & Marshall, I. (2000). *Spiritual intelligence: The ultimate intelligence*. London, England: Bloomsbury Press.

ABOUT THE AUTHOR

Laurel H. Campbell is an Assistant Professor of Art Education and Director of Art Education at Indiana University-Purdue University Fort Wayne. She has been an art educator since 1996 and a metalsmith since 1974. Her research interests include reflective practice, preservice teacher education, and holistic art education.

Multiple Facets of Holistic Art Education

Young artists, through their self-directed work in art class, connect with significant relationships and events to integrate meaningful aspects of their lives into their artwork.... Making meaning is central to artistic process, whatever form it takes. Through feeling, intuiting, perceiving, and knowing, children articulate bold visual statements about who they are and what they value.

—*Diane B. Jaquith, p. 165*

CHAPTER 9

Thinking Complexly in Art Classrooms

Juan Carlos Castro

Jon entered my high school art classroom, his face a mix of confusion and excitement. He had just returned from New Orleans, post-Hurricane Katrina, and his arms were full of just-developed 4x6-inch prints. Jon shared that he had just spent the morning going over his images and was not sure where to begin. I suggested we would take the first part of class to look as a group at Jon's images. After laying out his prints, the class and I began moving, shifting, and discussing the photographs. We began to see the editing challenge Jon faced because of all the possible stories that could be told. I am not sure who started picking out images of walls marked with spray paint messages left by search and rescue teams and survivors, but what we did know is that we could collectively see a theme emerging. Quickly, we began arranging them, finding all the images that fit this theme. Up to this point Jon's artworks were primarily focused on graffiti art. The thematic choice of grouping together the images of spray-painted messages, which Jon enthusiastically approved, reflected his evolving style. We were learning not only about what happened in New Orleans from Jon, but also how to recognize meaningful patterns in our artwork.

The trajectory of Jon's artistic growth is familiar to many artists. There are patterns and characteristics to an artist's work that unfold, grow, and emerge through time. Every twist and turn is shaped by a history of embodied experiences. Why is it then that we structure our art curricula as separate and disparate experiences? Why are our art curricula so often designed merely as standardized series of "fundamentals" and "essential skills?" On the other hand, why is the inquiry of an art student seen as an individual endeavor? This chapter offers a way of thinking holistically by considering all of the facets of an individual in relationship to a group of learners. I describe these relationships through complexity thinking.

COMPLEXITY THINKING

The approach addressed here draws on recent advances in theories about self-organizing phenomena (Waldrop, 1992) referred to as complexity thinking (Davis & Sumara, 2006), which challenge both common-sense, as well as philosophical notions of boundaries between the self and the animate world, revealing instead that we are tied far more closely to our environment than we ever thought (Humphries, 2009). Continuities in this regard include human consciousness and cognition. As Merlin Donald (2001) stated, "although we may have the feeling that we do our cognitive work in isolation, we do our most important intellectual work as connected members of cultural networks" (p. 298). Knowing can thus no longer be considered an isolated act, separate from society and culture, nor is learning an isolated phenomenon (Vygotsky & Cole, 1978). Yet this is nothing new, considering what we have long understood about the social nature of art and artmaking (Hagaman, 1990; Kindler & Darras, 1998; Wilson, 2004; J. Wolf, 1993). Here, too, knowing identities are sensed to be singular, and yet can also be understood as part of a collective. These theoretical understandings of complex dynamic systems with underlying scale-free and decentralized network structures, begin to describe the dynamics between different levels of phenomena, from neurological to cultural to ecological, which have profound implications for teaching and learning.

Perhaps most under-theorized and misunderstood in accounts of the social and cultural influences on learning are the dynamic characteristics of learning across scales. An important concept in thinking complexly about our classrooms is the relative extent of a system of relationships. For example, there is the scale of the individual in all of her or his complexity. Then there is the scale of the classroom made up many individuals. Rather than seeing learning as existing on one scale, complexity thinking frames learning as dynamic, where individuals and social relations are co-specifying—in other words, each is relationally shaping the other. It is then a question of scale, of where our attention is drawn to and where we place and describe agency and power. Though we consider each scale as being bounded—a human body bounded by skin and a classroom bounded by walls and class roster—each is in fact a system of relationships, which is itself porous, nested, and interdependent.

In art education, the theory of systems relations has been used to provide understandings of nonlinear learning in the visual arts. This, in turn, challenges traditional notions of developmental endpoints (Kindler, 1999; D. Wolf & Perry, 1988) and established ideas of developmental stages, suggesting instead that pictorial representation evolves in a more fluid manner as children are able to access multiple pictorial systems based on the educational, social, and cultural contexts in which they, as learners, are situated (Wilson, 2004).

In fact, complexity thinking actually extends nonlinear systems understandings of learning art, which are thus complementary to systems views of creativity in art education (Csikszentmihalyi, 1988; James, 1996, 1997). In systems understandings of artistic learning, diagrams usually show a field in which the individual, social structure, domain knowledge, and context are of equal size and distribution. By contrast, complex dynamic systems are nested (Davis & Sumara, 2006), providing a transphenomenal understanding of learning–one that treats learning as being possible across scales of phenomena. In other words, it provides an understanding of learning that addresses the nonlinear, inefficient, causal dynamics between individuals, collectives, societies, and ecosystems.

Complexity thinking thus provides a new and more nuanced metaphor for thinking of learning systems as nested and scale-independent. *Nested* means that you need a whole web of interdependent systems, whose dynamic relationships give rise to the character of a particular ecosystem. *Scale-independent* means that there will always be a level of irreducible detail, no matter what level of phenomena you look at. Simply put, the dynamics used to describe a society or a learning environment cannot be collapsed or reduced to describe the actions of one particular individual. Complexity thinking offers a way to hold these understandings of dynamic phenomena in conversation.

Flocks of birds, the stock market, cultural fads, and the evolution of human consciousness are all examples of emergent complex phenomena. Jon's story is also an illustration of an emergent complex learning system at work. In education, complexity thinking has been defined as the study and support of learning systems (Davis & Sumara, 2006). As such, it involves learning as a simultaneously individual, social, and cultural phenomenon, where students and teachers are engaged in open-ended learning, inquiry and artmaking, both on individual and collective levels (Wilson, 2003). As I will argue, thinking about the art classroom, students, teachers and curricula as a complex learning system is key for educating artists in the 21st century (Sweeny, 2008).

DESIGNING CONSTRAINTS THAT ENABLE ARTISTIC INQUIRY

Complex systems arise from individuals' dynamic interactions that result in an interdependency among the individuals and that give rise to possibilities for action and patterns of activity not available to individuals separately. The implication, here, is that individuals can in fact become more creative in a dynamic environment, a fact that has obvious implications for teaching art. Beyond the dynamics of the classroom, a further implication of complex systems for creativity in art has to do with the role of constraints. Typically, creativity in art is assumed to involve complete, or nearly complete freedom, meaning the absence of constraints. Yet as Juarrero (1999) explains, complexity (and, by implication, creativity) is not possible without constraints: "[In]a situation of complete randomness where alternatives are equiprobable you could say anything, but in fact say nothing" (p. 133). Having a landscape of equal possibilities is equivalent to a state of equilibrium. It is like the hiss of static, a wall of equal probability of a meaningful message, which ends up being meaningless. In creating a landscape of possibilities, prior actualities must be referenced because without such there can be no possibilities for future action. As artists, we work within constraints—from the limitations and possibilities of art materials to our personal histories. They shape how we inquire through art- making. We do not work in a vacuum as artists, rather we work from within and through constraints that are context sensitive (Juarrero, 1999), involving all of the factors that make up a given complex system: individuals, society, an historical period, etc. Such constraints are necessary and inevitable, because the history of a complex system shapes its future possibility interdependently with the context in which it is embedded.

These constraints are also enabling. Metaphorically, they provide the first marks on the blank canvas to which artists can then react. For art teachers, constraints that enable include how we ask students to engage with artmaking, whether it is as an elegant problem (Kay, 1998) or questioning about an enduring idea (Walker, 2003). The constraints we create in our classrooms should be dependent on personal experiences and understandings. They can be reflective questions and/or prompts that ask students to reevaluate personal and cultural ways of interpreting the world. As such, constraints serve as invitations to extend and reshape how we interpret the world. Many times they can act as a "burr" in our thinking, creating enough discomfort to shift around, while not enough to avoid engaging with the question altogether (Doll, 1989). It is this "shifting around" that enables a reevaluation of personal understandings. For example, the first question asked in my Photography I course was, "If you were to be struck blind tomorrow, what vision of the world would you leave?" Students would shift uncomfortably and often silence would permeate the room. After class, more often than not, I would be asked, "Do you have any examples that I can look at?" There were no examples presented, no master artist to look at; instead I asked them to think about how they saw the world, not what they would last want to see, how they would communicate, with their cameras, how they saw the world. The constraint of leaving the world an image that communicates how one sees the world, coupled with the finality of never seeing again, enabled me and my students to focus attention directly and powerfully to their particular "how of seeing."

The fact that, in this instance, I did not show a master artist does not mean that I believe authentic artmaking should not include the study of master artists. Working in context, whether it is referencing visual culture or the history of art, is essential. On the contrary, Dorothea Lange, the Farm Security Administration photographer who documented the narratives of migrant workers in the 1930s Depression era United States, inspired the constraint used for this assignment. Lange once stated that she photographed every day as if she were to be struck blind tomorrow (Coles, Heyman, & Lange, 1998). The urgency of this quote resonated with me as an artist, leading me to think: What visual statement would I make today if I were to be struck blind tomorrow? At the end of this project, I shared information about Dorothea Lange with my students, such as her work, her narrative, and how she inspired me to create this constraint.

Considering creativity through constraints from a curricular perspective, each constraint builds upon and folds into the next. This approach to curriculum follows from the more general concept that complex learning systems are recursively elaborative (Davis, Sumara, & Luce-Kapler, 2008). In other words, a complex learning system's future action is primarily dependent on past action. This means, in our field, that the end of one work of art is the beginning for the next, so that ideas and insights generated by students build and elaborate through time. This, at any rate, is how I structured the series of constraints that made up my curriculum, nesting and arranging them to engage students in examining how they see their world, from being in the world to becoming an agent of change in the world. Other constraints in my classroom would come in the form of prompts such as, "Create a self-portrait without showing yourself; photograph what you love and fear and juxtapose the two; create an artwork for a public space that asks us to see that space with different eyes." These prompts were not made in isolation—rather they were structured to help students connect to what they had previously experienced, and they provided a means to expand in unexpected ways upon what students already knew.

Equally important, these prompts and questions demonstrated how art curricula can be designed to engage with enduring ideas and contemporary issues. They depended on the expert knowledge of students, knowledge of their own lives, given form in ways that are diverse and divergent. Returning to Jon's narrative, we can see how his own artistic development evolved and took surprising turns as he engaged intensely in what mattered to him most, not just sharing what he already knew about, but extending and elaborating his understandings through artmaking.

In response to the question, "If I were to be struck blind tomorrow what image of the world would I leave?" Jon's first photograph looks down from a bridge at a drainage stream flanked on one side by railroad tracks and on the other side by a wall of graffiti (Photo 1).

FIGURE 1. Jon's response to "If I were to be struck blind tomorrow..."

 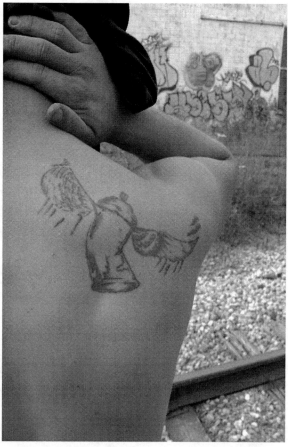

FIGURE 2. (left) Jon's response to "What places are special to me?"

FIGURE 3. (right) Jon's response to "What is family, who is my family?"

This was not, admittedly, entirely unexpected. Throughout his first year, it was apparent that Jon showed an interest in photographing those people and places associated with graffiti art.

In his response to "what places are special to me," he photographed inner city graffiti (Photo 2). When working through the questions, "what is family, who is my family," he responded with images of graffiti artists (Photo 3).

Initially, it seemed the culture of graffiti would be his path of inquiry when it came time to work independently in his senior year. However, things changed when, in the fall of 2005, Hurricane Katrina ravaged New Orleans. Jon's aunt was living there at the time, and when Jon went to New Orleans to help his aunt, he took his camera along to photograph the aftermath. In this new context, Jon's response was not necessarily about photographing graffiti, yet it was a response to the markings and messages made on the built environment. This interpretive framing of the world was expanded from photographing graffiti culture to the spray paint markings of search and rescue teams, both ways of communicating with others about experiences and events (Photo 4).

In the class critique of his final portfolio, it was clear to all that while the content of Jon's work seemed dissimilar to what he had done before (graffiti culture vs. the aftermath of a disaster) his way of interpreting and engaging with the world was dependent upon his previous experience and shaped by his established interests. I did not tell this to Jon, neither did any one person in the classroom that day; rather, it emerged from our interactivity and attention to each other within the class.

THE CLASSROOM COLLECTIVE

Jon's artistic journey was shaped and influenced by those working alongside him. His classmates developed a diversity of ideas. Each student's direction of inquiry was different, and their artwork explored ideas ranging from abstraction to critical documentaries. Examples included abstract color compositions; challenging Asian stereotypes, the scars and stories behind them; documentaries of emergency rooms; and even still life images of fruit. What the students did share was an interest in each other's inquiry, a commitment to dialog, and a desire to see everyone succeed.

The "intelligence" of a collective emerges when individuals are deeply committed to their own expert forms of knowledge and experiences in what on first glance seems self-centered (Surowiecki, 2004). Intelligence defined here means that the diversity of ideas embodied in a group self-generates more ideas.

FIGURE 4. A selection of Jon's independent series: From Post-Katrina.

There are two important conditions necessary for the exploitation and cultivation of this kind of intelligence. The first is that there must be enough diversity in ideas to stimulate thought and evoke the vast range of possibilities in any assignment. The second is the need to create a space where each individual's expert knowledge can be exposed and interact with that of others in structured as well as spontaneous ways. It is thus important to stress that complexity in the art classroom today is strictly opposed to learning as it is generally conceived, as converging around certain standardized pieces of information, or established strategies for solving problems. Perhaps in the past when art training was more tradition-bound and academic, learning was about creating a unified work of art, a single understanding, or uniform idea. Today, however, reflecting both the art world and the actual world of experience, it is more a collection of diverse and divergent ideas interacting dynamically. Walk into an undergraduate university or art school group studio and you will probably find a collection of artists seemingly working away on individual paths of inquiry, yet look closer and you'll see them interacting dynamically, learning through discussion and observation of each other's art works. They are learning about what it means to inquire as an artist and how to research, work through tough problems, and develop methods for representing ideas visually. In this way, the art room becomes a model for the way learning should occur in every subject and at every level, especially in a dynamic democracy.

Thus conceived, the art classroom is a network of relationships. It is made up of individual behaviors, ideas, and actions that create a range of possibilities not available to any one individual, including the teacher. The irony (and the significance for democratic and subsequently holistic art education) is that for a classroom to become a robust complex learning system, it requires the personal investment of each of its members. It is about working from a space of self-interest, while also trusting that the collective has her or his best interests in mind. It is about students taking the responsibility to support and critically challenge each other by asking questions such as "Is this what you want to say with your work, because this is what I see?" or "Have you looked at this artist, I think you might get some ideas to solve this problem?" The interactive dynamic around individual work is only one example of effective group learning in the art room. Others include group projects in which many students (and many disciplines) may be involved. Such assignments may, and often are, implemented by the teacher from the top down. However, alternatively, students could decide for themselves if it is in their best interest to collaborate on a project. The difference in this approach, for either individual or group projects, is the role of the teacher in setting up and facilitating interactions between individuals. These interactions should be specifically nurtured so that there is always the possibility for collaboration, either toward a common goal or in support of each other's diverse ideas.

What we know about networks is that communication between individuals who already have a lot in common is not necessarily the primary thing that enables a robust, complex learning system (Watts, 2003). Rather, the major stimuli for learning are encounters between individuals who do not share much in common. Thus, the art teacher seeking to foster such learning should actively seek to bring together individual students who might not usually talk to each other outside of the classroom, providing opportunities for them to share their experiences of artistic inquiry and creating a respectful, yet dynamic, environment in which such encounters can thrive and expand.

TEACHING AND LEARNING IN COMPLEX TIMES

As it has been described here, complexity thinking in the art classroom is not an argument for broad curricular content change. It embraces the innovations and insights made by art educators over the years about what we should teach in our classrooms. Rather, arguing for complexity thinking is a reordering of attentions and attitudes toward teaching and learning. It sees the art teacher's role as building relationships between students, curricula, culture and the world; creating constraints that enable diverse and innovative insights and ideas; and becoming a learner alongside students. This represents a shift in thinking that organizes curriculum and pedagogy to enable bottom-up emergence of new knowledge. These ways of learning are not new, they are not restricted either to art or to formal education. Today they are represented, among other things, in how businesses are organizing themselves (Tapscott & Williams, 2006), and how teens are learning and teaching each other through online social networks (Jenkins, Clinton, Purushotma, Robison, & Weigel, 2007). Thinking about our art classrooms in this way expands our understandings of holistic practice to include not only the facets of an individual but how those overlap with others dynamically. It expands the metaphor of the whole body of an individual to the collective body of a classroom where everyone plays a role in learning. Understanding and embracing the art classroom as a complex learning system means providing a space that is not just about the students, teachers and curricula alone, but all of these things interacting dynamically to create an environment of unimagined possibilities.

REFERENCES

Coles, R., Heyman, T., & Lange, D. (1998). *Dorothea Lange: Photographs of a lifetime*. New York, NY: Aperture.

Csikszentmihalyi, M. (1988). Society, culture and person: A systems view of creativity. In R. Sternberg (Ed.), *The nature of creativity* (pp. 325-339). Cambridge, MA: Cambridge University Press.

Davis, B., & Sumara, D. (2006). *Complexity and education: Inquires into learning, teaching, and research*. Mahwah, NJ: Lawrence Erlbaum Associates.

Davis, B., Sumara, D. J., & Luce-Kapler, R. (2008). *Engaging minds: Learning and teaching in a complex world* (2nd ed.). Mahwah, NJ: Erlbaum Associates.

Doll, W. E. (1989). Complexity in the classroom. *Educational Leadership, 7*(1), 65-70.

Donald, M. (2001). *A mind so rare: The evolution of human consciousness*. New York, NY: W. W. Norton & Company.

Hagaman, S. (1990). The community of inquiry: An approach to collaborative learning. *Studies in Art Education, 31*(3), 149-157.

Humphries, C. (2009). The body politic. Retrieved from http://seedmagazine.com/content/article/the_body_politic/

James, P. (1996). The construction of learning and teaching in a sculpture studio class. *Studies in Art Education, 37*(3), 145-159.

James, P. (1997). Learning artistic creativity: A case study. *Studies in Art Education, 39*(1), 74-88.

Jenkins, H., Clinton, K., Purushotma, R., Robison, A. J., & Weigel, M. (2007). Confronting the challenges of participatory culture: Media education for the 21st century. Retrieved from http://digitallearning.macfound.org/atf/cf/%7B7E45C7E0-A3E0-4B89-AC9C-E807E1B0AE4E%7D/JENKINS_WHITE_PAPER.PDF

Juarrero, A. (1999). *Dynamics in action: Intentional behavior as a complex system*. Cambridge, MA: MIT Press.

Kay, S. I. (1998). Shaping elegant problems for visual thinking. In J. W. Simpson, J. M. Delaney, K. L. Carroll, C. M. Hamilton, S. I. Kay, M. S. Kerlavage & J. L. Olson (Eds.), *Creating meaning through art: Teacher as choice maker* (pp. 259-288). Upper Saddle River, NJ: Prentice Hall.

Kindler, A. M. (1999). "From endpoints to repertoires:" A challenge to art education. *Studies in Art Education, 40*(4), 330-349.

Kindler, A. M., & Darras, B. (1998). Culture and development of pictorial repertoires. *Studies in Art Education, 39*(2), pp. 147-167.

Surowiecki, J. (2004). *The wisdom of crowds: Why the many are smarter than the few and how collective wisdom shapes business, economies, societies, and nations*. New York, NY: Doubleday.

Sweeny, R. (2008). Unthinkable complexity: Art education in networked times. In M. Alexenberg (Ed.), *Educating artists for the future: Learning at the intersections of art, science, technology and culture* (pp. 85-101). Bristol, England: Intellect Books.

Tapscott, D., & Williams, A. D. (2006). *Wikinomics: How mass collaboration changes everything*. New York, NY: Portfolio.

Vygotsky, L. S., & Cole, M. (1978). *Mind in society: The development of higher psychological processes*. Cambridge, MA: Harvard University Press.

Waldrop, M. M. (1992). *Complexity: The emerging science at the edge of order and chaos*. New York, NY: Simon & Schuster.

Walker, S. R. (2003). What more can you ask? Artmaking and inquiry. *Art Education, 56*(5), 6-12.

Watts, D. J. (2003). *Six degrees: The science of a connected age*. New York, NY: W.W. Norton & Company.

Wilson, B. (2003). Of diagrams and rhizomes: Visual culture, contemporary art, and impossibility of mapping the content of art education. *Studies in Art Education, 44*(3), 214-229.

Wilson, B. (2004). Child art after modernism: Visual culture and new narratives. In E. Eisner & M. Day (Eds.), *Handbook of research and policy in art education* (pp. 299-328). Mahwah, NJ: Lawrence Erlbaum Associates.

Wolf, D., & Perry, M. (1988). From endpoints to repertoires: New conclusions about drawing development. *Journal of Aesthetic Education, 22*(1), 17-35.

Wolf, J. (1993). *The social production of art*. London, England: Macmillan.

ABOUT THE AUTHOR

Juan Carlos Castro is Assistant Professor of Art Education at Concordia University. His research focuses on the dynamics and qualities of knowing, learning and teaching art through new and social media as understood through complexity thinking, network theory, hermeneutics and phenomenology. He is also a practicing artist whose current inquiry explores place, ecology, and learning.

Juan is a National Board Certified Teacher and taught at Towson High School in Maryland, where his teaching and curriculum was awarded a Coca-Cola Foundation Distinguished Teacher in the Arts award from the National Foundation for the Advancement in the Arts, and he was twice awarded the U.S. Presidential Scholars Teacher Recognition Award.

CHAPTER 10

Restoration of Sight Through Contemplative Practice

Sally Armstrong Gradle

This chapter explores a contemplative approach to seeing that aligns the practices of mindfulness, reflective observation, and appreciation with educative goals that are essential in holistic teaching. The careful looking and thinking that are necessary for the inner growth of a teacher are recognized here as the necessary point of departure for successful relationships with students, inquiry into art, and the connections that a cultivated practice of seeing contributes as restoration for the teacher and the discipline of art education.

Through three simple examples related to the practice of teaching art (mindfulness, *shikantaza*, and appreciative listening), I explore the potential for a deeper visual engagement with the world through artful contemplative practice. The practical recovery of this intuitive vision is at the heart of art education's purpose. Restorative sight in teaching, and subsequently in learning, spurs active contemplation for an awakened life.

Many decades ago when philosopher Josef Pieper made his first trans-Atlantic voyage between Canada and Rotterdam, he expressed amazement when his fellow passengers remarked how little there was to see from the ship's deck in the evenings. He observed that they missed "magnificent fluorescent sea creatures whirled up to the surface by the hundreds in the ship's bow wake" (1990, p. 32). Pieper used this incident and others from his trip to make a point: There is actually so much to see and understand that we often turn our senses off and overlook images and experiences that could add tremendous meaning to our lives. As we take an active, creative role by seeing with intention and then looking within to ponder what it means, we restore our sight with "a patient openness for all things quiet and inconspicuous" (p. 36).

CONTRIBUTIONS OF RESTORATIVE SIGHT TO EDUCATION

This work is about the recovery of [in]sight as an active, but patient contemplation for holistic teaching practice. I begin with current discussions about the restorative power of seeing through the practical cultivation of sensory and experiential awareness. Part of this is aimed at a necessary goal: Without a clear understanding of why we need to see with mindful sensitivity, we cannot restore our sight in a way that opens us to others' views of the world. While outside the scope of this work, there are many emergent educative viewpoints that suggest that a caring, ethical, holistic and sustainable approach to teaching can make significant changes in culture (Noddings, 2005; Gruenewald & Smith, 2008; Kessler, 2000, Riley-Taylor, 2002). In the field of art education, London (2007), McKenna, (2006), Hamblen, (1993), and Carroll (2006) all ask that we revisit the importance of such neglected opportunities in our domain. Art educator Graeme Sullivan (2005) notes that the paradigms are changing, and we must discover ways to become increasingly conscious of the works that precede us, those works whose stories we pick up as a vital thread of continuity in the preservation of culture and world studies. Here, I add an additional dimension to this essential discussion: that of *artful contemplation-as-action* as a necessary component to sustain the spiritual health of art educators *and* the field of inquiry.

RESTORATIVE SIGHT AND CONTEMPLATIVE ACTION

I define *restorative sight* as the empathic, intuitive insight that frequently joins teachers and learners with common goals: those of caring for the whole person and the whole earth. We accomplish this by looking for the connections among what is barely known and often hidden from our conscious understanding with what is observable when one's attention is cultivated. In art education for example, we might observe that learners have worldviews that may not be consciously known to them, but through a mutual inquiry into art, may be better understood and articulated. The practice of restorative sight engages a way of thinking for the teacher that encourages students when existential concerns surface about the world and human values. For most inquirers of artmaking and viewing, it does not end there. Questions often linger as we consider how visual works challenge us to better understand the whole person, his or her unique perceptions about the purposes of art, and the ways future artmaking might contribute to a restorative vision of the learners' place in the world—and our own place in the world. As these questions take shape in future discourse, it becomes possible to draw from the deep well of daily experiences cultivated through several contemplative methods and apply them to artmaking and viewing for better understanding.

Through art-based contemplation, the educative goals of developing attention and care for others and the earth emerge with greater clarity. An art education of this nature readies us to consider what is essential, even as it expands the discipline with a kind of anticipatory knowing (Heidegger, 1993) that prepares us to make a difference in the world through the practice of seeing and expressing in words and/or images. Several exemplars have considered the role that mindfulness can have as a practice that prepares one to receive, and thus restore, one's vision—in relation to art, or, more frequently, to a greater perception of one's life within the larger context of our relationships (O'Reilley, 1998; Brantley & Kabat-Zinn, 2007; Lictmann, 2005; Allen, 2005; Corbin, 1969). This in turn contributes to a better understanding of the world and the empathic, receiving-self that creates.

In the following discussion, I offer three explanatory sections about contemplative ways of knowing and how these practices can restore a teacher's sight. While the practical end to such a discussion grounds the learner in potentially mindful art practices, the journey to such a goal first necessitates a detour of inner growth that is needed by all teachers. For this reason, my main discussion will encompass recovery of sight in the heart of the educator, in the interior space that Parker Palmer has referred to as the "inner teacher" (Palmer, 2006, p. 36).

DISCUSSION OF TERMS: SIGHT AND CONTEMPLATIVE PRACTICE FOR THE INNER TEACHER

A restoration of sight (insight, gnostic wisdom, intuitive awareness—it is known by many terms) awakens with the intention of seeing and the belief that there is something worth searching for in the act of visual engagement. Like Pieper on his voyage, there is careful looking and thinking that must occur for insight to take hold, and for the conception of an idea to emerge as a complete visual work or a thought form. It is a hopeful beginning and relies on the desire of the viewers to develop their own sight through practice. To understand this theoretically as a teacher and an artist, I began with a study of Dustin and Ziegler's text, *Practicing Mortality* (2007). In this work, the authors anchor their discussion by explaining that it is not only the study of art and philosophy that enables us to comprehend what it means to be fully human, but also the fact that our own engagement in the process of looking and thinking are *participatory*. Connecting with the content of what one sees demands the action of daily practice. Dustin and Ziegler propose a "practical recovery of the intuitive vision" (p. 13), established when one dwells in the presence of the seen in order to behold something yet unknown. With practice, the appreciation of similarities, differences, and the inter-relational qualities that comprise our humanness enables us to become mindful of our capacity for insight as one of the most important teaching and learning components of our time.

DAILY PRACTICES IN A WIDE AWAKE LIFE

Contemplative educator Jackie Seidel (2006) notes that in teaching and learning, mindful practices are capable of holding us within the present moment, binding our journeys to those of others. Teacher Maria Lichtmann (2005) reveals that a contemplative approach to seeing is "letting *what is* unfold its levels of meaning before us" (p. 13) so that the chambers of our hearts become the restorative center of sight. We find ourselves able to deeply engage in understanding another, of mining the stillness that comes from this centered place of wisdom if we also add to our quiet observations *reflection and application*.

What I will talk about here are only a few spiritual practices for contemplative teaching through simple ideas that are readily available to anyone. I begin with a discussion about eating a cookie with awareness and intention, yet this is a mere preamble. Reflection-in-action (Schön, 1987) and the inclusion of memories, knowledge, and application of this knowledge to a teacher's spiritual life are essential, and expand upon this brief mindful eating encounter and how it connects to a larger sphere of associative practices in teaching art.

The second experience builds on reflective observation: *shikantaza*, a Buddhist teaching which is also known as the practice of "just sitting." This practice invites the participant into cultivating the kind of stillness necessary so that a relationship, an image, or an object speaks. This practice has connections to the Hindu concept of "going for darśan," (Eck, 1981) and also the experiential knowing that we attend to when we give our attention wholeheartedly to each other.

The third and final practice springs from what I suppose to be a very Midwestern, mid-century upbringing based upon a cautious, pragmatic optimism. This last contemplative orientation has taken me farther in teaching and life than I ever thought it would, and I can only describe it as this: *appreciating one small thing about one small thing*. On days when insight fails me and restoration of my own consciousness flutters and sags like a wet curtain near an open window subjected to a torrential downpour, appreciating small things allows me to restore a more holistic vision to my teaching, the study of art, and the revival of relationships.

CONTEMPLATIVE ORIENTATION TO THE PRACTICE OF LIVING A LIFE

The Buddhist teacher Thich Nhat Hanh (1975) has written about various approaches to cultivating mindfulness. He describes a state of awareness and focus in which disciplined practice enables one to connect more completely to all of life. Paying attention to one's slow, deliberate breathing, for example, or observing one's actions while doing daily tasks such as cooking, cleaning, or sorting laundry become opportunities to remain in the moment and savor the details of experience. Another of Hanh's examples, one that I have implemented periodically in teaching and life, is mindful eating. By focusing on the experience of taking small, deliberate bites, it is possible to explore food's visual complexity, its smell, its texture in the mouth, the sound of one's chewing, and the taste of each particular bite (Hanh, 1975; Brantley & Kabat-Zinn, 2007). In so doing, we stay in the moment. We begin again—we know the phenomenon as if for the first time, for each bite has a different feel on the ready palate when one is fully attentive.

For example, students and I have tasted, and then written about, eating cookies baked according to a recipe supposedly derived from St. Hildegard of Bingen's creative ingenuity.

I really can't verify the source of the recipe; it is handwritten in my mother's script, and has been enthusiastically endorsed as authentic for several years in our family. The cookie has withstood slight adaptations in the ingredients over the years, such as my mother's substitution of lard with "oleo," which probably appeared on the saturated-fat-timeline somewhere between animal fat and the low-fat margarines available today. It is a robust cookie, with a longevity most likely admired by the original consumers.

However, I digress. Hildegard the saint, the natural observer of life, the seer of divine visions and earthly portals, collector of herbs and remedies, created recipes to soothe, sustain or invigorate as needed. Her cookies crunch in the mouth, the spices slowly separate and are savored, the nuts provide a tantalizing texture, and the entire experience when repeated with each act of mindful chewing and swallowing keeps one in the moment. And yet... the experience of being in the moment means little without reflection and application of what this simple act might mean in one's life, and this seems most particularly true when I think about teaching.

As I reflect on eating one of Hildegard's cookies now, a host of ideas flutter around this mindful experience as the vivid, incarnational material that often triggers associative insights connected to knowledge about the subject. I muse about how St. Hildegard, in her observations of life, noted *viriditas,* or greenness, as the operative spiritual force in the universe and that this difficult translation of 'the greening concept' has baffled and delighted scholars of her work for centuries. What did she mean? What does it mean now to *become green*? Much like Thales the Miletian whose literary fragments suggested that the origin of life suggested itself through observation, Hildegard felt *viriditas* was an observable phenomenon in daily life (King-Lenzmeier, 2001; Flanagan, 1989). In a very physical way, the subtle, undeniable evidence that life was still *present* after a long dry spell or a trying winter was the proof that the spirit of God had not forsaken the earth. Life renewed, restored, and opened its celestial whole through seeds full of intention, and likewise through her visions of the physical/spiritual world. The sun-centered cosmos, wreathed with the productive winds and changing vapors of a universe that was constantly moving through a cycle of birth and death, explained *viriditas* visually. While her visionary descriptions recount what some would call the metaphorical, the spicy sustenance of a simple cookie was meant to revive and sustain a (w)holy body and spirit, which contributed to the *viriditas* of humankind in its own way. We think of 'going green' as something we must *do* in the 21st century, yet perhaps Hildegard would pronounce our greening as already accomplished, and not by our own doing. For her, *viriditas* was the life-restoring awareness that we exist as a gift: those receiving-selves who are capable of noticing and creating through active contemplation. In a sense, then, opening to what is life-giving and life-sustaining makes us green, fleshy, in-the-world participants who are also completely spirit.

Contemplative knowing, however, requires more than being in the moment and eating a cookie, or intuitive moments of awareness about a saintly artist's diverse life. In her writing on mindfulness in teaching, Lichtmann (2005) suggests that contemplative awareness must be reflexive if it is going to open the teacher to connections and depth with both students and subject matter. In other words, the next step to restoring a teacher's [in]sight has to be looking within, and seeing what active contemplation and appreciation might mean in relation to teaching, beyond the subject of an artist's work or the experience itself.

COUNTING THE GREENS: A STORY FOR THE TEACHER WITHIN

Several years ago in another city, I volunteered some time to assist a woman I will call Mildred, a paraplegic now deceased. It was her dream to learn from an art teacher how to paint "correctly." For Mildred, painting correctly meant replication of every possible green in a photographic panorama with an exacting palette, mastered because of a teacher's careful tutelage.

"Greens are so difficult to paint because there are so many possible variations," I recall saying, trying to simplify things. "Just look around this room!" I gestured broadly at the communal dining hall where we worked each week, cloaked with a shimmery dark green lower wall and a speckled greenish-gray carpet. The well-worn shag appeared to be a composite of colors that cleverly disguised stains and worn footpaths. Thomas Kinkade-like scenes punctuated the pink upper walls at regular intervals, each one a seeming reminder that this space of communal recovery was temporary—there were other scenes to dream about, and each one had a lit, inhabited cottage, a lush green garden, and a pathway home that was obvious and purposeful—like Mildred's search for greens.

I felt troubled over my lack of enthusiastic, direct instruction for Mildred's quest. Why wasn't I more engaged in her color matching? Did I sense the great divide between what she expected in an art teacher and what I was—a fumbling art student who used no particular formulas to paint with precision? Mildred must have sensed she had work to do on her own behalf if a correct painting was going to develop, since I was clearly not much help. By the next week, she had observed each print on the dining room wall and counted the shades of green in each cottage scenario. This was no small feat for an individual in a wheelchair with limited mobility. It probably took several days to tally up the greens. When she told me that there were never less than 20 greens in each painting, I thought about her process of discovering that knowledge on her own, the obvious respect that she had for studying something in great detail, and then my own attempt to recover a sense of insight into the teaching and learning process. I observed with wonder as Mildred applied what she took away from her discovery: Her painting task suddenly became far more exploratory in nature than it was a study in precision of greens. She painted scenes from her collection of glossy magazine images, then abandoned them as she envisioned places from her childhood farm, and finally gravitated toward the depiction of Bible stories that stuck in her memory over the years. We were both aware that she no longer required the same kind of teacher she originally thought she wanted; the boundaries of teaching and learning appeared to be shifting. Mildred observed with the heart-felt necessity of someone who aimed to see with intention; her participatory vision, which I call active contemplation, allowed access to insight, a way to identify and call forth the gift that was within her. This experience from a very determined student still teaches me decades later, challenging me daily to observe in greater detail, to savor the various greens when I am lost in a problem, and to trust that the greening is also occurring within me just as it does around me.

This small episode also carried me forward, marking my call toward contemplative life in teaching: those baby steps in which I struggled with my inability to know it all and teach it all, followed by a greater reliance on and respect for the student's visual conception to become form. The story itself connects me back to the quality of greenness, so sought after by Mildred, so revered by Hildegard, that the experiences I recall even now when I think of eating Hildegard's spicy cookies can open floodgates of associative rivulets. Cultivating a mind that participates in its own learning involves the "mixing of sensory and symbolic data" (Sewall, 1999, p. 55) a weaving of visceral knowledge, subject knowledge, and the keenly felt awareness that there is more to the moment than just the moment. Sewell, who writes about the seamlessness of our interior and exterior perceptual worlds, highlights the intuitive spirituality we often bury about sight: we 'see' with touch, taste, smell, and sound.

EXPERIENTIAL VALUE AND SHIKANTAZA

Sometimes our senses are challenged to 'make sense' of what one thinks of as experience. Philosopher David Abram (1996) watched several spiders spin webs across the mouth of a cave, each with its own particular center, where pattern upon converging pattern was his introduction to being "alive, awake, and aware" and the experience that enabled him to see "worlds within worlds that spin in the depths of this world that we commonly inhabit" (p. 19). An awareness of our experiences as artist-teachers is often missed due to the scholarly and well-honed focus of working in a particular medium over time (McNiff, 2004). Looking attentively in another medium is possible, as artist-teachers like Pat Allen (2005) have explored in their workshops. Like Abram (1996), or naturalist and conservationist Aldo Leopold (1949) whose observations were closely aligned to the animated world, place, and the interconnection of life within sight, one could give the same attention to any viewing experience, even one that is recalled from the past, and witnessed once again in consciousness. The daily practice of restorative sight occurs as visual particulars are remembered. "Insightful beholding and illuminating wonder, with extraordinary awareness and gratitude" (Dustin & Ziegler, 2007, p. 15), in turn, awakens the heart.

As I wrote this, I was thinking about my rather recent ventures into filming student performance art, and the shocking restoration of sight that occurred as a personally embodied experience in which I eventually learned to "see" with more than one sense. I filmed a student's lengthy performance during which she sawed flaps in a large box. Throughout the drama, she was enclosed in the box, only reaching a hand through the opened flaps to take in food and then discard its waste. While I was cognitively aware that I was filming her performance, I was not aware of how intently I was also recording my own experience of it. Unfamiliar with a tripod, I held the camera tightly in my novice hand, and it became my eye, my gesture, my body. My breath was recorded as part of the sound of the performance, and the motion of my breathing in and out—sometimes quite sharply—became part of the (e) motion of the film as well. Always fearful of closeted spaces, wary of confinement and lack of air, the camera and thus the image on the film moved with me as though *the film itself* was a living, moving being. Since then, I have watched the film countless times as someone else's story, another's performance. Only now that several years have passed am I able to see that my embodiment of the film's major themes was present in the filming itself: those of enclosure and displacement were a very real part of what I was experiencing, feeling, and breathing throughout my own unnoticed performance.

Sociologist Meredith McGuire (2003) appropriately clarifies that feeling, thinking, breathing bodies do indeed matter—we are enmeshed in our own spiritual questing, never separate from our so-named vessel 'the body.' We are instead a woven substance of all our bodily practices, habits of being, and interpretations of the same—artists, teachers and students alike. The embedded senses of 'common' sense, the sense of taste, of wonder, justice, reality, and even aesthetics (to randomly select a few "senses") comingle in memory and lived experience like lovers or mud wrestlers, take your pick. We cannot afford the luxury of a trial separation from the body; for our understandings are as tied to its health as my breathing was to the film. As Alfred Schutz (1932/1967) would also indicate, we become immersed in the meaning of our experiences only reflectively, and this is what stays with us, through us, and even *as* us. It is a kind of enfleshment with the experience, as performance author Peter McLaren (1994) would say, a way of feeling within us the unexpected surprises juxtaposed with the ordinary preoccupations of human experience; the point where Schön (1987) explains that the tacit, knowing-in-action responses present an awakening that leads to reflection-in-action.

When studying a particular image, I believe it is possible to gradually thaw the analytical self that might initially count the greens and then slowly touch the deeper sense of wonder and appreciation that Pieper must have felt when he first saw the ocean's marvels while crossing the Atlantic. To cultivate this as an artist and a teacher, I began to use what Dustin and

FIGURE 1. *Useless Science or The Alchemist*, Remedios Varo, Spain 1908—Mexico 1963. Used with permission.

Ziegler (2007) referred to as the practice of contemplative seeing as a daily viewing habit that leads to greater appreciation and reflection. I wanted to make viewing a *ritual*, and by this I mean exactly what the authors referred to as invoking "the deepest essence of that activity, [in this case, seeing deeply], in which thought and action are inseparable, all the senses are at work, and the body becomes a primary locus of meaning" (p. 50).

As an example for teaching practice, I studied the work of an artist, Remedios Varo, who was unfamiliar to me. She was a 20th-century surrealist painter, a mystical, alchemical sort of thinker, and a keen observer of both the built and natural worlds (Kaplan, 1988). By making Varo's work into the wallpaper of my computer, it was ever-present, and even when I was physically away from its presence, its memory was there for me. I set aside time each day to view the details in Varo's *Useless Science or the Alchemist (1955)*, to look with wonder, to be present with no other intention than to let the image speak, in whatever way it would. This practice of *just sitting* and observing has an ancient precedent. Buddhist scholar and naturalist Stephanie Kaza (1993) briefly clarifies this method as she has applied it in her observational research about trees. She writes,

> I spent time in silence, close to trees, doing my best to be simply present with the tree as Other, aware of my thoughts, moods, and projections. I had no idea at first how this would work, but I persisted in the experiment. The writing became an excuse to listen for a call from the trees, in whatever form it took. I did not go to the trees with an agenda or story in mind, but chose rather to see what would unfold by being completely present in the specific place and moment. (p. 5)

Her methodology is informed by Zen Buddhist *shikantaza,* (just sitting), but it also seems grounded in something more. Kaza mentions *place* and *moment*. What are the moments when we inhabit a place of understanding, wonder, and deep appreciation in a work of art? What are the conditions of practice that enable us to give up the idea of retrieving a story about ourselves as the teller of the experience, and listen to what is present in the work itself, the tree itself, or our relationships? How do we write about an artwork, for example, as a moment of deep appreciation, an experiential connection to the Other?

These questions were uppermost in my mind when I viewed Varo's painting entitled *Useless Science or the Alchemist.* The repeated practice of viewing pulled me deeper into the background in which she has prepared an alchemist's domain full of details. I scoured the distance: Over time, I recognized the distillation of hope being funneled through vessels and alchemized by fire, caught drop by drop in bottles that are almost hidden from sight. The lone monk-like creature turning a wheel in the center of the painting is covered with a black and white checked cloth that seems to emanate from her skin, drapes her body, and spills to the ground as a blanket might. How interesting that the cloaked figure seems to be producing this embodied pattern from her head! Or is she pulling the checkered floor pattern free, cloaking her body, and by so doing, transforming a hard surface into something soft and pliable? Is the singular focus of concentration on the act of turning gears on the wheel her expression of hope, however useless others may perceive such as action? My eyes wander to examine the tower of swinging bells in the background—is there sound? Is there a moment of alchemical transubstantiation marked by unlikely auditory complements of wind, water, and the crackle of flames? When does the holy become an all-pervasive *place* of being, or am I already in it, as I am now supposing in reflection that Varo was suggesting here? And what was it that Varo's figure sat turning, if not the patient interwoven fabric of her own soul, the nurturing faith that makes sense of the world, even when no one else was watching?

These were the ruminations that occurred in repeated moments of journaling after employing the "just sitting" practice that Kaza (1993) mentions in her work with trees. Based on the ancient Mountains and Rivers sutra, this practice is deceptive in its simplicity. While one begins by recognizing that things are what they are (bell towers, monks, rivers, mountains), staying the course of one's inquiry suggests the inter-connective possibilities among individual components, which "informs and transforms the perceiver" (p. 11-12). Through looking at artworks, students and I have noticed that most of our writing has become an act of questioning that marvels over an artist's perceptions that are different than our own, or queries into other views of consciousness that restore our sight, even as they challenge what we may believe to be true. This is a useful, active, restorative participation that is self-renewing when employed as a daily contemplative practice.

Dustin and Ziegler (2007) explore this same concept through Henry David Thoreau's walking. Thoreau, the authors explain, walked more than 4 hours a day and then transcribed his observations from his pocket-sized notebook into lengthy journal accounts. He did this purposefully, absorbing many details of his environment. His walks had little in common with a casual stroll or meander: These were disciplined, sustained practices of moving and seeing with care. I think of the intention of a pilgrim who has watchful eyes for the divine when I picture Thoreau in the muck and brine, at the edge of the clear cut, pacing his steps in a seasonal rhythm according to New England's climes. In Thoreau's journaling, he calls attention to the fact that our survival demands the kind of participatory engagement that carries us from one act (in this case, walking) to another (which was, for Thoreau, the observation and then the writing).

Is this different for a teacher, striding through the inner woodlot, field, or farm? What do we observe of the images we teach about, the students we engage, our very acts of walking a profession which challenges us to behold with wonder, find a voice for our questions and our witnessing with no less intensity? Dustin and Ziegler (2007) contend that the particulars of the world are known most faithfully through contemplative *anticipation*—or perhaps we would use the word hopefulness—which the practice of just sitting, just walking, or just witnessing the Other mean. The intense listening to understand prepares the ground for creative beginnings. Spiritual teacher Mary Rose O'Reilley (1998), a self-proclaimed "one person committee" of Buddhist, Catholic, and Quaker beliefs, offers a similar idea about deep listening:

> Like all contemplative disciplines, it deals with the whole rather than with the parts: it attends not to the momentary faltering but to the long path of the soul, not to the stammer but to the poem being born. It completes the clumsy gesture in an arc of grace. One can, I think, listen someone into existence, encourage a stronger self to emerge or a new talent to flourish. (p. 21)

This is uniquely different from examining a work (or a student) in order to analyze their forms, critique execution, or assign a value to compositional balance. Reading an artwork or a relationship for restorative purposes means listening into existence the message of sacredness conveyed as a living presence in the moment. It is the kind of listening that I wish to convey through the final section of this exploratory work on contemplative teaching in art.

APPRECIATING ONE SMALL THING ABOUT ONE SMALL THING

I have discussed practices of active contemplation such as sitting and observing; and before that, simple mindfulness practices such as eating which can lead to greater inner awareness for the teacher. But there is something less frequently named, more subcutaneous in one's experiences of living and teaching that is shaped by a host of past encounters: sense perceptions, an awareness of mystery, childhood experiences, and the meanings that can be opened ponderously, like unexpected gifts. Perhaps it is a Midwestern sentiment to look at the world and find one small thing to value, or maybe it was my upbringing which reinforced the idea that I should look for the silver lining in whatever gray funk I frequently stormed around in, but the concept stuck with me. Some years later in my academic reading, I formed an unlikely alliance of thought with a scholar of Islamic mysticism (Henry Corbin, 1969) who valued the active imagination as an organ of our being that retrieves the invisible essence of experience through metaphor. He explained that not only is there a universe that can be perceived through the intellect, and also a world quite experientially available to us through our senses, but there is a third, intermediate world of "idea-images" (p. 4) or archetypes, in which the spiritual takes on a physical presence, and the dyed-in-the-wool physicality of being is also spiritual. The past and the future in this intermediate realm of being, are in fact, concealed in our own intuited experiences—and herein nests the conservation and preservation of the world, according to Corbin. We are involved in alchemizing education by recalling and remembering, by gathering into being, by witnessing and acknowledging the depths of the spiritual in our practice. Being a witness of consciousness, someone who recognizes the truth in another, or an image, or a worldview, is the sound of attention. It is listening that thinks, that is receptive to the Other (Gradle, 2007). So when the inner teacher opens the receiving-self who creates via metaphor, acknowledging this intermediary realm of imaginative possibility, it is possible to envision that entire worlds are just coming into being by merely turning the lens to appreciate one small thing about one small thing.

THE SNOWSTORM STORY

The November sky was thick as gray sheep's wool, uncombed and stacked in a precarious pile overhead. Inside the elementary school, the mood had shifted with the weather's impending changes and the noisy 2nd graders bounced from place to place, which challenged the new student teacher to keep them on track with her art lesson. I sat in an inconspicuous corner, under the windows, observing the energy combustion when suddenly a shout went up: "Look! It's snowing!" A hush fell over the room and I was startled to look into 27 pairs of huge, wondering eyes that were not looking at me, but beyond me, out the window where a fast falling snow had begun to blanket the world.

In those few seconds, the mood drifted to the imaginative provocations that the newness of the hidden terrain afforded children who had experienced first snows of the season only a few times in their young lives. I marveled at their sudden, silent introspection and sense of wonderment, and also appreciated one small thing this gave me. I felt as though I was transported back in time, to the snows of my youth, which always seemed deep and heavy in their silence. Dressed like an alien in a spacesuit, my small, encased body moved slowly but eagerly over snow-plow-created peaks; those escalations that I boldly refused to ignore on the long, slow hike to school. All mountains were to be scaled! Treacherous footholds, wet clothes, and perpetual tardiness were nothing in the face of such adventure. The school day could, and always did, go on without me as I explored the flocked trees, the footprints of creatures that had gone before me, the dazzling blue shadows that altered everything. The gift of recalling such memories of mystery and exploration, and the gift of understanding that similar possibilities awaited these 2nd graders restored my sight, that oracular intuition that the whole of life's happenings give instruction, provoke memory, raise questions, and offer epiphanies that crack the veneer of teaching to reveal the active inner teacher within each of us.

IMPLEMENTING CONTEMPLATIVE ACTION IN THE CLASSROOM: WHAT IS PRACTICAL?

I am sometimes asked if contemplative actions that open us to the inner teacher can be conveyed to students, who might also employ the technique in their coursework or in furthering their reflective teaching practice out of the university setting. I suggest the following as a daily participatory practice, alone or in the company of classmates.

If I were requested to make suggestions that could extend one's contemplative teaching practice, this is what I would offer. Take 5 minutes to focus on an image (no more than one a week, over 5 to 7 days' time). Notice what calls to you first in the image. (The subject matter, the formal details, the artist's conveyance of mood, for example.) Does anything suggest a similarity or difference to you with other works recently seen? What do you wonder about? What seems marvelous, mysterious, still beyond comprehension, yet curiously fascinating? What delights you? How have your ideas changed since the last time you viewed the artwork?

Many individuals find it most productive to become oriented by sitting quietly a few minutes before responding orally or in writing. While sharing these contemplative actions aloud can be useful at times, it is often more productive to dialog after a week or so, giving students ample time to examine their growth in understanding the image and themselves before participating with others. By so doing, this method seems to have a carry-over to experiences. As we notice what we can observe over time in an image, we also awaken to what we can notice about our teaching practices and daily experiences.

ARTFUL PRACTICE: CONTEMPLATIVE ACTION AS A KOAN

Although long since past, I once had an adult student who used to examine the artwork we studied by writing letters to the artists as her journal entries. The majority of her writing was not descriptive of the content of the artists' works, but rather questions that she posed to the artists. She would ask what they were reading that provoked their ideas; why they decided that this particular image among so many others was the crucial idea to paint; and who inspired them, fed them, and nurtured their perceptions so they could accomplish their work. Reflecting on her journal approach now, I am thinking that the questions we ask ourselves are so often like *koans*, the inner queries that we carry about like soon-to-be hatched eggs in the inner teacher's psyche.

O'Reilley (1998) clarifies that koans loosen our attachment to the analytical and allow us to meander off into a place where we nurture, water, and feed the depths of our souls. Each person carries such koan-like questions well below the level of consciousness, where they have the possibility of becoming alchemized by the artful contemplative actions we undertake. They are the existential questions of becoming, the greening of us all, and the bold metaphors that wrestle us to the ground with Corbin's (1969) awareness that there is an intermediate world, where spirit takes form, form is also spirit, and we are therefore engaged in a serious battle for the preservation of the world with every imaginative act. The artful contemplative actions of creating art, viewing art, sensing, caring, and retrieving what restores us is a journey that is imperative for the heart of art education today. Like Josef Pieper on his Atlantic voyage, or Hildegard of Bingen in her astute observations of the natural, sacred world, we cultivate and restore ourselves through the mindful participation that has always been part of holistic teaching practice, one that addresses a restoration of the teacher's inner wholeness.

REFERENCES

Abram, D. (1996). *The spell of the sensuous.* New York, NY: Vintage.

Allen, P. (2005). *Art is a spiritual path.* Boston, MA: Shambala.

Brantley, J., & Kabat-Zinn, J. (2007). *Calming your anxious mind.* Oakland, CA: New Harbinger Publications.

Carroll, K. L. (2006). Development and learning in art: Moving in the direction of a holistic paradigm for art education, *Visual Arts Research. 32*(1), 16-28.

Corbin, H. (1969). *Alone with the alone: Creative imagination in the Sufism of Ibn ʿArabī.* Princeton, NJ: Princeton University Press.

Dustin, C., & Ziegler, J. (2007). *Practicing mortality: Art, philosophy, and contemplative seeing.* New York, NY: Palgrave Macmillan.

Eck, D. (1981). *Darśan: Seeing the divine image in India.* New York, NY: Columbia University.

Flanagan, S. (1989). *Hilegard of Bingen, 1098-1179.* London, England: Routledge.

Gradle, S. A. (July 2007). "The Imaginal World: Sensing the Creative Imperative." *Imaginative Education Research Group 2007 Research Symposium,* Vancouver, Canada. Retrieved from www.ierg.net/confs/papers.php?first_letter=G&cf=4

Gruenewald, D. & Smith, G. (2008). Creating a movement to ground learning in place. In D. Gruenewald & G. Smith (Eds.), *Place-based education in the global age* (pp. 345-358). New York, NY: Lawrence Erlbaum.

Hamblen, K. (1993). Collected silences: Audible and unheard (Editorial). *Studies in Art Education, 34*(4), 195-198.

Hanh, T. N. (1975). *The miracle of mindfulness.* (Mobi Ho, Trans.). Boston, MA: Beacon Hill.

Heidegger, M. (1993). *Basic concepts.* (Gary Aylesworth, Trans.). Bloomington, IN: Indiana University Press.

Kaplan, J. A. (1988). *Remedios Varo: Unexpected journeys.* New York, NY: Abbeville Press.

Kaza, S. (1993). *The attentive heart: Conversations with trees.* Boston, MA: Shambhala.

Kessler, R. (2000). *The soul of education.* Alexandria, VA: Association for Supervision and Curriculum Development.

King-Lenzmeier, A. H. (2001). *Hildegard of Bingen: An integrated vision.* Collegeville, MN: The Liturgical Press.

Leopold, A. (1949). *A Sand County Almanac.* New York, NY: Oxford University Press.

Lichtmann, M. (2005). *The teacher's way: Teaching and the contemplative life.* New York, NY: Paulist Press.

London, P. (2007). Concerning the spiritual in art education. In R. Irwin & L. Bresler (Eds.), *The International Handbook on Research in Arts Education* (pp. 1479-1492). Dordrecht, The Netherlands: Springer.

McGuire, M. B. (2003). Why bodies matter: A sociological reflection on spirituality and materiality. *Spiritus 3*(1), 1-18.

McKenna, S. (2006). (2006). Art is possible. *Visual arts research. 32*(1), 53-63.

McLaren, P. (1994). *Schooling as a ritual performance: An introduction to critical pedagogy in the foundations of education.* White Plains, NY: Longman.

McNiff, S. (2004). *Art heals: How creativity cures the soul.* Boston, MA: Shambhala.

Noddings, N. (2005). Place based education to preserve the earth and its people. *Educating citizens for global awareness.* (N. Noddings, Ed.)(pp.57-68.) New York, NY: Teachers College Press.

O'Reilley, M. R. (1998). *Radical presence: Teaching as contemplative practice.* Portsmouth, NH: Boynton/Cook Publishers.

Palmer, P. (2006). *The courage to teach.* San Francisco, CA: Jossey-Bass.

Pieper, J. (1990). *Only the lover sings.* (L. Krauth, Trans.). San Francisco, CA: Ignatius Press.

Riley-Taylor, E. (2002). *Ecology, spirituality, and education: Curriculum for relational knowing.* New York, NY: Peter Lang.

Seidel, J. (2006). Some thoughts on teaching as contemplative practice. *Teachers College Record, 108*(9),1901-1914.

Schön, D. (1987). *Educating the reflective practitioner.* San Francisco, CA: Jossey-Bass.

Schutz, A. (1967). *The phenomenology of the social world.* (George Walsh, Trans.). London, England: Heinemann Educational Books.

Sewall, L. (1999). *Sight and sensibility.* New York, NY: Jeremy P. Tarcher.

Sullivan, G. (2005). *Art practice as research: Inquiry in the visual arts.* Thousand Oaks, CA: Sage.

ABOUT THE AUTHOR

Sally Armstrong Gradle is an Associate Professor in the School of Art and Design at Southern Illinois University, Carbondale. She has taught both undergraduates and graduates in her areas of interest, which are contemplative art forms, eco-art and community practices, and curriculum. Prior to teaching at the college level, she experienced a full life in the classroom for 25 years as either an art teacher or an elementary educator.

CHAPTER 11

Reflections on a Bowl of Tea

Jay Hanes

ichigo-ichie
one time, one meeting[1]

A JOURNEY

Aesthetic practice has the potential to holistically integrate behavior, belief, and values. The performance of ritual can metaphorically link an individual's values, cultural beliefs, and community behaviors. By connecting values and behaviors, aesthetic experience bridges mind and body, media and heritage, thoughts and actions. The following describes how the ritual actions of sharing tea in a traditional manner provide opportunities for aesthetic experience, personal development, and harmoniously resonating relationships with others.

The tradition of *chanoyu,*[2] or Japanese tea ceremony, provides a ritualized time to focus on the connection between one's introspective meditation and transactions with others as well as the natural environment. The history of chanoyu spans a millennium of ritual practice and aesthetic process with a significant pivotal point late in the 16th century. While the drinking of tea originated in China, there are many tea rituals from around the world. The Japanese word chanoyu literally means hot water for tea, and in the West it connotes Japanese tea ceremony. Jennifer Anderson (1991) suggests that in the West we might think of it, rather, as the Japanese tea ritual. This traditional art form significantly influenced the arts and aesthetic sensibilities characteristic of the Edo Period in Japan (1603-1868). In contemporary times, it is practiced across the globe as a ritual encounter to strengthen the relationship between guest and host. For the rare few, practice of chanoyu is a way of life.[3]

PREPARATIONS

The tea bush (*camellia sinensis*) originated in Southeast Asia and has been enjoyed by the Chinese for at least 2,000 years. Tea, or *cha,* first arrived in Japan about the 6th century with the opening of trade and an exchange of ideas. In 1191 Eisai, a Zen monk returned from China, began the Rinzai School of Zen Buddhism in Japan and brought seeds for cultivating the plant at his monastery. Tea rituals continued to develop with Zen practice while artists and intellectuals contributed the aesthetic notion of *wabi.*[4] A valid interpretation of the wabi aesthetic system is that it expressed discontent with conquest and the accumulation of material wealth during the civil wars in the Sengoku and Azuchi-Momoyama periods roughly from the middle of the 15th century to the beginning of the 17th century.

The practice of preparing whisked powdered tea, or *matcha,* and the understated practice of *wabi-cha* by monks and artists continued toward an ideal of rustic simplicity. Rituals and tools for the modern tea ceremony developed under Sen no-Rikyu (1522-1591). Rikyu also collaborated with Chojiro, a local potter, and together they pioneered the *raku chawan,* or raku-fired tea bowl, a simple utensil that becomes a focal point in the ritual (Pitelka, 2005). To Rikyu, the raku chawan epitomized the wabi aesthetic he envisioned. A hand-hewn raku chawan is simple and imperfect, and it combines the artistic process with forces of nature. A raku chawan is light and comfortable to hold, and it symbolically and intimately delivers the matcha that is prepared in it from the vessel to the person. For example, the rim of a raku chawan has peaks and valleys that meaningfully represent high and low points in the circle of life.

Rikyu trained students in his aesthetic vision and found in the tea ceremony the elusive moment of beauty and imperfection (Plutschow, 2003). One of Rikyu's students was his patron, the most powerful warlord in Japan at the time, Toyotomi Hideyoshi (1536-1598). Rikyu's preference for simple objects and austere tearooms challenged Hideyoshi's ostentatious taste based on aggressive aggrandizement and economic acquisition. Rikyu emphasized human equality and humility through the tea ritual. His aesthetic choices also implied his opposition to Hideyoshi's plans to invade Korea followed by China (Plutschow, 2003). As a student of the tea ritual, Hideyoshi was humiliated by Rikyu's art form and anti-war sentiment with its understated symbolic gestures of harmony, respect, purity, and tranquility. Later, Hideyoshi sentenced Rikyu to *seppuku*, or ritual suicide, for his dissent against the plans for war in 1591.

Rikyu had served as an advisory council member to Hideyoshi, who eventually unified Japan. To divert another civil war and with the intention to conquer Manchurian China, Hideyoshi invaded Korea twice between 1592 and 1598. He employed millions of trained warriors from a militarily developed culture and a fleet of 2,000 ships built a decade earlier. The military casualties from these invasions included 130,000 Japanese, 300,000 Koreans, and 13,000 Chinese. In retrospect, it is easy to see why Rikyu opposed Hideyoshi's tactics.

The onset of the 17th century in Japan was the beginning of a cultural renaissance. The wars in Korea brought Hideyoshi's clan to economic ruin and the end of Azuchi-Momoyama Japan (1568-1603). With the Tokugowa government, a new feudal system that followed during the Edo Period, Japan maintained an isolationist attitude over a century and a half. In this early modern culture, the arts built on aesthetic influences from Rikyu-style chanoyu and flourished from internal stability during the Edo Period.

Similar to the military history, chanoyu followed the development of religious thought. Religious influences on tea ritual included Shintoism, the native religion of Japan, Zen Buddhism in the 12th century, and Jesuit Christianity from contact with Portugese merchants in the 16th century. By the 13th century, Samurai warriors adopted the tea ritual as an entrance into Zen Buddhism for sharpening their focus. It is important to consider that the Japanese Zen tradition was built on Mahayana Buddhism from China, a practice that emphasized meditation as a way toward enlightenment. There is also evidence that Zen directly borrowed from Chán Buddhism (Grigg, 1999), a later development that reintroduced native Taoist philosophies from China relating to the forces of nature. "Zen was the last major innovation in Japanese Buddhism, and it may not be coincidental that Japanese art also changed little after the fifteenth century" (Anderson, 2004, p. 220).

Yet, in the era of unification under the Tokugawa clan that followed, tea practice became more popular and other Japanese arts flourished. Directly after Rikyu's execution, few would claim an association with his practice openly for fear that Hideyoshi would determine their fate. But soon after the Azuchi-Momoyama era closed with the death of Hideyoshi, Rikyu's grandsons preserved his work in founding the two main schools of chanoyu, Urasenke and Omote Senke, and the practice developed as a popular art form.

Though Rikyu drew on a number of religious practices, it is important to note that chanoyu is not necessarily a religion. Although many religious practices include ritual action, a ritual form is not always religious. Human ritual is common in various non-religious activities such as brushing teeth. However, ritual has a performative quality and oftentimes is associated with artistic practice (Dissanayake, 1990). Evidence in writings about Rikyu's intent demonstrated that his tea ritual was spiritually based. Stories about his purpose illustrated how his ritual tea served to change dispositions as in the relationship between the tea master and his patron, much like tribal activities of a shaman dispelling a harmful spirit. Later, when chanoyu continued in schools with hierarchical structures, an antithesis of Rikyu's intent in some ways, the leadership developed and maintained a priestly presence.[5]

SHARING A BOWL OF TEA

I have found personal value in being a student of tea and making opportunities to share tea ritual with others, including students of all ages. Through two decades of work with chanoyu, I have de-emphasized romantic associations by intent. Rather, my emphasis has been derivation of meaning from the aesthetic ritual of chanoyu. My experience with students has ranged widely through backgrounds and contexts. I have offered countless tea ceremony demonstrations and lectures, attended tea conferences, and traveled through Japan sharing tea with native groups and visiting significant tea sites. In this section I will describe classes and courses that I have taught, the content that was emphasized, and anecdotal results. These various courses and classes demonstrated for students the holistic concepts of identity, meaning, and purpose through individual participation in community ritual toward peaceful co-existence.

I began with a simple method. First, I have students make and raku-fire their own tea bowls. Then, I host a community member adept at chanoyu to perform the ritual with the students' bowls. As the culminating experience for my first instructional unit on chanoyu in 1990, I invited Kazuko Law, a native Japanese artist, to visit my class as a community resource (Hollingsworth, 2000). Her classroom visitation elicited a significant positive, affective response from at least one student, Jason, who was known to be a troubled youth. Jason gave Kazuko-sensei his hand-made tea bowl after the tea event. This was an unexpected sign of respect. In 2009, Kazuko-sensei mentioned to me that she warmly remembered the tea bowl that Jason had made and given to her at our gathering. This early teaching unit foreshadowed the impact that the study of chanoyu could have on my own personal experience as well as on curriculum writing and the lives of students.

Since then, I have developed skills hosting tea and expanded on this model in two undergraduate courses and in an intensive 3-week summer arts program for children. With each opportunity to teach chanoyu, my knowledge of the material deepens, and my understanding of how students meet the content and my skills in presentation expand.

I taught my first course of this kind in higher education three times in consecutive summers as a university raku pottery course. Chanoyu informed the course, yet the focus was pottery production and raku firing. I approached the curriculum as a pottery course because of the familiarity and fit that pottery has in a Western, academic based college studio curriculum. Also, at that point I was more comfortable teaching pottery than chanoyu because I did not have training in the tea ritual. Most of my knowledge of tea was based on library research and my first experience of teaching the content in the high school unit. For each group of students, I performed a tea ceremony after watching a short video many times, mimicking the moves but not knowing their manner or significance. It worked like theatre. In my home studio, I continued to explore making tea bowls.

Before I offered this curriculum again, I studied Asian martial arts and took an apprenticeship with Kaji Aso-sensei to learn the practice of preparing and making tea. Besides developing an ability to make tea properly, these experiences provided me with an understanding of the meaning attributed to postures, mannerisms, and selection of tea tools as well as insights into my own production of better tea bowls. I have found that new knowledge adds value and understanding to the ritual behavior.

Years later, from 2005 through 2007, I offered my curriculum to younger students in an intensive summer arts program (Hanes & Nintze, 2008). The *Creating Landscapes*® method focused on experiential learning through aesthetic education and was holistic in design. The mission statement for the organization is "an intergenerational and mutually supportive community of learners in the arts and sciences" that has developed young artists since 1990 (Hyatt, 2006). Faculty of artist/teachers assisted by undergraduate student interns developed interdisciplinary thematic curricula that celebrated and discovered depth of understanding through music, rhythm and dance, creative writing, visual arts, science, and math. Each year, learning situations focus on a thematic concept that is often as elusive as it is inspirational. Clearly the methods of study in chanoyu and related Japanese arts fit the philosophical framework of Creating Landscapes.

My contribution to the program through the tea ceremony course included study in martial arts, meditation, calligraphy, book binding, flower arranging, origami, haiku, and, of course, tea ceremony. It should be reiterated that many of these traditional Japanese art forms are closely associated with aesthetic developments in chanoyu. The benefits of these activities as a holistic educational model are many and involve investigations into human thought and action.

One example of a student who appeared to benefit from this course stood out. A 10-year-old boy asked his mother to take him to the local public library so that he could read more about Japan. As a student at risk, this was the first time that he had asked to visit the public library. His mother was impressed that her son was motivated to pursue this interest outside of the classroom. As another example, two sisters constructed a tearoom in a third floor closet in their home. Additionally, older students had quite different responses to the curriculum, but were similarly inspired. Some have reported that their experience with this content has meaningfully changed their lives.

CHANOYU AS A HOLISTIC EDUCATIONAL MODEL

My most recent offerings on the subject of tea ceremony have been at my current post. This university offers a first-year experience program to assist new first-year students in their transition into undergraduate academic life with intentions to assist with orientation, basic academic skill development, and student retention. Lessons from chanoyu have potential to shape students' behaviors, beliefs, and values regarding their awareness of and involvement in their education.

In the study and practice of tea ceremony and related arts, students and I explored the beauty of nature and human relationships through wabi sabi and the virtues of tea. The practice of contemplation, the crafting of tea bowls, and the writing of poetry journals provided us with opportunities to focus and balance, strategies necessary to channel proper energy when entering the tearoom and returning to the outside world. Altogether, our practices strengthened our posture and etiquette in performing all tasks as gentle persons.

Whereas chanoyu is the act of serving tea with a pure heart or intent and chado is the embodiment of virtue, themes of human values arise from the study of tea in the form of virtues. Students can observe and contemplate the four principles of the tradition Urasenke, harmony (和 *wa*), respect (敬 *kei*), purity (精 *sei*), and tranquility (寂 *jaku*). Through various disciplined and routine exercises in a *dojo*-like environment as a formal place or space for practice, participants can develop focus and concentration to monitor and regulate their flow of energy, *ki*, and its exchange with others. The study of chado offers a thematic forum for linking thoughts and actions as well as exemplifying a model of holistic education.

In each tea course, students practiced martial arts, calligraphy, and accepting ritual tea to physically explore the importance of balance, focus, and the harnessing and exchange of energy in one's mind and body. The forms presented difficult challenges for students, and participation was awkward at first. Mastery at this stage is typically learned from imitating the instructor and listening to verbal cues. Often students struggled with focusing, remaining still, and keeping a slow pace throughout these exercises. With repeated practice, groups increasingly became more comfortable and familiar with the sequence of movements, less dependent on verbal cues, more fluid, and tended to speed through the movements less often, eventually solidifying their practice.

Calligraphy is an art form that I introduced through study of the four tea ceremony virtues. Our goal was to embody the meaning of each character. This practice augmented the holistic comprehension of the tea principles and informed the students' physical and mental states of being during tea and life. At first, students practiced the forms with markers on newsprint. Later they were introduced to a brush on newsprint and gradually learned from the effects of a singular chance at mark making on fine rice paper. Their work became increasingly proficient the more they understood the sequence and technique of the ink brush. Practice with the brush relates to behaviors learned in martial arts and tea ritual. It was further enhanced when students practiced brushwork to capture the essence of items found in nature.

With *haiku*, learning an abstract poetic form is an attempt to capture elements of nature and value in human relationships. I introduced haiku as another way to deeply investigate tea virtues. In creating haiku poetry, students meditated upon and expressed concepts and principles in simple yet powerful words. Through these poems, the students explored abstract ideas and conjured text based on images. With undergraduate students, I introduced haiku with *haibun*, prose in the manner of a travel log or journal. Traditionally, conclusion of a haibun entry is synthesized as a haiku.

As in my first tea curriculum with high school students, my courses in tea ceremony always included students making and firing a chawan for later use in a tea ceremony. The ritual event meaningfully consecrated all of the practice and training for this very special situation. Students were often nervous, thinking that they would make a mistake and dishonor the tradition and possibly the host. However, the goal of learning to be present in the moment was usually accomplished. From interviewing students, I found that they more often claim to focus on the moment, unaware of outside distractions. Although it is irregular for guests to take tea in bowls they have fashioned for themselves, the opportunity to pay respect to their own handiwork was very fulfilling. At first many students disliked the taste of the tea, yet after multiple sessions they learned to enjoy the beverage and understood the metaphoric poignancy in the relationship between the bitter tastes of tea and the accompanying sweet.

A BITTERSWEET MOMENT

From my personal experience, developing culturally based aesthetic themes can be meaningful for both the teacher/guide and the students. In these times, students need exposure to non-judgmental study of unfamiliar cultural practices for deep understanding. Holistic study that incorporates making things, decorating self and space, exploring values and questioning assumptions—particularly those associated with ritual practice—provides opportunity to both reflect and make connections to others. According to Anderson and Milbrandt (2002), cross-cultural thematic curricula offer meaningful experiences in an increasingly multicultural world. They claimed:

This is so because the rituals that support cosmology and beliefs in all cultures—including our own—have many artistic elements and in fact are frequently inseparable from the arts. When students realize that art reflects and perpetuates cultural values, they can examine the art and visual culture of many societies to see how others have examined life issues. Students can also try out other people's ideas and forms, and then adopt as their own the ones that fit. (p. 170)

The Zen Buddhist and Taoist philosophy-based practice of tea ritual is ideally suited for this kind of curricular approach because it requires similar reflection. By studying tea ritual, students can learn about themselves and consider their participation in a global community.

Thus, on our journey we come to realize holistically a community aesthetic as derived from adherence to a socially agreed upon code of conduct and production. Other educators may find inspiration from a personally relevant focus of cultural study. This chapter has been a description of my journey with tea.

ABOUT THE AUTHOR

Jay Hanes is head of Art Education at Edinboro University of Pennsylvania. He is an organic gardener, raku potter, and tea practitioner. He continues to explore cultural values, issues of identity, and political implications of art and education.

REFERENCES

Anderson, J. L. (1991). *An introduction to Japanese tea ritual.* New York, NY: State University of New York Press.

Anderson, R. L. (2004). *Calliope's sisters: A comparative study of philosophies of art* (2nd ed.). Upper Saddle River, NJ: Pearson Education.

Anderson, T., & Milbrandt, M. (2002). *Art for life: Authentic instruction in art.* New York, NY: McGraw Hill.

Dissanayake, E. (1990). *What is art for?* Seattle, WA: University of Washington Press.

Grigg, R. (1999). *The Tao of Zen.* Edison, NJ: Alva Press.

Hanes, J., & Nintze, J. (2008). Cultivating peace in times of war: Lessons from chado. *Journal of Cultural Research in Art Education, 26,* 51-64.

Hyatt, J. (2006, August 23). Mission. *Creating landscapes.* Retrieved from http://creatinglandscapes.com/about.htm

Hollingsworth, T. (2000). Kazuko Law: Artist, educator, student. In P. E. Bolin, D. Blandy, & K. G. Congdon (Eds.), *Remembering others: Making invisible histories of art education visible* (pp. 201-202). Reston, VA: National Art Education Association.

Juniper, A. (2003). *Wabi sabi: The Japanese art of impermanence.* North Clarendon, VT: Tuttle Publishing.

Koren, L. (1994.) *Wabi-sabi for artists, designers, poets and philosophers.* Berkeley, CA: Stone Bridge Press.

Pandian, J. (1991). *Culture, religion, and the sacred self: A critical introduction to the anthropological study of religion.* Englewood Cliffs, NJ: Prentice Hall.

Pitelka, M. (2005). *Handmade culture: Raku potters, patrons, and tea practitioners in Japan.* Honolulu, HI: University of Hawai'i Press.

Plutschow, H. (2003). *Rediscovering Rikyu and the beginnings of the Japanese tea ceremony.* Kent, CT: Global Oriental.

ENDNOTES

1. There are many translations for the phrase ichigo-ichie. The term is linked with Zen Buddhism and the idea of transience is typically associated with the Japanese tea ceremony. The sentiment also implies these other translations: one encounter, one chance; treasure every encounter, for it will never recur; and, one opportunity, one encounter. My tea sensi, Kaji Aso, offered the translation one moment, together in friendship.

2. Chanoyu (茶の湯) literally means hot water for tea.

3. In this sense the term *chado* (茶道) is more useful where *cha* means "tea" and *do* from the Chinese *tao* means "way." Thus, according to Anderson (1991) "Chado is a 'way' of life and it assumes a lifetime commitment" (p. 1).

4. Wabi literally means imperfect quality of any object. Often, it is paired with *sabi*, rust. Together they refer to loneliness of living with nature coupled with the beauty or serenity that comes with age. Together they represent a comprehensive Japanese aesthetic system centered on the acceptance of transience and the art of impermanence. Wabi is also paired with *cha* meaning rustic tea. See Koren (1994) and Juniper (2003) for more details on wabi.

5. For a complete discussion on the semiotics of shamanism and the priesthood see Pandian (1991).

CHAPTER 12

A Pedagogy of Embodiment: The Aesthetic Practice of Holistic Education in a Taiko Drumming Ensemble

Kimberly Powell

We believe that taiko for us is not just the drum; but it's the connection between the drum and the player. So at a certain point if we concentrate too much on technicality, and we lose that feeling or that spirit behind the playing, then it becomes just the drum. They become separated. The player is just using the drum rather than creating the relationship with it.

—Wisa, San Jose Taiko performer (quoted in Powell, 2006)

Cultural institutions provide alternative spaces for teaching and learning that offer significant educational experiences. Consistent with the assumption in this book that the arts from around the world have much to contribute to art education, I discuss the pedagogical practices of Japanese-American *taiko* drumming. The arts play a central role in the Eastern philosophy of mind-body unity. Considering this, and using the theoretical framework of holistic education, I describe one particular taiko ensemble, in which I was involved in an ethnographic study and apprenticeship. I emphasize holistic means and goals for learning as embraced through the Japanese principles of *ki* (spiritual energy) and *kata* (physical, aesthetic form), as well as other explicitly assessed outcomes such as attitude and musical technique.

While any teaching and learning context could be analyzed in terms of embodiment, the teaching philosophy used by this artistic ensemble focus explicitly on the ways in which the individual body fuses with an aesthetic, physical form and engages the individual in spiritual practice. In so doing, the body occupies a liminal space—an in-between space where participants encounter a qualitatively different way of being in the world that breaks with everyday embodied experiences, and as such, offers transformative potential for those in the margins. Such experiences are characteristic of the arts and holistic education, educational frameworks that allow for aesthetic, sensory, and spiritual dimensions. Thus, while my focus is explicitly on taiko drumming, with examples drawn from this practice, I aim in this chapter to highlight the significance of embodied practice(s) for an art pedagogy more generally.

CONNECTEDNESS, RELATIONALITY, LIMINALITY

This spiritual relationship is important in an era in which the separation of church and state is being challenged by faith-based initiatives, creationism in the classroom, and school prayer. It is important to distinguish and define spirituality as it has been conceived through holistic education and related fields of practice, such as transformative education, emancipatory pedagogy, consciousness studies and peace education, which often intersect with one another,. Educators involved in holistic education emphasize, for the most part, a secular view of the soul based on the holistic view of being, including an interconnected understanding of mind, body, consciousness and experience (e.g., Orr, 2005). When viewed in this way, the aim of education is to facilitate a more integrated teaching and learning experience (Orr, 2005). Thus, the concept of spirituality within a holistic education framework is not associated with or focused on a particular religion but rather with the development of the whole person, including not only intellectual development but also emotional, physical, aesthetic and spiritual development (Miller, 2007). Frequently, this secular view of spirituality is concerned with the qualities of educational experience that promote mindful awareness. Quoting Ronald V. Iannone, Rita Irwin (2007), suggested that a curriculum that encourages play, contemplation and intuition were important aspects of an "education of the soul":

> A spiritual curriculum moves beyond the rational and analytic ways of understanding the world and favors intuitive and emotional ways of knowing as we focus our perceptions on building connections, seeking unity, and feeling centered; in other words, being mindful. (Iannone, 1999, cited in Irwin, 2007, p. 1401)

Educators have posited dimensions of holistic education that suggest a concern with connectivity, relationality and care as critical educational goals in education. John Miller (2007) addresses three principles of holistic education: *connectedness, inclusion,* and *balance* (Miller, 2007). As described by Miller, connectedness refers to facilitating connections at every level of learning, breaking away from the fragmented approach to curriculum that most students encounter throughout the day, and indeed, within the same classroom. Examples of connectedness include linking the body and mind, integrating analytic and intuitive thinking, integrating subjects, linking to the broader community, connecting to the earth, and connecting to soul and spirit. Inclusion refers to creating a class environment that accommodates all types of students and providing a broad range of learning approaches. Balance suggests that there are complementary forces and energies. In classrooms, Miller argues, a focus on rational thought and individual competition dominate, while intuition and cooperative approaches have been largely ignored.

Themes that have been identified in essays and research into holistic education include the concept of embodiment, critical perspectives such as emancipatory, transformative and anti-oppressive pedagogy, spirituality, and wholeness (Miller, 2007). As noted above, proponents within the field of holistic education have often suggested mindfulness techniques such as meditation and yoga as a means to access, integrate, and expand a student's lived experience; and, indeed, educational programs using such practices exist (e.g., Denton, 2005; Forbes, 2005; Garbarino, 1999; Kessler, 2002; Orr, 2002; Schiller, 2005).

Whether or not they are situated within an explicitly holistic framework, arts-based research practices, arts-based curriculum, and the arts disciplines themselves often constitute educative spaces in which the soul, body, and mind can "breathe," generating new visions of educational practice and research that support a holistic view of teaching and learning. The arts can also offer a means of introducing spirituality into education (Irwin, 2007). Along with the dimensions mentioned above—embodiment of critical perspectives, spirituality, and wholeness—activities and encounters with the arts can present a qualitatively ambiguous dimension of lived experience: liminality. Liminality is defined as thresholds, or the borders between ideas, cultures, individuals, or territories that one crosses. In everyday life, it is often a space in which one wishes to pass through quickly, as it is often an unstable, contradictory, in-between space (Schechner, 1982). But such spaces also present possibility, where people, cultures, and ideas come into contact with one another, creating "interstitial conditions for new communities of learning" (Conroy, 2004, as cited in Irwin, 2007, p. 1402). For artists, living for a time in such spaces is desirable (Garoian, 1999), just as it is for those involved in spiritual practices and in rites-of-passage activities (e.g., Feeney, 1984; Hill, 1992; as cited in Wilson, 2005).

Taiko drumming is one of many practices in which the arts unite with spiritual practice to create such liminal spaces for its participants. As I will demonstrate, the pedagogy and philosophy of taiko offers important insights into arts education practice based on a holistic perspective. First, however, I will provide a brief background about the art form in North America.

THE NORTH AMERICAN TAIKO MOVEMENT AND SAN JOSE TAIKO

Taiko's diverse beginnings in Japan can be found in the 6th-century Japanese Imperial Court music of *Gagaku* (literally translated as "elegant" or "refined"), the Imperial Court music of Japan dating back to the 6th century, as well as folk and religious music, as in traditional festivals tied to Buddhism and to Shintoism. The form and substance of Gagaku are integral to contemporary taiko practices and include such aestethic practices as a steady rhythm, "elastic" breathing, in which a piece and its meter are not conducted but rather felt and performed as the rhythm of breathing (Malm, 1977). Unlike Gagaku, which often uses one drum, festival music often uses a collection of drums to accompany *hagaku* (conch shell), *hayashi* (flute) and/or gong. Festival drumming can still be heard in many Japanese cities and townships today, such as at Buddhist *Obon* (a celebration of returning ancestral spirits) or at spring *Matsuri* (festival). Festival drumming is principally marked by its focus on the drum as a primary instrument (rather than flute, for example) and its ensemble collection of drums. Different Japanese prefectures often have drum patterns, or melodies, that are unique to a village or town. Along with distinguishing drumming styles and patterns are stylized movements and stances, so that certain styles of drumming are associated with certain regions even today.

In taiko, instruments are played gracefully and with purposeful movement, so that the visual aspect of music is emphasized as much as the aural aspect of music (Malm, 1977). Early visual forms of drumming, referred to as kata (form), incorporated some dance forms. In more formal settings, such as courts or shrines, movement was restricted to the arms, in accordance with Japanese court aesthetics of drumming (Kodani, 2000). More recently, martial arts have influenced the kata of contemporary taiko ensembles, in which, for example, performers stand in the traditional lowered hip position to lower the center of gravity. Many Japanese prefectures, as well as contemporary taiko groups, have developed their own particular kata and visual characteristics of drumming.

Contemporary taiko (sometimes referred to as *kumi-daiko*, or harmony drum) refers to the art of Japanese drumming, as well as to the actual drums used in the art form. Sociohistorical events in the United States, notably the internment of Japanese Americans during World War II, served as the platform for reconceptualizing taiko as an Asian *American* art. North American taiko has become a cultural project concerned with artistic and cultural expression and identity for Japanese Americans as well as other Asian Americans (Hayase, 1985; Hirabayashi, 1988; Uyechi, 1995). With estimates of up to 8,000 known contemporary taiko ensembles in Japan (Rolling Thunder, 2010) and 150 taiko ensembles in North America, taiko has become an international Asian diaspora based on an identifiable aesthetic and sound (Kobayashi, 1994).[1]

Stylistically, North American taiko is a hybrid art form, indigenous to North America in the same way that jazz and gospel music are, and yet it is rooted in Japanese artistic aesthetics found in court music, religious and community festival drumming. It is an art form that borrows from traditional Japanese court, religious and festival drumming as well as jazz and other cultural rhythms. Contemporary taiko ensembles generally consist of a collection of different drums, percussive instruments such as cymbals and gourds, and sometimes Japanese bamboo flutes *(shakuhachi)* or other instruments associated with Japanese music.

San Jose Taiko, established in 1973, is one of the founding taiko groups in North America. The co-founders of San Jose Taiko, Roy and PJ Hirabayashi (Roy is Managing Director, PJ is Creative Director), have developed their approach to taiko into a forum for social action, community development, and cultural preservation, characteristics that mark many North American taiko ensembles (Hayase, 1985; Hirabayashi, 1988; Uyechi, 1995). Over the years, the organizations' primary goals have been to develop a professional performance ensemble as well as community-based classes that focus on the artistic learning and practice of drumming. San Jose Taiko has developed a professional performance ensemble and a junior program in order to introduce new generations of youth to taiko, as well as to provide workshops to the general public. They perform regularly in concert halls and other performance venues as well as at community events of San Jose's Japantown, such as the annual *oban* festival.

San Jose Taiko has established a 2-year apprenticeship[2] they call the Audition Process (often referred to as AP) influenced by their work with the professional Japanese taiko group, Kodo. AP is a sequenced, 2-year program, in which new potential members are evaluated at regular phases during the first year, and those who are accepted are integrated into the professional ensemble the second year.[1] During my ethnographic study of the ensemble, and at their request, I engaged in part of this apprenticeship so that I could understand in and through my own body what it meant to learn taiko. The descriptions that follow are based on my participation and observations of their practice as well as interviews with the performing members.

EMBODIED PEDAGOGY

San Jose Taiko has developed a framework for teaching, learning, and ongoing evaluation of apprentices and performers based on four principles: *attitude*, which involves respect for one's self, other players, the instruments themselves, and a discipline of both mind and body; *kata* (form), structured movements based on martial arts stances, traditional Japanese drumming and other choreographed movements; *musical technique*, and *ki* (energy), an Eastern concept of spiritual unity of mind and body, an essential principle of martial arts and a basic element of kata (San Jose Taiko, 2001). Through these four principles—attitude, kata, musical technique and ki—San Jose Taiko hopes to attain what they call the "ultimate expression of taiko, when the art becomes a part of our personality, a way of being and life expression."

Embodying Attitude: Liminality and Interanimation in the Dojo

For San Jose Taiko, the development of an appropriate attitude toward taiko is considered an important part of their art form, viewed as necessary for building individual and group confidence. Two components of attitude defined by San Jose Taiko are respect and discipline. Respect for the instruments, for one's self, and for other players is considered crucial by San Jose Taiko for the overall betterment of the group and for the practice of taiko. One source of preparation for this attitude concerns certain culturally prescribed, ritualistic movements in the *dojo*, or place of learning. Before entering the space, an apprentice, performer, or visitor must bow at the doorway entrance. Before entering the matted stage area, members must remove their shoes and arrange them along the perimeter of the stage. Slippers are provided for performers and guests who choose to sit in the row of chairs in front of the stage.

There are also beginning and closing bows to those who are practicing together. As apprentices, one of the first formal activities we learned was to stand in a circle and bow to each other, saying the following in unison: "*Yoroshiku onigai shimasu,*" translating to "Please think well of me," or, "Please remember me well." We bowed simultaneously, thus beginning the first synchronized act we will do together as a group. Group practice is also closed with a bow—after the stage has been swept and instruments put away with the following: "*Oskare sama deshita,*" a closing statement that roughly translates to "I honor you for your hard work."

Attitude was quite literally embodied through much of their training. Discipline, as they defined it, involves dedication to the rigorous, physical training involved in becoming a performer. Discipline is also of the mind: San Jose Taiko explicitly states in their guidelines that members should let go of the ego and self-consciousness to release the "inner spirit," pushing beyond one's own limits: "In this manner, a sense of spiritual unity is achieved through our continuous efforts to focus our minds, bodies and energies as one." Before each rehearsal as well as outside of group practice, members physically trained their bodies in order to develop the stamina and strength required for performing, often engaging in a full hour of exercise and stretching before rehearsing with the drums. Throughout my apprenticeship with San Jose Taiko, we engaged in a pre-set series of physical warmups. Calisthenics were a regular part of practice; apprentices worked up to 50 pushups and 250 sit-ups, the required amount for the performing members. Following a cooling down period, again led as a group, we engaged in a meditation exercise. Sitting in *sei-za* (legs folded), we were instructed to close our eyes and focus for a few minutes on the work we had just done and the work we were about to do.

These ritualized movements and routinized physical exercises served as a critical transition period from the outside world to the world of taiko, providing a liminal experience in which participants moved from one way of being into another, marked by cultural gestures such as bowing and merging physical training with synchronization that was also essential to ensemble-based practice. These ways of moving our bodies—the bow at the studio door, removing our shoes, bowing to each other, stretching, running, and counting together—all served as ways in which we experienced a place called taiko. More explicitly, we engaged in a process of "interanimation" (Basso, 1996), in which a sense of place is integrated into our bodies. The liminal experience marking this interanimation, which literally began with a bow at the literal threshold of our experiences, provoked an embodiment of social norms that broke with most of our secular, routinized social practices embedded in everyday life. These rituals synchronized us to each other in terms of movement and voice, serving as a warm-up in which we might begin an ensemble practice.

Ki: The Embodiment of Spirit

Ki is an aspect of an Eastern philosophy of cosmology that refers to a unity between the physical and spiritual, "the spiritual unity of the mind and body" (San Jose Taiko, 2001). Ki is also present in Eastern medicine, martial arts, and the arts of poetry, calligraphy, and music (Matsunobu, 2007). Matsunobu (2007) described the ways in which sound has historically been associated as means for tapping into ki, arguing that this link between sound and ki constitutes an "aesthetics of cosmology," in which certain qualities of sound (noise, single notes) are valued because of their connection to the natural world.

San Jose Taiko feels that ki is the "ultimate challenge that each member... must meet." Along with kata, musical technique, and attitude, members are evaluated formally on this dimension as well as the others. Through ki, oneness with the taiko, with other members, and even with the audience is achieved through sound and energy—what San Jose Taiko calls a "physical communication." Two aspects of ki are explicitly taught, learned, and evaluated for successful membership in San Jose Taiko. One form is known as *kiai* (pronounced kee-eye), shouted syllables, the most audible form of creating and maintaining ki. In some cases, kiai are actually part of a song, becoming a noticeable part of the texture of a piece in terms of volume and placement.

Because kiai involves producing sound, the focus of teaching and learning is on quality of sound as it is produced and felt in the body. In my observations and participation, finding the right moments to kiai was an important aspect of understanding the elusive nature of ki (Powell, 2006). Practicing, we were encouraged to kiai while hitting the drums, accenting silent moments with syllables like "*hip*" or "*yo*" while never being explicitly taught any right moments to kiai. In this way, kiai served an aesthetic purpose: accenting drum sounds, adding to the overall texture of the song, and serving to create a soundscape punctuated by shouted syllables.

One of the significant qualities of learning taiko that brings to mind holistic arts education in general is the sense of connectedness and relationality that the practice fosters and encourages. One dimension of this connectedness is the way in which learners have to coordinate instruments, other people, and the spaces in and around the drums, a quality that underlies the concept of ki. Another aspect that relates to holistic education is that learning to play taiko in many ways requires an individual to think beyond the immediate physical self, to integrate these various environmental features into one's playing. To play taiko thus requires an expanded, or relational, sense of self, a self that is always conscious of instruments, people and spaces. Ki calls for a blending of elements, a spiritual unity between player and drum and between players fostered through an aesthetic use and awareness of the body. In the process, participants learn to coordinate a variety of external and internal elements, bringing to the forefront a conception of art and artistry that differs radically from Western conceptions, in which the individual artist is often placed above the ensemble, and where art is often separated from other aspects of life. This integrative dimension in taiko is also present in the kata, which will be discussed in the following section.

Kata: Fusing Form to Body

Japanese arts have been preserved and transmitted through the concept of kata (form or mold) through which students learn not only the physical structure or movement in relation to art, but also patterns of artistic, social, and cultural behaviors, and moral and ethical values within a prescribed system of rules governing movement (Matsunobu, 2007; Powell, 2004). The key pedagogical strategy involves repetition, imitation, and slow motions so that the form is imprinted upon the body. The goal of kata is "to fuse the individual to the form so that the individual becomes the form and the form becomes the individual" (Yano, as cited in Matsunobu, 2007). Discipline and training are intended to harmonize the mind and body so that the mind's movements correspond with the body's (Yasuo, 1987). Through "cumulative training" with a disciplined practice, art is embodied so that "one comes to learn an art *through* one's body" (Yasuo, 1987, p. 105, emphasis added).

Kata is integral to and inseparable from taiko drumming technique. In relation to the taiko, kata dates back to an aesthetic convention originating in a form of Japanese court music that accompanied dance. Many taiko groups also root kata in martial arts practice, with posture marked by a lowered stance. One contemporary style, for example, referred to as *Sukeroku* style,[3] is characterized by identifiable movements that correspond with a slanted drum configuration in which the drum and the drummer's stance are aligned on a diagonal plane. Drum strikes typically have prescribed arm movements that correspond with particular sounds. Generally, strikes that are intended to generate a loud noise or that signify the major "notes" of a song begin with arms raised straight upward or diagonally out, making a diagonal movement across the body toward the drum face as the wrist snaps the end of the *bachi* (drumstick) on the drum's surface. Depending on the position of the player, the opposing arm may or may not cross the body in order to hit the drum.

Repetition, imitation, imagery, patterning, and slow-motion movement were the most often-used pedagogical devices of San Jose Taiko and are techniques that are cited in other Japanese artistic practices such as pottery (Singleton, 1998), the popular music genre of Enka (Yano, 2002), Noh drama (Yasuo, 1989), as well as in meditative practices (Yasuo, 1989; Shusterman, 2008). These are all processes that allowed participants to embody the form, internalizing, mastering, and then enacting these movements and drumming techniques on a less conscious level, a process of what David Plath (1989) calls "cultural inscription."

Kata presents an interesting aesthetic category for analysis, with evident differences between contemporary artistic practices in the West. Whereas arts education in Western culture are typically characterized by the search for ever-increasing freedom of expression, kata must seem excessively dictated and prescribed. As such, kata would seem to necessarily create a fixed performance. Yet it is precisely in such prescriptive moments that opportunity arises for agency, because it is the process of repetition that creates a space for improvisation and the potential for authoring new forms. Members of San Jose Taiko, for example, created their own kata through their own compositions, often blending the conventional aesthetics of movement with other forms from personal experience, such as classical dance, hiphop, hula, or other gestures evocative of a certain emotion or idea underlying a song. Kata is a means of moving beyond conventions and extending the genre while staying in it (Yano, 2002). Indeed, kata has been theorized as an emancipatory process, confronting and challenging racial stereotypes of Asian American men and women in taiko (Powell, 2008; Wong, 2004) and as a means to view tea ceremony as a metaphor for healing and transformative learning. (Mayuzumi, 2006).

Repetitive practice of kata and musical techniques allowed participants to build muscle-memory for well-practiced movement, which was a necessary precondition for effortless playing that led to a quality characterized as spiritual by several of the ensemble members. This experience was described as moving out of one's body, of spiritual unity with sound, drum, and with other players, becoming a conduit for the music, and/or a sense of participating in something larger than oneself. Visceral attention to mechanics, drills, and details, in other words, encode these movements in the body that, ironically, led to out-of-body experiences (Powell, 2004) that were characterized by relationality, or what Thich Nhat Hanh calls "interbeing" (cited in Mayuzumi, 2006, p. 20). In this sense, there is emancipation from the physical body toward an interconnectedness, a body without borders.

Beyond rehearsal, repetition is present in the final performance itself. Since the rhythms and melodies are repetitive, so is the kata, and both player and audience member are involved in familiar patterns that invoke anticipation. Trinh T. Minh-ha (1991) wrote about the transformative powers of repetition in film and media when it is used as an intentional practice and strategy. As an aesthetic device, repetition serves to establish expectations; we anticipate what we will see and hear, taste and feel next. In anticipation, we begin to pay attention to the spaces between the repeats. Trinh T. Minh-Ha wrote that "the element brought to visibility is precisely the invisibility of the invisible realm, namely the vitality of intervals, the intensity of the relation between creation and re-creation" (Minh-ha, 1991, p. 191). As such, the body in performance somaticizes identity through bodily forms that are simultaneously gendered, racialized and nationalized for an audience (Yano, 2002, p. 114), yet may break from convention and therefore destabilize these identity categories.

Embodied Experience as Emancipatory Pedagogy

It has been argued that transformative learning requires new educational practices (O'Sullivan, 2002; O'Sullivan, 2005). Among those suggested are arts-based research, education for the soul, spiritual practices such as meditation, modified martial arts, and forms of teaching and learning of indigenous peoples. Such movements, congruent with and based upon Paulo Freire's pedagogy of hope (1996), are concerned with radical transformation of pedagogical practices. Aesthetic philosopher Maxine Greene (2000) also wrote about transformations through conscious, active participation with the arts, saying,

> Art breaks open a dimension inaccessible to other experience, a dimension in which everything no longer stands in laws of reality. Art contradicts the established or the given, and leads those willing to risk transformations to the shaping of a social vision. (p. 30)

Key to such transformation in taiko and other Eastern spiritual/artistic practices is the mindful body. More specifically, taiko sets forth a potentially emancipatory pedagogy of hope and celebration as it seeks to transform Asian American identity and experience, primarily through the aesthetic forms of kata, composition, and the spiritual practice of ki. Embodiment is a related theme that connects taiko with much that has been written about holistic education (Miller, Karsten, Denton, Orr, & Kates, 2005). Placing primacy on an embodied experience that is aesthetic and spiritual not only opens a way for the marginal, for the liminal, it also opens one up to an acceptance of cultural diversity that is not currently present even in much that passes for multicultural curriculum.

In an educational world where the Cartesian view of knowledge privileges mind over body, many of the concepts described above may strike us as foreign. Yet, a current critique of critical and other forms of anti-oppressive pedagogy is that the Cartesian view of the mind and body privileges concepts and values related to rationality and logic that potentially serve to alienate students from other aspects of the self and creates distinctions between self and other (Orr, 2002, 2005). In an essay on mindfulness, Orr (2002) suggested that education must help students understand the dualistic forms of thinking that ground oppression, and confront behaviors and attitudes that are internalized in what Wittgenstein referred to as "language games" of oppression (see also hooks, 1994). This calls for pedagogical techniques that integrate and implicate the whole self.

A cultural analysis of an educational setting such as taiko also inevitably raises questions about the culturally valued, Western assumptions embedded in pedagogy, such as constructivist practices. Whereas many arts educators oppose structured instruction as restrictive of creativity, apprenticeship models of teaching and learning are often marked by extensive and demanding periods of directive teaching and "legitimate peripheral participation" (Lave & Wenger, 1991), in which learners are often given tasks to do, with difficulty and centrality increasing as they move toward expertise. In the taiko ensemble, improvisation and the chance to construct/compose followed 2 years of apprenticeship, in which improvisation was slowly introduced over time. Mimesis, repetition, and directive teaching are seen as critical to the initial learning and development of performers. Only after demonstrated mastery and competence occurs are members encouraged to then create and transform the ensemble itself through their improvisations and original compositions.

This difference in pedagogical approach can be explained in part through philosophical writings on the Eastern view of the relationship between mind and body, which emphasize disciplined training. Philosopher Yuasa Yasuo (1987) posited that the Eastern view of the body was incommensurate with Western philosophical categories in that Asian traditions do not treat the mind and body as ontologically distinct (Kasulis, 1987). Mind-body unity in Eastern philosophy is an *achievement*, rather than a given, approached through disciplined practice and mastery. In Western philosophical approaches such as phenomenology, psycho-analysis, and neurophysiology, the mind-body connection is viewed as constant rather than developed and universal rather than variable across individuals. These views do not consider "exceptional achievements" (Kasulis, 1987). Western philosophy thus views mind-body unity as a given, a conceptual and "theoretical possibility rather than a state that is actualized through religious or artistic masters" (Kasulis, 1987, p. 2). In Eastern approaches to mind-body unity, disciplined, artistic pursuits are central to achieving this unity, positioning art as a focus of and for study.

Cultural portraits of alternative educational settings like the one discussed in this chapter are critical for advancing a conception of educating the whole person. Looking across cultures can suggest unimagined possibilities for implementing more comprehensive approaches to education and human development that include multicultural perspectives on teaching and learning. From this close study of taiko, which draws upon Eastern concepts of mind-body unity, I draw four implications for the field of art education. The first concerns educational reform and policy. According to the Japanese holistic scholar, Atsuhiko Yoshida (2005), Japan's 2002 government reform plan included education for the heart and soul *(kokoro-no-kyoiku),* integrated learning *(sogo-gakushyu),* and the uniqueness of each school and individual person *(tokushyoku, koseika).* Without idealizing this Japanese educational reform, such a structure raises questions for the American No Child Left Behind educational policy and practice of testing and corresponding meritocracy. Elliot Eisner proposed that the aim of education might be the preparation of artists in terms of the modes of thinking and dispositions that the arts engender, such as flexible purposing, tacit knowing, and aesthetic satisfaction, calling for "...the creation of a new culture of schooling that has as much to do with the cultivation of dispositions as with the acquisition of skills" (Eisner, 2002, p. 213). The dispositions presented in this chapter extend our conceptual understanding of dispositions fostered in and by the arts to include cross-cultural perspectives on aesthetics, the body-mind connection, and interbeing that connects not just people but also objects (drums) and the ephemeral (spirit).

Second, the concepts described in this chapter raise possibilities for an art education that might seek to examine not just specific cultural artistic practices but also forms of embodied pedagogy that integrate such aspects of holistic education as mindfulness, interconnect-edness, disciplined practice, and attention to aesthetic form as valued aspects of critical multicultural understanding. Taiko is an art form that challenges representations of Asian American identity even as it attempts to create it. More broadly, it serves as an example of the ways in which concepts such as identity or culture are not static categories applied to social practices, beliefs and conventions; rather, identities and culture are actively created and refashioned in ways that reflect individual and group experiences, talents, and beliefs, brought about through embodied experiences with the spiritual and the sensuous—in this case, sounding—aspects of art. Culture and identity are constantly in flux as result of this embodied engagement. Moving beyond cultural specificity, art educators might consider the work of other artists who fixed categories through active engagement, and the ways in which the liminal, the spiritual, and the intangible are always at play and in critical relation to/with social constructs.

As art educators, our approach to research in and of art educational practice is also impor-tant. Research methods that are responsive to embodied knowing, sensory engagement, liminal states and other qualities of experience that mark the physical, spiritual, or aesthetic development of persons might underscore and produce a "sensuous scholarship" that mixes head and heart, providing "an opening of one's being to the world" (Stoller, as quoted in Denton, 2005, p. 82). An embodiment of such approaches underscores a corresponding research approach that is holistic and responsive to experiences that might otherwise not be included in the study of arts teaching and learning. Such a quest is not aimed *at* certainty, but, rather, toward knowledge of human experience that is informed through ambiguity, spirituality, complexity, and the intangible. It is the (re)search for forms of representation that can most adequately and substantively render the lived reality of participants. It is an orientation toward engaging aesthetic and/or artistic modes of inquiry and alternative epistemologies in order to investigate compelling phenomena. Sensing, we might indeed remain open.

REFERENCES

Basso, K. (1996). *Wisdom sits in places: Landscape and language among the Western Apache.* Albuquerque: University of New Mexico Press.

Conroy, J. C. (2004). *Betwixt and between: The liminal imagination, education and democracy.* New York, NY: Peter Lang.

Denton, D. (2005). In the flame of the heart. In J. Miller, S. Karsten, D. Denton, D. Orr, & I. C. Kates (Eds.), *Holistic learning and spirituality in education: Breaking new ground* (pp. 181-192). Albany, NY: State University of New York Press.

Eisner, E. W. (2002). What can education learn from the arts about the practice of education? In *The encyclopedia of informal education.* Retrieved from www.infed.org/biblio/eisner_arts_and_the_practice_of_education.htm

Forbes, D. (2005). In da zone: Meditation, masculinity, and a meaningful life. In J. Miller, S. Karsten, D. Denton, D. Orr, & I. C. Kates (Eds.), *Holistic learning and spirituality in education: Breaking new ground* (pp. 153-160). Albany, NY: State University of New York Press.

Freire, P. (1996). *Pedagogy of hope: Reliving the pedagogy of the oppressed.* New York, NY: Continuum.

Garbarino, J. (1999). *Lost boys: Why our sons turn violent and how we can save them.* New York, NY: Free Press.

Garoian, C. (1999). *Performing pedagogy: Toward an art of politics.* Albany, NY: SUNY Press.

Greene, M. (2000*). Releasing the imagination: Essays on education, the arts, and social change.* San Francisco, CA: Jossey-Bass.

Hanh, T. N. (1991). *Peace is every step: The path of mindfulness in everyday life.* New York, NY: Bantham.

Hayase, S. (1985). Taiko. *East Wind* (winter–spring), 46-47.

Hirabayashi, R. (1988). Odaiko Newsletter. San Jose, CA: San Jose Taiko.

hooks, b. (1994). *Teaching to transgress: Education as the practice of freedom.* New York, NY: Routledge.

Iannone, R. V. (1999, Summer). Toward spirituality in curriculum and teaching. *Education.* Retrieved from http://findarticles.com/p/articles/mi_qa3673/is_4_119/ai_n28736400/

Irwin, R. (2007). Plumbing the depths of being fully alive. In L. Bresler (Ed.) & R. Irwin (Section Ed.) *International handbook of arts education (Vol. II)* (pp. 1401-1404). Dordrecht, The Netherlands: Springer.

Kasulis. T. (1987). Editor's Introduction. In T. Kaulis, (Ed.). N Shigenori & T. Kasulis (Trans.), *The body: Toward an eastern mind-body theory* (pp. 1-16). Albany, NY: State University of New York Press.

Kato, E. (2002). The sword behind the chrysanthemum: Modern Japanese tea ceremony practitioners' self-empowerment through explicit and implicit motifs. *Semiotica,* (141), 111–144.

Kessler, R. (2005). Nurturing adolescents' spirituality. In J. Miller, S. Karsten, D. Denton, D. Orr, & I. C. Kates (Eds.), *Holistic learning and spirituality in education: Breaking new ground* (pp. 101-107). Albany, NY: State University of New York Press.

Kodani, M. (N.d.) Gagaku. Unpublished paper.

Kobayashi, T. (1994). Heartbeat in the diaspora: Taiko and community. *Fuse, 12*(5-6): 24-26.

Lave, J., & Wenger, E. (1991). *Situated learning: Legitimate peripheral participation.* New York, NY: Cambridge University Press.

Malm, W. (1977). Northeast Asia and the island countries. In *Music cultures of the pacific, the near east, and Asia.* Upper Saddle River, NJ: Prentice-Hall.

Matsunobu, K. (2007). Japanese spirituality and music practice. In L. Bresler (Ed.) & R. Irwin (Section Ed.). *International handbook of arts education (Vol. II).* Dordrecht, The Netherlands: Kluwer Press.

Mayuzumi, K (2006). The tea ceremony as a decolonizing epistemology: Healing and Japanese women. *Journal of Transformative Education, 1*(4), 8-26.

Miller, J. (2007). *The holistic curriculum* (2nd ed.). Toronto, ON: Ontario Institute for Studies in Education.

Miller, J., Karsten, S., Denton, D., Orr, D., & Kates, I. C. (2005). *Holistic learning and spirituality in education: Breaking new ground.* Albany, NY: State University of New York Press.

Minh-ha. T. (1991). *When the moon waxes red: Representation, gender, and cultural politics.* New York, NY: Routledge.

Orr, D. (2002). The uses of mindfulness in anti-oppressive pedagogies: Philosophy and praxis. *Canadian Journal of Education, 27*(2), 246-267.

Orr, D. (2005). Minding the soul in education. In J. Miller, S. Karsten, D. Denton, D. Orr, & I. C. Kates (Eds.), *Holistic learning and spirituality in education: Breaking new ground* (pp. 69-78). Albany, NY: State University of New York Press.

O'Sullivan, E. (2005). Emancipatory hope: Transformative learning and the "strange attractors." In J. Miller, S. Karsten, D. Denton, D. Orr, & I. C. Kates (Eds.), *Holistic learning and spirituality in education: Breaking new ground* (pp. 69-78). Albany, NY: State University of New York Press.

O'Sullivan, E., Morrell, A., & O'Connor, M. A. (2002). *Expanding the boundaries of transformative learning: Essays on theory and praxis.* New York, NY: Palgrave.

Plath, D. (1989). *Long engagements: Maturity in modern Japan.* Stanford: Stanford University Press.

Powell, K. (2004). The apprenticeship of embodied knowledge in a taiko drumming ensemble. In L. Bresler (Ed.), *Knowing bodies, moving minds: Embodied knowledge in education* (pp. 183-185). Dordrecht, The Netherlands: Kluwer Press.

Powell, K. (2006). The ensemble art of the solo: Improvising art, self and culture in a Japanese American taiko ensemble. *Journal of Arts and Learning Research, 21,* 273-295.

Powell, K. (2008). Drumming against the quiet: The sound of Asian American identity politics in an amorphous landscape. *Qualitative Inquiry, 14*(6), 901-925.

Rolling Thunder, 2010. Retrieved from www.taiko.com

San Jose Taiko (2001). San Jose taiko philosophy. In "San Jose Taiko class notes and articles." San Jose, CA: San Jose Taiko. Unpublished paper.

Schechner, R. (1982). *The end of humanism: Writings on performance.* New York: Performing Arts Journal.

Schiller, S. (2005). Contemplating great things in the soul. In J. Miller, S. Karsten, D. Denton, D. Orr, & I. C. Kates (Eds.), *Holistic learning and spirituality in education: Breaking new ground* (pp. 161-166). Albany, NY: State University of New York Press.

Shusterman, 2008. *Body consciousness: A philosophy of mindfulness and somaesthetics.* New York, NY: Cambridge University Press.

Singleton, J. (1998). Craft and art education in Mashiko pottery workshops. In J. Singleton (Ed.), *Learning in likely places: Varieties of apprenticeship in Japan* (pp. 122-133). Cambridge, England: Cambridge University Press.

Uyechi, L. (1995). University Taiko: Roots and evolution. Paper presented at Symposium on North American Taiko, Stanford University Invitational.

Wilson, L. O. (2005). Listening to ancient voices. In J. Miller, S. Karsten, D. Denton, D. Orr, & I. C. Kates (Eds.), *Holistic learning and spirituality in education: Breaking new ground* (pp. 167-180). Albany, NY: State University of New York Press.

Wong, D. (2004). *Speak it louder: Asian Americans making music.* New York, NY: Routledge.

Yano, C. (2002). *Tears of longing: Nostalgia and the nation in Japanese popular song.* Cambridge, MA: Harvard University Asia Center.

Yasuo, Y. (1987). Theories of artistry. In *The body: Toward an eastern mind-body theory* (pp. 99-110). In T. Kaulis, (Ed.), N. Shigenori & T. Kasulis (Trans.). Albany, NY: State University of New York Press.

Yoshida, A. (2005). Interface of holistic changes in Japanese schools and Waldorf education. In J. Miller, S. Karsten, D. Denton, D. Orr, & I. C. Kates (Eds.), *Holistic learning and spirituality in education: Breaking new ground* (pp. 129-136). Albany, NY: State University of New York Press.

ENDNOTES

1   The development of taiko in Canada has dealt with similar concerns in terms of using the art form as a cultural rebirth in the wake of US and Canadian immigration policies, helping to support the diaspora of not only Japanese Canadians but also other Asian Canadians (Kobayashi, 1994).

2   O Edo Sukeroku Taiko developed in 1959 at Yushima Tenjin Shrine in Tokyo in order to preserve the heritage of traditional Japanese drumming and to create a new contemporary style (Oedo Sukeroku Taiko, 2002). Unlike many other festival drumming styles, which involve little body movement, this style requires extensive, and often dramatic, leg and arm movements to accommodate the diagonal plane formed with the drum.

ABOUT THE AUTHOR

Kimberly Powell is dual associate professor in the Language Culture, and Society program in the College of Education and the Art Education program in the College of Arts and Architecture at The Pennsylvania State University. Her research and publications focus on embodied and sensory experience, the arts as critical forms of social, cultural, and political practice, place-based learning, and arts-based research.

CHAPTER 13

Korean Students' Holistic Engagement with Visual Culture

Jae-young Lee

We face both various conflicts and substantial potential regarding the intersection of visual culture art education and holistic art education. Despite the ongoing argument regarding the educational credibility of visual culture art education, the dazzling impact of popular images (specifically comic books for this chapter) on students' lives has pushed art education toward a child-centered approach in a responsive way that goes beyond our interest in teaching fine art. More art teachers, presumably not just in Korea, are becoming more aware of students' interest in popular culture. They investigate the influences of this ardent preoccupation and feel the need to incorporate these sources for educational purposes in an appropriate manner. One of the most enticing areas of inquiry, which has not been fully articulated in scholarly research, is the need to measure students' holistic growth because popular culture images create inner experiences that are spiritual and holistic. Beyond mere imitation, students' comic drawings reflect various aspects of the students' selves, shaped by the influences of the images.

However, there is insufficient research that approaches this intersection of visual culture art education and holistic art education. It is unknown how popular culture images specifically impact the self. If this assumed impact exists, is it not essential for us to seek how the images impact students' inner experiences in order to capture a deeper and more holistic understanding of the impact on the self? This influence occurs at an early stage, and this overwhelming task should not be ignored. Beyond our theoretical foundation of spiritual and holistic approaches in art education (Campbell, 2003, 2006; London, 2004), we need to seek more practical evidence depicting how a student's inner mind evolves holistically under the influences of popular images.

In an effort to seek this practical evidence, this chapter[1] presents the portraits of two 6th-grade Korean students who exhibited their holistic unfolding through a 10-week after-school art program organized for my dissertation research.[2] The vignettes in the portraits reveal the students' holistic understanding of the self and their favorite popular images in order to enhance the students' critical consciousness and empowerment, as Purpel (1998) addressed in conceptualizing his holistic approach. The stories of these participants are presented to exemplify how art education can facilitate students' critical awareness in a holistic manner. That is, it explicates all aspects of the students, who exhibit their physical, sensory, cognitive, affective, social, cultural, moral, and even spiritual wholeness and integration during the instruction as elements of their critical reflections on themselves as well as their favorite popular images. These practical portraits will open our discussion and understanding of the value and power of art education to enhance students' holistic development for their critical consciousness and empowerment.

PORTRAIT 1: YEON'S[3] CRITICAL REFLECTION AND A TOUCHED HEART

Yeon was a very sociable female student who desired to be a comic book artist like Arina Tanemura, a Japanese *manga* artist whom she admires. Yeon showed initiative, was self-confident, and was outgoing, like her favorite comic characters. She developed exceptional ability in drawing manga by imitating Tanemura's work after seeing the cartoons on TV when she was 7 years old (Figure 1). The influences of the comic book on Yeon were evident in the following statements:

> I would like to be in the comics. I really like to hear it when someone says to me that I look like the main character.... (With a big laugh) I am behaving like my favorite protagonist at school.... I had a friend. She was an ideal girl. She was really beautiful, had a beautiful hairstyle, wore beautiful clothes, had a good character, was tall enough, talked fast, and was very cheerful, like a protagonist in comics. I envied her a lot. Therefore, I am trying to be like her.... I wish I had long hair, earrings, necklaces, rings, bracelets, and beautiful clothes.... I want to have long wavy hair like many comic characters.

The character, as Yeon's stereotypic idol, seemed to shape her values, biases and stereotypes of what it means to be a beautiful girl.

The ideology of this visceral attraction seemed to overwhelm her. Yeon was not aware of her stereotype of a beautiful female character. Her awareness did not reach to the tremendous influence of her favorite *manga*, which was evident in her own appearance, personality, behaviors, and desires. Without critical awareness of the stereotype, she wanted to invent her own creative style so that she could escape from Tanemura's style and technique.

> I was really a fanatical admirer of the comic.... There was a lot of beautiful stuff.... I used to copy... the comic.... I have more stress these days.... I tear up my drawing and throw it in the trash when I am not satisfied.... When [my friends] see my drawing they say they can easily see Tanemura Arina's comic in it. There is no more progress in my technique for drawing my comic because I do not create my own character.... Considering that, I am now trying to find a character for my own comic.

FIGURE 1. (left) Yeon's comic drawing.
FIGURE 2. (right) Yeon's first self-portrait.

Her comic style and technique depicted very similar stereotypes of beautiful female characters. Finding a "technique" to create her own comic took over her mind, but she was not able to recognize and articulate how much of her value for beauty was influenced by *manga*.

In Yeon's first self-portrait (Figure 2), which aimed to introduce herself, she depicted various aspects of herself. The smiling face of the person and several clocks in the self-portrait represented her interests in and focus on drawing comics.

> [T]his reveals me drawing a comic because I like comics.... There is a brain, eyes, nose, and a mouth but no ears. That means I cannot hear any noise from outside when I draw comics.... I do not care what things happen when I draw comics. You can see the same picture my hand is drawing as if you can see it in my brain. That means I only think of my drawing when I draw comics.... My big smile presents that I am really happy when I draw comics.... You can see the stars and moon in my drawing. These indicate I feel like having everything in the world whenever I draw a comic.

It seemed that she thought this concentration on and interest in drawing comics was the most distinguishable feature for differentiating herself from others.

It is interesting to note that she did not draw herself in the self-portrait in a manner of the comic character she liked. It seemed that some changes happened in her mind throughout the instruction, and they inspired her:

> [During your presentation] There was an old woman, animal bone, easel, and mountains in the background.... When I first saw it, I was a little astonished. ... How can she draw her self-portrait with those things? At the beginning of the class I thought I was just drawing my face beautifully. However, after I saw the painting I thought differently.... I remembered the last painting that depicted an old man and a woman connected to a tree trunk in a rice field or a dry field. It was the last painting that touched my heart though I saw it very quickly. [The interviewer asked how the painting touched her heart.] Trees in a dry field cannot grow a lot within a short time. However, the trunk was really big, so I understood that the painting showed a strong affection between the dry field and them. It reminded me of my grandmother.... When I thought about a self-portrait, I thought about a person who is beautiful and has a good character. However, ... I realized that I could use my face connected to a big trunk in order to express that I had an intimate affection.... This [self-portrait] is a valuable work of art because I made it with this different thinking.

FIGURE 3. Yeon's first artwork.

We should not have any bias.

I changed only the face.

How do you think about your appearance? Tell us your opinion about it.

What this passage seemed to indicate was that she personally understood the power of the exemplar image. This personal reflection started to challenge her mindset, which had previously stuck to a stereotypical drawing style.

This change in her mindset kept unfolding throughout the subsequent lessons. Juxtaposing two characters in her first artwork (Figure 3) created a good contrast that revealed her critical awareness of her bias. In the upper left side of her artwork there is a beautiful character from Tanemura's *manga*, while many news reporters were on the bottom left side. On the opposite side there is a beautiful character whose face has been replaced by a middle-aged woman's face, an outcast from reporters and society. Above the juxtaposed characters, Yeon wrote, "I changed only the face. We should not have any bias."

> I had an idea of putting two people side by side and replacing the face of one of the people with an old person's face.... [M]any people wore the same clothes as

comic characters and their body shapes were similar. However, I felt they were really ugly when I saw them on TV.

Her artwork and explanations seemed to reflect this intellectually critical awareness. Talking about the meaning behind her first artwork during the interview, she elaborated upon her stereotype and articulated how the *manga* shaped her bias to judge others with their appearance and how equity in our society could fall into crisis:

> I thought that all beautiful characters had long hair, beautiful eyes, big eyes, and small noses.... I had a bias for beautiful people. I had not realized why having such a bias could be problematic. However, I knew that the stories and images from my favorite *manga* were related to my idea of what was beautiful. I also knew how the bias could destroy our society. Then, I could think I was doing something that destroyed our country.... I think *manga* can be bad because they make me have biases.

She became reflective and felt "regret" for the stereotype and bias she had held.

Yeon's second artwork (Figure 4) manifested more emphasis on this critical response by highlighting individual differences. One person had a different hairstyle and clothes from many people dressed in an identical manner as the beautiful *manga* character; this person was on the upper right corner and was hanging her head down, as if she was guilty. Others around her glared at her, whereas ugly Shurek in the bottom right had a big smile while saying that he was so popular even though he did not share the fashion. God in the upper left admonished the identical people for their loss of individuality and inner beauty. The text in the center of the artwork, "You know that your inner mind is the most important thing," overarched her critical awareness. Yeon became aware of the value of inner beauty and depicted the social issue that emerged from her favorite popular images.

Moreover, during the fourth interview, her voice contained her emotional responses that touched her heart.[4] When she expressed her great regret that Tanemura had firmly influenced her bias regarding the standard of beauty, she could no longer control her genuine regret. With moist eyes and a sad voice: "I am so sorry for Tanemura's *manga* and I do not know what I should do now." Her disappointed face was enough to reveal her broken heart, which was so

FIGURE 4. Yeon's second artwork.

pure, wandering, and struggling with her frustration from losing her ideal model in her mind. This despondent voice and gloomy mood were an extreme change from her initial upbeat, confident voice when she explained how much she blindly respected Tanemura. In this sense, her critical awareness seemed to shake her impregnable belief, agitate her emotion, touch her mind, and bring a change to her mindset. Through this critical self-reflection, she was able to feel and articulate from her heart how the stereotype yielded serious social problems, such as bullying, suicide, discrimination, and the excessive boom of plastic surgery, as well as how many people struggled with these problems.

It seemed that Yeon, over the course of this art program, realized the problem of the stereotype she acquired from her favorite comic. She also facilitated her own capacity for critical awareness. It was interesting to see how this critical capacity related to her holistic responses and yielded a heart-touching moment that held the potential for significant changes in her life. Her critical eyes were opened and stimulated her intellectual and emotional journey for spiritual exploration. She was able to both feel the value of inner beauty by self-reflecting on what she had done and contemplate what she should do now. It seemed that all the critical questions in her mind converged on a spiritual question, a search for the value of inner beauty and the meaning of life, which was invisibly saturated by the influences of popular images in which she blindly indulged.

PORTRAIT 2: EUN'S[5] IMMERSION AND SYMPATHY

Eun, a female student, loved to read the Japanese comic book, *Naruto*. The primary subject of the comic focuses on sword fighting and the adventures of the main character, Naruto, in a Ninja training school. Eun usually drew the character throughout her several volumes of sketchbooks. In her free time, she visited others' blogs to appreciate their drawings of Naruto and sword fighting as well as upload her comics involving sword fighting. By imitating *Naruto*, Eun taught herself how to draw comics. She was proficient in drawing and painting in cartoon style (Figure 5).

FIGURE 5. Eun's comic drawing.

During the interview with Eun about her first self-portrait (Figure 6), she indicated that it depicted various aspects of the self, such as her personality, interest in Naruto and sword fighting, preferences, appearance, and so on. Her interest in sword fighting dominated the first interview. Explaining how the comic book and character could be related to her, she said that she was trying to overcome a fear in her life:

> Since the 1st grade, I have usually gone out and played at night. In these days, after finishing private Taekwondo (martial arts) lesson, I go out and play.... I finish the lesson at 9:00 pm. Then, I go in-line skating and wander all around my neighborhood.... It is dark and dreary outside at that time.

Keeping her teeth tightly closed suggested that she was taking on the world and overcoming any fear and adverse circumstances.

Her second self-portrait (Figure 7), in which she sought to express herself by incorporating her favorite popular images, further clarified her interests in sword fighting. The self-portrait included a realistic sword fighting moment followed by violent scenes such as those shown in comic books. Two of the eight

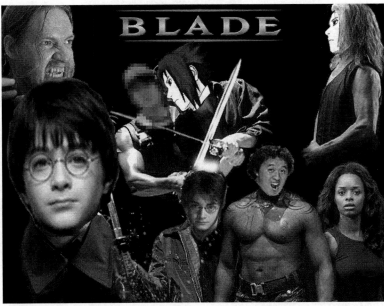

FIGURE 6. (left) Eun's first self-portrait.
FIGURE 7. (right) Eun's second self-portrait.

people in black clothes were sword fighting in the middle of the image. Eun put the image of her face and a comic character on top of the two warriors.

Despite lots of allusions in this artwork, one of the evident issues was Eun's desire to sword fight with the comic character in the center. It is, however, important to note that this interest in sword fighting was not only for entertainment. What she obtained from the comic was not a fantasy. She did not believe that sword fighting in *Naruto* was as violent as I felt it was. "Cruel? (snorting) My parents and older sister think so, but they believe that way because they have not read it." Eun explained that she liked Naruto because he overcame all difficulties, including unequal treatment from people in his hierarchical clan, by becoming the strongest Ninja after crossing swords and defeating all strong enemies. She added that the comic was not fun until she realized the story of "challenge and adventure to achieve [Naruto and Sasuke's] dream." It seemed that this awareness was her motivation to try to overcome any fear or difficulty in her life, such as playing outside at night and stomping on bugs:

> Playing outside at night is dreary, but I think I have to overcome the fear.... It is really difficult to overcome something dreary. It is really, really difficult.... I am going out intentionally because I really want to overcome my fear of night.... It is somehow difficult to stomp on ants. It is somehow creepy for me. I feel bad when I stomp on them. It is creepier when I stomp on earthworms.... I often try to kill bugs.

Although her artworks and majority of her explanation during interviews focused on how much she liked sword fighting, it seemed that there was something more about the connection between her and the comic.

After two more sessions and one intensive in-depth interview about why Eun liked sword fighting and the challenging story as well as how she could make personal connection with *Naruto*, her awareness and thoughts evolved, and she seemed to be transforming. Her struggle to catch my intention and answer my barrage of questions provided her with a more reflective moment in order to create personal meaning behind her interests in the comic. She realized that she was interested in how Naruto overcame unequal treatment through sword fighting. Reading the comic *Naruto* more carefully, I found that sword fighting in the comic book was an essential purpose for realizing Naruto's dream, which was to become the next Hokage—the most powerful and admirable Ninja—to keep peace and equality in the village.

FIGURE 8. Eun's second artwork.

Eun's second artwork (Figure 8) evidently revealed this unfolding. In her second artwork, she cried for equality in society. On the left half, she vertically placed three images that symbolized equality, friendship, and mutuality. On the other side were three images that represented inequality in South Korea: Two images depicting a woman who set a table for a big family (in traditional Korean society, women eat separately from their family, usually eating while squatting in the kitchen after setting the table for their family), and a moment of sacrificial rites (a woman traditionally was not allowed to participate in this memorial service), the gulf between the rich and poor (the "₩" symbol on the platform where the man is standing is analogous to the dollar sign), and a handicapped child, according to Eun's explanation. On the border, Naruto said in a speech bubble, "I hate any inequality."

Eun explained that this artwork aimed to visualize her voice crying for equality in our society while she responded to the mistreatment Naruto experienced. A transformation toward critical consciousness seemed to sprout. She explained that the adverse story of the comic was something about inequality. Gaining more knowledge to critically see *Naruto* made it possible for her to realize the dominant social issues emerging from the comic—namely, inequality, not sword fighting or violence.

More meaningfully, what I got from her voice, which was confident and affirmative, seemed to come not only from intellectual sophistication. Pauses, agitated tone, a trembling and resentful voice, a frown, and so on, hinted at her emotional agitation and burst when she explained how Naruto's story was "hers." She became reflective about her life story:

> Always my older sister first!... [My mother] loves only my older sister.... Whenever I have quarrels with my older sister, my mother always scolds me only.... My mother purchased a new desk for her.... My older sister took my bed.... (Eun heaves a sigh of grief). It is resentful.... I cannot live with such treatment.... I really hate it.... I asked myself whether I have to suffer from unequal mistreatment at home because I am the younger sister.... I feel it is my real problem.

Her resentment, hate, and anger were clearly articulated. Her critical reflection, internalization, and immersion extended to her parents' discriminatory treatment of her at home. (They loved their oldest daughter most, which is common in South Korean culture under Confucian tradition). This critical reflection and emotional engagement was related to her sympathy and pity for Naruto's struggles.

> He (Naruto) is so pitiable.... I am in the same situation as Naruto. The comic is also my story. This is why I like it." Her intense feeling sometimes reached a climax. "It (mistreatment) is not right.... I cannot live under the unequal treatment anymore.

From this passage, I understood why she was so interested in Naruto overcoming his agony and how the story could be related to her efforts to overcome any fear and difficulty in her life.

Eun's unfolding continued through her third artwork (Figure 9). She depicted more social consciousness based on moral[6] values and attitudes. In the artwork, she included a picture of a cityscape as the background. On top of this, she put a hand holding a magnifying glass zooming in on a detail of the city. She superimposed an image of a King from the Chosen Dynasty, when Confucianism was socially and culturally prevalent, and a maid on both sides, maintaining balance on top of the zoomed-in city image. The peaceful ending scene of the Naruto comic, many different people in line holding hands with their neighbors, appeared in the speech bubble attached to the magnifier. All these components were integrated into the entire composition in order to create a metaphor for equality among people:

> [I made my artwork] in order to reveal inequality in our society.... It depicts how we can see the social problem... when we see our society carefully like zooming in on something through a magnifying glass... unequal social problems such as sexual discrimination or disparity in the social standing.... I was treated impartially at home. My older sister is treated more warmly than I because she is the first-born.... Naruto was excluded from all the people in his village, and he was left alone until he became a powerful Ninja.... This artwork cries for equality in our society for all people.

Eun articulated how she immersed herself in her life story and in her favorite comic in order to call for social resistance and promote greater social goodness.

Looking back at her unfolding, it seems that her artworks were related to her "holistic" perspective. The process of delving into the influence of Naruto was a vehicle for her sympathy and morality in relation to equality, social justice, mutuality, and caring. Recognizing and feeling Naruto's suffering, Eun's sympathy and emotional engagement in herself, as well as her inner goodness, values, attitudes, and morality for greater social goodness, were the mixture of her critical investigation of her favorite popular images. Based on this immersion and profundity, she sympathized with Naruto's agony and amplified her inner goodness, developing her moral value toward a larger ethical goal. Part of this holistic connection among the intellectual, emotional, and moral unfolding seemed to be closely related to her critical consciousness of morality to care for anyone facing difficulties, as Lipman (2003) argued by conceptualizing the connection between critical thinking and caring thinking.

FIGURE 9. Eun's third artwork.

CONCLUSION

From the two portraits, we see the value and benefits of art classes that focus on students' interests in their favorite popular images. If it develops students' reflection and initiates students' deeper self-awareness within the cultural contexts of students' lives under the influences of popular images, visual culture art education can be overlapped with holistic art education. My students exhibited ways in which their critical reflection encouraged them to form the inner experiences and facilitated their unfolding in a holistic manner. Responsive pedagogy was an inspirational strategy for students to go beyond their superficial understanding of the images. This reflective and analytical study of comics in a responsive manner also demonstrated how to encourage students to go beyond mere imitation of their stereotypes to more genuine artistic expressions.

The feasibility of other art teachers adopting this approach, however, seems to be a different issue. The special situation of how the interviewer and researcher enhanced students' unfolding and growth should be considered. Art teachers should consider how they can make their teaching more dialogic and reflective for students. Art teachers should also set up a plan to incorporate thoughtful interviews and data analysis as part of their teaching. Another apparent point made within examination of these portraits is the impact of the attitude, character, and values of the art teacher who seeks these kinds of reflective opportunities for students to explore themselves and who possesses a holistic lens with which to gauge students' growth through art lessons.

REFERENCES

Campbell, L. (2003). *Portraits of visual artist/teachers: Spirituality in art education.* Unpublished doctoral dissertation. University of Illinois at Urbana-Champaign.

Campbell, L. (2006). Spiritual reflective practice in preservice art education. *Studies in Art Education, 47*(1), 51-69.

Lee, J. (2009). *Developing a responsive curriculum for 6th grade art students' critical consciousness and empowerment.* Unpublished doctoral dissertation. University of Illinois at Urbana-Champaign.

Lewis, J. (2000). Spiritual education as the cultivation of qualities of heart and mind: A reply to Blake and Carr. *Oxford Review of Education, 26*(2), 263-284.

Lipman, M. (2003). *Thinking in education.* Cambridge, England: Cambridge University Press.

London, P. (2004). Toward a holistic paradigm in art education. In *A report from the study group for holistic art education* [Monograph #1] (pp. 1-6). Baltimore, MD: Center for Art Education, Maryland Institute College of Art.

Mustakova-Possardt, E. (2003). *Critical consciousness: A study of morality in global, historical context.* Westport, CT: Praeger.

Purpel, D. (1998). Social transformation and holistic education: Limits and possibilities. In H. S. Shapiro & D. E. Purpel (Eds.), *Critical social issues in American education: Transformation in a postmodern world* (pp. 355-369). Mahwah, NJ: Erlbaum.

ENDNOTES

1   This chapter does not aim to discuss the research itself and the curriculum instruction; instead, it focuses on introducing a holistic picture of students' growth. Please check my dissertation for the research and curriculum (Lee, 2009). Readers should know that the dissertation did not discuss this holistic perspective because the holistic picture is recently emerging while reflecting on the research.

2   My dissertation research, a case study, was designed to investigate how 6th-grade students understood their favorite popular images and considered the influences of the images in their sense of self.

3   This name is a pseudonym.

4   This heart touching can be understood as one of the essential features that needs spiritual education, as Lewis (2000) addressed.

5   This name is a pseudonym.

6   Mustakova-Possardt (2003) pointed out the connection between critical consciousness and morality. Eun's story seems to elaborate upon this point, indicating the need for a holistic perspective to understand students' critical consciousness.

AUTHOR'S NOTE

All images used with permission.

ABOUT THE AUTHOR

Jae-young Lee is Assistant Professor in the General Studies division at Ulsan National Institute of Science and Technology in South Korea. He earned his PhD in art education from the University of Illinois at Urbana-Champaign. His research continues to center on curriculum and instruction, teacher education, holistic approaches to art education, and interdisciplinary research crossing Art, Science, and Technology.

CHAPTER 14

Quadratic Pedagogy

Steve Willis

This chapter addresses the structural components of a Native American sweat lodge as a basis for suggesting similarities to experiences found in the art classroom. By discussing the characteristics of *The Four Directions*, "a Native American pathway... for keeping order and a sense of purpose in... life," (Mails, p. 258) comparisons are developed that impact curriculum and pedagogy in art education. The author makes suggestions that a more balanced approach might establish a foundation for multidirectional practices in the art classroom.

HISTORY OF THE SWEAT LODGE

The practice of a sweat lodge or purification lodge can be found globally, both historically and contemporarily. For this writing, only the sweat lodge structure common within Native American cultures found in the United States, and specifically from The *Hocq'reila* Dance, will be discussed for comparison with constructs commonly found in the arts education classroom. I will argue that the art education classroom, like the sweat lodge, should offer experiences that provide a holistic way of knowing that includes the body, emotion, intellect and spirit.

Even though types of purification ceremonies can be found in many places throughout the globe, people attribute the Native American sweat lodge as originating with the Sioux People, as it is considered one of their Seven Rites.

From *Lakota Belief and Ritual*, Walker (1991) included Burt Means's translated conversation with George Sword about *Ni, Ini* and *Initi*. Sword stated, "The white people call it a sweat lodge. The Lakota do not understand it so. The Lakota think of it as a lodge to make the body strong and pure. They call it *initi*" (p. 100). Brown (1953), who recorded and edited conversations with the revered Lakota Elder Black Elk, cited that "The rite of the *onikare* (sweat lodge) utilizes all the Powers of the universe; earth, and all the things which grow from the earth, water, fire and air" (p. 31). Similarly, according to Mails (1988), who honored noted Native spiritual leaders Frank Fools Crow, Archie Sam, Renzie Gordon, and the Pueblo People in his acknowledgement, indicated that the Four Directions emphasized in a sweat lodge are found throughout Native American spiritual structures, and noted, "A Native American pathway ... for keeping order and a sense of purpose in your life is that of calling in power from the Four Directions" (p. 258). Deloria (1992) pointed out that Native American construction of the universe is considerably different from Western and Near Eastern paradigms, and explained that "...Indians pray to the 'four directions,' lay out elaborate sand paintings to represent the cosmos, and see in pipe bowls and sweat lodges a model of the larger cosmic whole" (p. 154).

Before going deeper into this subject, however, it must be made clear that discussion of the sweat lodge is understood by many Natives as encroaching on particular restricted areas, so many things cannot be written about the spiritual and ceremonial aspects of a sweat lodge. My traditional teaching also prohibits sharing ceremonial information. Moreover, I am sensitive to the misappropriation of Native American ceremonies, rites, and rituals, and therefore, I must honor the Elders' request not to share ceremonial information through text. In this manner, I will not refer to the experiences I have collected as a Firekeeper, Sun Dance supporter, Sun Dancer, and Sun Dance Helper that originated on and around the Rosebud Reservation in South Dakota. However, I can share societal, cultural, and historical information as well as personal anecdotal insights. In this regard, I will exclusively address the understandings I have of the sweat lodge from the *Hocq'reila* Dance where I help as a leader.

HOCQ'REILA LODGE

The Star Dance, known as *Hocq'reila*, maintains specific traditions and protocols, and the use of the sweat lodge, or *Ootah*, is integral to the understanding and success of the dance. Through this dance, circles of the community and culture grow progressively larger. Like other sweat lodges, the *Ootah* emphasizes the Four Directions, east, west, north and south, as a horizontal platform on which the earth is below and the sky is above, making in actuality, six directions with the participants being in the center—the seventh relational component. It is in this reference that I will discuss the experiences of the *Ootah* and the parallel experiences found in the classroom with students and teachers. Similar to other types of sweat lodges, the *Ootah* uses an altar, fire, water and heated stones, all of which are sacred and essential. In the same manner, there are protocols in the art classroom, such as curriculum, pedagogy, resources, and preparation, which are all essential for teaching and learning.

As suggested above, the *Ootah* must be experienced firsthand to be fully understood, so any attempt to explain the experiences may merely be an exercise in frustration. Nevertheless, I will attempt to create a bridge, enter into the lodge, and try to discuss the invisible and sometimes incomprehensible experiences with words. Though I know in advance it will be inadequate, I will attempt to act as a guide. In this, I seek the blessings of the Elders. As a matter of convenience, I will refer first to the West Direction. Like all the directions, the West is full of mystery and nuance.

The West: *Waa-Nicq*

The West Direction is oriented to emphasize the emotions of the participant and focuses on all aspects that are known through the heart, both the joyous and the difficult. This is not easy to discuss and is laddered with layers of knowledge and understanding both in personal and communal memories, some of which may be filled with anguish while others are abundantly ecstatic. In this, intellectualism cannot capture the mercurial aspects of the emotions that surface and reveal many aspects of reality. Therefore, many of the things that are understood in the West Direction cannot be discussed; the emotions are denser than can be communicated with the limitations of words.

Similarly, in the art classroom, there are emotional qualities that are actively encouraged and simultaneously discouraged. For example, it is not uncommon to find a teacher encouraging students to paint emotionally; to respond to some external stimulus such as music, sports, poetry, war, hunger, abuse, or a myriad of other catalysts. But here one can also find conflict between the artist, environment, and instruction. Creating an emotionally-based art form is one thing, discussing it is another.

As Herberholz and Herberholz (2002) stated, "Although each individual artist's creative spirit is unique and personal, the culture in which he or she lives places special values on specific activities, providing the need, the format, and the materials for individuals to fashion art objects" (p. 7). Typically, if the student-artist paints something emotional and finds that within the classroom culture the teacher or the other students do not understand or *like* the image, then the tendency is to paint something that garners recognition, not emotional honesty. The student strives to be accepted into the culture and achieve a status that demonstrates those special values.

Also, as with the West Direction in the Lodge, emotions can defy discussion, as language is in the East Direction with the intellect. As discussed in Edward's (1999) *The New Drawing on the Right Side of the Brain*, the language common in one function is absent in another; "Seeing is the problem, or, to be more specific, shifting to a particular way of seeing" (p. 4). The manner in which one *sees* is important in the West Direction, as seeing is part of knowing. Yet teachers commonly expect students to be able to discuss and explain the image. The in-process discussion between the teacher and student or among students may be of formative value, but the demand on language requires spoken or written comments similar to those found in the ubiquitous critique. If the expectations are truly emotional, then a spoken or written conversation by the artist, regardless of age, may be extremely limited.

I have often wondered if a student who speaks logically and intellectually receives a higher evaluation on the emotional image than the student who responds emotionally as instructed but cannot intellectually describe or even discuss the image. Is it possible that the spoken language receives more emphasis in the evaluative process because it is a common form of communication? If the intent is to ask a student to paint emotionally and to be able to intellectualize the image, all is well. But, if the expectations are truly emotional like ones found in the West Direction, then the response and potential evaluation of that mercurial moment or *feeling* may be difficult, as this is not easily captured by vocabulary words or experiences learned during previous critical or analytical conversations.

The North: *Aer-Nicq*

The North Direction is a place of faith and faces the invisibility of Divinity, a place where things are known through indirect observation such as the play of the wind on fields of tall grass. One knows there is wind even if it is invisible, and understands this through observation of the action of the wind on the field of grass. The North is also a place of conversation with personalities not seen. It is a place where neither emotion nor intellect can be used for comprehension, though there are occasionally strong emotional reactions and an abundance of internal dialog in many acts of faith. The North can thus be a place of great epiphany as well as sadness. The North can also amplify an empty, vacuous experience, which can be misunderstood through human frailty.

When facing the North and the experience is not understandable, it may be because prior intellectual experiences limit the occurrence, and emotional understanding is inadequate. I have been told by Elders that "What is experienced in Spirit World may not be translatable into a physical reality." The North is a place of non-thinking and a knowing that, like emotional expression, may defy the intellect.

Frequently, in what I might cautiously label as a standard art classroom, the attributes of the North may not be found. In this classroom, when an image is created that cannot be intellectualized for discussion nor understood by feeling, it is frequently discredited and ignored. Thankfully, Simpson et. al. (1998) remind us that, "The notion of art as a way of knowing, thinking, and feeling focuses attention on the ways art makes thought visible" (p. 79). This suggests that, when an artist adventures into the North Direction and experiments with those characteristics to create an image, perhaps *this image just is* and, although difficult to understand and embrace in a classroom at any level, it nevertheless may be quite valuable for the artist and community.

This type of image is created in the intuitive space that exists between the emotional and intellectual, between feeling and thinking. It is from this place of knowing that the artist creates deliberate images with personal certainty, confidence and courage. Goldsworthy (2003) commented about his creations in *Rivers and Tides: Andy Goldsworthy Working With Time*, saying that "words do their job, but what I am doing here says a lot more." This conveys that his images come from his place of knowing, personal certainty, confidence and courage.

Thinking about this personal 'place,' I am reminded of a confident and courageous story that was shared with me over 3 decades ago. The story has not lost its potency. I was told

> As the elementary art teacher walked about the classroom while the students had free drawing time, the teacher noticed one student who was enthusiastically creating a very large purple scribble. The teacher approached and asked, "What is that you are drawing?" and the student, without looking up, said, "A cow." The teacher promptly replied, "I've never seen a purple cow." To which the student responded, "That's too bad."

Unfortunately, as I mentioned above, after such an image is created in the meditative personal space of conception, it is frequently altered to meet external requirements, social interaction, and group dynamics. This is especially the case as students get older. So one question is: How can art teachers help protect the sacred space within each person, and support the art that comes from it? Although discussing multiculturalism, Bates (2000) makes an important parallel point that refers to the creative characteristics of the North understanding: "However, their [teacher's] primary focus is on the 'outside.' Individual instructors must use these resources in creative teaching strategies that connect with the 'inside'" (p. 173). Hopefully, artists and art students who create with attributes of the North will have the courage to let the image remain unaltered even though they may not be able to articulate its importance with logic or language. Nonetheless, this type of image by its very nature resides in an area that can be challenging for both the educator and society.

Can this be experienced in a standard art classroom? Will teachers be able to create an environment where this activity is recognized and valued? Can students enter the North, perceive the potential, and confidently and courageously create images, knowing that they may not be accepted in the classroom culture? And, if this happens, will critiques and assessments be appropriate when these educational activities are not included in the realm of the North? This is similar to brain hemisphere divisions where one side is non-verbal and intuitive while the other is verbal and logical. Can non-verbal and intuitive art be embraced? These are difficult questions, and the experiences in both the *Ootah* and the classroom can only be understood and answered by a person who has experienced the North Direction firsthand. Like in the Lodge, the rapport of experiential artistic commonality must be established in support of what Ram Dass (1985) called an environment conducive to learning.

As I pointed out in *The Four Directions* (2005):

> The paradox for many non-Natives is that there is a need for them to define visual symbols and cultural experiences with words when the Native experience is personal as well as communal and is essentially non-verbal. This presents a serious problem for non-Natives as the breadth and depth of the Four Directions cannot be compressed into words. It can only be completely understood through multiple personal experiences. (p. 39)

In this quote, 'non-artist' can easily be substituted for 'non-Native,' which may add clarity to how understanding the North Direction is constructed. And, for the artist, these experiences can clearly be non-verbal and exclusively visual. This is an area in the educational system that is problematic and requires insight by the teacher so that this potential and all its corresponding attributes can find value in the classroom and in the artistic process.

The East: *Fii-Nicq*

The East Direction ignites the intellect with the light of the rising sun and brings illumination to a dark night. For many, the characteristics of the East are the easiest directions to discuss because it is primarily intellectual and potentially easier to comprehend. In the East one moves from darkness of apprehension, fear, or ignorance into the light of knowledge, clarity, and enlightenment.

Since intellectualism drives the interaction in this direction, and since communication is a major part of the experience, one *can* talk about the environment and interaction. In the classroom, this important component underpins many activities by introduction, verbal demonstration, procedure, process, and assessment. Even in the visual arts classroom, teachers use spoken and written language as a primary form of communication. It is learned and rehearsed to perfection. Among other things, art teachers like to talk about the images they select as exemplars, mentioning issues like the precision of technical acuity, and the relationship of the artist to history and culture. Similarly, art teachers teach strategies to assist their students in talking about art forms, like Barrett's (2003) connotation and denotation.

Questions remain about the relationship between words and images. Howard Gardner introduced seven intelligences in the early 1980s, and among the seven, discussed visual imagery with the category of "visual-spatial intelligence." As Gardner (2006) stated, "An intelligence must also be susceptible to encoding in a symbols system—a culturally contrived system of meaning that captures and conveys important forms of information" (p. 8). Discussing visual images leads to an interesting paradox—can art exist independently from words? Or, more importantly, can the art classroom culture become independent and encode its meaning in visual language and use the visual language exclusively or at least primarily to convey important information, so art-knowing is understood and experienced in many ways other than those typically taught in schools?

Discussing human experiences, whether visual or not, is an important aspect of culture and history and should not be minimized in the educational process. Students need to develop a visual, as well as spoken and written language common in the artistic community. Both of these have been designed to support personal investigation and synthesize deeper artistic knowledge. Thinking about images, thinking about making images, and thinking about how images are important to the individual and group are all valuable components, but, like in the lodge, the intellect of the East must be balanced with the emotion of the West, the divinity of the North, and the humanity of the South.

The South: *Eeaar-Nicq*

The South sits low and solid on the Earth. It is a place of quiet contemplation. It is a place of introspection that allows Divinity to speak directly to the person. The South is a gentle and powerful place of truth and honesty. In the South, deceit, lies, and ego are not acceptable. It is a place of fulfillment and celebration. The South provides the threads that weave together the other Directions. It is where courageous independence and compassionate interdependence interact for the benefit of the individual and group.

In the art classroom, the characteristics of the South are paramount to the development of the individual and the corresponding art discipline. In this Direction, quiet reflection, meditative in form, allows the artist to see the gestalt uniting the environment and the individual and how that gestalt is reflected in the image being produced. This is also when the understanding surfaces that the artist and the image are not separate, but are bound together through common creation. Conversations in the art classroom should introduce the idea that *the art form also creates the artist.* This bi-directional conversation is important for every artist to understand. Teaching this delicate conversational nuance through compassionate pedagogy and engaging curriculum allows for individual experimentation that is crucial in the development of balanced artistic processes and should be available in every classroom.

Although ultimately, the South Direction represents resolution of oppositions, in the Lodge, the South is experienced initially, at least, in terms of oppositions. It is a place of both exaltation and conflict, a place of excitement and fatigue, a place of knowing and doubting, a place where one confronts oneself and one's contradictions. I would suggest that these characteristics are also present in the artmaking processes and in the art classroom. With the characteristics of the South, the student understands and celebrates, or misunderstands and lets frustration and disappointment become a powerful adversary of self-empowerment and self-recognition. This delicate but potent conversation with oneself, one's classmates, and with the teacher is most important. This is beyond the dialogue of the East and the emotions of the West; it is the place that balances the North. It is a place of weaving experiences; a place where, thanks to the effort to understand oneself and resolve one's inner conflicts, the tapestry of personal identity is secured and the design is created.

THE PARTICIPANT

When entering into the *Ootah*, as suggested in the previous section, one must come prepared to move beyond previous limitations. The energy of Four Directions that enters the Lodge with the participant is powerful and can be gentle or aggressive depending on the person and the needs that are consciously or subconsciously brought into the Lodge. But ultimately, the Energy is positive in all situations and weaves the logically and intellectually understandable with the intuitive and non-lingual experiences. In the Lodge, as in the art classroom, some experiences are understandable in the heart/emotion while other information comes for the mind/intellect. This relationship with the Four Directions supports the Seventh Direction—the participant. This type of knowing encompasses multiple dimensions, and is only complicated because complication seems to be a by-product of the 21st-century human. We make it more difficult than it needs to be. And, to add to the complications in the classroom, each individual learns through different catalysts and at different cadences. Though the Lodge is limited in physical dimensions, it is boundless in other dimensions and each participant can have personal experiences not shared communally. Thus, even though two people sit next to each other in the Lodge, they may have very different experiences. I would suspect that this is also found in the art classroom. This is difficult to understand and more difficult to communicate.

THE CLASSROOM

Translating an experience from the *Ootah* to ordinary life situations is difficult. But, with experiential commonality and careful comparison, the experiences from the Lodge can be understood to mirror similar qualities found in the modern art classroom. As Barry (1995) stated, "Significance isn't a kind of core or essence *inside* things; rather, meaning is always *outside*. Meaning is always an attribute of things" (p. 39). In the art classroom, as suggested earlier, the reliance on the intellect may, at times, overpower the other components of a balanced approach to artmaking, because, often, meaning is tenaciously attributed to artmaking through language about art, not through the art itself. Moreover, as Trend (1992) stated, "far from being a neutral carrier of ideas and images, language establishes hierarchies in form as well as content. It shapes the acquisition of culture" (p. 19).

Being aware of these situations, this chapter proposes that the logical/linguistic functions used in the creative process and the educational setting of the art classroom must be balanced with the other less verbal forms of communication, because, as Anderson and Milbrandt (2004) discussed, "When we express ourselves through making art, we create something tangible to look at, hold, reflect upon, feel, and try to understand mentally and physically" (p. 139).

With the awareness of multiple intelligences (Armstrong, 1994; Gardner, 2006), many art educators embrace the multiple proclivities presented in each learner as well as the diverse opportunities provided by each learning situation, but a search of even the most active classrooms rarely reveals the acceptance of non-verbal experiences as a final product. This tendency becomes even more of a concern in a time of accountability and assessment, where 5-year plans, program assessment, unified curriculum, student performance on standardize tests, and financial constraints make it difficult for educators to accept other forms of artistic communication, much less to actually put these into practice as a teachable and knowable form of visual communication. Non-verbal artistic activities are not measurable by standard methods of assessment, which are increasingly important in each classroom, school and district today. Knowing this, can we, as art teachers, support non-verbal art-thinking and artmaking as an integrated part of the holistic artistic experience, balanced with the existing specific language, codified symbols, and mutually agreed upon processes and procedures needed in the arts classroom?

CONCLUSION

Perhaps an understanding of the Four Directions and the corresponding characteristics might add other opportunities for ways of appreciating, encouraging, and cultivating individual differences and preferences in the arts classroom. To refer to the West, one finds the emphasis on the emotions. This is not new to the creative arts and has gained notable attention throughout much of the recent artistic history shared by many. But, like the West Direction in the Lodge, these emotions speak a language unto themselves that may not align with the intellectual properties of the East.

Perhaps it would be useful to illustrate the limitations of language to explain an essentially non-verbal form of communication through a creative medium that is, itself, based on language. U.S. Poet Laureate Billy Collins (2002) in *Sailing Alone Around the Room: New and Selected Poems* presents in his poem, "Introduction to Poetry" that perhaps poetry, like a visual image, is complete within itself and a critical posture and discussion are unnecessary for a meaningful experience.

>   ### Introduction to Poetry
>
>   I ask them to take a poem
>   and hold it up to the light
>   like a color slide
>
>   or press an ear against its hive
>
>   I say drop a mouse into a poem
>   and watch him probe his way out,
>
>   or walk inside the poem's room
>   and feel the walls for a light switch.
>
>   I want them to waterski
>   across the surface of a poem
>   waving at the author's name on the shore.
>
>   But all they want to do
>   is tie the poem to a chair with a rope
>   and torture a confession out of it.
>
>   They begin beating it with a hose
>   to find out what it really means. (p. 16)

Even in the visual realm of art education, written and spoken languages are so endemic and ubiquitous that they become invisible. Without recognizing the opportunity for other methods and other sets of educational lenses, language not only guides, but may also restrict the learning environment and limit many other approaches. There are, of course, other options for communication in the classroom, including the use of diagrams, demonstrations, and non-verbal language such as body and facial expression. These are not new to the art classroom as formative methods, but I propose that there should be a summative opportunity appropriate for the artistic experiences that is understood and appreciated for itself, for its qualities both obvious and subtle that is independent of other forms of communication. I have experienced paintings and dances and music and poetry that have opened portals to personal epiphanies that I cannot verbalize. I would hope as art educators that we could provide an opportunity for similar experiences for our students.

If these experiences are possible and acceptable, then a small bridge is constructed between the individual's learning and the educational environment that they cannot talk about, so that one does not feel alone, lonely and isolated by the limitations of their language. At the same time, such experiences open the possibility for a more holistic approach to art education, one that incorporates body, emotion, mind and spirit. This can happen in both the *Ootah* and the classroom. These more holistic experiences are individual moments, but recognition is reflected communally. Moreover, these moments should not be experienced occasionally, for it is only through consistent and repetitive holistic experiences that personal and communal knowledge can be fully understood and shared. This is not necessarily an easy journey, but an important one.

In the *Ootah*, what we say is less important than what we do. It is equally important to understand what is in our heart and emotion, and balance that with what is in our mind and intellect, thereby recognizing the multidirectional conversations that are possible only when multiple capacities within the individual are engaged and integrated. Perhaps there is a potential for these experiences to be delivered in the classroom through a combination of significant curriculum and compassionate pedagogy. Together, these can allow us, as teachers, to discover broader, more holistic, approaches to individual empowerment in the art classroom and beyond.

ABOUT THE AUTHOR

Steve Willis is a Professor of Art Education at Missouri State University in Springfield. He taught art in public schools in Florida for 23 years prior to coming to Missouri State. His interests include research concerning indigenous knowledge and tribal cultural construction especially in the arts, issues of equity, Native American practices, arts assessment, service learning and community engagement, and spirituality in art. As a contemporary artist, he creates images concerning spirituality.

REFERENCES

Anderson, T., & Milbrandt, M. (2004). *Art for Life*. New York, NY: McGraw-Hill.

Armstrong, T. (1994). *Multiple intelligences in the classroom*. Danvers, MA: The Association for Supervision and Curriculum Development.

Barry, P. (1995). *Beginning theory: An introduction to literary and cultural theory*. Georgetown, ON: UNIpress.

Barrett, T. (2003). Interpreting visual culture. *Art Education, 56*(2), 6-12.

Bates, J. K. (2000). *Becoming an art teacher*. Belmont, CA: Wadsworth/Thomson Learning.

Brown, J. E. (1953). *The Sacred Pipe: Black Elk's account of the seven rites of the Oglala Sioux*. Norman, OK: University of Oklahoma Press.

Collins, B. (2002). *Sailing alone around the room: New and selected poems*. New York, NY: Random House.

Dass, R. (1985). *Journey of awakening: A mediator's guidebook*. New York, NY: Bantam Publishing.

Deloria, V. (1992). *God is red*. Golden, CO: Fulcrum Press.

Edwards, B. (1999). *The new drawing on the right side of the brain*. New York, NY: Penguin Putnam.

Gardner, H. (2006). *Multiple intelligences: New horizons in theory and practice*. Jackson, TN: Basic Books, Perseus Books.

Goldsworthy, A. (Producer) & Thomas Riedelsheimer, T. (Director). (2003). *Rivers and tides: Andy Goldsworthy working with time*. Germany: Skyline Productions.

Herberholz, D., & Herberholz, B. (2002). *Artworks for elementary teachers: Developing artistic and perceptual awareness*. New York, NY: McGraw-Hill.

Mails, T. E. (1988). *Secret Native American pathways: A guide to inner peace*. Tulsa, OK: Council Oaks Books.

Simpson, J. W., Delaney, J. M., Carroll, K. L., Hamilton, C. M., Kay. S. I., Kerlavage, M. S., & Olson, J. L. (1998). *Creating meaning through art: Teacher as choice maker*. Upper Saddle River, NJ: Prentice-Hall.

Trend, D. (1992). *Cultural pedagogy: Art/education/politics*. New York, NY: Bergin & Harvey.

Walker, J. R. (1991). *Lakota belief and ritual*. Lincoln, NE: University of Nebraska Press.

Willis, S. (2005). The four directions. *The International Journal of Art & Design Education, 24*(1), 31-42. London, England: Blackwell Publishing.

CHAPTER 15

"Soft Stuff": Community, Identity, and Contemporary Craft in Education

Courtney Lee Weida

This chapter explores cognitive, sensory, and emotional dimensions of contemporary craft education. I have often overheard ceramics and craft teachers lament not only adolescent students' inability to model clay, knit, and/or crochet—but also express concern for adult students who have scarcely ever worked with their hands in a direct engagement with tactile art media. Learners who encounter warm, soft, and time-honored materials of craft can engage not only with craft histories and hand-made sensibilities, but can also "get in touch with" a sense of their own development and the embodiment of internal transformations. This chapter juxtaposes historical voices of M. C. Richards and Seonaid Robertson concerning wholeness and holistic education with commentary on contemporary DIY cultures and digital communities renewing and revising craft. Within this chapter, I will also investigate uneasy connotations of culture, gender, and status surrounding craft materials, including characterizations of "soft" scholarship and "hobbyist" status in artists' engagement with felt, fabric, fiber, clay, and other soft, sensory "stuff." I will consider examples from my own work teaching children about craft and clay, projects of the International Fiber Collaborative, and online craft groups geared toward adolescents and young adults as rich and varied learning examples exploring identity and community.

POSSIBILITIES OF CRAFT FOR THE WHOLE STUDENT

To discuss craft in art education is to touch on issues of sensory materiality, collective and individual consciousness, and a balancing of histories and traditions within the individual maker's constructed meanings. Historian Glen Adamson (2007) observed that *craft* is a term that applies not only to objects, but also describes approaches, attitudes, and actions of craftspeople that make those objects. Works of craft, thus understood, can be uniquely linked with the functions, cultures, and traditions of their makers and users. One adage of the crafts that expresses an awareness of these connections is: "We are what we make." Parenthetically, a contemporary, consumer-driven note to this adage might read: "We are what we use." Along this vein, this chapter will address the complexities of students' artistic development and holistic personal growth in terms of when and how they engage with craft practices and objects today.

In considering craft education from a holistic perspective, a central voice I will introduce is the renowned poet and potter, Mary Caroline (M. C.) Richards (1916-1999), who once noted that one "cannot talk about the crafts without appealing to the evolving spirit of man" (1989, p. 27). Richards taught in a variety of educational settings, including K-12 education, universities, and community workshops for learners across the lifespan. She discovered pottery when she came to Black Mountain College to teach writing and literature from 1945 to 1951. She later went on to teach poetry and pottery for special needs populations, and was also involved in sensory and arts-rich Waldorf education. Richards described the educational philosophy derived from her rich experiences as an "interdisciplinary study" and "search for wholeness... through the ordeals of life" (1973, p. 157). Her renaissance approach to teaching was a quest "to integrate poetry, pottery, inner development, community, and education" (1973, p. 3). Disenfranchised by colleges and universities, Richards sought to incorporate her passions for philosophy, ecology, ceramics, and poetics into a specialized curriculum honoring the student as a whole person. She initially proposed this educational framework in her classic book, *Centering: in Pottery, Poetry, and the Person* (1989).

One can locate philosophical threads from Richards' writing on crafts and holism in contemporary research in craft and education. For example, Canadian psychologist Darlene Clover and New Zealand sociologist Joyce Stalker (2008) recently noted, "quilts in particular have important therapeutic and healing properties associated with things such as comfort, warmth and protection" (p. 81). Richards provided a groundwork for such interrelations between objects, people, and communities in craft; stating in her 1973 address to artists and craftspeople: "there's a connection we ought to make between what we 'profess' as creatures sensitive to form, and what we practice in community" (p. 9). The creation of craft and the construction of communities can be compared in this way.

Building upon this broader, humanistic understanding of craft, this chapter will explore how craft objects and materials can contribute to both embodied learning experiences in studios and more conceptual explorations of communal and personal values. In so doing, I will initially examine some nostalgic (and even negative) art historical attitudes about craft. I will also describe varied contemporary crafts objects and their makers, consider the meanings of tactile encounters with materials, and investigate the communal aspect of making crafts (both past and present). Finally, I will conclude with some reflections on the notion of craft as a metaphor for education itself.

HISTORICAL FOUNDATIONS OF CRAFT: THE HAND AND MANUAL ARTS IN EDUCATION

While craft education has a history perhaps as long and rich as craft history, this chapter is specifically concerned with haptic sensibilities within craft education. Researcher John Howell White (2004) contextualized 19th- and 20th-century education in the US as a period of interest in the human hand in its connection with the mind. Opposing simplistic stereotypes of craft, Lecturer of Creative Craft Seonaid Robertson (1961) characterized the interest of practitioners of craft education in the hand (as in *hand*icraft), and with the entire body creating an "expressive rhythm relating mind and material" (p. 27). Early on, the paradigm of craft's therapeutic potential extended primarily to a population of children, women's clubs, and veterans. Within K-12 schools, crafts were contextualized in programs for Manual Training, Industrial Arts, and Applied Arts. (Teachers College Columbia University, for example, still bears signage referring to "Manual Arts"). Craft has thus often straddled many areas of human experience, as well as the terminologies needed to explain it, from hands to minds to hearts.

Writing of artistic-aesthetic development in children and adolescents, Judith Burton has noted the sensory and dialogic dimensions of artmaking through "interweaving levels out of which... dialogue between maker and material is formed" (2001, p. 37). She later (2009) emphasized the embodied, holistic conceptions of Viktor Lowenfeld about creative practice "as the place where the thinking, feeling, and perceiving of the *whole* individual could be attended to and developed" (p. 329). The writings of Howard Rissati (2007) similarly highlighted a sustained manual and bodily connection in craft work as opposed to machines, within a somatic process of making and communicating through craft materials. I have been intrigued by the connections and discords between making and machines in craft education. As recently as the 1970s and 1980s, my older siblings and I took public school classes in industrial/mechanical drawing and woodworking. Within this context, we engaged with line and form as precise and mechanical representations that translated into a combination of drawing and operating power tools to create smooth wooden objects. These odds and ends included lamps, boxes, and old fashioned children's toys and puzzles all intended for practical use, yet endowed with a certain aura of antiquity, nostalgia, and the "homemade." Even then, however, these classes were a dying breed in the curriculum, like culinary arts and home economics, which have widely disappeared from the schools in those particular incarnations.

More recently, a renewed interest in craft is observable in the ongoing "Craft in America" series in *School Arts* magazine. This series ran from 2007 to 2009 as an Educator Guide for the PBS show, "Craft in America." Craft activities, such as making friendship bracelets and doing macramé (which I remember from my own camp experiences as a young person) have evolved into a full-scale fiber art curriculum in some school art classes, including classrooms where my own student teachers facilitate learning today. As craft has begun to reemerge, it has embraced diversity and complexity within interdisciplinary curriculum; thereby being re-envisioned as practical, yet sometimes ironic, often personal, and even political. Further, a certain rebellion against the machine and mass-production is often observable.

One prime example of mixing public and personal expression is found in projects of the International Fiber Collaborative, a group with which my pre-service art and art education students and I have worked for the past few years. This collaborative, founded by artist and educator Jennifer Marsh, encourages craftspeople and students to design fiber patches or panels by hand that are joined to form monumental cozies installed over gas stations, rockets, and other large objects. By covering a site with messages and images of the artists, both the makers and the viewers can construct meanings around ecological, political, and aesthetic issues. For example, as a result of their involvement with Marsh's projects, art education students and art teachers I worked with in Virginia began to take more notice of abandoned gas stations in their communities, and then engaged with questions about the ecological impacts of fuel consumption, as well as the economic and communal implications of run-down plots of land. As they explored artistic responses as makers, they were dually involved in new ways of seeing and of investigating social and environmental questions.

TEACHING CRAFT CURRICULA: CRAFTSPEOPLE IN MANY CONTEXTS

Marsh's project not only spans many areas of thoughts, but also extends across several spaces. The International Fiber Collaborative takes place in classrooms, community groups, and individual homes, with a very strong and connective web presence. Despite the function and practicality originally associated with craft objects that initially connected it closely with schoolwork, today's craft projects are often as likely to exist beyond school walls, within informal learning environments. Often, these circumstances evolve from mentoring of teaching artists to extended apprenticeships. M. C. Richards greatly valued these sorts of learning situations, and even mused (1989) "all the arts we practice are apprenticeship" (p. 41).

An example of an apprenticeship model outside of school walls can be found in Billie Sessions' (2000) writings on another famed ceramicist with Black Mountain College affiliation, Marguerite Wildenhain. Sessions' research explores Wildenhain's pedagogical work in clay outside of traditional art education, indeed outside of conventional society in many regards. Pond Farm, the environment Wildenhain crafted as home, studio, and school, served as a specialized space for learning the craft and philosophy of making ceramics in a small community. Whether craft occupies a physical space outside of the classroom or not, learners may experience techniques and traditions reaching beyond purely cognitive considerations and traditionally academic locations.

Wildenhain was especially remembered as a teacher and mentor whose teaching techniques emphasized precision through repetition in ceramics. In contrast, M. C. Richards honored a more spontaneous and imperfect approach to forming pots. However, there is a point of connection in their appreciation of craftsmanship within the process of creating multiples. Richards (1989) emphasized both the nuance and continuity to be found in repetition: "to make a lot of things alike is as exciting as to make one surprise after another... and of course the rewards of sustained working rhythms are marvelous" (p. 29). Sustained learning towards an artistic practice of craftsmanship is an important experiential aspect of craft education.

As we consider the daily routines and practices of the studio apparent in Wildenhain's community pottery model, we might also examine craft theorist and educator Seonaid Robertson's views on the educational potential of the physical contexts of pottery. In 1961, Robertson addressed the United Nations' Educational, Scientific, and Cultural Organizations as a potter and educator, addressing the vast potential of craft in education. She advocated that learning through craft enables students not only to engage with well-made objects in terms of balance, form, and function; it also facilitates important and unconventional learning experiences such as digging, constructing, and operating a simple kiln (p. 13). Robertson noted the connective interdisciplinary potential of clay to touch on geography, archaeology, history, and botany. Within my graduate school years, these educational connections were particularly relevant in mental and physical learning experiences. As I studied ceramic archaeology and art history by day, I tended to the physical labors of the ceramics studio by night, with heavy physical lifting of clay, chemistry explorations in mixing glaze materials, and the alchemy of actions involved with firing of kilns.

M. C. Richards extensively addressed transfer or application of learning from one discipline to another, in a manner that honors the integrity of both. Working within community settings, Richards taught courses with students ranging from age 5 to age 15, and with parents and teachers dropping in as participants. Within these communities, learners were encouraged to discuss and explore the relationships of clay with geology, chemistry, ancient civilizations, writing development, and agriculture (1973, p. 57). Richards primarily worked with the pedagogical interrelationships of poetry to pottery and of pottery to poetry, characterizing both writing and ceramics as forms of handcraft. Richards wrote, "the intersection between writing and handcraft seems to me really to lie... in the quality of caring... an ability to respond humanly" (1973, p. 22). This cultivation of humanity and caring is central to holism, but also can become an academic and rigorous process. Specifically, Richards formed philosophies of pottery externally through "questions of meaning and technique" and internally within the potter's "inner activity... towards rebirth" (1989, p. 99). She proposes education that synthesizes many different aspects of the evolution of one's humanity through engagement with discourse and making.

Contemporary researchers are also exploring different dimensions of perceiving, making, and knowing through the crafts. Moving beyond traditionally narrow conceptions of craft in fiber art, researchers Tarja-Kaarina Laamanen and Pirita Seitamaa-Hakkarainen (2008) classified students' sources of inspiration in textile design with interesting coding categories. The multisensory and conceptual codes they identified in their data describe a range of responses to tactile engagement: *poem, story, artifact, picture, nature, expression, skill, challenge, composition, impression, material, touch, illusion, memory,* and *movement* (p. 110). These words suggest a very rich landscape of evocative and interdisciplinary possibilities. Textile professor

Sara Kadolph (2008) wrote of other connections (or threads) in the use of natural dyes of fiber with aspects of history, science, mathematics, and art I, too, have observed interdisciplinary possibilities in the compositions of Jennifer Marsh's fiber project, from embroideries that mathematically chart gas prices to fabric collages that advocate for animal rights with a focus on the sciences.

CRAFT CROSS-OVER: COMMUNITY AND CULTURE CONNECTIONS

As an artist and teacher, I have worked with all manner of media, but I have always been particularly drawn to older craft materials, such as baskets, ceramics, and fiber. This "soft stuff" has attracted and comforted me, and I realize that my ongoing engagement with craft has also helped me to make sense of deeply personal experiences, including those from my youth. My childhood separation, not only from my father, but also from my parents' families, contributed to my interest in issues of artistic origins and familial histories that wove themselves into the writing, teaching, and making of baskets and pots throughout my life. On a related note, Kathleen Keyes and Melanie Fales (2007) proposed art lessons that investigate personal family histories, pointing out that students can explore connections to traditional arts and crafts and discuss their roles within family and/or community structures (p. 25). Speaking of family craft collections, craft researcher J. Zimmerman (2003) observed "there is a reason beyond their monetary value that we pass heirlooms from one generation to the next" (p. 14). Those objects that we save reveal personal and communal aesthetics, indeed, a sort of familial curatorship. The identification of meanings surrounding these objects make them uniquely suited to contribute to the learning processes of students who are trying on the roles of archaeologist and ethnographer in order to better understand themselves and others.

Arts researchers have also identified diverse benefits of working in craft media across the lifespan and over extended periods of time. For example, Karen Heid (2007), in her study of multiage art learning, noted how important it is for teachers to be aware of the sensory and communal dimensions of learning so that we can measure aesthetic and cognitive development. In this way, craft can develop our sense of what we perceive and how we appreciate, as well as our shifting understandings of the social meanings of preferences and ideas about objects. Craft practices today often involve not only an adherence to traditions, but also a process of personal innovation and cultural (re)construction. We can become aware of the unfolding nuances of history, from memory to imagination and nostalgia, including the interplay of these various values.

It is important to be aware of ways in which craft practices are mediated by community, media, and individual perceptions. Seonaid Robertson (1961) wrote, "crafts are such a fundamentally human activity that they are more basic than any one language, and I have found a bond with craftsmen of all the countries where I have journeyed." (p. 13). While this statement may seem overly essentializing in today's diverse academic atmosphere, it still serves to highlight how craft connectively touches on widespread human needs for aesthetic and practical objects such as artful blankets, rugs, serving vessels, and clothing, as well as beautiful objects of design. On the other hand, considerations of craft education carry with them longstanding sources of tension and contradiction, particularly with regard to the politics of culture and gender.

Researcher of the senses Constance Classen (2005), for example, suggests that historically, "through craftwork women could explore alternatives to the dominant masculine visual aesthetic and at the same time remain safely within the bounds of acceptable feminine practice" (p. 229). F. Graeme Chalmers and Andrea Dancer (2008), in discussing ways art education can neglect male students, examined how some craft materials and techniques can also be gender-coded and noted that some educational activities around woodcrafts have coincided with romanticized notions of Native Americans via activities such as the Boy Scouts. Chalmer and Dancer's reflections on preconceptions of race and gender in craft have indicated some of the tensions that people may encounter if and when they choose to engage (or to not engage) with craft techniques and terminology. For example, I remember questioning my own interest in craft media when a studio professor told me my preference for clay and fiber was "suitable" because it was "soft," like me.

However, these concerns and obstacles take attention away from the profound benefits gained from experience with craft materials, not only in addressing the holistic developmental needs of the individual, but also in connecting the individual with various communities. Clover and Stalker (2008) have observed interesting contradictions between the desire to work individually in quilting, and to collaborate and be a part of a group among adult artists. M. C. Richards (1980) also wrote of collaboration: "to enter into the world of forming, to be co-creator speaks to our sense of creativity, our artistry, and our sense of adventure. We wish to be fully ourselves and at the same time, as a part of a self-realization, to offer and share with others" (p. 77). These nuanced statements coincide with my experiences as a middle school teacher and as a researcher of adult ceramic artists (Weida, 2008). A sense of ambivalence between individual expressive tendencies and collaboration in craft communities contains potential for interpersonal growth and change. Learners of any age can begin to negotiate when they will work communally and when they need to express an individual voice. In questions of collectivity and community, critical notions of ownership, authorship, and meaning also emerge for educational discussion.

Other important questions relevant to the exploration of craft in art education have to do with hierarchical attitudes about the relative status of craft versus art, as was mentioned at the beginning of this chapter. Clover and Stalker have noted self-depreciations among quilters that parallel concerns of ceramic artists in my research (Weida, 2008). These artists observed that their work is sometimes taken less seriously, both because of gender issues and due to attitudes about ceramics as craft versus art form. Another avenue of prejudice against craft is indicative in the often communal, social, and perhaps less serious nature of its creative activities, such as "quilting bees." Educational experiences with craft materials in schools, especially at the high school level and above, may introduce such controversies to students. However, it is important that educators not reinforce negative stereotypes through their curricula.

One way to introduce communal activity would be to provide significant opportunities for expression and creativity with crafts materials. Another is to encourage meaningful collaborations with craft media, while making students aware of other instances where collaboration was essential, whether in art or in craft. In the realm of art, we need only to look to ateliers, or to compare and contrast communities of Marsh's large-scale fiber projects with the huge wrapping projects of the Christos. In terms of straightforward examples of craft or community folk art, the collaborative *AIDS Memorial Quilt* also comes to mind. The cooperative, communal experiences characteristic of many of the crafts provide a socially and politically engaged alternative to the myths of the isolated artist creating in a vacuum and the master artist directing the production of unknown assistants and apprentices.

CONTEMPORARY CRAFT ISSUES IN EDUCATION: CONCLUDING COMMENTS

Within my research here, I discovered a wonderfully mystical sense of phraseology concerning the "craft" of teaching and learning, which often had relevant considerations in terms of the goals of this chapter. A library search of the keyword *craft* reveals myriad publications emphasizing the craft of research, the craft of writing, crafting one's voice, and numerous examples of craftsmanship across many human endeavors. This universality of the quality of craft emphasizes the importance of skill, practice, and personal connection that originates in the craft media but extends to other areas. I sensed a delightful resonance between this work and others, akin to what Richards (1973) called "a hidden or occult resonance in all things" (p. 150).

Another major consideration in addressing craft education is temporal, since tools and techniques alter with emerging technologies. Thus what was once necessary and central for daily life (like making quilts) and a viable means for earning a livelihood (such as production pottery) have been reduced to hobbies (or at best art forms) by the proliferation of mass-produced goods. Nonetheless, the very notions of crafting and craftsmanship retain an aura of timelessness. As I have noted in my recent research (Weida, 2009), emerging digital craft communities not only look forward to celebrate new ways of making, but simultaneously reflect upon traditions, providing spaces for historical inquiry among craftspeople. One area of the past's persistence in the crafts can be located in the renewed relevance of Richards's interest in the environment and deep ecology. Environmentalism is clearly a central topic for crafters and craftspeople today as well, as mentioned with regards to Marsh's International Fiber Collaborative and ecologically concerned artistic responses to abandoned gas stations. Sarah Kadolph (2008) has similarly observed how our contemporary ecology-sensitive culture has revivified interest in lost traditions of utilizing natural dyes in craft.

Another aspect of the enduring values of the crafts can be seen when craft is considered as a framework for human growth. In the words of M. C. Richards (1989), "the experiences of centering... through the crafts, the arts, educated perception—may foster a healing of those inner divisions which set man at war with himself and therefore with others" (p. 61). A poet by training, she further related pottery and education to poetry via metaphor, proposing "we must carry in our soul a picture of creating little by little the vessel of our humanity" (1996, p. 26). Richards also noted that each person may be viewed as a sort of "living vessel" (1989, p. 7). Going deeper, she pointed out the underlying linguistic link between vessels and cells, as the Greek word for cell translates into "hollow vessel" (1973, p. 56). In this way, Richards leads us to envision and embody our visions of craft and wholeness within micro and micro levels.

Ultimately, Richards strongly relates pottery to pedagogy: characterizing her "own style of teaching [as]... based upon the physical foundation of the clay body" (1964, p. 104), and adding educational dimension to the meaning of the vessel of the body and the vessel made of clay. This chapter has served to offer similar connections between wholeness in our teaching and our learning, as we work within the crafts and with a sense of craftsmanship. Through explorations of materials, histories, and philosophies of craft with a holistic perspective, we can begin to engage thoughtfully with our students as evolving craftspeople and develop communities in which creativity can be understood as a richly collaborative experience.

REFERENCES

Adamson, G. (2007). *Thinking through craft*. Oxford, England: Berg.

Burton, J. (2001). Lowenfeld: An(other) look. *Art Education, 54*(6), 33-42.

Burton, J. (2009). Creative intelligence, creative practice: Lowenfeld redux. *Studies in Art Education, 50*(9), 323-337.

Chalmers, F. G., & Dancer, A. A. (2008). Crafts, boys, Ernest Thompson Seton, and the woodcraft movement. *Studies in Art Education, 49*(3), 183-199.

Classen, C. (2005). *The book of touch*. New York, NY: Berg.

Clover, D. E., & Stalker, J. (2008). Feisty fabrics: Women's education, learning and activism through fabric arts in Canada and Aotearoa New Zealand. *Studies in the Education of Adults, 40*(1), 80-95.

Craft in America series. *School Arts (2007-2009)*.

Heid, K. (2007). Seeing feelings through shared art making. *Kappa Delta Pi Record 43*(3), 110-116.

Kadolph, S. (2008). Natural dyes: A Traditional craft experiencing new attention. *The Delta Kappa Gamma Bulletin, 75*(1), pp. 14-17.

Keys, K., & Fales, M. (2007). Traditions told and broken: Stories of family and community. *Art Education, 60*(5), 25-32.

Laamanen, T. K., & Seitamaa-Hakkarainen, P. (2008). Sources of inspiration and mental image in textile design process. *Art, Design and Communication in Higher Education,7*(2), 105-119.

Richards, M. C. (1973). *The crossing point: Selected talks and writings by M. C. Richards*. Middleton, CN: Wesleyan University Press.

Richards, M. C. (1980). *Toward wholeness: Rudolph Steiner education in America*. Hanover, NH: University Press of New England.

Richards, M. C. (1989). *Centering in poetry, pottery, and person*. Middletown, CT: Wesleyan University Press.

Richards, M. C. (1996). *Opening our moral eye: Essays, talks, and poems*. New York, NY: Steinerbooks.

Rissati, H. (2007). *A Theory of craft: Function and aesthetic expression*. Chapel Hill, NC: University of North Carolina Press.

Robertson, S. (1961). *Craft and contemporary culture*. London, England: United National Educational, Scientific, and Cultural Organizations.

Sessions, B. (2000). Marguerite Wildenhain: The Visible core. In P. Bolin, D. Blandy, & K. C. Congdon (Eds.), *Remembering others: Making invisible histories of art education visible* (pp. 11-25). Reston, VA: National Art Education Association.

Weida, C. (2008). Ambivalences of art: Nuance, contradiction, and duality in the words and works of women in contemporary ceramics. (Doctoral Dissertation, Columbia University Teachers College, New York, NY).

Weida, C. (2009). Subversively discursive digital communities of craft. In A. Arnold, E. Delacruz, A. Kuo, & M. Parsons (Eds.), *Globalization: Art & Education* (pp. 111-117). Reston, VA: National Art Education Association.

White, J. H. (2004). 20th century art education: A historical perspective. In E. Eisner & M. D. Day (Eds.), *Handbook of research and policy in art education* (pp. 55-86). New York, NY: Routledge.

Zimmerman, J. (2003). *Made from scratch: Reclaiming the pleasures of the American hearth*. New York, NY: Free Press.

ABOUT THE AUTHOR

Courtney Lee Weida is an Assistant Professor of Art Education at Adelphi University in Garden City, NY. She has taught within studio art and craft programs for pre-K through 12th grade within schools and community programs in Boston and New York. She is licensed in Visual Art, English, and Elementary classroom teaching. She completed her doctorate in Art & Art Education at Columbia University Teachers College. She earned an EdM from Harvard University. Her BA (Northeastern University) included a double major in Visual Art and English Literature. Her dissertation and recent publications address ceramic art, studio craft, and gender issues in art education. As a practicing ceramic artist, she possesses a unique background in English literature and archaeology museum work that has informed her art and research in ceramics and craft. She welcomes dialogue about craft in education.

CHAPTER 16

The Short Order Cook: Emotive Learning Among Two Young Schoolgirls and Their Teacher

Vicky Grube

When I started school, I was as small as the tiniest acorn in the
world, and I needed the tiniest paintbrush—the size of my head.
—Audrey, age 4

This is a qualitative study about the interaction between two 4-year-old girls. As their art teacher and the researcher of this study, I am faced with a crisis of representation. As a teacher, I support the relationships between the girls and inspire learning. As researcher, I am shaping and assembling a story. Often, these roles become blurred. In both positions I am firmly in the text, my concerns are the voice of the piece. Both of my roles are affected by a heightened self-consciousness. Olive, Audrey, and I share much. We all experience emotive ways of knowing, which are linked to memory, perception, intersubjectivity and the imagination of desire. The action takes place in the art room, an environment that invites cultural mediation and polysemic learning.

Audrey and Olive wave the tiny plush animals above their heads. Olive's animals seem to be washcloths with neckties. Her fist-sized bunny and dog wear pajama print material that matches what's lining their ears. The bunny sports a bow tie made of a red shoelace. Audrey's bear, the size of a sock ball, is unclothed with only his fuzz covering his polyfoam torso. This fuzz is matted around his eyes, reading as ferocious. The girls seem delighted and surprised to both have their stuffed animals at preschool today. As chummy mothers exit the preschool, arm in arm, waving goodbye, the girls giggle and skip into the art room, cheering at my suggestion to paint portraits of their plush toys.

Like a short order cook, I'm called on to serve the 4-year old painters. Olive asks for beige paint to be mixed, and Audrey needs brushes. Within minutes, the girls have their animals' silhouettes outlined on the large easel paper. The portraits are rich in detail. Olive paints and remarks, " I know there are little baby bottles on the pajamas. I just made little black flicks so it would be easier to draw." Olive knows to use the tip of her paintbrush with only a light soaking of paint to create the delicate marks of the fabric. Bunny's sidekick, Doggie, does not fare so well, watery white paint weeping down the paper (Figure 1). Olive becomes frustrated, so Audrey and I suggest reasonable explanations for the drippy snout: the dog has tremors and is crying or shaking while the portrait is painted. "No, no, no!" says Olive. I see her irritation with the drippy canine as her eyebrows gather. None of the narrative solutions satisfy. Olive sighs, "I like it this way."

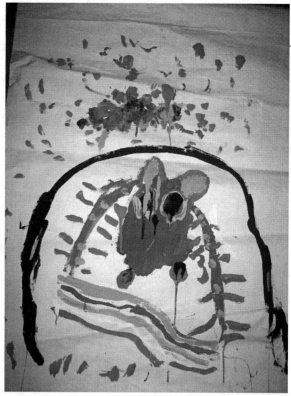

FIGURE 1. (left) Olive's Bunny and Doggie.

FIGURE 2. (right) Audrey's Bear.

A lot is happening in this small corner. The runny paint sabotages Olive's desire for a lucid portrait. The oozy snout buffaloes her, and Olive comes up with no satisfactory solutions. Her emotional connection with the doggie reminds me that feeling lodges in the visual symbol (Langer, 1953). A logjam of drooling paint leaves Olive disappointed despite Audrey's narrative explanations. Olive resigns herself to the drips. I suppose if Olive did not have so much faith in the paint, she would not expect clarity and feel less disgruntled. Yet she knows paint as an apt tool and is annoyed. Perhaps this symbol cannot be her doggie if he is oozing down the page?

I stand immobile watching the little girls use inexpensive horsehair brushes swollen with paint to describe their world. I am not the boss of the art room but a bowled over art teacher. Olive and Audrey are faced with a series of self-imposed challenges with no guidebook, clumsy materials, and a teacher who learns as she goes along. For 10 years, I have watched very young children use art materials as a fulcrum to teeter-totter with their peers. Appropriating images and techniques that their friends have used seems a common kind of copying in the art room. This is an active business; paint, glue and paper can expand, fly high, and release meaning. Not only does art provide the possibility for the self to express and uncover feeling, but once the image is out in the world, this form can be transformed into other's meanings.

I am debating whether to offer Olive a paper towel to catch the streaks when Audrey notices her own easel paint dripping. The bear's pink ear bleeds down a forehead almost obscuring the eye. Audrey's solution is to touch up the drips by painting over them with the underneath color. Curbing the streaming paint the best she can, Audrey pushes forward and draws ears and their lining, eyes, irises, toes and their nails (Figure 2). Bear drools like a teething toddler but Audrey, unlike Olive, shrugs it off.

The process of Audrey's artmaking, using a gooey liquid to depict a three-dimensional object on a piece of paper, forces the artist to make decisions. What do I put in and what do I leave out? Shall I use all the paints or just two? How do I paint clothes? Questions such as these, posed by challenges met in the art room, invite interaction, collaboration and the borrowing of images and techniques. Audrey observes her peers in this environment and is provoked, stimulated by the work of others. The array of possibilities suggests to her: "This is an idea I might try." The decisions, whether self determined or linked to the possibilities of another, are riddled with emotion in an activity like finding-your-way-while-uncovering-what-you-want. "Emotions are essential elements of human intelligence, rather than just supports or props for intelligence... deepening and refining our grasp of ourselves as beings" (Nussbaum, 2001, p. 3).

WHEN I WAS NINE

Cindy is looping the lace around the bow on her second shoelace. From down the hallway I hear Cindy's mother, "Damn Vicky and her grandmother's big fancy car! She thinks she is something! I am sick of that whole family!" I am 9 years old standing in the center of Cindy's bedroom, 20 minutes before the morning school bell. Picturing Cindy's mother whipping knives over head, I dash into Cindy's closet, yank the door closed, and hold my breath. My heart starts to burn. There's the whine of the bedroom door, then the bounce off the door jam. Cindy's mother slurs, "You'd better hurry. That girl Vicky will be here soon to pick you up. That girl with her richy rich grandmother." From inside the closet, the door slats blink blue and black, flickers of the figure in the familiar stained bathrobe and shoulder length oily hair weaving in the center of the bedroom. There too is the thick smell of a cigarette. Cindy's mother is an alcoholic and I know her as a ghoulish form that lurches down the hallway, never without soiled bathrobe and yellow gray smoke. "Let's meet tonight after it's dark to see if we can watch my mom hiding her liquor down in the basement" was Cindy's plan last night.

Every morning I stop by Cindy's house and we walk to school together. I often wait, watching Cindy pull on her white bobby socks and tie her tennis shoes. I don't know why I am mesmerized by Cindy's sock and shoe routine. It seems fascinating to me. I notice her socks are different than mine, softer and easier to slide on. It won't be long till Cindy's mother leaves the room and even this life. When Cindy is 12 her mother dies, and Cindy moves to Alabama to live with her grandmother. I am devastated and lonely. But until then, we have our friendship.

Cindy and I had a history that extended from her house to the neighborhood and to the school. The school was there to educate us and recognize our reading scores, our textbook fees and our attendance. We walked into school still radiating energies from wracked out, defeated parents. Our emotional lives were tangled in our learning, but the whole child, with emotional, spiritual qualities was never acknowledged. In school we were expected to control our emotions, which were roadblocks to learning. Traditional education saw emotions as "adversarial to reasoning of any sort" (Nussbaum, 2004, p. 185) and, except for the morning Pledge of Allegiance or weekly music class, within the school walls, emotions were suspended until after school.

AND NOW ON MY PORCH

I am outside sitting on my front porch feeling the soothing warm wrap of an evening wind. Any day the sun will turn to the fall solstice. The garden is drying out. The afternoon winds are slapping the pages of Dewey's book, *Art as Experience* (1934), fluttering the book leaves like a revolving door. The days are slowing down. Even the slugs that banquet on my hostas are becoming less rambunctious. A once yellow chrysanthemum has thrown in the towel, looking drained and exhausted. In a fit of energy, I yank the dead thing out of the soil, flinging it deep into the woods and leaving behind a dark cool socket.

Standing in the overgrowth of nettles, ferns, jewel weed and thorns, I gaze into the brush. I think of the friendship between the girls, the affective ways of knowing. I am curious about how much Audrey and Olive's feelings are connected with their painting. Dewey wrote, "emotion acts like a magnet drawing to itself appropriate material... it is selective of material and directive of its order and arrangement "(Dewey, 1934, p. 69). Dewey embraced the theory that in artmaking there can never be too much emotion, concluding, "the more intense the emotion, the more effective the "expression" (p. 69).

While painting, Olive expresses not actual feeling but ideas of feeling much like dialogue, language. Words similarly do not express "actual feeling, but ideas of them" (Langer, 1953, p. 59). The luminous sun in the corner resembles Olive's handprint, a golden palm with fingers outstretched, a stamp of her spirit. What is the relationship between back-flipping emotion and the serious business of cognitive thought? Does the elimination of one leave us with only partial knowledge? Isn't emotion tied to perception, a barometer of how life is working out? (Prinz, 2004)

EASEL AS EDGE

I remember watching Olive at the easel. She is careful to look at her toys before painting. She observes their shapes, colors, and textures. She adds a swing set and sky. As she shapes a narrative with images, Olive's activity seems bound to memory—the momentary glance away from the subject as the artist faces the paper, the image that emerges from the unconscious, or the metaphor that reminds one of the past. She conjures up a blue sky and a double swing set, painting true to the best of her knowledge, alluding to what was but is no longer. How reliable is her memory? Isn't memory partial, and with the glance away, the mind forgets? How does a swing set balance on the grass? Olive desires clarity, so she must visualize what she cannot remember. It's the imagination of desire that fills in the blanks. Imagination of desire, wish fulfillment, or *feelings of what one wants to believe* that are tied to memory.

The work at the easels has become a combination frontier and rumpus room for the girls. They are physical and risky. They are silent and forthcoming. They speak in non sequiturs, listen like modernists, and are companions for one another. To her swing set story Olive adds a picnic table loaded with dog biscuits and carrots. Her images are a language of self, which holds in its freedom an elasticity to imagine that a dog can sit on a swing and a bunny can wear pajamas. Olive narrates while she paints. Her images spring from direct observation, tied to brief memory—the looking at, then looking away and remembering what was just observed, and merging with more distant memories from the unconscious.

A paint brush saluting from each jar, a large sheet of white paper clipped to a sturdy broad easel, four large easels clustered near a child-sized sink, the painters relive past experiences and are in this moment constructing more. All their forms are metaphors for experience and are vessels of feelings (Dewey, 1934). In brief, their experiences are internalized, and from this emotional state, they create external metaphors of their memories.

The image becomes more than a stand-in for that moment but an acute mark of the past in dialogue with the present. The children paint from memory, but the image emerges in the present, which is situational, incomplete and interpretive. Through art the girls remember their past, turn life into language, and reveal to themselves the truth of their experiences (Ellis, 2004, p. 117).

By snack time, Olive's painting is pinned to the wooden drying rack. It still has the glistening sheen of wet tempera. A sun beams down from the upper right hand corner, illuminating the two friends, bunny and dog. This is a happy scene, and an informative one. How Olive uses materials to portray the picnic table, where it fits in her composition and even the decision to include a table, tells the viewer something about Olive. One might glean that Olive has a picnic table at home, it is outside, it can hold food, and has been part of a cheery occasion. In short, Olive has formed perceptions about art materials, her subject matter, and the activity of artmaking, all of which can be seen in her choices at the easel. Olive's perception of the bunny's pajama color affects her decision to use a pinkish orange color to paint her toy's likeness and her brush dabs represent her perception of the print. These perceptions are, themselves, based on past experiences or memories that are recalled in large part because they are charged with feelings. While Olive may not be conscious of her emotions, they are her Cyrano.

Audrey's painting is clipped to the easel and seems to be built from her own images but also those of Olive's. She has borrowed Olive's idea of a grassy yard and picnic table. Audrey must have peered around her easel or overheard Olive's question, "What is the color of dog biscuit?" Is Audrey just copying a good idea or is there something more going on? Perhaps Olive's picnic table triggered a memory in Audrey? Or maybe Audrey's appropriation is broader? If perceptions are influenced by emotions, the image borrowing could be influenced by Audrey's perception of Olive. Olive is important for what she means to Audrey's life. Audrey appropriates Olive's images because Audrey values what Olive means to her, as an important role in her life (Nussbaum, 2004).

There are plenty of physical signs of this emotional bond. Olive and Audrey often touch each other, they lean in when they talk, their toys are always having conversations, they share language like nicknames for things (the sink in the art room is dubbed "the pink sink"). At the easels, images are shared. For Audrey, Olive's picnic table is a pure symbol of Olive, an "intentional object" (Bilimoria, 2004, p. 217; Nussbaum, 2001, p. 27), a point of view or a constructed reality that embodies a feeling that Audrey holds for Olive. Like the griever coming across the deceased's hand-scribbled note, the object has emotional significance acting as a stand-in for the Other. The grieving find value in this physical artifact as a reminder of the Other's essence. So too the appropriated visual metaphor stands for the feelings of a friend.

ARTIFACT OF MY FATHER

Last week I opened the cover of a book I had brought back from my parent's house. I was there for my father's funeral and at one moment found myself in his small den. I guess I wanted to be with him a little longer and, in this cramped, book-lined room, I could smell and see him all over the place. While soaking him up, I spied a book I had given my father 2 years before. Always curious about the book, I knew he would no longer miss it, and who would I ask anyway? I packed the book in my suitcase. The other day, I rediscovered the book where I had taken it out of my bag. Nestled near the inside flap lay a public library bookmark with Vin Grube written in a shaky script across the top. I was flooded with emotion and felt great sadness, an ache I have come to know well, leaving my body bruised from the inside out.

There in that handwritten name I saw my father's presence, I realized how old he had become, how sweet and slow his life must have grown to be. His essence for me was there in that blue unsteady line. That bookmark meant everything and was my link to his most recent life.

There was a week that Olive and Audrey experimented with printmaking techniques. Olive first painted stripes onto a Styrofoam donut and pressed the plastic pastry onto her paper. Audrey, herself, preoccupied with making something look like it was in front of something, worked on a winter landscape with skier, four small cabins, four fir trees and a snowman. She struggled to place the cabins behind the snowy horizon. In the small corner in the busy art room, I pointed out "something is always in front of something," and illustrated how Olive is standing in front of an easel, and the chair is in front of Olive. Audrey growled like a dog, "Hey, the paper is in front of the easel!" Across the room, a child shouted for help with the typewriter drum; I left Audrey and Olive to untangle a tiny plastic sheep from the type bars.

Audrey abandoned her landscape to watch Olive make rainbow donuts using a Styrofoam ring. Enamored with Olive and the technique, Audrey appropriated the Styrofoam printing method and covered her own paper with multicolored circles.

"Are you painting your fingers?" Audrey began, hopping back and forth.

"And palms!" shouted Olive, " I'm painting my whole hand, painty, painty, painty." With fingers and palms coated with thick tempera and flattened onto the paper, their bodies became stamps.

Best friends together at the easels, Audrey and Olive create paintings that exhibit solidarity through the mutual appreciation of materials and the scaffolding of techniques. While I realize that what has meaning for one might not have the same meaning for another, Olive and Audrey have a common language that affects an intersubjectivity, or mutual knowing. They come to know themselves by knowing the other (Behar, 1996; Denzin, 1997).

Feelings run rampant throughout the preschool. You can hear it in the children's voices before you can see it. A child worries, "I thought it was in my pocket;" "Oh, no, its broken;" "This is my last one." While feelings apparently don't accomplish anything, they motivate us. When wondering, "How can Audrey with her own feelings born from her own history enter the life of Olive's painting?" I imagine the body like a specter, ghostlike, moving through the artwork of another. To me the capability of art to allow another to join in is like the sharing of the imagination or the partnership of desire, "the very essence of intersubjectivity" (Percy, 1954, p. 525).

Martin Buber described intersubjectivity as "imagining the real" (Buber, 1992, p. 75). Intuiting, according to Buber (1992), is an intimate dwelling place where one's spirit flutters within the life of another. In an "intersubjective experience," phenomena either *have, could have,* or *lack* intersubjective validity (Russell, 2006). In other words, truth learned on our own falls short. Others have the potential to affirm our experience. Like a centrifuge, we separate the likelihood of mutual truth, and as sediments range from heaviest to lightest we assess an echelon of possible meaning with others. Husserl dubbed the layered debris "appresentational stratum" (1963, p. 125).

Intersubjectivity does not jeopardize each child's authenticity. The self is the starting point. Entering into a shared experience, children hold to their idiosyncratic natures even though they become enamored with another. Through intersubjective activity, each discovers openness to life, more choices, more ways of being. There is an emotional need to have the Other. Emotions are the harbinger "of neediness and lack of self- sufficiency" (Nussbaum, 2004, p. 185). We perceive that we need another to know ourselves (Husserl, 1936/1970, 1929/1969). It is feeling entwined with belief, thought or perception. The emotions are about something. I ask Olive and Audrey to tell me about their portraits of the stuffed animals. Olive tells me, "I got them (her animals) in Germany. I was born in Germany. But I was actually born in Stuttgart. I keep them in a basket. I keep all my stuffed animals in a basket. They are just swinging on their swings. They are friends." And then, thinking more, "They are sisters."

When I ask Audrey how many stuffed animals she has at home, she answers, "A gazillion."

"What about your mouse, Audrey, where did she come from?" Audrey's voice drops two octaves, growls like an animated demon or a longtime football coach, "This is a bear, not a mouse!" She kisses bear's portrait smack center, and har-de-har-hars.

And what of my emotion? In this school for young children I inhale the breath of the children and exhale what they undergo through my own spongy epithelium. I wonder if what I notice is real or a delusion frayed by my own emotional memory? Derrida (1972) believes we are never awake to others except after the processional has passed. Besides, I am surveying a cultural group that left me in the dust years ago. This population carries toys in their pockets and are intrigued by cellophane tape. They learn ten times as fast as I do and are much more limber. When I ask 4-year-olds to interpret their actions, I scribble down their observations but have to ask again and again what they said. It's like I am deaf. I ask the room, "Do you always paint what you like or what is good? Have you ever painted anything that is very, very scary to you?? I mean really scary. Mean even?" There is stunned silence, minus the tinkley sound of little brushes stirring in small glass jars. Am I ever present, even to myself?

"I would be really good at painting butterflies because I am good at symmetrical."

Audrey leans over the "pink sink," passing the wet bar of soap back and forth between her hands. "Sometimes I have dreams about what to draw. Like a fountain maybe. Sometimes I follow through with my plan but sometimes I forget. Sometimes I see it in my head and I action it in my brain. Sometimes I don't see it. But sometimes I'm too afraid because I see it and I say, 'This is not going to work, but I just have to try it. It looks easy but I know it's not.'" She puts the soap on the counter. "My friend Riley had a picture of a beautiful girl and I thought of a mermaid."

In my notes, photographs, sketches and stories, the life of feeling as tied to memory, perception, intersubjectivity, and imagination of desire seems present in this art room, a space where children express themselves in other ways besides oral and written language. This polysemic learning recognizes emotive ways of knowing and is not hurried work. Learning here is sensuous and embodied. Through memory, perception, intersubjectivity, and imagination of desire, children create an emotive illusion to the unpresentable. This is the integration of the mind, body, and spirit. In a year or two they will begin public school.

Public schools must gain respect for the whole person. To ask children to uncouple from the darkness of a summer night, to never throw a hat up into the air, to forget about ballooning all out of proportion, or to watch the wrong thing is the main problem. Classrooms lined with laminated portraits, television sets mounted in the corner twelve inches from the ceiling, rules taped to the wall by doors with no windows strains the idea of a "socially constructed lived experience" (Kincheloe & McLaren, 2000, p. 280). All kinds of feelings, life histories, running through yards past your time to be home, are what happens here on earth. It is how we make sense.

REFERENCES

Bilimoria, P. (2004). Perturbations of desire: Emotions disarming morality in the "great song" of the Mahabharata. In R. Solomon (Ed.), *Thinking about feeling* (pp. 214-230). Oxford, UK: Oxford University Press.

Behar, R. (1996). *The vulnerable observer*. Boston, MA: Beacon Press/Collins Publishers.

Buber, M. (1992). *On intersubjectivity and cultural creativity*. Chicago, IL: University of Chicago Press.

Denzin, N. (1997). *Interpretive ethnography*. Thousand Oaks, CA: Sage Publications.

Derrida, J. (1972). Structure, sign, and play in the discourse of human sciences. In R. Macksey & E. Donato (Eds.), *The structuralist controversy: The languages of criticism and the sciences of man* (pp. 247-265). Baltimore, MD: Johns Hopkins University Press.

Dewey, J. (1934). *Art as experience*. New York, NY: Paragon Books.

Ellis, C. (2004). *The ethnographic I*. Walnut Creek, CA: AltaMira Press.

Husserl, E. (1963). Cartesianische mediationen. In S. Strasser (Ed.), *Husserliana I* (2nd ed.) (pp. 89-148). The Hague, The Netherlands: Martinus Jijhoff.

Husserl, E. (1970). The crisis of European sciences and transcendental phenomenology (D. Cairins, Trans.) Evanston, IL: Northwestern University Press. (Original work published 1936)

Husserl, E. (1969). Formal and transcendental logic. The Hague, The Netherlands: Martinus Nijhoff. (Original work published 1929)

Kincheloe, J. & McLaren, P. (2000). Rethinking critical theory and qualitative research. In N. K. Denzin & Y. S. Lincoln (Eds.), *Handbook of qualitative research* (pp. 279-324). Thousand Oaks, CA: Sage Publications.

Langer, S. (1953). *Feeling and form*. New York, NY: Charles Scribner's Sons.

Nussbaum, M. (2001). *Upheavals of thought*. Cambridge, England: Press Syndicate of the University of Cambridge.

Nussbaum, M. (2004). Emotions as judgments of value and importance. In R. Solomon (Ed.), *Thinking about feeling* (pp. 183-200). Oxford, England: Oxford University Press.

Percy, W. (1954). *The message in the bottle: How queer man is, how queer language is, and what one has to do with the other*. New York, NY: Farrar, Strauss and Giroux.

Prinz, J. (2004). Embodied emotions. In R. Solomon (Ed.), *Thinking about feeling* (pp. 44-58). Oxford, England: Oxford University Press.

Russell, M. (2006). *Husserl: a guide for the perplexed*. New York, NY: Continuum International Publishing Group.

ABOUT THE AUTHOR

Vicky Grube is an associate professor in art education at Appalachian State University. She has two National Endowment for the Arts grants for her painting as well as a Master of Fine Arts degree in Theater Arts. Her artmaking involves performance, painting, and building a tiny house inside her house that surrounds characters inspired by Paul Klee's puppets. These inhabitants were filmed and voices dubbed from an old recording of her grandparents. She has published a graphic narrative about the death of her father using ink and brush to render memory. She is keenly interested in the authentic artmaking of children, organizing art programs in North Carolina for children modeled on Room 13 in Scotland.

CHAPTER 17

Teaching for Artistic Behavior: Holistic Practice

Diane B. Jaquith

The complex, rich lives of children are discernible through their curiosity and knowledge, experience and skills, beliefs and awareness, fears and resilience, imagination and dreams, compassion and hopes. Such qualities, arising in predictable or surprising combinations, are revealed to attentive teachers who provide guidance for children's growth. Childhood forms the foundation for understandings, inclinations, and passions that carry into adulthood. When art education is holistic in practice, it can address unique aspects of the whole child *and* meet universal standards for teaching and learning. These apparent opposites are not, in fact, mutually exclusive.

Holistic curriculum is inclusive curriculum: diversity in ability, learning style, culture, and disposition are all taken into consideration in the planning stages of instruction. Differentiation opens paths for cognitive growth and inquiry and promotes relevant connections; this is what Miller (2007b) called "whole teaching." Whole teaching also would insist that the physical, emotional, intellectual, and spiritual dimensions of children all merit a place in the visual art curriculum. Holistic in practice, Teaching for Artistic Behavior pedagogy recognizes the whole child and supports young artists as they choose ideas and media for artmaking. Learners engage in meaningful work, examine relationships, and construct deep understandings while intrinsically motivated by topics of personal relevance.

In this chapter, I will explain the philosophy and principles of Teaching for Artistic Behavior, distinguishing it as a foundation for choice-based art education. This pedagogy is framed in a carefully designed structure that promotes creative thinking through self-directed learning. Choice-based art education affirms the whole child by challenging students to look within, choosing content and media that have personal relevancy. Although choice-based art education shares a focus on child-centered learning with "laissez faire" programs of the last century, it differs because the teacher assumes a highly active role to plan, instruct, assess, and reflect on student learning. As I will demonstrate below, this is a challenging but profoundly rewarding approach to art education for the teacher as well as the student.

Children turn to significant relationships in their lives for inspiration in their self-directed artmaking. Inspired by topics of interest and curiosity, classroom curricula, or inviting art materials, young artists draw from internal resources to create, question, and communicate. The child's inner self embodies multiple dimensions: physical, emotional, intellectual and spiritual. These evolving systems, shaped by innate as well as external factors and conditions, integrate in unique patterns that are accessed experientially during the stages of artistic process. According to Nokes (2005), the child's inner self, or "egosystem" is shaped by "exosystems" including nature, the built environment, objects, technology, the earth, the universe, and social forces. These powerful external influences are frequently featured in self-directed artwork, while the internal reserve provides ample resources for making connections, developing relationships, and constructing understandings. Classroom teachers, despite sincere efforts, often feel the pinch of frustration as they struggle to balance academic and logistical demands with the real needs of their students. Rigorous curricula, large class size, and too-tight schedules diminish the teacher's ability to acknowledge the whole child. Writing in 1984, Neal had noted missed opportunities to enhance learning through skills developed outside of school, and stated that "Children are robbed of the wonderful journeyman's bag of tools that has served them so well in creating and revising their own theories about the world" (p. 309). A quarter century later, opportunities to work with hands and hearts have diminished even more in schools bound up by standardized testing and similar constraints. Art class is the one place left in many such schools where the child's "bag of tools" still sparks imagination, gives rise to intuition, elicits compassion, and ignites initiative.

Art class is also one place where the holistic learning environment summons the inner child's spirit to relate and respond to the world through ideation, exploration, collaboration, and creation. Sesto (2009) described this inner spirit in terms of children's natural creativity:

> Without instruction, children naturally move to music before learning the waltz, they move their fingers through paint before learning how to draw a house, and so often burst spontaneously into song without knowing the words. This is a reflection of the creative heart we all carry within us. (p. 13)

Innate though such children's creativity certainly is, all too often it withers as children find themselves forced to conform to schooling. Creativity requires sensitive and stimulating teaching, even in arts classrooms, if it is to develop beyond the early elementary years. Classrooms that cultivate creativity and nourish the inner spirit may differ in superficial ways, but at their core, they share a set of common values:

- Respect for the child's point of view
- Authenticity in art experiences
- Differentiation for ability, learning style, and personal interests
- Flexibility with time, space, and resources

These values are at the heart of a holistic art program that prioritizes creative thinking. In choice-based art programs, curiosity, zeal, wonder, and play ignite imaginations and propel self-directed learning. These authentic problem-finding and solving experiences stimulate divergent thinking, innovation, and reflection to deepen awareness about one's life in relation to the world.

A HOLISTIC LEARNING ENVIRONMENT

The following anecdote illustrates how one child in a structured, yet open, classroom like those described above moved gradually from the safety of familiar choices to risk-taking. Mikayla was new to her school in 1st grade, joining children who had already completed 1 year in a choice-based art program. She glanced anxiously about the room, casting her eyes toward each of the various studio centers. When it came time to make a choice about the day's work, a classmate led Mikayla to the drawing studio center, set up with drawing materials and references. Mikayla's first drawings were filled with schematic representations. Her teacher recognized that she had limited drawing experience and enthusiastically praised her efforts. Dubious, Mikayla persisted with her work and returned to the drawing studio center the following week. While building confidence, Mikayla continued to shadow one classmate, first to the clay studio and much later, to the painting studio. After weeks of experimentation with color mixing, brushstrokes, and techniques, Mikayla felt comfortable in the painting studio long after her classmate had moved on to other art activities. As an older student, Mikayla

FIGURE 1. A painter states: "This is a house filled with people inside. I chose pink for the house because it's kind of beautiful. The trees are tall and bushy. There are two green birds flying into each tree."

learned to embrace new media, but she returned occasionally to the painting studio center. Her cheerful songs, sung in a low voice, resonated with contentment while she painted pictures of houses, her favorite motif to express the warmth and security of home (Figure 1).

Choice-based pedagogy, as exemplified by Mikayla's experience, establishes a vibrant artistic learning community based on the principles of teaching for artistic behavior. The core belief is in the child as the artist who self-directs his or her work and develops a unique repertoire of artistic behaviors (Douglas & Jaquith, 2009). Each class begins with a focused lesson or demonstration and then children decide whether or not to incorporate the information into their day's work. Time, space, and resources are carefully arranged in studio centers to promote inquiry through artmaking experiences. Learning is facilitated through whole-group, small-group, and one-on-one instruction, as well as peer coaching. Consistency in the learning environment enables children either to arrive with a plan or to work intuitively through problem finding and solving in art class.

Choice-based classrooms encompass both physical and emotional spaces that invite imagination and intuition. According to Palmer (1993), the ideal holistic learning environment supports three requisite criteria, "openness, boundaries, and an air of hospitality" (p. 71). The reference to boundaries may seem out of place, even antithetical to choice. Yet, stable structures like predictable routines and accessible resources are necessary to help establish clear understandings about parameters for self-directed activities and behavior. For example, when kinesthetic learners who perceive through movement know that they are not confined to an assigned seat; they choose a working style that comfortably fits their needs. Children will take risks in the public arena of the classroom if they feel safe and trust that they will not face criticism or ridicule by their peers or teachers. A 5th-grade boy in the following example explained how he made media choices based on his own strengths and weaknesses:

> I like to come to the 3D Sculpture Center because this is what I am good at—challenging myself. I am not as graceful as most kids. Here you don't have to be graceful; you just have to have good ideas.

This student has internalized beliefs about visual art—that it serves multiple purposes to the maker and can be both elegant and innovative. Authentic artmaking thrives when the learning environment meets the diverse needs of students. The whole child is present when learners respond with visual language to feelings and beliefs central to their existence.

TRUST AND AUTONOMY

Along with stable structures and routines, trust between teachers and students is essential to support student-directed learning. In a climate of trust, students are granted autonomy to make critical decisions about their work and learn to pursue their ideas with purposeful attention. Similarly, research by Amabile (1996) demonstrated positive connections between autonomy and intrinsic motivation, leading to high levels of student engagement. In sum, autonomy in classroom activities increases engagement because students feel entrusted to make choices about their learning and safe to take risks with new media and content.

Opportunities for autonomous learning grounded in trust are important for all children. It is especially necessary for those who struggle in school but find solace in art class, where verbal skills are not a prerequisite for success. Equally, for those who experience stressful family situations, or who suffer the loss of a beloved grandparent or cherished pet, trust lessens feelings of vulnerability in the school setting. Considering the needs of such children, it is helpful to consider the way Wuthnow (2001) described the holistic and spiritual healing powers inherent in the arts by citing their capacity to cultivate both creativity and a sense of inner connectedness:

> Creativity requires drawing connections among aspects of artists' experience that have previously remained separate. Ideas about spiritual connectedness and spiritual wholeness acquire special meaning in these contexts. Indeed, one of the important contributions of artists in any period is creating narratives and images of wholeness in the face of undeniable brokenness. (p. 9)

In a stable learning environment where trust is highly valued, the broken child has the chance to become whole through self-directed artmaking. Opening up to emotions in a safe situation provides comfort for those who experience loss, loneliness, or diminished health. Empathetic classmates often respond with kindness to soothe life's hurts and trauma. Gifts of artwork (Figure 2) are acts of empathy or adoration, presented with compassion to a friend, family member, or teacher. When the healing process can be integrated into the art program, not as an isolated activity but as core, students access and respond to their emotional states through artmaking.

Situations like those described here may seem more akin to art therapy sessions than to typical art classrooms; yet choice-based art education is, in many ways, far more "authentic" than much of what has passed for school art in recent years. London (1992) denounced formalist art education and argued instead for transformative practices that activate "multi-dimensional mindfulness" (p. 13). One such pedagogy, Teaching for Artistic Behavior, models its principles on the habits of established artists. Consider that adult artists follow a direction until they are satisfied that every angle has been exhausted; serious young artists may feel compelled to do the same, especially if they have autonomy to direct their work. In kindergarten, a student formed her self-portrait out of clay and continues this practice each

FIGURE 2. (left) This girl attaches wings to a clay angel that will function as a bell, a gift for a family member.

FIGURE 3. (right) A student reflects on her clay self-portraits, which she is arranging for an art exhibit.

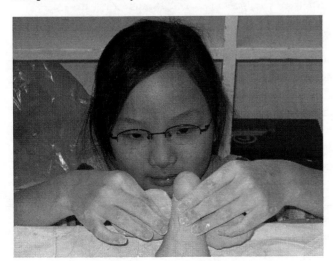

year without prompts or reminders. Her family keeps her portraits on display and she relates them to her artistic growth each year (Figure 3).

Establishing a line of inquiry provides learners with a compass; along the way they engage, examine relationships, construct knowledge, and refine understandings through reflection and self-evaluation. Speaking of this call to persevere, Szekely (1988) observed:

> Making art is a continuing process, with the artist seeking to develop ideas from one work to the next. Ending a work of art is thus only a temporary break, a time for reflection that inspires further ideas and further works. Artists assess what they have accomplished; they review their journey, so to speak. (p. 126)

Autonomous learning allows concepts to spiral, incubate, and return later with new insights. Recurrent themes connect artists with their past and future, affirming long-standing relationships.

COMMUNITIES OF LEARNERS

No amount of autonomy, as previously discussed, can propel learning in isolation. Instead, as Vygotsky (1978) demonstrated, learning becomes internalized after interactions with peers and teachers; in other words, independent thought develops through collaborative efforts. Choice-based art education, therefore, supports students at different developmental levels as they work side-by-side in communal studio centers. When students arrive, the art classroom transforms into a community; learners interact at studio centers through play, negotiation, collaboration, and informal sharing of inquiries. Differentiation in choice of media, content, pacing, and working style provides learners with flexibility to self-direct their work. Students examine relationships from within and make connections to the external world. Relationships like these are central aspects of holistic education, as described by Miller (2007a):

> The focus of holistic education is on relationships: the relationship between linear thinking and intuition, the relationship between mind and body, the relationships among various domains of knowledge, the relationship between the individual and community, the relationship to the earth, and our relationship with our souls. (p. 89)

Holistic learning communities respond to students' physical, emotional, intellectual, and spiritual dimensions by facilitating open-ended learning opportunities to examine relationships. Addressing this topic, Stout (1999) observed that education builds awareness of the "interdependence between self and other" (p. 33) and Palmer (1993) spoke of "rounder ways of knowing" (p. xxiv).

Yet learning to make connections does not happen on its own. It must be creatively facilitated through instructional strategies, such as activating knowledge or modeling problem solving, to encourage transfer (Perkins & Salomon, 1988). It also depends on qualities of character established as part of the classroom culture. In the choice-based learning environment described in this chapter where ideas, beliefs, and meanings are freely shared, community values of respect and cooperation are essential. The open system supports multiple relationships, including

- *Collaborative:* A drawing cohort self-selects to meet for weekly discussions on developing techniques and style.
- *Student as Teacher:* A technology enthusiast instructs his teacher about digital images.
- *Cross-curricular:* Several boys design an intricate marble maze, synthesizing a 4th-grade science lesson on ramps.
- *School Leadership:* 5th graders assume leadership for the all-school art exhibit through planning, promotion, and set-up for the exhibition.

- *Home/School:* Families collect and deliver recycled objects to be used for constructions and inventions.
- *Cultural:* A new 1st-grade ELL student from Japan teaches origami to her classmates.
- *Ecology:* Older students collaborate on animation movies to teach younger students about the environment.

These relationships, nurtured through shared interests, may or may not extend beyond the artistic learning community. Students seek peer coaches for advice based on the peer's expertise as described by Holt (1972): "What is speaking here is not the authority of age, but the authority of greater experience and understanding, which does not necessarily have anything to do with age" (p. 47). Adults are also learners in this holistic setting, observing innovative techniques with art materials and novel ideas presented by students. Role reversals are common as students educate their teachers about their passions, such as the life cycle of butterflies or the subtle differences between catapults and trebuchets. Teachers become acquainted with the whole child as meanings emerge in student work. In one case, flowers feature prominently in many artworks by Gina, whose painting titled "My Masterpiece," appears in Figure 4. She reflected:

FIGURE 4. An acrylic painting of a flower represents "a whole story on one small canvas."

> This isn't just a flower—it's a bunch of ideas in a flower. At first, I thought of a flower that wasn't very interesting. It reminded me of a sun so I tried to make the flower like a sun. I got other ideas from the girls working at the painting center. I added green leaves to show that the flower is happy. My painting reminds me of things that I would not expect to see. It is a whole story on one small canvas.

Gina looks inward and her spirit is renewed through her artmaking; she looks outward and finds support among her peer community. This exemplifies a need for heightened awareness by educators, as London (1992) advocated: "Art is, and Art Education could become, a powerful instrument through which we may and primal people have always, transformed the quality of their lives, from inherited states of being to preferred states" (p. 9). The positive impact of artmaking on Gina's well-being exemplifies the potential for holistic art education to sustain the whole child through trust, respect and cooperation. Without trust between teachers, students, families, and administrators, there is no community and without a sense of community, education cannot be whole.

HOLISTIC TEACHING AND LEARNING

Teachers who empower children to self-direct their learning must find ways to balance instruction with measured restraint because independence is the goal of learner-directed pedagogy. Teachers who relinquish control and entrust students with important decisions are not abandoning their responsibilities. Just the opposite! They assume the challenging task of facilitating students' discovery of meaning by providing them with authentic art experiences while serving as a guide and mentor (Jaquith, 2011). Giving up control means not knowing what the outcome will be, allowing surprises, and even failures to happen, but turning them into learning experiences. For example, unexpected outcomes from self-directed learning can encourage students to embrace ambiguity in their work, as described by Szekely (1988): "Each artwork is a culmination or summary of the numerous visions and ideas generated during the artmaking—most of which could not have been predicted by anyone, even by the artist, in advance" (p. 43).

The teacher-student relationship that reinforces student-directed learning is necessarily highly collaborative; the adult works in concert with the child to facilitate cognition and skill building. Writing about this kind of educational collaboration, Neal (1984) noted similarities between holistic teachers and their inquisitive students:

> The difference between the holistic teacher and the nonholistic teacher is infinite, but the difference between the primary-school child and the holistic teacher is only about 20 to 40 years and a more conscious awareness of what learning is—its relationship to theory, to immediacy, to life and to the possibilities of growth and change—that peculiar combination of the careful eclectic and the conscientious iconoclast who never stops observing, learning, and growing. (p. 313)

Holistic teachers recognize multiple benefits gained through learning interactions in the classroom. For example, Hathaway (2008) noted the opportunity to highlight a student's level of accomplishment through facilitated peer coaching. This is especially significant for children who do not shine elsewhere in the school, enabling them to build both interpersonal skills and confidence. In the choice-based art class, student coaches can address classmates' needs when their teacher is busy; in fact, some learners prefer peer assistance. These varied relationships challenge the traditional roles of teacher and student, with shared responsibility for teaching and learning. As noted above, education for student choice poses demands equal to or greater than those of a regular classroom, but rewards the extra effort with benefits to both the student and the teacher. Miller (2007a) enumerated these challenges and benefits when he cited levels of accountability that lead to strong and caring educational practice, including responsibility to the whole student, the school and its community, the municipality, and the universe. The visual art curriculum, designed on a holistic framework, scaffolds learning to broaden empathy and knowing in each of these domains without losing sight of individual artistic pursuits.

Responsibility for accountability also causes teachers to reflect on their practice and ensure that, while meeting student needs, the curriculum reaches learning targets set by their districts and states. Assessment in choice-based classrooms relies heavily on teacher observation, checklists, and conferencing with students to monitor progress (Douglas & Jaquith, 2009). Dialogue about the work is one way to facilitate students' efforts to create art from personal experience. Another way is to have students write or dictate artist statements. As well as facilitating and giving further evidence of learning, these statements also provide information about the students' creative process and ideas that may be obscured in the final artwork. The following artist statement reveals a 2nd-grader's thought process as she reflects on her mixed media artwork (Figure 5), classifying it as abstract:

> My painting is called *The Abstract Girl*. It is a garden and it is also the face of a girl. If you look up close, you can see dots and a head without the lips. When you look from far away, it is a garden.

Children's interests naturally grow and become refined as their knowledge of the world expands. To foster this growth, experienced teachers who focus on student choice must

FIGURE 5. The metaphor of self as garden is apparent in this painting titled "The Abstract Girl."

anticipate expanding sophistication in student preferences and be prepared to increase challenge when students show readiness. Such is the case with Amy, a 3rd-grade girl, who has a strong inclination toward architecture and a history of successfully managing long-term projects. She arrived at school one day with a comprehensive plan for a tree house scaled to fit her American Girl dolls. This authentic project spanned home and school, fulfilling a real need, and challenging the learner to think like an architect. Fortunately, most students do not work on the same scale as Amy! Their ideas, though, are also inspired by play and compel them to develop skills for the things they seek to accomplish. Toys, mini golf courses, and replicas of laptops and cell phones hold great fascination for young inventors in the same way that color mixing for landscapes and portraits attract child painters and pottery satisfies young ceramic artists. Teachers who appreciate childlike humor, play, and exuberance as expressed through students' artmaking affirm students' value systems and let them know that their ideas have a place in the art class. A course of study that develops around student-determined activities like these is called an "emergent curriculum."

THE EMERGENT CURRICULUM

Every art curriculum must address state standards and district requirements; the holistic art curriculum does the same while remaining open to emergent topics. Students' artistic behaviors and work provide a framework through which teachers can highlight key concepts and skills, essential understandings, art history, and connections that surface in the context of their endeavors. Even unexpected diversions in the curriculum can be used to bring validity to the art program because through them, students can be led to witness diverse relationships that art fosters beyond the classroom. In preschool, Dustin exhibited an interest in birds and taught himself intricate bird songs. It is not surprising that birds are featured in his drawings, paintings, and clay sculptures (Figure 6). Building upon Dustin's interest, his teacher

FIGURE 6. (left) A naturalist comments: "I am very interested in birds and other animals and almost all the time I draw animals. In my painting, a barn owl in the night is hunting a mouse in the field. I decided that the brown would be lighter if I painted white over it."

FIGURE 7. (right) Relationships between art and music inspired a collage with drawing by a 4th-grade boy.

encouraged a cohort of dedicated artists in the class to share their strategies and techniques while studying nature.

In like manner emergent art history, based on students' interests, introduces students to relevant artists whose work connects with their own (Hathaway, 2009). In 4th grade, Adam worked on a collage for many weeks (Figure 7) and then added drawing reminiscent of Kandinsky. Adam explained that he had seen similar drawings at a museum and was interested in the relationships between art and music. Just as Dustin's interest in birds inspired other students' interest in nature, Adam's artwork prompted a whole-class inquiry into Wassily Kandinsky, which was facilitated by their teacher.

These two examples demonstrate that the lives of children are replete with an aesthetic sensibility, which is shaped by sensory experiences, perceptions, and imagination (Spitz, 2006). They are eager to connect their inner lives, brimming with feelings, dreams, ideas, and memories with authentic schoolwork that has personal relevance. Teachable moments abound if teachers watch for educational possibilities. Spitz (2006) noted:

> When significant adults pay close attention to what is capturing the eyes and ears of young children, when we allow the rustlings and cracklings of leaves or the warbling of summer birds to become focal points of delight, then youthful aesthetic proclivities are nourished. Budding sensitivities can blossom. (p. 14)

Choice-based teachers encourage children to bring experiences like these from home in service to their artmaking. When they do, imaginations soar with insights cultivated far beyond the school walls. Emergent art curriculum, so described, thus resembles Anderson's (1981) organic view of art education: "a verb, as a process, as a vital, living, changing procedure which leads to wherever the inquiring critical mind may take it" (p. 38). Choice-based art education demonstrates that this is indeed possible in the school setting.

WHOLE CHILD, WHOLE SCHOOL

Art education has an opportunity to engage students' physical, emotional, intellectual, and spiritual dimensions more readily than most other areas of the school curriculum. In choice-based teaching and learning art programs, meaning is naturally made as students look within to examine relationships and construct understandings. These young artists, through their self-directed work in art class, connect with significant relationships and events to integrate meaningful aspects of their lives into their artwork. Making meaning is central to artistic process, whatever form it takes. Through feeling, intuiting, perceiving, and knowing, children articulate bold visual statements about who they are and what they value. Holistic art education pedagogy, including Teaching for Artistic Behavior, provides compelling models for caring school communities to provide all students with a whole education.

REFERENCES

Amabile, T. M. (1996). *Creativity in context*. Boulder, CO: Westview Press.

Anderson, T. (1981). Wholes and holes: Art's role in holistic education. *Art Education, 34*(6), 36-39.

Douglas, K., & Jaquith, D. B. (2009). *Engaging learners through artmaking: Choice-based art education in the classroom*. New York, NY: Teachers College Press.

Hathaway, N. (2008). 10 teaching and learning strategies in a "choice-based" art program. *Arts & Activities, 144*(1), 36-37.

Hathaway, N. (2009). Connecting from the inside out. *School Arts, 108*(7), 12.

Holt, J. (1972). *Freedom and beyond*. Portsmouth, NH: Heinemann.

Jaquith, D. B. (2011). When is creativity? *Art Education, 64*(1), 14-19.

London, P. (1992). Art as transformation. *Art Education, 45*(3), 8-15.

Miller, J. P. (2007a). *The holistic curriculum*. Toronto, ON: University of Toronto Press.

Miller, J. P. (2007b). Whole teaching, whole schools, whole teachers. *Educational Leadership, 64*(9), Retrieved from www.ascd.org/publications/educational_leadership/summer07/vol64/num09/Whole_Teaching,_Whole_Schools,_Whole_Teachers.aspx

Neal, C. (1984). The holistic teacher. *Learning Disability Quarterly, 7*(4), 309-313.

Nokes, C. (2005). Holistic integrated design education: Art education in a complex and uncertain world. *Journal of Aesthetic Education, 39*(1), 31-47.

Palmer, P. J. (1993). *To know as we are known: Education as a spiritual journey*. New York, NY: Harper.

Perkins, D. N., & Salomon, G. (1988). "Teaching for transfer," *Educational Leadership, 46*(1), 22-32.

Sesto, C. (2009). *Sticks: Building ideas and self-confidence in the Montessori elementary art room*. Raleigh, NC: Lulu.com.

Spitz, E. H. (2006). *The brightening glance: Imagination and childhood*. New York, NY: Anchor Books.

Stout, C. J. (1999). The art of empathy: Teaching students to care. *Art Education, 52*(2), 21-34.

Szekely, G. (1988). *Encouraging creativity in art lessons*. New York, NY: Teachers College Press.

Vygotsky, L. (1978). *Mind in society: The development of higher psychological processes*. Cambridge, MA: Harvard University Press.

Wuthnow, R. (2001). *Creative spirituality*. Berkeley, CA: University of California Press.

ABOUT THE AUTHOR

Diane Jaquith is a K-5 art teacher in Newton, MA, and a co-founder of Teaching for Artistic Behavior, Inc., a grassroots organization that advocates for choice-based art education. She is co-author, with Katherine Douglas, of *Engaging Learners Through Artmaking: Choice-Based Art Education in the Classroom*. She can be reached at dbjaquith@gmail.com.

Art Teacher Preparation

Art teacher educators committed to promoting a holistic approach for young people should implement a holistic curriculum in their own teacher preparation programs, an approach that encourages art education students to continue to develop as artists and to use their artmaking interests as inspiration for their own future curriculum planning and classroom-based research.... as preparers of art teachers, we need to practice what we preach, to actively model those values and behaviors that we want our preservice and in-service teachers to develop. Only if we model highly effective art educator behaviors for our college-level students will they in turn be able to model those same behaviors for their P-12 learners.

— *Pamela Harris Lawton, p. 179*

CHAPTER 18

Artist/Researcher/Teacher: A Holistic Approach to Art Teacher Preparation

Pamela Harris Lawton

A holistic and narrative orientation to teacher education acknowledges the connectedness of the learner's prior experiences, current purposes, and future goals. It locates the learner at the heart of the meaning-making process and recognizes the interrelatedness of the intellectual, emotional, social, moral, and aesthetic dimensions of the individual who is becoming a teacher.

—Mary Beattie

This chapter briefly examines the roots of holistic art education as it relates to artists/ researchers/teachers, followed by questions addressed through interviews with college art educators and experienced art teachers. The following questions are explored:

- How might art educators incorporate their own personal artmaking interests and experiences into teaching and classroom/community research?
- What are some effective ways in which art educators have achieved balance among their roles as artist, teacher, and researcher?
- How do college-level art educators bridge the disciplines of studio art and art education?
- What types of research have art educators done that utilizes this holistic approach?
- How are art educators perceived as makers of art? As researchers?
- What can be done to help preservice art educators synthesize their personal artistic practice, and inquiry interests successfully into their professional lives?
- In what ways have art teachers incorporated the ideals of holistic education into their own teaching praxis?

One of the reasons I became an art educator was because I enjoyed making art myself. I was an artist long before I became an educator, and as such my teaching practice is firmly rooted in the belief that art educators need to be practicing artists themselves. By practicing artist, I mean that we need to regularly give ourselves challenging, creative problems to solve, because as active participants in the creative process, we gain greater insight into what our students experience, think, understand, learn, and have difficulty with. By discussing our own struggles as artists with our students, we help them realize that fear is a natural and healthy part of finding and solving artistic problems. In addition, these discussions demonstrate that artists at every level of expertise experience struggle and doubt. Thus, the process of artmaking and reflexivity share a correlative relationship with teaching and learning.

In their book, *Contemporary Issues in Art Education*, Gaudelius and Speirs (2002) quote art educator Ed Check, who "suggests that as teachers we should approach the teaching of art from the context of our lives, fueled by our own personal experiences" (p. 20). This would include our experiences as learners, as teachers, and as artists. Additionally, Graeme Sullivan (2002) discusses the importance of studio experiences for graduate art education students as a basis for developing their professional profile as researchers and art educators: "For these contemporary artists, the process of producing art for public display is an educational act that continually opens up new possibilities for art learning and art teaching." (p. 29)

For several years, I worked in a group printmaking studio, exhibiting my work and on occasion teaching art classes to adult students. I found these brief forays into teaching satisfying and a way of connecting my own struggles as an artist with those of my students, opening a dialogue between teacher and student that provided mutual insights into the creative problem solving process. My training and practice as an artist have since helped me immeasurably in teaching both high school and college students. Currently, I work with graduate art education students who, in addition to a written thesis, must create and exhibit a body of visual work for exhibition. The visual work is based on both prior art experiences and studio classes taken over the course of the degree program. Helping students see the interconnectedness of their studio and art education research opens new and greater possibilities for them as effective art teachers and solidifies, for me, the importance of a holistic approach in developing art education professionals.

HOLISTIC EDUCATION—A BRIEF OVERVIEW

Although it has only recently emerged as a prominent educational paradigm, holistic education has deep historical and philosophical roots. The concept is based in Aristotle's theory of "holism" whereby "the whole is more important than the sum of its parts." More recent influences include the theories of Jean-Jacques Rousseau, Ralph Waldo Emerson, Henry Thoreau, Bronson Alcott, Johan Pestalozzi, Friedrich Froebel and Francisco Ferrer. Progressive education scholars like Maria Montessori and John Dewey, followed by psychologists Howard Gardner and Abraham Maslow, as well as political theorist Paulo Freire, among others, expanded and further refined upon these earlier philosophies (Forbes, 1996).

Building upon this well-established foundation, holism as a contemporary educational philosophy blossomed following the cultural revolution of the 1960s and the holism (Gestalt) psychology movement of the 1970s. These events resulted in "an emerging body of literature in science, philosophy and cultural history" providing a framework for understanding education known as "holism" (Miller, 2000). Among the leading voices in contemporary holistic education is Ron Miller, founder of the journal, *Holistic Education Review*, now entitled *Encounter: Education for Meaning and Social Justice*. According to Miller, "A holistic way of thinking seeks to encompass and integrate multiple layers of meaning and experience rather than defining human possibilities narrowly." Miller further writes, "Holistic education is based on the premise that each person finds identity, meaning, and purpose in life through connections to the community, to the natural world, and to spiritual values such as compassion and peace" (Miller, 2000).

The goal of holistic education is thus to teach the "whole child" within a broader conception of education, one that encompasses mind, body, and spirit. Yet it does not view the child in isolation, as the term *child-centered* might have once implied. Instead, it establishes the learner as interdependent with others and the environment. With this broader view in mind, current scholarship on holistic education points to four teaching strategies or principles that address how to teach holistically and how students learn holistically: transformation, connections, meaningfulness, and community (Holistic Education Network Tasmania [HENT], n.d.).

The *transformative* approach is based in John Mezirow's (1991) theory of transformative learning, described as "learning that involves reflectively transforming the beliefs, attitudes, opinions and emotional reactions that constitute our meaning schemes, or transforming our meaning perspectives" (p. 223). Cranton (1994) adds, "transformative learning occurs when, through critical self-reflection, an individual revises old or develops new assumptions, beliefs or ways of seeing the world" (p. xii).

Holism understands knowledge as something that is constructed through the context in which a person lives. Therefore, it is essential not just to teach students the facts or skills they will need to know for some standardized test, but also to prepare them to reflect critically on how we come to know or understand information. As a result, if "we ask students to develop critical and reflective thinking skills and encourage them to care about the world around them they may decide that some degree of personal or social transformation is required" (HENT, n.d.).

The idea of *connections* relates to the curriculum. Rather than taking a traditional, more narrow, fragmented view of curriculum as a series of separate disciplines, holistic education perceives curriculum integration as the best means to teach the whole child—how does science relate to art, math and language? How might one unit of instruction seamlessly integrate all of these disciplines to some extent and relate them to the child's experience of the world? "Holism sees the various aspects of life and living as integrated and connected, therefore, education should not isolate learning into several different components" (HENT, n.d.).

The concept of *meaningfulness* in holistic education speaks to the motivation and engagement of learners. Students are likely to learn better, to understand more deeply when the teacher encourages them to construct and make their own meaning, to think metacognitively and see the inter-connectedness between their own ways of knowing and those of the classroom community, including the teacher.

Finally, incorporating *community* is an important aspect of any holistic approach to education. If, as progressive education theorizes, the goal of education is to produce socially responsible citizens, then any effective system of education will encourage students to view their learning as a communal endeavor, being open and responsive to a multiplicity of perspectives and understanding that their classroom community is a microcosm of the school community, which resides within the larger community of a neighborhood, which lies within a town or city or region, which by extension lies within the global community of the world.

HOLISTIC ART EDUCATION

An examination of the research and teachings of German émigré artist-educator Henry Schaefer-Simmern exemplifies how holistic teaching and learning are applied in art education. Schaefer-Simmern (1970) believed that "the unfolding of artistic activity cannot be separated from the nature of man: It must grow out of him as a unified process" (p. 7). This is a wonderful example of holistic art education—connecting mind, body, and spirit wherein learners are encouraged to reflect critically on the self, to pay close attention to their daily life encounters, and to both problem-solve and problem-find through art. Far from the caricature of *laissez-faire* art teaching, which critics have used to depict child-centered approaches, Shaefer-Simmern's methods were demanding both of the student and the teacher. Particularly important in this process was the role of questioning and dialogue through which Schaefer-Simmern (and others who followed his lead) assisted students in resolving their artistic problems. These questions are posed to challenge, lead, suggest, inform and encourage self-discovery and self-evaluation (Gradle, 2009). In this, and other ways, Schafer-Simmern "directed students to examine what they might see—through their artmaking—in their daily lives that had meaning to them" (Gradle, 2009, p.9).

Like other holistic art educators today, I engage my graduate students in this same form of conscious inward/outward looking in deciding what to pursue artistically for their capstone exhibition and in finding connections between their artistic and teaching interests in formulating their research thesis—taking a more holistic approach to their education, personal, and professional lives.

Similarly, Hetland, Winner, Veenema, and Sheridan (2007) exhort art educators to model artistic behaviors for our students, behaviors that encourage them to develop "studio habits of mind," a series of dispositions that participation in the arts engenders. Once developed, these habits of mind *may* then manifest in transdisciplinary thinking and inquiry, eliminating the division between art and other disciplines. Hetland et al. have identified eight such behaviors: develop craft, engage and persist, envision, express, observe, reflect, stretch and explore, and understand the art world (2007). In order to effectively model these behaviors for our students, we must live these dispositions ourselves.

The approaches just cited suggest ways the four holistic education principles (transformation, connections, meaningfulness and community) can be applied to holistic *art* education, as well as to education in general. Schaefer-Simmern's theory of visual conceiving provides an example of this connection. Visual conception refers to "that which is conceived or begotten in the mind and which causes the birth of a visual configuration of (artistic) form" (Schaefer-Simmern, 1970, p. 13). "Visual conceiving must occur in addition to intellectual inquiry if the artmaker is going to form an artistic vision that results in visual work" (Gradle, 2009, p. 4). This "visual conceiving," similar to the studio behavior of "envisioning," (Hetland et al., 2007) results from a "natural unfolding of development that occurs only as an integration of visual structures also occurs" (Gradle, 2009, p. 5). Schafer-Simmern further theorized that "to bring an artwork into being involved artistic cognition that came from solving problems, organizing structures into wholes, establishing a figure-ground relationship, and therein creating unity" (Gradle, 2009, p. 6) or holism.

> As visual conceptions become unified, the process of visually organizing the work results in the simultaneous transformation of the artist who gives the form visibility... this wholeness in the image is mirrored as a transformational sense of wholeness in the artist. (Gradle, 2009, p. 7)

Thus, the concept of "visual conceiving" exemplifies the holistic education principle, transformation, as manifested in holistic art education.

The principle, connection, as a teaching strategy within holistic art education, plays a similar role to that of holistic education in general through designing curricula that integrates the arts with other academic subject content, such as language arts, social studies, math and science. Understood in this way, curriculum integration through visual art is easily accomplished since the broad realm of art has links to virtually every domain. However, for the purposes of this chapter, connections has a somewhat different focus. It refers to envisioning how one's art practice is connected to one's teaching and research concerns.

Meaningfulness, like the studio behaviors of *Engage and Persist* and *Reflect,* defined by Hetland et al. examines the importance of intrinsic/extrinsic motivation and engagement with an artistic task. For artmaking to be meaningful, one needs motivation to engage and persist at a task that leads to the self-construction of knowledge and meaning making. *Meaningfulness* further involves metacognitive reflection on the task at hand, learning to think about and judge one's own work, process, and the work and process of others (Hetland et al., 2007, p. 6).

Lastly, the principle of community in terms of holistic art education can be related to *Understand the Art World* (Hetland et al, 2007) or "learning to interact as an artist with other artists in classrooms, local arts organizations, and across the art field and within the broader society" (p. 6). In the field of art education this would include community-based art education research and the practice of art education, as well as studio art and artmaking.

PERSONAL VS. PROFESSIONAL: MAKING ART AND MAKING ART TEACHERS

In her book, *Work, Pedagogy and Change: Foundations for the Art Teacher Educator*, Lynn Beudert (2006) presents vignettes of the personal and professional narratives of art educators. Several address the struggle art educators face in creating a balanced and more holistic life. Often art education faculty may be required to teach, not only art education courses, but art appreciation and studio art courses, as well. Yet their studio colleagues more often than not disrespect the art education program "since they believe that art education students are not committed to the art program and are often not among the talented students. These attitudes also seem to extend to the art education faculty" (p. 41).

In some cases, these assumptions may be correct; however, in many instances art education faculty not only possess the same studio education and exhibition credentials as their studio counterparts, but they also hold advanced degrees in art education. These negative attitudes will persist as long as we aid in their perpetuation by not modeling studio habits of mind with our art education students and failing to encourage them to improve and expand upon their studio praxis.

Seug-Ryul Shin's narrative speaks to the pressures attendant in teaching both studio and art education within a small art department, leaving little time either for keeping abreast of innovations and scholarship in the field or for personal artmaking. Shin wrote,

> Even though it is tough to teach two subject areas, there are great advantages, too. Teaching experience in computer graphics and new media can lead to research possibilities for applying computer technologies within art education. I plan to cooperate with a public school computer art teacher on a research project. Thus, experience and skills in art multimedia design, web design and animation, and digital movies might be some of the most gains I have had through teaching. I find comfort in reminding myself that such skills are, and will be, very useful for art education as a field. (Beudert, 2006, p. 42)

College art educators may find themselves operating within a netherworld. Those teaching in art departments/colleges are often not considered artists and those teaching in colleges of education are often not considered teachers, whereas most art educators see themselves firmly as both (Beudert, 2006).

> Another important aspect related to preparing art teachers is to promote being an artist. Why it is assumed that someone can teach the higher levels of thinking that the arts uses, without continually making art themselves is an interesting notion... Skill, meaning, and imagination are not only important in producing art and teaching art, but also in creating active art lessons for students that relate to the art world, to the students' lives, and to expanding a student's connection to life. (Elisabeth Hartung in Beudert, 2006, p. 81)

The sentiments expressed in these narratives are echoed in the recently revised standards for art teacher preparation published by the National Art Education Association (NAEA). These standards reflect the importance of artmaking and research in the development of highly qualified and effective art educators, advocating a holistic approach to art teacher preparation that includes the growth and development of effective pedagogical, research, and artistic skills in preservice, novice, and experienced art teachers.

NAEA STANDARDS FOR ART TEACHER PREPARATION

Standard I: Art Teacher Preparation Programs Focus on the Content of the Visual Arts

Teacher education programs in the visual arts should enable candidates to study and engage in the processes of artmaking involving traditional and contemporary studio approaches. Basic concepts and skills related to processes, structure, technical aspects, expressive content, social functions, communicative qualities, and technical knowledge are developed through these comprehensive studio experiences (NAEA, 2009).

Standard III: Art Education Faculty Have Expertise in Theories and Practices of Art Education

Art education faculty responsible for preparing art teacher candidates should have extensive knowledge and practice in art and art education and demonstrated competence in teaching in preK-12 and/or other educational settings. Supervisory teachers and part-time and adjunct faculty should also be well-qualified individuals with formal training and experience in studio teaching who demonstrate known competencies in art subject matter.

Art education faculty should also have well-developed communication and inquiry skills that enable them to approach learning new skills and understandings in flexible and creative ways (NAEA, 2009).

VIGNETTES OF HOLISTIC PERSONAL AND PROFESSIONAL ART PRACTICE

In an attempt to conceptualize an effective pedagogical approach to holistic art teacher education, I posed the following questions to myself and three other artist-educators ranging from young adult to middle to old age, to better understand how artist/researcher/teachers embody the concepts and teaching strategies of holistic art education in their personal and professional lives. The following questions were asked in written and oral interviews/questionnaires:

- How have you incorporated your own personal artmaking interests and experiences into teaching and classroom/community research?
- What are some effective ways in which you have achieved balance among your roles as artist, teacher and researcher?
- As a college art educator, how have you bridged the disciplines of studio art and art education?
- What type of research have you done that utilizes this holistic approach?
- How do you think art educators are perceived as makers of art? As researchers?
- What can be done to help preK-12 art educators synthesize these aspects of their persona successfully into their professional lives?
- In what ways have you incorporated the ideals of holistic education into your own teaching praxis?

Each vignette touches upon one or more of the four holistic education principles (transformative, connections, meaningfulness, community) as it relates to art education and to art teacher preparation and development.

Pam Lawton (Age 51)

When I began teaching high school, I had very little preparation in terms of educational coursework and theory. However, I did have many years of artmaking behind me and spent much of my free time in a group studio creating prints. These art experiences greatly influenced what and how I taught. The high school where I taught did not own a printing press and I wanted to provide my art students with a more enriching printmaking experience. With the help of a colleague and a small traveling press, we were able to teach collagraph (relief)

FIGURE 1. Pam Lawton. *The Adventures of Pamela*—a collaborative altered book inspired by the Artstories dissertation research that then inspired an altered book project in my art education methods courses.

printing. Students created self-portrait collagraphs that they printed on both paper and cloth. The cloth squares were sewn together into artful quilts that the principal then co-opted for his office. Since he liked them so much, I suggested to him that our students could do more such projects if the school possessed its own printing press. He agreed and provided the money for the purchase of a printing press and invited me to develop printmaking courses. This is one small example of how my own studio interests *connected* to my teaching practice.

As I settled into teaching high school, I noticed that many of my students, both male and female, gravitated toward me, older-aged school volunteers, and many of the teachers who were empathetic and caring—adults who took the time to listen to them. I remember reading somewhere that the average adolescent only receives about 2 minutes of undivided attention from an adult per day. I know that for many of my students I was that one adult. I also noticed that "Grandma," one of our school community volunteers, wanted to feel needed. She provided a sounding board for the students while simultaneously exercising her need for "generativity." Generativity is Erik Erikson's term for the desire older adults have to share their wisdom and experience, garnered through living, with the future of the community (youth) (Erickson, Erickson, & Kivnick, 1986). Their concern for the future is manifested in narratives on life and living, and provides them with a way to contribute to something larger than themselves.

These observations, coupled with visits to an elderly aunt in a nearby assisted living facility, preyed upon my mind, plaguing me with questions. As an art teacher, what could I do to facilitate a meaningful intergenerational connection between students and seniors in the community who do not have the benefits of contact with an extended family network of their own? And was there a way of connecting these isolated members of the school community through arts learning? (Lawton, 2004, 2008).

Inspiration came from my art practice. My own artworks, prints, artist books, and assemblages that I refer to as "artstories," are visual/textual pieces that re-count, re-visit and reveal family history through intergenerational interaction and narrative. By expanding the notion of art story making from the individual and personal to the collective and general, artstories could be adapted into an arts learning research project for teens, middle-aged and senior participants unknown to one another. This idea became the basis of my doctoral dissertation research. Working with intergenerational groups of teens, middle and older-age adults on

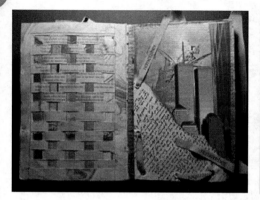

FIGURE 2. (left) Pam Lawton. *Adventures of Pamela.*

FIGURE 3. (middle) Kryssi Staikidis. *Adventures of Pamela.*

FIGURE 4. (right) Lisa Hochtritt. *Adventures of Pamela.*

artist's books (art/story/making), narratives that provided the opportunity for strangers to listen to one another and learn from one another was a *transformational* learning experience which would not have been possible if I had not been open to seeing the interconnectedness of my artistic, teaching and research selves. Holism is for me intuitive, a way of living and being personally and professionally that is both conscious and subconscious.

As a holistic art education professional, it is not difficult to find opportunities to exercise holism and model it for my own students. In fact, the students are often the impetus for new directions in my teaching, artmaking, and research. Almost every research project I have initiated since completing my dissertation has been a holistic one, combining my art, teaching, and research interests.

Lilian Burwell (Age 82)

FIGURE 5. Lilian Burwell. *Paradisaea.* Acrylic on canvas over wood. www.burwellstudios.com

It never ceases to amaze me how the people we meet, places we go, things we do, all seem purposefully interconnected. Such is the case with Lilian. The first time I encountered her was 42 years ago. She was my art teacher in elementary school and though I did not have art often because she divided her time between two elementary schools and many grade levels, I remembered her name and the projects we did. Lilian's teaching inspired and motivated me to make art—all the time. When I moved back home 1 year ago and began meeting my neighbors, I was thrilled to discover that Lilian lived just around the corner. I had not seen or spoken with her in 42 years, but our serendipitous re-encounter, in tandem with an experience I had in my teaching at the Corcoran College of Art & Design, led to my current art/teaching/research project and an interview with Lilian.

Lilian is the embodiment of holistic art education; the intersection of mind, body and spirit in art-making, art teaching and art-based research. She was a Depression Era child whose family migrated North to New York City for better economic opportunities. Her artist/educator parents integrated creativity into all aspects of family life, demonstrating for Lilian the seamless integration of art and life. Because they were poor, they used their artistic talents to create a home full of beautiful handmade things.

> The whole mentality of most of the world was how to make something out of nothing [during the Depression]. I mean the material nothing. All this feeds into what makes you creative. Everyday life is a process of making and becoming. It's about more than making pretty pictures. It's part of the education of the whole person. (L. Burwell, personal communication, September 29, 2009)

Lilian's mother worked in the garment district and saved everything that was thrown out, recycling it in some form in their home. Lilian recalls her mother making beautiful curtains from the silk pongee bags that the silks were shipped in from Japan. She decorated them with linoleum block print designs. She made lovely dresses for Lilian from worn, discarded bed sheets that she appliquéd with flowers cut from scraps of discarded material. Lilian made her own toys from wooden produce boxes, she collaged paper dolls cut from old magazines and wrote and illustrated her own stories using cut-up magazines for color.

Lilian had the good fortune to attend the "Little Red School House" in Greenwich Village from 1932-1937. The Little Red School House was one of the first successful schools founded on the principles of progressive education espoused by the school's founder, Elizabeth Irwin and inspired by her mentor, John Dewey. Irwin's school sought to tailor the curriculum to the child and to educate the "whole child" through hands-on, project-based experiential learning. Thus Lilian's home and school life embodied holistic principles and encouraged her to see her artistic interests and activities as integrated with everyday life. " I learned my color wheel from picking through colors of discarded clothing [that her mother used to make her clothes]. If you don't have it and you feel the need for something or you have an idea, then you learn to create it" (L. Burwell, personal communication, September 29, 2009).

Lilian's childhood experiences are a perfect example of the holistic principle of *meaningfulness*. Being surrounded in both family and school life by creativity and artistic expression provided intrinsic and extrinsic motivation to create her artworks, for both pleasure and purpose. These habits of mind have helped Lilian persevere in her development and evolution as an artist and educator.

Lilian attended Music and Art High School in New York City and later attended Pratt Institute from 1944 to 1946. It was at Pratt that she developed a strong child-centered foundation for teaching art. What I find most remarkable is that Lilian had these extraordinary experiences at a time when most women were not encouraged to seek art careers, let alone attend college, and for an African-American woman these accomplishments are even more remarkable.

What Lilian most wanted was to make a living as an artist; however, finances necessitated that she work, and with her educational experiences teaching art was a natural fit, one that she came to love:

> As I studied art education, as I began to teach, it became equally as important to me as making the art. Everything that I did in my art more convinced me that the creative spirit is in every single one of us (in some form). There is no other form of creativity that's more important than giving another human being hope.(L. Burwell, personal communication, September 29, 2009)

Her first teaching job was as a classroom teacher at a Catholic school where she developed a program for students designated as "hopeless non-readers." Lilian conducted her own research with these students using art experiences to help them "recall" the words they had already been taught, but were "locked away inside of them." This research provided her with an opportunity to teach art and use it to successfully teach these students to read. Lilian took the children outside to observe their surroundings and construct simple verbal sentences of what they saw. She then told them she would let them paint what they saw if they could spell it for her. These 3rd-grade students were motivated to recall what they had really already learned because she was able to engage them. They created art storybooks and learned to read in the process. Lilian later published the results of her research and would like to write a book about her holistic teaching experiences.

In addition to painting and exhibiting her works, writing and publishing her poetry and giving talks, Lilian is busy developing a curriculum for older adults for a creativity course she has been asked to teach at the local community college.

FIGURE 6. Kryssi working on Latino Community Center Mural.

Kryssi Staikidis (Age 51)

I met Kryssi when we were doctoral students at Teachers College, Columbia University. As artist educators we developed a deep friendship through our shared philosophies on art and teaching. Kryssi teaches at a research institution and finds it difficult to balance scholarship, on which tenure is weighted, with the need to create art. However, she firmly believes in art-based research and her published work reflects how her art praxis drives her teaching and research. Kryssi's work as an artist/researcher/teacher embodies the ideals of the principle of community in that she wants her students to see art and art-based research as a means of becoming socially responsible citizens, to view their learning as a communal endeavor, being open and responsive to a multiplicity of perspectives, understandings, and ways of knowing and making meaning:

As a painter I taught art for nearly two decades on the K-12 level in New York City. So my art studio practice was essential to my life as a teacher of children, a teacher who wanted her students to feel a vibrant love of art. To communicate passion to students, I felt I needed to be making artwork myself. And because I eventually began to miss study and scholarship, I decided to pursue a doctoral degree in art education. I was ready and eager to be a student once again. The new path that lay ahead was research, unfamiliar terrain, and when I searched my soul, I realized I wanted to be involved with research that emerged out of painters' studios.

The work of my mentor Graeme Sullivan (2005, 2006, 2008) speaks to studio practice as a legitimate site for transformative research. As Graeme and I discussed possibilities for doctoral work, and with the help of colleagues (particularly Pam Lawton, who sent me in the direction of Central America), I decided to study with Mayan painters as mentors. They would teach me painting outside of a Euro-American academic model, from inside their studios, one-on-one.

After several years of study, I learned that the pivotal points of teaching in two Mayan painting studios were the following:
- the relationship formed between teacher and student;
- a diffusion of the teacher as expert model that relied on students gaining expertise and teaching each other alongside the mentor;
- the inclusion of personal and cultural narrative;
- collaboration; and
- beginning with the learner's needs.

Through studying with Mayan mentors in their painting studios, I was transformed as both painter and teacher. Therefore, I sought ways to infuse my research discoveries into my higher education classrooms with young art educators. My students and I began to talk about our studio practice and the concepts that spurred our artmaking as the impetus for designing lessons. I also let students take on the roles of expert and novice, teaching each other through facilitation in small groups. Outside of the classroom, we designed a mural project based on a Mexican Aztec theme. Pre-service art education students collaborated with members of the local Latino community center. Our artistic, teaching, and learning processes involved the teaching methods that came out of Mayan pedagogy.

As I progressed along the professorial path, I naturally included aspects of my research to help students understand democratic teaching practices. I am currently working on a book with Mayan mentors that will be a collaborative ethnography in which we, as three painters from different cultures, co-author our trans-cultural pedagogical and artistic experiences. There seems no reason to separate my love of painting and teaching from the desire to produce research that focuses on issues of inclusion and diversity in the art classrooms of higher education. My approach as a painter, teacher, and researcher in the three areas is necessarily holistic: my artistry, teaching, and research are inseparable as each organically informs the other. (K. Staikidis, personal communication, November 19, 2009)

Kate Elkins—Graduate Student

Kate is a graduate student in the Corcoran College of Art & Design's Master of Arts in Art Education program. She taught art at the elementary level for 8 years and was feeling somewhat creatively drained when she enrolled in our program. Her enthusiasm for teaching was rekindled after she completed an identity map assignment I give students the first week of class. This assignment is based on the research of Congdon, Stewart, and White (2002), who developed an identity-mapping project to assist teachers in becoming more critically aware and self-reflective practitioners who understand how their own identities and biases influence the curriculum they develop. Through mapping their identities, "participants consider how their community identities impact the decisions they make in their curriculum work (and artmaking, when appropriate)" (p. 111). Kate perceived her identity map as a color wheel. The identity map diagram that Congdon et al. present is circular and has 12 identity sections, so envisioning it as a color wheel made sense. This assignment so influenced Kate that she created a similar assignment for her 5th graders which turned out to be very successful. In the fall, 2009, Kate began teaching art at the high school level.

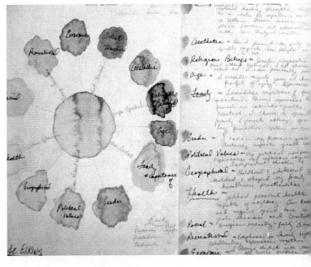

FIGURE 7. Kate's Color Wheel Identity Map.

Pam: *How have you incorporated your own personal artmaking interests and experiences into teaching and classroom/community research?*

Kate: My initial art education research emerged from personal reflections after being asked about my own early art experiences. I'd respond with stories about Shrinky Dink snowmen, hand turkeys, poster contests and teacher-directed mini-masterpieces. "Draw a line at the top of your paper. Now, paint a blue dot overlapping that line..." After a series of instructions, voila, I'd created a copy of a masterwork. However, I didn't make any of the decisions, so the work mattered little to me. Very few of these early art education experiences resulted in meaningful personal inquiry. Realization that these experiences were often detrimental to a student's holistic growth as a creative, unique individual prompted my investigation into a shift from traditional methods of delivering art instruction to a content-rich, issues-based approach. Fortunately, this research also positively impacted my own artmaking. My personal identities, as well as my community connections, influence the content direction of my art. Furthermore, now before designing a lesson, I ask myself, "how will my students relate to this activity? Will they create a memorable, meaningful connection? By participating in this exercise, will my students have a chance to put their own voice in their work?"

Pam: *What are some effective ways in which you have achieved balance among your roles as artist, teacher and researcher?*

Kate: A cohesive balance is achieved by not isolating these three roles into separate identities. My artmaking influences the direction of my research, which I then bring into my teaching curriculum. My research, artwork, and students benefit from the integration of these three components into one whole persona, each impacting the other.

Pam: *As an art educator how have you bridged the disciplines of studio art and art education?*

Kate: For many years, these two roles were very disconnected and because I separated these identities, the demands of teaching overwhelmed the physical act of visual expression. The realization that I was an art teacher who didn't produce art initiated my personal exploration into how my art might influence my teaching. I now find it equally imperative to be a teacher who creates art as well as an artist who teaches.

Pam: *What type of research have you done that utilizes this holistic approach?*

Kate: Multiple cultures and socioeconomic groups are represented in my art classroom. As a result, my research investigates how the students' art experiences can contribute to individual and cultural awareness. I research how integrating local resources, student interests regarding community and global issues, and local exhibits or contemporary installations impact their overall awareness of self and personal expression. My priority is to connect students with the cultural arts found in their own backyards. I have discovered that when students are engaged and encouraged to develop their sense of identity in this world, meaningful art experiences emerge. My goal is to offer opportunities for developing insightful connections between a student's individual world, his community, and the broader world around him through art. One example is a year-long project that my 9th graders are participating in: Personal Identity Sketchbooks. The students are arranging and prioritizing "Identity Issues" within a sketchbook format based on a color symbolism guide. They are exploring how to record their ideas and reflections through the use of imagery, symbolism-metaphors, visual vocabulary, and journaling. Ultimately, the sketchbooks are providing a venue for exploring feelings, thoughts, ideas, hopes, fears, and concerns. By exploring these issues, the students are gaining a clearer definition of personal identity.

Pam: *In what ways have you incorporated the ideals of holistic education into your own teaching praxis?*

Kate: To paraphrase from Maxine Greene, "The only way to really awaken to life, awaken to the possibilities, is to be self-aware." While teaching at the elementary level, I discovered the importance of introducing my students to the concept of personal reflection. After first discovering my own identity and prioritizing my community connections as a teacher, I developed an awareness of self that caused me to reflect on the identities of my students. I then became more aware of their individual and collective perspectives. Once the students' personal experiences became relevant, it was a natural progression to request their input when deciding which direction our lessons would go (K. Elkins, personal communication, November 26, 2009).

Kate's responses reflect the principles of connectedness and community. By connecting her own identity-mapping process to her curriculum, Kate was better able to join her artistic and teaching selves and to better connect with her students as individuals and makers of art. In turn, she was able to create a more aware, empathetic and self-reflective community of learners in her classroom.

CONCLUSION

Following what has been said above in both the text and the interviews, holistic education is a matter, not just for P-12 art teachers, but also for those who prepare them. Art teacher educators committed to promoting a holistic approach for young people should implement a holistic curriculum in their own teacher preparation programs, an approach that encourages art education students to continue to develop as artists and to use their artmaking interests as inspiration for their own future curriculum planning and classroom-based research. It is also important for teacher education faculty to maintain their own holistic development as artists and researchers, and, in other ways, sustain our own holistic development through life-long learning. In other words, as preparers of art teachers, we need to practice what we preach, to actively model those values and behaviors that we want our preservice and in-service teachers to develop. Only if we model highly effective art educator behaviors for our college-level students will they in turn be able to model those same behaviors for their P-12 learners.

REFERENCES

Beattie, M. (2007). *The art of learning to teach: Creating professional narratives*. Upper Saddle River, NJ: Pearson Education.

Beudert, L. (2006). *Work, pedagogy and change: Foundations for the art teacher educator*. Reston, VA: National Art Education Association.

Congdon, K. G., Stewart, M., & White, J. H. (2002). Mapping identity for curriculum work. In Y. Gaudelius & P. Speirs (Eds.), *Contemporary issues in art education* (pp. 108-118). Upper Saddle River, NJ: Prentice Hall.

Cranton, P. (1994). *Understanding and promoting transformative learning: A guide for educators of adults*. San Francisco, CA: Jossey-Bass.

Erikson, E., Erikson, J., & Kivnick, H. (1986). *Vital involvement in old age*. New York, NY: W.W. Norton & Company.

Forbes, S. (1996). Values in Holistic Education. Retrieved from www.putnampit.com/holistic.html

Gaudelieus, Y., & Speirs, P. (Eds.). (2002). *Contemporary issues in art education*. Upper Saddle River, NJ: Prentice Hall.

Gradle, S. A. (2009). Another look at holistic art education: Exploring the legacy of Henry Schaefer-Simmern. *International Journal of Education & the Arts, 10*(1), 1-21.

Holistic Education Network, Tasmania, AU, (HENT), (n.d.). Transformative learning. Retrieved from www.hent.org/transformative.htm

Holistic Education Network, Tasmania, AU, (HENT). (n.d.). Why Holistic Education. Retrieved from www.hent.org/hent/fundamental.htm

Hetland, L., Winner, E., Veenema, S., & Sheridan, K. M. (2007). *Studio thinking: The real benefits of visual arts education*. New York, NY: Teachers College Press.

Lawton, P. H. (2004). *Artstories©: Perspectives on intergenerational learning through narrative construction amongst adolescents, middle aged and older aged adults*. Unpublished doctoral dissertation. Teachers College, Columbia University, New York, NY.

Lawton, P. H. (2008). *Artstories©: Narrative construction in intergenerational and transformative learning*. Saarbrucken, Germany: VDM Verlag.

Mezirow, J. (1991). *Transformative dimensions of adult learning*. San Francisco, CA: Jossey-Bass.

Miller, R. (2000). What are schools for? holistic education in American culture. Retrieved from www.infed.org/biblio/holisticeducation.htm

National Art Education Association (NAEA). (2009). Standards for Art Teacher Preparation. Retrieved from http://alumniconnections.com/olc/filelib/NAEA/cpages/9009/Library/NAEA_Teacher_Prep_Stds.pdf

Schaefer-Simmern, H. (1970). *The unfolding of artistic activity: Its basis, processes and implications*. Berkeley, CA: University of California Press.

Sullivan, G. (2002). Ideas and teaching: Making meaning from contemporary art. In Y. Gaudelius & P. Speirs (Eds.), *Contemporary issues in art education* (pp. 23-38). Upper Saddle River, NJ: Prentice Hall.

Sullivan, G. (2005). *Art practice as research: Inquiry in the visual arts*. Thousand Oaks, CA: Sage.

Sullivan, G. (2006). Research acts in art practice. *Studies in Art Education, 48*(1), 19-35.

Sullivan, G. (2008). Painting as research: Create and critique. In J. Knowles & A. L. Cole (Eds.), *Handbook of the arts in qualitative research: Perspectives, methodologies, examples and issues* (pp. 239-250). Thousand Oaks, CA: Sage.

ABOUT THE AUTHOR

Pamela Harris Lawton is an Assistant Professor of Art Education and Director of the Education Studies Programs at the Corcoran College of Art & Design. She holds an EdDCT in Art Education from Teachers College, Columbia University, an MFA in Printmaking from Howard University, and a BA in Studio Art/Sociology from University of Virginia. She taught art at the high school level for 3 years and for the last 7 years has taught in the art education programs at Bank Street College of Education, Tyler School of Art, Temple University, and the University of North Carolina at Charlotte.

CHAPTER 19

Cultivating the Self: Journals as a Path for Contemplative Inquiry

Sheri R. Klein

Gradually by writing you will find more and more of your true self.
—Brenda Ueland

An increased emphasis upon the quantification of performance and/or meeting standards within teacher preparation programs in a current climate of academic corporatism (Ettin, 2005; Johnson, Johnson, Farenga & Ness, 2005) has made it challenging for teacher educators to advance the notion of teaching as complex and teacher development as a holistic process that requires personal inner work and relational thinking, or "the ability to understand the interdependencies and interactions of an event" (Gallegos-Nava, 2001, p. 84).

Many educators, however, now believe that we can no longer afford to ignore the development of whole person in teacher education for we are in an "integrative age... [and] the solution to the challenges ahead demands collaborative approaches instead of extreme fragmentation" (Scott, 2000, pp. 23-36). As Daniel Pink (2006), in *Whole New Mind*, and others have suggested, we are leaving the information age and entering an age where the qualities necessary for survival and success are not so dependent upon learning a fixed body of knowledge but "where learning can be a relational endeavor" (Miller, 2000).

Similarly, Campbell (2009) wrote, "students' relational selves are at stake and a holistic approach to art education can solve many problems" (p. 126). According to holistic educators, developing the relational self involves practices that advance self-awareness and an understanding of relationships—between "thought and intuition, mind and body, various kinds of knowledge, the individual and society, the individual and the planet" (Gallegos-Nava, 2001, pp. 139-140). Moreover, Gallegos-Nava (2001) reminded us that, first and foremost, relationships with others must begin with "profound self-knowledge and attentiveness to inner life and one's own interests, needs and goals" (p. 140), for that guides and influences our actions in the world. That is not to say that logical reasoning and critical thinking are not important; however, one must have an awareness of self and one's thoughts before one can think critically about them.

As an art educator, I have looked to numerous educators and philosophers to inform my pedagogical practices with undergraduate preservice teachers and to guide the construction of learning engagements that can assist students in developing their relational self, self-awareness, and a clearer articulation into their way of seeing through the act of writing. In *Education and the Significance of Life*, Krishnamurti (1953) wrote, "Education should awaken the capacity to be self-aware" (1953, p. 15). Similarly, Parker Palmer (2007) and others have suggested that teaching is a spiritual journey that requires self-awareness through contemplative practice and inner work. Finally, the work of Ken Wilber, particularly his writings on Integral Theory (2008, 2002, 2000) provide a framework for understanding and developing human consciousness and learning engagements that can facilitate the development of the relational self.

In my practice, I also acknowledge the principles of the scholarship of teaching and learning (SoTL), in that "to take learning seriously, we need to take learners seriously" (Schulman, 1999, p. 12). This chapter focuses on the process and outcomes of one scholarship of teaching and learning project: introduction to holistic reflection through journaling within two sections of a freshman/sophomore level teacher education course (Foundation of Education) that included art education majors. The journal framework, based on Ken Wilber's Integral Theory (2008, 2002, 2000), provided a structure for looking inward and engaging in holistic reflection with a "focus on intuition, imagination, and contemplation" (Klein, 2008, p. 112).

Findings from an analysis of students' responses to select journal questions will be shared to illustrate how journals may foster the development of contemplative inquiry with the aim of greater self-awareness. Benefits and limitations of the journal assignment, lessons learned, and recommendations for holistic reflection practices within teacher preparation will be offered.

FRAMING THE STUDY

While there are varying differences among holistic educators regarding methods and approaches, developing the whole person is a guiding principle of all holistic educators (Gallegos-Nava, 2001; Glazer, 1999; Halpin, 2003; Krishnamurti, 1953/1981; Miller, 2000). Freshmen "often arrive at the university with unsophisticated, dualistic understandings" (Ciccione, Myers, & Waldmann, 2008, p. 311) and have many unexamined assumptions about teaching, learning and schooling. Reflective practices are widely used in teacher education to unpack and examine students' assumptions and beliefs; yet, approaches often focus on logic/analysis, to the exclusion of other paths for understanding, such as, contemplation—a process that requires looking inward. Contemplation, or "contemplari... [means] to observe, consider, or gaze attentively" (Haynes, n.d., p. 2). Haynes (n.d.) defined contemplative inquiry as

> an epistemology based not on data, information, and the separation of subject and object, but on knowledge, wisdom, and insight about the interconnectedness of all things... contemplation is at the heart of knowledge, for to contemplate deeply is *to see*" [author emphasis]." (p. 5)

Learning engagements that allow teacher candidates to observe self through contemplative inquiry may lead to deeper insights as to what lies within one's heart and mind. One such engagement is journaling.

Journal writing has long been used as a format for reflection with college students in humanities, liberal arts, and teacher education courses. McKinney (2005) reported the value of using learning journals as they present "students' point of view and via their own words" (p. 2). Keller and Helferbein (2007) have utilized art and written narrative as a means for reflection. To understand preservice teacher thinking and beliefs, journals have been used widely in methods courses across disciplines using a variety of different approaches (Cohen, 2005; Grauer & Sandell, 2000; McKinney, 2005; Roland, 1995; Zimmerman, 1994). For example, journal entries may include responses to course content as well as "students' ideas, experiences, attitudes, and feelings" about the subject (Cohen, 2005, p. 145).

In our digital age, when students tend to engage in heavy multitasking and computing that results in less ability to focus (Tamkins, 2009; Thielfoldt & Scheef, 2004), journal writing also allows for an opportunity to focus and develop a mindful presence or "moment by moment present awareness" (Haynes, n.d., p. 2) through writing in class. As Haynes (n.d) explained, "teaching students techniques of awareness, concentration, and means of disciplining their attention is absolutely essential in our era of fragmentation, ever-increasing speed, multi-tasking, and continuously interrupted attention" (p. 2).

Keeping these aims in mind, this project set out to answer three questions: (1) What are students' beliefs and feelings toward issues relative to teaching and American public education? (2) What are students' perceptions toward journaling? (3) What do students say they learn from journaling? It was anticipated that the results from these questions could determine "what is" and "what works" (Hutchings, 2000, p. 4) regarding reflection strategies within undergraduate education courses. This chapter will address findings relative to research Question 1.

CONTEXT/METHOD

A total of 55 students in two sections of a Foundation of Education course at a small Midwestern public university in the spring of 2009 were required as part of course credit to respond to instructor-generated journal questions over the course of a semester. The assignment constituted 40% of the final grade. Class met twice per week for 50 minutes each. Approximately 20 minutes out of a 50-minute period and a total of 16 out of 32 class periods were devoted to responding to journal questions. Institutional research approval was garnered prior to collecting and analyzing data. Across both sections, 42 students gave permission to have their journals copied and their responses analyzed. Identifiers (names) were removed and journals were numbered. A nine-item Likert scale survey was distributed at the end of the semester to solicit responses regarding students' perceptions of the journal assignment. All students gave permission for survey analyses. Analyses of journals and surveys (48/55) were conducted after the semester ended and grades were submitted.

The Foundation of Education course is a required freshman/sophomore level course focusing on the social, historical, and philosophical foundations of American education. Within these two sections, students represented the following disciplines/majors within the school of education: art education, early childhood education, family and consumer science education, marketing and business education, special education, and technology education. In addition, there were several graduate students in each section from the school counseling program. The assignment was posted in D2L, a course management tool, used by the university for online teaching and learning. Students could access the course materials and journal assignment at any time.

Most students had some prior experience with journal writing in university classes; however, some did not. With the exception of one student, the students had no prior knowledge about holistic education theory, methods, and strategies. As the approved course text (Webb, Metha & Jordan, 2007) did not address holistic education principles and theory, I presented information about the historical foundations of and current approaches to holistic education. This occurred in the third week before students were asked to respond to questions that addressed spiritual, ethical, and moral issues in teaching.

The journal framework was explained as occurring in four sections with the intent to develop awareness of self and others' behaviors and an understanding of cultures and systems relative to education. It was also explained that the journal assignment was an opportunity to connect theory, beliefs, and practice, as well as to better understand course material, improve written communication skills, engage in self- and peer reviews of writing, express and voice opinions, engage in reflective thinking about issues in education, and contemplate and imagine solutions to problems in education.

FIGURE 1.

JOURNAL FRAMEWORK

SECTION 1

Correlates to course text Chapters 1-4

Correlates with Wilber's Upper Left Quadrant with emphases on the individual and inner experience

1. What life experiences have guided me toward becoming a teacher?
2. What human or spiritual values are important to me in being a teacher and why?
3. What is my philosophy of life?
4. What is the purpose of education?
5. What are the roles of teachers?
6. What are the roles of students?
7. What are the roles of parents and family in K-12 education?
8. What is my philosophy of education?

SECTION 2

Correlates to course text Chapters 5-14

Correlates to Wilber's Upper Right Quadrant with emphases on individual actions and behaviors

Given the diverse student body today in education,
1. What kinds of intelligences should teachers possess?
2. What kinds of skills should teachers possess?
3. What kinds of behaviors should teachers possess?
4. What criteria of the heart are important for teachers/teacher candidates to possess?
5. Mid term question: In your review of Chapters 5-10, in what specific way(s) do you think education in America has improved since its inception? In your estimation, how has it not improved? (You may use your book to answer this).
6. What federal laws regarding education do you think have significance and why?
7. What laws regarding students do you think are significant and why?
8. What approaches to curriculum in your respective discipline would you take and why?

SECTION 3

Correleates to course text Chapter 15-16

Correlates to Wilber's Lower Left Quadrant and emphases on cultures and interactions with cultures

1. What kinds of instructional approaches would allow you as a teacher to connect with diverse learners?
2. What is the role of technology in connecting learners with learning communities for the 21st century?
3. What is your vision for education for the 21st century? What does it look like?

SECTION 4

Correlates to course text Chapter 16

Correlates to Wilber's Lower Right Quadrant and emphases on systems and interactions with systems

1. Review the following list. Which issue or issues do you think are the most pressing for K-12 education today?
Economics/funding
Changing Demographics
Political
Religion
Curriculum
Standards
Testing
School architecture
School safety and violence
Legal issues
Vouchers and Parent Choice
Home Schooling
Lotteries for funding schools
Tenure
Moral or character education
Corporal Punishment
Teacher training
Globalization
Technology
Other
2. Final exam reflection question? What is creativity or creative thinking? Why is it an important skill for learners and teachers to possess for the 21st century?

The journal framework is shown in Figure 1. Based on Ken Wilber's Integral Theory, it focuses on four ways of knowing through individual experience, behaviors, and awareness of cultures and systems. The main components of the Integral Theory (IT) Model, known as AQAL (All quadrants, All levels), represent the core of Wilber's work.[1] Beyond this core, Wilber has identified other layers, such as levels, lines, stages, states, and types that are nested into each of the quadrants.[2] What this suggests is that, as individuals, we have unique and personal experiences, yet we are also part of collective cultures and systems that influence us so that our "self" develops within all these systems. This is in keeping with the notion of identity development as a spiral process discussed by Wilber and others, in that we can re-visit assumptions and beliefs at any stage of development because identity is never static (Flannery, 2000 in Tisdell, 2003, p. 127).

While the journal framework embraced Wilber's four quadrants, or four sections, the kinds of questions included were not able to, or intended to, address all quadrants with the same kinds of emphases. There were multiple aims for framing the journal questions. The breadth and kinds of questions allowed for reflection on course content and the self. As Wilber, Patton, Leonard, & Mitchell (2008) wrote, "particular practices will often emphasize one quadrant more than others" (p. 29). This is true in the case of the journal assignment that emphasized the quadrants relating to inner experience and outward behaviors (Quadrants Top Left and Top Right and Journal Sections I and II).

Another resource used for this project was Esbjorn-Hargens's work as an integral educator, which supports journaling as a path for contemplative inquiry through a focus on individual experience. Esbjorn-Hargens (2007) wrote that "integral education should take into consideration: cognitive (sensory, perspective, interconnections), emotional (feelings, impulses, awareness), moral (duty, responsibility, compassion)" (p. 81). The journaling process offered opportunities for activating many of these lines of development. His journal format, based on Wilber's model, also provided a sound model for adaptation with undergraduate students.

Two-thirds of the survey questions (14/21) addressed issues relative to the text and chapter content. One-third of the questions (7/21) addressed personal experience, memory (inner life), and the moral and spiritual dimensions of teaching. (See Figure 1.) These questions included:

- Section 1, Questions 1, 2 and 3: What life experiences have guided me toward becoming a teacher? What human or spiritual values are important to me in becoming a teacher? What is my philosophy of life?
- Section 2, Question 4: What criteria of the heart are important for teachers/teacher candidates to possess?
- Section 3, Question 3: What is your vision for 21st-century education?
- Section 4, Question 2: Why is creativity an important skill for the 21st century?

Process

The process included: (1) students' responses to journal questions, (2) peer review, (3) revision of journal entries, and (4) instructor review and assessment of journals. Two of the journal questions (Section 2, Question 4, and Section 4, Question 2,) also functioned as the midterm and the final exams that were completed in class and uploaded to the course drop box.

The journal process began with Section 1 and we moved through each of the three remaining sections sequentially throughout the semester. Responses to questions required a 100-word minimum and a 250-word maximum response with the aim of clear, complete, and insightful responses; most students responded with 100-150 words. Students worked on their journals in class and could access the journal documents that were posted in D2L, or the web-based course management system. Students were encouraged to prepare a draft prior to class to facilitate the writing process. After they completed their draft, they engaged in peer review in class. They were required to then revise their journal entry outside of class.

Paralleling their work in journal Sections 1 and 2, that correlated with Wilber's quadrants of individual actions and behaviors, I read selected poems about teaching at the beginning of class since poetry assists in the "service of turning inward" and "challenges us to examine whether we are living the life we most want to live" (Intrator & Scribner, 2007, p. 194). I hoped that the poetry would inspire students and help them to think not just practically and literally, but poetically and metaphorically about issues. Toward these ends, I also used quotes from philosophers about education—Dewey's *Experience and Education* (1938) and Krishnamurti's *Education and the Significance of Life* (1953). Finally, I selected film clips/scenes from inspirational Hollywood "teacher" films. *Pay it Forward* and *Freedom Writers* were viewed in class during Week 4 as a point of departure for discussing educational theory-in-action and responding to the journal Section 1, Question 8, What is my philosophy of education?

Prior to responding to journal Section 1, Question 2, and Section 2, Question 4, we discussed differences between human and spiritual values—that human values may be more universal and spiritual values may be associated with theological or religious traditions. Students in both classes engaged in brainstorming a potential list of responses to these questions. In addition, my term *criteria of the heart* (Klein, 2008) was explained as potentially useful in thinking about teacher dispositions related to attributes often associated with the "heart," such as feelings and emotions, as well as personal and ethical qualities. Examples of criteria of the heart that emerged through the process of student brainstorming included courage, compassion, forgiveness, fortitude, generosity, hope, inspiration, integrity, joy, justice, kindness, love, and tact. Students were encouraged to draw examples from this list or create new ones.

Time and space constraints limit a complete reporting of students' responses to all the journal questions. However, two particularly relevant journal questions (Section 1, Question 2 and Section 2, Question 4) will be discussed: What human or spiritual values are important to me in being a teacher and why? What criteria of the heart are important for teachers/teacher candidates to possess? It was anticipated that these questions would provide the most opportunities for contemplative inquiry. In keeping with the nature of SoTL work, "quoting students' comments as evidence" (Olson, 2009, p. 13) makes "student thinking more visible" (Ciccone et al., 2008, p. 310).

Journals were collected at the end of the semester, copied, graded, and returned to students. Identifiers were removed and journals were numbered. Responses to the two questions selected for analysis were read several times and at different intervals to "avoid a trap of finding what you are looking for" (Ciccone et al., 2008, p. 313). Key words and phrases were coded/circled and the responses were counted according to frequency.

FINDINGS: SELECTED JOURNAL QUESTIONS

What human or spiritual values are important to me in being a teacher and why?

Students provided numerous examples of human or spiritual values, such as compassion, courage, empathy, faith, forgiveness, goodness, happiness, honesty, hope, humility, inspiration, integrity, justice, kindness, love, openness, patience, respect, trust, and understanding. Of this list, the following were listed with the greatest frequency (10 + times): compassion, courage, love, and patience. Those values listed with some degree of frequency (5-10 times) included faith and humility. Those values listed infrequently (1-4 times) included empathy, goodness, happiness, honesty, hope, inspiration, justice, kindness, respect, trust and understanding. Some of the values listed might also be considered Cardinal Virtues, such as courage and faith, and are associated with theological virtues. Happiness might also be considered a state of being as well as a value.

The top five values in the order of frequently mentioned were love, patience, compassion, courage and faith. Of all the values represented, love was mentioned the most. Students expressed that teachers need to show love for children, the classroom, for teaching, for learning, for subject, and that "your heart must be in teaching" and you should show "love for the job." Students placed a high importance on having and demonstrating patience as "each student learns differently" and "kids have short attention spans." Moreover, they reported that patience is needed "to teach," "for all learners," and "to understand students' feelings and emotions."

About patience, students wrote, "Patience is needed for times when everything seems to be out of control" and "Patience allows me to understand my students, their feelings and emotions and most importantly their opinions." About compassion one student wrote, "Being compassionate is important because it means that I truly care for those who I impact in my life." Another wrote that compassion is needed to "let students know you care" and that it "can be demonstrated by giving students [the] gift of time and listening to them when they demand it," and "giving advice."

About courage, students wrote that courage "allows teachers to have the will power to go out and try new things or teaching strategies." Other students wrote that teachers "will need to stand up for their actions, their beliefs and their students," that "Courage is essential, you need courage to uphold [and] be strong in your decisions." Regarding faith, students commented, "It is important to have faith in your class.... If the students know that you have faith in them that they can learn, they will be much more motivated." Another student wrote, "Faith is very important to me, not as in a religious sense, but as having faith in every person that walks through the door." Another student wrote that "Faith is what makes us succeed in life." These comments supported a view of faith as not so much based on religious beliefs, but seen as "a person's way of finding coherence in and giving meaning to the multiple forces and relations that make up our lives" (Fowler, 1981, p. 4).

About humility one student wrote, "Teaching is a learning process and admitting mistakes and continually searching for more successful ways to teach is one, if not the most important, aspect in teaching." Yet another wrote, "It's difficult for a teacher to show humility and take constructive criticism from peers when they don't respect them."

What criteria of the heart are important for teachers/teacher candidates to possess?

There were some distinct overlaps in responses to this question as students indicated that compassion, courage, love/passion, and patience were important for teachers to possess. In addition, being creative, empathetic, generous, honest, hopeful, inspiring, joyful, kind, open, and understanding were also mentioned. Of all the responses noted, being hopeful, inspiring, and passionate were mentioned with the greatest frequency.

On being hopeful, students wrote "Hope is the light at the end of a dark tunnel," "You must have hope for students," and "Hope your presence will affect every child," "Hope students learn to love and respect themselves," "Having hope for the future is what all teachers should possess and strive for, " and "You need to have the hope that every student can change and achieve great things while in school." On being inspiring, students wrote, "Inspiration is necessary in working with students who lack resources and support necessary for positive development" and "You need to inspire students to be the best they can be." Another wrote "Teachers need to be inspired to teach... I think that part of teachers' and teacher candidates' jobs are to inspire the next generation and to make a difference in the world." Inspiration was mentioned in 7/42 journal responses for this question. This student captured the essence of Criteria of the Heart in writing that "A teacher should possess an open heart that lets love in—love from students, administrators, [and] parents."

DISCUSSION

There were some strong overlaps across the responses relative to the selected questions. Among these, love/passion and compassion were mentioned with the most frequency as important for teachers to possess as a value and a disposition. The following student's comment illustrates this: "A truly great teacher can command respect not through intimidation but by being a source of love and generosity."

It is important to think about how values and dispositions associated with the heart can be better addressed within current teacher education programs, particularly given the realities of the first years of teaching. It is timely to ask how we can provide learning engagements that may assist teacher candidates to become more loving, compassionate, and passionate toward self, others and about their chosen profession.

Hope and faith were also frequently mentioned as important for teachers. Typically, hope and faith are not discussed within teacher education, as they are typically associated with theological virtues. However, given the continued challenges facing teachers, perhaps it is timely to address hope and faith within preservice teacher education. Halpin (2003) argued about the significance of hope as a guiding force in the educational process. He wrote, hope is "a way of living prospectively in and engaging purposefully with the past and present" (p. 14) but adds, "to lack hope is to lack a vital spiritual energy and to run the danger of lapsing into lethargy and indifference" (p. 26). It is the notion of engaging purposefully and without indifference that also speaks to Palmer's (2007) call for moral courage.

Finally, students at the freshman/sophomore level are keenly aware that "Teachers are role models to hundreds of children and could be [the] one to leave a foot print in their heart." This insight suggests the awareness that teachers can and do impact students both positively and negatively. As such, it is important that preservice teachers develop self-awareness and habits of being and doing that are reflective of values and dispositions that may eventually leave gentle and loving footprints within others' hearts.

BENEFITS AND LIMITATIONS

It is clear that from survey findings that the majority of students found that the journal assignment provided them with a path for connection to their feelings and beliefs. Feedback on the process suggests that the journal does hold promise; however, some adaptations to the journal may be required to accommodate the variance of students' writing abilities and learning styles. For example, the journal could include more opportunities to respond to questions with art, poetry and/or music and could similarly allow for contemplation in different media.[3] Other formats for journaling could also be considered, such as web-based journal formats (e.g., livejournal.com), or having students create their own blog journals.

CONCLUSION

As Gallegos-Nava (2001) wrote, "Our culture does not nurture the best and most noble of the human spirit... It does not cultivate compassion, generosity and love" (p. 111). In reaction to this trend, there is growing interest in finding wholeness and making connections evident in the fields of psychology (Wilber, 2008, 2002, 2000), education (Gallegos-Nava, 2001) and art education (Campbell, 2009; Klein, 2008). The introduction of holistic reflection methods and strategies with both preservice and inservice art teachers that include opportunities for creative writing and reflection in a variety of media about their values and beliefs will not only contribute to their personal and professional development, but may also reinforce methods of reflective practice within K-12 art classrooms, and that may contribute to the holistic development of K-12 students.

Without concern for developing the teacher as a whole person, we are likely to see a continual rise in teacher burnout (Conway, Hibbard, Albert & Hourigan, 2005, p. 5) and especially high attrition rates among beginning teachers who are not equipped to deal with the range of issues and problems facing them and their students. Addressing such problems, as this chapter suggests, will require that teacher educators consider holistic approaches and strategies that foster self-awareness and understanding. In this regard, Wilber's work and model may assist teacher educators in creating engagements and courses for both preservice and inservice teachers that "increase awareness in small ways" (Melnick, 2005, p. 21). One such small but meaningful way is through cultivating the practice of reflective journaling.

ACKNOWLEDGMENTS

Thanks to my students for always enriching my understanding of the teaching and learning process. I would like to express gratitude to Dr. Ramon Gallegos-Nava for deepening and enriching my understanding of holistic education. I am grateful to Dr. Sean Esborn-Hargens for his clear and insightful scholarship on the application of integral theory for higher education contexts. Thanks also to Dr. Isabella Colalillo-Kates and R.S. for always engaging me in thoughtful and inspiring dialogue.

REFERENCES

Campbell, L. (2009). Spirituality in holistic art education: Preventing violence among youth in the United States. *Journal of Cultural Research in Art Education,* 121-130.

Ciccione, A. A. Myers, R. & Waldmann, S. (2008). What's so funny?: Moving students toward complex thinking in a course on comedy and laughter. *Arts and Humanities, 7*(3), 308-322.

Cohen, R. (2005). Journal writing in mathematics education. In J. Miller, S. Karsten, D. Denton, D. Orr, & I. Colallio-Kates (Eds.), *Holistic learning: Spirituality in education* (pp. 145-152). Albany, NY: State University of New York.

Conway, C., Hibbard, S., Albert, D., & Hourigan, R. (2005). Professional development of arts teachers. *Arts Education Policy Review, 107*(1), 3-9.

Dewey, J. (1997). *Experience and education.* New York, NY: Macmillan. (Original work published 1938)

Esbjorn-Hargens, S. (Summer 2007). Integral teacher, integral students, integral classroom: Applying integral theory to graduate education. *Journal of Integral Theory and Practice, (2)*2, 72-103.

Ettin, J. (Summer 2005). Contingent teaching, corporate universities, and the academic labor movement. *Radical Teacher,* 73, 26-32.

Flannery, D. (2000). Identity and self-esteem. In E. Hayes & D. Flannery (Eds.), *Women as learners* (pp. 53-78). San Francisco, CA: Jossey-Bass.

Forbes, S. (2003). *Holistic education: An analysis of its ideas and nature.* Brandon, VT: Foundation of Educational Renewal.

Fowler, J. (1981). *Stages of faith: The psychology of human development and the quest for meaning.* San Francisco, CA: Harper and Row.

Gallegos-Nava, R. (2001). *Holistic education: Pedagogy of universal love.* Brandon, VT: Foundation for Educational Renewal.

Glazer, S. (Ed.). (1999). *The heart of learning: Spirituality in education.* New York, NY: Putnam.

Grauer, K., & Sandell, R. (2000). *The visual journal and teacher development.* Paper presented at the Annual Convention of the National Art Education Association.

Halpin, D. (2003). *Hope and education.* London, England: Routledge.

Haynes, D. J. (n.d). Contemplative practice and the education of the whole person. Retrieved from www.contemplativemind.org/programs/academic/Haynes.pdf

Hutchings, P. (2000). Approaching scholarship of teaching and learning. In P. Hutchings (Ed.), *Opening lines: Approaches to scholarship of teaching and learning* (pp. 1-10). Menlo Park, CA: Carnegie Foundation for the Advancement of Teaching and Learning.

Intrator, S. M., & Scribner, M. (2007). *Leading from within: Poetry that sustains the courage to lead.* San Francisco, CA: Jossey-Bass.

Johnson, D. D., Johnson, B., Farenga, S., & Ness, D. (2005). *Trivializing teacher education: The accreditation squeeze.* Lanham, MD: Rowman & Littlefield.

Journal of Integral Theory and Practice [online], 2(2), 72-102. Retrieved from www.aqaljournal.org

Keller, D. B., & Helferbein, R. J. (Spring 2007). Art as reflection/art as reflective: Service learning. Preservice teachers and use of the aesthetic. *Mountain Rise: Journal of Scholarship of Teaching and Learning.*

Krishnamurti, J. (1981). *Education and the significance of life.* San Francisco, CA: Harpers. (Original work published 1953)

Klein, S. (2010). Exploring hope and the inner life through journaling. *Encounter, 23*(2), 48-52.

Klein, S. (2009). Issues in contemporary K-16 education [Web log post]. Retrieved from www.talkaboutk16education.blogspot.com/

Klein, S. (2008). The use of dispositions in preservice art teacher evaluation. *Studies in Art Education, 49*(4), 375-380.

Klein, S. (2008). Holistic reflection in teacher education: Issues and strategies. *Reflective Practice, 9*(2), 111-121.

Klein, S. (Fall 2000). Spirituality and art education: Looking to place. *Journal of Multicultural and Cross-Cultural Research in Art Education,* 18, 77-66.

McKinney (2005). Reflections on learning sociology: Analysis of learning log entries. *MountainRise, 2.* Retrieved from http://facctr.wcu.edu/mountainrise/archive/vol2no1/html/reflections_on_learning.html

Melnick, J. (2005). "The willing suspension of disbelief: Optimism" *Gestalt Review, 9*(1), 10-26.

Miller, J. P. (2000). *Education and the soul: Toward a spiritual curriculum.* Albany, NY: State University of New York.

Olson, K. M. (2009). Assessing student learning and perceptions in an upper level general education requirement argumentation course. *International Journal for the Scholarship of Teaching and Learning, 3*(1). Retrieved from www.georgiasouthern.edu/ljsotl

Palmer, P. (2007). *The courage to teach: Exploring the inner landscape of a teacher's life.* San Francisco, CA: Jossey-Bass.

Pink, D. (2006). *Whole new mind: Why right brainers will rule the world*. New York, NY: Riverhead/Penguin.

Roland, C. (1995). The use of journals to promote reflective thinking in prospective art teachers. In L. Galbraith (Ed.), *Preservice art education: Issues and practice* (pp. 119-134). Reston, VA: National Art Education Association.

Scott, D. K. (2000). Spirituality in an integrative age. In H. Kazanjian, Jr. & Peter L. Laurence (Eds.), *Education as Transformation Religious Pluralism, Spirituality, and a New Vision for Higher Education* (pp. 22-36). New York, NY: Peter Lang.

Shulman, L. (1999). Taking learning seriously. *Change, 31*(4), 11-17.

Tamkins, T. (2009, August 26). "Drop that Blackberry: Multitasking may be harmful." CNN Health. Retrieved from www.cnn.com/2009/HEALTH/08/25/multitasking.harmful/index.html

Thielfoldt, D., & Scheef, D., (2004). Generation X and the Millennials: What you need to know about mentoring the new generations. Retrieved from www.abanet.org/lpm/lpt/articles/mgt08044.html

Tisdell, E. J. (2003). *Exploring spirituality and culture in adult and higher education*. San Francisco, CA: Jossey-Bass.

Ueland, B. (1987). *If you want to write*. St Paul, MN: Grey Wolf Press. (Original work published 1938)

Webb, D. L., Metha, A., & Jordan, K. F. (2007). *Foundations of education*. (5th ed.). Upper Saddle, NJ: Pearson.

Wilber, K., Patten, T., Leonard, A., & Morelli, M. (2008). *Integral Life Practice*. Boston, MA: Integral Books.

Wilber, K. (2002). *Boomeritis: A novel that will set you free*. Boston, MA: Shambala.

Wilber, K. (2000). *A theory of everything: An integral vision of business, politics, science, and spirituality*. Boston, MA: Shambala.

Zimmerman, E. (Sept. 1994). Concerns of preservice art teachers and those who teach them. *Art Education, 47*(5), 59-67.

ENDNOTES

1   Ken Wilber's work has been described as being epistemologically pluralistic with a personal growth focus through integration of the mind, body and spirit. His work has been cited by scholars in psychology, spirituality, criminal studies, politics, and holistic education, yet little application, until recently, (Forbes, 2003) has occurred within education. See the *Journal of Integral Theory and Practice* [online] at www.aqaljournal.org.

2   To see a comprehensive diagram of Wilber's AQUAL model see Wilber (2000, 2002, 2008).

3   Revisions to the journal assignment in fall 2009 included opportunities for musical, visual, and poetic responses to journal questions. See (Klein, 2009) and (Klein, 2010).

ABOUT THE AUTHOR

Sheri R. Klein is a Professor (Ret.) of Art Education at the University of Wisconsin-Stout, Menomonie, Wisconsin. She has taught in K-16 art education contexts for over 20 years. Her scholarship has focuses on holistic approaches to teaching, learning, curriculum, and assessment.

CHAPTER 20

The Margaret Grauer Teaching from the HeART Program: A Teacher Education Perspective

Alex de Cosson and Kit Grauer

I was called to teach and I answered that call somewhat grudgingly. "What about my art?" I wondered. I had not yet learned that we tend to practice what we preach, that in unblocking others I would unblock myself, and that, like all artists, I would thrive more easily with companionship, with kindred souls making kindred leaps of faith. Called to teach, I could not imagine the good teaching would bring to me and, through me, to others.

—Julia Cameron

A (RE)ENVISIONING OF ELEMENTARY TEACHER EDUCATION

For the past 4 years, the University of British Columbia (UBC) has offered a unique holistic arts-infused teacher education program specially geared to elementary teacher candidates who have no background in the arts. These students have already completed a Bachelors Degree and join our program, as a cohort, for a 1-year specialization in teacher training. Our program provides an opportunity for student teachers to prepare for work as a teacher by working with artists as part of their student teaching experience. This prepares them for a lifetime of integrating the arts into the curriculum. Toward this end, candidates in this cohort work with a dedicated team of artist/researcher/teachers who believe in heart-felt teacher education and have taken to our acronym of HeART with vigorous delight.

Unlike many arts programs for this population, which concentrate solely on one art form such as visual art or music, this program exposes students to several domains, including music, dance and the visual and performing arts. Moreover, students' exposure comes directly from working with professional artists who have long experience in schools as artists-in-residence. Previous research with Learning Through The Arts™ (LTTA)[1] found that, among other things, artists-in-residence change pedagogical understandings of teachers and teacher candidates by allowing for an expanded understanding of how the arts can be used in the classroom (Kind, Irwin, Grauer, & de Cosson, 2005; Irwin, Wilson Kind, Grauer, & de Cosson, 2005; Grauer, Irwin, de Cosson, &Wilson, 2001).[2] In this chapter, we explore the development of this newly created project in elementary teacher education that is grounded in our LTTA research. Figure 1 shows a teacher candidate's hands as she works on a painted mural with one of the artists-in-residence.

Planning Day

The project, entitled the Margaret Grauer Teaching from the HeART cohort in the elementary teacher education program at UBC, is a professional development model that sees teacher education as a lifelong and life-wide journey. Thanks to the generous support of an outside donor and the Dean of Education, the project is able to provide funding to pay the artists-in-residence to work with the teacher candidates throughout their 1-year program. We are also able to provide a release day for an on-campus Planning Day for the sponsor teachers who support our program to work with their teacher candidates and meet the artists. This on-campus Planning Day provides an opportunity

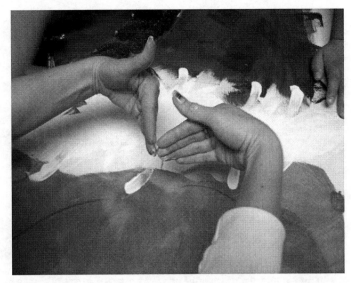

to expand the sponsor teachers' understanding of holistic arts education and its integration across the curriculum.

We also use the Planning Day to plan the artists' visit to the practicum classroom. Critical issues come into sharp focus for the candidate teachers as they fit their artists' visit into their 12-week practicum model. They must consider such issues as school time-tabling, space requirements, materials needed, and curriculum connections.

Integration of Art Forms, Artists in Residence, and Institutions

As noted above, one of the fundamental differences between this program and others is that it involves several different art forms. In addition, we integrate direct experience with artists and cultural institutions into the full year learning program of our teacher candidates. In part, this is meant to prepare these teachers to include experience with artists in their future class-rooms. According to Kind, de Cosson, Irwin, and Grauer,

> Inviting artists into schools is seen as a way to enrich and support curriculum, enhance school reform efforts, and also frequently act as professional development opportunities for teachers wishing to improve their arts education knowledge and practice. The latter is often the case in elementary schools. (2007)

With these ends in view, from the first week of the HeART program the teacher candidates were invited into a holistic and arts-infused learning space that was both innovative and transformative, that engendered learning through doing; a place of negotiated meaning making. In this paper we concur with Peter London's (2003) statement, "Art is a holistic language that is uttered from the mind, body and spirit. In this way, art is a perfect form of expression with which to imagine, investigate, propose and engage in a new worldview." We envision an arts-infused curriculum to be one in which the arts of all kinds permeate the entire day's activities for learning, from the math unit to the science unit, and that a place for negotiated meaning making is found along the day's journey from teacher to student / student to teacher. As one of our teacher candidates, with a BA in English literature and a minor in philosophy and no arts background, said, "(It) is one of the misconceptions about arts based learning that it is about teaching kids how to do art; (when really) it's about using arts to teach, not to teach them art." The activities that the teacher candidates did in the Teachers' Museum and Gallery Institute is an excellent example of how they learned first-hand the power of negotiated meaning making.

FIGURE 2. 'Artists Day' teacher candidates dance their signatures.

The HeART program engendered an attitude of openness among the candidate teachers, while also helping them to become a research-focused cohort of learners. Throughout the year-long program, they were engaged in an active research study, focusing on the use of artists-in-residence programming.

The Research Study: Artist Days

Throughout their 1-year teaching education program, the teacher candidates were given the structured opportunity to work with three internationally exhibiting/performing artists. For this study there was one visual artist, one dance artist and one musician. These three artists developed programming that integrated curriculum-specific learning through day-long hands-on arts workshops called Artist Days. For instance, in the first Artist Day, teacher candidates learned to dance their signatures, embody the correct stance for taiko drumming, and create a visual art collaged banner that visualizes the entire activity, thus engaging in learning through praxis. Figure 2 shows teacher candidates dance their signatures at an Artists Day.

In this study, the Artist Days were scheduled three times prior to the teacher candidates' 12-week long practicum session that occurs approximately three-quarters of the way through their program. These were augmented with additional artist workshops in specific methods classes in math, social studies, science, and language arts. (An example of a Science Methods course with arts integration is discussed later in this chapter). These additional artists' workshops are intended to help the student teachers unpack the concept of arts integration across the curriculum.

Also in this study, the artists went into the schools with the teacher candidates during their long practicum. The sponsor teachers were included in this study by participating in interview and debriefing sessions, as the teacher candidates progressed through their 12-week practicum. The artists participated as artists-in-residence, working through a curriculum integration unit that had been developed by the teacher candidates and supported and enhanced by the artists' unique experience and knowledge.

The researchers photo-documented the teacher candidates in their classes as they participated in arts integration with the artists. Researchers took observational notes, collected curriculum materials that supported arts integration, and facilitated interview sessions with the participants.

The researchers visited the practicum sites on a regular basis to observe the teacher candidates and their sponsor teachers and to photo-document the artists-in-residence process.

Photo-documentation assisted the teacher candidates, sponsor teachers, artists and the researchers in understanding the impact of teaching practices that were intended to use the arts as an integrative tool for learning.

This research study was self-selective, as it is specific to the established HeART cohort in the One Year Teacher Education Program in the Faculty of Education. All 36 members of the cohort took part in the study. All 36 sponsor teachers and the 3 artists were aware of the planned research study and chose to join the cohort with this prior knowledge.

This research was done as a collaboration between teacher candidates, teachers, artists, and researchers. It was enhanced by providing the candidate teachers with data collection capabilities, such as digital cameras and portable flash drives. In this artful action research model, the teacher candidates were encouraged to share with the researchers and become student researchers.

OUR COMMUNITY ARTISTS

Throughout their year-long program, our teacher candidates were fortunate to work with three exceptional community artists. In the program we are about to describe, the artists were Bonnie Soon, a taiko drummer; Richard Tetrault, a mural artist; and Kathryn Ricketts, a contemporary dancer. The teacher candidates met the artists and were engaged with pedagogically grounded hands-on art activities early in their program. For example, in their second week, our 'arts-shy' teacher candidates spent 3 days at The Vancouver Art Gallery and 2 days at the Museum of Anthropology, where they joined an art-focused graduate teacher institute: The Teachers' Museum and Gallery Institute. This intensive course focused on art, teaching, and interpretation in museums and community contexts. The program includes in-gallery exploration and interpretive activities; tours and demonstrations; lectures and panel discussions by artists, curators, art historians, and educators.

As an example of negotiated meaning-making, one of the topics at the institute was TATAU. The unit began with a visit to the exhibition on Samoan Tattooing and Global Culture at the Museum of Anthropology. This was a prelude to meeting and speaking, through the technological marvels of Skype, with the New Zealand-born, Pacific Islander of Samoan descent, artist Rosanna Raymond. Rosanna is a performance/installation/body adornment artist and writer currently living and working in London, UK. She allowed the teacher candidates to 'virtually' enter the world of body tattooing in a unique and inclusive way that calmed what, for many of them, was a sense of trepidation towards the medium. Through such exposure, they were also helped to develop a greater understanding of, and become more accepting of, cultural traditions very different from their own. This virtual arts-immersion challenged many of the teacher candidates' preconceived notions of what art can be, and suggested new curricular thinking for the classroom of the future. After working with a variety of different artists in The Teachers' Museum and Gallery Institute, our teacher candidates were eager to work with "their" artists in the fall course work and practicum experiences in the schools.

PLANNING AN ARTS INFUSED CURRICULUM

As discussed earlier in this chapter, teacher candidates go on to student teach in schools where they have the opportunity to work with their artists-in-residence, whom they know well from having worked with them on numerous occasions prior to being in the schools. These artist workshops create bonding and trust between the artists and the candidate teachers that engender experimentation in the curriculum delivery. The teacher candidates collaborate with their sponsor teacher, artist, and university researcher to plan an art-infused curriculum. Figure 3 illustrates just such a curriculum delivery.

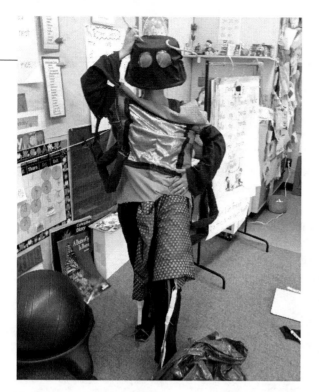

FIGURE 3. (left) A teacher candidate made this full size insect outfit from recycled materials for her kindergarten class.

FIGURE 4. (right) The Science Methods project reinterpreted in a kindergarten/grade one classroom.

To concretize the overall arts infused curriculum for the teacher candidates, two Faculty Associates facilitate our team. These associates have strong ties to the public schools. These exceptional women, Heather MacKay and Helen Robertson, organize our practicum placements and supervise the teacher candidates in the schools. We work collaboratively in planning the entire program and they teach the Principles of Teaching and Communication courses to the cohort. They provide continuity throughout the program and are an integral part of the success of the experience. Both believe strongly in the value of the arts and bring their unique areas of specialization to integrating the arts throughout the curriculum. Heather MacKay is a literature specialist and brings her love of children's literature and language literacy into all that we do. Helen Robertson teaches the visual arts methods course and implements the reflective visual journal project that starts on the first day of the program and continues to teacher candidates' final post-practicum reflections. (The importance of the visual journals is discussed in greater detail later in this chapter.)

Complementing these activities, the artists also work within the methods courses to help envision an arts-infused, holistic curriculum. For instance, Richard Tetrault, the visual artist, worked with the science methods course instructor to develop a project called *Small Worlds Projected Large* to integrate a unit on 'seeing' organic forms found in nature. The raw material consisted of a collection of objects gathered by the science methods instructor and used to help students develop an inquisitive eye and to realize the importance of visual research in the classification of objects. How we contemplate, reflect upon, and understand objects such as shells, tree roots, rocks, bones, etc., some of which are difficult to identify when found in nature, requires exact powers of observation. Richard worked with the teacher candidates to further develop their powers of observation by having them draw the objects they had chosen onto mural-sized paper, thus magnifying their object many times over. For this activity, the cohort was broken into groups of six to eight, and working collaboratively, they drew the chosen object with charcoal, while maximizing the use of the paper. This outline sketch formed the underlying 'shape' of the mural design and became an emphasis of the overall image, which was then augmented by another linking form that had a biological connection to the initial image, for example a spiraling shell fragment may be linked to the gnarled spiral of an old petrified tree branch. The mural was then further developed by adding Styrofoam prints of this additional form, which was integrated into the color and texture to become part of an over-all visual composition. Figure 4 illustrates a science project interpreted through an artists-in-residence project in a kindergarten/grade one class.

As the Science instructor said,

> I love the way the candidate teachers may not even know 'what' the object is that they are drawing, and many do not, but through the process of manipulating it, and the observation needed to draw it onto the mural paper, they have a much stronger understanding of it as an object. There is also a fascinating relationship of the transformation of an object, through the artistic medium, which nature does all the time but students often want to be fixed. (Field notes, Sandra Scott, March 16, 2009)

Visual Journals

To facilitate the process of observation and reflection, each teacher candidate is expected to keep a reflective journal of his or her journey into becoming pedagogical. On the first day of the program, candidates are introduced to the idea of a "visual journal," an artist's journal that combines image and text to explore ideas, feelings and curricular connections. It is more than a diary, more than a sketchbook. Their visual journals become the place to experiment with image and text together or separately, to collage, draw, paint, print, and manipulate their own and others' images, to "speak" to the process of learning to teach. Here they keep notes, visual artifacts, possibilities for artistic products, reflections on their readings and research into ideas for practice. By using such artistic habits of mind, they learn to unlock preconceived notions about the value of the arts to our understanding of the world. Figure 5 is an example of a teacher candidate adding a Styrofoam print to her visual journal.

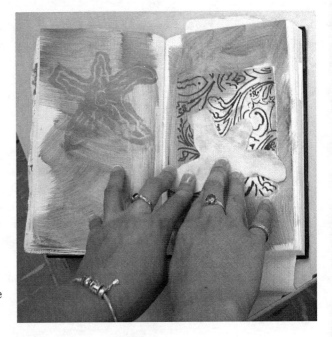

FIGURE 5. Visual Journal entry.

As the use of the journal suggests, we believe that everything that the teacher candidate experiences has or should have an experiential basis, and that this orientation makes it possible to blend research and practice. In addition, we hope that the power of using a variety of materials, the act of creating, and the glimpses into the creative processes of artists will combine to provide these beginning teachers with insights into teaching and learning that will profoundly shape their sense of what is possible in an arts-infused class room. Moreover, we want them to see the potential for authentic reflection and expression, away from the tyranny of one right answer.

Every Classroom Transformed

The artists-in-residence in our program not only work with our teacher candidates throughout their year-long program and practicum to co-facilitate an arts-infused curriculum, they also bring their considerable expertise to provide professional development to our sponsor teachers.

Artist-in-the-schools programs frequently serve as an attempt to bring new life to depleted arts programs (Hanley, 2003). With the ongoing budget cuts to schools in British Columbia, where dedicated art specialists are often laid off, it is important that our future elementary school teachers have ongoing and quality exposure to the power of art in their teaching. Programs such as HeART prepare teachers to bring arts-infused curriculum into the classroom; our teachers-to-be have also learned early in their careers the importance of artists as partners in education in their classrooms. Figure 6 reflects the work of a candidate

FIGURE 6. A teacher candidate made this full size cow for her kindergarten class after a class trip to the farm. The kids could 'milk' the cow just as they had seen at the farm.

teacher who made a full-sized cow for her kindergarten class after a trip to a farm. The kids could "milk" the cow just as they had seen done at the farm.

Many of our sponsor teachers have returned to the program specifically because they are exposed to a different artist each year, and over a 3-year cycle they enrich their teaching practice. We therefore intend to regularly renew the artists in the program; for instance, in our current year we have replaced the dance artist with a drama specialist, to continue to provide a variety of learning opportunities for our sponsor teachers.

Our sponsor teachers are, in fact, an extraordinary group of dedicated individuals who allow for the growth of their HeART teacher candidates in unique and varied ways, and we provide support for them, as well. For example, as mentioned at the beginning of this chapter, we facilitate an on-campus 'Planning Day.' This allows time for planning for the sponsor teachers and the teacher candidates approximately 6 weeks prior to the beginning of the practicum. On the Planning Day, the artists-in-residence are present to showcase the sort of work the sponsor teacher can expect in their classrooms, and to plan which days will work for the artists to come into the schools.

It is also an opportunity for the teacher candidates to demonstrate examples of their new artistic understanding and how this will fit into their curriculum planning. They show examples of their holistic integrated artistic learning with taiko drumming and dance sessions and exhibitions of the science murals referred to earlier in this chapter. They also share their visual journals and talk about how to incorporate visual journals into their practicum experience.

This year, two exceptional teacher candidates, Meghan Mitchell and Dan Coghlan, presented a PowerPoint introduction to the HeART cohort as a rehearsal for the presentation they were taking to the Western Canadian Association for Student Teaching (WESTCAST) Conference at Lethbridge University, in our neighboring province of Alberta (February 18, 2010).

The sponsor teachers are encouraged to join in with their teacher candidate/artists' projects during the practicum. With Kathryn, they may enact the chicken dance after the farmyard visit, or play a part in sock-animated, student-written, video production. With Richard, they may paint a large format mural based on nature themes, or learn about printmaking that can be added to a mural once dry. With Bonnie, they may lead a taiko drum circle of *"garbage cans turned taiko drums"* that then are piled, turned on their sides, and reconstructed into elements of an enacted classroom unit on the fish life-cycle. Using the "taiko drums" as fish, the children dance and mime their new understanding of this cycle of life.

This playful intermingling of artist/teacher/student goes a long way toward solidifying the teacher candidate's understanding of life-long holistic learning, which is the living pedagogy of a teacher becoming.

Learning Through Doing

The pre-practicum workshops with the artists also enable the teacher candidates to forget their apprehensions about art and to see their abilities as potential creative teachers. In thinking about children's artistic development, Walsh (1999), proposed that the purpose of art education was not to create "artists" but rather to create individuals with well-developed artist selves. Kind et al. also insist that

> This applies also to artists and teachers who each need support in finding ways to develop artist selves *and* teacher selves. In shifting understanding of identity from a single fixed entity to multiple selves and expressions, teachers can develop "artist selves" and move beyond the outward "how to" or project-focus of art education to a deeper, more personal exploration of their individual creative potential. (Kind et al., 2007)

Margaret Grauer's Public Bench on Galiano Island

The philosophy behind this cohort experience can be appreciated by reading Kit Grauer's (2006), "My Mother Wore Pink." In it, Kit remembers that her mother, Margaret, "never called herself an artist, but her life revolved around art" (p. 72). Moreover, her sense of art as a conduit to deeper understanding also plays itself out throughout our year long program.

FIGURE 7. Margaret Grauer's Public Bench on Galiano Island.

> They sing with joy as the sun shines and they are invited to run outside to follow artist Andy Goldsworthy's example of non-intrusive environmental artmaking. They are asked to embrace their emotions, to student teach with an open heart. (de Cosson, Grauer, Irwin, & Kind, 2005)

Margaret Grauer's Public Bench on Galiano Island, British Columbia, Canada, invites everyone to sit and stay awhile, to sit quietly and contemplate the beauty that is unfolding (Figure 7).

Based on this philosophy, we passionately believe that the inclusion of artists will help these teachers-to-be see the joy of teaching and learning through a holistic practice. As Peter London (2003) reminds us, "the artistic process is not merely a vehicle to represent our current state of mind and affairs, more significantly it is a powerful practice by which we can work towards the achievement of desired states of mind and work." We must be open to all artistic practices to open our teacher candidates to the full potential of holistic, arts infused curriculum. Our research demonstrates that given the chance to teach with the help of professional artists many more teachers could become more creative in their own classrooms. The teacher candidates from the HeART cohort therefore demonstrate how a model of an artists-in-residence program brought in at the beginning of a teacher's career can work wonders for creative classrooms in the future.

COMING FULL CIRCLE (THE LAST DAY)

Our artists, researchers and teachers introduce aesthetic ways of knowing throughout the year-long program. We strike early and methodically.

The teacher candidates dance, paint and drum curriculum from Day 1 of their program, visual journals at their sides, to their last day before graduation. In the process, our 'arts-shy' teacher candidates are transformed into 'arts-enthused' teachers, ones eager to enact holistic

ABOUT THE AUTHORS

Alex F. de Cosson is an a/r/tographer who has worked as a professional sculptor exhibiting nationally and internationally for over 25 years. Alex has an MFA from York University and was on the faculty of the Ontario College of Art and Design from 1989–2006. He is an adjunct professor in the Department of Curriculum and Pedagogy and MET Programs at The University of British Columbia.

Kit Grauer is a professor of art education at the University of British Columbia in Vancouver, Canada. She has written extensively and given numerous presentations, in-service, and keynote speeches. Her current research includes the use of artistic pedagogical strategies in both preservice and in-service teacher education, museum education, and community-based new media education. She has also been part of two research/creation grants which produce art as research and continues to be involved in her own artistic practice.

arts-infused curriculum. Moreover, through the eyes of teachers becoming, we refresh our own desire to enrich children's classrooms with holistic knowing. The teacher candidates are an inspiration to all of us. A renewal of the spirit that is teaching is found in these young and eager minds. As recorded in one of our field notes,

> The images beckoned me to peer deeper into my photographic practice and to see with new eyes the incredible splendor that is our yearly intake of extremely talented teacher candidates to the HeART cohort. Their year with us is a transformational one for all. They come in as raw individuals ready to make a difference as teachers but unsure of their way to succeed. They leave us assured educators ready to creatively tackle what the world throws at them. (de Cosson, Field notes, November, 2009)

We dedicate this chapter to our teacher candidates' continued success, knowing that they will meet challenges head on, and infuse their curriculum and lives with arts of all kinds. As one of our teacher candidates, with a Bachelor of Arts in Kinesiology with a minor in Geography and no prior arts background said, with newly understood joy only a few weeks from the end of the practicum, "Through this program we have begun to channel the artist within."

REFERENCES

Cameron, J. (2007). *The complete artists way: Creativity as spiritual practice.* London, England: Penguin Group.

Coghlan, & Mitchell, (2010). HeART: A teacher education model. Paper presented at WESTCAST (Western Canadian Association for Student Teaching). Lethbridge University, Alberta.

de Cosson, A. F., Grauer, K., Irwin, R. L., & Kind, S. (2005). Oneiric glasshouse walking (A sculpted (s)p(l)ace): Found walking an artist-in-residence or a/r/tography in praxis. *Education Insights, 9*(2). Retrieved from http://ccfi.educ.ubc.ca/publication/insights/v09n02/exhibits/artography.html

Grauer, K. (2006). My mother wore pink. *Visual Arts Research, 32*(1), 86-95.

Grauer, K., Irwin, R., de Cosson, A., & Wilson, S. (2001). Images for understanding: Snapshots of learning through the arts. *International Journal of Education and the Arts, 2*(9). Retrieved from http://ijea.org/v2n9/index.html

Hanley, B. (2003). The good, the bad, and the ugly—Arts partnerships in Canadian elementary schools. *Arts Education Policy Review, 104*(6), 11-20.

Irwin, R. L., Wilson-Kind, S., Grauer, K., & de Cosson, A. (2005). Integration as embodied knowing. In M. Stokrocki (Ed.). *Interdisciplinary art education builds bridges to connect disciplines & cultures* (pp. 44-59). Reston, VA: National Art Education Association.

Kind, S., de Cosson, A. F., Irwin, R. L., & Grauer, K. (2007). Artist-teacher partnership in learning: The in/between spaces of artist-teacher professional development. *The Canadian Journal of Education, 30*(3), 839-864.

Kind, S., Irwin, R. L., Grauer, K., & de Cosson, A. F. (2005). Medicine wheel imag(in)ings: Exploring holistic curriculum perspectives. *Art Education, 58*(5), 33-38.

London, P. (2003). *Drawing closer to nature.* Retrieved from www.peterlondon.us/5articles.html#draw

Walsh, D. (1999). Constructing an artistic self: The historical child and art education. *Visual Arts Research, 25*(2), 4-13.

ENDNOTES

1. This program is sponsored by the Royal Conservatory of Music, Toronto, Canada, and is designed to be a professional development model for generalist elementary classroom teachers wishing to learn how to integrate the arts into all subject areas within the curriculum. The program brings three different artists into a school to work with each teacher and, progressively over a 3-year period, classrooms are added so that at the end of the 3 years the whole school is involved.

2. We thank the Social Sciences and Humanities Research Council of Canada for their generous support of our research program entitled "Learning through the Arts: Artists, Researchers and Teachers Collaborating for Change."

AUTHORS' NOTE

Dr. Kit Grauer provided envisioning and mentoring for this program. Dr. Alex de Cosson served as artist and program coordinator, and Cohort leadership was provided by Heather Mackay and Helen Robertson. Artists included Kathryn Ricketts, Bonnie Soon, and Richard Tetrault. We wish to thank the artists Kathryn Ricketts, Bonnie Soon, and Richard Tetrault for their dedicated commitment to this project. Without them none of it would have been possible.

CHAPTER 21

Classroom Culture: Fostering Relationships in the Art Classroom

Karen Cummings

In 11 years of teaching high school art, I have come to recognize the importance of classroom socialization and a sense of belonging to student development as artists and as individuals alike. My students' actions revealed the value of community in the classroom, and the significance of my actions on the students' learning experiences. The following excerpts from my students and my own journal entries provide insight into the influences of a caring, supportive environment on my students' learning, and the strategies I employed to create a sense of community in my art classroom.[1]

Teachers may not have complete control over the actions of their students; they can, however, make changes to teaching practice and curriculum activities that will shape the classroom environment. Holistic educators (Berger, 2003; Kessler, 2000; Miller, 2007; Miller, 2000; Noddings, 1992; Olson, 2009; Pariser, 2001) advocate for encouraging students' sense of belonging, a classroom culture based on respect and compassion, and supportive relationships. Each school year, I face the challenge to encourage meaningful relationships and create an environment respecting the contributions each student brings to the classroom—an environment honoring the heart as well as the mind—while emphasizing the importance of art in the lives of my students. Through teacher/student relationships, peer interactions, and curriculum activities, I have found that I can foster a sense of belonging as I encourage tolerance and promote individuality through art-related discussions and activities (Cummings, 2010). At the same time, I challenge students to do their best work and to continue to develop as artists. To begin my discussion, I present the importance of developing a caring classroom environment and how this can be accomplished. I will conclude with some thoughts on the role of standards in students' artistic and personal development.

TEACHER-STUDENT RELATIONSHIPS: OPENNESS AND HONESTY

High school for Erica was troublesome. She did not struggle academically; the challenges she faced were psychological. She lacked friends, she was lonely, and she felt ridiculed by her classmates…. Erica's high school artwork did not visibly reflect her mental anguish, but the creative processes she encountered played a significant role in her adolescent development.

> *[I met with Erica at an exhibition of her most recent artwork]* Six years after her graduation from high school, Erica spoke fondly of the relationships that she developed during her art class. At the gallery opening, she reminisced about sitting at one of the tables in the classroom sharing her troubles and working on her art. Erica told of coming into the classroom, even when she was scheduled to be elsewhere, to talk and work because the room had become a refuge for her when her life proved difficult and more stressful than normal.[2]
>
> —Personal journal entry

Listening to my students provides insight into knowing and understanding them on a deeper level. The learning atmosphere is safe, so my students feel free to make mistakes and to raise questions. They are given opportunities to try new things, allowed to fail, and encouraged to reflect and assess their progress. I am candid and honest with them; I make myself accessible throughout the day. I greet my students at the door, speak with them in the hallways, and encourage them to come in my room before and after school. I talk *with* my students, not *at* them. I am open to the topics of conversation they feel are necessary. Once the class begins, however, dialogue shifts to a focus on the curricular topics.

I make time to talk with each student daily. Sometimes only a few words are spoken and on other occasions, several minutes are shared—these conversations focus on the projects and issues that students are addressing at the time, yet the students often choose to personalize the activity; therefore, conversations frequently take on a more personal tone. When face-to-face time is not available, I often add written comments to journal entries, including notes of encouragement, advice, and questions supporting further growth. As I engage in meaningful and valuable dialogue with my students, I never lose sight of my role in their lives—I am their teacher. I acknowledge and respond to the responsibilities and expectations that come with this role. I reveal my passion about art and teaching, and express my interest and caring about their lives; in response, my students share their concerns, their dreams, and their desires.

How teachers teach and what they teach play integral roles in developing relationships with students (Birdsey, 2009; Wolk, 2003). Students have a need to connect with others in the classroom (Kessler, 2000) and to talk with teachers and peers about things that are important and meaningful (Beattie, 2007). Fulton (2002) contends, "...teaching is relationship building, creating family within the confines of a classroom and a curriculum" (p. 138).

Building teacher/student relationships is not easy. In some instances, establishing a rapport is a year-long effort; however, building a classroom community is a worthwhile endeavor.

PEER RELATIONSHIPS: FRIENDSHIP AND SUPPORT

> In other classes, there are popular girls and stuff; when I am in here I am seen as a person, instead of a body in a chair. I feel like I am an insider, [*being in art class*] is a social thing.
>
> —Sara, grade 11

I encourage my students to ask questions and take an active part in the learning process. To promote interaction, I arrange the classroom so that students sit in groups of three to four. Students engage in activities in both small and large groups; activities include in-progress critiques, brainstorming sessions, discussions, and final project critiques. I establish the following criteria for all group activities:

- partners are at the students' discretion unless unfavorable behaviors occur;
- all students must belong to a group;
- each group member must contribute to discussions; and
- students are to remain attentive and respectful during the entire discussion activity.

Before working in groups, students are reminded of my expectations and are informed of the assigned tasks to be completed during the activity.

In many instances, I develop a series of questions relating to the curricular unit that students are to discuss. I ask students to write their ideas before sharing responses in their groups; working in this manner alleviates anxieties and makes it easier for students to speak out loud. When a student is having a difficult time sharing with his or her peers, I volunteer my own comments or listen to the student, as this encourages all students within the group to participate. As the students engage in their group activities, I monitor interactions. I find it necessary to interact with each group to encourage specific behaviors and to offer guidance in their progress at the beginning of the year. As the year continues, I am able to interact with each group, focusing on the content of discussions rather than on procedural and behavioral expectations. I encourage students to challenge and question their peers, but to remain respectful and tolerant of differing points of view.

The learning atmosphere is safe; students feel free to make mistakes without ridicule or embarrassment. As Kessler (2002) argues, a safe, non-judgmental, and compassionate environment within the educational setting can foster students' friendship, their willingness to challenge external influences, and the questioning of self and others. Students therefore see themselves as partners in the learning process, and recognize the significance of socialization in learning.

CURRICULUM DEVELOPMENT: CHALLENGING AND MEANINGFUL

> I learned more about the people in my class and how they feel. You can tell a lot about people's likes and the kind of person they are. I think that no matter what, people should accept others' beliefs. I mean they don't have to agree with them.... I guess the most important part should be asking questions like why you do the things you do.... After seeing everybody's project yesterday, it just really made me think about getting outside of my own world and all the other issues people face. I don't know, it just sort of made me feel connected to everybody else, that no matter what, each of us is different and that is really what matters.... We all felt different things but we had that link.
>
> —Meredith, grade 10

My art curriculum engages students in topics and inquiries based on their interests. I designed curriculum activities to encourage students to share personal values, attitudes, beliefs, strengths, and insights on a regular basis, and to allow students to know each other on a personal level. Toward those ends, I survey the students at the beginning of each year and develop curricula from their responses. Past survey responses have illustrated interests in topics such as stereotypes, power dynamics, personal identity, relationships, and media bias; therefore, these topics became themes investigated within the curriculum.[3] As the year progresses, I modify topics and activities to reflect students' changing views. I introduce lessons through teacher-directed inquiries. This is followed with further discussion of relevant artists and artworks, as well as additional inquiries and investigations into the topics. Students are asked to further their investigations of the topics from their unique perspective and to create studio projects illustrating their understandings and changes in points of view. I frequently remind students of my expectations and the standards of artistry expected in their studio artwork. At the end of each unit, the class conducts critiques, self- and peer assessments, and self-reflections. In the latter, students are encouraged to reflect on their new understandings, evaluate personal growth, and respond to their artwork and that of their peers. Through this process, they form a greater understanding of themselves as individuals and as artists.

At times, changes to the curriculum and to my teaching practice are not easily implemented and may lead to further concerns. When this happens, I solicit students' ideas and opinions in resolving difficulties, and incorporate their advice into the solutions. As students become active in resolving such difficulties and guiding the curriculum, they come to a new understanding of education as a domain in which they can be active participants, not just passive victims. As they come to appreciate the role they play in the outcome of their learning experiences, they also learn to trust each other and work together; they feel responsible for each other's learning as well as their own. In addition, by establishing a classroom culture based on honesty and respect, my students seem more willing to confront issues in a personal manner, such as questioning the social influences on their identity development. As the following quote suggests, however, this is not always an easy or comfortable thing to do, at least early on.

COMMUNITY: BELONGING AND ACCEPTANCE

> With every project, I see myself change from it. At the beginning of the year when we started doing personal projects, I didn't like it. I was scared to let people know the real me and I was scared I didn't know the real me. I think when we did the first few projects, I let myself out a little bit. I started expressing myself more. It helped me feel like it's okay for someone to know you and to not be scared to show how you feel.
>
> —Kara, grade 10

As noted, developing a sense of community in the classroom encourages students to take risks like Kara describes. Ideally, this sense of community should be part of the entire school environment. Lawrence-Lightfoot (2009) suggested that "[s]chools should be caring and compassionate places where relationships of love and trust permit people to feel safe; where risk-taking is encouraged; where failure, generosity, and forgiveness allow people to discover their unique gifts and capacities" (p. xi).

Even when this is not the case throughout the school, individual classrooms can become "safe havens." The examples shared in this chapter suggest that this may be especially possible in the art room, where projects can allow personal expression and communication about meaningful matters. Yet giving opportunities for self-expression is not enough by itself. Equally important is the attitude with which projects are given and received. Teachers who want their students to become invested in their artwork must genuinely care about understanding their students, learn who they are as individuals, and examine how to assist them in their personal discoveries. Based on this understanding and knowledge, teachers can then engage students in activities of interest, while also encouraging deeper understandings of issues of social significance and inviting students to question issues like self-identity. Through curriculum activities that are holistically conceived, teachers can challenge students to create artwork that is personal and meaningful, that illustrates creativity and skill, and that demonstrates thought and sensitivity.

The reference to creativity and skill is important. It is assumed on occasion that allowing students to express themselves means letting them do whatever they want, holding the potential to lower expectations and ignore standards. Just the opposite is true, as Berger (2003) argues in his book, *An Ethic of Excellence*. Although Berger is not an art teacher, his project-based teaching, ongoing class-critiques, and emphasis on public display of student work describe the kind of classroom culture that cultivates quality work in an atmosphere of cooperation and mutual support. Berger also talks about the justifiable pride students get from doing good work, and the democratic values that are taught when students work together to help each one achieve his or her highest potential. In addition, Berger's subtitle, "Building a Culture of Craftsmanship with Students," suggests a lot about expectations for art students. To do artwork that is personally meaningful, it is all the more important that the work succeed in expressing the student's intent as well as possible. This requires using the skills and knowledge necessary for the task at hand, including art history, criticism, and aesthetics as well as artmaking itself. Only by drawing upon the full range of standards that make up the content of the visual arts can teachers truly focus on the learning process of students both as individuals and as members of a group. Teachers must devote themselves to designing criteria to honor changes in students' artistic development and fostering their personal growth. Establishing a strong foundation of content-area competence as well as community in the classroom in the ways described in this chapter does take time and effort, but the benefits are immeasurable.

REFERENCES

Beattie, M. (2007). Creating a self: A narrative and holistic perspective. *International Journal of Education & the Arts, 8*(13). Retrieved from www.ijea.org/v8n13/

Berger, R. (2003). *An ethic of excellence: Building a culture of craftsmanship with students*. Portsmouth, NH: Heinemann.

Birdsey, T. (2009). *A room for learning: The making of a school in Vermont*. New York, NY: St. Martin's Press.

Cummings, K. (2007). *Webs, windows, and reflections: Experiences in a secondary art classroom*. PhD Dissertation, University of Illinois at Urbana-Champaign, United States, 2007. *Dissertations & Theses: A&I*, Publication No. AAT 3290213.

Cummings, K. (2010). 'So what.' 'Who cares.' 'Whatever.' Changing adolescents' attitudes in the art classroom. *Visual Arts Research, 36*(1), 55-67.

Deiro, J. (2005). *Teachers do make a difference*. Thousand Oaks, CA: Corwin Press.

Fulton, L. (2002). Finding the courage to be seventeen in forty-four-year-old skin. In S. Intrator (Ed.), *Stories of the courage to teach: Honoring the teacher's heart* (pp. 132-138). San Francisco, CA: Jossey-Bass.

Kessler, R. (2000). *The soul of education: Helping students find connection, compassion, and character at school*. Alexandria, VA: Association for Supervision and Curriculum Development.

Kessler, R. (2002) Nourishing the inner life in schools. *Paths of Learning, 12*, 27-31.

Lawrence-Lightfoot, S. (2009). Foreword. In K. Olson, *Wounded by school. Recapturing the joy in learning and standing up to old school culture* (pp. xi-xiv). New York, NY: Teachers College Press.

Miller, R. (Ed.). (2000). *Creating learning communities: Models, resources, and new ways of thinking about teaching and learning*. Brandon, VT: The Foundation for Educational Renewal.

Miller, J. (2007). *The holistic curriculum*. Toronto, ON: University of Toronto Press.

Noddings, N. (1992). *The challenge to care in schools: An alternative approach to education*. New York, NY: Teachers College Press.

Olson, K. (2009). *Wounded by school. Recapturing the joy in learning and standing up to old school culture*. New York, NY: Teachers College Press.

Pariser, E. (2001). Relational education: An open letter to an educator. *Paths of Learning: Options for Families & Communities, 8,* 35-42.

Wolk, S. (2003). Hearts and minds. *Educational Leadership, 1,* 14-18.

ENDNOTES

1   The names of the individuals in this manuscript have been altered to retain their privacy.
2   These recollections originally appeared in my 2007 dissertation entitled *Webs, Windows, and Reflections: Experiences in a Secondary Art Classroom.*
3   Survey, students' survey responses, and curriculum are available in the aforementioned dissertation.

ABOUT THE AUTHOR

Karen Cummings is an Assistant Professor of Art Education and Art Education Coordinator at University of Missouri, Saint Louis. She received her PhD in Art Education at the University of Illinois, Urbana in 2007. Her research focuses on adolescents' behaviors and attitudes in the art classroom; other areas of interest include teacher preparation and retention. Currently, she is involved in developing a support group in the St. Louis area for art educators in their first 5 years of teaching. Cummings was a high school art teacher for 11 years before becoming a university professor.

CHAPTER 22

Tibetan Mandalas, Curriculum Sketches, and the Spiritual Dimensions of Art Education

Mark A. Graham

Educators who are wary of including religious material in public school classrooms often ignore the spiritual dimensions of students' lives (Barrett, Blackson, Daiello, & Goffos, 2006). Nevertheless, the spiritual is an essential part of human existence and neglecting this topic leaves essential parts of both art history and human experience unexamined (Campbell, 2005; London, 2007). Even when teachers attempt to explore religious or spiritual meanings in art, difficult questions emerge. For example, How is it possible to consider sacred artwork or subject matter in secular classrooms? How can a teacher who is outside of a tradition of sacred art incorporate those beliefs into the classroom in an authentic manner that honors the intent and substance of the tradition?

This chapter considers these questions in the context of a study of Tibetan Mandalas with high school and college art students, using a holistic approach toward teaching and curriculum. Spiritual dimensions of learning are closely associated with holistic approaches to education that seek to integrate the fragments of experience into a coherent whole and that see education as a collaborative, liberating, and transformative process (Campbell, 2011; Miller, 2003). In order to cultivate this kind of learning in high school and college classes, curriculum was structured as a sketch of emergent possibilities rather than as a set of predetermined outcomes. The curriculum sketch created pedagogical support for divergent artistic responses and interpersonal engagement among the students and teacher by fostering hospitality both for students and for unexpected ideas. (Davis, 2004; Palmer, 1993). This liberating structure created openings for students to engage with sacred and spiritual aspects of art and artmaking and to reflect on issues of personal importance in their own artwork.

The notion of the sacred has deep roots in the visual arts, mythology, and human thought. Religious and sacred art are explicitly concerned with the spiritual dimensions of existence, defined by the quest for compassion, wholeness, and meaning. Yet beyond art history, contemporary life is itself filled with accounts of religious faith, religious conflict, and spiritual concerns. Moreover, as Mircea Eliade (1959) observed, even the most secular societies preserve traces of a religious valorization of the world and transcendent experience has always been a part of human culture. Modern civilization, however, views mythology or religious symbolism as superstitious fables that reflect outmoded forms of thinking. Nonetheless, properly framed, the sacred dimensions of existence can have a meaningful place in scientific, technological societies and even in our factory-like schools.

One way of addressing this topic is by introducing myths and religious symbols to provide an orientation toward archetypical, spiritual realities of human existence, including those that give life a perspective beyond material existence. Taken in this way, art that addresses the sacred, mythological, and spiritual dimensions of life can be viewed as one of the many ways

FIGURE 1. Yama-Chamunda Symbol Mandala Eastern Tibet, Gelukpa order, late 18th century, Tangka; sized pigment on cotton. The Shelley and Donald Rubin Collection. © Rubin Museum of Art / Art Resource, NY. Yama, as a representation of death, is a synonym for the endless suffering of cyclic existence.

visionaries of the past have attempted to find different possibilities for being in the world. From this perspective, the notion of the sacred as expressed through art can be understood as foundational to holistic education, giving experience greater wholeness and meaning by considering the fundamental values and purposes of life (Wright, 2000).

TIBETAN MANDALAS

Mandalas are symbolic images used as an aid to meditation in Buddhist and Hindu traditions (Figure 1). Mandalas are generally designed around circles inscribed within squares; however, they can also assume other forms, including three-dimensional constructions. Whatever their form, mandalas are intended to reflect the underlying structure of reality. Because of this larger purpose, the terms, 'cosmic maps,' 'sacred precincts,' 'temples,' sacred mountains,' 'sacred circles,' and 'states of enlightenment' are all terms that have been used to describe mandalas (Grotenhuis, 1999). Mandalas are therefore symbolic models of the world that reflect the need for psychic wholeness or the urge to reside at the center of creation (Eliade, 1991). They exemplify the transformative power of art and the search for meaning and purpose that characterizes the spiritual dimensions of life and teaching (Campbell, 2006). Mandalas are compelling because of how they connect form and function, connect the inner life to the outer life, and create a link between the personal and social. For example, when Tibetan Buddhist monks create the Kalachakra Mandala, they focus on social cohesion and harmony, rather than on individual artistic expression. They see themselves as selfless conduits for something larger than themselves. Collaboration, pure motives, and altruistic intentions are considered to be more important than creativity. When the initiation and artwork are finished, the mandala is ceremoniously destroyed, the sand blended together and returned to a nearby body of water (Anderson, 2002). The construction and destruction of the mandala creates a vivid contrast with teaching that emphasizes personal expression and the inherent value of the art object.

The mandala is also an excellent metaphor for what might happen in holistic art classrooms, where the focus is on the meanings and purposes of artmaking and the transformative possibilities of education. The Tibetan word for mandala is *Kyikhor*, meaning *center and surrounding environment*. The mandala is thus understood as a sphere of nurturing, a magical and sacred realm created in order to cultivate development toward enlightenment and to understand the true nature of reality. In Tibetan Buddhism, enlightenment refers to the process of gaining freedom from craving, sorrow, and delusions, including freedom from the compulsive patterns imposed by culture (Thurman, 1999). This is consistent with critical holistic pedagogy that seeks a transformative experience by making a break with conditioning in order to consider other ways of seeing and acting (Campbell, 2006; Miller, 2003). Enlightenment is a personal transformation characterized by the desire to abide peacefully and to help others. Even without adopting a Buddhist world view, notions of enlightenment resonate with a holistic emphasis on connection, the search for meaning, personal transformation, and the integration of self and experiences into a coherent whole (Parsons, 2004). As a metaphor for holistic education, the process of gaining enlightenment challenges students to stretch their understanding beyond cultural conditioning and to transcend fixed notions of self.

Carl Jung, who had an interest in Tibetan psychology, saw in mandala paintings profound psychological archetypes and an inward awareness of deity (Thurman, 1999). However, alongside these religious/spiritual concerns, Jung also recognized the mandala's psychological functions, which might be more comfortably addressed in public schools. For example, Jung felt that meditating on the mandala could function as an antidote for chaotic states of mind, and he also thought they expressed an archetypical structure of the inner self; this explained why mandala-like structures are found in many cultures throughout the world (Brauen, 1997).

Nonetheless, to fully appreciate these sacred works, it is important to understand them in the devotional context for which they were intended. This, too, is important in art education, for students may look at mandalas as simply beautiful or weird images, and forget that their function is more than decorative or narrative. Rather, they are intended to change consciousness and are objects of contemplation that signify an aim to shift or alter understanding and awareness. The use of 'enabling constraints' and 'curriculum sketches' is an effective way to engage students with both the artwork and new ways of thinking about artmaking.

ENABLING CONSTRAINTS, CURRICULUM SKETCHES, AND HOLISTIC PEDAGOGY

Enabling constraints are the parameters applied to learning experiences or creative activities, such as the media being used, the subject to be studied, the approach, style, or problem to be solved. As such, they describe a set of conditions that are both limiting and liberating (Davis, 2004). They allow for unforeseen, divergent, and imaginative possibilities within certain boundaries, traditions, or conventions of artmaking. Curricular enabling constraints are, thus, like the rules of a game: They describe the boundaries of action, yet allow for infinite variations of play (Ackerman, 1999). Another way of looking at enabling constraints is to say that they provide a structure or language for improvisation and creative action. This idea is particularly relevant to the study of an art form such as Tibetan mandalas, which use structure to gain the freedom of enlightenment. Similarly, a teacher can organize curriculum and teaching to accomplish the transformation associated with a holistic educational experience.

The idea of enabling constraints opposes the Romantic notion that the creative process must be wholly free from all restrictions. On the contrary, more recent research shows that, absent constraining rules, there is no context for creative discourse or means of expression. An effective enabling constraint is equally important in terms of education. It creates conditions for the emergence of complex learning and complex learning communities by balancing sufficient organization with enough openness to allow for a diversity of interests and experiences among students (Davis, Sumara & Luce-Kapler, 2008).

A curriculum sketch is a set of enabling constraints that will be tested with students (McKernan, 2008). It contains the possibility of surprise and the negotiation of content and methods in teaching. The curriculum sketch creates hospitality toward new ideas, possibilities for collaboration, and unanticipated outcomes. It suggests that student interests, concerns, and progress can shape what happens in school (Wilson, 2007). In drawing, the idea of a sketch connotes a lack of definition and openness to revision. Similarly, a curriculum sketch, as opposed to a fully developed curriculum, is the rough plan of an art project, which is open to change as things happen in the classroom. In contrast to instructor-directed projects directed toward clearly defined end-products, teaching becomes an ongoing conversation and quest for knowledge and enlightenment that focuses on expanding what is possible without pre-specified outcomes (Davis, 2004).

Curriculum sketches complement enabling constraints. They expand what might be possible rather than defining predictable outcomes (Rolling, 2006). In the process, curriculum and teaching emerge as a kind of collaborative research project with emergent possibilities that are not pre-scripted (Rinaldi, 1993). The ideas of emergent planning and enabling constraints in the form of a curriculum sketch are thus useful ways to consider the balance between structure and creative freedom.

MANDALAS IN A PUBLIC HIGH SCHOOL

Imagine walking into my high school classroom on a Monday morning in January. The lights are off and a circle of candles lights the table. The sounds of waves are playing quietly in the background. The students quietly slip off their shoes and sit in a circle on the floor. I begin by saying, "Close your eyes and take a deep breath..." Then I ask myself, "What am I doing? Do I dare close my eyes? I am no yogi; I hardly know anything about mediation. Let me think, I went to a yoga class once and I listened to a tape about breathing, but what am I doing leading a meditation? This is a lot like prayer! I could get fired. Enlightenment is what I need. Well, it's too late now." I had to be serious.

Actually, it was great just to have some quiet to ponder what was truly important. It gave me a moment to take a 'holistic snapshot' of the young people in my art room, to remember how my students are gifted with ideals, emotion, feelings, beloved by parents, and jeweled with traditions. We breathed deeply, and I asked them to imagine an artwork that might lead them to enlightenment and inner peace. This is how I stumbled through my first meditation with students and began our study of mandalas.

These 11th- and 12th-grade Advanced Placement students in a public high school in New York were about to begin their concentration projects. The concentration project requires students to investigate a theme or idea that is important to them. It seems like this would be easy, however, in reality, the lack of structure can be daunting. In preparation for the challenge that lay ahead, the study of Tibetan mandalas began as a curriculum sketch that combined the search for meaningful artistic themes with the quest for mindfulness and enlightenment suggested by mandalas. It also introduced a formal, visual structure into the quest for personal expression. The idea of a meditative journey to gain enlightenment, though drawn from

FIGURE 2. Josette Urso Collage.

a non-western religious tradition, was not at all religious in its approach or intent. Instead, it fit nicely with our search for sustained, artful investigations that were personally important. Before our day of meditation, I asked the students to gather collections of special images and photographs that were important to them. We also spent a few days painting paper using tempera paint. The students were instructed to use three colors plus white and black in order to create complex and improbable colors. These simple constraints allowed students to create an enormous variety of color swatches, as well as encouraging impassioned painting practice.

The images and painted paper were gathered into neat piles on the tables. The mandalas were constructed using a series of increasingly complex collage compositions. The first collages were simple three by three grids. These soon gave way to circular collage constructions that incorporated mandala designs and gave the collages a sense of order. I got the idea of collage mandalas from my friend Josette Urso, who constructs collages from both photographs and drawings (Figure 2). She said, "The circular pieces really started with a vague notion I had about making a paper quilt. For me, the circles do hold the universe—the tangle of the "everythingness" of our lives" (Urso, personal communication, May 22, 2009). The images in the student collages represented themes of importance and the "everythingness" they might incorporate into their own work. The encompassing formal structure of the mandala gave the collages coherence. These conceptual and design constraints were defined within the overarching purposes of exploring themes of personal importance.

Before we talked about the sacred artwork of Tibet or began working, I wanted to connect our work with a larger context that I hoped students would understand and relate to. I asked them to consider the mythical and spiritual dimensions of art and life and to consider what was important in their own lives. This was also the reason for the morning of meditation: to make a break with the ordinary patterns of school and to consider issues of meaning and purpose. After our moment of calm and reflection, we discussed Tibetan mandalas and how sacred art might function as a direct experience of inner peace or a path to enlightenment. We discussed enlightenment and what it might mean. We further noted that mandalas are used to establish a sacred space and to focus attention, to orient the viewer toward important realities, and to encourage inner healing. The ultimate idea behind this preparation was for students to consider what was truly important to them, as well as to expand their ideas of how a work of art might function in pursuit of a deeper meaning or purpose.

Such concerns remind us of the deeper, holistic purposes of education. For, just as a mandala points toward transcendent realities, teaching is about orienting students to notice things they may have not been aware of (Davis, Sumara, & Luce-Kapler, 2008). In this case, teaching was about orienting students toward notions of the sacred and the possibilities of considering issues of consequence in their own work.

After we had finished the concentration projects, we created a collaborative mandala mural. Each senior contributed one square to the painting. Before painting, we designed a color scheme based on concentric circles inscribed by a square. Students voted on the one they liked best. Each individual painting conformed to the color and shape of the circle where it would fit. The pattern and colors unified the final piece, however the individual paintings were highly varied (Figure 3). The process focused on integrating our individual experiences into a cohesive whole through a carefully planned collaboration. The final mandala transcended each individual's effort and created a compelling artwork.

USING ENABLING CONSTRAINTS AND CURRICULUM SKETCHES AT THE COLLEGE LEVEL

I also studied mandalas with my college art education students. Whereas the public school setting was characterized by diversity of beliefs within a secular institution, the church-sponsored university was characterized by shared beliefs within an institution that encouraged the discussions of spiritual ideas. However, the students were less familiar with non-Western approaches to spirituality, creating an entirely different set of boundaries and possibilities. This time I invited my yoga teacher to do the meditation and yoga practice. The character of the classroom changed completely when we were all quietly focused on breathing and mediation around one very calm teacher.

Subsequently, each student was asked to investigate Buddhism, mandalas, and meditation and to lead a meditation session with the class. One student taught an Indian dance, another a martial art breathing technique, and another a yoga healing technique. When these students constructed personal mandalas, they readily abstracted their experiences and created strong visual themes for their works. Nature, family, and relationships were among the subjects that featured strongly in the students' images. For example, Carlee placed herself and her husband at the center of the mandala (Figure 4). This was reminiscent of the union of

FIGURE 3. Mandala Mural.

FIGURE 4. Carlee's Mandala.

FIGURE 5. (left) Chelsea's Nature Tree Mandala.

FIGURE 6. (right) Amy's Mandala.

male and female deities found in many Tibetan mandalas. Chelsea focused on her feelings about nature (Figure 5), and Amy focused on her best friend (Figure 6). The final images suggested an intimate mixing of the profound archetypical structure of the mandala with themes of personal importance.

The teachings associated with Tibetan Buddhist mandalas have many counterparts in both religious and non-religious writings that focus on self-improvement or transformation. During our study of mandalas, I gathered numerous books that discussed paths to enlightenment. Authors included Jack Karouac, Sakyong Mipham, Twyla Tharp, and Thich Nhat Hanh, as well as Christian writers with which my students were more familiar. I wanted to create a mandala of infinite meditation that contained all this great advice in one large painting. I imagined it as a series of intricate lines with these profound instructions carefully woven throughout the piece.

I soon realized that I lacked both the obsessive attention to detail and the time needed to complete the project, so I enlisted the aid of my students. Some students worked on reading the texts and transcribing the parts I had underlined into a document. They printed out the compilation for the class on rough newsprint and rice paper. The class wrote their favorite passages from this compilation using sticks or branches dipped in ink. They also added some of their own favorite texts and we soon had a sizable collection of advice about life and enlightenment. The final mandala was constructed on large pieces of printing paper using acrylic polymer, ink, and gold thread (Figures 7 and 8). The entire process was shaped by student choices, collaboration, and a culture of experimentation, with the overarching purpose of personal and social transformation. The final piece was different from anything I had envisioned; however, it was the significant conversations and personal bonds developed in the shaping of the mandala that mattered most.

CONCLUSION

The study of Tibetan Mandalas illustrates, among other things, the tension between the constraints of artistic conventions and the freedom of personal expression. Students were asked to investigate things of importance, including the sacred and spiritual dimensions of art and life, and to consider how a work of art might function. At the same time, the design constraints of the mandala imposed a structure on the compositions that gave the students visual and

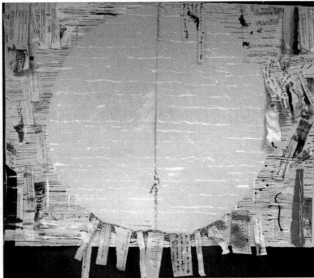

FIGURE 7. (left)The Mandala of Infinite Meditation (detail).

FIGURE 8. (right) The Mandala of Infinite Meditation.

conceptual languages with which to express their ideas. The study of mandalas also created a dialogue between a largely foreign spiritual tradition and the diverse beliefs that already existed in the classroom.

These projects were facilitated by working with the notion of curriculum as a sketch or experiment, which defined some parameters of artistic exploration while allowing openings to discuss student ideas as well as the spiritual dimensions of art. Student knowledge, experience, and research thus became important, but unpredictable, parts of the curriculum. This is consistent with holistic educational goals of transformative pedagogy that affirms the wholeness of students and connects students and curriculum by giving them space to shape both content and methods (Campbell, 2011).

Another one of the challenges involved in this kind of lesson was teaching about an artistic tradition less familiar to either the teacher or the students. Here, as noted at the beginning of this essay, there is the danger that the tradition will be oversimplified or trivialized. When addressing sacred images, even in Western art, it is all too easy to drain the work of its power to enlighten and transform by removing it from its culture of ritual and belief (London, 2007). Equally important, to entertain notions of spiritual enlightenment, the dominating force of Western scientific skepticism and rationality may need to be set aside. Approaching sacred traditions from an artistic vantage point using a holistic approach made it possible for students to gain a sympathetic understanding of the significant issues surrounding religious art and to work with issues of importance in their own work, as opposed to teaching students explicitly about other cultures' religious beliefs, which may either provoke scientific skepticism or cause conflicts with the students' own religious views (Anderson, 2002). The curriculum sketch facilitated an open-minded response and allowed students to explore an unfamiliar artistic convention while encouraging divergent outcomes, playfulness, and conversation. Through this strategy, the study of mandalas enabled us to explore the intent and substance of this sacred tradition and consider the spiritual dimensions of art and life. At the same time, the lesson was an excellent way to orient students toward issues of personal importance including the role of spirituality in art, while providing the means to make such issues a part of their artistic lives.

REFERENCES

Ackerman, D. (1999). *Deep play*. New York, NY: Vintage.

Anderson, T. (2002) Mandala: Constructing peace through art. *Art Education, 55*(3), 33-39.

Barrett, T., Blackson, B., Daiello, V., & Goffos, M. (2006). God, the taboo topic of art education. *The Journal of Social Theory in Art Education, 26*, 58-83.

Brauen, M. (1997). *The mandala: Sacred circle in Tibetan Buddhism*. Boston, MA: Shambhala.

Campbell, L. (2005). Spiritual reflective practice in preservice art education. *Studies in Art Education, 47*(1), 51-69.

Campbell, L. (2006). Spirituality and holistic art education. *Visual Arts Research, 32(1),* 29-34.

Campbell, L. (2011). Holistic art education: A transformative approach to teaching art. *Art Education, 64*(2), 18-24.

Davis, B. (2004). *Inventions of teaching*. Mahwah, NJ: Lawrence Erlbaum.

Davis, B., Sumara, D., & Luce-Kapler, R. (2008). *Engaging minds*. New York, NY: Routledge.

Eliade, M. (1959). *The sacred and the profane: The nature of religion*. New York, NY: Harcourt Brace Jovanovich.

Eliade, M. (1991). *Images and symbols: Studies in religious symbolism*. Princeton, NJ: Princeton University.

Grotenhuis, E. (1999). *Japanese mandalas: Representations of sacred geography*. Honolulu, HI: University of Hawaii Press.

London, P. (2007). Concerning the spiritual in art education. In L. Bresler (Ed.), *International handbook of research in arts education, Part two* (pp.1479-1494). Dordrecht, The Netherlands: Springer.

McKernan, J. (2008). *Curriculum and imagination*. London, England: Routledge

Miller, R. (2003). Education for a culture of peace. *Encounter, 16,* 3.

Palmer, P. (1993) *To know as we are known: Education as a spiritual journey*. San Francisco, CA: Harper San Francisco.

Parsons, M. (2004). Art and integrated curriculum. in E. Eisner & M. Day (Eds.), *Handbook of research and policy in art education*. Mahwah, NJ: Lawrence Erlbaum Associates.

Rhie, M. M., & Thurman, R. A. (1999). Worlds of transformation. In M. M. Rhie & R. A. Thurman (Eds.), *Worlds of transformation: Tibetan art of wisdom and compassion* (pp. 12-45). New York, NY: Tibet House.

Rinaldi, L. (1993). The emergent curriculum and social construction. In C. Edwards, L. Gandini, & G. Forman (Eds.), *The hundred languages of children* (pp. 17-34). Norwood, NJ: Ablex.

Rolling, J. H., Jr. (2006). Who is at the city gates? *Art Education 59*(6), 40-51.

Thurman, R. A. (1999). Worlds of transformation. In M. M. Rhie & R. A. Thurman (Eds.), *Worlds of transformation: Tibetan art of wisdom and compassion* (pp. 12-45). New York, NY: Tibet House.

Wilson, B. (2007). Third site bioquiry: Meditations on biographical inquiry and third site pedagogy. *Journal of Research in Art Education, 8*(2), 51-76.

Wright, A. (2000). *Spirituality in education*. London, England: Routledge Falmer.

ABOUT THE AUTHOR

Mark A. Graham is a professor in the Department of Visual Art at Brigham Young University. Graham is also an artist and illustrator and has illustrated more than 20 children's picture books. He continues to create various kinds of art objects, including mandalas. He spent most of his professional life in New York City where he studied at the Art Students League of New York and Columbia University. His research interests include Tibetan mandalas, place-based approaches to education, ecology and art education, and the role of teaching artists in K-12 schools.

CHAPTER 23

A Collage of Holistic Discoveries in Art Education

Barbara Caldwell

This chapter presents selected goals, methods, and applications of holistic art education. I describe the rewards of devotion to education that bring self-actualization, compassion, and community. Holistic, student-centered teaching methods that foster authentic creative development, engage multiple intelligences, and build social community are described. I share independent and collaborative aspects of a creative activity along with ways of fostering related student reflection, formative and summative assessments, and celebration of growth. My holistic approach is applied in examples drawn from art education courses for general elementary education and art education majors.

Faith Ringgold inspired the multidimensional lesson I developed that is described in detail. Art education that fosters creative authenticity, inspires empathy and collaboration, and builds a sense of global community is emphasized. Original photography illustrates this collage of learning in holistic art education.

FIGURE 1. Art: A path of holistic growth.

In nearly 30 years of teaching, learning, and artmaking I have come to recognize and engage essential elements of my own approach to holistic art education. As an example of this approach, I will describe a multidimensional lesson based on the quilts of Faith Ringgold, drawn from art education courses for general elementary education and art education majors. First, however, I will review some of the basic principles and benefits of holistic education, as I understand it.

Holistic teaching acknowledges the interplay of body, mind, emotions, and spirit in learning and in life, as captured in the portrait of a young boy immersed in the rustling of fall leaves, shown in Figure 1. Therefore, when applying a holistic approach to art education, the goal is to intentionally nurture student development on myriad levels: aesthetic, cognitive, perceptual, kinesthetic, creative, empathic, affective, social, multicultural, and spiritual. This rich mix of varied, interrelated areas of growth expands the art experience beyond simply learning about art or participating in art activities. It invites the learner, saying "Come as you are. Rise to become all that you can be."

So described, holistic art education can have lifelong benefits, furthering multidimensional growth through opportunities to explore identity; to relate to diverse people, media, and perspectives; and to experience a wide array of dynamic human commonalities. There are many ways to implement such an approach, allowing each teacher to use his/her own strengths to help students connect holistically to themselves, their art, and their world. Nonetheless, there are also some common features of holistic learning environments. For example, in such environments, teachers nurture openness and respectful interaction in order to promote positive personal change—physical, emotional, social, multicultural, and spiritual. This, in turn, begins with knowing, being, and sharing who we are as teachers, artists, and caring individuals. Only in this way can we create spaces where our students can do the same.

In my teaching of future and current teachers, art and design majors, and many other kinds of students, I promote a global, holistic, and pluralistic approach, as advocated by Chalmers (1996) and Caldwell (2003). Moreover, following Gardner, I aspire to nurture "minds for the future" through creativity, ethics, respect, and synthesis skills (Gardner, 2006) and engage multiple intelligences (Gardner, 1999). Among these, I focus especially on intrapersonal intelligence, through which students gain self-knowledge, and interpersonal intelligence, which leads to compassion. Along with creativity, these personal qualities are equally central in a holistic approach to student development and are a natural outgrowth of an expansive, compassionate learning environment. As teachers in such environments help students reflect upon and share their creativity, there is a continual need to accept both our own gifts and imperfections as well as those of others.

Based on these values, my ultimate teaching objective is to foster the unfolding of student individuality and potential (Maslow, 1971). Such development, however, is not at the expense of traditional art education emphases. Rather, holistic and artistic objectives can and should work in concert. For instance, expressiveness and creative growth most readily occur when one experiences a climate of trust and regard for human dignity (Rogers, 1961/1989). In this regard, I particularly strive to demonstrate respect for diversity and so infuse my teaching with multicultural examples from myriad artists and art forms; thus it is "whole child; whole world" art education.

My courses, therefore, begin with experiences that reveal both individuality and commonalities as students make and share collages incorporating personal values and interests. Over time, other activities contribute to building a respect-filled community essential to learning. There, my students grow in both creative authenticity and empathy. Art and the art process experienced in such caring communities changes lives, as illustrated by the lesson described below.

SHARING OUR STORIES: FAITH RINGGOLD QUILT BLOCKS

General education majors and preservice art education students alike enjoy and grow from experiencing my lesson inspired by artist Faith Ringgold. Following her example, students create individual collaged "quilt blocks" and story panels, which are then combined in a communal class quilt. Although class members come up with unique quilts based on their different experiences, the format is essentially similar, with central images surrounded by patterned borders that extract or combine significant childhood memories into creative adaptations as seen in Figure 2. This lesson is

FIGURE 2. Erin's quilt block and story panel.

holistic in its methods, process, and outcomes. It is also pluralistic. The description that follows details how intentions, implementation methods, and teaching considerations foster multidimensional growth while addressing art education goals and standards. In particular, this lesson supports helping students respond to, interpret, and create meaning in art while also encouraging the use of symbols and art media in expressive ways. At the same time, it strives to build understanding of and empathy for socially and culturally diverse populations through the inspiration of a world-famous African American artist, Faith Ringgold. Ringgold, as my students learn, has impacted the trajectory of fine art in combining painting and quilting while also publishing fine art in children's books. In many of her works, Ringgold imaginatively uses reconstructed childhood memories, tailored to encourage positive social change and achievement of one's potential, regardless of circumstances.

These qualities are illustrated in Ringgold's well-known children's book, *Tar Beach* (Ringgold, 1991), which was the initial inspiration for the teaching activity described in this vignette. *Tar Beach* is the story of a young girl who enjoys joining her family and neighbors atop her Harlem home for picnics high above the city and away from problems of everyday life. She soars over the rooftops claiming as her own all that she flies above: the wondrous George Washington Bridge, the ice cream factory, and the building her father helped build for a union that he was prohibited from joining because of his race. Despite such real-life hardships, the girl's aspirations make her able to transform things, and she shares her powers with others. She tells her brother, "Anyone can fly. All you need is somewhere to go that you can't get to any other way. The next thing you know, you're flying among the stars." In much the same way, I use this book and project to encourage students to face personal or social challenges, to help change injustice, and to use art experience to help themselves (and their students) overcome limiting beliefs or conditions.

To introduce the unit, students "meet" Faith Ringgold in the video, *The Last Story Quilt* (Freeman, 1991), which I have found is inspirational for future teachers. Students are impressed with Ringgold's art, as well as her perseverance and positive attitude. As they learn, Ringgold found innovative ways to show her work in a time when the art of women and African Americans was rarely exhibited. She also encourages leaps of faith. "I am inspired by people who rise above their adversity. That's my deepest inspiration," Ringgold declares with radiance and conviction. "And also I'm inspired by the fact that if I really, really want to, I think I can do anything" (Ringgold, Freeman, & Poucher, 1996, p. 3).

THE PROCESS OF INTEGRATING MEDIA AND MESSAGE

Faith Ringgold infuses her work with colorful patterns, so I introduce students to vegetable and object printing just before they learn about Ringgold and my story quilt lesson. Images from various fiber arts traditions, including Amish quilts, Guatemalan clothing, and Navajo weavings provide a motivational display behind me as I demonstrate multiple techniques of printmaking. On 10 strips of colored 6″ x 24″ construction paper, students create fold-over butterflies, string prints, and stamps using lemons, apples, and personalized symbols cut into halved potatoes. They enjoy layering symbols and textures, innovating with sponges, rollers, and finger prints as seen in Figure 3. I encourage them to make a variety of prints and not throw any away, as later they may be able to rescue a cast off, turning disappointment into an asset! I intentionally hint that some prints will be cut, so students are not too attached to the whole print. Making the prints first seems to fire innovation, while it also limits intentional creation of literal textures and colors in their collages. For example, tree tops created with pink lemon stamps or purple potato stamp stars are much more childlike and creative than are the usually leafy variations of green.

FIGURE 3. (left) Fingers used creatively in printmaking.

FIGURE 4. (right) Tonya's tribute to grandpa, swing, and dog.

Next, students create sketches of childhood memories in their journals in preparation for making the story quilt block collages. I still haven't told them about the project itself, but I do tell them that memories, along with aesthetic experiences in nature, creative imagination, and life observations, are rich resources for artwork content. I believe that keeping the actual assignment a surprise will foster innovation in imagery, so I wait until they have made their sketches of childhood highlights before they hear the story of *Tar Beach* read in class. Also, having made their own memory drawings may help them better relate to Ringgold's story, while avoiding the possibility of being too influenced by her images and ideas.

When the students finally are introduced to Ringgold's artwork and her inventive story, which effectively combines fact and fantasy, they are challenged to innovate, using new imagery inspired by memories as well as imagination for a personally empowering quilt block as shown by Figure 4. As suggested earlier, the project provides for lots of creative freedom but the steps of the lesson are well structured to help ensure that everyone succeeds. On a 22" x 22" poster board, students measure a 6" border that frames a 12" x 12" memory collage constructed in the center. The measurements are uniform, but borders and pictures vary widely. Incorporating some concrete objectives with room for personal creativity provides a balance of limits and freedom.

Even within these guidelines, students approach the creative aspect of the process in a variety of ways. Some begin planning, measuring, and cutting their paper prints for a border design. Others revisit their journals and extract or combine childhood memories to create uplifting center images. In addition, multiple art and design techniques are employed as students bring their reflective visions to life. For example, perspective is implied in a world of bookshelves, gesture is used in a ballet pose, and shades of brown are created to differentiate family faces. Many consult with me as they shape and reshape their ideas. In-process, informal formative assessment used in this way is a powerful aid in creative, holistic education. As students work, it is important to encourage them and to circulate around the room giving help and freedom as needed. As I do, sometimes I'm asked questions regarding technical or drawing assistance. I also respond to requests for mixed media, like glitter or yarn, or provide help with emergent thematic content dilemmas.

Although the majority of students enthusiastically recall positive memories, I have been challenged by students whose childhood memory sketches reveal a troubled past. Without

FIGURE 5. Quilt blocks united for display.

judgment, I try to steer such students to look at how they dealt with that situation, or how they reached where they are. In this way, I hope to help them turn despair into inspiration and excitement. I also share anonymous stories of students with challenging childhoods to help prepare these future teachers. I teach for similar "pop quizzes" that will someday provide opportunities for them to foster emotional growth and confidence in their own students.

The story quilt block and story panels are engaging and challenging for art majors, but they can also be expansive as well as highly attainable projects for those with little art or design experience. In both cases, students bring a wide variety of memories to their work. Themes represented in Figure 5 include such treasured experiences as the cozy surprise of an unexpected snow day, the magic of daydreaming while gazing in a mirror, the exhilaration of being pushed in a tire swing by Grandpa, and the joy of becoming a princess along with a beloved cousin. Besides the enjoyment provided by this particular project, lessons like these taught as part of a rich learning environment are intended to foster personal, emotional, and social growth. They may also encourage creative confidence and a valuing of a more balanced life in future teachers and artists.

To bring out students' memories, I encourage relaxation as part of a deep aesthetic experience. Students enjoy relaxing music and conversation as they "quilt" at tables seating four or five. They share opinions and decision making as well as happy discoveries. Students then compose their written story on a 6" x 22" panel, which can be displayed with their quilt block. Seeing their work hung together strengthens a sense of personal pride and class community.

Assessments of the story quilt block lesson occur in several ways. In-process communication helps students know and reach firm criteria (size of block and border, inclusion of imagery inspired by childhood memories, incorporation of original prints, and neat craftsmanship). Summative evaluation occurs through reflective "critiques" when each block of the displayed class quilt is explained to the class. Students also tell the story communicated in their quilt block. As they do, they must articulate ways symbolism and design convey their quilt's meaning and point out two of their favorite innovations in border and image creation. Classmates can then highlight other strengths. The focus is positive, so confidence as well as camaraderie grows. Part of the course final exam is also devoted to this project: Students sketch their quilt block, explain its meaning, and describe two ways their creation was inspired by Ringgold's work.

Joy is the most common outcome of this experience. Wonder and pride in their own creativity also emerges as students find diverse ways to infuse personal meaning and cultural influences into their quilt blocks. The importance of the themes they recall and invent helps them persevere as they carefully add elaborate details expanding the work's aesthetic quality. Other meaningful aspects of holistic art education in such activities include a sense of personal authenticity in art and empathy gained from sharing the meaning of one's work with others in a welcoming environment.

A Legacy of Holistic Convictions

A couple of years ago, I had the amazing opportunity to meet Faith Ringgold. I asked her what she hoped her legacy would be—what her influence would be. Her response was something like this: "I want people to see that they can be who they are. I want them to have the courage to rise and be all they can." I am grateful for her influence and, by way of her story and quilt blocks, to be able to continue her legacy, providing a holistic educational experience that my students can carry forward in their teaching and nurturing of artistic creativity.

ABOUT THE AUTHOR

Barbara Caldwell, Associate Professor of Art and Design at Iowa State University, teaches art education and photography. A passionate, creative teacher and mentor, she advocates a holistic, pluralistic approach to both teaching and scholarship. Caldwell has exhibited and published photography internationally and received numerous honors for teaching, mentorship, and service, including the Kathy Connors Award, the NAEA and AEI Outstanding Service in the Field of Art Education Award, and the Alumni Hall of Fame Award from Illinois State University where she gave the keynote speech for its 150th anniversary.

REFERENCES

Caldwell, B. (2003). Enduring coterie of soul friends: Photographs in authentic teaching. In K. Grauer, R. Irwin, & E. Zimmerman (Eds.), *Women art educators V: Conversations across time* (pp. 228-236). Reston, VA: National Art Education Association.

Chalmers, F. G. (1996). *Celebrating pluralism: Art, education, and cultural diversity*. Santa Monica, CA: Getty Center for Education in the Arts.

Freeman, L. (Director). (1991). *Faith Ringgold: The last story quilt* (Video). Chappaqua, NY: L&S.

Gardner, H. (1999). *Intelligence reframed*. New York, NY: Basic Books.

Gardner, H. (2006). *Five minds for the future*. Boston, MA: Harvard Business School Press.

Maslow, A. (1971). *The farther reaches of human nature*. New York, NY: Viking Press.

Ringgold, F. (1991). *Tar beach*. New York, NY: Crown.

Ringgold, F., Freeman, L., & Poucher, N. (1996). *Talking to Faith Ringgold*. New York, NY: Crown.

Rogers, C. (1989). *On becoming a person*. New York, NY: Houghton Mifflin. (Original work published 1961)

CHAPTER 24

Exploring Interconnections: Holistic Arts Education and the Arts in Community Building

Linda Melamed and Maureen Heffernan

The program Family Arts and Creativity (FAC) was conceived in 1998 by The Center for Family Involvement at Rutgers University in partnership with the Institute for Arts and Humanities Education (IAHE). In 2000, IAHE inherited the program, developing it in collaboration with New Jersey teachers and artists and the generous support of the Geraldine R. Dodge Foundation. FAC is now housed at Young Audiences NJ. FAC's initial goals encompassed a vision of families involved in the school community; engaged in personally meaningful, educationally sound, fun art-making experiences; and better attuned to the important role the arts play in their children's education.

Safe, accepting environments created in these workshops, and opportunities for meaningful exchange among classroom teachers, arts specialists, teaching artists, parents and children, allow a sense of community to flow, breaking down personal barriers to create sacred space. With family as one source of inspiration for their work, participants share memories that connect generations and forge bridges between cultures. They explore favorite pastimes and diverse family identities, giving their visions voice though visual arts, movement, music, and word. FAC nurtures collaboration, inventive self-expression, and shared reflections. The vision of holistic arts education as a fluid integration of mind, body and spirit provides a compatible lens through which to reflect on FAC, its structures and beliefs.

This paper describes FAC and examines ways in which the program gives life to core ideas in holistic arts education, comparing these attributes to qualities of FAC that support the development of a sense of community among workshop participants. It then outlines program evaluation strategies to document and communicate these effects, focusing in particular on the role of the program in creating a sense of community. Considering the importance to arts education programs of demonstrating such results to funders and other stakeholders, this approach to program evaluation, as well as the program itself, may provide a model for adaptation to other holistic education contexts.

OVERVIEW OF FAMILY ARTS AND CREATIVITY
Program Structure
In FAC, 3rd- or 4th-grade students come back to school in the evening accompanied by a parent or other significant adult and participate together in arts workshops. After the first week of the series, students and parents know to get right to work at the various "warm-up activities" awaiting them. Through these activities, that warm-up and awaken their creative minds, they are invited to explore materials and ideas that will be central to the work of the evening. For example, they might be invited to

- make clay pieces that describe prepositional words—under, around, between or through—as one of the warm ups for a collaborative clay landscape;
- collect rubbings from around the room whose line qualities, directions, and patterns will help inspire a movement piece; and
- capture facial expressions associated with different emotions, using a few simple lines, in preparation for a workshop on mask making.

After exploring the warm-up activities, families are brought back together for a warm-up exchange to share their solutions, celebrate the diversity of possibilities, ask questions, exchange information, and discuss plans and materials for the evening's main activity.

The main activity may involve an individual project, a parent-child challenge, or a collaborative small group exploration. The FAC facilitators—two teachers from the school (a classroom teacher and an arts specialist) and a collaborating artist—are available to ask and answer questions, provide assistance as the process unfolds, and participate as partnering risk-takers and investigators.

Finally, the group reconvenes for a wrap-up to reflect on their results, hear stories behind the pieces, share revelations and challenges, and revisit the core arts-ideas and materials that shaped the evening. In this interactive, non-competitive environment, parents affirm their children as competent, inventive, active learners within a social context. Children enjoy working with their parents. As one student said, "I didn't know how creative and silly and fun they could be."

An Inter-Arts Focus

FAC is an inter-arts program; it invites participants to tell their stories about family, neighborhood, favorite pastimes, and memories while engaging them with core, introductory concepts from the domains of dance, music, visual art, and theater. Students and parents are invited in, through welcoming entry points, exploring sound before music, mark-making before image, ritual before performance, movement before dance. Explorations in one domain become the catalyst for immersion in the next. Artists and teachers working together have created workshops that explore

- sound and sound effects and their importance in helping to tell a story, set a mood, and elicit an emotional response;
- the visual and emotional impact of the painted line when you take a paintbrush for a walk in response to music from diverse cultures and with diverse rhythms;
- wire sculpture and the suggestion of mass, weight, and motion when you bend, twist, and wrap a wire and take a line into three-dimensional space;
- collage and the juxtaposing of colors, textures, and found objects and images to tell a family story; and
- Tableau Vivant (living pictures) or a series of body sculptures, developed by a group, to convey their collaborative story, inspired by five photographs and a handful of words.

Fostering Family Involvement

This is a family involvement program. All of the families at a school's selected grade level are invited to apply. The facilitating teachers reach out to families that represent a cross-section of the school's diversity, and who might not be the regulars at school events. They also leave spaces for a family new to the district, or just learning English, or with a special education student, or a family undergoing divorce or illness. In this way, FAC aims to expand the network of families who feel comfortable in the school and acquaint them with other families in a meaningful way.

Providing Authentic Arts Experiences

Foremost, it introduces families to the important role the arts can play in learning and in life; the potential for self-expression and joyful parent-child interactions; the development of deep thinking skills; the ability of the arts to touch our spiritual core. Participants are invited into a non-judgmental, safe, and accepting environment while at the same time challenged to take risks, to explore materials, and to share personal experiences and beliefs. They engage in activities that are both structured and open-ended, compatible with their level of technical skill, and invite self-expression and creative exploration of core ideas in the arts. As an integral part of their physical engagement in art making activities, parents and children are also encouraged to reflect on and share what they are thinking and feeling. Participants are asked to respect and honor others' opinions and relish having their own ideas carefully considered.

Impacting School Day Teaching and Learning

It is the participating teachers and arts specialists who then embed the FAC experiences into their classroom practice. Much of the strength of Family Arts and Creativity comes from the in-depth professional development that the artist-teacher teams from diverse school sites share. They come together as participants in arts workshops; develop workshops tailored to their own school community; pilot them on one another and get collegial feedback before taking the workshops to their schools. Artists, arts specialists, and classroom teachers, working together as equal contributors, exchange a wealth of knowledge and experience.

Participating teachers find the program especially rejuvenating. It helps them remember how important it is to leave room for awe and discovery, for exchange of ideas and celebration, for false starts and shared strategies, for community building and collaboration—while skills and domain knowledge are being established. In their school day classrooms, they use the idea of FAC warm-ups and open-ended explorations of ideas and materials as they are beginning a new unit; they also incorporate questioning strategies they have revived with their FAC colleagues. More time is preserved for sharing discoveries, allowing students to tell the stories of their work and studio process. Teachers tell us that after immersion in FAC, they cede more control to their students, trusting the artistic process and their own skills as facilitators, welcoming the unexpected. They explore an idea from the perspective of several disciplines. Teachers integrate collaborative projects into their lessons, understanding that it is a way for their students to share knowledge, expand options, and build respectful community, even as an individual relationship grows between each child and an arts medium. They remember how helpful it is in teaching the whole child to get to know parents, to watch them interact, and invite them into the learning circle.

EMBEDDED ASSESSMENT
Exchange of Ideas, Strategies and Intentions

As summarized above, the workshop structure encourages and supports participants not only to experiment, but to reflect on and share their working process, including ideas, strategies, and intensions. This ongoing self assessment and exchange is implemented as they celebrate and build on diverse solutions, learning from mistakes and surprises, and finding links between ideas from their lives and experiences and ideas that arise from their interaction with the materials and methods of the various arts domains.

At the end of each professional development training day and after each family workshop, facilitators are asked to respond in writing to a brief series of reflective questions. Similarly, parents and children are asked to respond in writing and in conversation to a few open-ended questions. At the beginning of the program, feedback was collected at the end of each family workshop. Eventually, the written feedback was solicited only after the first and final workshops in a series.

This feedback is used to revise and improve the program, highlight program impact and accomplishments for publicity and grant proposals, and provide site-specific interventions when needed. It is assessed by reading through the complete responses of individual respondents, by collating answers to questions within a school site, and finally by collating question responses across school sites. In the 7th year of Family Arts and Creativity, when we set out to evaluate the program's impact and especially to focus on better understanding the oft mentioned response that FAC "created a wonderful sense of community," we relied on the information and specific language of these on-going assessments.

PROGRAM EVALUATION
Focusing on a Sense of Community

We embarked on a study of the impact of the Family Arts and Creativity (FAC) program on participating parents and their 3rd to 5th-grade children, focusing particularly on the program's ability to create a sense of community among participants. We wanted to look more closely at the feedback we had gotten over the years from participating families, who often spoke with enthusiasm about the "wonderful community-building experience" the FAC workshops provided. Of course, the 8 short hours that participating families come together for a series of four family workshops doesn't create an actual community, one that stays intact after FAC. Rather it creates a strong *sense* of community.

Concerns such as creating a sense of community are often used to justify programs like FAC to funding agencies, parents, and other stakeholders. Yet these results (like 'increasing creative thinking, holistic engagement, appreciation of art, or understanding), are both hard to define and difficult to prove. We set out to do both. Initially, we tried to better define the conditions that created this sense of community and how it impacted participants. We then sought to develop an instrument to measure, or at least better operationalize, *sense of community*. With these goals in mind, we looked to four sources for input:

- Research literature for descriptions of sense of community and for instruments that had been effectively used to capture sense of community through the arts (please see resources list);
- Conversations with the families at one alumni school site at the end of their family arts workshops to extend their feedback about FAC as building community;
- A focus-group discussion about the relationship of the FAC program to community building, with artists and teachers who were FAC facilitators; and
- Review of the program feedback from questionnaires that had been collected over the last 6 years, particularly looking for language used by participants when referring to its ability to create a "sense of community." In preparation for this study, with the help of a Rutgers University student intern, we compiled responses across years and school sites so we could take a broad look at the content as well as the language used.

Developing a Questionnaire

We developed a questionnaire for parents (adult participants) and one for students including feedback from participating artist-teacher facilitators. Each questionnaire had a first section of open-ended, unfinished sentences for the participant to complete which sought to identify the major areas of impact of FAC as defined by participants' qualitative responses.

The second section for each was a Likert Scale—statements that respondents were asked to rate from 1 to 5 to show their degree of agreement or disagreement with each item presented to them. The statements developed for the Likert Scale sections of the questionnaires were intended to delineate those characteristics that people described when talking about FAC's ability to "create community." The data analysis of this section focused predominantly on testing the series of statements to see if they fit together statistically as a description of sense of community. These statements had to do with:

- Experiencing a safe, accepting environment
- Making personal connections to the workshop activities
- Talking about and sharing their own ideas and (art) work
- Thinking creatively, trying new things
- Getting to know other people in a more personal way
- Listening carefully to the ideas and discoveries of the other participants
- Looking at things from someone else's perspective
- Observing and interacting with other parents and children
- Working as part of a group where
  - Ideas are heard and appreciated
  - No one person dominates
  - Participants benefit from the ideas and skills of other group members
  - Multiple ideas are integrated into one collaborative plan of action
- Having fun

Appendices A-D present the blank questionnaires and mean scores. A doctoral student of Psychology from Rutgers University was engaged to enter the data and analyze it. Linda Melamed, FAC project director, and Igda Martinez, the data analyst, met numerous times to discuss the emerging results, define coding categories for the open-ended questions, and determine what other analyses would be useful.

IMPACT STUDY RESULTS
Likert Scale Questions: Adult Responses

The FAC impact questionnaire was administered to a new group of families who had not participated in the activities used to develop the questions. Across the six impact study sites, 50 adults responded to the feedback form at the end of their final Family Arts session. The questionnaire included 13 statements that participants were asked to rate from 1 (strongly agree) to 5 (strongly disagree). Of these 13 statements given to the adult participants, 9 were affirmative statements (i.e. "My ideas were heard and appreciated"); 3 were negative statements (i.e. It was difficult to reach consensus); and 1 was stated contrary to the hoped-for responses (i.e., One or two people dominated our group process.) The data were compiled and the mean scores were calculated for each question. Given the 1-5 scale, the closer the mean is to 1, the more agreement there is among respondents in strong support of the statement. Among the nine affirmative statements, all mean scores fell between 1.04 and 1.56.

As hoped, among the three negative statements the means were much higher, moving toward the strongly disagree end of the scale; these included:

- difficult to make a personal connection to the activities, 3.76
- difficult to condense many ideas into one coherent idea, 3.29
- more difficult to have a collaborative vision than to make art alone, 2.32

The one "contrary" statement received a mean of 3.47. More than half of the respondents strongly disagreed that one or two people dominated their group process.

Likert Scale Questions: Student Responses

The student responses were slightly less cohesive, though still statistically significant with more use of the whole range of response options. Fifty-eight students responded to the questionnaires. The student questionnaire included 11 statements. A response of "1" again showed strong agreement and "5," strong disagreement. Of the 11 statements, 10 were positive and 1 was a "contrary" statement ("I would rather work by myself on my own art work."). Among the 10 positive statements, the mean scores varied from 1.47 to 2.72 although the mean responses to 8 of the 10 stayed under 2. The one "contrary" statement still received a much higher mean of 3.41.

Open-Ended Statements for Participants to Complete

Adults and students were each given a list of unfinished sentences to complete. The list given to adults was slightly different from that given to students. All responses were coded by identifying overarching categories of response. These categories were defined by having several evaluators read the open-ended responses and individually group the responses to create coding categories. Then the categories were compared across evaluators and any discrepancies were discussed and revised. For example, in completing the statement "The arts are a good way to..." 42% of the respondents said something about self-expression. These responses (express yourself, express the way you feel, express yourself in an appropriate way, release emotions, show feelings, allow children to express themselves) were all grouped in the data summary as "The arts are a good way to: express yourself." Supported by similar responses to other open-ended questions, Self Expression became one of the areas of impact in the program evaluation. Using this process, the open-ended section of the questionnaire, intended to identify the broader impact of the Family Arts program, identified categories to understand the data that included:

- Building Community
    - Creating a Sense of Community
    - Engaging in Group Process/Collaboration: understanding rewards and challenges
- Strengthening Family Relations
    - Enhancing Interactions
    - Developing New Realizations
- Learning In and Through the Arts
    - Experiencing Diverse Arts Activities, Media and Disciplines
    - Thinking and Learning Through the Arts
    - Expressing Oneself
    - Engaging in Creativity
    - Having Fun

Role of the Facilitators

As a result of the study, we are better able to articulate the characteristics that define sense of community. We also became more articulate about the behaviors of the workshop facilitators that nurture it. In our focus-group discussion with artist-teacher teams, the members of the alumni consortium spoke about the things they do to facilitate the development of this sense of community. These include:

- Recruiting families that represent all of the diversities of the school community at a given grade level;
- Developing a collaborative rapport among the three facilitators: classroom teacher, arts specialist, and artist;

- Creating a safe and interactive atmosphere for participants;
- Selecting the four arts workshops and the order in which they will be presented, to gradually increase the amount of group work or collaboration, risk taking, and performance required as the workshops progress;
- Encouraging parents and children to be equally active participants as they create, reflect, share ideas, and develop solutions;
- Moving activities progressively from parent-child interactions to small group projects to larger collaborations;
- Selecting families to work together in group activities who might not normally have the chance to interact, but would complement one another's strengths and working styles; and
- Making time throughout the 2-hour workshop for participants to exchange ideas, brainstorm, share solutions, and look at one another's creations, whether or not they are working on a group product.

CONCLUSIONS

The impact study succeeded in producing a preliminary scale to measure sense of community in a family arts program, which proved to be statistically significant when given to a new group of Family Arts and Creativity participants. Adults and children alike told us that the opportunity to share ideas and possibilities, to see how other people think, to hear about and tell about their art making process, and to celebrate the diverse outcomes in a non-competitive environment, created community. The majority of participants valued the exchange even more when they were asked to work together on a piece, to collaborate on the artistic solution to a shared challenge. They remarked: "The way creative ideas flow when you are working with others is awesome." "You learn from each other and create something wonderful." They were also able to reflect on the challenges of collaboration, which they identified as: "more ideas that you can use; different ways of thinking and working; need to listen and to speak up; need to put people's strengths to work and support their weaknesses; need to compromise to get things done."

The study allowed us to profile the behaviors of the teacher/facilitator that help to establish a collaborative classroom, as well as the benefits to the teachers themselves from participating in this type of training and implementation project. In addition, the evaluation results helped to define the major areas of impact of the Family Arts program.

The evaluation strategies used to assess the impact of the Family Arts program, as well as the creation of a scale to better illuminate one aspect of a program's impact, may be used by other types of arts-in-education programs. The results can be used to foster program development, as well as to facilitate pursuit of funding and advocacy efforts. If other programs choose to use the Sense of Community scale, we would love to receive feedback about the results, as it is newly created and ready to be tested and revised in a wider arena.

Many of the attributes that participating FAC family members, artists and teachers described as central to creating a sense of community in the arts classroom are also core to a holistic learning environment. In a safe and trusting environment, students share ideas and discoveries whether working individually or on a collaborative endeavor. Private and public reflection on process and intent allows for a celebration of multiple perspectives and diverse solutions. Students are encouraged to draw on life experiences and to find and share both personal and universal meaning in their art making. Connections are made among individuals and arts disciplines and between generations. FAC facilitators nurture creative exploration and a reconnection to a sense of awe and intuition, a holistic vision of arts education as a fluid integration of mind, body and spirit.

APPENDIX A. BLANK FEEDBACK FORM GIVEN TO ADULT PARTICIPANTS

Family Arts and Creativity Parent Feedback

School_____

Your Name (optional)_____

Please answer the following questions based on your experiences in the Family Arts and Creativity workshops. There are no wrong answers.

Please fill in the blanks to complete the statements. Thank you!

What I liked best about the Family Arts workshops was _____

_____

I realized that the arts are a good way to _____

_____.

Working as a part of a group was rewarding because _____

_____.

Working as a part of a group was challenging because _____

_____.

Seeing my child working as a part of a group, I realized _____

_____.

Something that I learned about the school community is_____

_____.

Something that I learned about the arts is _____

Please respond to the following statements.

Using the scale from 1-5 <u>below</u> each question, circle one number for each answer with 1 being Strongly Agree and 5 being Strongly Disagree

The workshop leaders created a safe and accepting environment for us to work in.

Strongly Agree **1 2 3 4 5** Strongly Disagree

From these *Family Arts and Creativity* Workshops, I realized how much my child learns from hands on experiences where he/she is actively involved.

Strongly Agree **1 2 3 4 5** Strongly Disagree

It was difficult to make a personal connection to the workshop activities.

Strongly Agree **1 2 3 4 5** Strongly Disagree

When we worked in groups I felt that my ideas were heard and appreciated.

Strongly Agree **1 2 3 4 5** Strongly Disagree

One or two people tended to dominate in our group process.

Strongly Agree **1 2 3 4 5** Strongly Disagree

When we worked in groups we benefited from the skills of other group members.

Strongly Agree **1 2 3 4 5** Strongly Disagree

It was difficult to condense the many ideas of our group into one coherent idea.

Strongly Agree **1 2 3 4 5** Strongly Disagree

This experience allowed me to look at things in another person's way, from perspectives that I would have not considered otherwise.

Strongly Agree **1 2 3 4 5** Strongly Disagree

I got to talk about my ideas and art work.

Strongly Agree **1 2 3 4 5** Strongly Disagree

The projects made us think creatively, analyze and reflect.

Strongly Agree **1 2 3 4 5** Strongly Disagree

I found that having a collaborative vision is far more difficult than making art by yourself.

Strongly Agree **1 2 3 4 5** Strongly Disagree

I got to know other families from the community in a more personal way. We got to see how other people think and work and how they interact with their children.

Strongly Agree **1 2 3 4 5** Strongly Disagree

These workshops reinforced that learning can and should be fun.

Strongly Agree **1 2 3 4 5** Strongly Disagree

APPENDIX B. AVERAGES OF LIKERT SCALE RESULTS FOR ADULTS

Averages for each of the Likert Scale Questions

Parent responses:

Question	Number of valid responses	Minimum	Maximum	Mean
The workshop leaders created a safe & accepting environment for us to work in.	50	1	2	1.04
From these workshops, I realized how much my child learns from hands on experiences where he/she is actively involved.	50	1	4	1.20
It was difficult to make a personal connection to the workshop activities.	50	1	5	3.76
When we worked in groups I felt that my ideas were heard & appreciated.	50	1	3	1.56
One or two people tended to dominate in our group process.	49	1	5	3.47
When we worked in groups we benefited from the skills of other group members.	50	1	4	1.22
It was difficult to condense the many ideas of our group into one coherent idea.	49	1	5	3.29
This experience allowed me to look at things in another person's way, from perspectives that I would not have considered otherwise.	49	1	5	1.53
I got to talk about my ideas & art work.	50	1	3	1.32
The projects made us think creatively, analyze & reflect.	50	1	2	1.16
I found that having a collaborative vision is far more difficult that making art by yourself.	50	1	5	2.32
I got to know other families from the community in a more personal way. We got to see how other people think & work & how they interact with their children.	50	1	3	1.38
These workshops reinforced that learning can & should be fun.	49	1	2	1.06

APPENDIX C. BLANK FEEDBACK FORM GIVEN TO STUDENT PARTICIPANTS

Family Arts and Creativity Student Feedback

School_____

Your Name (optional)_____

Please answer the following questions based on your experiences in the Family Arts and Creativity workshops. There are no wrong answers.

Please fill in the blanks to complete the statements. Thank you!

What I liked best about the Family Arts workshops was _____

_____

I discovered that the arts are a good way to _____

_____ .

Something I learned about my parent(s) was _____

_____ .

When we worked with ___(fill in for specific workshop series) _____ I learned how to

_____ .

To create a _____(fill in for specific workshop series) _____ I had to think about

_____ .

Working as a part of a group was fun because _____

_____ .

Working as a part of a group was hard because _____

_____ .

I learned that the arts are not just drawing and painting; you can also _____

_____ .

An idea or activity from Family Arts that I would like to continue to work on at home is _____

_____ .

Please respond to the following statements.

Using the scale from 1-5 <u>below</u> each question, circle one number for each answer with 1 being Strongly Agree and 5 being Strongly Disagree

The workshop leaders created a safe and accepting environment for us to work in.

Strongly Agree **1 2 3 4 5** Strongly Disagree

From these *Family Arts and Creativity* Workshops, I realized how much my child learns from hands on experiences where he/she is actively involved.

Strongly Agree **1 2 3 4 5** Strongly Disagree

It was difficult to make a personal connection to the workshop activities.

Strongly Agree **1 2 3 4 5** Strongly Disagree

When we worked in groups I felt that my ideas were heard and appreciated.

Strongly Agree **1 2 3 4 5** Strongly Disagree

One or two people tended to dominate in our group process.

Strongly Agree **1 2 3 4 5** Strongly Disagree

When we worked in groups we benefited from the skills of other group members.

Strongly Agree **1 2 3 4 5** Strongly Disagree

It was difficult to condense the many ideas of our group into one coherent idea.

Strongly Agree **1 2 3 4 5** Strongly Disagree

This experience allowed me to look at things in another person's way, from perspectives that I would have not considered otherwise.

Strongly Agree **1 2 3 4 5** Strongly Disagree

I got to talk about my ideas and art work.

Strongly Agree **1 2 3 4 5** Strongly Disagree

The projects made us think creatively, analyze and reflect.

Strongly Agree **1 2 3 4 5** Strongly Disagree

I found that having a collaborative vision is far more difficult than making art by yourself.

Strongly Agree **1 2 3 4 5** Strongly Disagree

I got to know other families from the community in a more personal way. We got to see how other people think and work and how they interact with their children.

Strongly Agree **1 2 3 4 5** Strongly Disagree

These workshops reinforced that learning can and should be fun.

Strongly Agree **1 2 3 4 5** Strongly Disagree

APPENDIX D. AVERAGES OF LIKERT SCALE RESULTS FOR STUDENTS

Averages for each of the Likert Scale Questions

Student responses:

Question	Number of valid responses	Minimum	Maximum	Mean
I got to do things that I had never done before.	58	1	4	1.74
I learned that people have different ways of seeing things.	58	1	4	1.52
I found that working together in groups and sharing ideas is fun & you can get a lot done.	58	1	5	1.60
I would rather work by myself on my own art work.	58	1	5	3.41
My mom, dad, or grandparent & I can work on the same project together & have fun.	58	1	5	1.47
In this program the students get to be the leaders sometimes & help the grownups.	58	1	5	1.81
When we worked in groups, it was easy to agree on one idea.	58	1	5	2.72
I realized that when we make art we get to solve problems & share ideas.	58	1	4	1.76
I enjoyed talking about my ideas and art work.	57	1	5	1.82
I got to make friends with students from school who I had not known well before.	58	1	5	2.29
I learned that I can do things in art that I didn't think I could do.	57	1	5	1.96

RESOURCES USED TO DEVELOP QUESTIONNAIRES

Allard, A., & Cooper, M. (2001). Critically interrogating classroom constructions of 'community' and 'difference.' Paper presented at the Australian Association of Research in Education National Conference, Fremantle, Western Australia.

Chavis, D. M., & Pretty, G. M. H. (1999). Sense of community: Advances in measurement and application. *Journal of Community Psychology 27*(6), 635-642.

Chipuer, H. M., & Pretty, G. M. H. (1999). A Review of the sense of community index: current uses, factor structure, reliability, and further development. *Journal of Community Psychology 27*(6), 643-658.

McKinney, J. P., McKinney, K. G., Franiuk, R., & Schweitzer, J. (2006). The college classroom as a community: Impact on student attitudes and learning. *College Teaching 54*(3), 281-284.

McMillan, D. W., & Chavis, D. M. (1986). Sense of community: a definition and theory. *Journal of Community Psychology, 14*(1), 6-23.

Rovai, A. (2002). Development of an instrument to measure classroom community. *The Internet and Higher Education 5*, 197-211.

Rovai, A., Wighting, M., & Lucking, R. (2004). The classroom and school community inventory: Development, refinement, and validation of a self-report measure for educational research. *The Internet and Higher Education 7*, 263-280.

Solomon, D., Battistich, V., Kim, D., & Watson, M. (1997). Teacher practices associated with students' sense of the classroom as a community. *Social Psychology of Education, 1*, 235-267.

Stemler, S. (2001). An overview of content analysis. *Practical Assessment, Research and Evaluation, 7*(17).

Wilson, B. G. (2001). Sense of community as a values outcome for electronic courses, cohorts, and programs. Paper written for VisionQuestPT3 Conference in Denver, Colorado.

ABOUT THE AUTHORS

Linda Melamed has worked with Family Arts and Creativity since 1998, as a team artist in the initial pilot project, as the Project Director from 2000 through 2007 at the Institute for Arts and Humanities Education, and most recently as a consultant to Young Audiences NJ. For more than 25 years, she has worked on projects that bring teachers, arts specialists and teaching artists together to develop and implement school-based arts programs and authentic assessment practices. As a studio potter and ceramics instructor, Melamed has been the recipient of individual artist grants from the Connecticut Commission on the Arts, and was an artist-in-residence for the Massachusetts Cultural Council, and the Connecticut Commission on the Arts.

Maureen Heffernan serves as the Director of Arts and Education at Young Audiences New Jersey, and has been a leader in the New Jersey Arts Education community since 1977. She was associated with the Institute for Arts and Humanities Education for 25 years, initially as an artist and finally as the Executive Director, during which time she created many interdisciplinary programs like Family Arts and Creativity. Heffernan was twice the recipient of the New Jersey Governor's Arts Award as a Distinguished Teaching Artist, and teaches Integrated Visual and Performing Arts at The College of New Jersey.

CHAPTER 25

Cultivating Creativity in Art Education and Art Teacher Preparation: A Holistic Perspective

Seymour Simmons III

Teaching and teacher education naturally reflect the historical moment and societal context of which they are a part. In periods of relative peace and stability, educators can comfortably reinforce established standards and even encourage standardization. But desperate times, as it is said, call for desperate measures, and faced with unprecedented challenges, teachers at all levels must respond with innovative strategies in order to prepare their students to think and act creatively. This was the situation in the 1950s, when the US and the USSR were locked in the Cold War and a related Race for Space. Emphasis on creativity then continued through the '60s and '70s, responding, in part, to the social revolution brought about by civil rights and other cultural/political movements. It is also the case today, as crises in every sphere—from economics to the environment—cause us to realize the limitations of previous ways of doing things, and in turn, force us to form new attitudes and find new solutions.

Given such conditions, questions about whether or how to cultivate creativity in schools are no longer left up to teachers and teacher educators to decide; they become matters of national concern. For example, a July, 2010, *Newsweek* article, "The Creativity Crisis," reports that a "recent IBM poll of 1,500 CEOs identified creativity as the number one 'leadership competency of the future.'" Yet the article also notes that for the past 20 years, "research shows that American creativity is on the decline." Among the causes: "lack of creativity development in schools." Highlighting the urgency of this situation, the article then compares our educational system to that of our competitors on the world market, especially China. Whereas China has moved from emphasizing standards to emphasizing creativity, we have gone in the opposite direction.

Current concerns over cultivating creativity in schools recall conditions in the middle of the last century. When the Soviet Union launched the first satellite, Sputnik, in 1957, a chorus of voices called for greater creativity in science education (Vernon, 1971, p. 11), while others argued equally for the arts, claiming that art classes "enable creative problem solving skills to develop long before they can develop in other areas" (Efland, 1990, p. 237). Recent events have prompted similar responses. For example, President Barack Obama is quoted on the National Art Education Association (NAEA) website as saying: "The future belongs to young people with an education and the imagination to create" (Obama, 2009), while former presidential speech writer Daniel Pink proclaimed that "art is the single most important class that students can take because the art class is one of the few places in schools where creativity is being nurtured" (Rushlow, 2008, p. 1). Responding in kind, art education as a field is turning its attention once again to creativity, with numerous publications (e.g., Zimmerman, 2009), as well as the 2011 National Art Education Association conference theme, devoted to the topic.

This chapter supports that renewed commitment by reviewing ways to cultivate creativity in teaching art and art teacher preparation.

In so doing, I call into question certain established beliefs, or "myths," that have interfered with teaching for creativity in the past, including the most potent myth of all, that creativity cannot be taught! Instead, I argue the opposite, and derive from the myths in question a set of criteria that can contribute to creative development for students at all levels. These include: *mastery* of materials and processes; *attention* to qualities of experience; *self-knowledge* related to interests and creative goals; *integration* of functions in the creative process; and *connections* with others, the natural world, etc. Assuming their importance for creative development in students, I further suggest how these criteria can also contribute to art teacher preparation. Finally, I argue that creativity for both art students and their teachers should be understood as a holistic endeavor, one that engages, develops, and integrates the range of human attributes: physical/sensory, emotional, intellectual, social, and spiritual.

IMPEDIMENTS TO CREATIVITY

To begin, however, I must acknowledge several other factors that could impede art educators from living up to claims such as those made by Daniel Pink. Some of these impediments may be well known within the field, but are not necessarily mentioned in public discussions about teaching creativity in art. They include alternative priorities in art education, matters of time, and issues of teacher preparation.

Alternative Priorities

First is the fact that, despite widespread interest in creativity in the mid-20th century, many art educators have since pursued other goals and developed new paradigms, such as "Discipline Based Art Education" (e.g., Dobbs, 1988) and "Visual Culture Art Education" (e.g., Duncum, 2006). These have enriched the field and strengthened art's standing in regard to the overall curriculum. Nonetheless, as reflected in the National Visual Arts Standards (Consortium of National Arts Education Associations, 1994), the combination of approaches has significantly expanded the list of objectives art teachers now are expected to meet, thereby potentially taking time away from cultivating creativity.

The Question of Time

Earlier in this anthology, Lindström (2012) addressed the importance of time in developing students' creative ideas, saying: "In order to further creativity, students should be given enough time to investigate, test and revise, to reflect and speak to peers, and to make critical assessments of their own work (p. 85)" Finding time for such activities is especially difficult at the elementary level, where art classes are usually short and infrequent. However, even secondary level teachers may have trouble focusing on creativity due to the need to address alternative art standards or concerns extrinsic to our field, such as using art to teach literacy and other skills meant to improve academic achievement (Winner & Hetland, 2000).

Issues in Teacher Training

Given this combination of scheduling constraints and competing curricular concerns, relatively little can be done to control how much time public school art classes can devote to creativity. However, there are also other factors that affect teaching for creativity, especially in regards to pre-service art teacher preparation. These factors include the extent to which art education students are enabled to develop their own creative art abilities, and how much they learn about transmitting creative strategies to others.

Such preparation, however, reflects educational priorities of particular programs and particular periods. If university art education programs in the '80s and '90s focused less on creativity than before, teachers trained in this period may be less prepared than their predecessors to teach for creativity. Yet, even where there is genuine interest in preparing art education students to cultivate creativity, this goal may still be impeded by long-standing myths about the subject. Some of these associate creativity with positive traits like talent and originality, while others link it to negative conditions like suffering, irrationality, and alienation.

THE MYTHS OF CREATIVITY

Myths associated with creativity have long been matters of concern, not just in art education, but also in such diverse spheres as psychology and business (Amabile, 2001). Addressing the topic, David Perkins (1984) wrote, "creativity is so myth-ridden and messy a subject that it's essential to clear the underbrush before seeking a sound characterization" (p. 1). In contexts like these, however, the term *myth* may refer less to genuine myths than to simple misunderstandings, like the assumption that creativity is primarily a property of the arts, or that whatever happens in the arts is, by definition, creative. On the contrary, following Runco (2007), creativity can be seen as a vital part of every domain from science and engineering to parenting and politics, while the arts can be practiced largely through imitation, involving no creativity whatsoever.

Compared to such common misconceptions, real myths like those handed down from ancient Greece embody fundamental truths, ones that transcend particular places and periods, but which can easily be misconstrued. Beliefs—both true and false—derived from such myths may be so deeply embedded in our culture or our psyches that we are hardly aware of them, yet they still can influence us for good or ill. In discussing each myth, I will begin by exploring some possible ancient origins, then highlighting their essential truths as well as common misinterpretations that may have negatively influenced art education in the past. Next, I will offer alternative interpretations based on the myth's basic truth. These are then translated into "Pedagogical Implications" to help art teachers more effectively address creativity in the future.

The Myth of Talent

The first myth actually brings together two myths of creativity that Perkins (1984) claims "perhaps do more mischief than the others": the beliefs that "creativity reflects a kind of special ability" and that "creativity depends mostly on talent" (p. 1). Ignoring distinctions between the two, both myths imply that creativity is an inherent capacity that a few special people have and most do not. I have therefore merged them for the sake of convenience into "the myth of talent." Having done so, however, I realize that talent and creativity are not synonymous and, in fact, may conflict with one another. As the composer, Robert Schumann, put it: "Talent labors, genius creates" (1946, p. 44). An example from visual art would be a student talented in drawing from observation who is unable to do anything inventive with it. More importantly, such students may feel content with their success in the tried and true, while fearing the leap into the unknown that creativity entails.

Despite this caveat, there is still an obvious truth to the myth that people do vary in the degree to which they think or act creatively, and this difference seems to be, at least in part, innate rather than learned. As to the source of this inborn ability, the Greeks thought talent was a "gift of the muses," the nine daughters of Zeus and Mnemosyne (memory), who inspired mere mortals to create in poetry, dance, music, etc. (Stewart, 2005). There was, however, no muse for the visual arts, which, from ancient times until well into the Middle Ages, was considered merely a craft, not worthy of divine inspiration. Today, we make no such distinction, but consider talent in the arts and elsewhere the result of "good genes." Whatever the explanation, the myth that equates creativity with innate talent has important pedagogical implications. Among these, it could be used to justify a laissez faire approach to teaching, based on assumptions that those who are creative don't need to be taught, and those who are not creative won't benefit much from teaching anyway. By contrast, Perkins (1984) presents creativity as more a matter of intentional effort, motivated by interest and aided by education, therefore potentially available to all.

Another argument against the myth of talent is the creativity universally evident in child's play. Whatever their background, children everywhere seem to come into the world with the impulse to invent stories, play act, make pictures, dance, and sing in their own individual ways. From this perspective, it would seem that the people we call "creative" are the ones who don't lose the spark as they grow older. But this explanation is too simplistic, for long after the playful impulses of childhood have vanished, many adults retain a creative imagination in the form of daydreams and fantasies; they just can't make anything out of them. Therefore, truly creative people must have other attributes that enable them to realize their ideas. According to Perkins (1984), these attributes include a commitment to do creative work, combined with the propensity to plan and the willingness to persevere. "Creative results," he says picturesquely, "do not just bubble up from some fecund swamp in the mind." Instead, creative people strive for certain creative goals and qualities, and "try quite straightforwardly and calculatingly to achieve them" (p. 4). Equally important, Perkins emphasizes that those who wish to be creative in a particular medium must acquire the technical means to pursue their goals. Perkins then directly opposes laissez faire teaching, arguing instead that,

> some efforts to impart creative problem solving may falter not so much because they do not give enough emphasis to the specifically creative side of the matter as because they do not provide sufficient guidance and experience on the competence side. (p. 12)

Pedagogical implications. Creativity may well be an innate capacity, but one that, nonetheless, does not develop on its own. Instead, like language, motor control, and other natural aptitudes, creativity in art is dependent on conscious cultivation. This gives the lie to laissez faire art instruction and urges art teachers to, once again, emphasize the importance of skills in the service of creativity. The question remains: How do we develop skills in a way that supports, rather than restricts, creativity? One formula might be a combination of media experimentation and repetitive practice, monitored and guided by reflection. The balance would depend upon various factors, including the requirements of the media, the degree to which the individual student is already inclined to creativity, and especially the developmental level of the learner. In reference to the latter criteria, Judith Burton (1980) focuses primarily on media experimentation complemented by reflective questioning to foster creative skills, as well as concept development, among preschool students. Josef Albers (Horowitz & Danielowitz, 2009), teaching at Black Mountain College and Yale, emphasizes repetition, but still encourages creativity, while teaching college students how to draw perfect circles and perfectly straight lines! In each case, balance is maintained as students learn to reflect on their efforts in light of their goals, a process modeled and encouraged by the teacher.

In art, development of skills in the service of creativity is particularly important in the middle years, when adolescents abandon the imagery that had satisfied them in childhood and instead aspire to more adult forms of art, whether these are found in museums or comic books (Wilson & Wilson, 1977). Thus, the first of my "criteria for creativity" is the pursuit of *mastery:* students' efforts to develop a level of ability in their medium of choice high enough to allow them to work creatively.

Important though it is, however, mastery of skills is not enough to ensure that students fulfill their creative potential. A more comprehensive approach includes multiple attributes such as those described by Hetland, Winner, Veenema, and Sheriden (2007) in their book, *Studio Thinking: The Real Benefits of Visual Arts Education.* As summarized on the Harvard Project Zero website, these include concerns for skill under the heading, "Develop Craft," as well as other foundations of creative work, notably "Express," "Observe," and "Reflect." Another category, "Engage & Persist," refers to the attitudes mentioned by Perkins (1984) as necessary to pursue creative problems. Admittedly, such habits of mind could apply equally to non-creative artmaking. However, two others address aspects of creativity specifically: "Envision," meaning "to picture mentally what cannot be directly observed and imagine possible next steps in making a piece"; and "Stretch & Explore," which means "to reach beyond one's capacities, to explore playfully without a preconceived plan, and to embrace the opportunity to learn from mistakes and accidents." The last studio habit, "Understand Art World," is perhaps more controversial than the rest. It involves "learning about art history and current practice," as well as "Learning to interact as an artist with other artists ... and within the broader society." These suggestions invite reflection on the next myth, which associates creativity with uninfluenced originality.

The Myth of Originality

Like the previous myth, this one, which equates creativity with originality, also contains an essential truth: That creativity necessarily involves something new and unexpected. The idea is evident in common definitions of creativity, e.g., as an "imaginative activity fashioned so as to yield an outcome that is of value as well as original" (Craft, 2001). The problem arises when the term "original" is interpreted to mean not simply novel, but instead "completely new and so not copied or derived from anything else" (Encarta, 1999). Classical nomenclature for this idea is *creatio ex nihilo,* "creation from nothing." The concept is memorably depicted by Michelangelo on the Sistine Chapel ceiling, by showing the bearded Jehovah with mighty arms outstretched bringing forth from the void the heavens and the earth—simply by pointing. Based on such ideas and images, the myth of "creativity as originality" gained popularity in the Romantic Era, when, according to Benton and DiYanni (2008), divine and artistic creativity were considered one and the same. Similarly, theorists at the time claimed that, "no painter or author should ever imitate any other. The new Romantic genius stands alone, different from the rest, and unsurpassed—a true original" (p. 449).

More down-to-earth examples of uninfluenced creativity include "folk" artists, many of whom demonstrate remarkable creativity, even though they have little formal education. Victor Lowenfeld (1957) referred to such artists when arguing for his approach to art education, which sought to protect children's creativity from all adult imagery, writing:

> If children developed without any interference from the outside world, no special stimulation for their creativity would be necessary. Every child would use his deeply rooted creative impulse without inhibition, confident in his own kind of expression. We find this creative confidence clearly demonstrated by those people who live in the remote sections of our country and who have not been inhibited by the influences of advertisements, funny books, and "education." Among these folk are found the most beautiful, natural, and clearest examples of children's art. What civilization has buried, we must try to regain by recreating the natural base necessary for such free creation. (p. 12)

Beliefs about the innocent creativity of children were reinforced by modern artists like Picasso, who purportedly rejected his own precocious capacities, as well as his rigorous academic training. Attending an exhibition of children's art, he famously said: "When I was their age I could draw like Raphael, but it has taken me a whole lifetime to draw like them" (Gardner, 1993, p. 145).

Based on statements like these, art educators for decades took the position that a child's natural creativity must never be compromised by copying, referencing adult art, or demonstrations by their teacher. Even observational drawing was considered suspect, de-emphasized by Lowenfeld to accommodate students with a non-visual (or *haptic*) orientation, and assumed by others to be something children either could not or would not do (Smith, 1983). The result was a total reversal from the way visual art had traditionally been taught. Moreover, while Lowenfeld's arguments were initially made in reference to early childhood art education, the same principles and practices were applied to elementary and secondary levels, as well as to college and even graduate art studies, where student artwork apparently influenced by another artist was often criticized as being *derivative*.

The impact of this paradigm shift can still be felt today, if not in art education classes per se, at least in many studio art classes where future art teachers are learning the skills and creative strategies they will one day go on to teach. It is, therefore, worth considering whether such dramatic changes were appropriate, based on either child development theory in art or the example of famous artists. In terms of development, both critics of Lowenfeld (Wilson & Wilson, 1977) and his admirers (Burton, 2001) have questioned his claim that exposure to the work of others, copying, and observational drawing necessarily curtail creativity. Instead, they cite research suggesting that children and young people use observational drawing and "drawing from the motif", in Burton's words (2001, p. 35), to enrich their "graphic repertoires" and facilitate "the continuity of experience of self and world," thus evidently supporting their creative development. Such findings are confirmed by a closer look at Picasso.

Even if he did aspire to childlike innocence, Picasso's actual life and work stand in stark contrast to the Romantic ideal of uninfluenced creativity. On the contrary, one could argue that Picasso's formidable inventiveness was largely possible precisely *because* of his exposure to so many influences. The masterly draftsmanship evident in his innumerable drawings, paintings, and prints would have been impossible were it not for the rigorous training in academic rendering techniques he received as a youth. Moreover, according to Norman Mailer (1995), when Picasso arrived in Paris from Spain in his late teens, he "proceeded to paint... in response to the work of Corot, Courbet, Daumier, David, Delacroix, Ingres, Manet, and a host of Impressionists" (p. 39). He then "absorbed" the work of Toulouse-Lautrec and other more contemporary artists (p. 40), before turning to the art of Africa and Oceania as stimuli for his early explorations of Cubism, a style which itself was developed in close collaboration with Georges Braque (Gardner, 1993, p. 160). Actually, Picasso made no pretense of being completely original, saying instead that "good artists borrow, great artists steal!" (Genn, 2008).

One possible way to reconcile the conflict inherent in the myth of originality, as outlined above, is to distinguish between different levels of creativity, such as the common distinction between small *c* creativity, and Creativity with a capital *C*. The former might otherwise be called *ordinary* creativity, because it applies to activities like child's play, everyday problem solving, and home decoration, that nearly anyone can do more or less creatively. Writing about this level, Robert Schirrmacher (1998), in *Art and Creative Development for Young Children,* can rightly claim that, "creative expression begins early in life. Babies manipulate toys, explore space, discover their body parts, test hunches about the immediate world, and even solve problems" (p. 4). Creativity such as this, found among virtually all children, is a gift of nature. By contrast, Mihaly Csikszentmihalyi (1996) views creativity as "any act, idea, or product that changes an existing domain, or that transforms an existing domain into a new one" (p. 28). His definition refers to Creativity with a capital *C* and is largely, though not exclusively, a product of culture.

Pedagogical implications. Significant creative development beyond childhood clearly does not happen without immersion in an established domain, which includes studying existing works, both great and not so great. Csikszentmihalyi (1996) addressed this issue, writing:

> A person who wants to make a creative contribution... must learn the rules and the content of the domain, as well as the criteria of selection, the preferences in the field... a painter cannot make a creative contribution without looking, and looking, and looking at previous art, and without knowing what other artists and critics consider good and bad art. (p. 47)

Applied to art education, this idea recalls the value in integrating creative artmaking with the study of other "art disciplines," including art history, art criticism, and aesthetics, as well as "visual culture." Yet, the question remains of how this can be done while avoiding the threat of undue influence raised by the myth of originality. One answer might lie in framing the study of art as a matter of developing *attention*, my second "criterion for creativity." For one thing, the processes of description, analysis, interpretation, and judgment or other systems of art criticism (Payne, 2010) teach students to attend to characteristics and effects of various media, and to discover different ways art elements and principles can be used effectively for depiction, expression, and design. Equally important, informed exposure to works of art can make students increasingly aware of and sensitive to aspects of direct experience that might otherwise escape their notice. Elliot Eisner, in *The Arts and the Creation of Mind* (2002), makes this point, saying:

> We learn to see, to hear, to discern the qualitative complexities of what we taste and touch. We learn to differentiate and discriminate, to recognize and to recall. What first was a reflex response, a function of instinct, becomes a gradual search for stimulation, differentiation, exploration, and eventually for meaning. Our sensory system becomes a means through which we pursue our own development. But the sensory system does not work alone: it requires for its development the tools of culture: language, the arts, science, values and the like. With the aid of culture we learn to create ourselves. (p. 2)

Art history lessons could also encourage students' creative evolution by focusing less on the finished masterpieces (which might discourage students because such works are obviously far beyond their abilities) and more on how these works came into existence. Opposing the idea of *creatio ex nihilo*, lessons could begin with notes on the education of the artist, then trace the developmental arc of her or his work (Wolf, 1988), including early failures as well as later successes. Equally important would be documenting the *problems* the artist set for her or himself, the creative *process* used to pursue these problems, and the cultural *context* that provoked and supported the artist's creative development. These topics will be addressed in reference to the following myths.

The Myth of Suffering

The third myth associates creativity with suffering of various kinds. It assumes that creative people suffer more than most, and that suffering is a necessary cause and/or effect of creative acts. A legendary example is Daedalus, the mythic sculptor and architect, who, after murdering an apprentice in a jealous rage, was forced to build King Minos the Labyrinth to house the horrid Minotaur, half-man and half-bull. Daedalus was then trapped in the Labyrinth for helping Theseus slay the beast, but escaped on waxen wings, only to lose his son Icarus, who flew too close to the sun, melted his wings, and fell into the sea (Charmandaris, 2006). A similarly unfortunate, but true, story, recounted endlessly in art classes, is the one about Van Gogh cutting off (part of) his ear. The link between creativity and suffering is reinforced by popular films about creative individuals, particularly in the arts, who led difficult lives and died tragic deaths. Visual artists portrayed in this way include Rembrandt, Goya, Van Gogh, Jackson Pollack, Picasso, Andy Warhol, Frieda Kahlo, and Jean-Michel Basquiat. Irving Stone (1961) alludes to it by titling his biography of Michelangelo, *The Agony and the Ecstasy.* In music, this myth is expressed in the familiar phrase, "you have to suffer to sing the blues."

Beyond these examples, it is hard to deny that creative people, not only in the arts, do sometimes suffer—from illness, injury, emotional or mental problems, lack of recognition, poverty, etc. Sadly, this may also be true for students, some of whom use art to express the difficulties of their lives or else to escape them. Reaching out to these students, we, as art teachers, may want to tell them about artists, such as Kathe Kollwitz, who were able to convert their personal suffering into profoundly expressive works. Doing so, however, we should also be careful to discourage self-destructive tendencies, negative feelings, or nihilistic thinking that students might also associate with being a suffering artist. On the contrary, we could remind them that personal suffering is not a prerequisite for being creative and note that, until rather recently, artists weren't particularly known for their suffering. According to Wittkower & Wittkower (2006), suffering only became associated with artists in the Renaissance, when the anonymous craftsmen of the Middle Ages were replaced by strong personalities like Leonardo and Michelangelo, who took on the mantel of "genius."

Another way of approaching this myth is to acknowledge a still more fundamental truth: Genuine creativity involves some degree of suffering, because it only happens in response to genuine problems. As Csikszentmihalyi (1996) contends:

> The creative process starts with a sense that there is a puzzle somewhere, or a task to be accomplished. Perhaps something is not right, somewhere there is a conflict, a tension, a need to be satisfied. The problematic issue can be triggered by a personal experience, by a lack of fit in the symbolic system [the domain in which the problem arises], by the stimulation of colleagues, or by public needs. In any case, without such a felt tension that attracts the psychic energy of the person, there is no need for a new response. (p. 95)

By the same token, lack of need and the related absence of suffering may actually impede creativity. Those who live in comfort have little reason to do anything new and may even see change as disruptive or threatening. This natural, conservative tendency serves a purpose, giving order to life and stability to society. On the other hand, people faced with difficulties have an equally natural inclination to relieve their suffering and restore a sense of equilibrium through a creative act, whether self-expression or problem-solving. One might also argue that, even in the best of conditions, there are always potential problems and new possibilities waiting to be discovered. Indeed, Getzels and Csikszentmihalyi (1976), in an early study of art students, described the most creative ones not simply as problem-solvers, but as problem-finders.

Pedagogical implications. Based on what has been said above, art teachers interested in encouraging creativity must, to some extent, serve as "provocateurs," challenging students, through problem-based projects, to take risks, "get out of their comfort zones," "stretch the envelope," etc. Teachers also should be preparing more mature students to find and solve their own problems. Toward these ends, teachers might benefit from understanding what kinds of problems are more likely to provoke a genuinely creative response, as well as what types of problems artists set for themselves. Such problems, according to Stokes (2006), are "ill-structured," meaning they have no single correct answer and so invite multiple diverse responses. Ill-structured problems are the ones artists choose for themselves, like the Cubists' problem of how to show objects from different angles at once. By contrast, "well-structured problems" have one correct answer and generally a predetermined way to find it. In art, this would be a "paint by numbers" kit.

Nonetheless, creative problems are not entirely open-ended. Stokes (2006) explains that, instead, they are, of necessity, subject to constraints in at least two ways: one set of constraints limits the media, theme, and/or style in which the artist will work; another set blocks him or her from using tried-and-true solutions. Stokes uses, as an example, Monet in his development of Impressionism. Monet's positive constraint, according to Stokes, was his focus on the effects of light, while his negative constraint was to do this while avoiding the academic emphasis on value. Instead, the artist kept a limited value range, using cool colors for shadows and warm colors for lights. It must be remembered when teaching that solving such genuine problems can involve frustration and painful struggles against old habits and beliefs; moreover, students should be made aware that creative solutions do sometimes provoke resistance from other people by threatening the status quo. Like many innovators, Monet was, himself, initially mocked for his work. In fact, the term "Impressionism" came from a derogatory comment made by a critic about his painting, *Impression: Sunrise*.

Another implication of this myth has to do with creative self-expression. Like other aspects of creativity, self-expression has been less of a concern in recent years than it was in the past, where it was deemed by Lowenfeld (1957) and others as fundamental for "creative and mental growth." Indeed, teachers may avoid addressing issues of self-expression for fear of the disturbing imagery that might emerge (Henley, 1998). Despite such valid concerns, it might be argued that the need for self-expression is actually growing as children and adolescents face increasingly difficult personal and family crises, along with daunting social, economic, and/or environmental challenges. Moreover, because self-expression has long been a leading motivation for and theme of Western art, to neglect it opposes both curriculum-centered *and* student-centered concerns (Dewey, 1960; Clark, Day & Greer, 1987).

In regard to creativity, one might say that genuine self-expression is of necessity creative, because each individual, and each experience, is to some degree unique. Still, there are plenty of examples of so-called expressive works that are, indeed, derivative, or simply ill-conceived, and thus ineffective in communicating the intended feeling. The challenges suggested here include identifying feelings genuinely in need of expression, then channeling and shaping them into a successfully expressive and original (in the common use of the term) artistic imagery. Admittedly, expressive concerns stand at the often uncomfortable intersection between art education and art therapy, but therapeutic methods are not necessary to invite self-expression. More suitable to an educational setting would be for students to keep a reflective journal, in which they record dreams, feelings, experiences, and so on, that might be of expressive interest (Winner & Simmons, 1993). Toward this end, journals serve the third "criterion of creativity," *self-knowledge*. Self-knowledge supports the creative impulse in several ways, including helping to determine problems of compelling interest and enabling students to determine their strengths and weaknesses in relation to their goals. Defined by Gardner (1983) in terms of "intrapersonal intelligence," self-knowledge is increasingly essential in contemporary democratic societies, where expanding opportunities for choice increase the need for self-direction. It is all the more important for those in the arts, where independent thinking and self-expression are necessary criteria for success.

Beyond their more general purpose in supporting self-knowledge, journals can also be used as practical tools for creative problem solving, what John-Steiner (1997) calls "notebooks of the mind." Toward this end, journal/sketchbooks have been used by creative individuals in all domains (McKim, 1972; Picasso, 1986) to gather inspirational words and images, generate and work out ideas in thumbnails, and keep process-notes and reminders. Based on such journal entries, teachers can guide students in the effective expression of feelings, as well as in their efforts to solve problems or create products. Together, these steps are part of a comprehensive "creative process," as discussed in the following section.

The Myth of Madness

The fourth myth associates creativity with abnormal mental or emotional states, picturing the creative individual as someone strange and eccentric. An early statement of this myth comes from Plato, who described creativity as a kind of divine madness (Plato, trans. 1956). Speaking specifically of the poet, Plato claimed he could only create when he is "inspired and is out of his senses, and the mind is no longer in him" (*Ion*, 534b). Irrationality and creativity in ancient Greece were also linked in the Dionysian revels, wildly intoxicated celebrations of the god of wine, which gave birth to the theatre. More recently, research by psychologists such as Sass (1992) seems to confirm correlations between creativity and mental illness today. Examples include "outsider artists" classified as clinically insane, as well as established artists like Salvador Dali, who appeared to be mad, even though he claimed he was not (Ludwig, 1995).

As with the myth of suffering, the association of creativity with abnormal mental states has both its facts and its fictions. There are indeed many artists who have suffered from schizophrenia, bi-polar disorder, depression, and so on, at some point in their lives, and who have responded to these conditions in their creative work. Moreover, as suggested in the previous section, art is recognized as an effective means of diagnosing and treating various forms of mental illness.

Setting aside the link between creativity and mental disorders, there is another element of truth to the myth in question that is far more common and far less troubling: The fact that creativity almost always involves non-rational elements, those we refer to as intuition, insight, and imagination. Recent research in neurophysiology has acknowledged these subtle and mysterious events as legitimate mental functions, locating them on the right hemisphere of the brain. This same research, as is now well known, has similarly added legitimacy to art education, due to the fact that visual/spatial functions have also been located on the right side of the brain, (Edwards, 1979; Pink, 2005). Yet, according to Brewster Ghiselin (1952), irrational/non-rational elements are found in every discipline, even supposedly left-brained fields like science and math. Based on his review of the working methods of noteworthy creators from across the spectrum, Ghiselin claims that, "Production by a process of purely conscious calculations seems never to occur" (pp. 14-15).

Creative people may, indeed, "think different," as the Apple computer ad puts it. Some may also look and behave in eccentric (literally 'off-center') ways. But that need not imply they are any less sane than others. Moreover, "positive psychologists" like Csikszentmihalyi (1996) argue that creativity represents not a pathological condition, but an optimal psychological state, characterized by a sense of "flow" (1990). Such views correspond with the writings of potter and poet, M. C. Richards (1964), for whom creativity was connected to spirituality and personal transformation. Similar statements have been made by those who view creativity within the context of religious traditions, such as Zen or Taoism (Chang, 1970; Sze, 1956).

One way to understand this more positive interpretation of the present myth is to see creativity as a holistic activity, involving, among other things, both sides of the brain. This view is reinforced by descriptions of "the creative process" (Goleman, Kaufman & Ray, 1992) in which creative leaps associated with mental functions below (or above) the level of ordinary consciousness (Freud, 1958; Kubie, 1958) interact with and complement intentional, conscious acts, like gathering data, reflecting, analyzing, and critiquing. As discussed in the previous myth, the process is initiated by a genuine problem that provokes research and reflection. This is typically followed by a period of incubation, in which the issue to some degree works itself out below the level of consciousness, at which point it eventually re-emerges in the form of an "inspiration" or "insight." These must then be tested and either proved or disproved, in which case the process starts again.

Considering the impressive power of those "aha" or "eureka" moments, it is tempting to celebrate the seemingly irrational, or non-rational, aspects of creativity. For example, Albert Einstein is popularly quoted as saying, "Imagination is more important than knowledge" (IOP, 2000). Statements like this may in some sense be true, but, taken literally, they misrepresent the educational factors fundamental to cultivating imagination in the first place, as well as the psychological, neurological, and practical factors underlying each particular creative act. These several factors are succinctly captured in the common phrase, "inspiration only comes to those who are well prepared." Thus, Gardner (1993) points out that Einstein was well prepared to use his imagination to achieve insights like "$E = mc^2$," thanks to years of immersion and academic training in the physics of his day. Equally, according to Leher (2008), such insights may appear like a "bolt from the blue," but they would not be possible without previous periods of thinking and research. In terms of hemispheric functions, insights evidently come when the focused, left-hemisphere attention required for research finally relaxes, allowing the right hemisphere to do its work, making new connections and discovering unexpected possibilities.

Pedagogical implications. These findings reinforce the importance of preparation in cultivating creativity, e.g., developing attitudes, skills, and content knowledge within the domain of art. Equally, they define the way creativity can emerge as a process in response to a certain problem. This recalls the statement made in the previous section about teaching, not only the end-product of creative problem-solving (the final masterpiece), but the steps by which the result was achieved. This process is strikingly evident in the numerous drawings Picasso did for the painting, *Guernica*. Rudolf Arnheim (1973) carefully analyzed these preliminary drawings to illustrate his theory of creativity. Briefly, Arnheim, like Czikszentmihalyi, believes that creativity begins with a rough, intuitive sense of a problem to be solved or, in art, a feeling to be expressed. However, the sense of this problem or feeling must itself evolve throughout the course of the creative process, only to be fully realized when the work is done.

Although the painting *Guernica* was a unique and deeply personal creative effort, Picasso's process, as described by Arnheim, is similar to that of many other artists from various periods in history, including Renaissance masters like daVinci and Raphael (Bambach, 2002), as well as more modern artists, like Andrew Wyeth, who work in quite different ways than Picasso (Hoving, 1976). In each case, the work begins with an initial sketch or series of sketches (sometimes called "thumbnails"), in an attempt to catch a rough idea of what the finished composition will look like. These sketches are then followed by further compositional sketches, as well as studies of details and experiments with media, all leading up to work on the final piece, which, in turn, may require still more sketches and studies to achieve.

The artists' creative process described above reflects the mental traits identified by psychologist J. P. Guilford (1970) as common to creative people in every field. First is *fluency*—which involves generating innumerable possible ideas without inhibiting or judging them. Second is *flexibility*, in which ideas go in diverse directions, connecting with different types of thoughts, feelings, and experiences. Third is *originality*, the tendency to look at things in ways few other people would. Fourth is *redefinition,* the ability to improvise on the situation, to see it from different angles. A fifth habit, *elaboration,* allows development of ideas in depth and/or in breadth.

Equally important in this process, as mentioned earlier, is the trait of *reflection,* through which the creator monitors the process and evaluates the progress in light of initial or evolving intentions. John Dewey stressed the importance of reflection in artmaking in his book, *Art as Experience* (1934), noting important similarities between thinking in art and in intellectual spheres. In fact, Dewey characterizes such processes as "reflective thinking" (Dewey, 1910), using the term to describe the so-called "scientific method." The relationship between creating and reflecting (or "doing and undergoing," as Dewey puts it) brings to mind another supposed dichotomy, that between critical and creative thinking. Some, like Goleman et al. (1992), claim that critical analysis and criticism can impede creativity. However, Passmore (1967) argues that there is no necessary contradiction between the two, and instead merges the terms into "critico-creative" thought, to demonstrate their interdependence.

As suggested above, relationships between two forms of thinking and between right and left hemispheres are part of a much more comprehensive, or holistic, understanding of creativity, one that involves, not only the engagement, but the *integration* of physical/sensory, emotional, intellectual, and other functions. This is my fourth "criterion of creativity." Integration opposes the association of creativity with insanity, which is often characterized by a fragmentation of the personality. At the same time, it aligns with Dewey's concept of the aesthetic (1934, pp. 35-57), which unites the full range of human functions in experience. Integration in artmaking will, of course, take different forms, depending on the nature of the project. In work calling for creative self-expression, feelings are obviously central, but these must be linked to the physical/sensory capacities required for expression, as well as to intellectual capacities needed to guide the process and analyze the results. Conceptual art and design similarly require physical/sensory skills to give form to concept. However, even if these are primarily intellectual and/or practical endeavors, emotions also play a part. Conceptual art, for example, might engage what Scheffler (1991) calls "cognitive emotions." Applied originally by the author to the pursuit of knowledge in science, math, and similar academic domains, these include "a love of truth and a contempt for lying, a concern for accuracy in observation and inference, and a corresponding repugnance at error in logic or fact" (p. 4). Other emotions related to cognition are applicable to creative development in design. Following Scheffler, these include the "joy of verification" (pp. 9-11), when expectations are confirmed by the process of investigation, and "receptivity to surprise" (pp. 12-14), when efforts yield unexpected results. A fourth aspect of holistic involvement, the social dimension, recognizes that artists don't work in a vacuum, but rather are part of a creative community. This topic, along with the spiritual dimension, is addressed in the final myth, in which creativity is associated with alienation.

The Myth of Alienation

The fifth myth imagines the creative artist as a misunderstood visionary, a rebel against society, or simply someone who seeks isolation. An archetypal rebel was the Titan, Prometheus, the divine artist who first formed human beings out of clay, then stole fire from the gods to give life to his creations, a crime for which Zeus had him chained to a rock, then sent an eagle to repeatedly peck out his liver, which kept growing back. Humans continue to honor Prometheus by the word "promethean," meaning "boldly creative; defiantly original" (American Heritage Dictionary, 2007). The literal translation of the Greek word *prometheus* is "foresight," indicating the visionary role of creators in foreseeing future needs. However, Prometheus had a brother, Epimetheus, who created the beasts, but is best known for opening Pandora's box and letting all manner of evil loose on the world. In Greek, the word *epimetheus* means "hindsight," evoking the unforeseen negative consequences of ill-conceived creative efforts, another reason why creators may be alienated and spurned by society (History Source, 2000-2012).

Real life examples of misunderstood, rebellious, alienated, or socially isolated artists also abound. Among the misunderstood are innumerable painters who were only "discovered" after their death. Among the rebellious, alienated, and isolated, Gauguin was well known for having fled his family and career in banking to live in Tahiti, while Georgia O'Keeffe spent her later years alone in the deserts of New Mexico. In ordinary human experience, the myth of the creative person as alienated individualist is reenacted in the form of adolescent rebellion. Similarly, students who feel alienated from peers, parents, and the rest of society sometimes gravitate toward the art room, as one place they feel at home.

However, even in the art room, students may feel a sense of isolation due to the fact that visual art projects are largely done individually, unlike those in music, dance, and theatre.

It is true that art students, and, indeed, many artists, need time to themselves in which to work. Nonetheless, art is not necessarily an isolated activity. Up to a century ago, many established artists had busy *ateliers,* peopled by apprentices, who actually worked on the master's paintings or sculptures. Even the most cutting-edge artists usually had friends, colleagues, and allies. Picasso and Braques felt as if they were "chained together on a mountain," as they collaboratively developed Cubism (Gardner, 1993). More recently, Andy Warhol formed The Factory, a group of artists, writers, and musicians, who frequented his studio, along with many assistants, who helped produce his prints and other projects (Cale, 2002). That group artmaking is hardly a thing of the past is illustrated by glass artist Dale Chihuly (2010-2011), sculptor Jeff Koons (art21, 2001-2011), and environmental artists Christo and Jeanne-Claude (2008), all of whom require teams of assistants to accomplish their projects, not to mention the army of illustrators, animators, model-makers, and designers listed in the credits of every animated film.

Speaking in more general terms, Csikszentmihalyi (1996) claims that creativity is *never* just a matter of what goes on in any one person's mind (p. 23). Rather, it must be part of a complex system involving the *individual*, a *domain,* and a *field*. Domains, like the visual arts, consist of "a set of symbolic rules and procedures (p. 27)," which are used and modified by the creative individual to create new work. Such domains "are in turn nested in what we usually call culture, or the symbolic knowledge shared by a particular society or by humanity as a whole" (p. 28). The field consists of individuals who currently "act as gatekeepers of the domain. It is their job to decide if a new idea or product should be included in the domain" (p. 28). In the visual arts, "[t]he field consists of art teachers, curators of museums, collectors of art, critics, and administrators of foundations and government agencies that deal with culture. It is this field that selects what new works deserve to be recognized, preserved and remembered" (p. 28).

On the margins between particular domains are interdisciplinary arenas, such as theatre, where artists have long worked in creative collaboration with set and costume designers, directors, and producers. Other collaborative contexts include architecture, which links art and engineering, as well as more contemporary forms, such as those produced in places like the M.I.T. Media Lab (MIT, 2009) and the Stanford Humanities Lab (Stanford, 2009), where visual artists work with technology specialists, engineers, scientists, scholars, and others on social and environmental projects. In the future, Gardner (2008) argues, the capacity for synthesis required in such collaborations will be an increasingly valuable creative commodity. Similarly, Florida (2002) urges members of what he calls the "Creative Class" to work with other aspects of society, for the good of all. Taken together, these examples and arguments suggest that art teachers should challenge the association of artistic creativity with alienation, and instead prepare students to interact, not only among their artistic peers, but with their fellows in other disciplines. Doing so, however, requires reconsidering how and where art is currently taught.

Pedagogical implications. As with the myth of originality, assumptions associated with the myth of alienation might be hidden behind the tendency to emphasize individuality in art production, interpreting this to mean that students must do their work alone and on their own, with limited interaction except, perhaps, in group critiques. Art classes with this agenda tend to be quiet places, where concentration is encouraged—a worthy goal, especially in this age of endless distractions and instant gratification. But such models of creativity can also be contrasted to the examples of group art cited earlier, as well as to creative brainstorming sessions in business and other domains (McKim, 1972), where chaos seems to rule and the flow of ideas is loud and unimpeded.

Institutional alienation takes another form, when art classes are separated, literally or figuratively, from other activities in the schools. The segregation of art from academics can itself be contrasted to the approach taken in the Renaissance academies (Pevsner, 1973), during one of the most creative moments in history. Sponsored by wealthy patrons like the Medici, these academies opposed the insular practices of the medieval guilds by bringing together masters from many different disciplines, including the arts, the sciences, philosophy, etc., to find creative solutions to the problems of the day.

Such multi-faceted approaches are also essential in order to resolve today's daunting difficulties, which brings to mind the fifth "criterion of creativity": *Connections.* Along with the cross-disciplinary connections described above, creativity in general involves a sense of connectedness to the social and/or natural world, without which the creative effort would fail to meet one of its most important aspects: Usefulness or adaptation. These criteria can be addressed even with students in elementary school, through creative projects connected to community needs.

One model for interconnected-interdisciplinary learning comes from Ron Berger (2003), a 6th-grade teacher who received national recognition for his innovative project/portfolio-based curriculum. First of all, Berger ensures that all his projects are grounded as much as possible in authentic, "real world" tasks, involving interaction with the community. For example, a science project had students collecting and testing water samples from all the town's wells, then publishing the results in a local newspaper. A skilled carpenter, Berger also builds the design process into his assignments. Addressing synthesis, he tries wherever possible to bring together learning from different subjects, linking art, math, science, and English lessons. All of these were brought together when, following a field trip spelunking in a local cave, students wrote an imaginative mystery story that happened in a cave, then illustrated it with an accurately scaled and geological convincing section-elevation drawing of the cave in which the action took place. While many of these projects are done individually, the final project of the year had students work in pairs to research, design, and construct scale-models of a public institution, e.g., a pizza parlor, a college campus, or an airport. In each case, students began by going into the community to connect with people working in these institutions and/or experts in the area to determine needs and concerns; then they designed their projects with those issues in mind.

Even with projects done independently in class, Berger's assignments also involve public presentations to the school or community, where students must explain their work. There are also constant conversations about the work going on within the classroom, in the shape of formative critiques. Here again, as opposed to assumptions earlier attributed to Goleman et al., (1992), formal and informal critique sessions become vehicles for helping all students advance in their creative efforts. Toward this end, Berger has three rules to ensure that critique sessions are truly "episodes of learning" (Wolf, 1993): Be kind, be constructive, and be specific. In fact, such critiques are part of a more comprehensive procedure, integrating assessment and teaching. This approach, which served as a model for the Arts PROPEL project mentioned by Lindström in this anthology, has been characterized in a paper by Berger entitled, "Assessment *For* Learning—Key Strategies: Critique Protocols and Models of Work" (Berger, n.d.). Based on the work of Rick Stiggens (Stiggens, Arter & Chappuis, 2004) and the Assessment Training Institute (ATI, now a subsidiary of the Educational Testing Service, which also produces the Scholastic Aptitude Test), Berger's paper applies ATI strategies to teaching writing. But these same strategies can help foster creativity in any subject. Among them, teachers should

- Provide a clear and understandable vision of the learning target,
- Use examples and models of strong work and weak work,
- Design lessons to focus on one aspect of quality at a time,
- Teach students focused revision, and
- Engage students in self-reflection.

Beyond formative assessments, teachers are, of course, expected to provide summative evaluations of student work, which, from middle school onward, usually mean grades. Along with other aspects of art, such as self-expression, it is notoriously difficult to attach a number or letter to creativity. However, effective approaches to assessing individual creativity have been identified by Rostan (2005), while Lindström (2012), in this anthology, describes a holistic assessment of creativity on a national scale, addressing both processes and products. Maintaining both criteria, this system could be adapted for use in art classrooms at all levels. Large-scale assessments such as this serve another connective purpose, providing evidence, accessible to the general public, of the creative learning that goes on in the art room.

CREATIVITY VIEWED FROM A HOLISTIC PERSPECTIVE

The five myths of creativity understood in one way can combine to curtail efforts to cultivate creativity. However, they can also be re-interpreted to contribute both principles and practices that support such efforts. These principles are addressed under the "criteria of creativity": *mastery, attention, self-knowledge, integration,* and *connections.* Meeting these criteria also contributes to the holistic nature of creativity. Although mentioned in previous sections, this characteristic is worth examining in greater depth, especially when considering creativity in the context of holistic art education. Among the various aspects of artmaking assessed on standard rubrics, most are easily associated with one dimension of the person or another. For instance, craftsmanship and technique are naturally attributed to the physical dimension, including perception and hand skills while expression is obviously related to emotions, and concept development as well as composition are primarily the work of intellect. None of these dimensions, on its own, can account for the complexity of creativity. Moreover, creativity can apply to each aspect of artmaking listed here, but when it does, it connects physical, emotional, and intellectual facets, as discussed under the topic of *integration.* The social dimension, which we have already shown to be essential to creativity, itself involves a mix of other skills, notably the physical/sensory, emotional, and intellectual abilities required for people to work together.

All of these dimensions come together in the final aspect of holistic development, the spiritual. Based on the view articulated by Campbell in this volume, spirituality is understood, apart from its religious connotations, as a sense of connectedness, uniting all aspects of the individual, while connecting the self with others, with the community, with humanity, with nature, and ultimately with the transcendent, however that might be understood. Rollo May (1957) touches upon the transcendent when defining the holistic experience of creativity in terms of "ecstasy":

> The topic of ecstasy is one to which we should give more active attention in psychology. I use the word of course, not in its popular and cheapened sense of "hysteria," but in its historical, etymological sense of "ex-stasis"—that is, literally to "stand out from," to be freed from the usual split between subject and object which is a perpetual dichotomy in most human activity. *Ecstasy* is the accurate term for the intensity of consciousness that occurs in the creative act. But it is not to be thought of merely as a Bacchic "letting go"; it involves the total person, with the subconscious and unconscious acting in union with the conscious. It is not, thus *irrational*; it is, rather, suprarational. It brings intellectual, volitional, and emotional functions into play all together. (p. 49)

May's words are reminiscent of Csikszentmihalyi's characterization of flow (1990) as a "holistic experience that people feel when they act with total involvement" (p. 36). Based on these arguments, a clear case can be made for viewing creativity from a holistic perspective. It remains, then, to consider what this kind of holistic engagement might look like in practice, and to review possible implications of this perspective for teacher preparation in art.

A Model of Holistic Engagement

Following the principles outlined above, creativity for young people should build a foundation of skills, habits, and attitudes conducive to creative work in various media, complemented by immersion in the domain involving the other art disciplines and possibly additional studies in other related fields. Based on this foundation, students should apply skills and knowledge to age-appropriate problem solving and self-expression using a creative process and facilitated by a constructive, yet challenging, social environment. This type of holistic engagement is exemplified by the Advanced Placement portfolio of a student at Northwestern High School, Rock Hill, South Carolina. His theme, the Seven Deadly Sins, is illustrated in Figures 1-3.

Evident on the physical plane is *mastery* of technique with the chosen media, colored pencils. These are matched on the sensory plane by strong observational skills, as well as *attention* to qualities of work within the domain, notably the stylistic characteristics of

FIGURE 1. (left) Following the duality depicted in a self-portrait, the sin of wrath is represented here by a hand holding a knife, while compassion is depicted by an open hand held out to someone in need..

FIGURE 2. (right) This image reflects on possible causes of the character traits that lead to sin or its opposite: Is it nature, as depicted in the strands of DNA, or nurture (education, environment, family, etc.)?

Surrealism and sequential art. In terms of emotion and *self-knowledge*, several images express disturbing feelings, including self-doubt, anxiety, and rage. Intellectually, the concept is broadly conceived, intricately investigated, and imaginatively portrayed. At the same time, the various works demonstrate the *integration* of technical skills with emotional expression and concept. *Connections* in one form are made through the cross-disciplinary references to psychological, genetic, and societal issues as potential sources of the sins in question. The social dimension of this work should also be understood in terms of the *inter-connections* among students, as facilitated by their AP art teacher, Kim Grant. Finally, the spiritual dimension is reflected in the theme, based on the Christian doctrine of sin.

FIGURE 3. One possible cause of sin today is the pressure to get so many things done so quickly, leading people to cut corners and so make ethical and other kinds of compromise.

Holistic Teacher Preparation

This example demonstrates one form of addressing the attributes of creativity from a holistic perspective. Following the principles and practices presented in this chapter, art teachers can be prepared to cultivate creativity holistically for students of all ages and levels of ability. These guidelines for art teacher preparation listed below are derived from the five myths of creativity, as well as from discussions of the artist/teacher model by both Sullivan and Lawton and other topics addressed in this anthology:

- *Talent vs Teaching:* Based on the first myth, art teachers in training will need a solid foundation in studio art concepts and techniques, and then be challenged in more advanced classes to pursue *mastery* of particular media, in developing their own body of creative work. Toward that end, art education classes should also encourage habits and attitudes conducive to creativity, including curiosity, willingness to take risks, and perseverance in the face of difficulties.

- *Originality vs Immersion:* Following the second myth, art education classes should complement those in art history, art criticism, and aesthetics, by: 1) training future teachers to *attend* to qualities of art addressed in these disciplines; and, 2) preparing art education students to use these subjects to support their own and their future students' creative process.

- *Suffering vs Problem Solving:* Considering the third myth, art education students need opportunities to cultivate *self-knowledge* by regularly reflecting on their own goals and intentions; then to express personal feelings; and finally to face the challenge of genuine, ill-defined problems in the domain. These can begin in introductory studio and art education classes with teacher-directed problems, and proceed in more advanced classes to become increasingly self-determined. This process, recorded in a creative journal, may be of value in preparing students for the *Praxis II, Art Making Test,* especially the second part on "Documentation of Personal Art Making" (ETS, 2008).

- *Madness vs Method:* In developing their body of work, art education students should be trained to develop a creative process that *integrates* physical/sensory, emotional, and intellectual functions. Like the creative problems, the process, too, can be initially dictated by the course instructor based on a standard model, as described under the fourth myth. However, increasingly, students should develop their own unique approaches to creativity. Linked to this, art education students also need to be versed in the holistic development of students, PreK-12. A description of holistic development at various age levels is described in *Creating Meaning through Art: Teacher as Choice-maker* by Simpson et al. (1998). Finally, art education students should learn strategies such as those included in this anthology, for activating holistic creative development in students of different ages.

- *Alienation vs Connection:* From the fifth myth, art education students need to *connect* with a creative community, including professional artists, mentors, teachers, and more experienced peers. Crossing disciplines, they can also make contact with teachers and professionals in other fields, as well as connecting with state and national art education associations, community organizations, businesses, advocacy groups, and others that support the arts. Besides expanding teachers' creative opportunities and those of their students, such connections may provide opportunities for art teachers to share their knowledge of creativity with others, thereby helping to solve the challenges noted at the outset of this essay.

CONCLUSIONS

Creativity is described here as a natural part of being human. As such, it can be cultivated in all students, regardless of their innate talents or initial inclinations. In this way, creativity is akin to other uniquely human qualities, such as the abilities to speak, to reason, to use tools and symbol systems, and to thrive in all kinds of climates. Yet creativity is not just one significant capacity among the many; it is arguably the most important of them all. This is true, in part, because creativity allows us to apply our other abilities to new and useful ends, but also because it enables us to make art and to participate in other forms of meaningful expression that shape our cultures and define us as individuals.

Creativity, employed in these ways, has been essential to humanity since its earliest beginnings, making it possible to advance in a relatively short time from an animal-like existence—living in caves and eating roots and berries—to a world of space travel, computers, biotechnology, and continual change. If anything, the need for creativity is accelerating, especially in industrialized countries like the United States, where there is constant demand for innovation in every sphere. Unfortunately, however, many of the challenges that call for creativity today impact, not only the success of our society, but the very survival of life on earth. In this context, we have much to learn from those who initiated research into creativity half a century ago. Then, as now, the stakes could not have been higher. Nonetheless, many who wrote about creativity at that time did not focus solely on the practical benefits of creativity urged upon educators by external influences. Rather, they talked about the holistic development that creativity both entails and encourages—the integration of being, which is brought about through the creative act. Jerome Bruner, at the height of the Cold War, put it this way:

> Yet there is good reason to inquire about creativity, a reason beyond practicality, for practicality is not a reason but a justification after the fact. The reason is the ancient search of the humanist for the excellence of man: the next creative act may bring man to a new dignity." (1962, 1979, p. 17)

Bruner then goes on to speak about the nature of that excellence and dignity in terms that reflect the values and goals of this anthology: "It is implied, I think, that the act of a man creating is the act of a whole man, that it is this rather than the product that makes it good and worthy." (p. 18)

AUTHOR'S NOTE

This chapter is based on a web document, "Cultivating Creativity in Arts Education: Myths, Misconceptions, and Practical Procedures" published by the South Carolina Alliance for Arts Education to accompany *Teaching for Creativity using SC Standards.* (Hockman & Walling-Wohlford, 2008). (www.lander.edu/Libraries/SC_Art_Alliance/Teaching_Standards_Based_Creativity_in_the_Arts.sflb.ashx)

REFERENCES

Amabile, T. (2001). Beyond talent: John Irving and the passionate craft of creativity. *American Psychology, 54*(4), 333-336.

Arnheim, R. (1973) *The genesis of a painting: Picasso's Guernica.* Berkeley, CA: University of California Press.

art21, Jeff Koons. Retrieved from: www.pbs.org/art21/artists/jeff-koons

Bambach, Carmen. (Living document, 2000-present). "Renaissance Drawings: Material and Function." In *Heilbrunn timeline of art history.* New York, NY: The Metropolitan Museum of Art. Retrieved from www.metmuseum.org/toah/hd/drwg/hd_drwg.htm (October 2002) Source: Renaissance Drawings: Material and Function | Thematic Essay | Heilbrunn Timeline of Art History | The Metropolitan Museum of Art.

Benton, J., & Di Yanni, R. (2008). *Arts and culture: An introduction to the humanities.* Upper Saddle River, NJ: Pearson, Prentice Hall.

Berger, R. (2003). *An ethic of excellence: Building a culture of craftsmanship in schools.* Portsmouth, NH: Heinemann.

Bruner, J. (1962, 1979). *On knowing: Essays for the left hand.* Cambridge, MA: Belknap Press of Harvard University Press.

Burton, J. (1980, September). Beginnings of artistic language. *School Arts, 80*(1), 6-12.

Burton, J. (2001). Lowenfeld: An(other) look. *Art Education 54*(6), 33-42.

Cale, J. (2002) My 15 minutes. Retrieved from www.guardian.co.uk/culture/2002/feb/12/artsfeatures.warhol

Campbell, L. H. (2012). Five emerging themes of holistic art education. In L. H. Campbell & S. Simmons (Eds.), *The heart of art education: Holistic approaches to creativity, integration, and transformation.* Reston, VA: National Art Education Association.

Chang, C. Y. (1970). *Creativity and Taoism.* New York, NY: Harper and Row.

Charmandaris, V. (2006). *The myth of Deadalus & Icarus.* Retrieved from http://galev06.physics.uoc.gr/daedalus.html

Chihuly, Dale (2010-2011). Retrieved from www.chihuly.com

Christo and Jeanne-Claude (2008). Retrieved from www.christojeanneclaude.net

Clark, G. A., Day, M. D., & Greer, W. D. (1987). Discipline-based art education: Becoming students of art. *The Journal of Aesthetic Education, 21*(2), 129-193.

Consortium of National Arts Education Associations. (1994). *National Visual and Performing Arts Standards.* Reston, VA: Author.

Craft, A. (2001), *An analysis of research and literature on creativity in education.* Report prepared for the Qualifications and Curriculum Authority. Retrieved from www.euvonal.hu/images/creativity_report.pdf

The Creativity Crisis: For the first time, research shows that American creativity is declining. What went wrong—and how we can fix it? Retrieved from *www.newsweek.com/2010/07/10/the-creativity-crisis.html*

Creativity defined. Retrieved from http://psychology.ucdavis.edu/Simonton/GeniusCreativityTalent.ppt

Czikszentmihalyi, M. (1996). *Creativity.* New York, NY: Harper Collins.

Czikszentmihalyi, M. (1990). *Flow.* New York, NY: Harper Collins.

Dewey, J. (1910). *How we think.* Boston, MA: D.C. Heath.

Dewey, J. (1934). *Art as experience.* New York, NY: Penguin Putnam.

Dewey, J. (1960). *The child and the curriculum* and *The school and society.* Chicago, IL: Phoenix.

Dobbs, S. (Ed.). (1988). *Research readings for discipline-based art education: A journey beyond creating.* Reston, VA: National Art Education Association.

Duncum, P. (Ed.). (2006). *Visual culture in the art class: Case studies.* Reston, VA: National Art Education Association.

Edwards, B. (1979). *Drawing on the right side of the brain.* Los Angeles, CA: Tarcher.

Efland, A. (1990). *A history of art education: Intellectual and social currents in teaching the visual arts.* New York, NY: Teachers College Press.

Eisner, E. (2002). *The arts and the creation of mind.* New Haven, CT: Yale University Press.

ETS (2008). Educational Testing Service. *The Praxis Series: Art Making (0131):* www.ets.org/Media/Tests/PRAXIS/pdf/0131.pdf

Florida, R. (2002). *The creative class...and how it's transforming work, leisure, community and everyday life*. New York, NY: Basic Books.

Freud, S. (1958). *Creativity and the unconscious*. New York, NY: Harper & Brothers.

Gardner, H. (1983). *Frames of mind*. New York, NY: Basic Books.

Gardner, H. (1993). *Creating minds*. New York. NY: Basic Books.

Gardner, H. (2008). *Five minds for the future*. Cambridge, MA: Harvard Business School Press.

Genn, R. (2008). Pablo Picasso art quotes. In *The painter's keys*. Retrieved from http://quote.robertgenn.com/auth_search.php?authid=72

Getzels, J. W., & Csikszentmihalyi, M. (1976). *The creative vision: A longitudinal study of problem finding in art*. New York, NY: Wiley.

Ghiselin, B. (ed). (1952). *The creative process*. New York, NY: New Mentor Library.

Goleman, D., Kaufman, P., & Ray, M. (1992). *The creative spirit*. New York, NY: Dutton.

Guilford, J. P. (1970). Traits of creativity. In P. E. Vernon, (Ed.), *Creativity*. Middlesex, England: Penguin.

Harvard Project Zero (2010), Research: Studio thinking framework, eight habits of mind. Retrieved from http://pzweb.harvard.edu/research/StudioThink/StudioThinkEight.htm

Hetland, L., Winner, E., Veenema, S., & Sheridan, K. (2007). *Studio thinking: The real benefits of visual arts education*. New York, NY: Teachers College Press.

Henley, D. (1998). The art of disturbance: Provocation and censorship in art education. *Art Education, 50*(4), 45-49.

History Source (2000-2011). Creation of Man. Retrieved from http://historylink102.com/greece2/creation_man.htm

Hockman, S., & Walling-Wohlford, E., (2008). *Teaching for creativity using SC standards*. Greenwood, SC: South Carolina Alliance for Arts Education. www.lander.edu/Libraries/SC_Art_Alliance/Teaching_Standards_Based_Creativity_in_the_Arts.sflb.ashx

Horowitz, F. A., & Danilowitz, B. (2009) *Josef Albers: To open eyes*. London, England: Phaidon.

Hoving, T. (1976) *Two worlds of Andrew Wyeth: A conversation with Andrew Wyeth*. Boston, MA: Houghton Mifflin.

Institute of Physics (IOP). (2000): Einstein year: Did you know? Retrieved from http://einsteinyear.org/facts/physicsFacts/. From Calaprice, A. (editor), 2000, *The expanded quotable Einstein*. Princeton, NJ: Princeton University Press.

John-Steiner, V. (1997). *Notebooks of the mind*. New York, NY: Oxford University Press.

Kubie, L. S. (1958). *Neurotic distortions of the creative process*. New York, NY: Farrar, Straus, & Giroux.

Lawton, P. (2012). Artist/Teacher/Researcher: A holistic approach to art teacher preparation. In L. H. Campbell, & S. Simmons (Eds.), *The heart of art education: Holistic approaches to creativity, integration, and transformation*. Reston, VA: National Art Education Association.

Lehrer, J. (2008, July 28). The eureka hunt. *New Yorker, 44*(22), 40-47.

Lindström, L. (2012). Assessing and teaching for creativity. In L. H. Campbell, & S. Simmons (Eds.), *The heart of art education: Holistic approaches to creativity, integration, and transformation*. Reston, VA: National Art Education Association.

Lowenfeld, V. (1957). *Creative and mental growth (3rd ed.)*. New York, NY: McMillan.

Ludwig, A. M. (1995). *The price of greatness: Resolving the creativity and madness controversy*. New York, NY: The Guilford Press.

Mailer, N. (1995). *Portrait of Picasso as a young man*. New York, NY: The Atlantic Monthly Press.

May, R. (1975). *The courage to create*. New York, NY: Norton.

McKim, R. H. (1972). *Experiences in visual thinking*. Belmont, CA: Brooks/Cole.

M.I.T. (2009). MIT Media Lab. Retrieved from www.media.mit.edu

Obama, B. (2009). National Art Education Association. Retrieved from www.arteducators.org

Original. (n.d.) In *Encarta World English Dictionary*. Retrieved from www.encarta.msn.com

Passmore, J. (1967). On teaching to be critical. In R. S. Peters (Ed.), *The concept of education*. London, England: Routledge & Kegan Paul.

Payne, J. (2010). Teaching students to critique. *ArtsEdge*. Retrieved from http://artsedge.kennedy-center.org/educators/how-to/tipsheets/student-critique.aspx

Perkins, D. N. (1984). *Creativity by design*. Paper presented at the Wingspread Conference on Teaching Thinking Skills, *Association for Supervision and Curriculum Development*.

Pevsner, N. (1973). *Academies of art, past and present*. New York, NY: Capo.

Picasso, P. (1986). *Je suis le cahier* [I am the notebook]: *The sketchbooks of Picasso*. New York, NY: Grove Atlantic.

Pink, D. H. 2005. *A whole new mind: Why right-brainers will rule the world*. New York, NY: Penguin Books.

Plato. (1956). *Ion* (B. Jowett, Trans.) Retrieved from http://classics.mit.edu/Plato/ion.html

Praxis II: Retrieved from www.euvonal.hu/images/creativity_report.pdf

Prometheus: Retrieved from http://historylink102.com/greece2/creation_man.htm

Richards, M. C. (1964). *Centering in pottery, poetry and the person*. Middletown, CT: Wesleyan University Press.

Rostan, S. (2005). Educational intervention and the development of young art students' talent and creativity. *Journal of Creative Behavior, 39*(4), 237-261.

Runco, M. (2007). *Creativity: Theories and themes: Research, development and practice*. Burlington, MA: Elsevier Academic Press.

Rushlow, B. (2008). The future according to us. *NAEA News, 50*(3), 1 & 4.

Sass, L. A. (1992). *Madness and modernism: Insanity in the light of modern art, literature, and thought.* New York, NY: Basic Books.

Scheffler, I. (1991). *In praise of the cognitive emotions and other essays in the philosophy of education.* New York, NY: Routledge.

Schirrmacher, R. (1998). *Art and creative development for young children.* New York, NY: Delmar.

Schumann, R. (1946). *On music and musicians.* New York, NY: Pantheon Books.

Simpson, J. W., Delaney, J. M., Carroll, K. L., Hamilton, C. M., Kay, S. I., Kerlavage, M. S., & Olson, J. L. (1998). *Creating meaning through art: Teacher as choice-maker.* Upper Saddle River, NJ: Prentice-Hall.

Smith, N. (1983). Drawing conclusions: Do children draw from observation? *Art Education, 36*(5), 22-25.

Stanford Humanities Lab. (2009). Retrieved from http://humanitieslab.stanford.edu/admin/directory.html

Stewart, M. (2005). "The Muses," *Greek Mythology: From the Iliad to the Fall of the Last Tyrant.* Retrieved from: http://messagenetcommresearch.com/myths/bios/muses.html

Stiggins, R., Arter, J., Chappuis, J., & Chappuis, S. (2004). *Classroom assessment for student learning.* Portland, OR: Assessment Training Institute.

Stokes, P. (2006). *Creativity from constraints: The psychology of breakthrough.* New York, NY: Springer.

Stone, I. (1961). *The agony and the ecstasy.* New York, NY: Doubleday.

Sullivan, G. (2012). Art practice as relational and transformative. In L. H. Campbell, & S. Simmons (Eds.), *The heart of art education: Holistic approaches to creativity, integration, and transformation.* Reston, VA: National Art Education Association.

Sze, M. (1956). *The way of Chinese painting: Its ideas and technique.* Princeton, NJ: Bollingen.

Vernon, P. E. (1971), (Ed.). *Creativity: Selected readings,* New York, NY: Penguin.

Webster's new world dictionary of American English, 3rd College Edition, (1994). New York, NY: Prentice Hall.

Wilson, B., & Wilson, M. (1977). An iconoclastic view of the imagery sources in the drawings of young people. *Art Education, 30*(1), 4-12.

Winner, E. & Simmons, S. (1993) (Eds.). *Arts PROPEL visual art handbook.* Cambridge, MA: Project Zero and Educational Testing Service.

Winner, E., & Hetland, L. (2000). The arts and academic achievement: What the evidence shows. *Journal of Aesthetic Education, 34*(3-4), 2000.

Wittkower, R., & Wittkower, M. (2006). *Born under Saturn: The character and conduct of artists.* New York, NY: New York Review Books Classics.

Wolf, D. P. (1988). Artistic learning: What and where is it?" *Journal of Aesthetic Education, 22*(1), 143-155.

Wolf, D. P. (1993). Assessment as an episode of learning. In R. Bennett & W. Ward (Eds.), *Construction versus choice in cognitive measurement* (pp. 213-240). Hillsdale, NJ: Lawrence Erlbaum.

Zimmerman, E. (2009). Reconceptualizing the role of creativity in art education: Principles and practices. *Studies in Art Education, 50*(4), 282-399.

ABOUT THE AUTHOR

Seymour Simmons III is an associate professor of Fine Arts at Winthrop University, where he coordinates the undergraduate art education program and teaches drawing. Prior to coming to Winthrop, he taught at the Massachusetts College of Art, and did research at Harvard Project Zero (in particular, on the Arts PROPEL project).

Holistic Narratives from the Visual Arts Classroom

If adults who guide children could better understand the process for engaging the whole child through artistic pursuit, perhaps there would be more encouragement of children's inner creative necessities. By this I mean honoring and evoking curiosity, trusting one's own intuition, taking risks, instilling a passion for the world, and encouraging one's creative, constructive response to it. Such a process engages children—mind, body, and spirit—around work that is meaningful to them. It challenges and intrigues the logical, imaginative, and intuitive mind; activates the body and the senses by use of sumptuous media in a sensuous world; and nurtures the heart and human spirit.

—*Virginia K. Freyermuth, p. 269*

CHAPTER 26

Julie's Story: Letters From a Teacher Who Dares to Teach Art

*Anita Sinner, Julie Lymburner, Kit Grauer, Rita L. Irwin,
Carl Leggo, and Peter Gouzouasis*

INTRODUCTION

Julie's story is an intimate account of an a/r/tographic learning experience that infused her art education program and school community with the power of hope, courage, promise, and reconciliation. In her art classroom, Julie developed holistic learning opportunities for students to engage the mind, body and spirit in the richness of creative expression, making this story in part Emily's story of illness in her senior year, and a collective story of coming to understand social responsibility and broader social issues. Daring to teach in relation to social issues and student experiences of chronic or terminal illness, Julie recounts how a quilting project became the focus of her art class. Interpreting Julie's experience through an a/r/tographic lens highlights student engagement as renderings of living inquiry, metaphor and openings, and connects us with Freire's (1998) impassioned call to teachers as cultural workers. We adopt Freire's framework of letters in this chapter; Julie's 'letters' document her capacity to challenge the status quo of teaching, to disrupt the art curriculum and taken-for-granted roles of student and teacher, and to set the stage for change with her students, the school community, and the many individual lives they collectively touched through their acts of making art.

FIRST LETTER: IN-BETWEEN FOLDS AND SEAMS

There are in-between spaces in teaching, moments that rupture forth to make us pause and consider, why do we teach? When we reflect on our practice in such times, we may rightly wonder how we contend with all that we experience in a classroom. We may ask for strength when we are faced with situations involving life's essential questions, when we as teachers come to negotiate what being part of a school means day-to-day (Springgay, Irwin & Kind, 2005). Liminal spaces are not formally taught in teacher education. Indeed over our careers, we seldom discuss in-between spaces as the essence of a school where the pulsing heart of everyday experience forms the character of our community of learning. Yet in the folds and seams of our practice, there reside memories and experiences defined by sadness and even grief, bringing to our mission both dreams and beginnings, and regressions and endings.

We came to know Julie's story during our inquiry at a high school in the Lower Mainland of Vancouver, one of five sites that participated in our multi-year Social Sciences and Humanities Research Council of Canada[1] research undertaking known as the *Integration Project*. Julie is a member of our research group, a teacher-in-the-field with whom we teamed to investigate how educators conceptualize arts integration across a variety of arts programming models, and how these conceptualizations might change through ongoing teacher research.

The lead researcher at this site was Kit Grauer, an artist, researcher, and teacher with an ongoing interest in how teachers implement and assess teaching the arts as disciplines within particular programming structures, and how teachers' beliefs and practices about learning and teaching change through arts-based reflective research methods. Julie's classroom is in a large high school of Grades 8 to 12 that has an exemplary arts program nestled within an academically oriented school community. While we investigated our research questions, Julie lived with, in, and through another dimension of her life as a teacher. This story of Julie's teaching is the story of her Grade 9 art students, which is in part the story of a student at the school, Emily, who struggled with illness in her senior year. This is a collective story of coming to understand social responsibility and broader social issues. Working with Julie at this critical pedagogical moment in her teaching revealed the heart of learning through practice, and how participating in a community of a/r/tographers can facilitate spaces of sharing in the classroom in unexpected and rewarding ways for students, teacher, and researchers.

Julie's story of teaching art in in-between spaces is an intimate account of guiding her students and herself, in togetherness, through a learning experience that infused the environment of her classroom, her school and her community with the power of hope, courage, promise, and reconciliation. Julie's story of teaching extends beyond the form to the substance of the cycle of learning, where in the process, she too became one of the collective of "teachers [who] sit on our shoulders... their lives live in ours, and our lives live in theirs"—forever part of many stories of teaching and learning (Eisner, 2006, p. 44).

Daring to teach in relation to social issues and student experiences of chronic or terminal illness encompasses a realm of teaching that is perhaps too difficult for many to enter, given the limited literature available in the field of education. Instead of statistical assessments of grief and loss (Bailis & Kennedy, 1977; Pratt, Hare & Wright, 1987), counseling-based models of illness and grief (Munson & Hunt, 2005; Schlozman, 2002), formulaic curricular and/or step-by-step classroom approaches to illness and grief (Haggard, 2005; Moore, 1989; Naierman, 1997; Shaw, 2004), we engage in Julie's first-person account of real life events that unfolded in her art classroom. In Julie's narrative, we also find what is important to remember in our research practices in the academy: The questions we begin with in a study are often very different from the questions of significance we realize while conducting the research in the field.

We situate our understandings and discussion of this liminal space in teaching within a/r/tography[2], an approach to inquiry that is enacted in a series of renderings rooted in reflection and reflexivity (Irwin & de Cosson, 2004). A/r/tography brings our attention to "deep meaning, enhanced through perceptual practices that reveal what was once hidden," articulated in this case through renderings of living inquiry, metaphor and openings (Irwin, 2004, p. 36). Julie shares her experience as an embodiment of living inquiry, a rhizomatic journey through which she witnessed the situational transformation of students through visual art expression (Irwin, Beer, Springgay, Grauer, Xiong & Bickel, 2006). In her art classroom, Julie developed holistic learning opportunities for students to engage the mind, body, and spirit in the richness of creative expression (London, 1989, 2003, 2005; Denton, 1998; Ashton & Denton, 2006; O'Sullivan, Morrell, & O'Connor, 2002; Palmer, 2004). In the course of this a/r/tographic inquiry, we open conversations and relationships of friendship and compassion that exemplify teaching as living inquiry, and like Grauer (2006), we "provide a picture of a teacher in a portrait unlike what is common in our writings about teacher education" (p. 86).

We are informed by the philosophy of Paulo Freire (1998), who wrote in his letters to teachers like Julie that "the sharing of experiences must always be understood within the social praxis that entails both reflection and political action," for teachers are cultural workers (p. xiv). Freire (1998) believes "it is impossible to teach without the courage to love," for we learn and teach "with our entire body... with feeling, with emotion, with wishes, with fear, with doubts, with passion, and with critical reasoning" (p. 3). And this is certainly true of Julie's teaching life. In homage to Freire, we adopt a framework of letters in this chapter. These letters are shaped by Julie's art curriculum, and are composed as a referential quilting of images and text in an a/r/tographic approach to share her in-between spaces in teaching. This way of disseminating our research is different from the expected norms of reporting research in the academy. In doing so, we seek to disrupt educational research in both our mode—our approach to interpreting field research—and medium—our form in this chapter, for our research message also echoes Freire (1998): "Never reduce teaching to merely a feel-good process" (p. 4).

SECOND LETTER: THREADING A COMMUNITY OF CARING

In a/r/tography, living inquiry is a practice of rendering complex phenomena through processes of creating, searching, and learning in what Irwin (2004) describes as an ever-present convergence and divergence of understandings, explorations, perspectives, and knowledge. Gouzouasis (2006) describes living inquiry as:

> A process that includes the creation of images, music, movement, and text that are not separate or illustrative of each other, but contrapuntally connected and inextricably woven through each other to create enhanced meanings, new ideas, and a plethora of research questions...[it is] research as embodied in praxis. (pp. 30, 31)

Living inquiry involves "the processes by which one's life is lived," where issues and questions rooted in embodied ways of knowing construct meaning-making in a third space, generating a transformative experience between awareness and understanding (Springgay et al., 2005, p. 902). In this way, the interrelationships between artmaking and the lives of makers of art are intimately tied, spawning a continuous interrogation of self-in-the-world, leading to more questions, deeper reflection and a greater commitment to art practice. It is this fluidity that Irwin (2004) highlights as the essence of living inquiry, where "caring for the creation of self through aesthetic experiences" helps us "re-imagine our life in and through time" (p. 35).

In Julie's classroom, the act of making art with a social purpose presented students with an opportunity to engage in living inquiry and to discover meaning-making by creating together. As the teacher, Julie embodied living inquiry in the "co-production" of artmaking and teaching in a classroom as she responded to students in a reflective yet reflexive manner, and in how she engaged collaboratively with students in artmaking while the experience was underway (Springgay et al., 2005, p. 903). Julie's narrative reveals how quilts became a focus for her art curriculum and how her decisions led to the evolution of a new approach to teaching high school students through active engagement:

> In recent years, the British Columbia Ministry of Education has called on teachers to orchestrate experiences in which students might gain a heightened sense of social responsibility. Acting on this initiative, the Fine Arts department in my school, which includes music, theatre, visual arts, home economics, and culinary arts, has risen to the challenge year after year. Together we create through paint and clay, voice and horn, fibers, threads, theatrics, and culinary creations—we share the responsibility to lift the spirit and stir the soul of our school community. Each year we develop one shared vision, one fine arts celebration, one integrated event. We strive to awaken our youth to the world of social consciousness, drawing on our artistic talents to create a positive difference in the world around us.
>
> And so in August of 2004, the Comfort Quilts concept was born at our secondary school. We decided three of our quilts would be donated to three worthy agencies:

St. Paul's Hospital Palliative Care; the B.C. Transplant Society; and the Domestic Violence Program at Vancouver General Hospital respectively. The fourth quilt would be given to Emily, a graduating student and an integral member of the Music Department, who was fighting a courageous battle with leukemia.

The master plan seemed to ooze with potential. Art and textiles students would design and stitch quilts, music students would select and rehearse songs, drama students would compose and rehearse expository writings, and culinary arts students would prepare delicious refreshments. If everything went according to plan, the fruits of our labor would be shared at a grand quilt unveiling event in the school auditorium in February. The quilted gifts, along with a healthy donation from ticket sales, would be presented to four deserving recipients that night.

The teachers of visual art, music, theatre, culinary arts, and home economics signed on to support this special project, which would encompass and celebrate all of the arts. We each agreed to lead a group of students through a process in which they would endeavor to make a real difference in the world. Through their various art forms, they would send a positive ripple effect out into their community. Our Comfort Quilts project would be seamless. With 25 years of art education under my belt, a rich family tradition of textiles behind me, and a supportive cast of students and colleagues at my side, I was ready to rock the teaching world.

At first glance, I thought my role in this project would be so easy. For example, with the help of my 60 Grade Nine Multimedia students, I set out to make the first quilt for the Domestic Violence Program at Vancouver General Hospital. Our quilt would take the form of an "I Spy" game. Combined with a special handmade book, we hoped to create a quilt that would not only provide physical comfort and warmth, but would also serve as a pleasant diversion for families, and especially children, whose home life was in a state of upheaval. So with months of time ahead of us, a few stitches here and a few stitches there, we set off to make our vision a reality. This project truly had wonderful written all over it.

To make the project even more remarkable, I invited my mum to be part of the process in my classroom. I knew it would be fabulous to have her on board. Now a retired teacher, and a pretty "with-it" granny, I had watched in awe as she had masterfully handcrafted countless quilts over the years. This would be a wonderful occasion for me to see my mum interacting with kids again AND a great opportunity for my students to connect with a fun-loving senior in the community.

Yes, on the surface it all seemed too good to be true! I suppressed my prejudicial reservations about boys quilting and teenagers mixing with seniors and launched into the project. But deep down inside I knew this project would be unlike anything I had tackled before. Not only would I be delving into a lengthy textile design process for the first time since my undergraduate days, my own mother would be standing in the room next to me as the project began.

The a/r/tographic rendering of living inquiry was reinforced by the in-between spaces that emerged in the quilting project. Students and the teacher lingered with the immediate tasks of designing, constructing and developing quilts, while at the same time, they reflected on the purpose of the quilts and those who might benefit from their work and their giving.

At the back of everything, Julie and her students considered each quilt recipient, desiring to make a difference in their day and hoping for their well-being and recovery.

As the teacher, Julie had several courses of action available to infuse the curriculum with social responsibility. Because she chose to engage in an ongoing discourse with her students to artfully express the importance of belonging and contributing to society, Julie created an environment that brought forward "a critical awareness of our social and political responsibility as a civil society" (Freire, 1998, p. 11). As Julie envisioned, students would "socially construct" their understandings of artmaking and take "critical ownership" of the quilting assignments (Freire, 1998, p. 24). With the added layer of knowing that Emily, a student in their school, suffered with cancer, Julie's class would evolve into a community of caring centered on consciousness and relationships, in which, as Freire (1998) suggests, the "rich moments of learning in teaching" reside (p. 17).

THIRD LETTER: SASHING[3] METAPHORS OF MEANING

On our first day, we did introductions. My mum quickly engaged the class with stories of quilt lore and enlisted the help of many in stretching the already pieced quilt top over a quilting frame. I stood by and tentatively watched the students' reactions. They were smiling: their eyes alert, their heads nodding. In my art classes, when Mum asked for volunteers, the boys rushed forward to lend a hand.

I heaved a great sigh of relief at the close of the day. The introductory lesson seemed to be a success and it appeared that our quilt project would provide something for everyone: hands-on experience for the kinesthetic learners, clear techniques to be practiced and perfected by the more analytical high achievers, and, as an added bonus, endless days ahead for all of us to collectively "stitch and bitch" around the quilt frame.

Before heading home, I did a cursive sweep of the room, collecting wayward paintbrushes, lifting stools off the floor. In my travels, one small scrap of paper caught my eye from the corner table. It was a student's note, presumably passed in class earlier that day. As I peeled it open and unmasked the words I knew they were intended for a friend... jarring raw comments for a teacher. The scribbled words assaulted both the project as stupid and gay[4] and my mother (as an old grandma). I reeled as I read and re-read the cruel, heartless remarks. I realized there was a crack in my seamless plan.

My mind raced. Who wrote the note? How could someone be so abusive? Well, one thing was certain. I would dig to the bottom of this. I would launch a classroom investigation. I would publish an overhead of the note for all to see and I WOULD humiliate this person. No, I would vilify, berate, disparage, slander, scorch... No... No... hang on...

A few quiet moments passed. I sat down at my desk, broody and dejected, staring at the crumpled paper. A handful of disconsolate tears dropped onto the desktop below. While I knew that a communal flogging was not the answer, I acknowledged that the content of the note would certainly need to be addressed. This was a teachable moment... a crack... unlike any other; a moment for all of us to step back and reflect on the larger purpose of our project.

Following a weekend of contemplation, I strode into my classroom on Monday morning ready to talk calmly and openly about the quilt. Choking back tears, I explained to the class about the note and my feelings, and I asked students for their input. In as much as I wanted everyone to be a part of this project, I couldn't see anyone working on it if they truly felt it was "stupid." In fact, I felt false hands might somehow tarnish this precious creation. I explained that our quilt needed to be made by the hands of those who honestly cared and wanted to help others in need. Most students were aghast. Predictably, those who spoke up couldn't believe someone could write such a mean note. (There's nothing quite as melodramatic as a self-righteous 14 year old!) We talked over the situation as a class and then I spent a bit of time with each student, asking individuals if they wanted to continue with the project. They were all—100%—committed to staying the course.

The note incident was a critical turning point for the quilting project, and in some ways, for Julie as a teacher. Looking back, the relationship between Kit and Julie was central in defining this moment, an a/r/tographical shift, as Julie writes, a crack in the understood protocols and expectations of teaching art to high school students. Initially Julie did not want to confront the situation, and had Kit not been in the school, she may have taken another direction that may have resulted in very different outcomes for the quilting project. It was the convergence of Kit's inquiry through the *Integration Project* and Julie's practice through the *Comfort Quilts* that generated an open space where divergence within the student body was engaged as a positive opportunity, a source for progressive movement within the curriculum. This is the essence of a/r/tography, coming together to collectively be more than we are individually, to trouble differences, and to problematize questions and experiences within an a/r/tographic lens. Kit demonstrated and embodied this a/r/tographical way of being with Julie, and encouraged Julie to confront the situation to bring transparency to the artmaking process and to determine if there was a clear commitment to the project before the class began. Their ongoing dialogue and strength of communication wove a/r/tography into Julie's classroom in ways that were not initially anticipated within the context of the Integration Research Project.

Julie understood the conditions that shaped the rebellion expressed in the note. She asked for input, created choices for her students, and enabled their decision-making and autonomy in the classroom. It was Julie's democratic approach to teaching that created a safe space for a discussion about the note, recognizing that if we deny conflict, we will in fact only "preserve the status quo" (Freire, 1998, p. 45). She responded with lovingness, patience, permissiveness and tolerance instead of employing her authority, and as a result, she evoked courage in her students and a desire to nourish an ethical and progressive educational experience (Freire, 1998). Her actions modeled the "educator's task," as a "critically disciplined performance with which to challenge learners" (Freire, 1998, p. 43). The resulting conviction of students following the note incident solidified the social importance of the task they were to undertake. This made the curriculum and the pedagogical purpose of their art classroom an experience of educational transformation over the 4-month school term.

The demanding occupation of the task and the difficulty of being immersed in their handiwork, along with the needed discipline to work through obstacles had to be forged by individual students (Freire, 1998, pp. 28, 22). In time, students overcame their fears of undertaking a series of complex projects, each with significant goals, and committed themselves fully to a process they would not abandon once it began.

Through artful expression, Julie's class sought to make a positive contribution within their community. Her Grade 9 students, along with three other classes in the school, designed and created four comfort quilts in response to their increasing social awareness, demonstrating ways of knowing that "evolve through acts of deep engagement" (Springgay et al., 2005, p. 904). A/r/tographically, each comfort quilt represented a metaphorical relationship with textures, fabrics, colors and threads, doubling in meaning as a signifier of both violence and illness, and comfort and care. Metaphor as an a/r/tographic concept makes experience "accessible to the senses," and like the patterns evident in the designs of the quilts, metaphors open us to "fresh" perceptions of the world that embrace "complexity" in the process of making art and reflecting on questions of social consequence (Springgay et al., 2005, pp. 904, 905). As Wilson (2004) suggests, we need to "broaden the scope of education to include, embrace and even welcome dimensions of dependency and loss" as sources of "great value" and "of caring" (p. 43).

The movement of students' thinking around social issues and responsibility inherent in the comfort quilts effectively became a third space, encouraging a shift in perception and a means of bringing forward new ways of thinking about the act of making (Irwin, 2003). The comfort quilts were intended to "warm frail bodies" with fabric that "speaks of home," in a pedagogic inquiry that is "not just an investigative process... but a spiritual practice as well" (Wilson, 2004, pp. 48, 57). The comfort quilts created by Julie's class represent what Grauer (2006) describes as a "token of care," a "symbol of our spirit," a "metaphor... for the deeper meaning we want to teach" (p. 94).

FOURTH LETTER: PATCHWORK OPENINGS

Student engagement in Julie's classroom was both active and responsive, requiring "attentiveness to what is seen and known and to what lies beneath the surface" (Springgay et al., 2005, p. 905). In this way, the comfort quilts were, in a/r/tographical terms, openings. Openings invite "evocative and emotional" responses, and relational "issues of reciprocity" to emerge, in the act of creating, conversing, and negotiating meanings between self and others (Springgay et. al., 2005, p. 906). As an a/r/tographic rendering, openings describe experiences as transformational, where "cuts, cracks... tears" serve as a way to "deliberately seek out" that which ruptures "the uniform surface" (Springgay et. al., 2005, p. 905). Such spaces encourage connecting and composing, in "an aesthetic awareness open to wonder and surrender, while being attuned to what is unfolding," to sharing perceptions and knowledge while reciprocating with others in the process of making art (Irwin, 2003, p. 67). Wilson (2004) eloquently describes openings in a personal a/r/tographic inquiry of quilting that also explored questions of life and death:

> Moveable pieces, interchangeable, nothing fixed, maybe there are even some pieces missing, placed elsewhere, lost, and I haven't found others to fill the gaps yet.... Looking into the emptiness, living in the loss, and finding my way to being content and at peace with emptiness and absence, to letting go and letting be. (p. 41)

In Julie's *Comfort Quilts* project, openings are both spaces in the cloth—fibers woven and strands joined together—and spaces of student inquiry where students consider the scope of social issues that encompass their classroom project and define their individual roles in the making of the quilts. A/r/tographic openings are also what Julie describes as teachable moments, unexpected layers in the experience of teaching art, like the moment Julie found the student's note, a dis/juncture that continues to reverberate in our understandings and our ongoing reflective and reflexive practices long after the actual event (Leggo, 2005). Over the course of the year, Julie often returned to the note incident as a barometer of positionality, asking more and more questions about her role and the feelings and beliefs of students, and as a means of reassessing the quality and value of quilting as a holistic experience for personal growth and development (Irwin, 2006; Jardine, 1998, 2000; Kessler, 2000; Kind, Irwin, Grauer, & deCosson, 2005; Miller, 1999; Miller, 2000).

The *Comfort Quilts* project was a complex and sophisticated undertaking for Grade 9 students. The understandings inherent in Julie's curricular decisions about the project clearly resonated within a/r/tography, and remained deeply rooted in the a/r/tographic community formed primarily between Julie and Kit. Together, Julie and Kit entered into a dialogue specifically about a/r/tographic openings, bringing into focus the impact of the note on the lives of teachers and students, and the scope of actions that can constructively negotiate moments of tension in a classroom. The note is symbolic of the many ways spaces open in teaching, and how, a/r/tographically, such spaces hold the promise of learning in new and innovative ways.

As Julie's personal reflection reveals, her class was situated in the a/r/tographic rendering of openings as the project progressed, a generative space where "exchanges unsettle, create movement, collide, and nestle side-by-side" (Springgay et al., 2005, p. 906). Freire (1998) describes such knowledge production "as social, as open-ended, as unfolding," a space where learners engage in "critical dialogue in which their practice" helps inform their understandings (p. 47). In Julie's classroom, students faced their initial fears and overcame them by taking risks, resulting in the emergence of a sense of "deep trust" within their community of practice (Freire, 1998, p. 48).

Comfort Quilts Celebration[i]
February 17. 2005.

A Special Invitation to you...

This year, students enrolled in several textiles and visual art classes have collaboratively produced four quilts, each handcrafted with a unique design, each carefully prepared for a special destination. On Thursday, February 17th, the Fine Arts Department is planning a celebration at which each finished quilt will be unveiled and presented to its recipient, in concert with a showcase of music and drama. The evening will conclude with beverages and desserts, prepared and presented by our culinary arts students.

Three of our quilts will be donated to St. Paul's Hospital Palliative Care, the B.C. Transplant Society, and the Domestic Violence Program at Vancouver General Hospital respectively. The fourth quilt will be given to Emily, a graduating student and an integral member of the Music Department, who is currently fighting a courageous battle with leukemia. It is our hope that this project has provided our students with an opportunity to produce meaningful work and realize the difference they can make in our world.

As a key member of the education community, we invite you to support this very worthwhile project by attending our gala celebration. Clear your calendar if you are able, and plan to join us on Thursday, February 17th at 7:00pm. To help us plan for the evening, please RSVP via email or call the school office. We will reserve a complimentary seat for you and look forward to seeing you there!

Julie
Fine Arts Department Head

_____
[i] Specific details such as names and locations have been deleted from this letter

FIGURE 1. Julie's letter, Comfort Quilts Celebration.

Four months and thousands of stitches later, our finished quilt was unclamped from the frame and took on a new life. This soft cotton work of art was now padded full with caring and meaning. United in our purpose, we had stitched tirelessly across the surface of the quilt, and on the night that our work was unveiled, we witnessed a positive ripple effect moving out in our community (Figure 1). We made a real difference in the world. Our invitation was sent out to our school community, and to the community at large.

Art and textile students designed and stitched quilts, music students selected and rehearsed songs, drama students composed and practiced expository writings, and culinary arts students prepared refreshments. The fruits of their labors were shared with fellow students, parents, school staff, and community members at a unique "Comfort Quilts" evening in February, 2005. That evening, four grateful guests graciously accepted a handmade quilted gift as a symbol of comfort and support. It was a night I will never forget. I am certain that all recipients felt respected and honored, as they cherished that night. I am confident that my students, too, felt very special. For there, seated in the fourth row with her mother, was Kathy, the infamous note writer: smiling, proud, and satisfied with her accomplishment. Yes, unbeknownst to Kathy, her distinctive handwriting, as it permeated the pages of her sketchbook, had ultimately identified her to me as the author of the nasty note. But that night, together, we shared an evening replete with tantalizing color, powerful music, delectable treats, emotional speeches, and, above all, sincere caring. As hoped, both the learning processes and the culminating event raised the social consciousness of the students involved. Perhaps more importantly, however, this student collaboration provoked an emotional response from our community at large well beyond anything we could have fathomed.

. . .

Later that same year, following the earlier months of treatment and trauma, and then successive long weeks of hope and healing, we stood shoulder to shoulder at our June 2005 Valedictory ceremony bursting with unabashed joy. We were applauding the efforts of graduate Emily, one of our quilt recipients, now a cancer survivor and a remarkably strong young woman. Graduating with a 4.0 grade point average, she would be heading to university in the fall to follow her dream and study sciences. There was little doubt that her strength and determination came from within, but a caring circle of friends and family provided love and support along the way. As she endured a year seemingly plagued with illness and fatigue, I can only hope that our quilt provided Emily with comfort on her most melancholy days, warmth on her bleakest nights, and some light and color during her most somber hours. Emily's miraculous accomplishment was celebrated that evening with a thunderous standing ovation. Everyone there, whether they knew Emily or not, shared in the electricity of the moment. I'm sure that even those students who had contributed a few stitches to Emily's quilt were proud to have lent a hand and may have even felt a small personal connection with her that evening. I know that I did.

The "transaction" between students and the quilts parallels what Freire (1998) describes as reading a text, an encounter within a group where, in this case, the "difficulty" and "fascination" with the act of making is in part the "process of creating comprehension" (p. 30). This creative process is "gradually built in the dialogue between the different points of view about the challenge," and moves toward critical understandings of the object in question (Freire, 1998, p. 30). As Freire (1998) suggests, "it is important to underline the aesthetic moment" reflected in the ways students engage (p. 32). In Julie's classroom, this is evident in the willingness of students to experiment with their stitches, their dialogue about the quilting experience, and their ongoing interaction with each other and fabric over time.

According to Freire (1998), as teachers we must be prepared to participate in student development, to connect learners "in their process of discovery" and "to contribute to the gradual transformation of learners into strong presences in the world" (p. 33). Julie exemplified this practice, bringing her students into an experiential learning process over 4 months of their Grade 9 year that enabled the development of new understandings of social responsibility. Questions of domestic violence and terminal illness seldom form part of the curriculum, but Julie's personal philosophy that adolescents can make a difference by engaging through artmaking provided students a vehicle to explore such issues. Julie found a medium through which to raise awareness that was at the same time life affirming: The quilts were intended to bring comfort and support to recipients during times of loss, grief and suffering. Even though these issues did not directly affect the Grade 9 students who made the quilts, Emily's struggle made illness real rather than distant in their everyday lives. Her struggle with cancer became part of their personal experiences, their life narratives, because of the quilting experience. Quilting became a method of constructively embracing the liminal spaces in teaching and learning, and school and society, where critical social issues were integrated with sensitivity into interactions in the art classroom. As Grauer (2002) states:

> The art room becomes a safe haven in an impersonal school system. Art making and understanding personal aesthetic response are vehicles to analyze and construct personal identity. Providing a safe environment where the search for identity can be reflectively developed is one of the main themes in art education. (p. 89)

The inclusion of social issues in the art curriculum may help promote healthy attitudes and improve coping skills for students when they face the most stressful life experiences. Perhaps Julie's daring to teach in liminal spaces will evoke deeper understandings about lived experiences, the consequences of actions, as well as the life questions of mortality.

Through action, students came to understand they could make positive changes to social conditions in the world beyond the school, and perhaps more importantly, among their peers and within themselves. As Freire (1998) states:

> Teachers must give creative wings to their imaginations, obviously in a disciplined fashion. From the very first day of class, they must demonstrate to students the importance of imagination for life. Imagination helps curiosity and inventiveness, just as it enhances adventure, without this we cannot create. (p. 51)

FIFTH LETTER: SETTING RELATIONAL UNDERSTANDINGS

Julie had the capacity to challenge the status quo of teaching, to disrupt the art curriculum and understood roles of student and teacher, set the stage for change, for her students, the school community, and for the many individual lives they collectively touched through their acts of making art. She helped her students learn to "live a life of awareness, a life that permits openness to the complexity around us, a life that intentionally sets out to conceive and perceive things differently (Irwin, Gouzouasis, Grauer, Leggo, & Springgay, 2006, p. 7). Julie nurtured curiosity and taught her students humility in the process. Freire (1998) suggests such humility "requires courage, self-confidence, self-respect and respect for others" (p. 39). She demonstrated to students "that there is beauty in ethical struggle," and "ethics and aesthetics are intimately tied together" (Freire, 1998, p. 56). Freire (1998) reminds us that "education is a political act," and a "cultural expression," in which teachers who live authentically open students to the "contextual reality" of learning (pp. 63. 69, 74). In the course of discovery, we gain insight into many layers of learning that connect us together through ideas and concepts, relationships with one another in the classroom and with people in society as a whole, as "thinking subjects and knowing objects" (Freire, 1998, p. 75). A/r/tographically, as a teacher in the field, Julie continues to be a progressive and inspiring artist, researcher, and teacher who dares to teach that "the fundamental condition of life is the condition of relationship" (Freire, 1998, p. 75).

> *For our comfort quilts, the whole was greater than the sum of the p/a/r/t/s. When a group of impassioned artists band together to collectively learn and collaboratively create art pieces laden with meaning and purpose, it would stand to reason that the whole would indeed be greater than the sum of the parts. When it comes to staging an interdisciplinary arts event, however, a lot of its success rests with the original vision.*

> *In September, 2005, another school year began, and our comfort quilts still came up in conversations. Our first staff meeting of the year was about to begin. The anticipation of a new term hung in the room and we awaited all the good news: ample*

supplies, fresh faces, crisp ideas, and new beginnings. Instead, we were shocked by the opening announcement: Emily's cancer had returned.

While Emily valiantly battled further chemotherapy treatment and prepared for a bone marrow transplant, the sudden death of our drama teacher, Ken, in late September stunned us all. Then, falling on the heels of a difficult and emotional memorial service, came the stress of provincial job action; teachers were on strike as our only way to negotiate for the things we believed worth preserving in our schools. These cruel and unexpected realities helped me put my work and my life in perspective. As the next school year unfolded, I seized every opportunity to reflect and ruminate on the extraordinary days of my recent past. In the intervening moments, as I moved between the staff room and the classroom, I built and preserved a particular and exceptional knowledge borne from my experience.

Then in November 2006, Emily passed away.

Life is indeed fleeting. In the great scheme of things, I am not likely to venture this way again. So at school I am trying to make the most of each day. I focus, therefore, on forging positive relationships, reaching out to others whenever I can, and providing a safe environment where my students can speak their minds while accepting the ideas of others. I continued my reflective and reflexive practice, seeking ways to make sense of the day-to-day activities of teaching in the broader context of life and living.

Finding meaning in loss is at the core of grieving. Julie's desire to make a positive contribution is a way of coping with the reality of death in her school community just months after the successful completion of the quilting project. Her existential worldview brings a dimension to Julie's teaching in, with, and through the taboo spaces of pedagogic practice that suggests our known curricular approaches and patterns can be readily infused with the power of heartfelt caring through artful practices. Her actions demonstrate how teachers can bring forward often unspoken private matters into the public realm of teaching in ways that facilitate open expression and the sharing of personal perspectives to create change. The quilting project became a means of symbolically negotiating liminal spaces between illness and death, during the original project, and more recently, in a new school year. The quilts arguably took on an 'emotional life' for Julie in the midst of personal and professional distress, intimately connecting her with those lost.

Many of the same students who participated in the original *Comfort Quilts* project have now returned to Julie as Grade 11s in Senior Drawing and Painting. Our research interests turn to the present: *How are the students thinking about caring today? How does teaching continue beyond the classroom? How is the groundwork Julie laid 2 years ago now rendering transformation through the arts?* Perhaps it is in the continuity of the arts, in the outcomes of the quilting project, and in the lifelong effects for students that we may come to understand the essence of our Integration Project in terms of the intellectual discipline developed through acts of creating and in the evolving social relationships among students (Freire, 1998, p. 87).

When we unfold the situations and challenges that are behind our questions and outcomes as researchers, and when we hear the voices in the classroom and follow their lead, we inspire understandings of teaching and learning that are relational and collective, as in this case, understandings that are a/r/tographical. During the course of our field research on the Integration Project, we came to know of Julie's story as a powerful example of educating through the arts, and an exemplar to teachers across the curriculum. Interpreting her experience through an a/r/tographic lens highlights the depth and breadth of student engagement as renderings of living inquiry, metaphor and openings, and readily connects us with Freire's impassioned call to teachers as cultural workers.

Julie's story is a narrative of living deeply in the "fluid, uncertain, and temporal" spaces of the classroom, where meaning-making is generated through the "senses, bodies, minds and emotions," and "dis/comfort and struggle... allow one to conceive of possibilities unthought of before" (Springgay et al., 2005, pp. 908-909). A/r/tography was a pathway to new understandings of time and place in Julie's classroom, rooted in the emergence of a community of practice shared primarily by Julie and Kit during the Comfort Quilt project. As Kit informed Julie's experience concerning the openings and cracks of teaching, Julie informed the Integration Project of her powerful, holistic teaching and learning experience (Abbs 2003; Freire, 1997; hooks, 2000, 2003; Huebner, 1998; Miller 1998; Palmer 1998; Pelias, 2004). The reciprocity and mutuality of coming together, sharing possibilities and enacting change created a unique space during our research and enabled both teacher and researcher to open up their perspectives, and to revise and revitalize practices. Neither Julie nor Kit would have achieved these insights working in isolation. Julie prompted our research endeavors further by drawing our attention to the cracks in our research expectations and experiences, highlighting the importance of researchers responding with humility and attentiveness to the voices and stories that permeate the field, embracing stories like Julie's as the essence of our purpose and the reason for our a/r/tographic research journey to continue. As Grauer (2006) suggests:

> In the art classroom we need to see beauty and the best in all our students, to live by example so that the first greens of spring and the dead branches of winter all have their place in the cycle. We need to be able to reap the pleasure in giving and see the beliefs and values that make our work meaningful, creative and in harmony; simple sentiments but very powerful in their possibilities. (p. 95)

Julie tells us that in spite of the loss of Emily and Ken, they forged ahead with another interdisciplinary fine arts event that year. They linked an "Empty Bowls" dinner with the opening night of the spring musical, *Les Misérables*. Colleagues, students, and community once again witnessed an inspiring and triumphant evening of art, music, theatre, and cuisine. The proceeds were donated to the Deltassist Emergency Relief Fund.

As a tribute to Emily and Ken, Julie declares, "the show must go on," and in her commitment to her practice, she continues to dare to teach art in liminal spaces, affirming Freire's hope for teachers as cultural workers. As Julie passionately promises, "we will stage this year's event with the same mindfulness and conviction as we have in the past."

REFERENCES

Abbs, P. (2003). *Against the flow: Education, the arts and postmodern culture*. London, England: Routledge Falmer.

Ashton, W., & Denton, D. (Eds.). (2006). *Spirituality, ethnography, and teaching: Stories from within*. New York, NY: Peter Lang.

Bailis, L. & Kennedy, W. (1977). Effects of a death education program upon secondary school students. *The Journal of Educational Research, 71*(2), 63-66.

Denton, D. (1998). *In the tenderness of stone: Liberating consciousness through the awakening of the heart*. Pittsburgh, PA: Sterling House.

Eisner, E. (2006) The satisfaction of teaching. *Educational Leadership, 63*(6), 44-46. Retrieved from www.ascd.org/el

Freire, P. (1997). *Pedagogy of the heart*. (Trans. D. Macedo and A. Oliveira). New York, NY: Continuum.

Freire, P. (1998). *Teachers as cultural workers: Letters to those who dare teach*. Boulder, CO: Westview Press.

Gouzouasis, P. (2006). A reunification of musician, researcher, and teacher: A/r/tography in music research. *Arts and Learning Research Journal, 22*(1), 23-42.

Grauer, K. (2002). Teenagers and their bedrooms. *Visual Arts Research 9*(1), 86-94.

Grauer, K. (2006). My mother wore pink. *Visual Arts Research, 32*(1), 86-95.

Haggard, G. (2005). Providing school support for the grieving child. *The Delta Kappa Gamma Bulletin, 72*(1), 25–44.

hooks, b. (2000). *All about love: New visions*. New York, NY: William Morrow.

hooks, b. (2003). *Teaching community: A pedagogy of hope*. New York, NY: Routledge.

Huebner, D. (1998). *The lure of the transcendent: Collected essays of Dwayne Huebner*. Mahwah, NJ: Lawrence Erlbaum Associates.

Irwin, R. L. (2003). Towards an aesthetic of unfolding in/sights through curriculum. *Journal of the Canadian Association for Curriculum Studies, 1*(2), 63–78. Available at www.csse.ca/CACS/JCACS/PDF%20 Content/07_Irwin.pdf

Irwin, R. L. (2004). A/r/tography: A metonymic metissage. In R.L. Irwin & A. de Cosson, (Eds.), *A/r/tography: Rendering self through arts-based living inquiry* (pp. 27–38). Vancouver, BC: Pacific Educational Press.

Irwin, R. L. (2006). Walking to create an aesthetic and spiritual currere. *Visual Arts Research, 32*(1), 75-82.

Irwin, R. L., Beer, R., Springgay, S., Grauer, K., Xiong, G., & Bickel, B. (2006). The rhizomatic relations of a/r/tography. *Studies in Art Education, 48*(1), 70–88.

Irwin, R. L., & de Cosson, A. (Eds.). (2004). *A/r/tography: Rendering self through arts-based living inquiry*. Vancouver, BC: Pacific Educational Press.

Irwin, R. L., Gouzouasis, P., Grauer, K., Leggo, C., & Springgay, S. (2006). Investigating curriculum integration: The arts and diverse learning environments. Lisbon, PT: *United Nations Educational Scientific and Cultural Organization (UNESCO) World Congress on Arts Education*. Retrieved from http://portal.unesco.org/culture/en/files/30192/11415092521irwin_gouzouasis_leggo_springgay_grauer.pdf/irwin%2Bgouzouasis%2Bleggo%2Bspringgay%2Bgrauer.pdf

Jardine, D. (1998). *To dwell with a boundless heart*. New York, NY: Peter Lang.

Jardine, D. (2000). *Under the tough old stars: Ecopedagogical essays*. Brandon, VT: Solomon Press.

Kessler, R. (2000). *The soul of education*. Alexandria, VA: Association for Supervision and Curriculum Development.

Kind, S., Irwin, R. L., Grauer, K. & de Cosson, Alex (2005). Medicine Wheel Imag(in)ings: Exploring holistic curriculum perspectives. *Art Education, 58*(5), 33-35.

Leggo, C. (2005). The heart of pedagogy: On poetic knowing and living. *Teachers and Teaching: Theory and Practice, 11*(5), 439–455.

London, P. (1989). *No more secondhand art: Awakening the artist within*. Boston, MA: Shambhala.

London, P. (2003). *Drawing closer to nature: Making art in dialogue with the natural world*. Boston, MA: Shambhala.

London, P. (2005). *Toward a holistic paradigm in art education: Monograph #1*. Center for Art Education, Maryland Institute College of Art (Ed.). Baltimore, MD: MICA.

Miller, J. (1988). *The holistic curriculum*. Toronto, ON: OISE Press.

Miller, J. (2000). *Education and the soul: Toward a spiritual curriculum*. Albany, NY: State University of New York Press.

Miller, R. (1999). Holistic education for an emerging culture. In S. Glazer (Ed), *The heart of learning: Spirituality in education*. (189-203). New York, NY: Penguin Putnam.

Moore, C. (1989). Teaching about loss and death to junior high school students. *Family Relations, 38*(1), 3-7.

Munson, L. & Hunt, N. (2005). Teachers grieve! What can we do for our colleagues and ourselves when a student dies? *Teaching Exceptional Children, 37*(4), 48–51.

Naierman, N. (1997). Reaching out to grieving students. *Educational Leadership, 55*(2), 62-65.

O'Sullivan, E., Morrell, A., & O'Connor, M. A., (Eds.). (2002). *Expanding the boundaries of transformative learning: Essays on theory and praxis*. New York, NY: Palgrave.

Palmer, P. J. (1998). *The courage to teach: Exploring the inner landscape of a teacher's life*. San Francisco, CA: Jossey-Bass.

Palmer, P. J. (2004). *A hidden wholeness: The journey toward an undivided life*. San Francisco, CA: Jossey-Bass.

Pelias, R. J. (2004). *A methodology of the heart: Evoking academic and daily life*. Walnut Creek, CA: AltaMira Press.

Pratt, C., Hare, J. & Wright, C. (1987). Death and dying in early childhood education: Are educators prepared? *Education, 107*(3), 279–286.

Schlozman, S. (2002). When illness strikes. *Educational Leadership, 60*(1), 82-83.

Shaw, P. (2004). Death and divorce: Teaching dilemmas or teachable momens? *Kappa Delta Pi Record, 40(4)*, 165–169.

Springgay, S., Irwin, R. L., & Kind, S. (2005). A/r/tography as living inquiry: Through art and text. *Qualitative Inquiry, 11*(6), 897–912.

Wilson, S. (2004). Fragments: Life writing in image and in text. In R. L. Irwin & A. de Cosson.(Eds.), *A/r/tography: Rendering self through arts-based living inquiry* (pp. 41–59). Vancouver, BC: Pacific Educational Press.

ENDNOTES

1. We wish to thank the Social Sciences and Humanities Research Council of Canada for funding our research program entitled *Investigating Curriculum Integration, the Arts and Diverse Learning Environments (Rita L. Irwin, Principal Investigator; Peter Gouzouasis, Kit Grauer and Carl Leggo, Co-Investigators)*.
2. For more information on a/r/tography, see http://m1.cust.educ.ubc.ca:16080/Artography/
3. Sashing is the fabric that separates blocks in a setting, framing blocks and making the quilt larger. For more information see http://mccallsquilting.com/lessons/glossary/index1.html.
4. In this case, the term "gay" is used by the note-writer as a pejorative term suggesting the quilting project is boring, weak or a waste of time.

ABOUT THE AUTHORS

Anita Sinner is an assistant professor of Art Education at Concordia University in Montreal, Canada.

Julie Lymburner is an art educator and Fine Arts Department Head in the Delta School District in Tsawwassen, Canada.

Kit Grauer is an associate professor in the Department of Curriculum and Pedagogy at the University of British Columbia in Vancouver, Canada.

Rita L. Irwin is a professor of Art Education and Associate Dean of Teacher Education at the University of British Columbia in Vancouver, Canada. She is also the current President of the International Society for Education Through Art.

Carl Leggo is a professor in the Department of Language and Literacy Education at the University of British Columbia in Vancouver, Canada.

Peter Gouzouasis is an associate professor of Music Education in the Department of Curriculum and Pedagogy at the University of British Columbia in Vancouver, Canada.

CHAPTER 27

One Art Teacher's Search for a Holistic Approach

Virginia K. Freyermuth

As a new elementary school art teacher, I began my career by planning lessons around time-honored design concepts that resulted in thoughtful, well-composed works of art that would then be displayed in school corridors and parents' homes. My students looked forward to their 45-minute art class once a week, worked hard, learned the principles and elements of design, and for the most part, did what I requested. Before long, however, I became disenchanted with the predictable results and became bored with my own teaching. My career stretched before me as a long succession of directions and techniques.

I began to question myself and my teaching thus far. If I was bored, were my students bored, too? Were they just going through the motions to please me? I also began to pose deeper questions about my students: Who were these children anyway? What interested them? What were their lives like? What did they care about? What were their dreams? I became curious about these young people whom I didn't know and decided to try something new. I would relinquish my unilateral power in the classroom. Instead of building lessons only around art concepts, I would organize my teaching around the children by asking questions to which I did not know the answers. None of these questions would have one right answer, and each individual could answer in his or her own way. I would also give the children choices of art media with which to explore their own unique visual responses. They would demonstrate their expertise about the one thing they knew best—their own lives. In short, the children would become *my* teachers. I would become the student.

The prospect was intriguing though somewhat scary, but I did it despite my concerns. To begin, I asked questions to prompt visual work about matters of importance *to them*—the people they loved, the things they liked to do, the things they wondered about, what they hoped for, what they were curious about, places that were special to them. I told them that they could choose from the media available on my rolling art cart. There would be no value judgments; they could do what *they* chose to do in a way that *they* thought was best.

Mirroring my own mixed feelings, the students met this new way of approaching art class with a mix of initial uneasiness, suspicion, and excitement. Some were hesitant, but most jumped right in. After all, these were questions they could answer. Then *their* questions started pouring in. "Is it O.K. for me to use crayons *and* paint? Can I make it big? Is this right? Is this good? *Is this what you want?*" Their extreme eagerness to please was touching but troubling. So I replied, "Yes, you can use crayons and paint. It's not about good or bad. What do you think would work best for your idea? Is this what *you* want?"

Although I began these lessons without specific instruction, teaching naturally followed as their need to know grew. "I need purple; how do I make purple? I need to make fluffy clouds, how do I use chalk pastels? How do I make something look far away?" So we talked about color mixing, how to use different media, perspective, and concepts I would have otherwise taught as distinct, directed "lessons." But now *they* wanted to learn them because they were ready. They had a need and eagerness to know and were serious about their highly personal work.

Critics of learner-centered art education have often characterized this approach as laissez faire, an easy way out in which the teacher just stands back and lets the students do whatever they want. In fact, I strongly contend that it is very much the opposite, and may be the most challenging kind of teaching there is. For one thing, as students struggled with their own individual problems, I found it hard to respond to so many different questions and needs at once. There was a sea of hands in the air. I feared it would be too chaotic, that they would get frustrated, that I would become frazzled. I took a deep breath, consciously practiced calm patience, and asked for theirs. I told them that I would nod to acknowledge a student's need for help when I saw a hand. While they waited, I asked that they put their hands down, get back to work, and do the best they could as I moved about the room. By the time I made my way to each child, I often found they had solved the problem themselves. Before long those who were the first to learn something new or solve a problem were helping others. Collaboration between students happened naturally. Generosity expanded. My trepidations subsided. It soon became clear that the challenges of this type of teaching were more than compensated for by the rewards.

In addition, this type of teaching requires finely tuned perceptual and intuitive skills on the part of the teacher. One must be ever watchful for the subtle signs, passing remarks, body language, and manners of working that suggest what individuals may be struggling with, uncertain about, or tentatively attempting. The teacher must know when to intervene and when to allow the student space. The teacher must be highly observant, attentive, sensitive, compassionate, and understanding. Interaction between teacher and student is thus highly personalized.

The teacher must also be well-versed in varied ways of artmaking, ready to respond to the multitude of needs students may have in the media and processes of creation. This requires that the teacher be well versed in the content of both studio art and art history. An artist / teacher who has had experience solving similar problems understands the creative process from a personal and pedagogical perspective.

Another criticism of this type of teaching is that it focuses exclusively on making art, avoiding reference to art history for fear of influencing students. Nonetheless, before long I began to share images of great works of art with my students, not as examples of what they should do, but as a way to understand that people who preceded them in far corners of the world had pondered similar questions and solved similar problems. My intention was not so much to induce awe for these masters, but to establish a kinship with distant fellow creators who shared their sense of curiosity and dedication. These, too, became their teachers.

Then one day, a boy asked me the most courageous question. "Can I think up my own question?"

I paused. Was I ready to even relinquish control of lines of inquiry? Would it jeopardize what had been, up till now, a collective pursuit? I asked the student what he had in mind, saw his enthusiasm and anticipation, and could not say no. He poured himself into his work and, as I watched his personal investment in his work, I made it my goal to say "yes" as much as possible to any question that showed positive initiative, serious intent, and sincerity. They were taking risks. They were thinking outside the box. They were taking charge of their own learning. They were self-invested. They were becoming more courageous. They were becoming... empowered.

The process resulted in some works that might not be considered a "success," either in my terms or theirs. When they did things that didn't work out, they said, "I made a mess. I made a mistake." I asked them why they felt that way and pointed out that we can learn from our "mistakes." I told students I wouldn't even call them mistakes; they were simply opportunities to make changes or move in new directions. Struggles, as I explained to them, were chances to learn about what worked and what didn't, but more importantly, they could learn about and cultivate their own character as they faced discouragement and practiced persistence. Success was redefined in terms of the learning process and individual growth rather than a singular focus on the product.

On days when I needed to broadly address particular concepts, I gave them as many choices as possible and continued to frame instruction through open-ended questions. Over time, I honed my questioning techniques to keep the process as flexible as possible. As I have come to understand it, questioning strategies based on truly open ended, reflective questions are key to this kind of teaching. Framing questions in this way—a way that makes children really think for themselves—is just another of the challenges associated with this type of teaching. But, once again, for every challenge there were far greater rewards.

Even though I had 500 students per elementary school and taught in two schools, I connected with them in ways I had not thought possible and truly *saw* them as I had not seen them before—as individuals with particular points of view, feelings, needs, desires, and approaches. Teaching and learning became a shared enterprise. Visual art was the language through which they communicated and explored their distinctive inner and outer lives. As they better connected to themselves, they also developed a more natural affinity for media, a curiosity about other artists' questions, each other's work, and the world beyond. When they shared their work by speaking about the things they cared about, their struggles, their successes, and their reasons for making the choices they did, they learned to appreciate and be intrigued by the variety of stories of their classmates. They congratulated each other's efforts. The classroom became a compelling community of mutual respect. We shared a sense of passion. Teaching became an honor instead of a job. Art became a process of discovery instead of a product. It was liberating for them and for me, but it was not a free-for-all. The pursuits were focused, the intentions serious, and the means to explore them required their care to obtain the richest results and deepest satisfaction.

Given the rewards of this type of teaching, I brought it with me wherever I went. When I was fortunate enough to have an art room in a new school, I asked the children to bring old broken toys and other discarded found objects, images, and natural objects from home to keep in the room as a way of eliciting questions and inspirations. One long counter became filled with their finds: toy cars and trucks, broken dolls, shells and pine cones, clock gears, an old pair of ice skates, a baseball glove, feathers, and stones. What fascinated them? Why? What did it suggest? How could it engage their imaginations or their ability to really study something? The art room was a place of inquiry, and as artists, they set out to respond by the use of their own two hands, their curiosity, and whatever supply cabinets I opened that day.

The approach described above is based on a philosophical position, not just a pedagogical one. I believe there is an artist inherent in every person. The artist within has the capacity to wonder, to experience the world in fresh and surprising ways, to imagine things that could be, and to share a unique point of view with others through authentic work that arises from a personal sense of purpose. This has proven itself to me through 35 years of teaching people of all ages, experiences, and abilities, including many adults who initially told me they did not consider themselves the least bit artistic.

There are also psychological implications involved—the view of the child as an integrated whole, involving physical, emotional, and intellectual capacities, among others—all of which need to be addressed in art education. If adults who guide children could better understand the process for engaging the whole child through artistic pursuit, perhaps there would be more encouragement of children's inner creative necessities. By this I mean honoring and evoking curiosity, trusting one's own intuition, taking risks, instilling a passion for the world, and encouraging one's creative, constructive response to it. Such a process engages children—mind, body, and spirit—around work that is meaningful *to them*. It challenges and intrigues the logical, imaginative, and intuitive mind; activates the body and the senses by use of sumptuous media in a sensuous world; and nurtures the heart and human spirit. It connects us to ourselves, each other, nature, and generations of humanity from all corners of the world.

I have spent most of my professional life in public schools as a teacher, a K-12 Art Coordinator, and as an art education faculty member at a state university. I know it is possible for teachers to teach art in a holistic manner while meeting required standards and more importantly, exceeding them. Based on my engagement with holistic teaching practices, here is what I believe is necessary as a teacher of Holistic Art Education.

The teacher

- Models a passion for, love of, fascination with, and respect for life and learning
- Demonstrates and expresses genuine care for those she teaches
- Is willing to forego a position of "power over" and adopts an attitude of care in the role of facilitator, catalyst, guide, fellow-learner, and fellow-traveler
- Understands the vital need for and power of cultivating the whole person—mind, body, and spirit
- Welcomes imagination, intuition, and expressions of the heart
- Cultivates a learning environment that is abidingly safe, respectful, and supportive for all learners
- Promotes open-ended, deep questioning that encourages and is responsive to personal meaning-making
- Provides opportunities for choice on the part of learners that is appropriate to their developmental needs
- Seeks means for direct engagement with the world as a source of inspiration and a sense of wonder
- Values a sense of community and cultivates a spirit of collaboration and cooperation
- Pursues opportunities to authentically connect learners with traditions, histories, and concepts of art
- Is tolerant of ambiguity and encourages risk-taking and invention
- Promotes experiential learning
- Views all members of the class as both learners and teachers
- Believes that artistic engagement goes beyond "picture-making" and can be transformative

Even given their desire to teach in this manner, some educators tell me there is no time. They say there is precious little room for creativity with the current focus on high-stakes test results, external demands, and time limitations. I hear their frustrations and agree that the ways schools are structured today makes it an enormous challenge, but I also believe that with knowledge and commitment this work can be honored in meaningful ways. A widening gap between personal, educational, societal, and global needs endangers the artistic fulfillment of children in a world that so often misunderstands, marginalizes, overlooks, and devalues meaningful artistic development. As a means of personal, societal, and global transformation, it is time art educators take full ownership of this unique and extraordinary aspect of being human. Put simply, we must.

AUTHOR'S NOTE
An expanded version of this chapter appears in the book, *Ways to Your Child's Art: A Parent and Teacher Guide to Holistic Art Education*, ©2010 by Virginia K. Freyermuth, Inc.

ABOUT THE AUTHOR

Virginia K. Freyermuth was the 1994 Massachusetts Teacher of the Year and was named the 1995 National Outstanding Art Teacher by Walt Disney's American Teacher Awards. She holds BFA and MFA Degrees in Painting and a PhD in Interdisciplinary Studies with a Concentration in Art Education. A lifelong art educator, she is an assistant professor of Art Education at Rhode Island College. She is inspired by the writings of Peter London and Ron Miller pertaining to Holistic Education.
Her websites are www.artwhereyouare.com and www.virginiafreyermuth.com.

CHAPTER 28

Sugar and Spice: Envisioning Possibilities for Holistic Art Education Inspired by *Ace of Cakes*

Stephanie Harvey Danker

Within popular visual culture, a number of contemporary television series approach design challenges in a holistic manner, providing appropriate and exciting indicators for curriculum development in the visual art classroom. One such example is the popular Food Network program, *Ace of Cakes*, which aired from 2006 to 2011. Aspects emphasized within the show that resonate with classroom methodology include artistic creativity based on team meetings, small group collaborations, research, effective communication, thoughtful display, celebration, and reflection. The processes framed by this show afford a valuable model for secondary art teachers in efforts to balance facilitation of shaping self with artistic growth, for practical purposes stimulated by community engagement. This vignette will juxtapose aforementioned processes observed in *Ace of Cakes* with imagined possibilities and theory-informed practices within visual art classroom spaces.

Though it can be convincingly argued that popular visual culture such as commercial television often appeals more to the senses than to the mind (Duncum, 2005), the particular audiences and the social context in which these shows are viewed and interpreted combine to mediate the impact and effects that are possible (Rose, 2005). Similarly, while the commercial lure of television programming cannot be denied, some television shows can provide relevant examples for structuring learning environments within the art classroom (see Carpenter, 2006). These programs exemplify purposeful attention given to designing educational environments and curriculum, which embrace and integrate social, emotional, and intellectual domains, thereby inspiring educators to foster meaning through capitalizing on those connections in their teaching. Through such processes, it also becomes possible to eliminate distinctions between cognition and emotion (Eisner, 2005), and to connect them to creative as well as practical activities, in this case applicable to a business environment.

Duff Goldman leads the *Ace of Cakes* team at his business, Charm City Cakes, in Baltimore, Maryland. According to the way the Charm City Cakes staff represent themselves on the television series, it seems that they work cohesively as a team, enjoy the work they are involved in, and appreciate the people with whom they work. Each episode, viewers are able to watch several final products come to fruition through this collaboration and teamwork. These products celebrate human relationships (weddings, birthdays, organizational anniversaries and events) within, and sometimes outside of, the Baltimore community.

Creating a nurturing and supportive work environment amidst demanding deadlines and rigorous expectations of clients requires a special kind of leadership. Duff assembled his friends to work for him, friends who came to Charm City Cakes with various background experiences closely related to aspects of art education, including interior design, exhibition

FIGURE 1. Chef Duff Goldman, of Food Network's *Ace of Cakes*, unveils a replica 64 Box birthday cake as part of the 50th birthday celebration for the Crayola 64 Box, Wednesday, April 9, 2008, at Toys "R" Us Times Square in New York. The celebration also included the unveiling of eight "Kids Choice Colors"—*best friends, awesome, giving tree, happy every after, fun in the sun, bear hug, famous,* and *super happy*—which were chosen by nearly 20,000 kids through an online survey. Photo by Diane Bondareff, Insider Images.

design, engineering, and architectural model building. The bakery is their studio. There is also an atmosphere of encouragement. Duff once professed that if properly inspired, anyone can accomplish anything (Lewis & Rogan, 2006). Similarly, as in art education, he shows his staff a medium and demonstrates techniques, and from there individual artists add their own unique flair to the projects at hand. Following Duff's lead, the secondary art teacher assists student-artists when needed, but also fulfills roles that he or she models: facilitator, source of inspiration, and resource. Relationships between peers and mentors are seen as both source and topic of education (Forbes, 1996).

The Charm City Cakes staff holds team meetings during their busiest times, when the whole group gets together to discuss their multitude of projects, and then breaks out into smaller teams to tackle individual projects that are themselves cooperatively constructed. Like art students, the cake artists are always under deadlines to complete projects; but here, missing a deadline is not an option (as students sometimes imagine it is in an art class). As reminders of the non-negotiable expectations of the job, separate clipboards keep each project organized, with one wall being devoted to the clipboards, arranged by deadline. The clipboards are accessible to all staff members, and each presumably contains client information and communication, a contract, research, and sketches for the cake. Along with these clipboards, class meetings and a similar organizational system for deadlines could easily be mimicked in the art classroom. Creating collaborative artworks that are intended to celebrate relationships within the local community would certainly take more work on the part of both the art teacher and the students, but could foster (and/or sustain) meaningful community partnerships.

The show also gives clues for how to design and implement creative collaborations. Within the Charm City Cakes staff, everyone has a specialty and excels at different skills. Each team member comes to a project from a different perspective, with expertise in varying disciplines, funneling that knowledge into creating an artwork together. Decision-making is decentralized once the smaller team takes over a project and the clients' goals have been conveyed. Effective communication is then stressed between team members; now it is up to them to research and interpret together. Although the work challenges each team to do its best, there is no competition between the teams, since each project serves a different purpose. Working with deadlines becomes a group initiative; contributions come from staff members not originally assigned to the project when time limitations make it necessary. Translated for the art classroom, small groups working together strive to initiate and maintain meaningful dialogue and interactions between members, understanding individual strengths of each class member, and utilizing those strengths appropriately for the specific project. All parts of the artmaking process are interconnected, and every voice is acknowledged and considered.

Complementing the organizational structure and teamwork, success of the final products at Charm City Cakes depends on research to adequately know the client, to choose appropriate imagery, and to determine technical aspects, all while maintaining effective communication between the team members. In the art classroom, community-based arts projects could be similarly structured. They may begin by arranging interviews and social interactions with community leaders and school partners to research community needs, followed by whole class discussions to determine how the group might address those needs through visual representation in a collaborative artwork. In addition, service-learning initiatives could be encouraged. Together, such activities can foster communication between students, the school, and the community. Projects can be engaging for their own sake, while also leading students towards a life of active citizenship. No less important, this approach assists students to see that the artwork they create can serve a purpose and affect the community. In this way, real-world applications become a natural part of life in the classroom, and community spirit is bolstered. Charm City Cakes expresses such commitment to community in episodes of *Ace of Cakes*, as well as on their blog (Charm City Cakes, 2010).

Another important component of using shows like *Ace of Cakes* as examples for art students is that they suggest ways that skills acquired in the art room can be used to earn a living, sometimes in unexpected ways. They also reveal that art can take all kinds of forms and serve a variety of purposes. The artists at Charm City Cakes take their non-permanent artwork into the community to be thoughtfully displayed within the space of an event, as a focal point representative of many people coming together to celebrate relationships. The team members responsible for creating the piece are often invited to become part of the celebration.

Equally important, they exemplify the qualities of creativity and care that it takes to make a work of art, whatever the medium. The extraordinary details and time that the Charm City Cakes staff puts into their work makes each customized cake special, and provides a meaningful experience for those who are privileged to come in contact with the actual products. Documentation of the cake deliveries and celebrations on *Ace of Cakes* episodes shows clients who are pleased with outcomes, which must be rewarding for the artists. Finally, the visual symbolism that the cake represents is significant for the recipients and celebrants, just as more permanent works of art serve significant celebratory purposes in state and religious events.

One further dimension of the creative process exemplified by this program is worth attention for teachers and students of art. During the process, as well as afterwards, there is always a reflective component in *Ace of Cakes* episodes, recognizing what worked well, and techniques or communication strategies that could have improved the final piece. Reflective practice and acknowledgment of growth is viewed as essential to advancing professional skills in many creative fields and is an important part of learning in the arts. Following this model provided by Charm City Cakes for *Ace of Cakes* episodes, reflective video journaling could be implemented to facilitate documentation of the process of artmaking through collaborative team efforts.

During this process in the secondary art classroom, short clips could be filmed throughout the making of a project and woven together by the students in video editing software to result in a final short documentary. All group members should be featured (and encouraged to embark in a speaking role) in team-reflective video journals, with each taking on a specialized production role. The production roles could vary if more than one product or reflective video journal is created to enable students to experience unique communication aspects affiliated with each and assist in identification of individual strengths and weaknesses. Besides teaching students skills with making and editing videos, the process of creating a reflective video journal that accompanies the final art product would aid students in developing articulation skills. This would enable them to cultivate their artistic identities while preparing them for other real-world applications.

As a class, reflective video journals could be watched at the conclusion of the unit, for the purpose of understanding each team's collaborative processes. This would include learning from mistakes and advancing team skills for future activities, as well as critiquing technical aspects of photography and filming. Student-artists would also be well-served to keep their personal video journal files in a digital portfolio format for future reference and possible career preparation. Similarly, each team could be responsible for photographing their final art product for inclusion in their digital portfolio. Both of these activities would serve to assist students in recognizing the value of professional display of their work.

Assessment is meaningful and closely linked with curriculum. This interdependence can be made evident through reflective documentation of the process of collaborative artmaking. Another application occurs when, as suggested above, the completed video becomes significant for promoting the artists involved. Potential audiences range from peers at school to community public broadcasting and community-based social media sites. Thus, the art classroom becomes a space for multi-layered meaning making. Students learn through making art in at least two forms: a collaborative piece that celebrates relationships in the community, as well as a collaborative film documentary that features and promotes individual artistic identity and technical skills, with an undeniable emphasis on problem-solving and group communication.

On a personal level, emphasis on such projects is put on caring for each other as respected team members and utilizing individual strengths—values which may extend well beyond the walls of the school. In addition, collaborative art experiences facilitated through a methodological framework such as the one suggested may assist in cultivating connectedness between classmates, affording peer acknowledgement of positive individual contributions toward the completion of a successful project. Taking these aspects into consideration, when student-artists are motivated to create artwork which celebrates connections to the community in which they live, they are encouraged to develop intellectually, socially, and emotionally. This occurs in conjunction with development of technical skills and aesthetic sensibility—because, of course, the cake must be pleasing both to the eye and to the taste buds! Holistic art education such as this invites those involved to consider what is of value to them and how they will obtain purpose in their lives, which can be a life-changing process. Duff considers Charm City Cakes "a place where people come to be creative, be artistic and be awesome in a really cool setting" (Lewis & Rogan, 2006). Why shouldn't art educators take a cue from *Ace of Cakes*?

REFERENCES

Carpenter, B. S. (2006). Whose line is it anyway? Visual culture spaces as learning environments. *Visual Arts Research, 32*(2), 69-72.

Charm City Cakes (2010). Retrieved from www.charmcitycakes.com

Duncum, P. (2005). Visual culture and an aesthetics of embodiment. *International Journal of Education Through Art, 1*(1), 9-19.

Eisner, E. (2005). Back to whole. *Educational Leadership, 63*(1), 14-18.

Forbes, S. H. (1996, June). *Values in holistic education.* Paper presented at the Third Annual Conference on Education, Spirituality and the Whole Child at the Roehampton Institute, London, England.

Lewis, B., & Rogan, T. (Producers). (2006). *Ace of cakes: The complete first season* [Television series]. Baltimore, Maryland: Food Network.

Rose, G. (2005). *Visual methodologies: An introduction to the interpretation of visual materials.* London, England: Sage.

ABOUT THE AUTHOR

Stephanie H. Danker is assistant professor of art education at Coastal Carolina University, Conway, SC, and previously served as a middle school art teacher in Fairfax County Public Schools, VA.

CHAPTER 29

The Altered Book: Holistic Education in Action

Laura Gardner

Preservice art educators are "beings in the process of becoming" (Freire, 2000), in transition from being art students to artist-teachers. It is a transformation of identity. In the Winthrop University art education program, we utilize a holistic approach to help students make this transition. To this end, we embed reflective writing, dialogue, and collaborative activities into each art education course as a way to provide opportunities to address such questions as: *Who am I? What are my strengths and vulnerabilities? What do I value? How do I bring these qualities to my emergent teaching?* Students also lead discussions, work in community schools and museums, and share artwork and lesson ideas. Class, then, is less a place for lectures and listening, but serves more as a laboratory to practice active listening, speaking, leading, and sharing of tasks, helping students grow in confidence and in community. In these classes, we also hope to model the ways our art education students will interact with their future students.

In the elementary methods class that I teach, for example, course goals include: (1) use reflection as a daily practice; (2) make connections between artmaking and art teaching; (3) explore story and narrative as a way to gain an understanding of one's unique individuality and strengths; and (4) feel safety and trust in the classroom through ritual, sharing, and committee work. To further help my students know themselves and learn to teach from their strengths, I created a mid-term project on the theme of *change*, change in thinking or attitude as told visually in an "altered book" format. The book that was to be altered was a children's board book, which would be painted or collaged over to make a fresh surface, but one with a past. Initially students were asked to look inward at their lived experience and to document in their altered book the story of an experience that changed or transformed their lives in some way. The lesson assignment, student reflections, and findings follow.

THE ASSIGNMENT: ALTERED BOOK

The students in the class were given the following information:

- The form and the content of the book you will construct will complement each other. Both will reflect change: change in format and change in thinking or being.

Questions to consider:

- *Concept:* Does my book express a eureka moment in my life, an experience (or experiences) that changed the way I think, do, live, relate...?
- *Craftsmanship:* Has the board book been sufficiently changed (altered) so that it is no longer recognizable as the book I began with?
- *Communication:* Do the images and text clearly convey the experience? Is this an experience I am comfortable sharing?

How...

- Choose a 6-8 page children's board book, no larger than 6″ x 6″ or 6″ x 8.″ Spray paint with sandable primer to create a blank canvas on each page.
- Draw, paint, collage, stitch, sculpt, print, cut and reassemble—whatever medium or media you prefer except pastel or oil pastel (it may be mixed media).
- You may use images and text, images only, or text used in a graphic or unique way.

What the Altered Book is...

- Your narrative, a part of your life story, told in images and text, images only, or text with a strong visual design.

What the Altered Book is not...

- A scrapbook. No scrapbooking imagery material to be used. (Tools and hardware, yes.)
- A photo album—although you may use photos and other imagery.

SHARING THE ALTERED BOOKS

On the day we were to share our Altered Books, I placed the tables in a circle so that we would be facing one another during our presentation and explained that we would not critique the books in the traditional manner, as our focus was the meaning of the experience rather than the formal qualities of the work. Rachel started us off. She broke the tension with a book that dropped open vertically like a waterfall—full of images of Asian and Indian art, art she knew nothing of until a recent non-western art history course. Her enthusiasm was infectious. She put her peers at ease with the story of her new passion and way of seeing life. Rachel's classmates, spurred by Rachel's offer to go first, revealed stories that were often deeply personal: An account of the death of a brother and its effect on the family, of a trip to Eastern Europe and perspective gained, of what it's like to be a twin now living alone, of dating outside one's culture and how it has opened eyes, of recognizing and declaring one's identity as an artist, of the importance of recycling to the environment, of a father building the family home and its effects on the family, of winning a contest and the meaning of the win, and of choosing teaching as a profession. The room was hushed, each one in his or her seat, watching, listening with interest and respect as peers told stories only they could tell. Each was revealing to the others who they are, what they value. And all were aware that we were doing something courageous. Anne quietly noticed, "We had no idea. Then these things come out and we get to understand a little better. What they're sitting in there with isn't what you're sitting with... It's a whole different thing."

FIGURES 1 AND 2. Altered Book Projects.

STUDENT RESPONSES: REFLECTIONS ON ALTERED BOOK SHARING

At the next class, the 10-minute timed writing prompt for the day was: *What did you hear and see during the sharing of the Altered Books?* Rose saw clearly that no two altered books were the same, and noted the connection between content and form: "It was interesting to see how different they all turned out; *none* was anything like each other." Karen and Rachel recognized the initial discomfort of the group and the unfolding that took place. Karen had this to say: "Listening, watching... funny how much acceptance played a role in a lot of the books. Accepting other cultures, ourselves, losses in our lives... I really got a sense of community." Rachel reflected: "After the class, I could not stop thinking about how... people were bonding." Emily appreciated the depth of the sharing: "It opened my eyes to see the core part of each individual." Beth noted that it is conflict, or what Mezirow (1991) calls a "disorienting dilemma" (p. xvi), that is often the impetus for growth or change. Several recognized that for some, the point of discomfort became an opportunity for individual growth or family connection (Gilligan, 1982).

FINDINGS

After sharing the altered books, there were immediate changes in the tenor of the class: a general ease in relating, talking to one another and to me. Students reminded each other of due dates, collaborated on assignments, and went deeper in their reflective journal writing. We saw in the Altered Book Project that holistic classroom artmaking is not competitive (Berger, 2009). The work was uniquely individual and came from the students' lives; their own stories. It was evident as well that giving choices teaches us about how minds work differently: There is not just one way to do things. Bill expressed it this way: "[The Altered Book] exercise gave us the choice to create unique books to share our unique stories... I felt I couldn't do it wrong, which helped me see the importance of open-ended lesson planning." It was clear that by listening and by giving the students an opportunity to share, they revealed themselves.

Although the focus of the Altered Book Project was on the meaning of the experience and not the formal qualities, the quality of the books was generally high. Students were not directed to include specific National Visual Arts Content Standards, but clearly several were met: (I) Understanding and Applying Media, Techniques, and Processes; (II) Using Knowledge of Structures and Functions; (III) Choosing and Evaluating a Range of Subject Matter, Symbols, and Ideas: (IV) Understanding the Visual Arts in Relation to History and Cultures; (V) Reflecting upon and Assessing the Merits of Their Work and the Work of Others; and (VI) Making Connections between Visual Arts and Other Disciplines (National Art Education Association, 1994). Anne described the tacit standard and sense of safety in the class, "I never felt like I would be put on the spot if I messed up... yet quality was expected of us." At the end of the semester, in the final reflection, two students asked, "How can I do this in my future classroom?" They understood the engagement we all felt in the class was something worth carrying on with students of various ages.

I have assigned the Altered Book Project to several other art education classes, enough to see replications and patterns. As with this first class in all others, students have shared deeply personal issues: two people have come out to the class, others have shared the tensions of the immigrant experience and the desire to belong. Individuals have revealed stories about illness, death of a parent, divorce, moving, identity, and coming of age.

Beyond the challenges of this particular project are those inherent in holistic education, whether applied with children and adolescents or with future art teachers. First of all, going beyond the teaching of content, moving from a mechanistic accretion of discrete facts to a holistic view takes time, courage, and compassion on the part of all participants, teacher and students alike. Treating one another with kindness and respect, seeing one another as whole persons who bring more than their cognitive selves to class is, by definition, a key to holistic education. All of us come to class complete. We do not leave our beliefs, desires, connections, or fears at the classroom door. Related to this is the need to simply (and no, simply does not mean easily) be present with one another. What this means was evident as students in a recent class wrote that, in the sharing that took place during the Altered Book Project, they recognized bravery and fearlessness and saw past the superficial or the masks we wear into the hearts of their classmates. Some noticed the change in how the group interacted, that they were more connected, and that they felt closer to the others in the class. Or they wrote about changes in self, "I am less quick to judge because I don't know what another is going through right now."

The preservice art teachers who have experienced this holistic approach to teaching also feel empowered. One non-traditional student revealed that she would have dropped out of school had it not been for this class; that the recognition that we are whole persons who bring our emotional, physical, spiritual, cultural and social selves wherever we go was the welcome she needed to stay in school. Other outcomes are more interpersonal. Following the altered book project, students communicate with peers and with me more directly, they assist each other, they become active in class and the art education club. These values, which are at risk in many parts of our society, can be reinforced in the art classroom, drawing upon the traditional roles of art in fostering reflection, expression and communication; connecting self to others; and addressing the full range of head, heart, and hand as Ruskin (1893, p. 57) put it. Yet it is in no way inevitable that such connections are made in the course of ordinary teacher preparation. Instead, they must be intentionally cultivated by projects like the altered book. Moreover, students must be guided to find ways to apply these to their own eventual students, making age-appropriate modifications. Other concerns that must be addressed are the possibility of disturbing content (Mezirow, 1991; Gilligan, 1982) and the need to challenge students to apply principles of art, craftsmanship, and other standards without sacrificing individuality.

I am encouraged by my students' reflective responses. The work it takes to slow the pace down, to make time to attend to one another, is worth it, and can be seen as a way to mentor our students for success as individuals, as artist-teachers, and as contributing members in community.

REFERENCES

Berger, R. (2009). Holistic education: A brief introduction. Retrieved from www.pathsoflearning.com

Gilligan, C. (1982). *In a different voice*. Cambridge, MA: Harvard University Press.

Freire, P. (2000). *Pedagogy of the oppressed*. New York, NY: Continuum.

Mezirow, J. (1991). *Learning as transformation*. San Francisco, CA: Jossey-Bass.

National Art Education Association. (1994). *The national visual arts standards*. Retrieved from http://arteducators.org/store/

Ruskin, J. (1893). *The two paths: Being lectures on art*. New York, NY: Maynard, Merrill & Co.

ABOUT THE AUTHOR

Laura Gardner began her career teaching art to young children in the Hudson Valley. She moved down the river to New York City to attend Bank Street College of Education and teach art in Manhattan. Further south, in North Carolina, while raising her family, she worked in the design and furniture industries. She recently completed her doctoral work at Union Institute and directs graduate programs in arts administration and art education at Winthrop University in Rock Hill, South Carolina. She is a letterpress printer and book artist.

CHAPTER 30

A Holistic Approach to Teaching Art in High School

Karen Cast

This article describes one of my preservice experiences as an art educator when using a holistic approach to teach visual arts in a high school art class. It includes a brief theoretical framework, a proposed definition for a holistic approach to art education, and an explanation of how a particular art assignment aided in the positive transformation of a high school art class during the implementation of an art unit.

As a preservice art educator, I have a deep sense of connectedness with the universe and it is my goal to enable and nourish my students' own sense of connectedness. Agreeing with Miller, I believe that holistic education enables children to be "connected to knowledge, community, the environment, and to the cosmos" (Miller, 1993, p. 64). Ultimately, many students who pass through the doorway of the art classroom will not pursue a career in the arts; however, I believe their time spent in the art room can serve to strengthen them as individuals. As I incorporate each aspect of the self—mind, body and soul—in the learning process, I hope to afford my students a more complete education. I further hope that this holistic approach will be transformative in that it will enable students to experience a sense of interconnectedness within themselves and with others.

Art education through a holistic approach nurtures the student's inner life and allows significant connections to develop between the student and the subject matter (Miller, 1998). Addressing "big and small questions" about the human experience within the context of art can also help relate material to these personal questions, which Delacruz (1995) suggested are, "...questions that artists in every culture have asked (either directly or implicitly)" (p. 102). Yet holistic art education is not only a matter of individual experience. Instead, according to Gude (2009), "through art, the self becomes vitally interested in other selves, sensing the possibilities and problems of those selves within oneself" (p. 4). Issues of self-identity and connectedness addressed with a holistic approach, focus on intellectual development, but equally on emotional, aesthetic, moral, and spiritual growth (Miller, 1998). Because all of these aspects are integral part of the content of art, it might be imagined that such holistic learning would happen naturally in art education. However, as Campbell (2006) suggested, teachers need to intentionally create curricula that addresses these aspects of human development.

One aspect of a holistic approach to art education is the development of spiritual awareness. Art educators who have researched spirituality in education understand the potential of visual arts to allow students the chance to develop socially, academically, and spiritually (Campbell, 2006; Miller, 1998). In combination with the growth of artistic skills and creative thinking, spiritual awareness has practical implications. For example, it can transform students' understanding of such issues as diversity, multiculturalism, and social justice leading to more meaningful and effective actions in the world. In preparing students for engagement in these larger fields of action, participation within a school environment can be seen as a socialization process in which questions and issues of difference surface; thus, opportunities for collaboration and dialogue in the art classroom are potentially numerous (Gaudelius & Speirs, 2002). The lesson discussion that follows addressed the spiritual dimensions noted here as well as the more familiar aspect of the spiritual in terms of religion.

THE CONTEXT

Issues relating to holistic education, including the social and spiritual dimensions discussed here, were foremost in my mind recently when I began my last placement as a preservice art educator in relatively new Catholic high school under a seasoned, caring art educator. One of my teaching assignments was to design and implement a series of lessons appropriate for the Honors Art class, comprised of nine senior high students, three young men and six young women. The first 2 weeks, I observed my cooperating teacher as she conducted the art class. During this time, I did what was usually expected of interns: I took careful notes regarding seating arrangements, names, and reminders to myself on what to remember when I did begin to teach, as well as making other observations regarding interactions between the students themselves and between the students and the classroom teacher, Sarah. As I interacted with the students, I learned their names and they learned mine. However, I very much wanted to get to know each one of them better, so I frequently engaged in conversations with them, asking them all sorts of questions about themselves. They shared their future plans and aspirations with me as well as telling me what activities they most enjoyed. Sometimes they also talked about the situations they faced during the daily grind of the school day.

Once I became settled into the school routines, it was time to develop my own lesson. Sarah knew that I had a lot of experience as a practicing glass artist, so she asked me if it would be possible to teach a unit involving glass to this senior art class. She thought that her students would really enjoy the exposure to this new medium and she was confident that they would be responsible with the material. As I reviewed my field notes, I recalled that one of my students, Nejmun, was Muslim. Realizing that she didn't exactly fit in with her classmates, in my observational notes I had made a note to myself to find ways to bring her into the discussions more and to find ways that the other students could interact with her. Having spent several years working with glass, I realized immediately that a glass mosaic project would be a great idea. In addition, I had studied Arabic mosaics as research for several of my projects in the past, and realized that the mathematical precision and complexity of Arabic designs would be a challenge for this group, but one that they could certainly rise to. As I mulled over the project, I began to write out my lesson plan in detail; it was at this point I realized I had only a superficial and limited knowledge of Islam. I was, therefore, very concerned that I would in some way unknowingly offend Nejmun. As I collaborated with Sarah, we came up with a solution to this problem. This was the idea: to ask Nejmun if she would be willing to teach the class about Islam, Islamic calligraphy, and Islamic art, providing her fellow students with the background information that they would need in order to do the project. Besides providing a useful learning experience for all of us, I realized that this effort might serve a more personal purpose in helping to bring out this student and encourage closer connection with her Christian classmates, while perhaps also promoting greater appreciation among them for Islamic culture and art.

So I asked Nejmun if she would have time to meet with me after school, as I wanted to discuss the upcoming art lessons with her. She graciously agreed to meet with me that afternoon. I was a little nervous in asking her if she would mind teaching the class and me about Islam, Islamic calligraphy, and Islamic art. I didn't want to overload her with more work, nor did I want her to feel trapped into agreement. I therefore carefully explained the art project that I had hoped to bring to the class and acknowledged my dilemma: that I just wasn't knowledgeable enough about Islam to teach the project accurately. I then explained that the class would be asked to create a design for a glass mosaic tabletop. The design was to be based on traditional Islamic designs using the complex mathematical precision that they incorporate; also it had to include Islamic calligraphy, and the color choice had to be split-complementary. Despite my worries, Nejmun became quite excited about the project and, as I explained what her role would be, she readily agreed to the assignment.

The classroom teacher, Sarah, was also quite excited, and somewhat amazed, when I informed her that Nejmun would be willing to teach us. She noted that Nejmun, even though very personable, was for the most part an outsider in the class and very quiet. I assured Sarah that I had been careful not to exert pressure on Nejmun and I had certainly given her many opportunities to say no. Having helped ease her worries, Sarah gave me the go-ahead and so I informed Nejmun that she would be presenting the week after I introduced the project.

The next few days were filled with preparations for the lesson, amassing supplies, refining the lesson plan, creating handouts and an exemplar as well as preparing PowerPoint presentations just to name a few. Finally, the day arrived and I introduced the mosaic project to the students during a PowerPoint presentation, using many of the images that Nejmun had shared with me. I took extra time explaining to the students that I did not have a deep understanding of Islam or Islamic calligraphy and that that particular knowledge was essential for them to complete the assignment. However, I explained to the class that we did have a resident expert who had agreed to teach us all about her faith and its culture. I then introduced Nejmun and the class was pleasantly surprised and excited. Nejmun came prepared with colorful calendars displaying current Islamic artworks, a beautiful leather bound Koran, art history texts on Islamic art, and other books on Islamic calligraphy for her classmates to peruse at their leisure after her lectures. She also had a well-thought-out lesson plan and shared her personal insights and knowledge with the class. We were all enthralled by her style and the ease with which she led the class, and were impressed with the way she fielded questions from her classmates with such grace.

When the actual mosaic project began, the students were asked to draw three thumbnail sketches of designs that they might like to attempt. Once the thumbnails were completed, they were to meet with Nejmun so that she could offer advice on how to keep their design accurately within an Islamic framework. Each student carefully designed their thumbnails and came prepared with a list of words they wished to include in their design. Nejmun patiently met with each one and offered assistance in constructing their words using Islamic calligraphy. Two of the students had chosen designs that would not have been found within Islamic culture and Nejmun was quick to inform them that their choices would be inappropriate and why. The students quickly deferred to her and changed their designs so as not to be offensive.

Each student was given a 24" diameter round wood table, upon which to assemble his or her glass mosaic design. (Figure 1). Then the students were required to accurately draw their final design choices in full scale on the wooden tabletop. With the design elements approved, the students chose their split-complementary colors, which are formed by finding complements like yellow and purple and then choosing the colors on either side of the complement, like blue-violet and red-violet. I was the resident expert in glass, so when it came time for the students to begin construction of their mosaic tabletops, I took over and led the class. It was exciting to watch their faces as they rummaged through the boxes of glass that I had brought in searching for their split-complementary color choices (Figure 2).

Equally interesting, the dynamics of the class had subtly changed. Nejmun was no longer on the fringes observing rather than interacting; she had moved to a place of prominence and importance. Her peers now actively engaged her in conversation. They also became more

FIGURES 1 AND 2. Finished mosaic tabletops.

interactive in general as they began mentoring one another in the art of glass cutting. As a result, the atmosphere in the classroom felt friendly, focused, and yet lively and light-hearted. Students, including Nejmun, began sharing their plans and dreams. Nejmun openly shared her desire to attend medical school, which brought nods of approval from all her classmates, and she expressed her love for art as well. She had now become an important part of the group, while the group itself had bonded more closely together and taken on a new dynamic personality. They had become a community of student/artists.

CONCLUSION

This experience reflected the principles of holistic art education—balance, inclusion, and connection (Miller, 1993). The unit theme was chosen as a way for the students to make connections between their own views and those of the "other." The project inspired acceptance of Nejmun, thereby including her in the class community. And the unit provided balance in that the art classroom and activities highlighted or illuminated particular qualities of the student connection with others during the socialization process. As I reflect back on that project, I smile. It was truly a success. Yes, the students had created fantastic artworks, many of which brought in significant sums of money at the school's year-end fundraiser. But more importantly, the project served as a vehicle by which to build a bridge from one culture to another. All of us went away with a greater understanding and appreciation for those of the Islamic faith. Most importantly, Nejmun went from a being a wallflower to a highly respected member of the class, and all of us gained a greater understanding her, her faith, and her culture.

REFERENCES

Campbell, L. (2006). Spirituality and holistic art education. *Visual Arts Research, 32*(1), 29-34.
Delacruz, E. M. (1995). Multiculturalism and the tender years: Big and little questions. In C. M. Thompson (Ed.), *The visual arts and early childhood learning* (pp. 101-106). Reston, VA: National Art Education Association.
Gaudelius, Y., & Speirs, P. (2002), *Contemporary issues in art education.* Upper Saddle River, NJ: Prentice Hall.
Gude, O. (2009). Art Education for democratic life (Lowenfeld lecture). Paper presented at The National Art Education Association Annual Conference, Minneapolis, MN.
Miller, J. P. (1998). Making Connections through holistic learning. *Educational Leadership, 56*(4), 46-48.
Miller, R. (1993). *The renewal of meaning in education: Responses to the cultural and ecological crisis of our times.* Brandon, VT: Holistic Education Press.

ABOUT THE AUTHOR

Karen Bernier-Cast is a doctoral student at the University of Illinois at Urbana-Champaign. She has been a practicing artist, specializing in glass, for 20 years, and is the Assistant Director of the Saturday Art School program in the School of Art + Design, UIUC.

CHAPTER 31

How Am I Like a Tree?

Aileen Pugliese Castro

For a number of years, I have sought to design art educational experiences for elementary children that foster metaphorical and relational thinking. One particular exercise I used with elementary students I now use with preservice teachers. The exercise is called "How are you like a tree?" It was used with my elementary art students (Castro, 2004) to develop relational awareness with the "more-than-human" world (Abram, 1996). This involves developing a deeper relationship with the idea of self and the natural world. The following chapter is a demonstration of how this kind of relational thinking between the self and more-than-human world prompts opportunities for critical reflection for preservice elementary teachers. As with the elementary students, by asking preservice teachers to consider their relationship with the more-than-human, they have to consider their own internal interconnected relationships. At the same time, the exercise provided a space for them to reflect on their own beliefs, relationships, and goals as future educators. Another attribute that connects this exercise with holistic art education is that it invites reflection simultaneously on the individual's past and on his or her individual and on our collective future.

Like all worthwhile educational experiences, the exercise addressed in this chapter provided learning for students and teacher alike. I used this exercise initially with elementary students when I taught in Baltimore, Maryland. When I began teaching an art course for preservice elementary general classroom teachers at The University of British Columbia I was presented with an audience that was different in age as well as culture. I chose this exercise in part because I also wanted to know where these students were in their own lives, experiences, and knowledge. As such, it was one of the first activities on the first day of our course.

Before asking students how they were like a tree, I began by asking students to draw a self-portrait. They drew their face from memory on one half of a handout. On the other, I asked them to write about their strengths, weaknesses, and future goals. Since this was a course for non-art major preservice teachers, the portrait drawing provided me with an opportunity to assess their technical skills and personal goals. Not unexpectedly, students' drawings were mostly contour line, as they used the pencils or pens they brought with them to class. Their reflections ranged from describing their strengths as organizational skills to a fear of being in charge of a class of students. Most expressed that they wanted to be successful teachers.

At that point, I introduced the tree exercise, in part because I wanted to know still more about the students: their frames of mind, such as how expressive, creative, or imaginative they were; and the kinds of divergent thinking of which they were capable. I also wanted to get them thinking about their internal relationships with those of a more-than-human world. For some of the students, this was the first time they had used art materials since they were in elementary school. I introduced— and, for some, reviewed—the kinds of materials they had available to them in the classroom to use for the exercise, including different kinds of papers, coloring materials, tools, adhesives, and so on.

I began the "How am I like a tree?" exercise by asking students to close their eyes and imagine the day they were born. I stated that on the day they were born a tree sprouted up from the ground. I then asked students, "If you were to come across this tree today, what would it look like?" I then continued with this visualization: "You may or may not know where exactly this tree is, but it is as old as you are today. It has been growing just like you have and has faced challenges, both positive and negative, just like you." I guided them to specific details of their visualization: "Think about the kind of tree it is. How big is it? What color is your tree? Does it change colors with the seasons? What makes up your tree? What kind of leaves does it have? Does your tree grow fruit or flowers? What does your tree feel like? What does it smell like? Can you eat from this tree? Where do you think it is growing? Is there anything nearby or close to it? How is your tree like you?" I then asked students to open their eyes and select materials to begin representing their tree.

Students were able to select from a variety of papers and materials that would best express the image of the tree that they had visualized. I encouraged students to consider the expressive and metaphorical qualities of the materials and what meaning they would bring to their works. Some students responded immediately by selecting materials and started working. Some explored the materials first on scrap paper to see if it was appropriate to their ideas. Some searched for an image to reference from books, magazines, or the Internet. And some sat and reflected quietly before getting started. While students worked, I repeated the prompt. I asked them to consider the characteristics of their tree, and the similarities and differences between themselves and their tree. As the students finished their images, I asked them to write about their tree. Some students used an extra piece of paper, some wrote directly into their visual journals, and some students wove these words into their artworks.

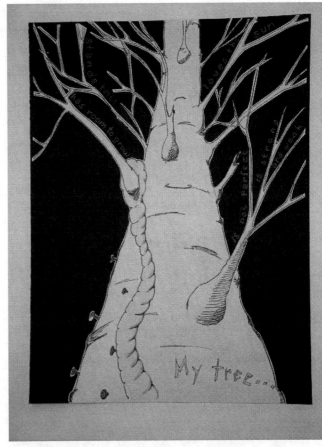

FIGURE 1. "My Tree." Photograph by Susan Brise, 2008.

In my elementary school classroom, a 1st-grader reported being "fast, full of energy and loves to play," or a 5th-grader commented, "I am similar to my tree because we are both lonely" (Castro, 2004, p. 19). I found that my elementary students focused their ideas on the present self and less on their future self. This was different from the university students, who reflected on their life history and how that shaped their future. Mike, an older preservice teacher, stated "I would never stop growing as a tree—the same as I would never want to stop growing in experiences as a person" (Mike Rourke, personal communication, January 6, 2009). Other students would note differences in themselves and their trees, such as "I am different from my tree because I am mobile and still finding my way, where as the tree is confident in where it is" (Glenda Meehan, personal communication, January 6, 2009). Susan described different characteristics about herself, stating "My tree... stands tall, has room to grow, loves the sun, is not perfect, is strong and weak" (Susan Brise, personal communication, September 4, 2008).

Some students, like Claire, communicated that they had difficulty with drawing, as well as with their self-images as teachers:

> Initially I found this activity stressful because as our class closed our eyes and imagined our trees, I could only visualize the roots and the trunk. I could not see if it would be an apple tree or an evergreen. I wanted it to bear all sorts of fruit, yet stay green in

the winter. But each time I tried to imagine what it would look like, I drew a blank. So I decided to illustrate exactly what I could see and think about why I couldn't see the rest. I feel like I am still changing and growing each year, and trying on all sorts of hats. It would be hard to pick one kind of tree to represent me. I feel a lot more confident with where I've been and where I have come from than where I'm heading, so the roots and trunk were easier to draw than the top of the tree. I like big bold shapes and colours when I create art—maybe because I knew I'd have to draw it I didn't allow myself to see lots of small detailed leaves. How can I gain more confidence in my self image? Is this really necessary to being a good teacher or is it perhaps good to acknowledge that all people are complex and ever-changing whether child or adult? (Claire Wells, personal communication, September 4, 2008)

Many students commented on their surroundings and not just the tree. Local landscapes, and the students' experiences in them, shaped their responses. Kevin stated, "My tree grows where I most like to be. Gazing out over the ocean, thinking about far off places. We were both raised at the ocean and have been influenced by its beauty and power" (Kevin Dimmick, personal communication, January 6, 2009). In one class, three students, all sitting at different tables, drew their tree growing off the edge of a cliff along the water. Jennifer expressed how others around her have had such an important impact on her throughout her life:

> Something that was just as important to me as the tree was the background. As a tree is partly a product of its surroundings and I know that I grew up the way I am because I grew up against a beautiful background. I am surrounded by wonderful people, numerous advantages and a favourable environment, and I wanted to represent that in my painting. (Jennifer Cowell, personal communication, January 25, 2007)

FIGURE 2. (left) "My Tree." Photograph by Kevin Dimmick, 2009.

FIGURE 3. (right) "How are you like a tree?" Photograph by Jacqueline King, 2007.

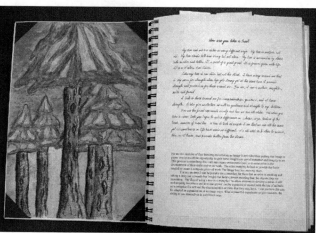

Jacqueline shared that her tree is surrounded and supported by others. By inviting these preservice teachers to reflect on their relationships with the more-than-human world, they were able to see their histories and possible future as interconnected.

At the end of a class, I asked my preservice teachers to reflect on ways in which they could use this lesson in their future classrooms. Many commented about how this would be a great introductory activity, as a way to get a glimpse of the whole student. Jacqueline stated that it could provide an opportunity for their students to make connections to telling meaningful stories in both words and images:

> My tree and me are alike in many different ways. My tree is mature, not old. My tree stands tall and strong but not alone. My tree is surrounded by others, both smaller and taller. It is part of a great forest. It is forever green with life. It is a Western Red Cedar. Like my tree I am older but not the oldest. I have many around me that I rely upon for strength when life gets stormy, yet at the same time I provide strength and protection for those around me. You see, I am a mother, daughter, sister and friend. I look to those around me for companionship, guidance, and at times strength. I also give protection as well as guidance and strength to my children. For me, the forest represents society and how we are all alike. Yet when you take a closer look, you begin to notice differences in shape, size, texture of the bark, numbers of branches. When I look at people I see that we are all the same, yet circumstances in life have made us different. We all need each other to survive, lean on at times and provide shelter from the storms. For my students I can help make the connection for them that an artist is speaking and telling a story not in words but images that hold a deeper meaning than the objects they are recreating. The idea of using a tree as a metaphor 'to allow student to develop a sense of self and empathy for others and how one grows' can be expanded in so many ways. What a powerful experience to give students the ability to see themselves in a different way. (Jacqueline King, personal communication, January 25, 2007)

FIGURE 4. "Snow Falling on a Maple Tree." Photograph by Kelsey Singer, 2007.

Kelsey stated that "this lesson would be useful in a classroom near the beginning of the year in a grade seven class when the students are considering their lives so far, and the daunting idea of life after elementary school" (Kelsey Singer, personal communication, January 25, 2007). This could also be an opportunity for elementary-age students to reflect on how elementary school could prepare them for what they will become in the future.

After one of my classes, a student turned to me and said, "I have never done a self-portrait before, and here you had us do two in one day." From my experience in working with the diverse range of learners from elementary to high education students, I see this as a way for artists to express themselves visually and metaphorically. This holistic exercise allows me to get to know my students, but it also allows them to get to know themselves in relation to the more-than-human world and their relationships with each other in a safe, non-judgmental, and expressive environment. Every dimension of a person is considered through relationships of personal identity and ecology and metaphors of self. It is important to understand these connections as they influence our own teaching. Teacher identity, of who we are, affects not only our own artmaking, but also our own teaching and classroom environment.

It is interesting to compare the students' reflections from one assignment to the other as a way of considering the nature and benefits of holistic education. In the case of the self-portrait, students did write about themselves, but admittedly the reflections did not go very deep and were more or less concentrated on themselves in isolation: that is, after all, what a self-portrait is. Perhaps another reason that the reflection was limited was due to the fact that the students may have been intimidated by having to portray themselves directly as they appeared.

The exercise with the tree was a totally different type of experience. First, they were working not from something real and observed, like their own faces, but an imaginary tree. Also, they were able to address the tree as a metaphor *for* the self, rather than as a representation *of* the self. This could also be liberating because it gave the students a chance to create associations that go beyond obvious solutions. Finally, and perhaps most importantly, the tree was part of a larger environment, encouraging students to think of themselves as connected, part of a larger whole. As seen in the captions and illustrations, the responses from students show this kind of connectedness as part of a deeper reflection about themselves, their lives, and their goals as teachers.

Holistic education is exemplified by this exercise in several ways: first, in the way that it enables students to reflect on themselves in multi-dimensional ways; second, in the way it engages word-making combined with picture-making; and third, in that it helps students identify ways in which they are interconnected, not isolated.

The challenge would be to carry this kind of expanding, and increasingly complex, sense of self throughout the course, while at the same time encouraging students to apply their self-discoveries to even more engaging interdisciplinary activities, connecting art to other fields of study while connecting them all back to the students themselves.

REFERENCES

Abram, D. (1996). *The spell of the sensuous: Perception and language in a more-than-human world.* New York, NY: Random House.

Castro, A. P. (2004). *Introducing metaphorical thinking to children.* Baltimore, MD: Maryland Institute College of Art.

ABOUT THE AUTHOR

Aileen Pugliese Castro is a Visiting Assistant Professor at Concordia University, Montreal. She has more than 13 years of experience working with elementary students, and more than 4 years in higher education in the US and Canada.

CHAPTER 32

The Ethic of Caring Holistically for Art Students: Esmeralda's Boutique

Laurie A. Eldridge

Good art education involves more than outstanding pedagogy, sound content knowledge, or exemplary student products. It involves understanding students as complete beings and meeting their holistic needs so the above can take place. This can involve understanding the kinds of stresses that students experience outside of school, and the kinds of basic needs that are not being met, thus preventing them from optimal learning. This level of caring requires art educators to reflect upon how we have traditionally understood and approached students versus how we may holistically perceive students. In this chapter, a practicing art educator applies the principles of care theory and reflective practice to her involvement in a community outreach program at her high minority, low socioeconomic level school, and so demonstrates how this experience improved her pedagogy, her relationship with students, and her sense of self.

CARE THEORY
The Most Vulnerable Students

Why students become at-risk for low academic performance or failure has been linked to family systems, low-quality education, and poverty. Students who live in communities that experience joblessness or low paying jobs, housing problems, little or no access to health care, and racism live with these stressors every day. Students in these communities are more likely to experience the effects of addiction on families and on individuals, defiant peer subcultures such as youth gangs, and children who rear themselves even in the presence of parents. These vulnerable children are most likely to attend schools that are under-funded and under-performing. The physical and emotional condition of schools, especially in deteriorating or devastated communities, has an impact on educational achievement. Students who encounter ill-maintained, inadequately equipped and unaesthetic campuses, one-size-fits-all teaching, insensitive and ineffective teachers, oppressive school policies, and poor school climate have additional challenges to gaining an education (Bowker, 1993; Taylor-Dunlop & Norton, 1994; Phuntsog, 1998; Valenzuela, 1999; Sanacore, 2000; Nieto, 2006).

Minority students may also encounter difficulty in school because their home cultures are substantially different from the cultures of their schools. When home cultures and school cultures are different, or even clash, students' risk for academic failure is intensified because they do not have the types of experiences that schools expect they should (Sanacore, 2000). Finally, students who experience a long series of life stresses may opt out of school through a variety of behaviors including dropping out, self-destructive behaviors such as drug and alcohol abuse, and seemingly self-affirming attitudes of defiance (Taylor-Dunlop & Norton, 1994; Conchas, 2001; Delacruz, 2008).

There is, however, hope for even the most challenged populations when the right conditions exist within the school, community, and/or family. For example, Conchas (2001) reported that low-income students of Mexican origin can succeed when they find supportive ties within schools and seek out mentors or advocates to help them. Similarly, Bowker (1993) found that academic success among Native American females was associated with a caring adult, often a teacher who was a personal advocate. Other factors included a strong sense of spirituality and low family stress (Bowker, 1993). The research cited above does not imply that minority students and students in poverty are innately at risk for failure, but it does indicate that they are compromised in an at-risk context. Helping these vulnerable students be successful learners is, therefore, an equally complex, nuanced process that involves understanding the distinctive needs of these unique learners (Reyes, 1997; Sanacore, 2000). This process includes developing caring schools and caring art educators who are part of these schools.

What are the Qualities of Caring in Academic Settings?

It is important not to confuse care with sentimental emotion as opposed to thoughtful and conscious action. The concept of caring in academic settings moves beyond an individual who is seen as a caring person to the establishment of a cultural norm of caring relationships (Neal, 1999). This norm involves developing a community of people (teachers, administrators, and so on) who make an effort to empathize with someone else's life issues. Genuine caring communities are also places where there is a collaborative spirit, where all stakeholders feel a sense of belonging, where there is connection and trust between students and teachers, and where students see adults acting in caring ways toward each other. Here, there is genuine respect for students and their families.

Many researchers have found significant correlations between caring and learning. Tarlow's study developed a system to rate schools on their levels of caring. Schools with a higher caring rating were found to have higher academic performance and fewer behavior problems (Tarlow, 1994). Solomon and Battistich studied the effect of community on affluent and high poverty schools. Socialization theory basically postulates that children will adopt and feel committed to the norms and values of socializing agents, such as schools, when they feel bonded or attached to these agents. This happens when the agents satisfy basic needs for feeling supported, cared about, and listened to. The phenomenon of satisfying these basic needs is called *community*, a widespread opportunity to participate actively and meaningfully in community activities and decision-making. This study found that students in higher community-level schools exercised more autonomy, participated in more classroom decision-making and collaborated more with each other. Students in high poverty schools were found to have less opportunity to be autonomous and participate in decision-making, and they experienced less emphasis on both academics and pro-social values. Students in higher poverty schools were also less likely to experience a caring and supportive school environment. However, the negative effect of poverty level on students' attachment to school only occurred among schools with low community levels, and the evidence in this quantitative study showed that the positive effects of community were particularly pronounced in some instances. Students in high-community schools reported greater interpersonal concern, pro-social behaviors, interpersonal skills, and feelings of efficacy, along with less smoking and less delinquent behavior. The researchers concluded that a caring, supportive and responsive community may be particularly important in impoverished communities (Solomon & Battistich, 1993). The bottom line is simply that, when students feel cared for, affirmed, and supported, they do better in school. They have better chances of being knowers and learners, and, last but not least, they even score higher on standardized tests (Kang, 2006; Nieto, 2006; Larkin-Strathy & LaRocca, 2007).

Pedagogical caring in such communities is evidenced through meaningful, supportive, rewarding, and productive relationships that teachers have with students. At the same time, students have opportunities to help others and support one another. Furthermore, the cultural integrity of students is maintained through respecting diversity, creating inclusive environments, and using multiple instructional approaches and varied learning experiences that cross disciplines and cultures (Phuntsog, 1998; Lumpkin, 2007). High behavioral and academic expectations are also in place, along with discipline and order, but not oppressively so; students should feel free to ask questions and risk making mistakes (Taylor-Dunlop & Norton, 1994; Neal, 1999; Sanacore, 2000; Gallavan, 2005; Nieto, 2006, Larkins-Strathy & LaRocca, 2007; Lumpkin, 2007). A positive learning environment such as this can bind teachers and students across differences in race, gender, economics, and class. One important result is greater student optimism (Conchas, 2001). Vulnerable students need hope for their futures and must come to believe that school can be an avenue to success (Brown & Skinner, 2007).

Art educators can easily be part of caring school communities in ways similar to those described above. Delacruz (2008) encouraged art teachers to take the time to do the things that matter both in and out of classrooms. Her view is that by creating caring classrooms, art educators are helping to create more caring societies. She stated,

> Our art educational aims must embrace notions of a citizenry that is creative, caring, and connected and one that is imaginative, informed, and engaged with others toward our mutual goals of building the kinds of worlds we ourselves wish to inhabit. (p. 14)

Art educators must also find meaningful connections to the things that students care about (Delacruz, 2008). This can mean helping families with basic necessities like clothing and food.

Caring in this context is thus not just an inner attitude, but rather a set of behaviors that is recognized by students. Among other things, teachers who are perceived as caring by students are attentive, respectful, helpful, good listeners, and concerned about the social and academic welfare of students. These teachers are helpful with both schoolwork and the pragmatic aspects of life. Even young students can recognize the qualities of a caring community. A study of African American elementary students, for example, found that the children preferred learning environments where teachers displayed caring bonds and attitudes toward them, where they experienced community- and family-type classrooms and where teachers made learning an enjoyable process (Howard, 2001). Older students might say something like, "I want teachers who talk to us and not at us!" Caring teachers employ reflective listening skills, such as the listener paraphrasing what the speaker says, perception-checking, in which the listener states what she thinks the speaker is feeling, and non-judgmental or non-prescriptive listening, in which the listener responds not by prescribing advice but by helping students problem-solve. Teachers like these are perceived as trustworthy (Tarlow, 1994; Brown & Skinner, 2007).

While some teachers naturally seem to have the caring qualities listed above, others may be challenged to learn effective ways of caring that can positively influence their students (Kang, 2006). One means toward that end is to develop and maintain a sense of self-scrutiny and reflection. Through self-scrutiny, teachers can monitor their thoughts, feelings, actions, and frames of reference in their interactions with students. They can then reflect upon these phenomena in order to accept and understand, or to modify their own behaviors, in order to create safe, predictable, and equitable havens for learning (Scott, 1999). By contrast, the lack of introspection may mean that teachers are not challenging themselves (Phuntsog, 1998), and may not be creating the most effective learning environment for their students. While some may think self-scrutiny is a sign of insecurity, just the opposite is true. The disposition of self-scrutiny actually takes a degree of self confidence. Moreover, ego, anxiety, and fear, among other things, can interfere with teachers' efforts to engage in both clear-minded action and reflection (Tremmel, 1993).

Maslow's Pyramid

Maslow developed a theory of human motivation that posits a hierarchy of human needs based on two groupings: deficiency needs and growth needs. These are often expressed in the graphic of a pyramid. Each deficiency need must be met before moving to the next higher level, and once these are satisfied then the individual will be able to move on to growth needs. The first four levels are the physiological needs, safety and security, belongingness and love, and esteem—the need to achieve, be competent and to gain approval and recognition. Maslow stated that an individual is ready to act upon growth needs if and only if the deficiency needs are met. Individuals at the lowest level seek coping information in order to meet their basic needs, and information that is not directly connected to meeting these needs is simply left unattended. Maslow saw the main growth need as the need for actualization, which he differentiated into four levels: cognitive, aesthetic, self-actualization, and self-transcendence (Huitt, 2004). It is important to note that in, order to reach the level where someone can act upon the aesthetic need, as well as the cognitive needs to know, understand, and explore, all deficiency needs must first be fulfilled. This means that students need to be fed, clothed, clean, and housed, and feel a sense of safety and belonging in order for art learning to take place (Figure 1).

FIGURE 1. Maslow's Pyramid. Compiled from information at www.edpsycinteractive.org/topics/conation/maslow.html

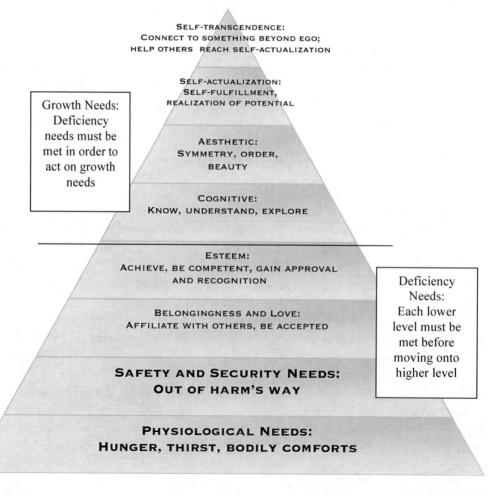

Moreover, as previously stated, learning in general, as well as aesthetic learning in art classrooms, will not be fostered until students, especially those from lower socioeconomic levels, are convinced that a teacher genuinely cares for them. This situation, in terms of schooling, may be understood in terms of another important concept: trust. Determining if someone cares for you is the first step in a trust relationship, and some level of trust is necessary to risk learning (Tarlow, 1994; Bulack, Brown & Potter, 1998). Tarlow found that when students perceived a teacher as genuinely caring for them, they experience a reduction in anxiety, which is often the result of life stressors such as the effects of poverty. Tarlow proposed a strong relationship between feeling less anxious, feeling good, and feeling safe, and this addresses students' security needs as defined by Maslow's pyramid (Tarlow, 1994). Again, the relationships are clear: When teachers genuinely care, students sense it and respond by optimizing their commitment to learning and putting forth greater effort to reach their potential (Lumpkin, 2007). Genuine caring meets students' needs for understanding and attention, which are part of "belongingness and love" on Maslow's pyramid (Tarlow, 1994). But students aren't the only ones who benefit from developing caring relationships within a school or community. Teachers may achieve their own self-actualization and self-transcendence through helping others, most significantly their students and their students' families (Clarken, 2008). I found this to be true when I became involved in the school program titled "Esmeralda's Boutique."

IMPLEMENTING ESMERALDA'S BOUTIQUE

I teach visual art to kindergarten through 8th grade students in a large metropolitan area in the southwest. In 2007, the school where I teach received a grant that provided school clothes for needy students. Although I did not know it at the time, this grant would have a significant impact on my teaching and my personal life. I had, to some extent, already begun to develop a holistic view of reflective practice, embedded in my world-view as a Native American person. In part as a result of the grant, I now see my life world as a teacher, my life world as a researcher, and my spiritual life as seamlessly melded together. I have learned that, to be a sensitive, aware, and reflective teacher I must practice what some Native American people call "Walking the Red Road." That means being aware that all thoughts, speech, and actions have reciprocations beyond what we can immediately see. Walking the Red Road also implies that we must always bring a "good heart" into our actions so that our words, deeds, and thoughts are not damaging to others. This means that in my interactions with others, including my students, I must try to stay aware of what I say and think and feel so that I can attempt to respond to others' actions and words with integrity. I endeavor to be attentive to how my thoughts, speech, and actions affect my students in their art learning and in their journeys to becoming caring, thoughtful adults. Before explaining what brought me to this point, I should give a little more background about the school where I teach and the grant that has influenced both my school and my life.

The elementary school where I teach is located in the highest crime rate district in the city. There is significant drug activity and gang presence in the neighborhood where the school is located. At this Title I school, 78% of the student body receives free or reduced breakfast and lunch, and the school is part of a program that offers free lunch and breakfast during summer vacation.

Poverty is a vicious cycle within the close-knit, often intergenerational and predominantly Hispanic households of the neighborhood. Many properties have recently been offered for sale due to the current economic downturn. Several of these homes are vacant and in disrepair, with weeds growing everywhere. The neighborhood has a general air of neglect, and even working people have few resources, but they are doing what they can to make it through rough times.

Responding to some of the most basic challenges faced by this community, the grant the school received provided funds for the purchase of school clothes, shoes, underwear, and socks for students in need. The school nurse, along with the intervention specialist (similar to a school counselor), decided how to purchase and distribute clothing. They were adamant that they did not want the students and their families who received this assistance to feel like they were charity cases to be pitied or looked down upon by others. Toward that end, the planners decided that, even though the clothing would be available at no cost, the space had to look like an upscale boutique clothing shop, not a bare bones thrift store. That was how the concept of Esmeralda's Boutique was born (T.H., personal communication, 7/2/2009).

I became involved when the nurse and the intervention specialist asked for assistance in renovating the spare office that was to become Esmeralda's Boutique. Several teachers helped paint the walls a warm buff color. Members of the school community donated shelves, cabinets, clothing racks, a mirror and a chest of drawers. I assisted with the painting of the walls, and helped members of the student council clean up the clothing racks. In addition, I used my art background to engage 4th graders in sponge painting the furnishings, and drew up the initial plan for arranging the space. Then, with the help of other teachers, I placed the furnishings, and tried to style-up the space with silk plants, baskets, and decorative items I had picked up at second-hand and discount stores. Clothing was purchased with the grant, and other donations were added such as gently used clothing, backpacks, and school supplies. The result is a pleasant, relaxing atmosphere where students and their families can come to "shop."

When her partner was no longer able to commit the necessary time, the school nurse became concerned that one person would not be able to manage the needs of maintaining Esmeralda's Boutique. That is when I got even more involved. Now, I assist with tasks such as sorting through donated clothing items, keeping the clothing racks and shelves organized and stocked and keeping records of donations and inventory. We also keep a record of which students and families receive assistance so that we can look for trends and either refer them for additional social services or put them on a list for additional assistance during the winter holidays. What has become the most meaningful task for me is helping students and their families select clothing and other items.

Esmeralda's Boutique has grown to include toiletries and hygiene items, basic household goods such as laundry soap, toilet paper, and light bulbs. Some basic pantry staples are also kept on hand. These last additions have obviously become increasingly important with the economic crisis. Also, we have added a new service: gently used and new dresses, dress shirts, and ties that students can borrow to wear for performing arts concerts and 8th-grade promotion activities. Complementing the initial grant, monetary donations for these items have begun to come from private individuals and civic groups. Teachers, support staff, community members, and administrators of the school also provide additional resources that are beyond the scope of the grant.

Despite all these efforts, we have found that occasionally a student is not comfortable receiving assistance from Esmeralda's Boutique or that what the student needs is not available in Esmeralda's Boutique. In such cases, the nurse, the principal, or the assistant principal will take the student shopping at a national chain known for low prices or a large discount store. Funds for these shopping excursions are often from donations; otherwise, the adults will simply use their personal funds.

Nonetheless, not all families want their children to receive help from Esmeralda's Boutique, so we are careful to contact parents to make sure that assistance is welcome. In addition, not all staff members seem supportive of the efforts of the people involved with

Esmeralda's Boutique due to their personal beliefs about charity. For my part, I have become increasingly committed to the Boutique, because of what it has done for the students, and for what I have gained from being a part of the project. For both of us, the experience has confirmed the research reported above about the importance of caring in education.

MY CHANGING RESPONSES TO STUDENTS

As I became more involved in Esmeralda's Boutique I noticed a number of changes in my experience at school. For example, some of the students whom I helped select clothes and other items became more talkative with me and paid better attention in class. If they had a behavior issue, they either monitored themselves better or they apologized for disruptive behavior. The texture of our student/teacher relationship in class was subtly changing.

For my part, I was becoming increasingly aware of students as more than just a physical presence in my classroom. Previously I would have noticed if a student had a shoe with a sole that flapped because I would have been annoyed by the noise. Now I ask if that student has other shoes at home that fit, and if not, I ask if they would like a new pair. I now notice when a student has shoes that are kicked off easily while playing soccer at recess because they are two or three sizes too big, or if a student wears shoes with the toes cut out or the sides sliced because they are too small. I notice if a student wears the same two outfits over and over. I have learned to listen for a stomach that rumbles or to look for a student holding her sides or looking faintly sick, and then ask them with a smile what they had for breakfast or lunch or dinner to find out if they had eaten recently. I have learned how to delicately talk with a student who has body odor and listen when she explains that her family doesn't have water and they have to carry water over from a neighbor's to wash themselves and their clothes. I have learned to pay attention, to really pay attention, to the children who walk through the door of my classroom.

I have looked into the lives of our students, and now have a better understanding of the many stresses that they face, and what causes some of the behaviors they exhibit. Even when a student displays behavior in my art class that is defiant, or too loud, or when he can't sit still, or she argues with others, or when she grabs all the crayons so others can't use them, I find a time in the lesson when I can quietly and privately ask them if they had a good morning or if something is going on at home. When I ask these questions, I have had students tell me that they do not have electricity, that they stayed up most of the night playing basketball outside so they would not have to listen to their parents argue, that their aunt and her children moved into their house because they lost their home and the little kids are sleeping four to a bed—three side-by-side and one crossways at the bottom who gets kicked a lot and does not get much sleep.

Equally, since becoming involved with Esmeralda's Boutique, I have become more reflective of my own actions and reactions. I am now more likely to check myself before I say things to make sure that I am not asking personal questions, such as "Does your family currently have utilities?" in ways that belittle or demean the child and her family. I am also much more committed to using listening skills such as paraphrasing and reflective listening. I make sure that I talk to each student individually, and somehow acknowledge that person separate from the group, at least with a look and a smile. I call that a "heart connection" because, along with that look into that student's eyes and my smile, I try to telegraph to that person the emotion of acceptance, that I feel joy that the person is in my classroom at that moment, and have no negative thoughts of any kind—even if she has just asked me to repeat everything I just said for the third time. When I do this, I find that even the least motivated students respond with some attempts at trying assignments, although they have been defeated again and again in their attempts to learn at school.

Yes, there are still the kids who are constantly irritating. There are still students who never seem to pay attention, the ones who are "too cool for school," the ones who try to be invisible. But, because of my involvement with Esmeralda's Boutique, I try not to let myself get hung up on the actions that make teaching harder and instead try to see the person inside that is hiding behind those behaviors. This helps me to address behavior issues with more calm and detachment, not taking what students say or do personally, or, when they do make an attack personal, I take a deep breath and don't attack back. I find that I am much more able to keep to high standards of behavior and high standards of learning with compassion. I now understand that there are days when some kid will need to chill out for half of the class before he is calm enough to focus on the assignment, so I keep a rocking chair in my classroom just for that purpose. I also understand that sometimes a student needs to be told in very clear language that a certain behavior will not be acceptable in my classroom. At the same time, I have learned to become more flexible and to let go of the notion that equality does not mean that everyone is treated the same.

To sum up, I now see each student more clearly as an individual. I am more open to their foibles and mistakes, more gentle in how I talk to and with them, more aware of how much support and what kinds of support it really takes to help these vulnerable students learn, succeed, and grow into happy, healthy, well adjusted young adults.

This growing understanding of my students' needs has also changed what I teach and how I teach it. First, I have increased my focus on bringing artworks into my students' lives— artworks that I think will help them to see themselves reflected in the school curriculum. I also help them to learn about the wider world beyond the small geographical area they roam on their bikes and their return trips to Mexico.

Second, I have begun to focus more on studio assignments that allow students to express a positive identity about themselves. I've found that this is possible, even when the topic of the lesson seems unconnected to their lives. For example, 6th-grade students study ancient China in social studies, so I developed an art lesson about China that connects to the social studies curriculum, meets state and national standards for visual art, and allows for positive identity development through goal setting. Initially, we discuss New Year traditions in China including the symbolism of the colors red (good fortune) and gold (wealth). Then students use bamboo brushes to write the phrase "gong hei fat choi" (happy new year) in simple Chinese calligraphy. Students next develop four to six goals for the new year, even numbers being the most auspicious during the lunar new year. Then they learn how to use Western calligraphy pens and write out their goals with the calligraphy pens, mounting them on red paper and decorating them with gold glitter. These are posted around the room.

Another lesson that focuses on students' development of self-worth starts as students do a detailed observational drawing of one of their own hands. Then, they surround their hand drawing with words that express who they are, including only positive things about themselves. To begin, students write out 50 words on lined paper so I can check for spelling. I also ask them to edit out negative words or statements. I help them think of positive qualities they themselves possess; when they are stuck, and I ask them to help each other to think of positive things about each other. I have become increasingly aware of what little self-esteem many of my students have as a result of living in poverty. It is as though they sometimes cannot see any positive qualities in themselves at all. I have found that some students cannot name even five good characteristics about themselves. Some students cannot name any, some only one. Then I have found that I need to tell them that I have watched them and that I know that they are good people with good hearts, and I name five character traits for them so they know for sure that I see them for the persons they truly are, and sometimes are afraid to be.

INVOLVEMENT WITH ESMERALDA'S BOUTIQUE AFFECTS SELF

Being with students and their families as they "shop" in Esmeralda's Boutique has affected my approach to teaching, and has changed me personally and helped shape me into a better person. Sometimes this can happen in unexpected ways. For example, the clothes purchased with the grant have the price tags on them, and several students have purposefully looked for clothes with price tags on them, including a young man who selected a pair of jeans and stated with great emphasis that these pants were just like from the mall, not Goodwill. I knew that I helped him feel a little better about himself because he did not have to wear hand-me-downs. Similarly, I learned about personal pride and identity both from the student who was deeply embarrassed to be in Esmeralda's Boutique but was there out of the necessity to shop for a younger sibling, and from the student who was jumping up and down at the excitement of being in Esmeralda's Boutique. I was deeply touched by the mother who hugged me with tears in her eyes after we provided clothes and shoes for her, her husband, and their children after their home burned. I loved watching the 8th-grade students getting ready for the pro-motion ceremony; a boy standing proudly in front of the mirror adjusting a tie looking more like a young man than a child, or a girl looking at herself in heels and a formal for the first time seeing herself as the woman she is becoming. I feel a touch of pride when students who enter Esmeralda's Boutique look around with a little bit of awe and say things like "this looks like a real nice store," because I know then that we have hit the mark in trying to take the stigma out of receiving assistance. I am also humbled when a student asks, "Can I pick out something for my little cousin?" or "My mother would love this, can I take it?" All these people, and many more, have helped me to become a happier person. I feel more fulfilled because I know for sure that I am making a difference in these kids' lives. In being of service to others, I feel that I am more committed to Walking the Red Road.

CONCLUSIONS, FUTURE STEPS

Becoming aware of the holistic needs of art students can be life changing and community changing and can transform pedagogy. Nonetheless, schools must expect conflict, difference, and contradiction to naturally arise when committed to an ethic of caring (Neal, 1999). For example, caring schools need to develop rules for offering specialized assistance in ways that recognize the complexity of "fairness." Fair for whom? Fair according to whom? Fair using what criteria and how are these criteria applied? Should school personnel respond to each person who receives assistance in the same way or respond on a case-by-case basis? Perhaps they should receive assistance according to their value to society or according to merit? Each aspect of distributing assistance can be weighed more heavily than another, depending upon the social philosophy of the decision maker (School Mental Health Project-UCLA, 1998). In response to such concerns, art educators in such schools need to be deeply reflective about their own personal beliefs regarding caring for others and providing assistance for others as they develop or extend caring classrooms. Similarly, art education professors who hope to prepare caring art teachers need to be aware of how they perceive the whole student in their classes, and how this influences their pedagogical philosophies. By changing how we teach, we just might be able to change the world.

REFERENCES

Bowker, A. (1993). *Sisters in the blood: The education of women in Native America*. Newton, MA: Women's Educational Equity Act Publishing Center.

Brown, D., & Skinner, D. A. (2007). Brown-Skinner model for building trust with at-risk students. *National Forum of Applied Educational Research Journal, 20*(3), 1-7.

Bulack, C. R., Brown, C., & Potter, L. (1998). Behavior that creates a caring learning community. *Journal of a Just and Caring Education, 4* (4), 458-470. Retrieved from www.westga.edu/~cbulach/sclimate/caring1.htm

Clarken, R. H. (2008). *Seeking a brain, heart and courage: On becoming a holistic teacher*. Paper presented at the American Educational Research Association Annual Meeting, New York, NY. (ERIC Document Preproduction Service No. ED502124)

Conchas, G. Q. (2001). Structuring failure and success: Understanding the variability in Latino school engagement. *Harvard Educational Review, 71*(3), 475-504.

Delacruz, E. M. (2008). From bricks and mortar to the public sphere in cyberspace: Creating a culture of caring on the digital global commons. *International Journal of Education & The Arts, (10)*5. Retrieved from www.ijea.org/v10n5/

Gallavan, N. (2005). Helping teachers unpack their "invisible knapsacks." *Multicultural Education, 13*(1), 36-39.

Howard, T. C. (2001). Telling their side of the story: African-American students' perceptions of culturally relevant teaching. *The Urban Review, 33*(2), 131-149.

Huitt, W. (2004). Maslow's hierarchy of needs. *Educational Psychology Interactive*. Valdosta, GA: Valdosta State University. Retrieved from www.edpsycinteractive.org/topics/conation/maslow.html

Kang, S. (2006). Identity-centered multicultural care theory: White, Black, and Korean caring. *Educational Foundations, 20*(3-4), 35-49.

Larkins-Strathy, B. K., & LaRocca, D. J. (2007, April). *Teachers as caring classroom leaders: A case study of practices that encourage the hearts of students*. Paper presented at the 39th Annual New England Educational Research Organization Conference, Portsmouth, NH.

Lumpkin, A. (2007). Caring teachers: The key to student learning. *Kappa Delta Pi Record, 43*(4), 158-160.

Neal, K. (1999, November). *Developing and sustaining teacher communities: Caring as central in teachers' negotiation of reading instruction and curriculum implementation*. Paper presented at Annual Meeting of the Mid-South Educationl Research Association, Point Clear, AL. (ERIC Document Reproduction Service No. ED436527)

Nieto, S. (2006). *Teaching as political work: Learning from courageous and caring teachers. The Longfellow Lecture*. Child Development Institute, Sarah Lawrence College, Bronxville, NY.

Phuntsog, N. (1998). The magic of culturally responsive pedagogy: In search of the genie's lamp in multicultural education. *Teacher Education Quarterly, 1999*, 97-111. Retrieved from www.teqjournal.org/backvols/1999/26_3/phuntsog.pdf

Reyes, A. (1997, October). *School productivity: teachers as resources*. Paper presented at the Annual Meeting of the University Council for Educational Administration, Orlando, FL. (ERIC Document Reproduction Service No. 423583).

Sanacore, J. (2000). Promoting effective literacy learning in minority students by connecting teacher workshops to the Comer Process. *Reading Psychology, 21*(3), 233-255. (ERIC Document Reproduction Service No. ED 438 541).

School Mental Health Project-UCLA (1998). Toward a caring school culture. *Addressing Barriers to Learning, 3*(2), 1998. Retrieved from http://smhp.psych.ucla.edu/lesson32.htm

Scott, R. (1999, February). *Literacy is about "teacher caring."* Presentation given at the annual meeting of the Wisconsin State Reading Association, Milwaukee, WI.

Solomon, D., & Battistich, V. (1993, August). *Students in caring schools and classroom communities*. Presented at Annual Convention of the American Psychological Association, Toronto, Canada.

Tarlow, B. A. (1994). Caring, a process that varies: A study of caring in families, schools, and voluntary agencies. *Dissertation Abstracts International, 55*(03A), 0754 (University Microfilms No. AAI9417714).

Taylor-Dunlop, K., & Norton, M. (1997). Out of the mouths of babes... voices of the at-risk students. *Clearinghouse, 70*(5), 274-278. (ERIC Document Reproduction Service No. ED 402523).

Tremmel, R. (1993). Zen and the art of reflective practice in teacher education. *Harvard Educational Review, 63*(4), 434-458.

Valenzuela, A. (1999). *Subtractive schooling: U.S.-Mexican youth and the politics of caring. SUNY Series, The Social Context of Education*. State University of New York Press.

ABOUT THE AUTHOR

Laurie A. Eldridge is an independent scholar who teaches art to elementary and middle school students in a Title I school in Arizona. Her research interests include care theory, Native American art, and cultural competency.

CHAPTER 33

Cultivating a Healing Classroom Environment

Camilla McComb

> "Good teachers join self and subject and students in the fabric of life"
> —Parker J. Palmer (1998, p. 11)

Parker Palmer is a writer who speaks to the spirit of teaching. In his book *The Courage to Teach* (1998), Palmer identified two truths of teaching: "The first is that what we teach will never 'take' unless it connects with the inward, living core of our students' lives"; the second is that "...we can speak to the teacher within our students only when we are on speaking terms with the teacher within ourselves" (p. 31). When I first read Palmer's words, they brought inspiration, along with a sense of curiosity. What does the teacher inside of me look like? How do I connect my knowledge of artmaking to students in a way that makes the knowledge and skills relevant to their daily lives? The drive to embody these two truths in my classroom was strong; I did not fully know what Palmer meant, however, until I considered the role of artmaking in the healing process.

THE JOURNEY WITHIN

On the morning of July 16, 2004, I learned what it was truly like to experience loss in my life. My mother was preparing to leave on our Friday morning shopping excursion when a pulmonary embolism ended her 60-year life. I heard my name, followed by a "thud" to the floor... motionless body... 911... flashing red lights... paramedics... doctors...a chaplain whisking Dad and me to a private room... phone calls to relatives... decisions... private tears.... The shock was instantaneous. One moment, Mom was greeting me with a hug at the door, and 90 minutes later the doctor was asking if I wanted to spend time with her body before leaving the hospital.

After a strong and measured public response to mom's death, I continued to privately feel overwhelmed with grief and regret, having difficulty comprehending the magnitude of the loss. I began to write notes, sketch images, and talk with friends who helped me realize that the angst of my grief and the persistent feeling of regret came from being denied the opportunity to say goodbye to my mother. To remedy the situation, I turned to painting.

Saying Goodbye (Figure 1) was created to visually represent the perception I had of my mother's transformation from this

FIGURE 1. *Saying Goodbye*, 2004, Camilla McComb, watercolor.

world to the next. The bottom figure, cuddled in a fetal position, represents her wounded body lying on the floor. Energy from her body radiates toward the outstretched violet figure, inviting the spirit to come and collect her for the journey. The green floral urn, while being a vessel for the crossing, cannot contain the spirit that continues moving toward the heavens and grows in the lives of those still living. Placing these images onto watercolor paper allowed me to ease their intensity, and gave my mind a new and refreshed perspective from which to see the memory. The creation of this painting allowed me to take a highly charged life event and channel the emotions and images lingering from the experience into a painting that now brings comfort and peace of mind.

While the creation of *Saying Goodbye* was cathartic, painting it also served to open a new realm of possibility for my work with students. I began to consider that, if painting could help me heal from the loss of my mother, then perhaps it could help 6th-grade students reflect on and heal from the multitude of hurts, disappointments, and struggles they face in their own lives. The *teacher within* spoke, suggesting a more mindful and holistic way to design lessons that would not only allow students to learn required artistic objectives, but also could facilitate a connection between 6th-graders and the lives they experience and imagine (Greene, 1995). As in my own case, I knew I would be touching upon realms of action, feeling, and thought not often addressed in the classroom setting, even in the art room. The process of doing so was more challenging than I expected, but also more rewarding.

IMPACTING THE CLASSROOM: TOUCHING THE LIVING CORE

This newfound understanding of painting and its ability to heal suggested two specific questions: In what ways do 11- and 12-year-olds need to heal? And could art curricula be designed to provide students the opportunity to explore and reveal meaningful aspects of their own lives? In order to know how students need to heal, I set out to design a "learning progression" (Popham, 2008, p. 24) that would connect students to issues pertinent to their lives.

The goal of the learning progression was to have each student produce a 16″ x 20″ narrative painting based upon life experience as a means of personal expression. The lesson sequence was built around autobiographical paintings of Marc Chagall, because I felt that the floating, abstract, and disjointed imagery used in Chagall's paintings would create a sense of intrigue that could easily capture the imagination of students. Chagall's choice of subject matter could also lead students to include both realistic, figurative subject matter and highly abstract imagery, allowing students to make a variety of strong connections.

I then created a PowerPoint presentation featuring several of Chagall's paintings, with emphasis on his 1911 painting, *I and the Village* (Walther & Metzer, 1993, p. 20). This presentation emphasized the principles of design, while providing a clear example of personal connectedness that would be pertinent to students as they related to the immediate relevance of their village, town, and city. Chagall's imagery was also unusual, with its references to Russian customs and culture unfamiliar to my students, which meant they would have to delve deeper into themselves in order to understand the digital images before them.

Having taken adequate time to prepare and research the artist and the paintings necessary for the lesson, I felt confident students would also be ready and willing to respond by making personally relevant artwork. I began the lesson sequence by showing students Chagall's work, engaged them in critical discussion, and then asked them all to create personal paintings just as Chagall did. I had a rubric so everyone knew exactly how the paintings would be assessed.

Contrary to what I anticipated, the lesson was a flop.

The completed paintings were beautiful, but when it came time to take the artwork home, several students asked the question that all caring art teachers dread: "Do I have to keep this?" My heart sank. Outwardly, I scolded students and explained how proud their parents would be to see their artwork. Inwardly, I cringed, realizing that, while the lesson sequence produced well-executed paintings worthy of display, it somehow missed helping students make the personal connection I was seeking. I further felt that, unless I could lead students toward making personal connections, I was never going to know if classroom artmaking activities could, in fact, be used to assist them in healing. To achieve that goal, something was clearly missing, and I knew I had to alter the sequence before repeating it. But what was the missing link?

I sat down with my plan book to reflect upon the classes that completed the painting project, and determined that they each seemed to relate to Marc Chagall and that they genuinely liked and appreciated the reproductions shown. Students replicated some of the dreaminess indicative of Chagall's work and responded well to the challenge to their skills required to execute the complex painting. Since the product being produced was visually strong and engaging to viewers, I decided that Chagall would stay.

Realizing that the exemplar was appropriate, I then examined the students' paintings more closely, asking the question, "What is missing?" The answer was obvious: Students had trouble relating images depicted in their paintings to their own lives, so they side-stepped the problem by simply mimicking the master. If Chagall included buildings in his work, then so did they. If he included religious imagery, they felt they should also. Because they were really only copying Chagall's idea, students could not adequately explain *why* they had included a particular image when questioned, nor could they determine any relevance the image had to their lives. Instead of creating personal narratives, students were creating images they thought they ought to create (Raider-Roth, 2005). What was missing was Haley's love of horses and Kayla's fear of spiders. Cody was a skateboard fanatic, yet there was no evidence of this love in his artwork. I now realized that students needed to understand that they had my permission to include the everyday aspects of their lives in their artwork, and that the things they love, hate, avoid, and covet could all be valid subject matter for artmaking.

The second time I taught this lesson sequence, I attempted to solve the problem by initially prompting students to think more explicitly about their own lives. Students were therefore asked to list responses to four categories: hobbies, dreams, relationships, and secrets. Students worked to list 10 items per category, and then shared responses with their peers. Many listed the sports they play, goals they have for the future, favorite relatives, or endeared pets. Many did not know how to respond to the "secrets" category. Students were cautioned not to reveal family secrets; instead, this category was designed to help them think of something that no one at school knows about them. To make this easier, I asked students to keep these responses private, unless they really wanted to share with others. One boy told us that he loved to knit with his grandmother, and a girl who seemed painfully shy in class revealed that she was a real blabbermouth at home. Conversations around these prompts created a spark of enthusiasm in the classroom, as students realized where they had commonalties and differences with their peers.

Once students had some concrete ideas about their lives, I took time to help them figure out how to represent these concepts by viewing, questioning, and creating symbols. Initially, each class worked together to determine popular, relevant symbols they encounter every day. Whether it was the Nike Swoosh™ in the middle of the chest or a logo representing the hottest skateboards, students understood the power and significance of being seen wearing the "appropriate" cultural symbols. They then began to design and draw six simplified symbols based upon their created lists. With these images in hand, we proceeded with the Chagall lesson as previously described.

Once again, students created strong paintings, only this time they wanted to keep them! Students peeked in the door on their way to recess, asking, "Have you graded our paintings yet?" They were genuinely connected to the works created, and were eager to take them out to show classroom teachers and parents alike. Early in my career, I would have called this response a success, and stopped there to relish the excitement of having created a lesson sequence that inspired students to want to keep and display their artwork. Now, however, as I stood viewing the collection of paintings, it became obvious that we were still brushing the surface. Students were connecting to general concepts, but there were no specifics. I could see that a student was connected to soccer, for example, but knew nothing more. What I wanted to see in these paintings was the lives of students represented at a deeper level. After these two attempts, I concluded that this task was going to require some outside assistance.

If I have learned one lesson in 20 years, it is when to ask for help! I took a couple of paintings along with my questions, to speak to the gifted specialist assigned to work with teachers in the building. She promptly adopted the concern; 3 days later, she popped her smiling face into the classroom with an armload of tangible ideas and resources. We sifted through the possibilities and found an activity that seemed a perfect fit to the lesson, one that could take student responses to a higher level.

Once again, I started the painting sequence with the symbol discussion—only this time, before introducing students to Marc Chagall, they completed Lesson No. 3 of Nancy Atwell's *Lessons that Change Writers,* titled "Mining Your Heart" (2002). Atwell's lessons are presented with accompanying handouts and the prompts are designed for written responses, which I modified to allow students to write *or draw* their responses. The premise of the activity was simple: Students were asked to draw a large heart in the center of their paper. Within the heart, they could either write about or draw images representing what lives deep in their hearts. Atwell called this "heart mapping." The word "mining" in the lesson title was critical: when questioned, students understood that, when we mine, we are looking deep, below the surface. Atwell's lesson suggested a series of prompts that I used:

> What stays in your heart? What memories, moments, people, animals, objects, places, books, fears, scars, friends, siblings, parents, grandparents, teachers, other people, journeys, secrets, dreams, crushes, relationships, comforts, learning experiences? What's at the center? The edges? What's in your heart? (Atwell, 2002, p. 16)

Students worked quietly for a good 20 minutes, then the noise level in the room gradually increased. I was about to redirect what appeared to be an unruly class, but then I realized the students were telling each other stories from their childhood. The most enthusiastic stories being told were responses to the "scars" prompt. Students were once again connecting to their peers, distinguishing similarities and differences as they had during the previous version of the lesson, only this time each student truly felt unique. Even if every one of them had a scar on his or her leg, each story of how that scar occurred and how he or she responded in the moment was distinctive.

To reinforce the truly personal nature of this assignment, I shared my own "heart" with the class, where they learned of the recent loss of my mother. Students took their "hearts" home and brought them back the next day with more stories from parents and relatives to add to the mix. I had not planned to have students present these hearts to their peers, but finally did simply because students insisted on sharing their work and sharing their lives.

The addition of this activity had another surprising effect: It impacted student discussion surrounding Chagall's work. Instead of waiting to be told what Chagall intended, students

seemed more eager and able to speculate. Once some students became comfortable expressing perceived connections, others would comment on the validity of the claim. I had always
encouraged students to offer visual evidence to support their interpretations, but here they
were holding one another accountable without intervention. After twice revising the learning
progression, I found that students were finally learning to view artwork and its purpose on a
personal level, understanding *why* an artist might create artwork based upon life experience.
Then, having viewed Chagall's paintings, students began designing their own, realizing that
their lives, too, could be the subject of artmaking.

Another surprise that emerged this time was a marked difference not only in subject
matter selection, but also in student work habits. Without being prompted, they began almost
from the outset working on compositions, considering how the arrangement of shape and
form helped to communicate ideas. Rather than jamming the painting full of symbols, students were carefully placing those images to depict specific stories from their lives. Moreover,
instead of asking for help drawing specific shapes and objects, students sought advice on how
to create a mood or feeling.

Finally, after three tries, I had found an instructional sequence that could make both the
study and creation of art relevant to students' lives. Still, there was more to making these personal connections than simple sequencing.

As this endeavor began, the question I asked was: In what ways do 11- and 12-year-olds
need to heal? The answer to this question became evident as students were exposed not only
to the lesson, but also to my own personal experience of loss. As I told my story, students
began to feel comfortable visually expressing their own sense of loss; for example, depicting
images of beloved family pets now deceased. A few students
represented parents who had divorced, grandparents who had
died, and two 6th-graders independently used the opportunity
to express their thoughts also associated with the recent loss
of a parent (Figure 2). The most unexpected work came from a
girl dealing with the concept of abandonment. Her mother was
addicted to drugs and alcohol, causing the girl to be removed
from the home at age 7. She was placed in foster care and later
was adopted by a couple she came to love. The painting process
allowed her to tell the story, and the act of visual representation
helped her to realize that, despite losing her mother, she was
much happier with her new family.

By joining a positive classroom climate with a curricular
sequence that allowed students to bring their lives into the artmaking process, I had created an atmosphere that Lucy Andrus
(2006) called a *therapeutic approach* to art education. Unlike
the one-on-one conversations that art therapists might have
with students to alleviate tension or resolve conflict, my role as
a therapeutic art educator was instead to "facilitate the process
of self-discovery that occurs in the special relationship between
the student, his or her mental images, and the use of media to
express these ideas" (Andrus, 2006, p. 181).

The healing component of this sequence manifested as
children were able and allowed to place tragic, even painful
events or memories into the context of their academic, creative
lives. They could write and draw about these painful events

FIGURE 2. *My Mom in Life and Death*, 2005, Megan Starrett, gouache. Used with permission.

or losses, and the images became embedded into an array of positive ideas, helping students begin to realize the complexity of human experience. In designing a lesson to help students heal, the door for subtle expression was also opened. The stories students told were far more sophisticated, and riddled with specificity. Paintings no longer featured merely a soccer ball; instead, they represented the thrill of the first goal. Imagery transformed from a collection of hobbies to a visual diary of emotion-laden experience. Finally, as a result of this particular lesson, I had inadvertently become a "holistic" art educator.

Children entering puberty search and struggle to find their place in the world. Knowing how to use artistic creation as a form of expression gives them one more tool in assisting their physical, social, and emotional development, helping them to heal and grow into mature adults who are able to communicate their most personal thoughts and ideas. As teachers, our curricular sequencing can assist children in learning to self-determine artistic subject matter, creating artwork that can teach them something more of their inner selves. Perhaps this experience will assist them one day as they, too, look toward the teacher within themselves.

SEVEN RECOMMENDATIONS FOR CLASSROOM TEACHERS

Should you decide to open your curricular design to the healing potential of holistic art education through personal expression, consider the following elements.

- *Build Trust:* Make sure the students in your class know one another, and that you have taken time to establish classroom rapport, especially when working with children. It can take one class period or an entire grading period to develop a positive, safe climate essential to creating honest, personal artwork. Students who trust one another are much more likely to be open and honest in their artwork. Sharing your own life experiences can also help build trust, by letting students know their experiences will be heard and respected.

- *Set Boundaries:* The purpose of this process is to connect students to deeper, more personal levels of artistic thought, not to delve into the personal lives of students' families. Be sure to establish these clear boundaries from the start of the curricular sequence by placing your lesson into an academic context. Explain that you are helping them connect to their deepest ideas, but make sure to caution students that family secrets are best shared with the school counselor.

- *Include Writing Prompts:* If you begin a lesson sequence by asking students to draw their ideas first, then they will draw what they are good at drawing. Instead, consider asking students to initially describe their ideas in writing. Written responses invite students to consider the details of their memory or thought, and can provide rich resources from which students can later create unique visual imagery. Writing open-ended prompts that cover a wide range of emotion will allow students who feel they have nothing to heal from to create very personal work by focusing on someone they love or a memorable experience.

- *Pair/Share:* You can make students feel more comfortable in sharing ideas by pairing students. Sharing a response with one person before sharing an idea with the entire class makes the sharing process less intimidating. Make sure students are paired ahead of time with individuals who will respect the artwork and ideas of their partners.

- *Individualize the Project:* Offer multiple media options to students. Some feel comfortable drawing, while others would rather select images to rearrange. Remember that, in the early stages, the focus is on creating substantial, personally relevant ideas. You can always offer design advice once a good idea is born.

- *Become Introspective and Reflective:* Think introspectively about what you can bring to the lesson from personal experience. It doesn't always need to be deep and painful, but it helps your students connect with you as a person, and potentially with themselves in similar ways. Then, when setting goals, be willing to reflect and examine the products created to determine whether students did in fact achieve the specified goal. Teaching is an art as well as a science. It requires experimentation, and trial and error, before landing on the right mix to reach the population of students you are serving. If the sequence does not evolve as hoped, then look around and be willing to rely on your colleagues for intellectual assistance and support.

- *Assess for Understanding:* Follow the artmaking process with informal formative discussions and, if time allows, conclude with a summative self-assessment. In this instance, students wrote a five-paragraph paper explaining the significance of the images in their painting. This writing helped students better articulate their thoughts, and assisted me in evaluating the success of their artwork, as well as determining the quality and depth of their reflective processes.

I never imagined that reflection upon my mother's death would make me a better teacher. Painting what weighed on my heart allowed my artistic spirit to shine so students, in turn, could see artmaking in a meaningful light. Such a holistic approach to art education begins in the heart: *your* heart. In allowing the content of your heart to shape curriculum, you begin to cultivate a healing classroom environment.

AUTHOR'S NOTE

Thank you, mom, for nurturing in me the reflective skills necessary to have the courage to teach... for having the courage to persevere in forging a connection to my students and their lives.

REFERENCES

Andrus, L. (2006). Art education, art therapy and therapeutic teaching: Definitions, distinctions and common ground. In B. L. Gerber & D. Guay (Eds.), *Reaching and teaching students with special needs through art* (pp. 177-188). Reston, VA: National Art Education Association.

Atwell, N. (2002). *Lessons that change writers.* Portsmouth, NH: Heineman.

Greene, M. (1995). *Releasing the imagination: Essays on education, the arts, and social change.* San Francisco, CA: Jossey-Bass.

Palmer, P. J. (1998). *The courage to teach: Exploring the inner landscape of a teacher's life.* San Francisco, CA: Jossey-Bass.

Popham, W. J. (2008). *Transformative assessment.* Alexandria, VA: Association for Supervision and Curriculum Development.

Raider-Roth, M. B. (2005). *Trusting what you know: The high stakes of classroom relationships.* San Francisco, CA: Jossey-Bass.

Walther, I. F., & Metzger, R. (1993). *Marc Chagall 1887-1985: Painting as poetry.* Köln, Germany: Benedikt Taschen.

ABOUT THE AUTHOR

Camilla McComb is a National Board Certified Teacher (2006 Art/EMC) committed to improving instructional practices in K-12 visual arts education. She was awarded Master Teacher designation by the Ohio Department of Education (2008), and was granted the Robert Rauschenberg Foundation Power of Art Workshop Award (2006) based upon her proven work with children with disabilities. Her doctoral thesis, *Think, Record, Reveal: Studio-Process Assessment and the Artistic Thinking it Reveals,* (2010) combined theory in studio thinking, assessment, multimodal literacy, and self-regulated learning to shed light on the artistic thinking of pre-adolescents.

CHAPTER 34

How Art Endures: Implementing a Holistic Approach to Art Education in High School

Stacey McKenna

In this chapter I will describe how I facilitated the transformation of a high school art program by attending to the whole learning situation and then setting out to alter the dynamics of that learning situation by responding to each of its four components: context, learner, content, and teacher. First, I will identify my understanding of a holistic approach to art education. Then I will describe what I did to alter the whole learning system. I will conclude with some observations of the transformation.

The root *holo* is of Greek origin meaning *whole* or *entire* and refers to integrated wholes that cannot be reduced to the sum of their parts (Miller, 1996). A holistic approach to education might therefore be thought of as the purposeful integration of all parts of the learning system,[1] wherein the teacher's role is to attend to and select from among those possibilities that present themselves to her or his awareness. In this sense, teaching is about *minding—* being mindful in, being conscious of, being the consciousness of—the collective (Davis, 2004).

A learning system can be described as involving primarily four components: context, learner, content, and teacher (Levine, 2006; Eisner, 2002; Schwab, 1969). I propose that an art teacher who practices a holistic approach to art education is simply one who reflects on the relationship of those four components as they manifest themselves in her particular situation and who then initiates art experiences that might bring the four parts into more dynamic relationship, creating a learning system from which meaningful experiences might arise for *all* participants, teacher included. In my interpretation of a holistic approach to art education, *art experiences are central* to the teacher's responses, and it is through art experiences that the learning system transforms.[2]

The transformation reported in this chapter emerged out of my involvement with The Study Group for Holistic Art Education, which was initiated at the Maryland Institute College of Art for the purpose of exploring what holistic art education might look like in everyday practice.[3] At an early stage of our research, The Study Group reviewed holistic teaching and learning theories, as well as situations in which teachers attempted to apply aspects of holistic educational theory to their teaching practice.[4] Within this larger context, The Study Group noticed that four teacher responses appeared in multiple art teaching situations: In each situation, the teacher facilitated a safe and trusting community of learners, understood the learners, created art experiences to which learners could bring their own experiences, and varied instruction (Carroll, 2004). It seems logical that these four teacher responses are closely tied to the four parts of the learning system.

In this chapter, I have embedded each teacher response within a particular quality of the learning system in order to better explore the relationship of the parts and their interaction with the whole.

THE CONTEXT: ART EXPERIENCES CREATE A SAFE LEARNING ENVIRONMENT

Of the 1,600 students in the public high school where I taught in an economically prosperous suburb of Washington, DC, 300 were enrolled in art courses. When I began teaching there, I tried to create a comfortable working atmosphere by facilitating group discussions, speaking individually with students, encouraging students to move freely around the studio, and sponsoring art activities—intuiting that, if the students felt at ease, then they would be more likely to take creative risks. Despite those attempts, juniors and seniors in my Portfolio Development class still elected to sit at worktables in cliquish groups, and many did not even know all of their classmates by name. To alter that studio dynamic, I crafted the following art problem: "Interview an assigned peer-artist, and then make an homage sculptural head using the three-dimensional medium of your choice that will express something about them in addition to what they look like." Constructed this way, the habits, information, skills, and attitudes I hoped students would learn were embedded in the problem itself. Elsewhere, I have described how I paired students, modeled a peer-interview process, facilitated the sculptural responses, and recorded student reflections on the experience (McKenna, 2004b, pp. 47-49).

The finished sculptures demonstrated that the students had a better understanding of the structure of the human head and had a working knowledge with materials that were new to them as a result of the exercise. In addition, a dramatic shift occurred in the studio dynamic, or *milieu*,[1] which was quite evident to those of us in the room. That shift was further illuminated by surveys students completed after the experience; 95% of students said before this art problem they did not know their assigned artist-partner "at all," and felt "indifferent" toward them. Furthermore, 65% enjoyed being interviewed. One student shared that "I liked it because I could have a reason to tell [my partner] things that I wouldn't just come out and tell people." Another observed, "[The interviewing] was the best part of this assignment because it was a great chance for the students to socialize... everyone talked and smiled much more than usual" (survey responses, 2002).

When describing the atmosphere of the classroom while work was in progress, all of the students used positive adjectives—such as "friendly," "focused," "lively," "unified", and "light-hearted." One student characterized the environment as "The atmosphere was really... pumped. Everyone was interacting with one another. No one was left out or alone. The room was just vibrating cuz [sic] of the talking and getting along. It was a great vibe!" Noted another, "The atmosphere changed immensely because even the different tables started to talk to each other, which previously had never happened." Ninety-five percent of the students stated that they "liked" their artist-partner whom they previously did not know. The studio was transformed into a place of connectedness and community. Thereafter, I began every semester with interactive art experiences so that students built relationships early, and felt safe and supported in taking creative risks throughout the year.

THE LEARNER: ART EXPERIENCES SHOW ME WHO MY LEARNERS ARE

Although general information about my students could be gathered from school and community data, to learn about individual students, I created art assignments that prompted students to connect their lives with the artmaking enterprise—most often through the use of visual metaphors, by actively attending to daily life, or in using visual narrative. In this way, I learned about their physical abilities, their prior understanding of art, and their personal values (body, mind, and spirit).[5] At each lesson's conclusion, students wrote about the decisions they made, such as how visual choices conveyed particular metaphors or communicated personal experiences, so that much of who they were and what they valued was revealed. For example, for my Art I class (made up of 34 students of varied ages, interests, and abilities), I asked students to collect detritus from their daily lives over several days. Additionally, in class I asked them draw rapid visual responses to 15 instructions: "In the next 5 minutes, make a drawing from memory of an object you might use when you are 'just hanging out' at home," or "Using only color, line, and shape—no pictures, symbols, or letters—make a drawing that represents the sound of your favorite piece of music." Then, I gave the assignment: "Using the found and hand-made representations of your life, construct a metaphorical self-portrait that feels like you more than it looks like you." In constructing this piece, students realized that self-portraiture could be a metaphoric rather than a perceptually realistic image, and students had an opportunity to think deeply about what made them who they were. In written reflections on the completed works, students identified the aesthetic and metaphoric choices they had made, and how those choices revealed something about their identities. Jacob, age 16, said of his piece (Figure 1) that

> My self-portrait depicts me in a very accurate way. It shows that I am very skinny and wearing my usual attire, jeans and a tee-shirt. The chaotic shapes emanating from my head show that I usually have a lot on my mind. The large, bright, bold guitar is dominant because, for me, music dominates my life, and I could hardly go a day without listening to some sort of music.

Sally, age 15, described her self-portrait (Figure 2) this way:

FIGURE 1. (left)
FIGURE 2. (right)

> I really love stars. I have an earring that has stars on it, a shirt and skirt that have stars, and all of my shoes have stars on them. This is why I drew lots of stars in the

background. Second, the swirl placed as my skirt represents my confused feelings. I feel so confused and not clear in this country since it has been just 10 months I've been living here. Third, the picture of two girls' backsides sitting on the beach represents my emotional stability and calm happiness. I felt really relaxed when I was in Korea if I was sitting on the beach with my best friend. Even though I cannot go there with my best friend now, thinking of that time makes me little happy and relaxed. My life had lots of changes and lots of events and things made me. My life can be described as a pizza, like my face in the portrait, since a pizza is a product of mixing all kinds of things.

THE CONTENT: ART EXPERIENCES ARE PERSONALLY MEANINGFUL FOR ALL ARTISTS

In developing a more holistic approach, I created new lessons like the collage self-portrait just described, but I also altered old assignments with the intention of creating more relevant, engaging problems. I wanted to provide opportunities for students to make personally meaningful art regardless of whether they were in introductory or advanced classes. Nevertheless, while giving students more autonomy, I still wanted them to learn fundamental art processes and techniques. One way I did this was by altering an abstract painting lesson. In its first incarnation, this Art I lesson had an Elements & Principles approach in which students illustrated pre-defined moods like happy, angry, or excited after defining organic and geometric shapes, making a color wheel, and experimenting with symmetry. The reinvented lesson was described in the following manner: "Create a painted composition that is a metaphor for your own personality. Select the colors, shapes, and lines that you believe best represent your personality traits, and organize them in such a way as to represent who (or how) you are." To assist the students in finding personal meaning in their selection of colors, lines, and shapes, I developed a series of provocative, interactive experiences before students began designing and painting. One experience involved all of the students in a group re-imagining of the television program *Survivor* using Color Aid paper and reflection of self and community (McKenna, 2004a, p. 41). To assess the paintings, students were asked to describe how their choices (e.g., color mixing, shape and line quality, paint application) metaphorically represented their personalities.

Jingya, an Art 1 senior, reflected on her visual choices for her piece, entitled *Flying Dreams* (Figure 3):

> A major part of my personality is a fanciful dreaming and freedom of imagination. Almost every single one of my lines is curvy and wavy because of the random flow of thought—it also exemplifies an easy-going, mellow mood. Most of my shapes are irregular for unpredictability. The orange and green background represents an excitement in creativity—the colors are bright, suggesting eagerness; the shape is narrow on the bottom left-hand corner and gradually grows wider—the expansion symbolizes opening up and flourishing surprises. There's a purposeful imbalance and lack of exact pattern to represent unconventional surprises. The swirls and squiggly lines add to this craziness and zest; yet, at the same time, there's also a more pensive "out-of the box" sense, as symbolized by the darker shades of red, violet, and green. Overall, there's not really an area of dominance—rather, it allows the eyes to go wild along with the design, and to discover the imaginative freedom of endless possibilities.

Students who took art classes over the 4 years during which I facilitated these changes became quite adept at making meaningful choices for their artwork. As seniors, those students were truly independent "Independent Study" students, as they were better able to initiate self-directed, technically proficient, and personally meaningful work after 3 years of practice doing so. Not only did these students come up with individual projects that were

FIGURE 3.

personally engaging, but they also identified general strategies that suited their interests and creative styles, thereby potentially sustaining their efforts in art for years to come.

One student, Joe, chose for his Independent Study to sculpt from nontraditional materials; this stemmed from an experience in his junior year when, during a found-object art-to-wear assignment, he had discovered that a materials-based, problem-solving process felt right for him. Joe's Independent Study included *Toilet Paper Toilet*, in which he "wanted to show the idea of using a disposable material to make a non-disposable object," and *Student Absence/Presence,* for which he cast clothing retrieved from a donation bin. He wrote, "Early on in [Art I], I had the idea in my head that 'good' art was what looked real or what someone of importance said was 'good.' Now that doesn't matter so much, it is about saying what I want to say."

Another student, Rachel, writing about her series of paintings and drawings based on the theme *Reflection,* explained, "I think the creative idea is the most important thing to me as an artist. There are many artists, and I think the only way to survive among many artists is creative idea and concept. I think handling material and skills do not matter—just practice a lot, and enjoy art a lot, then the skills will be improved soon."

THE TEACHER: ART EXPERIENCES BECOME VARIED THROUGH COLLEAGUE COLLABORATION

Over lunch or after school, my two art-teacher colleagues and I shared our lesson experiences; together, we figured out ways to make all of our lessons more context-sensitive, learner-centered, and content-rich. Sometimes we traded courses, and in so doing found a number of opportunities for collaborative planning and integrating disciplines (Shauck, 2005). As our sharing and collaborating continued, we developed an outline of expectations, experiences, and assessments proceeding vertically from the Art I level to the most advanced courses. Since the outline evolved from our own reflective teamwork, we found it to be a significant asset for future communication, planning, and teaching.

CONCLUSION: ART EXPERIENCES TRANSFORM THE WHOLE ART PROGRAM

Prior to the implementation of changes described in this chapter, none of our students took the AP Studio Art Exam, and only two seniors went on to study art at the college level. Significantly, a radical change occurred in our students' involvement with art and pursuit of external recognition such as the AP exam, beginning with the seniors who had been a part of the 4 years of changes described here. Of that group of seniors, 17 of 19 passed or excelled on the AP Studio Art Exam, and 23 seniors were awarded more than $600,000 in merit-based scholarships to attend college-level art programs, including top-rated art colleges. Perhaps more important to me as a teacher were the changes in the day-to-day reality. As the implementation of context-sensitive, learner-centered, content-rich lessons continued, and as my colleagues and I continued collaborative and varied approaches to instruction, we noticed significant—but unexpected—changes in our students' behaviors. They had a greater willingness to mentor one another, an eagerness to help us, an excitement about discussing ideas, and greater focus on making their artwork. Yet even while the work ethic became more intense and serious, there was more laughter and ease in the studio; the whole art program had become a community of artists.

REFERENCES

Carroll, K. (2004). Developmental theory in a holistic context. In *Toward a holistic paradigm in art education* (pp. 7-9). Baltimore, MD: Center for Art Education at the Maryland Institute College of Art.

Davis, B. (2004). *Inventions of teaching: A genealogy*. New York, NY: Lawrence Erlbaum Associates.

Eisner, E. (2002). *The arts and the creation of mind*. New Haven, CT: Yale University Press.

Levine, D. N. (2006). *Powers of mind: The reinvention of liberal learning in America*. Chicago, IL: The University of Chicago Press.

McKenna, S. (2004a). Assignment: Make art, make friends. In *Toward a holistic paradigm in art education* (pp. 47-50). Baltimore, MD: Center for Art Education at the Maryland Institute College of Art.

McKenna, S. (2004b). Changing the mood: How to add personal meaning to an ordinary design problem. In *Toward a holistic paradigm in art education* (pp. 41-46). Baltimore, MD: Center for Art Education at the Maryland Institute College of Art.

Miller, J. P. (1996). *The holistic curriculum*. Toronto, ON: Ontario Institute for Studies in Education Press.

Schwab, J. (1969). The practical: A language for curriculum. *The School Review, 78*(1), 1-23. The University of Chicago Press. Retrieved from www.jstor.org/stable/1084049

Shauck, B. (2005). Artful collaborations. *School Arts, 104*(7), 43-47.

ENDNOTES

1. Davis describes a complex phenomenon, like a learning system, as being the product of its parts *and* their interaction. See Davis (2004), Chapter 14 -17, for a more in-depth description of ecological and complexivist approaches to teaching and learning.
2. See Davis (2004), page 152, for more information about transformation of complex systems.
3. The Study Group for Holistic Art Education was initiated at the Maryland Institute College of Art by Dr. Peter London and Dr. Karen Carroll, and met during 2001 and 2002.
4. Eisner elaborates on this term in *The Arts and the Creation of Mind*.
5. For further information on conceptions of mind, body, and spirit, in relation to art-making, see *Toward a Holistic Paradigm in Art Education*.

ABOUT THE AUTHOR

Stacey McKenna is a painter and art educator who has been a college studio art instructor for nearly 20 years. She was also visual arts department chair for a large suburban high school that earned national and regional recognition for her department and students. In addition to presentations at national and regional conferences, Stacey has curated exhibitions, worked in museum education, served as a visual arts curriculum consultant, and published articles based on her research. Stacey was the curriculum specialist for the 2008 Maryland Institute College of Art MICA-in-Tuscany Pre-college program and is currently a full-time faculty member in the Center for Art Education, Maryland Institute College of Art, where she teaches and coordinates the Graduate Internship Program for MFA students. She is finishing doctoral studies at Teachers College, Columbia University.

Laurel H. Campbell and Seymour Simmons III

Approaching this project, we were made increasingly aware (by allies and critics alike) of problems or concerns associated with the concept of holistic education, as well as with holistic educational practices. Over the course of reviewing chapters and assembling them into sections, we found that many of these concerns had been addressed, if not fully resolved, by one author or another. Yet even where problems remain, we were all the more convinced by what we read that the value of holistic approaches to art education—the promise that such an approach holds for children and young adults—is worth facing the challenges. In this chapter, we outline perceived problems and the responses to them from our authors, followed by a synopsis of what we consider to be the important possibilities holistic art education holds in light of student needs and other aspects of society today.

PROBLEMS AND RESPONSES

**Problem 1: *What is it?* **The concept of holistic art education is vague and hard to define.

- **Response:** We admit that the concept of "holistic education" is not self-evident, and may be subject to misunderstandings. For that reason, several authors in this anthology, including Campbell and Lawton, provide clear, concise definitions of holistic education as an approach to educating the whole child, addressing and integrating the physical/sensory, emotional, intellectual, social, and spiritual needs of the individual, while connecting the individual to peers, teachers, the community, the wider society, the world, and the environment.

**Problem 2: *Too open-ended.* **By this definition, almost any kind of teaching approach could be considered "holistic."

- **Response:** Because holism aspires to address various needs of every student, it must encompass a diversity of content. Moreover, to reach this wide population, holistic art education must accommodate a variety of different teaching styles and methods. That doesn't mean, however, that "anything goes." Only approaches that have the comprehensive needs of students at the center of their concern can be considered "holistic." Additionally, holistic art education promotes integrative and transformative learning by creating curricula that utilize all dimensions of experience. Examples of non-holistic art education include curriculum focused on a particular dimension (e.g., skills in a specific medium, art history, elements, and principles), as well as lessons that address several dimensions but lack intentional effort to connect the learning to students' lives.

**Problem 3: *Divisiveness.* **Holistic art education seems to oppose established approaches, such as emphasis on art disciplines, visual culture, aesthetic education, and others.

- **Response:** Holistic education is, in fact, inclusive rather than exclusive. As suggested, any approach can be holistic if it addresses a diversity of human dimensions and makes students' needs the central concern. Johnson's chapter demonstrates how holistic approaches can address the study of art, while chapters by Lee and Danker apply holistic approaches to art education based on the study of visual culture. Weida shows how holistic concerns can be applied to traditional approaches, such as teaching crafts. By contrast, Juan Castro, as well as Lin and Bruce, apply holistic theory to such contemporary concerns as the use of computers, new media, and social networking in the classroom.

Problem 4: *Substance and sustainability.* Holistic education is more of a romantic ideal than a valid approach with research to back it up. As such, it is likely to be just another educational "bandwagon"—here today and gone tomorrow.

- **Response:** In truth, holistic education is informed and reinforced by a growing body of research from a variety of perspectives. Jeffers addresses the relationship of holistic education to contemporary research in neuroscience, while Weisman and Hanes deal with the influence of cultural transactions and aesthetics on holistic learning. Other authors refer to cognitive psychology, developmental psychology, and educational assessment. In regard to the short-lived "bandwagon" argument, the large number of authors interested in this topic suggests that holistic art education does indeed have a future. Equally important, as noted in several chapters, it also has a long and distinguished history in educational philosophy, going back to Plato and Rousseau, as well as more recent theorists such as John Dewey, Maria Montessori, and Rudolph Steiner.

Problem 5: *Legacy.* Referring to Rousseau and Dewey, contemporary holistic approaches are no different from earlier attempts at "child-centered" art education, such as those associated with Victor Lowenfeld. As such, they suffer from the same limitations and problems, especially in putting undue emphasis on the child as an isolated individual while leaving out the wider social context.

- **Response:** At the start of this anthology, Burton addresses the relationship between earlier approaches and more recent ones, providing a comprehensive theory built on past practices but grounded in contemporary research and understanding. Sullivan then shows how the holistic artist/teacher can model social engagement through art. Both authors emphasize the importance of experiential learning and working with art media as engaging the whole learner, whatever their age or stage of development. For Burton, the learner is a young child or adolescent; for Sullivan, the subject is a mature adult who has spent most of his life as a professional artist. In subsequent chapters, "child centered" is redefined in terms of "child connected" (Miller, 1993), where the educational experience intentionally strives to connect essential aspects of self while also connecting the individual with peers, family, school, community, and the environment. Vignettes demonstrate how the theory of connectedness translates into practice in a wide range of settings, with diverse populations, and at different ages and stages of development. For example, Grube applies holistic principles to early-childhood education, while McKenna and Castro address implementing a holistic approach to art education in high school.

Problem 6: *Laissez faire.* Holistic art education's focus on hands-on art activities, creative development, and self-expression suggests earlier child-centered approaches in which "teaching art" meant simply giving students materials and leaving them alone.

- **Response:** Lindström's research on the assessment of creativity and Simmons's discussion of the "myths" of creativity explicitly dispute popular assumptions about *laissez faire* teaching, while other authors acknowledge the fact that, in this era of accountability, holistic art classes must address the full range of National Visual Arts Standards. Most important, however, is the fact that committed holistic educators realize that they cannot address students' comprehensive needs without developing their knowledge and competence by teaching them the skills and the content of the subject matter. Cummings and McComb demonstrate how this is done through projects based on authentic problems in the domain, which also relate to students' lives and interests. Such projects also involve students in the construction of knowledge and use assessment as an episode in learning.

Problem 7: *Spirituality*. Holistic art education often explicitly includes the spiritual dimension, with its controversial associations with religion and transcendence.
- **Response:** There are good reasons to be concerned about addressing spiritual issues in public education, ranging from the laws separating church and state to the view that spirituality is focused inwardly and not outward, distracting people from opposing injustice and other "real life" problems. In response to the first concern, many authors who write about holistic education, including Campbell, explicitly distinguish "religious" from "spiritual." Where "religion" is generally defined as an established belief system based on devotion to a deity, "spirituality" implies personal experiences such as a sense of interconnectedness among people and between people and nature. Moreover, following Campbell, spirituality has direct societal implications insofar as it involves basing one's actions on one's deepest values for social good. Gradle, among others, provides a narrative on spirituality in holism that widens the conversation to include diverse perspectives.

Problem 8: *Anti-Academic*. A holistic emphasis on physical/sensory skills and emotional issues undermines efforts to affirm art education's academic stature.
- **Response:** Holistic art education, as previously indicated, does indeed address students' intellectual/academic development. Nevertheless, other aspects of holistic development are equally relevant to learning in several important ways. As Eldridge shows, unless students' personal lives are sensitively addressed, it is quite likely that negative feelings, attitudes, and behaviors will almost inevitably interfere with learning in the content area. Where holistic concerns are neglected, students not only fail to learn, but all too often become self-destructive or explode in violence. Moreover, constructive attitudes and positive feelings are essential conditions not only for responsible behavior in school, but also for good citizenship, success in the workplace, and other aspects of meaningful involvement in society. Unlike certain academic areas, where considerations such as those just mentioned might appear to be tangential, art content has always included personal and social issues, combining emotion with thought and action. Art also frequently addresses the domains of ethics and values. As such, art classes provide the most appropriate place for addressing such concerns in school, providing occasions for students to look more deeply into works of art while using art as a means to better understand their own lives.

Problem 9: *Diversity*. Holistic education ignores postmodern issues such as multiculturalism and cross-disciplinary learning.
- **Response:** Many authors in this anthology dispute such assumptions, including Willis and Hanes, who demonstrate how Native American and Japanese cultures address holistic concerns. Powell, as well as Melamed and Hefferman, show connections between visual arts and other artistic domains.

Problem 10: *Practicality.* Even though art teachers recognize and value holistic concerns, it is unrealistic to expect them to teach this way, given pressures to address the standards and teach literacy skills.

- Response: No one would deny that addressing students' holistic needs, while covering the range of content included in the Visual Arts Standards, is a daunting task, especially considering the economic pressures that increase class size while reducing budgets, planning time, and even salaries. These, and similar real-life concerns, were foremost in our minds as we selected the chapters to be included. We wanted to ensure that many of these chapters, no matter how theoretical, contained an element of practice. We therefore sought contributions from currently practicing art teachers or about practicing teachers, such as the chapter by Sinner *et al.,* to show how this kind of teaching can be done today at all levels, with a variety of populations, and in a myriad of situations. In offering examples of actual projects or curriculum, such as those described by Aileen Castro, Caldwell, and Cast, we acknowledge that holistic activities come in a variety of shapes and sizes, according to the needs and interests of the student audience being addressed. Holistic art education has no "recipes" or easy-to-replicate formulaic approaches; instead, as Jaquith explains, holistic education almost invariably demands some degree of inventiveness on the part of the teacher, followed by ongoing individualized instruction to help ensure that students are being inventive as well. Evidently, implementing this kind of engaged, responsive instruction on a regular basis requires teachers' deep commitment to students. It also requires genuine content/skill expertise willingly placed in the service of student needs.

PROMISES AND POSSIBILITIES

After acknowledging the challenges of a holistic approach to art education, it is appropriate to summarize the promises of this approach in light of students' needs, and what this anthology attempts to provide in order to make holistic art education possible.

As previously indicated, the chapters in this anthology were chosen because they combined holistic principles, values, and goals with strategies to put the theory into practice. Freyermuth describes the atmosphere in a holistic classroom, while several others provide concrete examples of holistic curricula, lessons, and learning environments. Other chapters are devoted to implications for teacher preparation, with diverse perspectives offered by Grauer and deCosson, as well as Gardner, Klein, and Graham.

Based on this array of writings, it is possible to highlight certain goals and values associated with holistic education, as well as strategies to pursue them. For example, two goals discussed in this anthology are transformation and connectedness, both of which can be applied on personal and social levels. Values mentioned include respect for the student's point of view and authenticity in art experiences. Among the prominent means cited to achieve these ends were differentiation for ability, learning style, and personal interests, as well as flexibility with time, space, and resources. Additional strategies that were discussed include the following:

- Choice-Based Learning, Teaching for Artistic Behaviors, and Emergent Curriculum;

- Keeping journals for reflection and creative development;

- Taking advantage of new technologies for communication to provide students with more options and opportunities;

- Building community connections to address underprivileged students;

- Teacher preparation through holistic methods involving multicultural and cross-disciplinary perspectives;
- Holistically cultivating and assessing creativity;
- Using holistic art education as a means of healing both the person and the society;
- Restoring and holistically re-framing the model of the artist/teacher; and
- Addressing craft and design as domains of holistic art education.

CONCLUSION

The pressures and problems of contemporary society make student-connected, holistic art education more of a necessity than ever, yet there are difficulties to overcome in implementing a holistic art curriculum. Among these, American public education still places priority on academic achievement, as demonstrated on high-stakes standardized tests, thereby leaving little time and providing little encouragement for holistic concerns. Moreover, even in the art room, where such pressures are often not directly felt, art educators may be ill-prepared to teach holistically and/or may have apparently conflicting concerns.

Though necessarily limited in size and scope, this anthology is intended to address these issues. It demonstrates ways holistic education can be pursued in complement to (rather than in conflict with) academic, standards-based learning. It also offers indications for preservice and in-service art teacher preparation in holistic principles and practices. Finally, it proposes theoretical and practical advances that have recently emerged to make teaching holistically more attainable. Given this wide-ranging background, the primary concern is to help teachers find their *own* ways to approach holistic art education. Ultimately, there can be no recipes—no common way—to teach holistically. Teachers must each find their own creative approaches in light of their individual abilities and interests, and in response to their particular contexts and their students' unique developmental needs.

Building upon the references in this anthology, a further step toward meeting the needs of holistic art teachers and their students might be to develop networks of communication by which individuals could connect to one another, enabling them to share ideas, insights, and information. Such a network could also link art teachers to holistic educators in other domains, as well as to organizations such as the National Art Education Association that provide resources and support. Here again, new technologies can be a tremendous asset, as is the multiplicity of materials available in print and digital format on the Web.

Whatever the method, whether through contemporary applications or traditional media, the challenge of holistic teaching in our field remains the same: to reach, teach, develop, and integrate the whole student, while simultaneously connecting that student to others and to the environment through authentic and meaningful experiences with art content and skills. This, we believe, is "the heart of art education."

REFERENCES

Miller, J. P. (1993). *The holistic teacher*. Toronto, ON: The Ontario Institute for Studies in Education.

ABOUT THE EDITORS

Laurel H. Campbell is an assistant professor of Art Education and Director of Art Education at Indiana University-Purdue University Fort Wayne. She has been an art educator since 1996 and a metalsmith since 1974. Her research interests include reflective practice, preservice teacher education, and holistic art education.

Seymour Simmons III is an associate professor of Fine Arts at Winthrop University, where he coordinates the undergraduate art education program and teaches drawing. Prior to coming to Winthrop, he taught at the Massachusetts College of Art, and did research at Harvard Project Zero (in particular, on the Arts PROPEL project).

Jerome J. Hausman

The literature of art education is full of references to "holistic" orientations for the work we do. We speak of the education of the "whole child." We acknowledge that judgments and actions need to be seen and understood in context, part of a total (or whole) configuration. Yet, in more recent years, pressure has built for establishing definitions and criteria for assessing the specifics of what our students know and are able to do. Greater specificity in outcomes has resulted in more-focused formulations regarding teaching practice.

Of course, there have been other "pressures." New media and technologies have enlarged the repertoire of possibility. Major social issues have forced reappraisals as to the functions of art and artists. The framework for describing and evaluating the work of the art teacher has expanded to encompass a larger and wider array of "content possibilities." The territories to be covered are incredibly broad and diverse. What's an art teacher to do? Assuredly, we can't do it all!

In editing *The Heart of Art Education: Holistic Approaches to Creativity, Integration, and Transformation* Laurel H. Campbell and Seymour Simmons III have responded to the need to clarify the nature and purpose of holistic art education, today. They have assembled and skillfully juxtaposed the writings of art educators at different levels and with different backgrounds to provide theoretical foundations for the concept, while viewing the challenges of contemporary holistic education through a variety of lenses: aesthetic education, visual culture, globalization, ecology, social justice, and multicultural studies. The larger challenge, however, involves figuring out the dynamics of coordination, connection, and collaboration in the education of real students in a multitude of settings and circumstances. How can we become more holistic in thinking and practice? Thus, along with the theory, they have included concrete examples of what that theory might look like in various classrooms as well as in alternative situations.

In summing up the ensemble of these chapters, I am left with a number of generalizations that capture ideas and values, and give direction to a holistic orientation.

- Art education needs to move beyond previously defined disciplinary boundaries.

- Radical transformations are necessary to reorient thinking and find new solutions.

- The availability of digital media makes possible new approaches to be balanced with spiritual and holistic concerns.

- The distinctive focus of art education is still its emphasis upon creative thought and visualization processes. These center upon the quality of experience.

- Art educators need to make the case for broader meaning-of-art processes and the transformation of human consciousness. Art activity based upon qualitative thinking turns life back on itself.

- The broader community needs to be brought into the thinking and actions of art instruction. We can expect support only if what we do is understood and valued.

- Thinking like an artist invites insightful and multivalent ways of seeing. We need to hold to a vision that defines education in terms of the ensemble of body, mind, and spirit. We need to think and act holistically.

- Artists are drawn to the positive intrinsic rewards of creating aesthetic forms. This kind of involvement leads to a transformation of consciousness.

- Many approaches and avenues lead to artistic creation. Art is always being redefined by changes in our ways of knowing and acting.

- Art can involve the combining of seemingly unrelated ideas that result in novel forms. The creation of new forms can give rise to expanded or altered criteria for the evaluation of these forms.

- Art education should be linked to a total learning process. The teaching of art is informed by learning in other disciplines. In turn, the teaching of art should extend or enhance learning in other areas.

- Attention to the qualitative dimensions of thinking and the experiencing of art changes our modes of thought. The artist focuses upon ongoing consciousness about doing. For students, doing and consciousness are potentially one (holistic).

- Visual perception involves multi-sensory experience: We "see" in ways connected to touch, taste, smell, and sound. Prior knowledge and expectations influence what we consciously "see."

- Aesthetic distance enables the seeing of larger patterns and textures. Yet distance distorts, too. The "truth" of experiencing depends on distance as well as closeness to the "center."

- The art process can be likened to a "dialogue" that brings new understanding into experience. Conflict and contradiction can occur on the way to understanding or realization. The process is both reflective and reflexive.

- Creating or responding to art extends the qualities of the immediate present to another level of consciousness. We need to "extend" our attention to look not only at the finished work of art, but also to include attention to motives, reasons, and contexts of artists themselves.

- Media and materials possess particular qualities, and impose their own limits and possibilities for use.

- New media and technologies are transforming our visual environment. Real and virtual realities need to be understood as part of our knowledge of "now." Holistic approaches acknowledge the importance of an individual's experience in the present.

- Technical skills can and should be taught. In rare instances, technical skill can be seen as an end unto itself. In most art, technique is instrumental to the expression and realization of an idea or feeling.

- Qualitative approaches that reference memory, imagination, and spirituality are admissible to the realm of art education.

- Creative visualization, conceived holistically, is crucial to the art process (perceiving, making, and judging). This involves the expansion of consciousness.